ORACLE®

Ora

Oracle VM 3 Cloud Implementation and Administration Guide

Second Edition

About the Authors

Erik Benner is currently an Oracle ACE Director and Enterprise Architect serving as a lead strategist for federal, state, and local government and commercial customers throughout the United States. These customer engagements include enterprise cloud transformations, data center consolidation and modernization efforts, and Big Data projects and implementations of Oracle Engineered Systems. He is a board member of the Washington DC metro area's National Capital Oracle User Group as well as the Independent Oracle Users Group's Cloud Computing Special Interest Group (SIG), and he is actively involved with the Oracle Enterprise Manager SIGs. Erik presents frequently at conferences, including Oracle OpenWorld, Oracle FedForum, COLLABORATE, and other user groups and conferences around the United States. He has worked with Oracle and Sun Systems since the mid-1990s and is experienced with most of the core Oracle technologies. Erik also actively blogs at TalesFromTheDataCenter .com. When not flying to the far corners of the country from the Atlanta metro area, he enjoys spending time with his family at their observatory, where the telescopes outnumber the people.

Edward Whalen is the founder of Performance Tuning Corporation (www.perftuning.com), a consulting company specializing in database performance, administration, virtualization, and disaster recovery solutions. Prior to starting Performance Tuning, he worked at Compaq Computer Corporation as an OS developer, and then as a database performance engineer. He has extensive experience in database system design and tuning for optimal performance. His career has consisted of hardware, OS, and database development projects for many different companies. Edward has written four other books on the Oracle RDBMS and five books on Microsoft SQL Server. He has also worked on numerous benchmarks and performance-tuning projects with both Oracle and Microsoft SQL Server. Edward is recognized as a leader in database performance tuning and optimization.

Nic Ventura has specialized in computer systems as a technical solutions architect with real-world comprehensive experience in most aspects of the IT lifecycle—from concept and design to data center and enterprise deployment, including post-implementation support and performance engineering—for over 30 years. He is highly skilled and is certified on micro, midrange, and mainframe architectures and is often asked to lead teams in the analysis and documentation of complex business and technical requirements, to deliver results to executive management, and to assist with the implementation of recommended solutions. Nic was also awarded two USAF coins and is a recipient of the USAF Enterprise & Technology Management Award on the largest ERP in U.S. Air Force and Oracle history.

About the Technical Editors

Gregory King has over 27 years of experience in systems administration, professional services, software development, and product management. Gregory is currently a sustaining software developer for Oracle VM, responsible for identifying and fixing problems with server-side components of Oracle VM and Private Cloud Appliance, such as the agent, networking, and storage.

Prior to that Gregory spent five years with Oracle VM product management where he focused on creating and documenting best practices and solutions for Oracle VM, including the Oracle VM disaster recovery solution using Oracle Site Guard. In addition, he spent eight years as a senior Unix/Linux systems administrator in production data centers at Oracle.

Simon Hayler is currently a technical product manager looking after the Oracle Enterprise Manager systems management integration between the Oracle VM Server product and Oracle VM Server–based engineered systems. He previously worked on the infrastructure management team for Oracle Ops Center and before that had many roles in systems pre-sales, support, and professional services in the field.

Simon has over 27 years of experience with systems, storage, networking, and systems management, starting his career at British Telecom and moving on to Sun Microsystems and then Oracle.

ORACLE®

Oracle Press™

Oracle VM 3 Cloud Implementation and Administration Guide

Second Edition

Erik Benner
Edward Whalen
Nic Ventura

Mc
Graw
Hill
Education

New York   Chicago   San Francisco
Athens   London   Madrid   Mexico City
Milan   New Delhi   Singapore   Sydney   Toronto

Library of Congress Cataloging-in-Publication Data

Names: Benner, Erik, author. | Whalen, Edward, author. | Ventura, Nic, author.
Title: Oracle VM 3 Cloud : implementation and administration guide / Erik
    Benner, Edward Whalen, Nic Ventura.
Description: Second edition. | New York : McGraw-Hill Education, [2018] |
    Includes index.
Identifiers: LCCN 2017035527 | ISBN 9781259643866 (alk. paper)
Subjects: LCSH: Virtual computer systems. | Oracle (Computer file)
Classification: LCC QA76.9.V5 B466 2018 | DDC 005.4/3—dc23 LC record available at
https://lccn.loc.gov/2017035527

McGraw-Hill Education books are available at special quantity discounts to use as premiums and sales promotions, or for use in corporate training programs. To contact a representative, please visit the Contact Us pages at www.mhprofessional.com.

Oracle VM 3 Cloud Implementation and Administration Guide, Second Edition

1 2 3 4 5 6 7 8 9   LCR   21 20 19 18 17

ISBN   978-1-259-64386-6
MHID   1-259-64386-7

Sponsoring Editor	**Technical Editor**	**Production Supervisor**
Wendy Rinaldi	Gregory King and Simon Haylor	Lynn M. Messina
Editorial Supervisor	**Copy Editor**	**Composition**
Janet Walden	Barton D. Reed	Cenveo® Publisher Services
Project Editor	**Proofreader**	**Illustration**
LeeAnn Pickrell	Claire Splan	Cenveo Publisher Services
Acquisitions Coordinator	**Indexer**	**Art Director, Cover**
Claire Yee	Karin Arrigoni	Jeff Weeks

The authors would like to dedicate this book to the developers of Oracle VM and the Xen hypervisor.

Contents at a Glance

Contents

PART I
Introduction to Oracle VM

PART V
Installing and Configuring Enterprise Manager Cloud Control for IaaS

PART VI
Disaster Recovery, Maintenance, and Troubleshooting

Acknowledgments

W e would like to thank Greg King and Simon Hayler for their hard work editing this book from a technical perspective. They not only did a great job editing but also offered suggestions along the way. Technical editors can either make or break a book. Greg and Simon put a lot of effort into making this book what it is.

Thanks also to Claire Yee, Wendy Rinaldi, and all the staff at Oracle Press/McGraw-Hill Professional for their hard work and professionalism. This publishing company is excellent to work with.

—The authors

I'd like to thank my wife, Erin, and my son, Ethan, for putting up with all the time I spent working on this book. I'd also like to thank some of the people who have encouraged and supported me professionally over the years: Paul Seifert, Kimberly Borden, Eddie Soles, and all the Oracle Linux and Oracle VM product managers I have had the pleasure of working with, including Honglin Su, John Priest, and Simon Coter.

—Erik

I would like to thank my parents for inspiring me to be the best that I can be. I'd also like to thank all of the people at Oracle Press who have helped make this book great.

—Ed

I would like to say thanks for the educational guidance I received from Norman Dria and Lyn Paladino as well as for the never-ending support from my wife of 30 years, Deanna.

—Nic

Introduction

In the last decade, we have seen virtualization evolve from the standard way of doing business in the data center to a new model called the cloud, where resources are dynamically allocated and managed by the developers, users, and application managers. Cloud technology has changed how data centers are built and managed, as users can now directly provision not only virtual machines but entire applications via a few mouse clicks. The basis of this in an Oracle technology stack is Oracle VM, which is based on the Xen hypervisor. Oracle VM was introduced at the Oracle OpenWorld conference in 2007, and after Oracle purchased Sun Microsystems in 2010, Oracle VM was rebranded as Oracle VM Server for x86, and the Sun Solaris virtualization technologies were renamed Oracle VM Server for SPARC. The latest version of Oracle VM integrates with Oracle Enterprise Manager to provide full technology stack integration.

A cloud architecture provides several benefits over the traditional hardware system. Most of the benefits are economic, in that server consolidation, performance improvements, and speed of provisioning all provide value. Here are some of the main reasons companies choose virtualization:

- **Server consolidation** Many heterogeneous servers can be configured on the same virtual host, thus providing an economical server platform.

- **Provisioning** Virtual machines can easily and quickly be deployed, by administrators, developers, or even end users.

- **Functional separation** Whereas multiple applications might have had to share the same operating system in the past, they can now be configured on separate operating systems. They can be expanded in a private cloud, where applications that cannot be hosted in a public environment can now leverage the cloud technologies to improve agility and reduce expenses.

■ **Performance** Some applications simply don't scale well with many CPUs and large amounts of memory. For better performance, a larger server can be broken down into smaller operating systems where the sum of the parts is greater than the whole.

■ **Resource management** System resources can be tracked to the organization that consumes them, allowing for a fair allocation of the expenses in supporting the environments.

This book covers not only the advantages of using virtualization, but also how to install, configure, size, and administer a private cloud virtualized environment using Oracle VM.

PART I

Introduction to Oracle VM

CHAPTER
1

Introduction to Virtualization and Cloud Computing

*C*loud computing is the term used to describe services provided to your application either from within your environment or outside of your environment. Anything from storage services to onsite and offsite services is included in cloud computing. The original use of the term referred to providing computer services within a corporation or outside of a corporation in order to deliver additional resources. This in turn started out as virtual computing, or virtualization.

Virtualization became the technology that allowed providers to create resources that could then be offered to internal or external clients, including guest systems. This idea expanded and became the basis for cloud computing. In most cases, virtualization is still the key component of cloud computing, but other services such as cloud backup, applications and other technologies as a service have been included in cloud computing. However, virtualization is still the main component of cloud computing.

Virtualization has changed the way we look at computing. Instead of using many different computer systems for different tasks, with virtualization we can use a single system to host many applications. Not only has virtualization increased in popularity, but it has also influenced new hardware CPU innovation, including Intel VT-x and AMD-V technologies. Since its introduction, virtualization has become a core technology in every data center. Oracle VM, as one of the virtualization platforms, is based on stable and proven technology.

This chapter provides an overview of virtualization technologies, including the various types of virtualization and their typical uses. The reasons why companies choose to use virtualization and how they use it are also discussed. Subsequent chapters discuss the mechanics of installing, configuring, and managing Oracle VM 3.x.

What Is Virtualization?

Virtualization is the abstraction of computer hardware resources. This definition is very general; however, the broad range of virtualization products, both hardware and software, makes a more specific definition difficult. Virtualization can consist of storage, CPU resources, or a combination of resources. Virtualization can also include virtual tape devices used for backup and recovery. For the sake of this book, virtualization is primarily focused on virtual computer systems (specifically Oracle VM).

There are hardware products that allow for virtualization, software products that create virtual systems, and hardware options that assist with software virtualization. All of these products and options perform essentially the same function: they separate the operating system and applications from the underlying hardware.

A number of different types of system virtualization are available, including the following:

- Hardware virtualization
- Full software virtualization
- Paravirtualization
- Hardware-assisted software virtualization
- Component or resource virtualization, including storage and backup virtualization

As this book progresses, you will learn about these types of virtualization and their attributes. You will also obtain the information you need to decide which type of virtualization to use.

Although virtualization allows you to abstract resources away from the hardware layer, there are some limitations. With today's commercially available technology, virtualization—or at least the most popular types of virtualization—allows you to abstract only like architectures. For example, if you use software virtualization that runs on x86 or x86_64 architecture, you can run only virtual hosts with either an x86 or x86_64 operating system. In other words, you can't virtualize a SPARC system on an x86 or x86_64 architecture.

At this time, several major virtualization products are on the market:

- VMware was one of the first companies to offer a fully virtualized hardware platform environment, including a range of products with fully virtualized environments. VMware was founded in 1988 and was acquired by EMC in 2003. In addition to hardware virtualization, VMware also offers some paravirtualized drivers.

- Microsoft Hyper-V was released in 2008. Hyper-V provides both fully virtualized and guest-aware virtualization (if you are running a Windows guest). Hyper-V has been enhanced and now supports Linux as well as Windows clients.

- Xen Hypervisor is an open-source standard for virtualization and runs on multiple platforms. The first public release of Xen was in 2003, and the company was acquired by Citrix in 2007. Xen currently supports both hardware virtual machine (HVM) and paravirtualized machine (PVM). Xen does not offer any paravirtualized drivers.

- Oracle VM is a free, next-generation server virtualization and management solution from Oracle that makes enterprise applications easier to deploy, manage, and support. The Oracle VM hypervisor is an open-source Xen project with Oracle enhancements that make it easier, faster, and more efficient. In addition, Oracle VM is currently the only virtualization product supported for the Oracle Relational Database Management System (RDBMS) and other Oracle products. Oracle VM supports both HVM and PV and provides a set of paravirtualized drivers for both Windows and Linux paravirtualized hardware virtual machines (PVHVMs).

In addition, numerous proprietary hardware and software products allow you to virtualize specific vendors' hardware and operating systems. Many products are also available to virtualize networks, storage, and so on; although some of these products are discussed in this book, as appropriate, the main focus is on Oracle VM.

Reasons for Virtualizing

There are many reasons for creating systems in a virtualized environment rather than using physical hardware. In general, if your applications allow for virtualization, a virtualized environment lets you allocate sufficient resources to your applications using less power and with fewer cooling and space requirements. If applicable, in a virtualized environment, many virtualized systems can run on one physical computer, thus consuming fewer resources. Here are the top reasons for virtualizing:

- Cloud computing
- Server consolidation
- Server provisioning
- Functional separation

- Performance improvement
- Backup/restore
- Hosting
- Training, testing, quality assurance, and practice

Cloud Computing

Cloud computing has become ubiquitous. Everywhere you look you find cloud computing services and products. Whether you are a cloud provider or a cloud consumer, it is everywhere. As mentioned before, the core of cloud computing is virtualization, and the core of Oracle cloud services is Oracle VM.

Cloud computing consists of more than virtual machines; however, for the purpose of this book, virtualization is the primary focus. Cloud computing can also consist of application services, backup services, and other application services. In fact, pretty much every service provided can be called a cloud service, even human resources.

Server Consolidation

Server consolidation is probably the top reason for virtualizing your environment. To consolidate servers, you take multiple computer systems and collapse them into (or consolidate them into) one server. Server consolidation is often, though not necessarily, accomplished using virtualization. From an Oracle database perspective, you can consolidate servers in multiple ways. You can consolidate servers by taking databases from several servers and putting them on a single server, each with its own instance. You can take databases from several servers and put them on a single database server within the same Oracle instance, either with or without partitioning. Finally, you can consolidate multiple Oracle databases onto a single server by creating multiple individual virtual machines on a single server and then creating a single Oracle database instance on each virtual machine.

Oracle VM is the only platform that allows the Oracle database to be licensed on a vCPU (virtual CPU or core) rather than on the physical cores in the underlying host system. This is true when using hard partitioning in Oracle VM or Trusted Partitions on the Oracle Private Cloud Appliance.

Single Server, Multiple Instances

This option allows you to migrate multiple databases to a single server. You then configure the memory and CPU resources for each instance, thus dividing resources among the various instances. With this option, you consolidate multiple instances onto the same database server and still have some control over how the resources are allocated. The downside, as with the next option, is that some system resources, such as open files and the number of processes, can be exceeded. In addition, a single instance can sometimes utilize a disproportionate amount of system resources.

Single Server, Single Instance

With this option, you run all of the data from all of the instances to be consolidated from the same Oracle instance. This way, you can share resources more easily. However, other problems, such as security issues, often arise. In addition, a single instance often utilizes a disproportionate amount of system resources. Performance issues can also occur because all logical databases must share a single set of initialization parameter values for the Oracle database instance. This option is usually not the one to choose when consolidating Oracle databases.

Multiple VMs, Multiple Instances

This option allows you to configure and manage each database separately, much like the first option. However, because each Oracle instance runs on its own virtual server, this option has a few additional benefits. Because you can move a VM dynamically between underlying VM servers, you have more flexibility with the resources. If a system needs more resources, you can move it or another VM sharing that server, thus lessening the load.

This option's downside is that the OS is duplicated, causing more overhead than with the first option. When consolidating an Oracle database, you'll find both this option and the first option are often good choices.

Single Server, Single Instance, Multiple Pluggable Databases

With Oracle Database 12*c*, an efficient way to consolidate is with a single virtual server with a single instance and multiple pluggable databases. This provides a more efficient way of sharing resources within the database instance while allowing separation of functions within the database. Also, by optimizing the Oracle instance for multiple databases, you minimize the amount of resources required by the VM.

Server Provisioning

One of the primary advantages of using virtual machines is the ability to provision servers quickly and efficiently. A virtual environment allows you to keep templates of various types of servers— such as application servers and database servers—and to deploy and put them into production easily in a matter of minutes or hours. The process of provisioning a server typically involves either copying a server or building a new server from a template. Once you have deployed this new server, you run scripts to rename it, change its IP address, and so on, getting it into production quickly.

By pre-staging servers and templates, you can quickly, efficiently, and precisely deploy them. By using a pre-staged server, you also avoid mistakes, which makes the provisioning process faster and more exact. You can easily pick what type of server to deploy from your library of templates and pre-staged servers. The Oracle VM architecture allows you to deploy the new server into any system in the server farm that you desire, creating a high-performance, scalable server in a very short period of time.

Functional Separation

Various applications don't work well together in an operating system. The reason is primarily due to resource contention in certain subsystems in the OS, such as the memory subsystem, the I/O subsystem, service ports, and the OS scheduler. Often, application servers do not scale (achieve higher performance) when additional resources such as CPUs or memory are added. In these cases, using several smaller servers (two CPUs, 2GB of RAM) is better than using a larger server with many CPUs and lots of RAM. This is especially true of Java, which doesn't scale very well with large amounts of memory and multiple CPUs.

Even when application servers don't scale well with large numbers of CPUs and lots of RAM, you can still take advantage of the cost effectiveness of these systems by virtualizing them. Scaling problems typically occur in the application itself and in the OS scheduler, where the system simply can't keep track of too many processes, or in Java. Java applications typically can't take advantage of more than 2–3GB of RAM. By virtualizing, you can assign each system a reasonable amount of resources that the application can handle. Because the process tables and application queues exist in the virtual server and not on the host, the virtual environment will continue to scale. Fortunately, the Oracle database server scales very well with CPU and memory resources.

In addition, you can use functional separation to split management responsibilities, provide additional security, and reduce contention. By virtualizing and splitting up applications by vendor or group, you can allocate a single application to a single server and still not waste hardware resources.

Performance Improvement

As mentioned in the previous section, application servers often perform better as several smaller servers rather than one large server. Therefore, virtualizing a large server into multiple smaller ones can often improve application server performance. By splitting up a large host system into multiple, smaller VMs, you can often achieve not only higher performance but also a greater level of scalability.

In addition, the virtual environment provides a feature that you can't find in physical servers: the ability to move the VM to another host. This gives you the flexibility and ability to alter the physical characteristics of the underlying host while the virtual machine is still up and running, giving you the benefits of live load balancing and performance improvements without interrupting service to the VM user.

By moving VMs from one host to another while live, you use resources efficiently and you can reuse them when needed. If a host becomes too busy, you can add another to the server pool and move VMs to it as needed.

Backup/Restore

An often-overlooked feature of virtual machines is the ability to back them up quickly and efficiently because a virtual machine looks essentially like several large files to the host OS. Most performance problems that occur during backups are due to the number of small files in a system. When backing up a small file, the backup software takes more time opening and closing the file and finding all the parts of the file than it actually takes to read the contents and back them up. The amount of data backed up per second drops significantly for small files.

When backing up an operating system, the backup software traverses the entire directory structure and opens, copies, and then closes each file. With large files, the software spends more time copying data. With small files, the software takes more time opening and closing files. Because each virtual disk is actually a large file in the OS, backups are very fast.

Backups from the VM can be problematic while the VM is running because the state of the files is constantly in flux (a file might only be halfway written when the backup occurs). Memory may also be in flux. Considering that most systems use hard drive files for swap, the backup could become corrupted using this approach. Therefore, you must consider a backup of a virtual machine file to be a "crash consistent backup." You should back up the virtual server image when the virtual OS is shut down.

If you're running backups from the VM itself in order to back up specific items or to back up the database directly using RMAN, then the advantages you achieve by backing up the entire VM image are not realized.

For the same reasons that backing up the entire virtual disk is much faster than backing up each individual file within the virtual disk, restoring is similarly optimized. Restoring one large virtual disk file is much faster than restoring each file individually within the virtual machine.

With newer versions of Oracle VM, creating a "hot standby" is now allowed. In fact, an entire standby VM farm can be created. This allows for live standby and quick recovery in the event of the loss of a data center or system.

Hosting

One of the most common uses of virtualized machines is for hosting environments. Both hosted environments and cloud computing use virtualized machines to provide on-demand computing to their clients. Depending on the underlying hardware, dozens of virtualized systems might be running on the same underlying host server(s). This model allows the hosting vendor to provide virtual systems to its clients using an on-demand model where virtual machines are automatically created as needed. In addition, the hosting vendor can easily size the system to the desired number of CPUs and RAM instantly.

Many vendors now offer hosted solutions and cloud computing. *Cloud computing* defines a type of computer resource that is available over the Internet or internally and is made up of resources that you know little about. These resources, usually in the form of a Linux or Windows cloud computer, are available to be used anywhere, and are provided with a set number of CPUs and a set amount of memory and disk space. Typically the end user doesn't really know anything about the underlying hardware or software, thus turning computer resources into commodities.

> **NOTE**
> *Two types of cloud computing are available: private and public.*
> *Private clouds are hosted using internal networks.*

Cloud computing has become more popular in recent years as many customers have decided to abandon expensive data centers and instead acquire just the resources needed to run their business. Cloud computing is less expensive than traditional computer systems—up to a point. The higher-end cloud computers tend to be a little pricey.

Training, Testing, Quality Assurance, and Practice

Some of the most popular uses of virtualization are for training, testing, quality assurance (QA), and, of course, just plain practice. Virtual environments are absolutely ideal for testing business systems because they are easy to set up, use, and refresh. All of these types of activities benefit from the ability to quickly refresh virtual machines.

Training

Training is by far one of the best uses of virtualization. Oracle employs a great deal of virtualization for training purposes. For example, you can reset the VMs for the next week's training classes by simply removing and replacing them with new copies. You can preconfigure the correct software, class exercises, and configurations and then redeploy whenever necessary. Oracle has an entire library of training classes, including the following:

- Oracle 11*g*
- Oracle 10*g*
- Oracle RAC
- Oracle on Windows
- Oracle Application Server

By storing several classes, you can easily repurpose your training facility to handle any class you need. Because many classroom environments are not CPU intensive, you can create several virtual machines on the same underlying host.

Training systems are easy to set up as well as access. By using technology such as Virtual Network Computing (VNC), students can access the systems and run X-Windows programs such as the Oracle Universal Installer (OUI) and the Database Configuration Assistant (DBCA); we will cover VNC in more detail later in this book. You can also create a training system assigned to individual students so they can experience managing an entire OS environment. When the class is finished, or if a student causes irreversible problems with the system, you simply remove and re-create the virtual machine using a preconfigured image complete with a preinstalled operating system and applications.

Testing

Testing is an important part of every system. Unfortunately, many companies do not have the resources to purchase test systems, thus leading to severe problems and risk to the production environment. I have actually been called in on occasion to assist with recovering from problems that resulted from an upgrade or patch that wasn't thoroughly tested on a nonproduction server before being put it into production. The reason for not having a test server is usually budgetary.

With a virtual environment, you can put a test system into place efficiently and economically simply by making a copy of the original virtual machines. For example, your database administrators (DBAs) can test upgrades, patches, installations, new configurations, and even undertake performance testing without impacting a production business system by using copies of the original virtual machines. Without a proper test system, the DBA might miss some step or important detail of a patch or upgrade that he or she might not otherwise notice. By testing installations, configurations, and deployments, the DBA will be more comfortable with and better at doing these tasks. Test systems are one of the most important resources you can have. And once you've finished testing, with one click, you can move the test system into production.

By using Oracle VM, you can create multiple test environments and also save these environments at various stages, so you can deploy the next step over and over again, thus testing exactly what you need to test. You can also preconfigure virtual machines with different versions of the OS and various configurations, including Real Application Clusters (RAC).

QA

Having a set of virtual machines for QA has many advantages. You can keep multiple versions of operating systems, databases, and applications, which allows you to test modifications multiple times using different variations with very little setup time in between attempts. You can also refresh and reset the QA system whenever a new code drop is released, which increases efficiency in redeploying systems for testing and validation.

Practice

Having a system to practice and test new things on is always a good idea. You can hone your skills and try new things such as backup methods, patching, and upgrades. Through practicing and testing, you improve your skills, leading to professional advancement and self-confidence.

Overview of Virtualization Technologies

Virtualization has been around for quite a while now; however, its mass appeal has only been realized with the extensive improvements that have appeared over the last few years. In virtualization's early days, you had to purchase very expensive hardware; now, due to its commoditization, you can use commodity PC servers and download free virtualization software to get started.

A number of different virtualization technologies are available in the market today, including the following domain types:

- Full software virtualization
- Hardware-assisted software virtualization or hardware virtual machine (HVM)
- Paravirtualization or paravirtualized machine (PVM)
- Hardware-assisted software virtualization with paravirtualized drivers (PVHVM)
- Component or resource virtualization

Depending on your situation, you might be able to take advantage of one or more of these virtualization types. In this section, we explore each virtualization type, along with its pros and cons. Each type has its own attributes that provide specific benefits. The type of virtualization you choose depends on your needs. Oracle VM supports hardware-assisted software virtualization, paravirtualization, and the hybrid hardware-assisted software virtualization with paravirtualized drivers.

Full Software Virtualization

In *full software virtualization,* all the hardware is simulated by a software program. Each device driver and process in the guest OS believes it is running on actual hardware, even though the underlying hardware is really a software program. Software virtualization even fools the OS into thinking that it is running on hardware.

One of the advantages of full software virtualization is that you can run any OS on it. It doesn't matter whether or not the OS in question understands the underlying host hardware. Thus, older and specialty operating systems can run in software virtualized environment. The architecture is very flexible because you don't need a special understanding of the OS or hardware.

The OS hardware subsystem discovers the hardware in the normal fashion. It believes the hardware is really hardware. The hardware types and features that it discovers are usually fairly generic and might not be as "full featured" as actual hardware devices, though the system is functional.

Another advantage of full software virtualization is that you don't need to purchase any additional hardware. With hardware-assisted software virtualization, you need to purchase hardware that supports advanced VM technology. Although this technology is included in most systems available today, some older types of hardware do not have this capability. To use this older hardware as a virtual host, you must use either full software virtualization or paravirtualization.

NOTE
Only hardware-assisted software virtualization requires advanced VM features; full software virtualization does not. VMware ESX works on older hardware that does not have any special CPU features. This type of virtualization is also known as emulation.

Unfortunately, full software virtualization adds a lot of overhead, which dramatically slows performance of the operating system and applications. This overhead translates into extra instructions and CPU time on the host, resulting in a slower system and higher CPU usage. With full software virtualization, the CPU instruction calls are trapped by the virtual machine monitor (VMM) and then emulated in a software program. Therefore, every hardware instruction that would normally be handled by the hardware itself is now handled by a program.

For example, when the disk device driver makes an I/O call to the "virtual disk," the software in the VM system intercepts it, then processes it, and finally makes an I/O call to the real underlying disk. The number of instructions to perform an I/O call is greatly increased. This process is diagramed and explained in further detail in Chapter 3.

With networking, even more overhead is incurred because a network switch is simulated in the software rather than running in hardware. Depending on the amount of network activity, the overhead can be quite high. In fact, with severely overloaded host systems, you could possibly see network delays from the virtual switch itself. This is why sizing is so important.

Hardware-Assisted Software Virtualization

Hardware-assisted software virtualization is available with CPU chips with built-in virtualization support. With the introduction of the Intel VT and AMD-V technologies, this virtualization type has become commoditized. It was first introduced on the IBM System/370 computer and is similar to software virtualization, with the exception that some hardware functions are accelerated and assisted by hardware technology. Similar to software virtualization, the hardware instructions are trapped and processed, but this time using hardware in the virtualization components of the CPU chip.

By using hardware-assisted software virtualization, you get the benefits of software virtualization, such as the ability to use any OS without modifying it, and, at the same time, achieve better performance. Because of virtualization's importance, significant effort is going into providing more support for hardware-assisted software virtualization. Hardware-assisted virtualization also supports any operating system.

Using hardware-assisted software virtualization, Oracle VM lets you install and run Linux and Solaris x86-based operating systems as well as Microsoft Windows without modifications to the operating system or device drivers. This technique also makes migrating from VMware systems to Oracle VM easier, as described in Chapter 21.

As mentioned earlier, both Intel and AMD are committed to supporting hardware-assisted software virtualization. They both introduced virtualization technology around 2005/2006, and their support has improved the functionality and performance of virtualization.

NOTE
Hardware-assisted virtualization is really the long-term virtualization solution.

Intel

Intel supports virtualization via its VT-x technology. The Intel VT-x technology is now part of many Intel chipsets, including the Pentium, Xeon, and Core processors family. The VT-x extensions support an input/output memory management unit (IOMMU) that allows virtualized systems to access I/O devices directly. Ethernet and graphics devices can now have their DMA and interrupts directly mapped via the hardware. In the latest versions of the Intel VT technology, extended page tables have been added to allow direct translation from guest virtual addresses to physical addresses.

AMD

AMD supports virtualization via the AMD-V technology. AMD-V includes a rapid virtualization indexing technology to accelerate virtualization. This technology is designed to assist with the virtual-to-physical translation of pages in a virtualized environment. Because this operation is one of the most common, by optimizing this function, you can greatly enhance performance. AMD virtualization products are available on both the Opteron and Athlon processor families.

NOTE
The virtual machine that uses the hardware-assisted software virtualization model has become known as the hardware virtual machine, or HVM. This terminology will be used throughout the rest of the book and refers to the fully software-virtualized model with hardware assist.

Paravirtualization

With *paravirtualization,* the guest OS is aware of and interfaces with the underlying host OS. A paravirtualized kernel in the guest understands the underlying host technology and takes advantage of that fact. This not only helps in runtime but skips many steps in the boot process, resulting in amazingly fast booting. Because the host OS is not running all the device driver code, the number of resources needed for virtualization is greatly reduced. In addition, paravirtualized device drivers for the guest can also interface with the host system, thus reducing overhead. The idea behind paravirtualization is to reduce both the complexity and overhead involved in virtualization. By paravirtualizing both the host and guest operating systems, very expensive functions are offloaded from the guest to the host OS.

The guest essentially makes special system calls that then allow these functions to run within the host OS. When using a system such as Oracle VM, the host operating system acts in much the same way as a guest operating system. The hardware device drivers interface with a layer known as the *hypervisor*. The hypervisor is also known as the *virtual machine monitor* (VMM).

Hybrid Virtualization Technology (PVHVM)

With *hybrid virtualization,* the guest OS uses HVM, but some device drivers are paravirtualized. HVM allows for hardware acceleration, and a paravirtualized device driver in the guest understands the underlying host technology and takes advantage of that fact.

Since Oracle Enterprise Linux (OEL5), Oracle has provided the ability to create an HVM that uses a few specific paravirtualized device drivers for network and I/O. This hybrid virtualization technology provides the benefits of a paravirtualized virtual machine with the additional hardware accelerations available within the HVM. This technology is still new but might be the future of virtualization. This type of virtual machine is known as a *paravirtualized hardware virtual machine*, or PVHVM. This virtual machine type has the benefits of both the HVM system and the PV system.

Component or Resource Virtualization

Component or resource virtualization has come to mean many different things, depending on the context. Probably the most popular form of component or resource virtualization is in the area of storage. Network resources can also be virtualized but are not as common.

Storage virtualization is simply the abstracting of logical storage from physical storage. This process has been going on for many years and is very popular. Storage virtualization has tremendous advantages as well as a few drawbacks.

Benefits of Storage Virtualization

Storage virtualization has many benefits because it allows storage to be highly available and highly scalable. Storage virtualization lets you add drives to a virtual disk while the system is live and running. Management of the storage system can be done external to the database and without system administrators. Storage virtualization also supports large numbers of disk drives and virtual disks.

Virtual disk systems have been around for a long time—especially if you consider Redundant Array of Inexpensive Disks (RAID) to be a virtual storage system. RAID meets the definition of a virtual storage system as an abstraction of logical storage from physical storage. RAID systems provide both performance (from multiple disk drives) and redundancy to protect the system from the loss of a component. As you can see, storage virtualization actually provides many benefits.

Drawbacks of Storage Virtualization

The drawback of storage virtualization is that you lose control of I/O resources. The I/O subsystem is one of the most important subsystems for database performance. If the I/O subsystem is overloaded, it can lead to high latencies, which, in turn, lead to slow query performance. The I/O subsystem's performance depends on several factors, including the number of disk drives (or spindles) and how busy those drives are.

In a virtualized storage environment, the storage presented to the server is abstracted from the physical storage. Logical unit numbers (LUNs), or virtual disks, are made up of multiple disk drives, and multiple LUNs can span the same disks. Unfortunately, this means you might not know exactly where your storage is coming from and how many other systems are sharing the same drives with that storage, which can cause unpredictable performance.

Because I/O performance is so important to the Oracle database, Oracle Automatic Storage Management (ASM) disks should be made up of LUNs with dedicated drives (that is, no other LUNs sharing the disk drives). In some virtualized storage environments, this is not possible, however. In fact, some storage systems automatically stripe all LUNs across all drives in the system.

Depending on the I/O subsystem's flexibility, different configuration options are available that might let you have more control over storage. In a theoretical environment, the abstraction of logical to physical shouldn't matter. Unfortunately, in the real world, the speed of the disk drives is finite and therefore must be allocated properly.

Backup Virtualization

Many sources of cloud backup are available that allow systems to back up directly to storage and/or APIs available in the cloud. Oracle has recently introduced the ability to configure a cloud backup where the cloud backup devices are configured as a tape drive within the Oracle RMAN utility. This provides a valuable resource for backups to be made directly to the cloud.

Miscellaneous

Other forms of virtualization exist that haven't been mentioned in this chapter. These virtualization methods typically involve expensive proprietary hardware. Because this book is focused on Oracle VM, which doesn't use any proprietary hardware, those technologies have been excluded from this chapter. This book will, however, discuss technologies that are similar to and share some of the same ideas as Oracle VM (primarily, VMware ESX Server and Xen). As you will learn in the next chapter, Oracle VM has its roots in Xen technology.

The Hypervisor

The hypervisor is what makes virtualization possible. The hypervisor is the component that translates the virtual machines into the underlying hardware. There are two types of hypervisors: The type 1 hypervisor runs directly on the host hardware; the type 2 (or hosted) hypervisor runs in software. In addition, some proprietary hardware has a hypervisor built into it. The type of hypervisors we are concerned with, however, are the type 1 and type 2 hypervisors.

Type 1 Hypervisor

The type 1 (or embedded) hypervisor is a layer that runs directly on the host hardware, interfacing with the CPU, memory, and devices. Oracle VM and VMware ESX Server both use the type 1 hypervisor. The hypervisor treats the host OS in much the same way as a guest OS. The host OS is referred to as Domain 0 (or dom0), and guests are referred to as Domain U (or domU), as shown in Figure 1-1. Here, you can see that all virtual machines must go through the hypervisor to get to the hardware. The dom0 domain is a virtual system just like the domU virtual machines (but it has more capabilities, as discussed later). Currently, the type 1 hypervisor is considered the most efficient and is the most recommended hypervisor.

NOTE
Even though Oracle VM and VMware both use a type 1 hypervisor, these hypervisors are significantly different. VMware handles device drivers directly in the hypervisor; Xen handles them in dom0 or a driver domain.

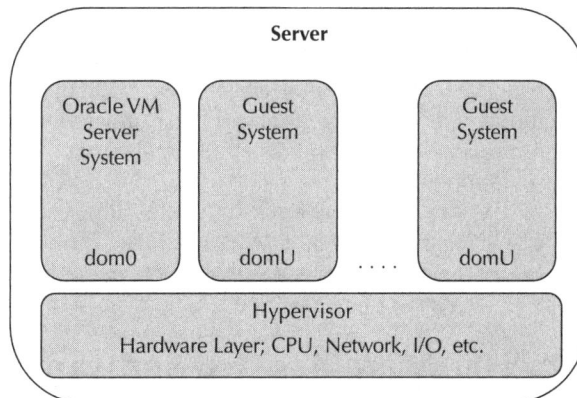

FIGURE 1-1. *The type 1 hypervisor represented graphically*

The dom0 domain does not differ much from the other domains in the virtual environment, except that you access it differently and it is always enabled by default. In addition, dom0 has unlimited rights to hardware, whereas domU only has access through a layer of indirection and only to what the hypervisor grants it. Because the type 1 hypervisor is essentially part of the OS, it must be installed on the hardware itself and support the devices installed on the system.

Type 2 Hypervisor

The type 2 (or hosted) hypervisor runs as a program and is used for software virtualization. Because the type 2 hypervisor runs as a program, it has neither the same priority as the type 1 hypervisor nor the ability to access the hardware directly. Its main advantage is that you can install it on a variety of host systems without modification. The type 2 hypervisor works with both full software virtualization and hardware-assisted software virtualization. VMware Server is an example of a type 2 hypervisor.

Oracle also has another x86 virtualization product called Oracle VM VirtualBox. It is a type 2 hypervisor-based product and is very popular for testing. I know many people who run VirtualBox on their PCs in order to quickly and efficiently spin up a Linux virtual machine.

Summary of Virtualization Technologies

Both hardware-assisted software virtualization and paravirtualization have benefits and drawbacks. With the recent changes in hardware, the software and the technology are changing at a rapid pace.

Currently, three domain types are supported by Xen and by extension Oracle VM: hardware-assisted software (HVM), paravirtualization (PVM), and paravirtualized hardware virtual machine (PVHVM). Full software virtualization and hardware-assisted software virtualization are very similar, as no additional coding or configuration is required (except perhaps to enable virtualization in the BIOS). The main comparison, therefore, really falls between hardware-assisted software virtualization and paravirtualization.

Benefits of Hardware-Assisted Software Virtualization

The main benefit of software virtualization is its flexibility. You can run any OS on the guest that is compatible with the underlying hardware. That is, if your underlying hardware is Intel or AMD, then the guest must run on Intel or AMD hardware. A number of combinations of 32-bit and 64-bit OSs can run in this environment.

With a 64-bit host, you can run 32-bit or 64-bit guests. Either type of guest is supported, and you can combine both 32-bit and 64-bit guests. When running a 32-bit host, a 64-bit is only available with hardware assistance. If the host system is a 32-bit server without VM technology (hardware assist), the host only supports 32-bit guests. This is described in more detail in Chapter 3.

Drawbacks of Hardware-Assisted Software Virtualization

The main drawbacks of hardware-assisted software virtualization are I/O and network performance. Because hardware calls are being trapped and processed in software, there is a great deal of overhead. The use of hardware assistance accelerates these operations if they are in the supported system calls (mainly memory).

Benefits of Paravirtualization

The primary benefit of paravirtualization is performance. Because the guest OS understands that it is actually running in a VM environment, it can bypass some software interpretations of hardware calls and go directly to the underlying host or hypervisor. Both the guest and host must be running the VM kernel so they understand and can communicate with the underlying hypervisor.

Drawbacks of Paravirtualization

The main drawback of paravirtualization is the restriction on the supported OS. Because the host and guest must both be running a VM kernel, at this time, paravirtual drivers support only Linux, Solaris x86, and Windows.

Another drawback of paravirtualization is the lack of hardware support. Currently, paravirtualization does not take advantage of the new VM hooks that hardware vendors are adding to their CPU chips. In the future, this is likely to change. When paravirtualization is accelerated with hardware, performance will increase dramatically.

Because the VM kernel must be used, converting a VMware or other image to Oracle VM is difficult. This shortcoming can be resolved, however, but you will find it is a little more difficult than converting a VMware image to a hardware-assisted software virtualization environment.

If you are running a Linux guest, paravirtualization is the recommended method of virtualization because of its performance benefits. Upcoming chapters provide information on creating both hardware-assisted software virtualization and paravirtualization guests.

Summary

This chapter has introduced you to the various types of virtualization. The information provided is intended to be fairly generic because specifics of Oracle VM are provided throughout the book. Both software and paravirtualization were described, as well as the benefits and drawbacks of both technologies. Because hardware support for virtualization is changing so rapidly, some of the information in this chapter may be obsolete by the time you read this book; however, the general principals and methods will remain the same.

This chapter compared hardware-assisted software virtualization and paravirtualization. This comparison is based on the technology as it exists today. Soon hardware extensions for virtualization will improve as well as hardware support for paravirtualization. Virtualization is now at the forefront of CPU technology and is leading the new technological revolution.

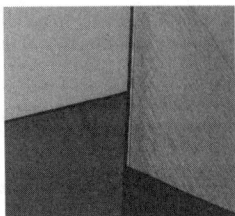

CHAPTER
2

What Is Oracle VM?

Oracle VM is no longer considered new to the VM marketplace, and the underlying Xen technology has been thoroughly tested and used. Oracle introduced Oracle VM at the Oracle World conference in 2007 and made the product available for download shortly after that. At the time, Oracle touted this as being one of its largest software announcements in the history of the company. The Oracle VM product consists of two major components: the Oracle VM Server and the Oracle VM Manager.

Since Oracle's acquisition of Sun Microsystems, the Oracle VM product, which is the subject of this book, was rebranded as Oracle VM Server for x86. At the same time, the virtualization products that were available for the Sun hardware product line were rebranded as Oracle VM Server for SPARC. In addition, Oracle has added desktop virtualization to its product line with Oracle VM VirtualBox. In this book, Oracle VM Server for x86 will be referred to simply as Oracle VM. Any of the other products will be referred to by their full name.

In this chapter, you will learn about the history of Oracle VM and Xen, its underlying technology, as well as some of the competition. This chapter also covers some of the key features of Oracle VM and the Oracle VM template library.

History of Oracle VM and Virtualization

Oracle VM was not the first virtualization product on the market, nor is it the last. VMware was introduced in 1998 and is majority owned by EMC. VMware introduced its first virtualization product for the desktop in 1999 and its first server product in 2001. Then, in 2003, VMware introduced the VMware Virtual Center, the vMotion, and Virtual SMP technology. These products made virtualization viable for server consolidation in the enterprise. Prior to that, VMware was primarily used only as a test or training platform. In 2004, VMware introduced 64-bit support. EMC also acquired VMware in 2004.

As with Oracle VM, VMware is supported on the Intel/AMD x86 platforms only. This, in part, has led to the race between Intel and AMD to focus their efforts on providing an extensive set of features that optimize virtualization on their platforms. With both Oracle VM and VMware, fully virtualized systems are now supported. In addition, Oracle VM supports paravirtualization, where the underlying operating system realizes that it is running on a virtual system and makes intelligent choices based on that knowledge. Although VMware provides replacement drivers for video and I/O, it isn't the same as paravirtualization. However, both products also support any OS that will run on the x86 platform in a fully virtualized guest.

The third major player in the virtualization market is Microsoft with its Hyper-V product. The Microsoft Hyper-V virtualization solution is a hypervisor-based virtualization product that was introduced in 2008. This product appears to be targeted primarily to the Microsoft Windows environment.

Another player in the virtualization market is KVM (Kernel Virtual Machine). The built-in virtualization for Linux has moved from Xen to KVM. Although Oracle maintains open-source compatibility with KVM, they have decided to stick with Xen as the basis of Oracle VM rather than moving to KVM. For the time being, Oracle is continuing to use Xen as its preferred virtualization technology.

One additional player in the virtualization market is Citrix. Citrix had purchased XenSource, but isn't pushing it as a dominant virtualization platform, as Citrix tends to focus more on the desktop replacement rather than the virtualization environment. Citrix continues to be a major player in the desktop virtualization market but does not participate in server virtualization.

In addition to the major commercial virtualization products, other virtualization products have been created specifically for cloud providers such as the Amazon AWS (Amazon WorkSpaces), which is developed and maintained by Amazon. Other commercial vendors have done the same. Oracle Cloud services are run on Oracle VM or a slightly modified version of Oracle VM.

These companies do not represent the entirety of the virtualization market and virtualization products, but they do represent Oracle VM's main competition. The focus of this book is Oracle VM; although many other virtualization products are available, including hardware virtualization products, they will not be covered here.

Virtualization technology is not new to Oracle. Oracle VM is based on the Xen Hypervisor, which is a proven and stable technology. To understand the history of Oracle VM, you must first look at the history of the Xen Hypervisor.

History of Xen

The Xen virtualization product began around the same time as VMware. It was created at the University of Cambridge Computer Laboratory, and its first version was released in 2003. The leader of the project then went on to found XenSource. Unlike both VMware and Hyper-V, Xen is maintained by the open-source community under the GNU General Public License. In 2007, XenSource was acquired by Citrix Systems.

Whereas VMware and Hyper-V only support the x86 architecture, Xen supports x86, x86_64, Itanium, and PowerPC architectures. As mentioned in Chapter 1, the Xen architecture is based on a hypervisor. This hypervisor originally allowed only Linux, NetBSD, and Solaris operating systems to operate in a paravirtualized environment. However, since the introduction of Xen 3.0 and hardware virtualization support in hardware, unmodified OSs can now operate in Xen.

Oracle VM 3.4 is based on the Xen 4.4 kernel. In order to fully appreciate where the Xen 4.4 kernel is, let's look at a brief history of the Xen Hypervisor. The following is a brief timeline of Xen's history:

2002	Development begins on the Xen Hypervisor.
2003	The first releases of Xen are made available.
2004	The second release of Xen is made available, and the first Xen developers' summit is held.
2005	XenSource is founded and version 3.0 is released.
2006	XenEnterprise is released. Linux begins adding enhancements for virtualization. VMware and Microsoft adopt paravirtualization as well. In addition, this year marks the launch of Amazon EC2 (Enterprise Cloud 2).
2007	Citrix acquires XenSource. Oracle announces Oracle VM, which is based on the Xen Hypervisor. The original version is Oracle VM 2.1.
2008	Xen begins showing up embedded in flash memory.
2009	Oracle releases Oracle VM 2.2 based on Xen 3.4.
2010	Oracle purchases Sun Microsystems.
2010	Oracle VM is rebranded as Oracle VM Server for x86.
2011	Oracle VM 3.0 is released based on Xen 4.0.
2012	Oracle VM 3.1 is released based on Xen 4.1.2.
2013	Oracle VM 3.2 is released based on Xen 4.1.2.
2014	Oracle VM 3.3 is released based on Xen 4.3.
2015	Oracle VM 3.4 is released based on Xen 4.4.

Let's look at a few of the major releases in more detail. Because Xen is the basis for Oracle VM, understanding where it is coming from and how the various releases have evolved is important.

Xen 1.*x*

Xen 1.0 was the first release of the Xen product and included all of the basic pieces needed to support virtualization. Xen 1.0 supported only the Linux operating system, but at the time of its release, the Xen development team was already working to enable Microsoft Windows to run in a virtual environment. The original release of Xen was based on paravirtualization, where the guest operating system is modified so that it's aware it is actually running in a virtualized environment. This awareness improved performance but did not allow the full range of OSs to run unmodified in a virtualized environment. Xen 1.0 reached its goal of allowing any application that ran on the guest OS to be able to run in an unmodified manner, however.

Microsoft Windows was the first non-Linux operating system ported to Xen, but Microsoft pulled support shortly after announcing its support to begin work on its own virtualization technologies.

Xen 2.*x*

The Xen 2.0 release again targeted the x86 market and included a number of substantial new features. The most impressive of these new features gave users the ability to perform a "live migration" of a virtual guest from one host to another with no interruption in service. This feature is known as vMotion in VMware and is one of the truly outstanding features of virtualization. Using this feature, users could adjust and manage the load on the underlying hosts without interrupting service to the guest OS. In addition, XenSource improved the manner in which virtual I/O devices were used and configured, especially in the area of networking.

Xen 3.*x*

Even though Xen 2.0 and, in some respects, 1.0 had significant features, it wasn't until Xen 3.0 that Xen was truly ready for the enterprise. The features enabled in this version made Xen viable as an alternative to physical servers and increased its popularity. These features have created the explosion in the virtualization market. In the past few years, the popularity and variety of virtualization have grown tremendously.

In this section, we cover the history of Xen 3.x in more detail.

Xen 3.0   Xen 3.0 included many features that were required for enterprise computing, including the following:

- **32P support**   Xen 3.0 added support for up to 32-way SMP guest operating systems. This support was important for larger applications such as databases.

- **64-bit**   Xen 3.0 provided 64-bit support for the x86_64 platform, including Intel and AMD processors.

- **PAE**   Xen 3.0 added support for the Intel Physical Addressing Extensions (PAE) to support 32-bit servers with more than 4GB physical memory. Although this was not as efficient as 64-bit support, it was better than nothing.

- **Fully virtualized**   When using Intel VT-x (or AMD's AMD-V), Xen 3.0 made it possible to run unmodified guest operating systems as hardware virtual machines (HVMs). This feature is sometimes known as *hardware-assisted virtualization*. It allowed for OSs such as Microsoft Windows and earlier releases of Linux and UNIX to run as unmodified guests.

- **Miscellaneous enhancements** Xen 3.0 added other enhancements, including improved utilities, graphics, and Advanced Configuration and Power Interface (ACPI) support.

Without 64-bit support, many people found it difficult to migrate their applications to a virtualized environment. This is probably the most significant improvement in the Xen 3.*x* family.

Xen 3.1 The Xen 3.1 release, although not as significant as the 3.0 release, added many valuable new features:

- **XenAPI support** Xen 3.1 added support for XenAPI 1.0. This API uses XML configuration files for virtual machines as well as VM lifecycle management operations.
- **Save/restore/migrate** Xen 3.1 added the preliminary save/restore/migrate support for HVMs.
- **Dynamic memory** Xen 3.1 introduced dynamic memory control for nonparavirtualized machines.
- **32-bit on 64-bit** Xen 3.1 added support for a 32-bit OS (including PAE) to run on a 64-bit host.
- **Raw partitions** Xen 3.1 added support for virtual disks on raw partitions.

Xen 3.2 Like the 3.1 release, Xen 3.2 was not as significant as the 3.0 release, but it added many valuable new features:

- **XSM** Xen 3.2 added Xen Security Modules (XSM) support.
- **Suspend** Xen 3.2 added ACPI S3 suspend-to-RAM support for the host system.
- **PCI passthrough** Xen 3.2 added the first preliminary release of PCI passthrough support (assuming supported hardware).
- **Bootloader** Xen 3.2 added a preliminary release for a wider range of bootloaders in fully virtualized (HVM) guests, using a full emulation of x86 "real mode."
- **Faster graphics** Xen 3.2 included faster standard (nonsuper) VGA modes for HVM guests.
- **Timers** Xen 3.2 added support for configurable timer modes for HVM guests.

Xen 3.3 Like the 3.1 and 3.2 releases, the Xen 3.3 release was not as significant as the 3.0 release, but it probably had the most new features of any of the minor releases:

- **Power management** Xen 3.3 added power management for P- and C-states to the hypervisor. In CPU terms, P-states are operational states and C-states are idle states.
- **PVGrub** Xen 3.3 added support for booting the PV (paravirtualized) kernels using the actual grub inside the PV domain instead of the host grub.
- **PV performance** Xen 3.3 improved paravirtualized performance by removing the domain lock from the pagetable-update paths.

- **Shadow3** Xen 3.3 optimized the shadow pagetable algorithm to improve performance.
- **Hardware assist** Xen 3.3 added hardware-assisted paging enhancements, including 2MB page support to improve large memory performance.
- **PVSCSI drivers** Xen 3.3 allowed for SCSI access directly into the PV guests rather than through a translation layer through PVSCSI drivers.
- **Device passthrough** Xen 3.3 added miscellaneous driver enhancements to allow device passthrough rather than through a translation layer, including multiqueue support on NICs.
- **Full x86** Xen 3.3 added full x86 real-mode emulation for HVM guests on Intel VT, allowing for a wider range of legacy guest OSs.

Xen 3.4 Xen 3.4 was the release used by Oracle in Oracle VM 2.2. The Xen 3.4 release did not introduce any major new features but did improve many existing features:

- **Device passthrough** Xen 3.4 added more enhancements started in the Xen 3.3 release.
- **Offlining** Xen 3.4 added support for CPU and memory offlining, where unused CPUs and memory can be "turned off" to save resources.
- **Power management** Xen 3.4 enhanced the power management features introduced in Xen 3.3, including scheduler and timers optimized for peak power savings.
- **Hyper-V** Xen 3.4 added support for the Viridian (Hyper-V) enlightenment interface.

Xen 4.*x*

As with the other major releases of Xen, the Xen 4.0 had a number of significant and minor features. These features increased the ability of Oracle VM to be an enterprise virtualization platform. The evolution of Xen has increased its ability to participate in the virtualization market as well.

This section covers the history of Xen 4.*x* in more detail.

Xen 4.0 Xen 4.0 added upgrades and features that create a more robust and improved platform. Xen 4.0 included many features that were required for enterprise computing, including the following:

- **Performance and scalability** Xen 4.0 added support for 128 CPUs and 1TB of RAM on a physical server. It also added support for up to 128 vCPUs and 512GB of RAM per guest operating system. This support was important for larger applications such as databases.
- **Hardware support** Xen 4.0 provided support for improved IOMMU PCI passthrough using hardware-accelerated I/O virtualization techniques for Intel VT-d and AMD IOMMU.
- **Online operations** Xen 4.0 provided support for online resizing of guest disks without reboot/shutdown.
- **Hot-plug** Xen 4.0 provided RAS (Reliability, Availability, and Serviceability) features such as hot-plug CPU and memory.

Xen 4.1 Xen 4.1 added upgrades and features that create a more robust and improved platform. Xen 4.1 is not as significant as Xen 4.0, but is still important. Its features include the following:

- **CPU pools** Xen 4.1 added support for CPU pools to allow for hard partitioning. This is very significant for Oracle database licensing.

- **AVX** Xen 4.1 provided support for x86 Advanced Vector eXtension (AVX), which allows for more complex CPU instructions.

- **Jumbo frames** Support for jumbo frames was fixed in Xen 4.1.

Xen 4.2 Xen 4.2 added some scalability and performance improvements:

- **Performance and scalability** Xen 4.2 added support for 4095 CPUs and 5TB of RAM on physical servers. It also added support for up to 128 vCPUs and 512GB of RAM per PV guests operating systems, and 256 vCPUs and 1TB of RAM for HVM guests. This support was important for larger applications such as databases.

Xen 4.3 Xen 4.3 added some new features, including an experimental feature:

- **Experimental support for ARM Virtualization** Xen 4.3 added development support for ARM processors; however, no production usage was supported because hardware for ARM processors was not available.

- **NUMA-aware scheduling** Xen 4.3 allowed the Xen scheduler to prefer a CPU that a process was previously run on, so the VM would at least try to run on the CPU where its memory resided.

- **Support for openvswitch** Openvswitch is a new networking bridging mechanism.

Xen 4.4 Xen 4.4 has added several new features aimed at improving performance and scalability:

- **Solid libvirt support for libxl** Xen 4.4 has improved the interface between libvirt and libx.

- **Improved Xen event channel** Xen 4.4 has added support for a scalable event channel interface.

- **Hypervisor ABI for ARM support** Xen 4.4 has improved the hypervisor ABI for ARM support, but it is still not available for production.

- **Nested virtualization** Xen 4.4 has improved nested virtualization so it is now ready for tech review and will soon be available in production.

This history of the Xen virtualization monitor shows the dynamic nature of virtualization technology and the care taken to provide the latest and greatest features possible. In addition to the features provided by Xen, Oracle has added a management console designed to assist with the use and management of Xen and Oracle VM. The next section describes the additional features provided by Oracle.

NOTE
Oracle VM does not immediately integrate new versions of Xen because the value of Oracle VM over the base Xen distribution is rock-solid stability for enterprise use. Oracle fully tests every new Xen feature before using it in Oracle VM. New features can be manually enabled by modifying the vm.cfg file or by using the Xen APIs directly. Oracle, however, does not support this.

Oracle VM Features

Oracle VM is based on the Xen Hypervisor, but there is more to Oracle VM than just the server software itself. Oracle has taken the Xen Hypervisor and added enhancements and fixes as well as improved the management of the virtualized environment. Oracle VM is made up of two components: the Oracle VM Server and the Oracle VM Manager.

Oracle VM Server

The Oracle VM Server has been enhanced to provide better manageability, scalability, and supportability. In addition to modifying the Xen Hypervisor for their own product, Oracle's engineering team contributes to the development of the mainstream Xen software.

Oracle VM Server Features

The Oracle VM Server is the application that actually manages and runs the virtual guests. The Oracle VM Server, which is installed on a bare-metal system, consists of the Xen Hypervisor, a dom0 guest that is used for management and monitoring, and includes the Oracle Virtual Server (OVS) agent that runs within dom0. As you will see throughout this book, the Oracle VM Manager is what really makes much of Oracle VM work. Features of the Oracle VM Server include the following:

- **High availability**   You can configure resources to restart guests on another host if the underlying host fails.
- **Live migration**   You can relocate guests from one host to another with no loss of service. This feature is great for load balancing as well as system maintenance. Oracle VM is the only virtualization technology that performs live migration using an encrypted connection, thus providing an additional layer of security.

NOTE
The server pool must be created with encryption, which does increase the time it takes to perform the migration.

- **Distributed Power Management**   The Distributed Power Management system allows VMs to be automatically migrated off of lightly used servers so that they can be powered off during light load times.
- **Distributed Resource Scheduler**   This allows VMs to be migrated in order to allow for busy servers to offload VMs to servers with more resources available.

- **Load balancing**   If configured, Oracle VM automatically load balances upon guest startup, thus providing the best overall performance to the VM farm by maximizing resource utilization.

- **Performance**   Oracle VM is optimized for performance, and the Xen Hypervisor is among the fastest forms of virtualization.

- **Rapid provisioning**   Through the use of cloning and virtual machine templates, Oracle VM can quickly and efficiently create new guest systems.

- **VM templates**   Oracle provides a wide range of preconfigured virtual machine templates that can take the guesswork out of configuration. These templates are available from Oracle.com. You can customize downloaded templates, and you can also create completely custom templates based on an Oracle VM guest you create on your own.

- **Fault tolerance**   Oracle provides a number of features to offer high availability and disaster recovery to both the host servers and the virtual machines. These features are covered in detail in this book.

These features and more are covered in detail throughout the remainder of this book. In the next chapter, the Oracle VM/Xen architecture is covered in detail.

VM Guest Support

Oracle VM 3.*x* supports a full range of guest operating systems using hardware virtualization, as listed in Table 2-1. Using paravirtualized drivers will improve the performance of the system by avoiding the execution of unnecessary code.

Guest OS	32-bit Virtualized Hardware	32-bit Virtualized Hardware with PV Drivers	64-bit Virtualized Hardware	64-bit Virtualized Hardware with PV Drivers
Oracle Linux (OL) 7.*x*			•	•
Oracle Linux (OL) 4.*x*, 5.*x*, and 6.*x*	•	•	•	•
Solaris 11.*x*				•
Solaris 10.*x*		•		•
Red Hat Enterprise Linux (RHEL) 7.*x*			•	•
Red Hat Enterprise Linux 6.*x* and earlier	•	•	•	•
CentOS 4.*x*, 5.*x*, and 6.*x*	•	•	•	•
SUSE Linux Enterprise Server 11.*x*	•	•	•	•

TABLE 2-1.   *Supported Linux and UNIX OSs Using Hardware Virtualization*

Guest OS	32-bit PV	64-bit PV
Oracle Linux (OL) 7.x		
Oracle Linux (OL) 4.x, 5.x, and 6.x	•	•
Solaris 11.x		
Solaris 10.x		
Red Hat Enterprise Linux (RHEL) 7.x		
Red Hat Enterprise Linux 6.x and earlier	•	•
CentOS 4.x, 5.x, and 6.x	•	•
SUSE Linux Enterprise Server 11.x		•

TABLE 2-2.   *Supported Linux and UNIX OSs Using Paravirtualization*

NOTE
On 32-bit CPUs, only 32-bit guests are allowed.

Oracle VM 3.x also supports a full range of guest operating systems using paravirtualization, as listed in Table 2-2.

NOTE
No Microsoft operating systems are fully paravirtualized. Although PV drivers are available for Windows XP/2003/Vista/2008, as shown in Table 2-3, having a PV driver is different from having a paravirtualized operating system delivered from Microsoft.

Guest OS	32-bit PV	64-bit PV
Microsoft Windows Server 2012 R2		•
Microsoft Windows Server 2012		•
Microsoft Windows Server 2008 R2 SP1		•
Microsoft Windows Server 2008 SP2	•	•
Microsoft Windows Server 2003 R2 SP2	•	•
Microsoft Windows 8.1	•	•
Microsoft Windows 8	•	•
Microsoft Windows 7 SP1	•	•

TABLE 2-3.   *Supported Windows OSs Using Paravirtualized Drivers*

Host Hardware Requirements

In order for Oracle VM to run effectively, there are some minimum requirements on the class of machine; however, most modern systems will work. Here are the requirements:

- **Host platforms**   Oracle VM currently supports Intel and AMD x86 and x86_64 platforms. The minimum CPU is the i686; however, to run HVM fully virtualized guests, you must use CPUs with virtualization acceleration. Intel CPUs indicate virtualization acceleration with the "vmx" flag and the AMD processors with the "svm" flag.

NOTE
This book covers Oracle VM for the x86 platform. Oracle VM is also available for the SPARC platform as well, but is implemented differently.

- **Memory**   The amount of memory should be proportional to the size and number of VMs. Currently, Oracle VM Server supports a maximum of 6TB of RAM. Of this 6TB of RAM, you can allocate 500GB to a PVM 64-bit guest, 1TB to an HVM 64-bit guest, 2TB to a PVHVM guest, and 64GB of RAM to a 32-bit guest.

- **CPUs**   As mentioned previously, having CPUs that support virtualization is advantageous. A minimum of one CPU is required, but this number is not suitable for more than one or two guests. A maximum of 384 CPUs is currently supported. The best practice is to reserve one core for dom0 and use the remaining cores/processors for the domU virtual machines.

- **Disk support**   Oracle VM currently supports SCSI, SAS, IDE/SATA, NAS, iSCSI, FC, and limited support for Fibre Channel over Ethernet (FCoE) storage.

Chapter 4 contains more detailed information on how to properly determine the number of CPUs and the amount of memory needed for particular applications.

Oracle VM Manager

A major feature of Oracle VM is the management console, which is called the Oracle VM Manager. The Oracle VM Manager is a web-based application that you use to monitor and configure the entire VM farm. You install and configure the Oracle VM Manager on a Linux system. This Linux host can be a standalone server or a virtual machine; however, if you choose to install the Oracle VM Manager on an Oracle VM guest, you will have to manage that VM manually. That is, you cannot start the guest via the console because it is hosting the console. Of course, the VM where Oracle VM Manager is installed can be managed by another Oracle VM server pool or even a VMware or KVM guest.

You can download the standalone Oracle VM Manager from the same location as the Oracle VM Server (www.oracle.com). Since release 5, Oracle VM Manager has also been incorporated into Oracle Enterprise Manager (OEM) Grid Control with the Oracle VM Management Pack. OEM Grid Control with the VM Management Pack allows for centralized management and monitoring of hosts, databases, applications, and virtual machines. You can see an example of the standalone Oracle VM Manager in Figure 2-1. The VM Manager console is where you perform operations such as creating, starting, stopping, live migrating, and deleting Oracle VM guests.

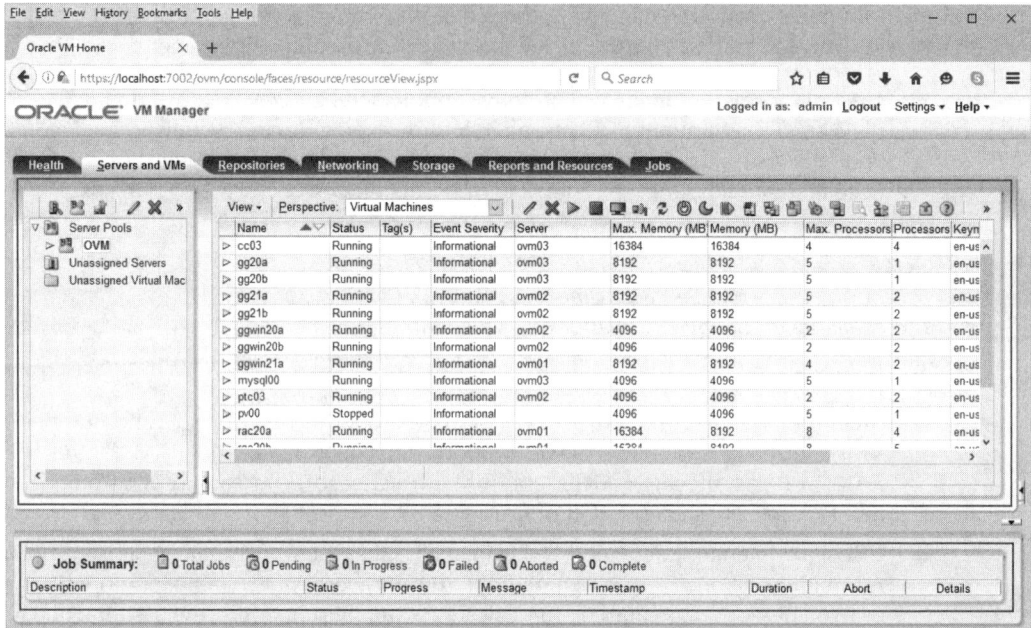

FIGURE 2-1. *Oracle VM Manager*

In addition to the Oracle VM Manager, command-line utilities are available. These command-line utilities let you script and easily modify and save operations. Later in this book, we cover the standalone Oracle VM Manager (Chapter 10), the command-line utilities (Chapter 11), and Cloud Control (Chapters 23, 24, and 25) in detail.

Oracle Support for VM

Currently, Oracle VM is available free of charge. Oracle derives its revenue from selling subscriptions for Linux support, which includes Oracle VM as well as other Oracle open-source products. You'll find both advantages and disadvantages to going the "single vendor" route with software deployments. By deploying Oracle VM, Oracle Enterprise Linux (OEL), and Oracle applications and purchasing Oracle support, you only have one place to go in the event of a failure. The disadvantage is lack of selection.

On the other hand, Oracle support is still available if you use Red Hat Enterprise Linux. If you purchase Oracle support for Red Hat Enterprise Linux, your updates will come from Oracle's servers, not Red Hat's. After running the up2date utility on the Red Hat server, you'll see no differences between the Red Hat installation and an OEL installation. Oracle keeps OEL in lock-step with Red Hat at all times.

As with all Oracle products, Oracle stands behind its software. In addition, to assist customers rapidly, Oracle offers Advance Customer Services. These services include assessment and planning services, deployment, and ongoing support and/or monitoring if you desire. The level of support you get is based on your individual needs.

Oracle is committed to ongoing virtualization support and to supporting the open-source community in this area. After all, with virtualization comes a whole range of advantages, including power and cooling reduction, centralized management, and optimized provisioning. All these advantages are covered in this book.

Oracle's VM Template Library

One of the most exciting advantages of Oracle VM is the extensive Template Library. Oracle not only supplies the VM system, but also the operating system, database software, applications, and so on, as well as preconfigured templates. These templates allow you to deploy applications rapidly because part of the work has already been done for you. The Oracle VM Template Library is available at Oracle.com in the software download section.

Oracle's preconfigured templates are easy to deploy and configure. Each template is designed for a specific application stack and, as such, has been tested and validated. Thus, these templates make downloading, deploying, and running applications easy.

After you've downloaded the templates from the Oracle website, you can easily import them into the Oracle VM Manager. Once these templates are imported into the Oracle VM Manager, you can configure new guests from them. We'll cover how to create guest systems from templates in Chapter 18. Once you have created the virtual machine, it is just a matter of configuring and deploying the guest.

The Oracle Template Library is divided into 64-bit and 32-bit templates. You might find it a little surprising, but a lot of software still has not been ported to 64-bit Linux. This includes some Oracle products as well. This section provides a brief overview of the 32-bit and 64-bit templates that are currently available at the writing of this book.

Most of the VM templates provided by Oracle are "Just enough OS" (JeOS) installations, based on the Oracle standard of installing just the components needed to perform the task at hand. This not only provides for an efficient OS deployment but also helps to meet security standards as well.

Oracle 64-bit VM Templates

The Oracle VM 32-bit templates are only available in archives and are not readily available for download any longer. All templates are now 64-bit.

The following 64-bit Oracle VM templates are available from http://www.oracle.com/technetwork/server-storage/vm/templates. The number of templates is always increasing, and there are too many to list. Therefore, only a sample of the categories and templates are listed here:

- Oracle Enterprise Manager 12c and 13c
- Oracle VM Manager
- Oracle VM Template Builder
- Oracle VM Server
- Sun Ray Software
- Oracle Secure Global Desktop
- Oracle VM Templates for Exalogic

- E-Business Suite (multiple versions)
- E-Business Suite for Oracle Exalogic (multiple versions)
- JD Edwards and Tools (multiple versions)
- Oracle Peoplesoft
- Oracle Business Intelligence Enterprise Edition
- Oracle Application Server
- Oracle Fusion Middleware
- Oracle Database 12c and 11g both Stand-Alone and RAC
- MySQL Enterprise Edition
- Oracle Linux (multiple versions)
- Oracle Solaris (multiple versions)
- Brocade Virtual Traffic Manager

Many 64-bit templates are available currently, and more are being added.

Oracle has provided an extensive set of preconfigured templates. These templates are built using the JeOS (Just enough OS) Linux software and configuration scripts necessary to deploy the system and the application. Specifics on how to use many of these templates and how to use templates in general are provided in Chapter 18.

Summary

This chapter continued our introduction to virtualization, and Oracle VM in particular. The chapter began by explaining more about what Oracle VM is. You cannot understand what Oracle VM is without also understanding what Xen and the Xen Hypervisor are. This chapter gave a brief introduction into those concepts and also touched on Oracle's support for virtualization and the open-source manner in which Xen is developed and supported.

The chapter concluded with an overview of the Oracle Template Library. This template library provides a way to download and deploy a complete virtualization environment quickly and easily. These templates are built using the Oracle JeOS Linux distribution. In addition, most of the templates include preinstalled applications that are ready to be configured and deployed. Of course, these templates might need customizing, which will be covered in Chapter 17.

The next chapter explores the Oracle VM architecture, including not only the architecture of the VM Server and VM Manager but the Xen Hypervisor architecture as well. By understanding how Xen and Oracle VM work, you will better understand how to configure and tune them.

CHAPTER
3

Oracle VM Architecture

D iscussing the Oracle VM architecture is difficult without also including the Xen architecture, the underlying technology. In this chapter, you learn about the different components of both. By understanding how the components work, you can administer, tune, and size the virtual environments within the Oracle VM system more effectively.

Oracle VM Architecture

Oracle VM is a virtualization system that consists of both industry-standard, open-source components (mainly the Xen Hypervisor) and Oracle enhancements. Oracle does not use the stock Xen Hypervisor. Oracle has performed significant modifications and contributes to the open-source Xen Hypervisor development. In addition to Xen utilities, Oracle provides its own utilities and products to enhance and optimize Oracle VM. Oracle also continues to acquire new companies that provide new technology to improve Oracle VM.

As discussed in previous chapters, the Oracle VM system is made up of two components: the Oracle VM Manager, which can be installed on either a standalone server or a virtual machine, and the Oracle VM Server, as shown in Figure 3-1.

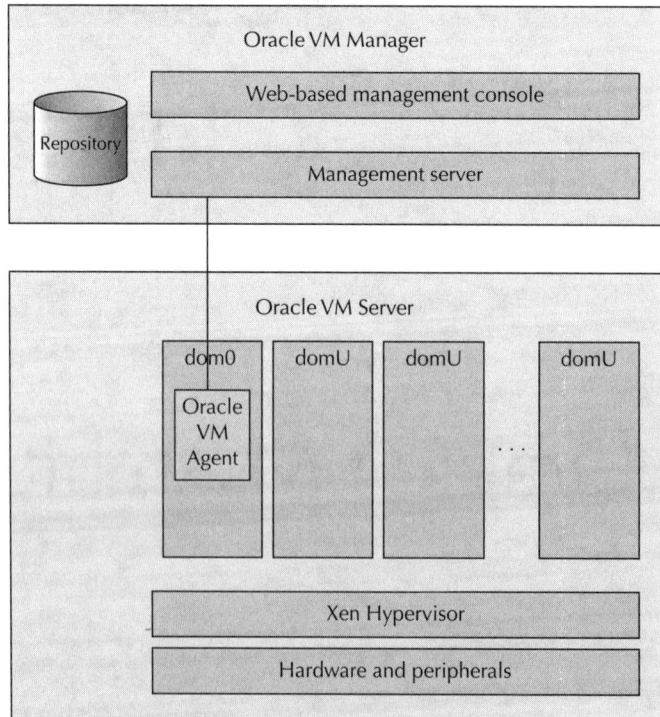

FIGURE 3-1. *Oracle VM architecture*

The Oracle VM Server consists of a bare-metal installation of the Xen Hypervisor, which is a lightweight hypervisor that sits between the virtual machines and the hardware. By default, a special virtual machine called dom0 is installed. This virtual machine has special access to communicate with the hypervisor. As you will see later, dom0 plays a vital role in controlling all other virtual machines.

Oracle VM allows for multiple hardware systems to provide virtualization services beyond what a single server can provide. Oracle VM does this by creating a set of servers that work together in a server pool. A group of servers providing services that far exceed the capabilities of a single server is known as a *server farm* or *data center*. In addition, Oracle has vastly increased the amount of resources that can be utilized by an Oracle VM Server and allocated to a single guest virtual machine. This continues to increase with each new release.

Servers and Server Pools

A server pool is made up of one or more virtual machine servers. Traditionally, a server pool master was required, however, beginning with OVM 3.4, the server pool master has been deprecated. Now the OVM Manager communicates with the OVM Agent on each server in the server pool directly. When using more than one server in a server pool, it is best practice to configure it as a clustered server pool.

NOTE
Although it is possible to set up multiple servers in a nonclustered server pool sharing NFS storage, this can lead to issues.

The server pool master (OVM 3.3 and earlier) controls the server pool, and the virtual machine server supports virtual machines. The server pool is a collection of systems that are designed to provide virtualization services and that serve specific purposes. A server pool is defined by a single Oracle VM Manager and shares some common resources, such as storage. By sharing storage, the load of running virtual machines (VM guests) can be easily shared among the virtual servers that are members of the server pool. Without a shared disk, a server pool can exist on only one server.

Server Pool Shared Storage

You can create a virtualization environment made up of multiple host servers as a single server pool or as multiple server pools. How you configure them is determined by several factors. As mentioned earlier, a shared disk subsystem is required. This shared disk system must have some type of hardware that can share disk storage safely—typically either SAN or NAS storage. When SAN storage is used, the disks are configured with the OCFS2 filesystem. Because OCFS2, which stands for Oracle Cluster File System 2, is a clustered filesystem, the sharing among VM servers functions properly.

When using Network Attached Storage (NAS) for Oracle VM guest storage repositories, you have a couple different options. NAS can be configured as either NFS or iSCSI. If NAS presents Network File System (NFS) storage, the Oracle VM Server can use that storage directly because NFS is inherently shared. If the storage is presented as iSCSI, then Oracle VM will format it as OCFS2, just like SAN storage. A clustered filesystem is required because of the shared nature of the VM server pool. When using NFS as a repository source, Oracle VM will use the distributed lock manager (DLM) from OCFS2 to handle file locking for cluster server pools. This locking service is called *dm-nfs*.

If you use a single host for the VM Server, you can use local storage. In a single-server environment, there is no need to share the VM guest storage. However, in a single-host environment, neither load balancing nor high availability is possible. By default, the Oracle VM Server installation uses the remainder of the hard drive to create a single, large OCFS2 partition for /OVS, where the virtual machines are stored.

Server Pool Requirements

In addition to shared storage, you must create the server pool on hardware that has the same architecture and supports the same hardware virtualization features. You cannot place a system with hardware virtualization into a server pool with a system that does not support hardware virtualization features. You can have up to 16 server pools controlled or owned by a single Oracle VM Manager, and each server pool can use servers from completely different manufacturers or that are completely different models.

NOTE
The Oracle VM Manager does not specifically prohibit the creation of a mixed environment. It is possible to create a server pool with mixed architectures. But when the time comes to restart a virtual machine, or to live migrate a virtual machine to a new host, Oracle VM will perform a runtime check and disallow restarting or moving to a different architecture, which is why a mixed environment is not recommended.

Although not required, it is a good idea to create a server pool of the same speed and number of processors per system. This setup allows for better load balancing. Mixing various performance levels of VM servers can skew load balancing. Therefore, creating a server pool of similarly configured systems is a good idea.

Always consider the requirements of the largest VM. In order for High Availability (HA) to work (or for live migration), you need another server with sufficient resources. If a virtual machine has been granted 32 vCPUs, and only one server in the pool has that many vCPUs, then the virtual machine cannot be restarted or moved. This is not an argument for using larger servers in the pool as much as it is an argument for using horizontal scaling. Databases can use Real Application Clusters (RAC), and middleware can use its own clustering to keep vCPU and RAM requirements per VM reasonable.

Configuring the Server Pool

You can create server pools based on both the available hardware and the type of business use. If no shared storage is available, you can create individual server pools. If the hardware is diverse, you can create individual server pools. You can also create server pools based on how the hardware and the VM guests will be used. The recommended approach, however, is to create one or more VM Server farms that can support the entire environment.

If the VM Server farm needs to support VMs for many different departments, you might find it beneficial to create a separate server pool for each group of virtual machines. This setup creates both a physical and logical separation of systems. In other cases, where each group only has a few virtual machines, sharing all of the virtual machines in one server pool might be beneficial. Planning and architecting an Oracle VM environment is covered in more detail in the next chapter.

The primary factor when designing server pools is normalizing the loads on the pool. For example, you should mix virtual machines with high CPU use but low disk I/O with virtual machines that need high disk I/O but low CPU. You can also design a server pool to handle one type of load (for example, a compute cluster). In this case, servers are provisioned with a lot of CPU and memory but with inexpensive Network Attached Storage instead of expensive SAN resources.

The Oracle VM server pool is made up of one or more virtual machine servers, one or more utility servers, and a single server pool master (OVM 3.3 and earlier). Let's look at these server roles in more detail.

Oracle VM Server   The virtual machine server is the core of the Oracle VM server pool. The virtual machine server is the Oracle VM component that hosts the virtual machines. The Oracle VM Server is responsible for running one or more virtual machines and is installed on bare metal, leaving only a very small layer of software between the hardware and the virtual machines. This is known as the *hypervisor.* Included with the Oracle VM Server is a small Linux OS, which is used to assist with managing the hypervisor and virtual machines. This special Linux system is called *domain 0* or *dom0.*

The terms *domain, guest, VM guest,* and *virtual machine* are sometimes used interchangeably, but there are slight differences in meaning. The *domain* is the set of resources on which the virtual machine runs. These resources were defined when the domain was created and include CPU, memory, and disk. The term *guest* or *VM guest* defines the virtual machine that is running inside the domain. A guest can be Linux, Solaris, or Windows and can be fully virtualized or paravirtualized. A *virtual machine* is the OS and application software that runs within the guest. Visit the Oracle virtualization website at http://www.oracle.com/us/technologies/virtualization/oraclevm/overview/index.html for the most up-to-date support information.

Dom0 is a small Linux distribution that contains the Oracle VM Agent. In addition, dom0 is visible to the underlying shared storage that is used for the VMs. Dom0 is also used to manage the network connections and all of the virtual machine and server configuration files. Because it serves a special purpose, you should not modify or use it for purposes other than managing the virtual machines.

In addition to the dom0 virtual machine, the VM Server also supports one or more virtual machines or domains. These are known as *domU* or *user domains.* The different domains and how they run are covered in more detail in the "Xen Architecture" section of this chapter. The Oracle VM domains are illustrated in Figure 3-2.

The VM Server's main responsibility is to host virtual machines. Many of the management responsibilities and support functions are handled by the Oracle VM Agent.

Oracle VM Agent   The Oracle VM Agent is used to manage the VM Servers that are part of the Oracle VM system. The Oracle VM Agent communicates with the Oracle VM Manager and manages the virtual machines that run on the VM Server. The VM Agent consists of two components: the server pool master and the virtual machine server. These two components exist in the Oracle VM Agent but don't necessarily run on all VM servers.

Server Pool Master (OVM 3.3 and Earlier)   The server that currently has the server pool master role is responsible for coordinating the actions of the server pool. The server pool master receives requests from the Oracle VM Manager and performs actions such as starting VMs and performing

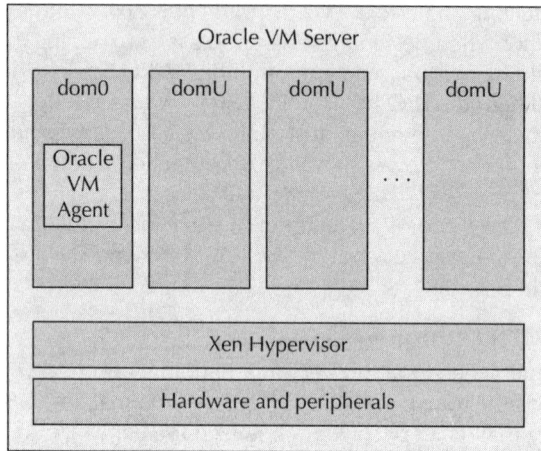

FIGURE 3-2. *Oracle VM domains*

load balancing. The VM Manager communicates with the server pool manager, and the server pool manager then communicates with the virtual machine servers via the VM Agents. As mentioned earlier, you can only have one server pool master in a server pool. In addition, the server pool master has been deprecated in OVM 3.4. Now the OVM Manager communicates with the OVM Agent on all virtual machine servers.

Virtual Machine Server   The virtual machine server is responsible for controlling the VM Server virtual machines. It performs operations such as starting and stopping the virtual machines It also collects performance information from the virtual machines and the underlying host operating systems. The virtual machine server controls the virtual machines. Because the virtual machines are actually part of the Oracle-enhanced Xen Hypervisor, this topic is covered in the "Xen Architecture" section, later in this chapter.

Oracle VM Manager

The Oracle VM Manager is an enhancement that provides a web-based graphical user interface (GUI) where you can configure and manage Oracle VM Servers and virtual machines. The Oracle VM Manager is a standalone application that you can install on a Linux system. In addition, Oracle provides another way to manage virtual machines via an add-on to Oracle Enterprise Manager (OEM) Cloud Control. Both options are covered in this book.

The Oracle VM Manager allows you to perform all aspects of managing, creating, and deploying virtual machines with Oracle VM. In addition, the Oracle VM Manager provides the ability to monitor a large number of virtual machines and easily determine the status of those machines. This monitoring is limited to the status of the virtual machines.

When using OEM Cloud Control, you have the additional advantage of using the enterprise-wide system-monitoring capabilities of this application as well. Within OEM Cloud Control, not only are you able to manage virtual machines through the VM Manager screens, but also you can add each virtual machine as a host target, as well as any applications that it might be running. In addition, OEM management packs can provide more extensive monitoring and alerting functions.

The VM Manager can perform a number of tasks, among which is virtual machine lifecycle management. Lifecycle management refers to the lifecycle of the virtual machine as it changes states. The most simple of these states are creation, power on, power off, and then deletion. Many other states and actions can occur within a virtual machine. The full range of lifecycle management states are covered in Chapter 4. The VM Manager is shown in Figure 3-3.

Users and Roles

A user account is required to access and use the Oracle VM Manager. Users can be assigned the following roles, each having a different level of privilege:

- **User**   The user role is granted permission to create and manage virtual machines. In addition, the user role has permission to import resources.

- **Manager**   The manager role has all of the privileges of the user role. In addition, the manager role has permission to manage server pools, servers, and resources.

- **Administrator**   The administrator role has all of the privileges of the manager role. In addition, the administrator role is responsible for managing user accounts, importing resources, and approving imported resources.

Administering users is done via the ovm_admin command-line utility.

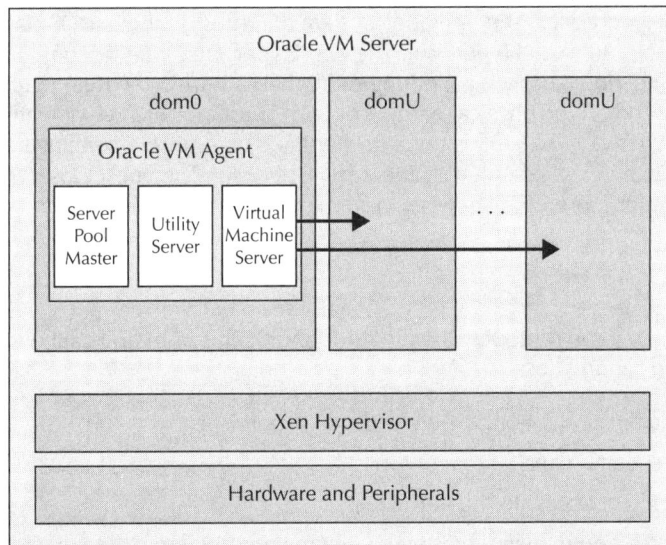

FIGURE 3-3.   *The VM Manager*

Management Methods

You have several options for managing Oracle VM Manager, including the Oracle VM Manager GUI tool and the Oracle Enterprise Manager Cloud Control add-in for Oracle VM. You can also use an Oracle VM command-line tool from Oracle. Finally, you can use the Xen tools built into the Oracle VM Server. Which tool is right for you varies based on what you are trying to do.

For monitoring the Oracle VM system, a graphical tool is often the most efficient and easiest to use. You can quickly see the state of the system and determine if there are problems. You can sort and group the virtual machines by their server pool and determine the current resource consumption on the underlying hardware easily. In addition, performing tasks such as creating virtual machines is very straightforward with the assistance of wizards.

Xen Architecture

The core of the Oracle VM system is the software that runs the virtual machines. This software is the Xen virtualization system, which consists of the Xen Hypervisor and support software. Xen is a virtual machine monitor for x86, x86_64, Intel Itanium, and PowerPC architectures (Oracle only supports the x86_64 architecture). At the core of the Xen virtualization system is the Xen Hypervisor.

NOTE
For the purposes of this book, the terms x86 and x86_64 are interchangeable. With OVM 3.x, only the 64-bit architecture is supported. The terms x86 and x86_64 both refer to the 64-bit architecture.

The Xen Hypervisor is the operating system that runs on the bare-metal server. The guest OSs are on top of the Xen Hypervisor. The Xen Hypervisor, after booting, immediately loads one virtual machine, dom0, which is nothing more than a standard virtual machine but with privileges to access and control the physical hardware. Each guest runs its own operating system, independent of the Xen Hypervisor. This OS is not a further layer of a single operating system, but a distinct operating system being executed by the Xen Hypervisor. The guest OSs consist of a single dom0 guest and zero or more domU guests. In Xen terminology, a guest operating system is called a *domain.*

Dom0

The first domain to be started is domain 0, or dom0. This domain has the following special privileges and capabilities:

- Boots first and automatically with the hypervisor
- Has special management privileges
- Has direct access to the hardware
- Can see and manage the storage where the virtual machine images are stored
- Contains network and I/O drivers used by the domU systems

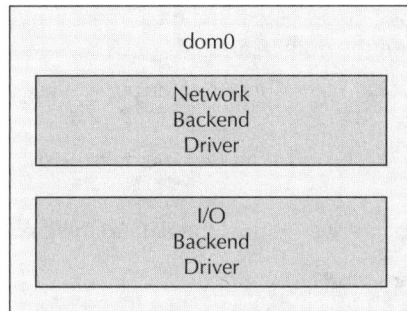

FIGURE 3-4. *Backend drivers*

The Oracle VM dom0 is a Just enough OS (JeOS) Oracle Enterprise Linux (OEL) operating system with the utilities and applications necessary to manage the Oracle VM environment. The Oracle VM Server installation media installs dom0, which is a 32-bit OEL system including the Oracle VM Agent. The 32-bit system is installed even on 64-bit hardware.

In the small Linux OS, dom0 contains two special drivers, known as *backend drivers:* the backend network driver and the backend I/O or block driver. You can see both in Figure 3-4. Oracle calls these the *netback* and *netfront* drivers and the *blkback* and *blkfront* drivers, respectively.

The network backend driver (netback) communicates directly with the hardware and takes requests from the domU guests and processes them via one of the network bridges that have been created. The block backend driver (blkback) communicates with the local storage and takes I/O requests from the domU systems and processes them. For this reason, dom0 must be up and running before the guest virtual machines can start.

DomU

All of the other guest virtual machines are known as *domU* or *user domain guests*. If they are paravirtualized guests, they are known as *domU PV guests*. Hardware virtualized guests are known as *domU HVM guests*. Access to the I/O and network is handled slightly differently, depending on whether the guest is a paravirtualized or a hardware virtualized system.

PV Network and I/O

The paravirtualized guest has a network and a block PV driver that communicates with the network and block drivers on the dom0 system via shared memory that resides in the hypervisor. The PV driver on the domU system shares this memory with the PV driver on the dom0 system. The dom0 system then receives a request from domU via an event channel that exists between the two domains. Here are a few examples for a PV read and write.

DomU Read Operation   A domU read operation uses the event channel to signal the PV block driver on dom0, which fulfills the I/O operation. Here are the basic steps to perform a read:

1. An I/O request is made to the PV block driver on the domU system.

2. The guest PV block driver issues an interrupt through the event channel to the dom0 PV block driver, requesting the data.

3. The dom0 PV block driver receives the request and reads the data from disk.

4. The dom0 PV block driver places the data in memory in the hypervisor that is shared between dom0 and the domU guest.

5. The dom0 PV block driver issues an interrupt to the domU PV block driver via the event channel.

6. The domU PV block driver retrieves the data from the memory shared with the dom0 PV block driver.

7. The domU PV block driver returns the data to the calling process within the guest.

This process is illustrated in Figure 3-5.

Even though this process seems sophisticated, it is an efficient way to perform I/O in a paravirtualized environment. Until the newer hardware virtualization enhancements were introduced, paravirtualization provided the most performance possible in a virtualized environment.

DomU Write Operation   The domU PV write operation is similar to the PV read operation. A domU write operation uses the event channel to signal the PV block driver on dom0, which then fulfills the I/O operation. Here are the basic steps to perform a write operation:

1. A write request is made to the PV block driver on the domU system.

2. The domU PV block driver places the data in memory in the hypervisor that is shared between the domU guest and dom0.

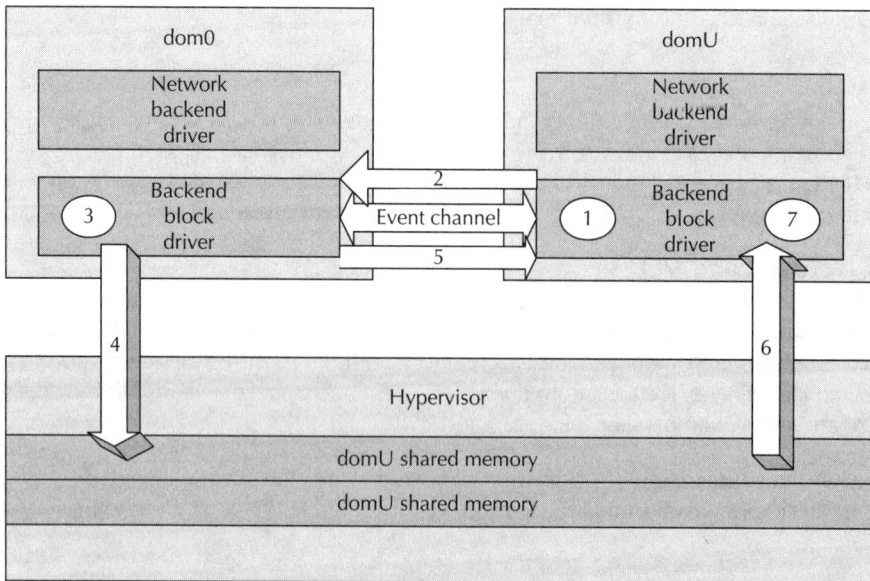

FIGURE 3-5.   *A domU read operation*

3. The guest PV block driver issues an interrupt through the event channel to the dom0 PV block driver, requesting the data be written out.

4. The dom0 PV block driver retrieves the data from the memory that is shared with the domU PV block driver.

5. The dom0 PV block driver receives the request and writes the data to disk.

6. The dom0 PV block driver issues an interrupt to the domU PV block driver via the event channel.

7. The domU PV block driver returns the success code to the calling process.

This process is illustrated in Figure 3-6.

Like the PV read operation, although this operation is somewhat complex, it is also efficient.

HVM Network and I/O

The HVM guest does not have the network and block PV drivers. Instead, a process (daemon) is started on the dom0 system for each domU guest. This daemon intercepts the network and I/O requests and performs them on behalf of the domU guest. This daemon is the Qemu-DM daemon, and it looks for calls to the disk or network and intercepts them. These calls are then processed in dom0 and eventually returned to the domU system that issued the request.

With hardware acceleration, the ability to access hardware at near native speed has been enabled. This is accomplished by taking the software interface that had been used to intercept I/O and network operations and processing it via hardware acceleration. Although it's an evolving technology, operations at nearly the speed of direct OS-to-hardware interaction have recently been performed.

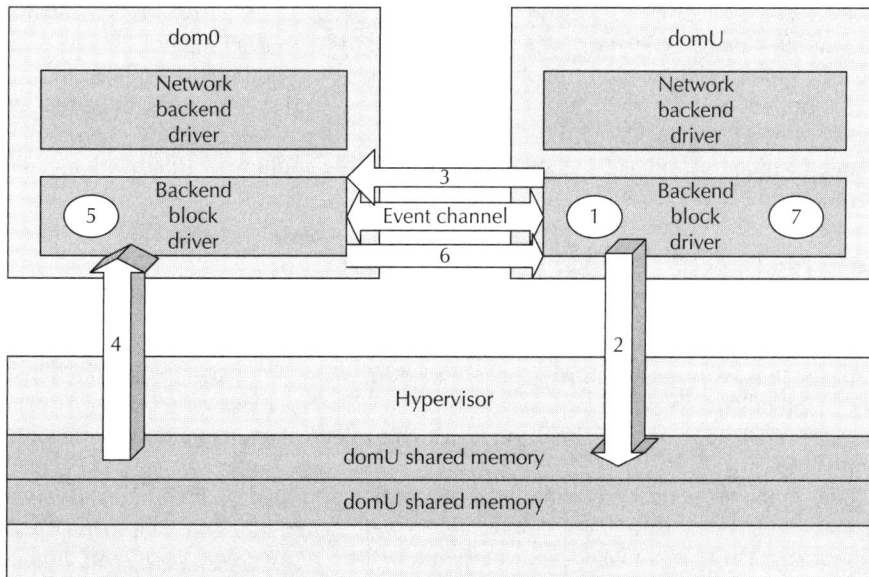

FIGURE 3-6. *A domU write operation*

Hypervisor Operations

The Xen Hypervisor handles other operations that the OS normally performs, such as memory and CPU operations. When an operation such as a memory access is performed in the virtual guest, the hypervisor intercepts it and processes it there. The guest has a pagetable that maps the virtual memory to physical memory. The guest believes that it owns the memory, but it is retranslated to point to the actual physical memory via the hypervisor.

Here is where the introduction of new hardware has really made today's virtualization possible. With the Intel VT and AMD-V architectures, the CPUs have added features to assist with some of the most common instructions, such as the virtual-to-physical translations. This advance allows a virtualized guest to perform at almost the same level as a system installed directly on the underlying hardware.

DomU-to-Dom0 Interaction

Because of the interaction between domU and dom0, several communication channels are created between the two. In a PV environment, a communication channel is created between dom0 and each domU, and a shared memory channel is created for each domU that is used for the backend drivers.

In an HVM environment, the Qemu-DM daemon handles the interception of system calls that are made. Each domU has a Qemu-DM daemon, which allows for the use of network and I/O requests from the virtual machine.

Networking

With Oracle VM/Xen, each physical network interface card in the underlying server has one bridge called an *xenbr* that acts like a virtual switch. Within the domain, a virtual interface card connects to the bridge, which then allows connectivity to the outside world. Multiple domains can share the same Xen bridge, and a domain can be connected to multiple bridges. The default is to map one xenbr to each physical interface, but through trunking/bonding, you can and should (it is recommended) take multiple physical NICs and present them as a single xenbr.

The bridges and Ethernet cards are visible to the dom0 system and can be modified there if needed. When the guest domain is created, a Xen bridge is selected. You can modify this later and/or add additional bridges to the guest domain. These additional bridges will appear as additional network devices, as shown in Figure 3-7.

Hardware Virtual Machine (HVM) vs. Paravirtualized Virtual Machine (PVM)

In this chapter and throughout the book, you will learn about the differences between fully virtualized and paravirtualized systems. Much debate remains over which is better to use. The fully virtualized system currently has the advantage in that you do not need to modify the OS to use this form of virtualization. In addition, both Intel and AMD have put great effort into optimizing for this type of virtualization.

Prior to the introduction of virtualization acceleration, using paravirtualization was much more efficient. Because the kernel and device drivers were aware that they were part of a virtualized environment, they were able to perform their functions more efficiently by not duplicating operations that would have to be redone at the dom0 layer. Paravirtualization, therefore, has always been seen as more efficient.

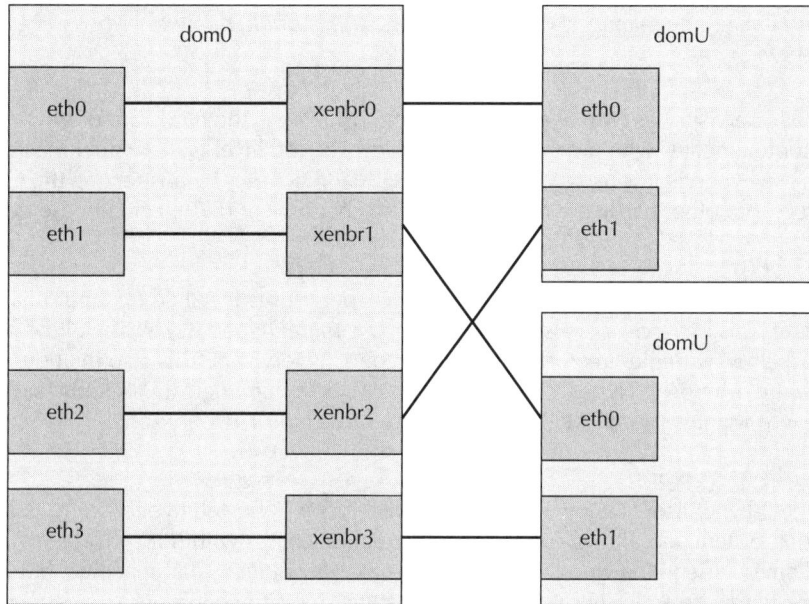

FIGURE 3-7.   *Xen networking*

With the introduction of the hardware assist technology, however, fully virtualized systems now have an advantage. Many of the traps that required software emulation are now done by the hardware, thus making it more efficient and perhaps more optimal than paravirtualization. Now work is being done to provide hardware assist technology to paravirtualization as well. The next generation of hardware and software might possibly create a fully hardware-assisted paravirtualized environment that is the most optimal.

At the current stage of technology, both paravirtualization and hardware-virtualized machine (HVM) are high performing and efficient. Choosing which to use most likely depends on your environment and your preferences. We recommend and run both paravirtualized and HVM (and now PVHVM) guests. Both choices are good ones.

Xen Hypervisor or Virtual Machine Monitor (VMM)

The Xen Hypervisor is the lowest, most innermost layer of the Xen virtualization system. The hypervisor layer communicates with the hardware and performs various functions necessary to create and maintain the virtual machines; the most basic and important of these functions is the scheduling and allocation of CPU and memory resources. This area is also where the most activity has occurred in recent years in terms of improving the performance and capacity of virtual host systems. The hypervisor abstracts the hardware for the virtual machines, thus tricking the virtual machines into thinking that they are actually controlling the hardware, when they are actually operating on a software layer. In addition, the hypervisor schedules and controls the virtual machines. The hypervisor is also known as the *virtual machine monitor (VMM)*.

NOTE
In some documentation, the virtual machine monitor is known as the virtual machine manager. *For the purposes of this book, the two terms are synonyms.*

The hypervisor has two layers. The bottommost layer is the hardware or physical layer. This layer communicates with the CPUs and memory. The top layer is the virtual machine monitor, or VMM. The hypervisor is used to manage the virtual machines by abstracting the CPU and memory resources, but other hardware resources, such as network and I/O, actually use dom0.

Type 1 Hypervisors

There are two types of hypervisors. The type 1 hypervisor is installed on, and runs directly on, the hardware. This hypervisor is also known as a *bare-metal hypervisor.* Many of the hypervisors on the market today (including Oracle VM) are type 1 hypervisors. This also includes products such as VMware, Microsoft Hyper-V, and others. The Oracle Sun Logical Domains (now known as Oracle VM Manager for SPARC) is also considered a type 1 hypervisor.

Type 2 Hypervisors

The type 2 hypervisor is known as a *hosted hypervisor.* A hosted hypervisor runs on top of an operating system and allows you to create virtual machines within its private environment. To the virtual environment, the virtual machine looks like any other virtual machine, but it is far removed from the hardware and is purely a software product. Type 2 hypervisors include VMware Server and VMware Workstation. The Oracle VM Solaris 10 container is considered a type 2 hypervisor as well.

Hypervisor Functionality

In a fully virtualized environment, the Xen Hypervisor (or VMM) uses a number of traps to intercept specific instructions that would normally be used to execute instructions on the hardware. The hypervisor traps and translates these instructions into virtualized instructions. The hypervisor looks for these instructions to be executed, and when it discovers them, it emulates the instruction in software. This happens at a very high rate and can cause significant overhead.

In a paravirtualized environment, the Xen-aware guest kernel knows it is virtualized and makes modified system calls to the hypervisor directly. This requires many kernel modifications but provides a more efficient way to perform the necessary OS functions. The paravirtualized environment is efficient and high performing.

The primary example of this is in memory management. The HVM environment believes that it is a normal OS, so it has its own pagetable and virtual-to-physical translation. In this case, the virtual-to-physical translation refers to virtual memory, not virtualization. The virtualized OS believes it has its own memory and addresses. For example, the virtualized environment might think it has 2GB of physical memory.

The pagetable contains the references between the virtualized system's virtual memory and its (virtualized) physical memory; however, the hypervisor really translates its (virtualized) physical memory into the actual physical memory. Thus, the virtual-to-physical translation call is trapped (intercepted) and run in software by the hypervisor, which translates the memory call into the actual (hardware) memory address. This is probably the most-used system operation.

This is also where the hardware assist provides the biggest boost in performance. Now, instead of the operation being trapped by the hypervisor, this operation is trapped by the hardware. Thus, the most commonly used instructions that the hypervisor typically traps are not trapped and run in the hardware, which allows for almost native performance.

Hardware Virtualization Support
Both Intel and AMD have been providing virtualization support for several years. AMD has created the AMD-V extensions to the x86_64 line, which include virtualization technology known as *Rapid Virtualization Indexing* (RVI) that allows for hardware translation of guest virtual memory. In addition, an *input/output memory management unit* (IOMMU) allows guests to use peripheral devices directly. This is accomplished through DMA and interrupt remapping.

Intel VT-x processors also include many virtualization features, including Extended Page Tables (EPT) that allow for hardware translation of guest virtual memory. Intel also includes I/O accelerations know as Virtualization Technology for Directed I/O (VT-d).

Both Intel and AMD continue to add additional support for virtualization for both performance and functionality improvements.

Features of Oracle VM

Oracle VM is a full-featured product. It is a fully functional virtualization environment that comes with an easy-to-use management console as well as a command-line interface. Here are some of the features of Oracle VM:

- **Guest support** Oracle VM supports many guests. The number of guests you can support on a single server is limited only by the memory and CPU resources available on that server.

- **Live migration** Oracle VM supports the ability to perform live migrations between different hosts in a server pool. This allows for both High Availability and load balancing.

- **Pause/resume** The pause/resume function provides the ability to manage resources in the server pool by quickly stopping and restarting virtual machines as needed.

- **Templates** The ability to obtain and utilize templates allows administrators to prepackage virtual systems that meet specific needs. The ability to download preinstalled templates from Oracle gives administrators an easy path to provide prepackaged applications.

These features make Oracle VM an optimal platform for virtualization.

Hardware Support for Oracle VM

Although the Xen architecture supports several platforms, Oracle has chosen to focus on the Intel/AMD x86_64 architecture. Since the Oracle acquisition of Sun Microsystems, Oracle has rebranded some of the virtualization technologies built into the Sun hardware and Solaris operating system as Oracle VM. The Sun virtualization technology is not covered in this book. For the purposes of this book, Oracle VM refers only to the x86 virtualization technology.

As with most software products, the Oracle VM documentation provides a minimum hardware requirement. This minimum is usually very low and does not allow for even basic usage of the product. Therefore, the hardware requirements provided in Table 3-1 include both the Oracle minimum requirements and the minimum requirements recommended by the authors.

Requirement	Oracle Recommendation	Author Recommendation
Minimum CPUs/cores	1/1	2/4
Maximum CPUs/cores	64 cores	64 cores
CPU type for paravirtualization	Intel AMD	Hardware with virtualization support, Intel VT-x, or AMD SVM
CPU type for hardware virtualized guests	Intel VT-x AMD SVM	Intel VT-x AMD SVM
Minimum/recommended memory	1GB/2GB	4GB/based on guests
Maximum memory	x86_64 (64-bit) 510GB	x86_64 (64-bit) 510GB
Supported disk type for VM files	SCSI, SAS, IDE/SATA, NAS, iSCSI, FC	SCSI, SAS, NAS, iSCSI, FC

TABLE 3-1.   *Oracle VM Actual Minimum Requirements*

The choice of hardware depends mostly on the type of virtual machines you intend to run as well as the number of machines. This is covered in much more detail later in the book.

Summary

This chapter provided some insight into the Oracle VM architecture. By understanding the architecture, you will find it is easier to understand the factors that influence performance and functionality. The beginning part of the chapter covered the components of the Oracle VM system—the Oracle VM Server, the Oracle VM Manager, and the Agent, the latter of which is a key component of the system.

Because of Oracle VM's use of the Xen Hypervisor, this chapter also covered the architecture of the Xen virtualization environment and the Xen Hypervisor. The Xen virtualization system is an open-source project that is heavily influenced by Oracle (since Oracle relies on it). This chapter provided an overview of the Xen system and Xen Hypervisor, as well as detailed some of the hardware requirements necessary to run Oracle VM and Xen. Although Xen runs on a number of different platforms, Oracle VM only supports the x86_64 environment at this time.

This book is about the Oracle VM products based on Xen technology and does not cover the hardware virtualization products available with the Oracle line of products.

The next chapter covers virtual machine lifecycle management. Lifecycle management is the progression of the various states that the virtual machine can exist in—from creation to destruction. Within lifecycle management, you will also study the various states of the lifecycle of virtual machines.

CHAPTER
4

Oracle VM Lifecycle
Management

Oracle VM lifecycle management describes the change in state of the virtual machine—from creation to destruction and every state in between. For example, the lifecycle of a virtual machine starts with the machine being built and then continues with it being started, suspended, resumed, stopped, and eventually deleted. Within the lifecycle of a virtual machine are four major states—nonexistent, stopped, running, and suspended—and a virtual machine can transition between these states, as this chapter describes. Also, various tasks take place within these states, and the transitions that can be made vary according to which state the machine is in. There are several ways in which transitions occur between each state of existence, all of which comprises the virtual machine lifecycle, as described in this chapter.

The Oracle VM Virtual Machine Lifecycle

A virtual machine built with Oracle VM has various states in which it can exist. For the purposes of this chapter, I will add an additional state: nonexistent. This state is used as the starting point and ending point of the lifecycle and describes a state of nothingness from which the virtual machine is created and where it is returned after it has been removed from the system and the system resources it utilized are released.

From nonexistence, the virtual machine is created and enters the lifecycle. It may enter many states within the lifecycle before returning to the state of nonexistence. This entire process is known as the lifecycle. Managing the lifecycle refers to how users transition between the various states.

The various states that a virtual machine can exist in consist of the following:

- **Nonexistent** This state is the starting and ending point, where the virtual machine does not exist. The virtual machine has no definition or state and uses no system resources. This is the state before the virtual machine is created and after the virtual machine has been removed from the VM Server. From the nonexistent state, you create the virtual machine.

- **Stopped** The virtual machine is defined in this state. Both a configuration file and data files exist. In the stopped state, the virtual machine consumes disk space but does not consume memory or CPU resources. From the stopped state, you can start, migrate or move, clone, edit, or delete the virtual machine.

- **Running** This is the operational state of the virtual machine from which tasks and processes are performed. When in the running state, the virtual machine consumes not only disk space but also memory and CPU resources. From the running state, you can stop/kill, restart, migrate or move, clone or suspend the virtual machine.

- **Suspended** This state preserves the machine's current settings and application states without releasing system resources, allowing the machine to resume this state with a short load period. In this state, the virtual machine consumes memory and disk resources but very little CPU resources. When in the suspended state, you can resume the virtual machine.

Figure 4-1 shows all the states that are possible in Oracle VM and the transitions that are available.

Creating and Deleting

The virtual machine is "born" when you create it. The virtual machine "dies" when you delete it. Everything that happens between creation and deletion is the virtual machine's lifecycle.

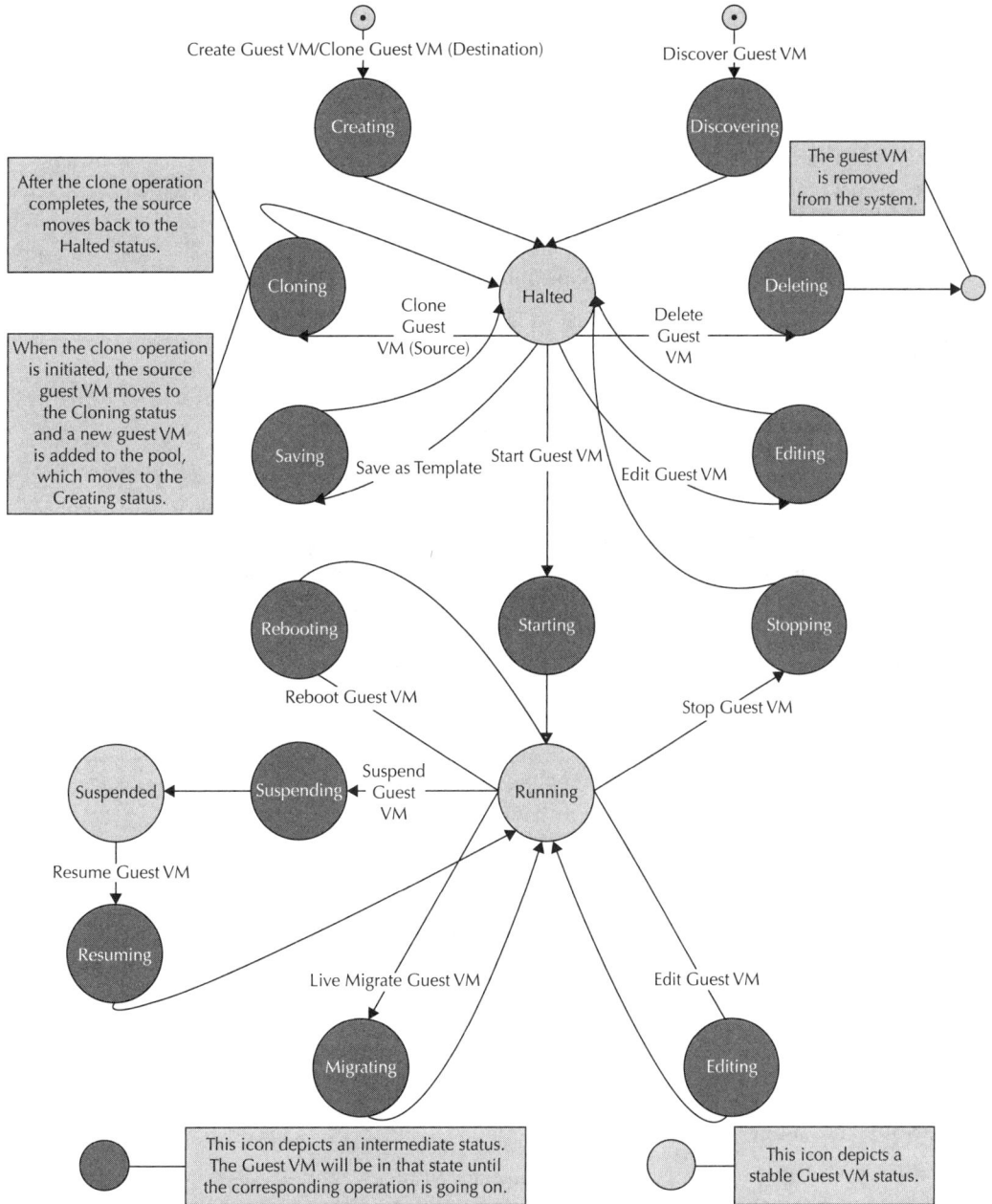

Create Guest VM/Clone Guest VM (Destination)

Discover Guest VM

Creating

Discovering

The guest VM is removed from the system.

After the clone operation completes, the source moves back to the Halted status.

Cloning

Clone Guest VM (Source)

Halted

Delete Guest VM

Deleting

When the clone operation is initiated, the source guest VM moves to the Cloning status and a new guest VM is added to the pool, which moves to the Creating status.

Saving

Save as Template

Start Guest VM

Edit Guest VM

Editing

Rebooting

Starting

Stopping

Reboot Guest VM

Stop Guest VM

Suspended

Suspending

Suspend Guest VM

Running

Resume Guest VM

Resuming

Live Migrate Guest VM

Edit Guest VM

Migrating

Editing

This icon depicts an intermediate status. The Guest VM will be in that state until the corresponding operation is going on.

This icon depicts a stable Guest VM status.

FIGURE 4-1. *The Oracle VM lifecycle*

The lifecycle is not complete until you delete the machine: its lifecycle does not end upon entering the shutdown or suspended state.

When you create or clone a virtual machine, it initially enters the stopped state. In this state, you can modify the virtual machine's configuration before starting it. A virtual machine is typically in the stopped state when you remove it from the system, thus allowing for proper resource cleanup.

When the virtual machine is in the stopped state, you can add resources to it, such as memory, vCPUs, network resources, and more disk space. You can modify a few resources while the virtual machine is running, but in order for them to become visible to the virtual machine, a reboot is often required.

In this state you can also migrate and/or clone the virtual machine. When migrating the virtual machine, you can move the virtual machine to a different server or server pool or you can move the virtual machine storage (or part of it) to another repository. In this state the movement is easier because no "live migration" is done.

> **NOTE**
> *Although a virtual machine can be created through several different menus, each method uses the same command: Create Virtual Machine. This command invokes a wizard to assist you with creating the virtual machine. You can choose to create a virtual machine from an existing template or a virtual machine from a virtual appliance, or you can choose to create a virtual machine manually. Creating a virtual machine from a template is covered in detail in Chapter 18. Creating a virtual machine manually is covered in detail in Chapter 19. Because creating the virtual machine is the first step in the lifecycle, it is a critical step.*

Starting and Stopping

In Xen (Oracle VM) terminology, starting a virtual machine is referred to as "creating a domain," and stopping or shutting down the virtual machine is known as "destroying the virtual machine." From the stopped state (shutdown), the virtual machine can move to the running state. You do this by starting the guest VM.

From the running state, you can stop the virtual machine. Depending on the command you use, this might be a hard stop (similar to pulling the power cord) via the **kill** command or a graceful shutdown using the **stop** command. Whenever possible, you should shut down the system gracefully rather than perform a hard shutdown. If you perform a hard stop, you might find it takes much longer to restart the virtual machine. For example, stopping a system might cause the database application running on that system to take much longer to restart because it has to perform data recovery.

Suspending

The suspended state offers the ability to stop the virtual machine in its current operating state and to return the machine to that exact state upon resuming. The difference between the two states is the manner in which the machine's settings are preserved and how the resources that the virtual machine uses are affected.

Putting a virtual machine into the suspended state simply stops the execution of further commands momentarily, much like a Windows desktop enters Sleep mode. In the suspended state, the machine's applications and settings are simply stopped (that is, they are kept the same as they were when the suspended state was entered). The settings and application states are not saved to files that are then used upon resuming the virtual machine; they are simply stopped and kept as they are. This allows for a fairly short load period upon resuming operation, but the virtual machine also continues to utilize (some of) the Oracle VM server's resources.

If your desire is to simply stop execution of the virtual machine for a short period of time and to restart it quickly, you should choose to suspend the virtual machine. This option provides a fast restart as well as holds system resources. If the VM Server were to fail, the suspended system will be lost and require recovery if applicable.

Cloning, Creating from a Template, and Migrating

Cloning a virtual machine involves creating a new virtual machine from a template or duplicating an existing virtual machine. A cloned virtual machine is an exact copy of the machine or template from which it is cloned; however, it is assigned a different MAC address for the network adapters. This option is great for creating a copy of a virtual machine. By copying a virtual machine that is already configured for the desired application, you save significant time by avoiding time-consuming tasks such as adding packages and installing and configuring applications.

Templates allow you to create virtual machines rapidly using preconfigured settings. Templates are not virtual machines themselves; rather, they are profiles that determine what resources the machine will use. The Template Library is one of Oracle VM's most significant features. Templates allow you to save a preconfigured system and reuse it over and over again to provision additional virtual machines quickly and efficiently. With a few configuration changes, you can quickly put the new virtual machine into production, allowing you to add more capacity in an efficient manner.

In addition to using the Oracle predefined templates, you can create a template of a virtual machine that you have created. This is done via the **clone** command. When you select the clone option, you will be asked whether to clone to a virtual machine or clone to a template. Cloning your own, already configured virtual machine to a template can be very efficient and useful because all of the software and updates you require are already installed.

Migrating a virtual machine involves moving the execution of an existing machine from one Oracle VM server where it's currently running to another Oracle VM server, server pool, or storage repository, without duplicating the virtual machine. Migration helps you balance resources as well as achieve high availability. With Oracle VM, you can migrate a virtual machine while keeping it in a running state. This way, you can also balance resources while the virtual machine is live. If you need additional CPU resources and/or memory and they are not available on the Oracle VM server the virtual machine is currently running on, you can move it live to a Oracle VM server that has sufficient resources. Once the migration is complete, you can add resources. In addition, if maintenance is required, you can abandon a VM server during the maintenance period and then return to it once the maintenance has been completed.

State Management and Transitions

The major states of the virtual machines were introduced earlier in this chapter. The transitions between the various states differ based on what state the virtual machine is in. This section describes these transitions and states. From each state, specific transitions can be accomplished. Of course, all states can move to the stopped state if the virtual machine server fails, and all states can move to the nonexistent state if the storage repository fails, but in this chapter, we are really only concerned with orderly and normal transitions.

For each state, there are a number of operations that are not mentioned in this section because they do not change the state of the virtual machine. These operations include gathering display information, creating a report, and viewing the parameter. Operations that change the state of the virtual machine are the ones covered in this section.

Stopped

In the stopped state, the virtual machine exists but is only consuming storage resources. The virtual machine is not running and is nonfunctional. The stopped state offers you the following options:

- **Start** From the shutdown state, you can start the virtual machine. This activates the system, taking it to the running state. Once the virtual machine has started, a Power-On Self-Test (POST) process runs and then the OS boots. At an early stage of the start process, the virtual machine console becomes available.

- **Clone** Cloning allows you to copy a stopped virtual machine to either the same or a different server pool. A cloned system is identical to the original. During this process, the virtual machine is not available. In this version of OVM, a *hot-clone* can be created while the source virtual machine is still running, but this process does not create a completely reliable clone and should only be used for backup purposes. It is best practice to create a clone while the source virtual machine is in the stopped state.

- **Clone to a template** In order for you to create a template of a virtual machine, it should be in the stopped state. A running virtual machine that you copy will most likely result in a corrupted image. The template process saves the virtual machine images as well as the virtual machine configuration file. The virtual machine configuration file is modified to reflect the template path. This template makes a great starting point for creating virtual machines. Creating a virtual machine, customizing it as needed, and cloning it to a template is an easy way to deploy custom virtual machines.

- **Delete** You can remove a virtual machine from the stopped state. You can probably delete the image files of a running virtual machine, but doing so might leave the VM Server in an unknown state. Of course, deleting a running virtual machine causes it to crash.

- **Edit** In order for you to edit a virtual machine, it should be in the stopped state. Modifications include adding disks, network adapters, and so on. In this state, you can add additional disks and/or modify the ones you have. You can modify a few options with the virtual machine running, but the underlying OS might not recognize those changes.

Because stopped systems are currently not running, they are in the ideal state for the operations mentioned here.

Running

In the running state, the virtual machine is available for users and can be accessed. In this state, only some changes can be made to the virtual machine configuration. The following state transitions are available from the running state:

- **Stop** Stopping the virtual machine moves it from the running state to the stopped state. You can do this either via an orderly shutdown or by killing it (similar to powering it off). An orderly shutdown is preferable, if at all possible. By stopping the system, you might have to perform recovery operations, resulting in performance problems on startup.

- **Restart**   The restart state is identical to a system reboot in Linux. The system is shut down and then restarted. However, it is important to note that the virtual machine configuration is not reloaded during a restart, so any manual changes to the vm.cfg file will remain unrecognized until the virtual machine is stopped and then started again.

- **Kill**   The kill state is identical to powering off a system in Linux. The system is immediately aborted.

- **Migrate**   You can migrate the virtual machine to another VM server without ceasing operation via live migration from the running state. There are many reasons for migrating the virtual machine, such as load balancing, maintenance, and so on. You can also migrate the virtual machine configuration file and any virtual storage to a different storage repository within the same server pool as long as the virtual machine is stopped.

- **Edit**   You can edit a few things while the system is in the running state, including memory (up to Max Memory Size). Regardless of whether Oracle VM allows the edit to occur while the virtual machine is running and whether the virtual machine recognizes the changes depends on the virtual machine itself. Not all operating systems recognize dynamic configuration changes.

- **Suspended**   Entering the suspended state preserves the machine's current settings and processes in memory without releasing system resources, allowing for quick resumption of the virtual machine's state. The suspended state can return to the running state via a resume transition.

The running state is where most of the work gets done and is the most useful state.

Suspended

Entering the suspended state preserves the machine's current settings and processes in memory without releasing system resources, allowing for quick resumption of the virtual machine's state. From the suspended state, the virtual machine can enter the running state or the shutdown state, and the following transitions are possible:

- **Resume**   Via the resume transition, the virtual machine returns to its previous state and processes at the point where the suspended state was entered after a short load period. Resuming results in the virtual machine entering the running state.

- **Kill**   In suspended mode, a **kill** command powers off the virtual machine and moves to the stopped state.

This state is only useful for short periods of time. In the event of a virtual machine server failure, the suspended state is lost.

Summary

The virtual machine lifecycle is defined by the various states in which it exists and operates in. Four basic states exist within the lifecycle, each one allowing for different tasks and configurations. The beginning of the lifecycle is the creation of the virtual machine. The end of the lifecycle is the deletion of the virtual machine. The states in between are known as the lifecycle of the virtual machine.

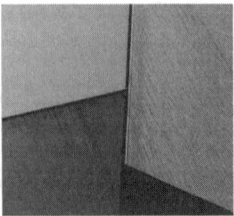

CHAPTER
5

Planning and Sizing the Enterprise VM Server Farm

Oo ne of the most important steps in configuring the Oracle Enterprise VM farm is *planning,* which involves all aspects of both sizing and configuration. *Sizing* is the art and science of determining the amount of hardware required for a system you are configuring. A mistake or underestimation of needed resources could cause significant problems later on when performance is an issue. In this chapter, you will learn how to plan and size the Oracle Enterprise VM farm.

Planning the VM Server Farm

You have several choices to make when planning the VM farm, including the number of servers, their configuration (server pool masters or virtual machine servers), and their sizing. Before getting started, let's look at the definition of a Oracle VM server farm.

Server farm is another term for data center. The server farm is a collection of systems used to serve an enterprise when the use of one system will not provide sufficient capacity needed to support the enterprise. Thus, the Oracle Enterprise VM farm is the collection of systems used to support the virtualization needs of the Oracle Enterprise. The Enterprise Oracle VM farm can be made up of one or more Oracle VM server pools, which are made up of one or more Oracle VM servers.

One Pool or Multiple Pools

From a high level, it might appear that putting all of the Oracle VM servers into the same server pool would be most efficient. This is certainly an efficient way to manage all of your resources with the least effort because all the VMs can now run on all the underlying hosts. However, a few other concerns might make this impossible.

When planning the server pool, keep in mind that there are nonclustered server pools and clustered server pools. Let's look at these different types of server pools.

Nonclustered Server Pool

The nonclustered server pool is made up of a collection of VM servers that use NFS for shared VM storage. The nonclustered server pool can be made up of one or multiple VM servers. If you chose to use shared filesystem storage, the server pool must be clustered. The nonclustered server pool does not support High Availability (HA).

Clustered Server Pool

The clustered server pool uses shared cluster storage and the cluster quorum to maintain the cluster. In the event of a server failure, the virtual machines from the failed server will automatically restart on existing servers in the cluster. As with the nonclustered pool, the clustered pool can be made up of one or multiple servers.

All the nodes of the cluster must reside on the same shared storage, thus maintaining the cluster. An interesting option is to locate some of the servers in another part of the data center or another building in order to create a stretched pool. As long as storage is accessible from the stretched nodes in the server pool, this will maintain a higher level of HA.

Although the stretched pool is not completely supported, it does work and can be implemented. Keep in mind that there might be some performance degradation for the remote nodes.

Server Pool Configuration

First, all the systems in the VM server pool should be running on the same hardware. The Oracle VM Manager will not prohibit mixed server pools, but they really aren't a good idea because of the problems you might run into. Some features, such as the HA Auto-Restart feature, will work even if the servers are not the same architecture because the HA enabled feature will start the system from a cold state; however, live migration will not work. Also, all the systems in the server pool must have the same basic hardware architectures.

Second, all the systems in the VM server pool should support the same level of hardware virtualization. Many systems remain in production that are 64 bit but do not support hardware virtualization. It is not recommended that the two processor types be configured in the same pool. If only paravirtualized guests are being used, mixing both systems with hardware virtualization support and hardware without hardware virtualization support is feasible. In addition, features such as HA enabled, live migration, and HVM will dictate whether a mixed environment can be used.

Sometimes it's not easy determining what type of processor you have and what support is available for virtualization. In the case of the Intel chipset, an easy-to-use web page that can help you is available: http://ark.intel.com. From here, you can determine the support available for your system. For example, I retrieved the following information from /proc/cpuinfo:

    Intel(R) Xeon(R) CPU   X5670 @ 2.93GHz

I then entered the model number X5670 on the Intel website and, among other information, obtained the following:

    Intel® Virtualization Technology (VT-x) ‡
    Intel® Virtualization Technology for Directed I/O (VT-d) ‡
    Intel® VT-x with Extended Page Tables (EPT) ‡

This information tells you that the processor on this system is capable of supporting hardware-assisted virtualization. You can find similar information on the AMD website at http://www.amd .com/en-us/solutions/servers/virtualization.

Once you've resolved hardware compatibility issues, you need to decide whether to create one large server pool or several server pools.

Single Server Pool

The primary reason for creating a single server pool is simplicity, which means easier configuration and administration. Because everything is in a single server pool, you have a single set of templates and images as well as a single storage system. Moving any virtual machine to another system in the server pool is easy, and failover is straightforward. A single server pool means less work to manage, seeing as you have one master and one or more VM servers all grouped together. The only real planning challenge is in the sizing of the server(s).

NOTE
With Oracle VM version 3.4, the idea of the master server has been deprecated. However, this book covers all the 3.x releases, so it is still discussed.

The downside of having a single server pool is that several maintenance tasks require the entire server pool to be rebuilt. These maintenance tasks can cause some loss of service to the server pool while the maintenance is being done. If you have multiple server pools, you can maintain one server pool at a time. These tasks include the following:

- Changing the OCFS2 cluster timeout
- Moving the OCFS2 cluster heartbeat to a different Oracle VM network
- Changing the NFS filesystem used for a pool file system
- Changing the SAN device used for the pool file system
- Changing the hostname/IP of an NSF file server used for a pool file system
- Recovering from a corrupt pool file system if no backup exists
- Converting a nonclustered sever pool to a cluster server pool

In the next section, you will learn the advantages of multiple server pools.

Multiple Server Pools

Using multiple server pools makes sense for a lot of installations for several reasons. Some of the reasons are technical, but others are purely a matter of politics and/or policy considerations. Having multiple server pools means having multiple sets of storage and multiple sets of servers; however, you can still manage them with the same VM Manager. You can also create multiple VM Managers if desired.

One of the primary reasons for separate server pools is separation of data. Many enterprise security policies require data from different departments or sometimes even require different projects to be stored separately. This is especially true in the government, where data secrecy might demand separation of data. This separation of data is accomplished by configuring separate server pools.

Another reason for having separate server pools is Quality of Service (QoS). Dividing components into separate server pools based on different levels of performance, uptime, monitoring, and management is quite common. The higher the QoS, the more you would typically pay for that service. It makes sense to pay only for the service level you require. For example, getting less service for testing, development, and training environments than for the production environment is okay.

To create separate service levels, split the virtual machines into different server pools. The various server pools might have different numbers and types of servers, different storage, and more networking equipment based on the level of service required. A server that guarantees a higher level of service might allocate fewer virtual machines per CPU than one with a lower guaranteed performance level. This is true of storage as well.

Another reason for separate server pools is to separate environments based on access and function. Thus, production, testing, and development can be allocated in separate server pools, which helps guarantee there is no unintended access or overlap. This allows you to create a barrier between environments. This architecture provides security as well as isolates performance issues into their own environments.

Regardless of your reasons, if you decide to create multiple server pools or a single server pool, you must plan. Planning must include sizing and determining the number of systems for the server pool master, utility servers, and virtual machine servers.

Planning the Server Pool

You have multiple ways to set up the server pool. The server pool is composed of one server pool master and one or more virtual machine servers. Even though the systems are configured as different server types, the software installed is identical; in fact, the server is not designated a server type until you've configured it. Therefore, each server starts out identically and is configured as a specific server type. The three server types are server pool master, utility server, and virtual machine server. A VM Server can be designated to perform a single server role, two roles, or all three roles.

Server Pool Master

One server is designated as the server pool master. As you'll recall, the server pool master is simply a specific component of the VM Agent. The server pool master is the communication conduit between the VM Manager and the Agent, as well as the interface to other Agents on other VM servers. The server pool master is automatically assigned and managed, with no manual intervention required. The server pool master manages load balancing, among other functions. When the administrator requests that a virtual machine start, the server pool master determines which virtual machine server is the least loaded and dispatches the request to start the virtual machine. Typically, the server pool master is also a utility server or a virtual machine server as well, unless it is a server pool master for a large and very busy pool.

With Oracle VM 3.4, the server pool master server role has been deprecated. In OVM version 3.4 and later, the agent communicates directly with the VM Agent on each of the OVM servers. However, because this book covers OVM 3.x, we will continue to refer to the server pool master role.

Virtual Machine Servers

The virtual machine server is really what Oracle VM is all about. This is the server that supports the hypervisor and runs virtual machines. All servers are VM servers by default. There are one or more virtual machine servers in a server pool. The number and type of virtual machine servers is determined by the number and type of virtual machines that need to be supported. When an administrator requests that a virtual machine start, the server pool master determines which virtual machine server has the most resources available and starts the virtual machine there. If a virtual machine server is not found with sufficient resources, an error is returned to the VM Manager.

Utility Servers

The utility server is a server that is chosen to perform more specific tasks in the VM server farm. This server performs tasks such as pool filesystem operations and updating the cluster configuration as well as importing virtual machine templates and virtual appliances and creating virtual machine templates from virtual appliances. It is also responsible for creating repositories. By default, all servers are utility servers. If a utility server is not available, a VM server will be used.

Server Pool Configurations

You can set up server pools in the following ways: All-in-One configuration, Two-in-One configuration, and the individual configuration. Which configuration you decide to use depends on the size of your configuration.

All-in-One Configuration

The All-in-One configuration is the most straightforward configuration. It is made up of the server pool master and virtual machine servers, all residing on the same VM server. This configuration

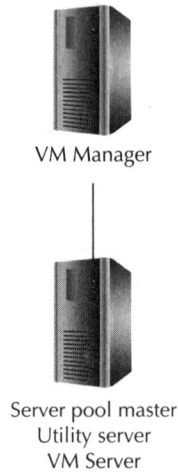

FIGURE 5-1. *All-in-One configuration plus VM Manager*

functions well for either a VM farm where there is only a single or a few servers or a configuration where many virtual machines are managed but there are very few changes.

The All-in-One configuration can consist of a single server, as shown in Figure 5-1, or of a single server that supports the server pool master, utility server, virtual machine server, and one or more additional virtual machine servers, also shown in Figure 5-1.

With Oracle VM 3.4, because there really isn't the concept of the server pool master, all VM servers use the All-in-One configuration.

The advantage of the All-in-One configuration is that configuring and managing it is easy. This configuration does have a disadvantage in that there is a single point of failure if the single Oracle VM Server were to fail (if there is only one). This configuration is becoming more common as hardware is released that is capable of supporting enormous numbers of virtual machines.

Because you can easily add additional virtual machine servers to a server pool (assuming the storage used is capable of being shared), you can always start with an All-in-One configuration and add to it as needed.

Large Servers and Oracle VM

Several hardware vendors have released new hardware with many multiple core processors and large amounts of RAM. These systems are now able to support 128 cores and up to 1TB of RAM. These servers are well suited for Oracle VM, and with a system this large and expandable, the All-in-One configuration is often the configuration of choice. Just make sure you have two of everything for the sake of redundancy, in case you experience a problem.

FIGURE 5-2. *The Two-in-One configuration*

Two-in-One Configuration

The Two-in-One configuration involves setting up the server pool master and utility server on the same server. The Two-in-One server configuration is for larger configurations where separating the virtual machine server from the server pool master is necessary. The Two-in-One configuration is shown in Figure 5-2.

The Two-in-One configuration makes sense where the VM server farm is moderately sized and you need to separate administrative functions from virtual machine functions. If the separation is for preference rather than load, you can configure the server pool master and utility server system as a smaller server than the virtual machine servers.

The type of configuration you choose is partially based on the capacity you need for the VM server farm and partially based on anticipated growth of the farm. Fortunately, if you decide to change things later, this is one area where modifications are easy. This configuration is no longer valid for 3.4 and newer versions of OVM since OVM 3.4 no longer uses the utility server.

Sizing and Capacity Planning

Perhaps more important than the configuration of the VM server farm is sizing and capacity planning for the farm. If the VM server farm is undersized, performance and capacity will suffer and your system will not run at the desired level of service or capacity.

Computer Sizing

Sizing is the act of determining the amount of hardware needed for an anticipated workload.

Capacity planning is the act of determining the amount of additional hardware necessary to add to an existing system in order to meet future workloads. This is used to determine if the existing VM farm can handle existing workloads and when additional hardware might be needed.

Both sizing and capacity planning are as much an art form as a science. They involve mathematics, monitoring and analyzing of existing workloads, and a lot of extrapolation. Probably more so than most activities, with sizing and capacity planning, the better the data input into the exercise, the better the end result.

In addition to the traditional variables used for sizing and capacity planning, such as the number of servers, number of CPUs, RAM, storage size, and I/O performance requirements, CPU virtualization acceleration features must now be taken into consideration as well. These new virtualization acceleration technologies allow for more virtual machines to be run more efficiently than ever before on the same hardware. In addition, server features such as Non-Uniform Memory Access (NUMA) technology affect performance.

Sizing and capacity planning are among the most challenging tasks you must undertake in planning the VM server farm. As such, they are two of the most important as well. As mentioned earlier, an undersized system will cause performance problems later. In the next sections, both sizing and capacity planning are covered.

Sizing

Sizing is the act of determining the amount and type of hardware needed for a new installation of an application. Sizing differs from capacity planning in that the hardware will be supporting a new application or a new installation of hardware, rather than an upgrade or addition to the existing hardware in a system. For example, if a computer system will be replaced by another system that has more resources or is faster, sizing is involved. If that same system will have more CPUs or more memory added to it, capacity planning is involved. Typically, the components that end up being the biggest bottleneck to the VM server farm are network and storage.

This section assumes that the sizing exercise is geared toward taking nonvirtualized systems and virtualizing them—in other words, taking standalone systems and sizing a virtualized environment to accommodate new virtual machines to run the applications formerly running on the standalone

NUMA Systems

Non-Uniform Memory Access (NUMA) systems use multiple memory controllers that are each assigned to a CPU or set of CPUs. This is different from a symmetric multiprocessing (SMP) system, where all CPUs share the same memory controller. NUMA allows you to add more CPUs to the system with better performance. Because a memory controller is a finite component, in an SMP environment, the number of CPUs supported is limited by the memory controller. OVM supports NUMA but does not support C-state power-saving features where unused CPUs can be shut down.

servers. The section on capacity planning is geared toward managing the capacity of an already virtualized environment.

The steps involved in sizing a new system are data collection, analysis, and design. The better the data collection, the better the design will be. Keep in mind that there will still be a lot of work to do in the analysis stage where you analyze and decompose the data.

Data Collection

Sizing the new system starts with collecting as much data as you can about the application and the expected workload. If the new system is a replacement for an existing system, much of this data is readily available. You can collect data by monitoring the existing system. If possible, create specific tests or conditions where a single virtual machine is running, so you can analyze a specific workload.

A few different types of data are collected. Data collection is used to gather information about the workload that will be run. In addition, data is collected about the number and type of virtual machines that will be deployed. Collect this data in a workbook that you can then use to determine the number and size of systems to include in the design.

Workload Data Collection   Collecting data about the required workload is typically done using tools available in the OS that is being deployed with whatever systems are available. If this is a completely new system and there are no available reference systems, sizing is more difficult. As mentioned before, the better the data, the better the result.

If you're modeling Linux systems, use tools such as sar, top, iostat, and vmstat. These utilities provide information about the system's current CPU utilization as well as memory utilization and I/O utilization. Collect data over a fairly long period of time, so you can gather both averages and peaks. Collect a minimum of one month of data, though longer is recommended.

If you're modeling Windows systems, use Performance Monitor (perfmon). Perfmon provides data on CPU, memory, and I/O utilization. You can use this data to help size the new system. Windows perfmon not only is capable of collecting a large variety of data but also is capable of saving it. Its major downside is its inability to export that data in text form.

Requirements Collection   Requirements collection involves interviewing management to determine the number of virtual machines needed and what they will be used for. Certain requirements, such as the number of systems, should be fairly easy to obtain. Other requirements, such as the needed amount of RAM, might be readily available due to specific requirements such as database size, or you might need to ascertain it from the workload data collection.

RAM is one of the most important requirements because Oracle VM does not over-commit memory. Therefore, you must size the host with sufficient RAM to support the sum of the RAM of the individual virtual machines. This differs from some other virtualization products such as VMware, which allow for the over-committing of memory. The designers of Oracle VM and the Xen Hypervisor felt that the over-committing of memory could lead to potential performance problems and that memory is inexpensive enough to make over-committing unnecessary.

Memory Over-Commit

Memory over-commit is when more memory is allocated to virtual machines than is available in the VM server. If more memory than is actually available is used, that memory is paged out, as is done in a normal virtual memory system. With Oracle VM, physical memory is allocated for each virtual machine when the virtual machine is created.

CPU Metrics Collection

The CPU metrics you collect should be the average CPU utilized during normal work hours. Why is this important? If you use the overall average CPU utilization, the value would be skewed lower in most cases due to the lack of off-hours activity. For example, let's say a system runs at 50 percent utilization between 6:00 AM and 6:00 PM and is idle overnight. This is a daily average of 25 percent. If 25 percent were used to size a system, the system would be dramatically undersized during normal work hours. In addition, not only should the system be sized based on a normal work-hours load, but also it should be sized based on peak load. Configure the system to handle a peak steady-state load with relative ease. *Peak load* is the highest load seen during the measurement period. The peak load is slightly different from a spike because the peak load is somewhat sustained, whereas a spike is a one-time event.

In addition to memory, you need to gather CPU requirements. The number of CPUs required for virtual machines might be determined by business rules or workload analysis. Typically, some business rules require a minimum of two CPUs. If no business requirements are available, you can figure out the number of CPUs by determining the workload that must be supported.

The amount of required disk space is usually determined by the group deploying the application(s). In addition to the amount of space, consider the performance capacity of the I/O subsystem. An underpowered I/O subsystem can result in performance problems from both the OS and the application standpoint.

Once you've gathered both performance data and physical requirements, you can then move on to the analysis stage. At this stage, the requirements and data you've collected is translated into physical requirements for each virtual machine. Once you've completed the analysis, you can design the sized system.

Analysis

The analysis stage of the sizing process involves taking the data collected in the previous step and using it to calculate the amount of resources needed to meet the requirements determined during the collection stage. You can split the analysis phase into several phases. The first phase is to take the requirements from both the collected requirements and, if available, the workload collection process. Enter that information in a spreadsheet and adjust it (that is, translate it to a single reference platform) if you used different systems for data collection.

Translated Performance

The reason to adjust or translate the performance information is to give you a standard metric to use. For example, adding 50 percent of a 1-GHz processor and 50 percent of a 2-GHz processor together is difficult. By adjusting the 50 percent of a 1-GHz processor to be 25 percent of a 2-GHz processor, you can compare the two. The danger is that the adjustment is somewhat arbitrary, especially if you are comparing unlike CPUs, such as Sun SPARC and Intel/AMD. In the following examples, I have chosen to adjust the performance to meet that of a basic CPU value. The assumptions and conversion should be documented.

VM	# of CPUs	Type	% Utilization	Adjusted CPU	Memory	Disk
1	1	x86_64 1 GHz	50%	0.25	1GB	8GB
2	2	x86_64 1 GHz	75%	0.75	3GB	20GB
3	2	x86_64 2 GHz	30%	0.6	8GB	40GB
Total				1.6	12GB	68GB

TABLE 5-1. *Sizing Information*

In the second phase, this data is summed over all of the systems identified in the requirements. This provides you with the data necessary to identify the total resources required for the host(s). Remember, hardware improvements allow the load on several slower CPUs to be replaced with fewer faster CPUs. Once you've collected the data and calculated the totals, it is time to start thinking about the potential solutions.

In the following examples, the process and some ideas are presented to illustrate how to put together an analysis spreadsheet.

Example 1 In the example shown in Table 5-1, data has been collected for several older 1-GHz systems and some newer 2-GHz systems.

NOTE
The CPUs are adjusted to 1 = 100% of a 2-GHz x86_64 CPU = 1.0. Therefore, two CPUs running at 75 percent is equivalent to 150 percent, but adjusted to the reference CPU, this translates back to .75.

Using this spreadsheet, you can then begin the design stage.

Example 2 In the example shown in Table 5-2, data has been collected for a half dozen very busy systems. This information will be used to analyze how much equipment is needed for the new installation. In this case, there are some holes in the data for new systems that don't have an equivalent running system to collect data from.

VM	# of CPUs	Type	% Utilization	Adjusted CPU	Memory	Disk
1	2	x86_64 2.2 GHz	80%	1.6	4GB	20GB
2	2	x86_64 2.2 GHz	75%	1.5	8GB	20GB
3	2	x86_64 2.2 GHz	60%	1.2	8GB	40GB
4	2 requested		NA		16GB requested	200GB
5	2 requested		NA		8GB requested	100GB
6	2 requested		NA		4GB requested	100GB
Total				4.3 + ?	46GB	480GB

TABLE 5-2. *Sizing Information*

NOTE
The CPUs are adjusted to 1 = 100% of a 2.2-GHz x86_64 CPU = 1.0. Therefore, two CPUs running at 75 percent is equivalent to 150 percent, or 1.5.

Using this spreadsheet, you can then begin the design stage.

Design

The design stage is where you choose the hardware for the VM Server system(s) and create a configuration. Sizing systems involves these components: the amount of memory, the number of CPUs, networking components, and the amount of disk space and storage performance required.

Sizing Memory   Because Oracle VM does not over-allocate memory, sizing memory is probably the easiest part of this exercise. Simply sum the memory required for each of the virtual machines to be supported and add an additional gigabyte for dom0. In the case of the preceding two examples, the required memory is pretty self-explanatory.

Sizing CPUs   Sizing CPUs is a little bit more challenging than sizing memory. This is mainly because CPUs are a shared resource and are always over-allocated. *Over-allocating* means it is common that more CPUs are allocated to the virtual machines than actually exist on the VM server system. Fully allocating CPUs to virtual machines is not feasible because they will not be fully utilized.

It is possible (and very probable) that virtual machines will utilize all of their allocated CPUs at one time or another, but it is very unlikely that they will run at that load for an extended period of time. This is why over-allocating CPU resources is possible. Because CPU resources are limited, if a one-to-one allocation of CPUs to virtual machines is used, the number of VM server CPUs would be much higher than really needed. The idea is to have as many as you need, but not to buy more than is necessary.

Sizing the Network   Sizing the network is another important component of sizing the VM server farm. The network is used for virtual machine network traffic as well as potentially for storage traffic (NFS). In addition, the network is used for live migration of virtual machines. The performance of the network is crucial in all of these tasks.

The network should be sized for peak utilization as well as for steady state operations. Peak utilization will occur during a live migration. A slow network could cause minutes or hours of additional migration time.

Sizing the Disks   Disk or I/O sizing has become much more difficult since most storage is virtualized now. That is, a disk or array is no longer allocated for a single purpose. Instead, pieces of the same array are allocated to many different purposes and potentially to different organizations and applications. Storage sizing is broken into two main components: sizing for capacity and sizing for performance.

Sizing for capacity is easy. In the example shown in Table 5-1, 68GB of storage is required. In the example in Table 5-2, 480GB of storage is required. That's the easy part. The more difficult part is identifying the performance characteristics needed and sizing properly for them. If the I/O subsystem is undersized, the entire environment might suffer.

Unfortunately, sizing for performance involves extensive monitoring and data collection, which often are very difficult to do. What's more, various storage subsystems provide additional features, such as caching and acceleration, that enhance performance. Each storage subsystem works differently and requires specific knowledge to be able to ascertain which features will benefit Oracle VM.

Capacity Planning

Capacity planning is the process of planning the capacity of the system in order to meet future requirements for increased workloads or adding more business systems. Capacity planning is different from sizing in that instead of dealing with a new system and a somewhat unknown workload, it directly involves the system currently being used, so more information is available. Capacity planning results in either adding more hardware (upgrading) or replacing the existing hardware with new hardware. Whether you're upgrading or replacing the hardware, the capacity planning exercise requires the same steps as with sizing: data collection, analysis, and design.

Unlike traditional servers, Oracle VM provides a straightforward, almost seamless, upgrade path. If the VM server farm needs additional capacity, add a new VM server to the server pool. With the addition of the new VM server, you can migrate virtual machines to the new VM server seamlessly, thus spreading out the load to a new server. If a specific virtual machine needs additional capacity, you can easily add CPUs and memory (as long as they are available on the VM server).

In addition, the Oracle VM Server farm requires capacity planning not only for the VM servers, but also for the virtual machines themselves. Capacity planning for the Oracle VM Server farm involves monitoring both the Oracle VM Server itself and the individual virtual machines. As mentioned earlier in this section, the basic steps involved in capacity planning are similar to those involved in sizing: data collection, analysis, and design.

Data Collection

In the section on sizing, the focus was geared toward collecting data from individual servers with the goal of sizing a virtualized environment to host them. This section is geared toward collecting data from an already virtualized environment.

Data collection from a capacity planning standpoint is a little different from a sizing exercise. Here, you already have existing systems that hopefully have long-term monitoring enabled on them. Oracle Enterprise Manager (OEM) Cloud Control is an excellent product for monitoring

OVM 3.4 Limitations

Oracle VM 3.4 supports Oracle VM Server (hypervisor) with up to 288 CPUs, but a single PVM virtual machine can have a maximum of 256 virtual CPUs assigned to it, or 128 virtual CPUs for HVM. The memory limit for Oracle VM 3.4 varies based on the type of virtual machine:

- 32-bit paravirtualized guest: 64GB
- 64-bit paravirtualized guest: 500GB
- 64-bit HVM guest: 1,000GB

Some of these limitations are likely to change in future releases. The limit for a 32-bit system will always be 64GB due to 32-bit limitations.

virtualized environments for capacity planning purposes because of the ability to save years' worth of data that you can then analyze.

In addition, tools such as the Xen Top command (xm top) will display resource utilization in an existing environment. An example of xm top is shown in Figure 5-3.

If only the memory and number of virtual CPUs for the various domains are desired, you can acquire this with the command xm list, as shown in Figure 5-4.

These statistics provide enough information to give you a good idea of how the individual virtual machines are performing and an idea of how things are currently running. Unfortunately, the xm top utility does not provide data in a tabular form that can be saved, unlike other OS utilities, such as sar.

Analysis

In the capacity planning analysis phase, you have to do more than in the analysis phase of the sizing exercise. When sizing, you design the system for the workload you have analyzed. When doing capacity planning, you analyze trends and determine future workloads. This involves extrapolation of existing data. Oracle Enterprise Manager (OEM) Cloud Control is an excellent tool for gathering long-term trend data for analysis.

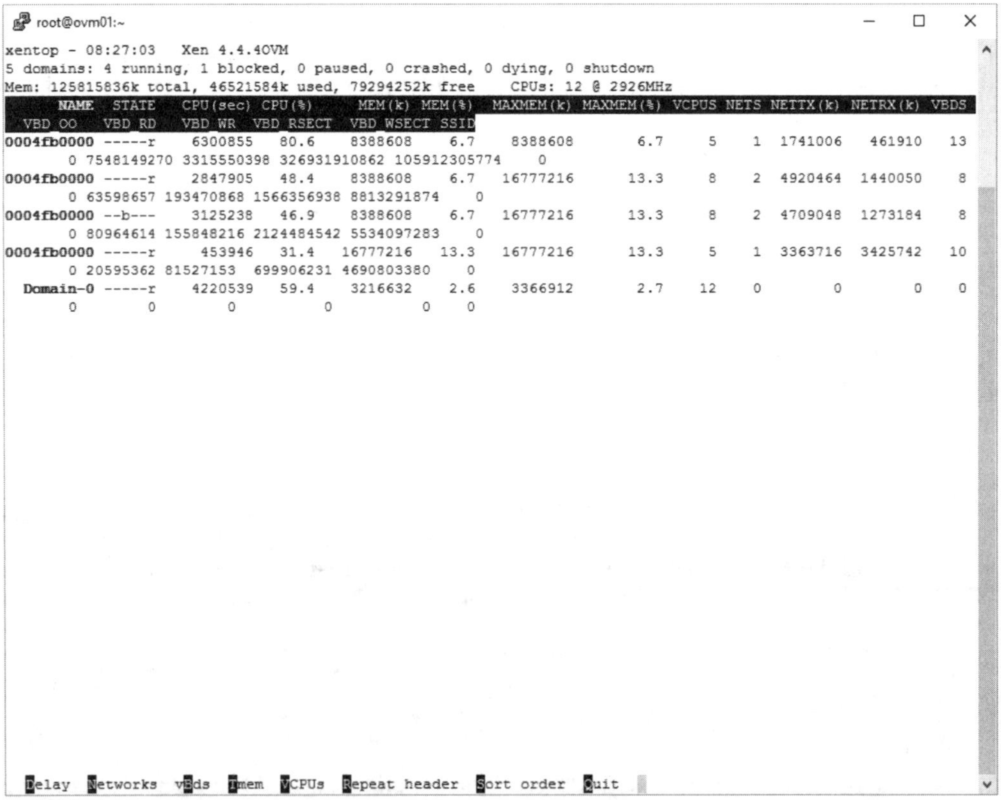

FIGURE 5-3. *xm top*

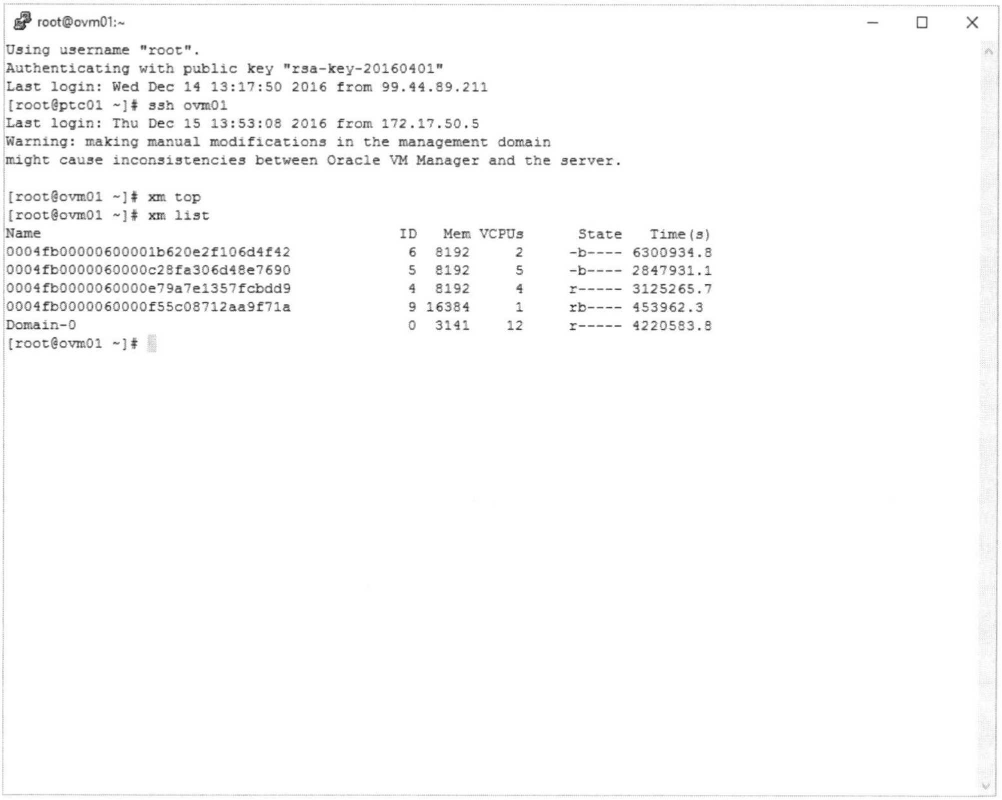

```
root@ovm01:~                                                          —   □   ✕
Using username "root".
Authenticating with public key "rsa-key-20160401"
Last login: Wed Dec 14 13:17:50 2016 from 99.44.89.211
[root@ptc01 ~]# ssh ovm01
Last login: Thu Dec 15 13:53:08 2016 from 172.17.50.5
Warning: making manual modifications in the management domain
might cause inconsistencies between Oracle VM Manager and the server.

[root@ovm01 ~]# xm top
[root@ovm01 ~]# xm list
Name                                    ID   Mem VCPUs      State   Time(s)
0004fb00000600001b620e2f106d4f42         6  8192     2     -b---- 6300934.8
0004fb0000060000c28fa306d48e7690         5  8192     5     -b---- 2847931.1
0004fb0000060000e79a7e1357fcbdd9         4  8192     4     r----- 3125265.7
0004fb0000060000f55c08712aa9f71a         9 16384     1     rb---- 453962.3
Domain-0                                 0  3141    12     r----- 4220583.8
[root@ovm01 ~]#
```

FIGURE 5-4. *xm list*

Because capacity planning involves trend analysis and extrapolation, gathering long-term data is absolutely critical. Plot this data and extrapolate it for future workloads. In addition to gathering performance data, you need to gather business requirements. Business requirements should include any information related to future workloads as well as future applications and user counts, such as new call centers opening, the addition of personnel, and so on.

The final area of analysis involves how far into the future to look. Some companies prefer to plan hardware upgrades to handle workloads for the next two years; others want to handle the next three or four years. This is a business decision that must be included in the capacity planning calculations.

Design

The design stage varies based on whether the capacity planning is for individual virtual machines or for the Oracle VM Server. If the design is for a virtual machine, the modifications could be as simple as adding CPUs and/or more memory from the VM Manager. If the capacity planning activity is for the Oracle VM Server itself, you may be adding hardware, but, probably more likely, more Oracle VM Servers.

Virtualization provides much more flexibility than traditional servers. Rather than you having to move applications to new servers and/or shut down the server to add new CPU boards or memory, Oracle VM provides the ability to add a new Oracle VM Server to the server pool and then live migrate virtual machines to that new server seamlessly. This is one of the primary advantages of a virtualization environment.

Servers, CPUs, and Cores   You have multiple options when adding hardware to a virtualization environment. Adding more servers to a server pool by sharing the storage and joining the pool is an easy matter. Once you have determined that a new Oracle VM Server is needed, you can actually add it to the pool without incurring downtime from the pool. Simply add the server to the pool and configure load balancing and/or HA, and the rest is easy.

A less costly approach is to add resources to an existing server. You can often do this by adding CPUs with or without multiple cores. There is now an abundance of CPUs with multiple cores— anywhere from two to eight. Multiple-core systems came about as a result the chipmakers' ability to add more and more components to a single chip.

A *core* is a CPU within a CPU. As integrated circuit density has increased, we now have the ability to add more compute power to the CPU by essentially creating multiple CPUs within the CPU chip. The local terminology for the CPU chip is a *socket,* whereas the individual compute engines within the chip are referred to as the *cores.*

The multiple-core CPU is an evolution of CPU technology. In the early days of the PC, the Intel/AMD architecture had a single core and appeared to the OS as a single CPU. PC vendors eventually developed multiprocessor systems that enabled more capacity within the same server. Later technology was known as *hyperthreading* or *hyperthreaded CPU.* This appeared to the PC as an additional CPU, but, in reality, hyperthreading was a method of taking advantage of CPU instruction cycles that might otherwise be wasted. Even though the OS thought that the hyperthreaded CPU was an additional CPU, it really only provided an additional 30 to 50 percent more performance.

The multiple-core CPU is actually an additional CPU built into the die of the chip. So the chip itself has multiple "CPUs" built in. These CPU chips also include the multiprocessor technology needed to maintain multiple CPUs and manage memory access between the chip and the RAM. Some designs even include a memory controller on the chip.

In addition to the multicore features, hardware acceleration for virtualization has been introduced to allow virtual machines to run at near native CPU speed. This has helped make virtualization very economical.

Regardless of whether additional CPUs/cores or entire VM servers are added to increase the VM server farm capacity, planning ahead is important. Planning for additional hardware when the system is out of capacity is too late. At that point, users will already be complaining.

A Little Bit of Computer History
The author of this chapter started out his OS/database career at a major computer manufacturer, where he personally experienced the introduction of the 80386 processor and 32-bit memory addressing. At that time, we used to joke that nobody would ever be able to afford 4GB of RAM. Since that time, the capacity of computer systems has dramatically increased while the price has dramatically decreased (known as Moore's Law).

NUMA Technology

Most newer CPU chips use NUMA technology. With NUMA technology, you have multiple memory controllers that service a specific set of CPUs or cores. This differs from an symmetric multiprocessor (SMP) system, which employs only one memory controller. Each CPU sees the same memory, so it is symmetric.

Storage   Storage is fairly easy to plan for from a capacity standpoint but is often difficult to plan for from a performance standpoint. This is because storage administration is often not done by the same personnel who manage the servers and the virtual environment. In addition, there are many factors to consider, such as I/O subsystem cache, storage channels (such as fiber channel switches), and storage virtualization itself.

Storage-size capacity planning is best accomplished by keeping long-term monitoring data about the size and usage of your storage system. It is impossible to perform capacity planning tasks by looking at a single data point. To project future growth, you have to have data regarding past performance. Tools such as OEM Cloud Control can assist with this by monitoring both the space usage of the individual virtual machines and the VM Server itself. Because Oracle VM storage uses OCFS2, obtaining space information is not difficult. If no tools are available, it is easy to create a crontab script to collect space information on a regular basis. This will provide valuable information for future capacity planning.

Monitoring and Capacity Planning

Monitoring is extremely important to capacity planning. The better the data, the better the outcome of the capacity planning exercise. The key to monitoring for capacity planning is to develop metrics. These metrics should be relevant, informative, and useful. A key initiative in many organizations is to develop enterprise metrics collection. The term *enterprise metrics* refers to metrics from all aspects of the business. These metrics might include business metrics as well as technical metrics. By gathering business metrics, you can anticipate future growth needs from the growth of the company itself.

Systems should be monitored on a regular basis, and statistics should be kept for as long as possible. This data should be stored in a database so you can view various reports in different ways. This allows metrics to be combined to produce relevant data. Without long-term monitoring and good data, future capacity planning will suffer.

In many ways, capacity planning is more challenging than sizing because it involves projection into the future. But if you've collected good data, the job will be much easier. In addition, good performance data will assist with performance tuning as well as capacity planning.

Summary

A lack of proper planning can often lead to a poorly performing system. Through proper sizing, the right hardware can be allocated for the right job. This chapter provided information on how to perform sizing and capacity planning for the Oracle VM Server farm. Included was some information on how to monitor the performance of the VM server farm. Performance monitoring is covered throughout this book as well.

In the next chapter, you will learn how to install the Oracle VM Server. In later chapters, you will learn how to install and configure the Oracle VM Manager and OEM Cloud Control plug-in for Oracle VM.

CHAPTER

6

What's New in OVM 3.x

Oracle VM Server for x86 version 3 is the latest virtualization product from Oracle and at the time of publication of this book was at version 3.4.2. Oracle VM Server for x86 is just part of the virtualization product line, which also includes Oracle VM Server for SPARC and Oracle VM Manager. This book covers both Oracle VM Server for x86 and Oracle VM Manager, but VM Server for SPARC is not covered in this book.

Introduction to OVM 3.*x*

OVM 3.*x* for x86 is the latest in the evolution of Oracle's virtualization products, and it represents a significant investment in virtualization and cloud computing from Oracle. Oracle VM 3 has added many new, easy-to-use features in order to improve its usability. The new features of Oracle VM 3.*x* are covered in the remainder of this chapter.

OVM 3.4.2 was released in September of 2016 and is the current release as of the writing of this book. Other versions of OVM 3.*x* were released according to the schedule listed here:

OVM 3.4.2	September of 2016
OVM 3.4.1	March of 2016
OVM 3.3	July of 2014
OVM 3.2	January of 2012
OVM 3.1	May of 2012
OVM 3.0	August of 2011

These releases continue to improve and enhance the Oracle VM product. As you will see in this chapter, Oracle VM is much improved from the previous version, OVM 2.*x*.

OVM 3.*x* New Features

Many new features have been added to Oracle VM 3 and are detailed in this chapter, including features of both the Oracle VM Manager and Oracle VM Server for x86. The Oracle VM Manager has been enhanced to work across both Oracle VM for x86 and Oracle VM for SPARC. This book, however, is written to cover Oracle VM for x86 only, and references to Oracle VM for SPARC will be provided only when necessary.

OVM Manager

The OVM Manager is the web-based tool we use in order to administer the Oracle VM environment. This tool is robust and is constantly being updated and improved. The OVM Manager consists of a database repository, a web server, and a user interface. The OVM Manager provides an API that allows other applications, such as the command-line interface (CLI), to communicate with it as well. In OVM 3.*x*, this API is implemented as a Web Services API that provides a REST interface into the OVM Manager.

WebLogic Server Built In

In OVM 3.x, the WebLogic server is built into the installation process. It is not necessary to install or configure WebLogic separate from the OVM Manager. The version of WebLogic installed with the OVM Manager varies based on the specific version.

The Oracle WebLogic server provides a stable and robust platform for running the OVM Manager. It is installed automatically with the OVM Manager, so no additional steps need to be performed.

MySQL Database Built In

The Oracle VM Manager repository database stores configuration and event information. This is now configured as a MySQL Enterprise database that is bundled with the OVM Manager installation process. As with the WebLogic installation, the version of MySQL Enterprise varies based on the OVM Manager version and is constantly being updated.

MySQL Enterprise provides a stable and high-performance database to serve as the repository for OVM. As with the WebLogic server, nothing else needs to be installed. Installation is automatic with the OVM Manager.

The use of MySQL gives Oracle better control over features, such as automated integrity checks, automated backups, and so on. Automatically installing MySQL as the repository database creates the OVM Manager as an appliance, where everything is included.

New Management Features

New management features are available within OVM Manager and OVM Server that are designed to help with the administration, troubleshooting, and maintenance of OVM. These features improve OVM and include the Xen 4.0 hypervisor, an updated dom0, centralized network configuration and management, and the OVM Storage Connect framework.

Xen 4.0 Hypervisor

OVM 3.x utilizes the Xen 4.0 hypervisor, which provides more hardware support, improved performance, and more scalability than previous versions of the Xen hypervisor. Oracle continues to stay in sync with the latest stable releases of the Xen hypervisor in an effort to provide the best features and capabilities from the Xen community.

Updated Dom0

Dom0, or domain 0, is critical to the Oracle VM system and has been updated with the latest Oracle Unbreakable Linux Kernel and device drivers. The role of dom0 is to be the interface between the administrator and the hypervisor. Unlike other domains, dom0 has direct access to the underlying hardware.

Centralized Network Configuration and Management

All network configuration is done via the OVM Manager, including network configuration, NIC port bonding, and VLAN network access configuration. Unlike in Oracle VM 2, you no longer need to perform any configurations outside of OVM Manager.

Storage Connect Storage Configuration and Management

The OVM Storage Connect framework allows for the easy configuration of storage within the OVM environment. This allows you to configure Storage Area Network (SAN), Network File System (NFS), and Internet Small Computer System Interface (iSCSI) storage all from within the OVM Manager. The OVM Manager will automatically discover available storage using this feature.

Performance, Scalability, and Security

With OVM 3.x, the OVM server is capable of supporting up to 160 CPUs and 2TB of memory. The per-machine limits of the OVM server have been increased to 128 virtual CPUs. The latest supported maximums for both Oracle VM servers and Oracle VM guests are documented in the release notes for each Generally Available (GA) or errata release of Oracle VM.

Job Management Framework

The new job management framework has improved the functionality of OVM Manager. Each operation is performed as a job. OVM Manager provides the status of a job as it is running, including percent complete, steps completed, and steps remaining. You can view the job through the GUI at any time and debug a failed job through the GUI.

Event Logging

New event logging is essentially a history that allows changes made to the OVM system to be logged and reviewed. Events can also alert you to issues or problems with the OVM jobs.

Easier Hard Partitioning

With OVM 3.x, it is now easier to set up hard partitioning than in previous versions. Hard partitioning allows physical CPUs in the underlying OVM server to be mapped to OVM clients. By using hard partitioning, you are able to guarantee that only those CPUs are used by the client. This is the only method that allows you to license virtual CPUs for Oracle databases and other Oracle software. In order to set up hard partitioning, download the OVM Utilities from My Oracle Support. The OVM Utilities contain ovm_vmcontrol, which can be used to configure hard partitioning.

Private Cloud Self-Service with OEM

Oracle Enterprise Manager integration with Oracle VM allows for more than just management of OVM. For example, it provides the ability to configure private cloud self-service. Oracle Enterprise Manager 13c provides all the support necessary to enable the private cloud. This also allows for management of Oracle Site Guard within OEM.

Manage Old OVM with New OVM Manager

Starting with OVM Manager version 3.4.2, you no longer have to update Oracle VM servers immediately during an upgrade. OVM Manager version 3.4.2 manages Version 3.4 and Version 3.3 Oracle VM servers. However, it is still a good idea to upgrade the servers as soon as possible to take full advantage of new features, capabilities, and fixes introduced with each subsequent release of the product.

Huge Page Support

Support for Huge Pages has been added to guests in OVM 3.3. This allows for Oracle databases running in OVM Guests to take advantage of this valuable performance feature. The Huge Pages feature allows Oracle database instances to access SGA memory using 2MB memory pages versus 4KB memory pages, decreasing memory management overhead and providing higher performance.

Topology Maps

From the VM Manager, select a VM either through server pools or via the VM server itself. Right-click on the VM and select Display VM Hierarchy Viewer in order to see the virtual machine hierarchy and dependencies. This gives you a graphical view of the VM components.

Support for OVF

OVM now supports Open Virtualization Format (OVF) software-based assemblies. This makes it easier to deploy prebuilt virtual machines.

OSWatcher

OVM 3.4 has enabled the OSWatcher utility to run at boot time on OVM servers. The OSWatcher utility collects valuable OS performance information that can be used to analyze the system.

Distributed Resource Scheduling

The Distributed Resource Scheduling (DRS) provides real-time monitoring of Oracle VM Server utilization to rebalance a server pool for maximum utilization and performance. DRS Live migrates VMs from higher utilized VM servers to less utilized ones.

Distributed Power Management

Distributed Power Management (DPM) optimizes a server pool for minimum power consumption by reducing the number of powered-on servers when there are periods of low utilization. DPM will automatically power up more Oracle VM servers as they become needed.

Disaster Recovery Using Oracle Site Guard

Oracle Site Guard is bundled with Oracle Enterprise Manager 12.1.0.5 and later. Oracle Site Guard orchestrates virtual machine failover and more, allowing databases and applications to be moved between Oracle VM Managers at the same site or even different sites if there is an issue with the primary system. Oracle Site Guard supports Active/Passive, Active/Standby, and Active/Active configurations. This is a needed component for disaster recovery (DR).

OCFS2 Filesystem

Oracle VM 3 supports the updated OCFS2 cluster filesystem. As new releases of OVM are released, the version of OCFS2 is constantly being improved. OCFS2 is used to provide clustering for the High Availability features of Oracle VM.

RESTful API

The RESTful Web Services provide a way of communicating between programs (REST stands for Representational State Transfer). The RESTful calls can use XML, HTML, JSON, or other defined formats. The RESTful API is implemented in the VM Manager and is available via the OVM Manager port.

Integration with Private Cloud Appliance

Oracle VM comes integrated with the Oracle Private Cloud Appliance out of the box. This Private Cloud Appliance is an Oracle Engineered System designed to provide high-performance and scalable private cloud services.

Virtual Appliances

Virtual Appliances are pre-built virtual machine assemblies. Examples of these "appliances" include Oracle VM Virtual Appliances for E-Business Suite 12.1.3 and Oracle Big Data Appliance Lite.

A Virtual Appliance is a virtual machine (or a set of virtual machines) that performs a specific function or service for a particular application.

NVME Support

With Oracle VM 3.4.2, NVM Express (NVMe) devices are supported and detected. NVMe stands for Nonvolatile Memory Express. These are essentially flash hardware devices that can be used to provide high-performance storage in the OVM environment.

Storage Live Migration

OVM 3.4 introduces storage live migration, which allows not only for live migration of virtual machines between servers but live migration of storage as well. This is a huge step forward in reducing downtime by allowing for live migration from systems that use local storage for storage repositories. This feature was introduced to provide nonclustered server pools with the ability to "live migrate" Oracle VM guests between multiple nodes without shared storage. This feature does not work with shared Oracle VM storage repositories using NFS, iSCSI, or Fibre Channel—only local storage.

Oracle VM Limitations

Oracle VM limitations vary slightly by version. In order to give you a complete picture of these limitations, they are provided and notated where subsequent releases have improved on them.

Oracle VM Server Limits

The limits on VM servers are impressive. Here, they are broken down into server maximums, network maximums, and storage maximums. Server maximums are provided in Table 6-1.

Network maximums are provided in Table 6-2.

Storage maximums are provided in Table 6-3.

Oracle VM Virtual Machine Limits

The virtual machine limits are also impressive. The maximums are listed in Table 6-4.

Item	Maximum	Notes
CPUs	160	Increased to 320 in OVM 3.3.
RAM	2TB	Increased to 6TB in OVM 3.3.
Virtual machines	128	Increased to 2,560 in OVM 3.4. (Ten virtual machines per server × 256 servers.)
Servers per server pool	32	With OVM 3.2, 64 unclustered, 32 clustered.
Virtual CPUs per host	Unknown	Increased to 900 in OVM 3.3.

TABLE 6-1. *Server Maximums*

Item	Maximum	Notes
Networks per bond	2	Increased to 256 in OVM 3.3.
Bonds per VM server	5	With OVM 3.1, this was increased to 10. Increased to unlimited in OVM 3.3.

TABLE 6-2.   *Network Maximums*

Item	Maximum
LUNs in a storage array	1,000
OCFS2 volume size	64 TB
Files per OCFS2 volume	30,000
Virtual disk size	10 TB

TABLE 6-3.   *Storage Maximums*

Item	Maximum	Notes
Virtual CPUs	128	In OVM 3.4, 288 tested and 384 designed
Virtual RAM (32-bit guests)	63GB	
Virtual RAM (64-bit guests)	1TB	Increased to 2TB in OVM 3.2 Increased to 6TB in OVM 3.4
Virtual NICs	31	Eight hardware virtual guests
Virtual disks	52	

TABLE 6-4.   *Virtual Machine Maximums*

Summary

This chapter has provided basic information about the new features in OVM 3.x. Some of the features highlighted here were introduced in OVM 3.0, and some were introduced in later versions. At the time of this writing, OVM 3.4.2 is the current version of OVM. However, newer versions of OVM could be out, possibly including OVM 4.x, by the time you've read this chapter. Regardless, many of these features will continue to be the core features of OVM in the future.

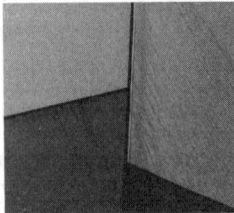

CHAPTER
7

Disaster Recovery
Planning

*D*isaster recovery (DR), as well as the common United States government term *continuity of operation plan* (COOP), refers to a set of policies and processes that enables systems to recovery from a failure of the primary data center. Disaster recovery is often confused with High Availability (HA), which in the most simple terms is the recovery from a failure within a data center. When you're planning for disaster recovery, two important metrics directly drive the time and cost for implementing the disaster recovery plan: the recovery time objective and the recovery point objective. Defining and testing the disaster recovery plan are also critical steps in the continuing operation of a system once the primary data center is considered no longer operational. When you're defining the recovery plan, it is important to understand that there will be a period when the system is completely unavailable and that some data may be lost.

The first critical metric, the recovery time objective (RTO), defines the acceptable amount of time within which the system must be restored after a disaster. The RTO normally involves the time needed to bring the disaster recovery system online, including recovery, testing, troubleshooting issues, and notifying end users. The time needed for leadership to declare a disaster traditionally is not included in the metric. The RTO metric is attached to the business process for the disaster and should not include the resources required to implement the process. Therefore, the process should be simple so that less senior staff can implement the plan. Short RTOs tend to lead to more expensive solutions, because in order to reduce the downtime, advanced technologies such as storage replication are usually required. In cases with a very short RTO, warm standby sites are required. In cases with a longer RTO, a cold site can be maintained, with systems built at the time of the disaster. This results in a lower cost to implement the plan. Many third-party companies provide cold site service, but numerous organizations are now leveraging the cloud to provide a warm disaster recovery site and simply scale from a small footprint (to maintain the replication) to the resources needed to continue operations when a disaster is declared.

NOTE
A warm standby is a site that is operational as a base level, usually with just the operating systems online and the database in a replication mode. Cold sites usually have no servers online and are built at the time of disaster recovery.

The second critical metric, the recovery point objective (RPO), defines the acceptable amount of data loss for the business, with smaller amounts quickly driving up the expense to implement the plan. As with the RTO, the metric is attached to the business process for the disaster and does not include the time needed by leadership to declare a disaster situation. An RPO is dependent on a data synchronization point, which defines the relationship between system activity and is defined as the point in time at which a set of backups exist that, when restored, can be synchronized to the same point of the business process. A simpler way is to compare the database backup to the application server on an imaging application. For example, if the database backup was completed at 2 P.M., but the images are not backed up until 4 P.M., then the restoration of services will include several hours of missing data for the application. This is a common mistake that disaster recovery planners make, because assumptions are often made at a large scale without understanding each application's needs. It is because of this that application-level disaster recovery plans are highly recommended—a one-size-fits-all approach to all the replication requirements often will not lead to the results expected.

$$,$$$

Recovery Point Objective Target

Recovery Time Objective Target

Weeks Days Hours Minutes Seconds $$$ Seconds Minutes Hours Days Weeks
Seconds

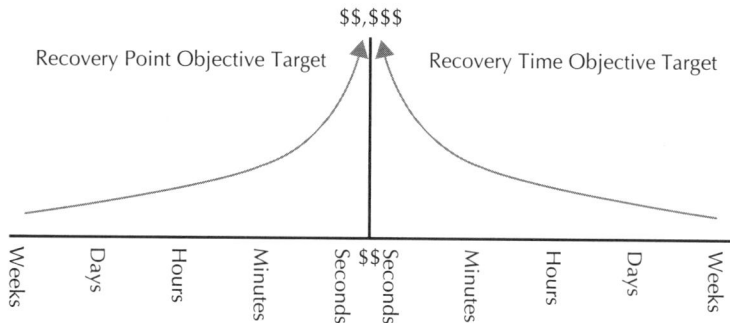

FIGURE 7-1. *RTO and RPO vs. expense*

As shown in Figure 7-1, the combination of RTO and RPO can mean the difference between a low-cost solution and a high-cost solution. A cold disaster recovery site, with a sample RPO of 48 hours and an RTO of 48 hours, would normally be significantly less expensive to implement and support compared to a solution with an RTO of 30 minutes and an RPO of 5 minutes, which would require a warm disaster recovery site with database replication combined with storage replication of application data not stored in the database. This chapter discusses different options as strategies for disaster recovery, for both the Oracle VM Manager and virtual machines within a VM farm.

Disaster Recovery for the OVM Manager

At the core of an Oracle VM farm is the Oracle VM Manager (OVMM), which is required in order to perform administrative tasks such as adding virtual machines, managing resources, and checking the health of the OVS systems. Two common strategies for recovery of an Oracle VM Manager are recovery offsite by reinstalling Oracle VM Manager and recovery using a hot-standby Oracle VM Manager.

NOTE
Although other options for disaster recovery are discussed, whenever possible, the best solution is to leverage Oracle Site Guard for Oracle VM. This solution integrates with Enterprise Manager Cloud Control and provides the best solution for disaster recovery challenges.

Recovery with a Reinstallation of OVMM

When you're using a cold standby site, recovering the OVMM is a simple task because you can simply reinstall a new OVMM and then, if storage is replicated, rebuild and reimport the OVS systems. This solution, shown in Figure 7-2, offers a lower cost than a full warm site, but it does require more time to bring the systems online. In addition, once systems are moved to the disaster recovery site, Enterprise Manager will need to be refreshed and all prior information in Enterprise

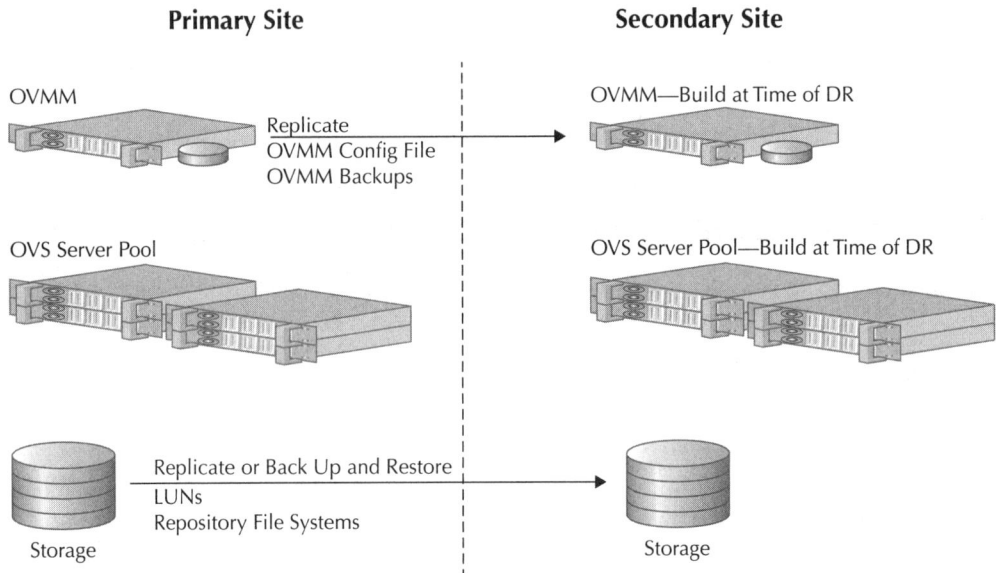

FIGURE 7-2. *Cold disaster recovery*

Manager will likely be lost. With this method, storage is replicated from the primary site, and if you're using a NAS-based repository, the files can be restored from backups. When preparing the Oracle VM Manager for this option, it is critical that you copy the /etc/sysconfig/ovmm.cfg file from the original OVMM to a secure location. It is also important to verify that the MySQL backups are saved before you install the Oracle VM Manager and copy the file to the new system. When the Oracle VM Manager installs, it will detect the file and configure its universally unique identifier (UUID) to match the original production system. Once the OVMM is restored, the MySQL backups are restored, the OVS nodes are discovered, and the storage repositories are then verified before the virtual machines are brought back online. Although effective, this method can take a fair amount of time to perform.

Recovery of Server Pools Using a Warm Standby OVMM

As shown in Figure 7-3, with a warm standby site, systems are left online at the disaster recovery site, which enables lower RTO and RPO metrics. When the Oracle VM Manager is installed, it will detect whether the file /etc/sysconfig/ovmm.cfg file exists, and if so, will configure its UUID to match the original production system. Once the OVMM is restored, the MySQL backups are restored, the OVS nodes are discovered, and the storage repositories are then verified before the virtual machines are brought back online. Although effective, this method will take more time to perform versus an application-based standby.

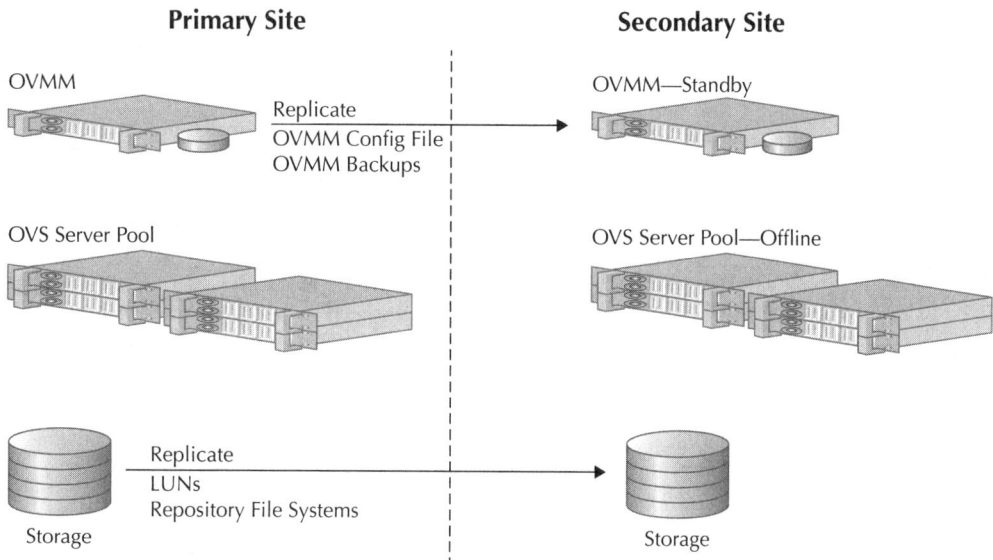

Primary Site

OVMM

Replicate
OVMM Config File
OVMM Backups

OVS Server Pool

Replicate
LUNs
Repository File Systems

Storage

Secondary Site

OVMM—Standby

OVS Server Pool—Offline

Storage

FIGURE 7-3.   *Warm disaster recovery*

Disaster Recovery for VMs: Application Level

Both of the previous methods require some sort of storage replication and, as a result, present a challenge in keeping the RPO and RTO metrics low. This is a result of several factors, including the time it takes to bring a cold standby online, the opportunity of data loss due to how often the storage is replicated, data synchronization issues between the database and application tier, and the time it takes to restore data and bring database and application systems online. In addition, there are challenges when restoring multiple applications, mainly due to conflicting priorities. These challenges can all be overcome by using a disaster recovery method that is application focused.

NOTE
Your disaster recovery site can be in the cloud, which is a great option due to the agility of most cloud solutions, the small footprint needed to enable replication, and the ability to expand that footprint when the system is needed.

As shown in Figure 7-4, application-aware disaster recovery is achieved by using a combination of technologies. For the database, the most common approach is to have a hot-standby system using Data Guard for replication. This provides for minimal data loss and a rapid recovery time. Data Guard maintains the standby databases as a copy of the production database. If the production database becomes unavailable—either for a true disaster or a planned maintenance event—the database administrator can use Oracle Site Guard to switch the standby database to the production role.

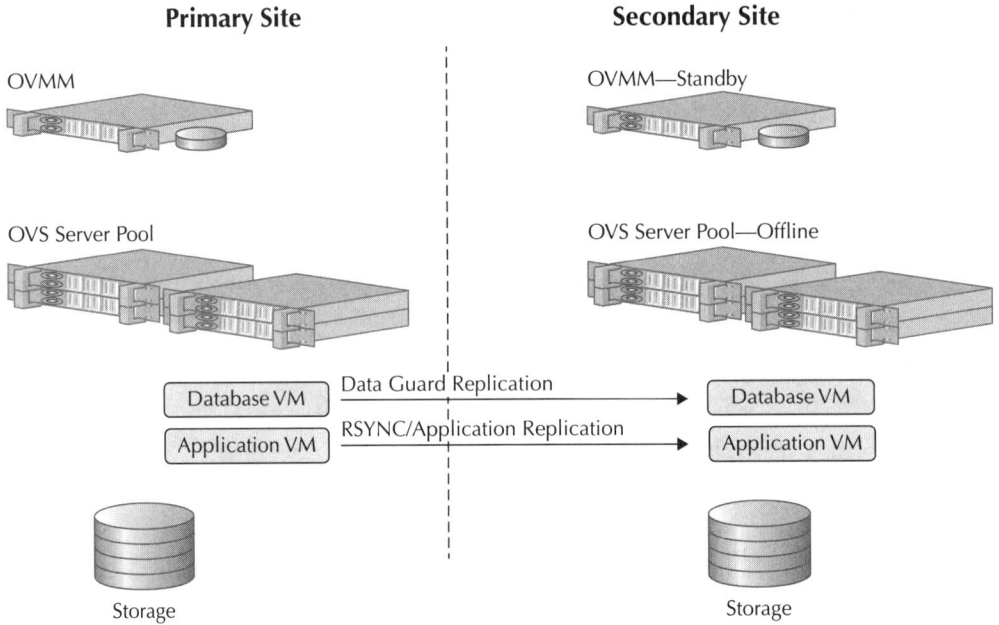

FIGURE 7-4. *Application-level disaster recovery*

This minimizes the downtime associated with the outage. Data Guard can also be combined with traditional backup and restore techniques to provide a high level of data protection and data availability.

Other technologies such as Active Data Guard and GoldenGate are also commonly used. Active Data Guard is similar to Data Guard, but it enables the standby database to be mounted as read-only, thus providing the ability to run reports against the standby system or backup jobs. This is used to offload these workloads from the production system. Oracle GoldenGate is another popular addition to this strategy, enabling real-time replication to the target system while the target database is mounted as read-write. GoldenGate can also be used for bidirectional replication, turning the disaster recovery solution from an active-standby solution to an active-active solution.

For the application tier, a combination of preinstalled and configure application servers and operating system–level replication is often used. Using this method, the application is installed at the disaster recovery site, with critical database files being replicated from the production site. For Linux systems, rsync is commonly used for synchronizing these files from the production site to the disaster recovery site. The advantage of this solution is the speed in which the disaster recovery site can be brought online. You simply bring the database online and then start the preconfigured application servers.

CAUTION
Not all applications will work with this method. However, applications such as the Oracle E-Business Suite work well because most of the data is stored in the database tier.

Disaster Recovery Using Site Guard for Oracle VM

A disaster recovery solution cannot be successful without the organization being able to implement the plan. A challenge that is experienced when faced with a true disaster is that key technical resources are often impacted by the same event that caused the data center disaster. Automation is a key methodology to help protect against a failed disaster recovery due to critical staff being unavailable to support the recovery. For disaster recovery, Oracle VM Site Guard, shown in Figure 7-5, provides automation capabilities for the more traditional storage-based method. Site Guard for Oracle VM is a powerful and flexible solution that can complement the application-level DR approach using Site Guard. Also, Site Guard can orchestrate the guest failover with or without automated application recovery logic, while at the same time integrating with Data Guard failovers at the database tier, thus enabling a controlled failover to the disaster recovery site without a guest failover. Unlike a nonintegrated storage replication-based disaster recovery solution, a Site Guard-based solution supports both a planned failover to the disaster recovery site as well as recovery in the event of a catastrophic failure of the data center; application and system owners will need to ensure applications are also protected with reliable and consistent backups. By leveraging Site Guard for Oracle VM, the process of replicating the storage, bringing the repository online, and importing the virtual machines is automated though a single Enterprise Manager instance, which is ideally itself protected with at least a Level 3 Enterprise Manager MAA setup to guide you to a successful end to this solution path. For more information about the available Enterprise Manager Maximum Availability Architectures, refer to the Enterprise Manager documentation.

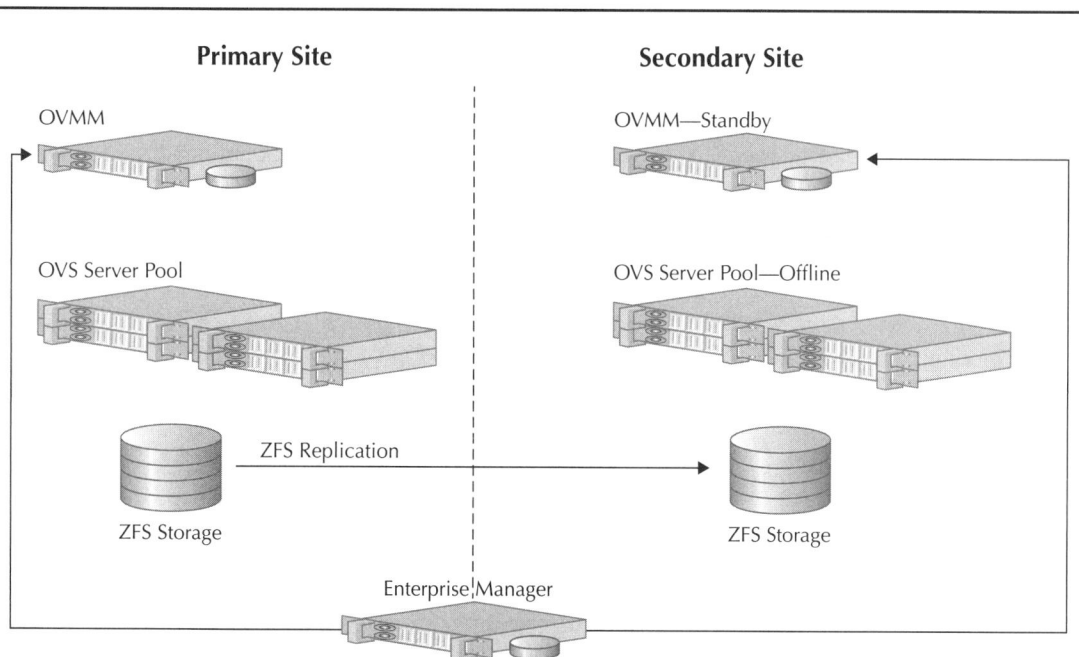

FIGURE 7-5. *Site Guard recovery for Oracle VM*

Site Guard for Oracle VM works by adding a management tier to the technology stack with Enterprise Manager. As shown in Figure 7-5, the Enterprise Manager system communicates to the Oracle VM Manager at the primary site as well as the secondary site. Oracle VM Manager is running at both locations, with Oracle VM Servers running at each. An Oracle ZFS storage array is running, and ZFS replication is used to replicate storage between the sites. Although each location has its own server pool, there is no requirement that they be the same types of servers, as long as the CPU architecture is the same. You cannot mix x86 and SPARC, for example. As with the first few examples in this chapter, storage replication is used, and the user can choose to integrate with a fully supported array like the ZFS Appliance from Oracle or to use custom integration with some shell scripts. Both storage replication and OVM management are controlled from the Enterprise Manager system, which will control the process moving forward. Site Guard for Oracle VM ships with several scripts that automate the transition of Oracle VM systems between sites. It also enables automation of both Oracle and non-Oracle workloads, including database, WebLogic, and third-party applications. In this example, there is a single Enterprise Manager system, but it is highly recommended that you use a redundant Enterprise Manager deployment. For more information on Enterprise Manager deployment methods, see http://www.oracle.com/technetwork/database/features/availability/em-maa-155389.html. Chapter 26 covers how to configure Site Guard.

Although the Oracle VM and Enterprise Manager infrastructures can be implemented separately, the Oracle VM environment must be complete and validated before you attempt to implement the Site Guard solution. The integration of the two infrastructures is the last step in the entire process and should be done only after the Enterprise Manager system is deployed in its highly operational configuration.

Summary

This chapter addressed the many different options you have for planning and providing a disaster recovery solution for your virtualized business. The key metrics needed to plan for an appropriate disaster recovery plan, RTO and RPO, were covered. You learned several different approaches to planning for disaster recovery, including the three major approaches: cold standby site, warm standby site, and application-level disaster recovery. The benefits using Site Guard as a tool to automate the disaster recovery process were covered. The next chapter discusses Enterprise Manager Cloud Control and how it can improve your private cloud operations.

CHAPTER
8

Overview of Oracle
Enterprise Manager
Cloud Control

E ver since computers became practical for business use, the industry has experienced a consistent trend of reinvention. Generally, once every decade, the industry reinvents itself to provide a better return on investment. Consistent architecture advancements have led to the modern concept of cloud computing, including private clouds, public clouds, and hybrid clouds. These advancements date back to the 1960s with the adoption of the monolithic mainframe as businesses started migrating workloads to computers. In the 1970s, the precursor to the modern public cloud—timeshare computing—saw widespread adoption as multiple organizations shared expensive mainframe time, each using a fraction of the mainframe and paying for the resources used. By the 1980s, client/server architectures became popular, with desktop systems processing the user interface and backend servers performing the compute workload, similar to how web browsers generate the user interface and the backend web and application servers perform the primary compute. In the 1990s, an explosion of IT services created more knowledgeable users as they were introduced to the World Wide Web, and the industry started to explore using systems on the Internet to provide services. In the 2000s, Software as a Service (SaaS) companies started to form, and at the same time mainstream IT organizations started to virtualize their commodity servers. This decade also saw companies such as Joyent and Amazon start providing virtual machines under an Infrastructure as a Service (IaaS) model to clients over the Internet. It was in this decade when the term *cloud* was adopted by larger Internet companies such as Google and Amazon.

In the 2010s, the public cloud started to make a significant impact to niche markets, with SaaS companies such as Taleo and RightNow cementing their market positions. At the same time, the IaaS providers set the standard for automated provisioning and easy self-service. This is also when Oracle released Oracle VM 3 and Enterprise Manager 12*c* (EM12*c*) as tools for building and managing private clouds. Private clouds also started to become common in the enterprise, focused primarily on IaaS offerings, though many Oracle customers started down the path for private clouds focused on a database tier managed by EM12*c*. At the end of 2015, Oracle released Enterprise Manager 13*c*, which coupled systems management with the database, middleware, and application management capabilities that EM12*c* provided for the cloud.

NOTE
In "The NIST Definition of Cloud Computing," Peter Mell and Tim Grance of the National Institute of Standards (NIST) define cloud computing as "a model for enabling ubiquitous, convenient, on-demand network access to a shared pool of configurable computing resources (e.g., networks, servers, storage, applications, and services) that can be rapidly provisioned and released with minimal management effort or service provider interaction."

The cloud architecture itself can be placed into one of three major buckets: private cloud, public cloud, and hybrid cloud. In a private cloud, all the components exist within an organization, including the hardware, software, and applications themselves. In a public cloud, a third party owns all the assets and provides the user a subscription to access the resources, usually over the Internet. A third, emerging model is the hybrid cloud, which consists of a mix of private and public cloud technologies. A common example is backing up a database to the Oracle public cloud, where the database and its supporting technologies exist under the control and ownership of the organization, but the backups for the database are provided by Oracle, with Oracle owning the backup target technologies, including the disks, servers, and related infrastructure software. The three types of clouds are summarized in Figure 8-1.

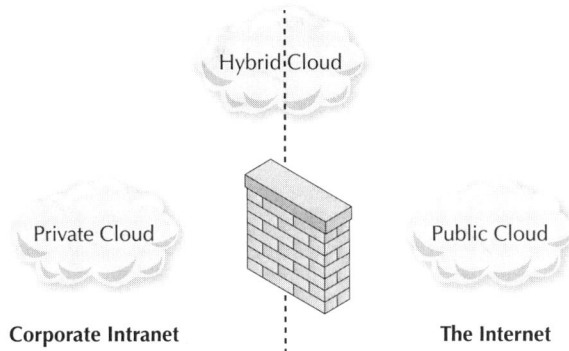

FIGURE 8-1. *Clouds*

As the industry continues to move through this evolution, IT is starting to move most (if not all) of the enterprise into a cloud, including custom-built applications and systems containing the most sensitive data—whether it is to a public cloud, hosted by a third party, or a private cloud, where the business owns and manages the hardware, software, and applications. This complex technology becomes even more difficult to manage when a mix of public and private clouds are deployed in the enterprise.

As private clouds are more widely adopted, a common problem faced by the enterprise is how to achieve efficiencies in this new cloud world without custom-building complex management and provisioning systems. Oracle VM plays a key role in enabling the transition to a private cloud. Simply implementing Oracle VM and placing just a few virtual environments on an existing server can significantly increase the administrative workload for IT staff if there is no automation, as the great efficiencies are achieved though the coupling of Oracle VM with the application technologies (database, operating systems, WebLogic, and so on) and the business processes. Any solution that paves the way to a private cloud needs to integrate directly into the hypervisor as well as with the other components of the application stack.

For architecting private clouds based on Oracle VM, three common toolsets can be used to build and, in some cases, manage the private cloud: Enterprise Manager, Puppet, and Open Stack.

Ways to Use Enterprise Manager Cloud Control

As the enterprise adopts the cloud, it starts to face several challenges in the new landscape. The first set of challenges involves the day-to-day management of the cloud and how different aspects are provisioned, patched, monitored, and decommissioned. Without some common management tools, any potential cost savings that the cloud architecture brings to the table are quickly lost.

With a multivendor approach, shown in Figure 8-2, multiple disparate systems need to be glued together to provide the servers, with each layer (operating system, database, middleware, and application) requiring a different tool and skillset. Due to the complexity of management systems built like this, maintenance of these systems becomes an expensive proposition because multiple developers and administrators are needed to keep the systems operational. A change to one component often causes unintended consequences with the customized integration, requiring the business to support a multitier development, sandbox, regression, and production environment to maintain the integration between diverse systems.

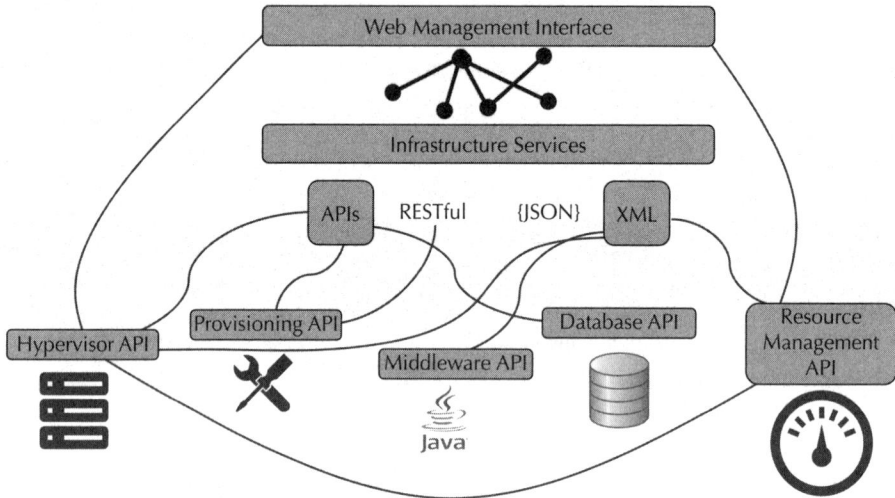

FIGURE 8-2. *Multiple-vendor cloud architecture*

Challenges arise when different systems can no longer communicate, creating provisioning issues that can require large amounts of time for even the most skilled admins to resolve. The problems quickly escalate when dependencies fail to provision correctly, causing the needed resource from being available to the users. Enterprise Manager 13c fills all of these needs. First, by integrating into Oracle VM Manager, it enables the cloud architect to provide a single system to manage the virtualization layer of the hardware, database, and middleware, as shown in Figure 8-3.

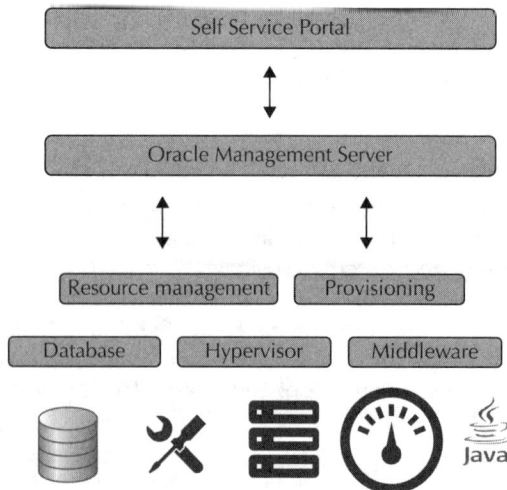

FIGURE 8-3. *EM13c cloud architecture*

Enterprise Manager 13*c* offers a wealth of features to enable end-to-end management and provisioning of private clouds. With Enterprise Manager, the cloud architect can enable privileged users to create virtual machines within a defined subset of the environment, with Oracle VM providing the core technology for IaaS. These virtual machines are based on the same custom templates created in Chapter 18. As machines are created using Enterprise Manager, they can be automatically registered to the system, thus enabling the monitoring of the virtual machines at a detail level beyond what Oracle VM Manager provides. A sample of the basic information provided by Enterprise Manager is shown in the following illustration. In this example, you see the general health of the virtual machine, along with a summary of the main metrics being monitored, such as name, operating system, CPU, memory, and filesystem distribution.

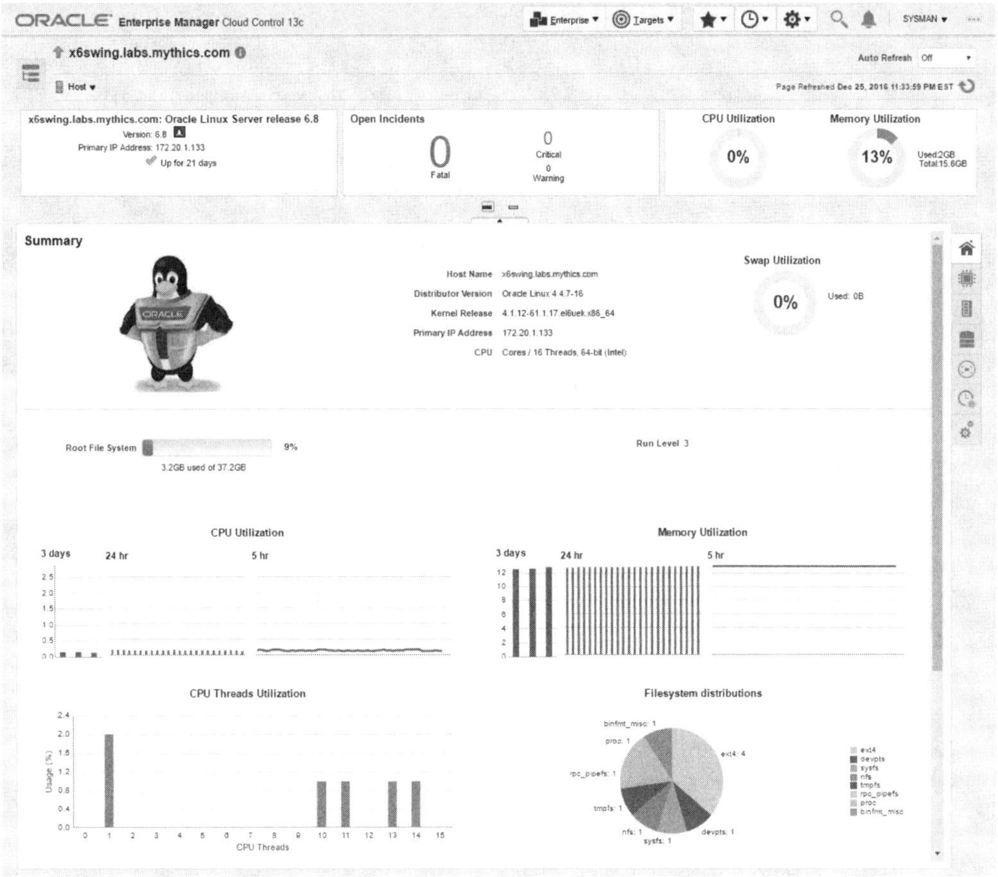

In this example, you can also see any jobs that were run against the virtual machine, along with the event history. Events can be as simple as a threshold being exceeded or a failure of the target.

With Oracle VM Manager, the administrator can look to see the status of any particular virtual machine, but when Oracle VM Manager is combined with Enterprise Manager, the administrator can receive notifications when a virtual machine is offline as well as look at detail metrics, such as the top processes for a host, as shown here.

Enterprise Manager not only enables self-service capability for IaaS, but it fully enables the complete lifecycle management for databases, virtual machines, middleware and even the application tier. A feature-rich security model provides access to developers, team leaders, database administrators, application administrators, and even end users, enabling each the access required to complete their task. This allows for a single tool to provision all aspects of the application, from the application itself, down through the middleware and database tiers, past the virtualization layer and into the storage and network layers.

The second challenge that the enterprise experiences with building and managing private clouds is monitoring them. Although it's not obvious, monitoring is a critical component to a successful cloud deployment. Monitoring involves not just reporting on the availability of the cloud, but also tracking how resources are consumed. The end goal for any cloud is end-user self-provisioning, meaning the user can easily subscribe to IT services, fulfilling the needs of the applications with user-directed provisioning for the entire technology stack, including the operating systems, databases, middleware, and even the applications themselves, to provide a highly available, scalable, and secure system.

A properly managed cloud must adjust to the capacity needs of the hosted applications, while at the same time hold these applications accountable for the resources they consume. Enterprise Manager enables this behavior through the operating systems, which allow Enterprise Manager targets to be assigned a cost center, with usage attributes based on resources consumed, software expense required to license the systems, and labor effort required to support the applications through their lifecycle. This complex billing model is based on the concept of a *service catalog,* which is a collection of documents and artifacts that describe the services an IT organization provides, as well as specifies how those services are delivered and managed. By defining specific combinations of service-level agreements (SLAs), software mixes, and capacity sizes, the IT organization is better able to define what is being offered to the users. Once a service is defined, the cost to provide that service can be calculated. Then, based on the user's subscription of services, a report can be generated that shows what resources have been consumed. This is commonly referred to as *chargeback* by the industry, a concept that has been used since the days of monolithic mainframes. Using a correctly accounted-for chargeback model, IT not only can monitor and report on resource usage, but can also use the data for internal cross-charge to enable funding of large-scale platforms that can host multiple applications, such as Exadata and the Private Cloud Appliance. Just like the mainframes of old, these new systems allow infrastructure to be shared by multiple applications, reducing the overall expense to the organization.

With the ability for users to rapidly deploy new virtual environments in the enterprise, there is a need to map the value of the resources to what the users are consuming, not only for accountability but also for resource planning. Without some form of showback, users will eventually consume all available resources in the cloud, with little-to-no business value. This has happened with large numbers of VMs sitting idle or barely being utilized.

NOTE
Showback is a new term that emerged in 2010 that focuses on the ability of IT to allocate resource usage to departments and cost centers.

Enabling this is both a simple and complex task. The mechanics are very simple. You just need to download and install the plug-in via the Enterprise Manager Extensibility feature using the Plug-in Manager. Once it's installed, you can set up a basic charge plan and assign it to your targets. This will provide you the basic showback capability.

NOTE
Configuring IaaS and showback/chargeback in Enterprise Manager is covered in Chapters 23, 24, and 25.

The complexity comes in configuring the rates for the charge plan to leverage the chargeback capability. This is where you may want to get some help, because calculating your costs can be a complicated task, as you need to factor in not only the capital expenses for your environment, but also the operational expenses and the impact that your SLAs have on the cost model. A common example of the complexity is the CPU cost for a RAC database server. Not only do you need to factor in the hardware expense and the Oracle license expense, but you also need to calculate the labor expense for the senior admin who built and supports the cluster, as well as the more junior admins who usually provide the daily care of and feeds to the database. Often this also includes the expenses for backups, disaster recovery drills, and processes unique to your organization.

CAUTION
Missing an expense item can quickly result in inaccurate rates for your charge plan.

Having the showback/chargeback functionality not only helps make IT more efficient through feedback, but it also may show consumers of resources how to better understand their technology footprint, and can act as a tool to provide a way to reinforce good behavior.

An added benefit of Oracle Enterprise Manager is its ability to help manage a cloud for all the components, from infrastructure components like operating systems, storage and hypervisors, up the technology stack to the database and middleware tiers. Enterprise Manager can even expand into the application itself, with prebuilt plug-ins for many different applications. An administrator can even use Enterprise Manager to move database workloads easily between private clouds and a public cloud. This ability to almost seamlessly migrate workloads is being expanded to other components of the Oracle Red Stack. Enterprise Manager can also be used to monitor resources in both private and public clouds, enabling it to act as the single tool for monitoring all aspects of the enterprise, also known as *single pane of glass* for all aspects of the enterprise.

OpenStack and the Private Cloud

OpenStack is an emerging open-source framework that was initially built for deploying IaaS workloads for Rackspace hosting and NASA, though many other companies have adopted the framework and its related APIs. With OpenStack, you can manage different kinds of hypervisors, network services, storage components, databases, and more, using an API that creates a data center fabric. Vendors can write plug-ins that implement a solution using their own technology. Because OpenStack is an open-source project, many features are consistently being added, which is both a strength and weakness of the technology. Because changes occur at an accelerated pace, new features are constantly being added. This rapid change also introduces some challenges when it comes to upgrading or mixing new features with older components.

As seen in Figure 8-4, OpenStack consists of six core components: Swift, Keystone, Neutron, Nova, Cinder, and Glance. These core components make up the minimum system, enabling a basic IaaS framework, and are often augmented with additional components.

- **Swift** The object store, where objects and files are written to storage. Swift can replicate the storage between active nodes, thus providing redundancy.

- **Keystone** The core identity service, which acts as the central directory for all users and privileges. It is commonly integrated with existing Lightweight Directory Access Protocol (LDAP) systems.

- **Neutron** Where the network is managed from. Neutron provides IP addresses, VLANs, and more.

- **Nova** The core compute fabric manager for OpenStack. Oracle VM can act as a Nova target providing for hypervisor management for the virtual machines for both the x86 and SPARC architectures.

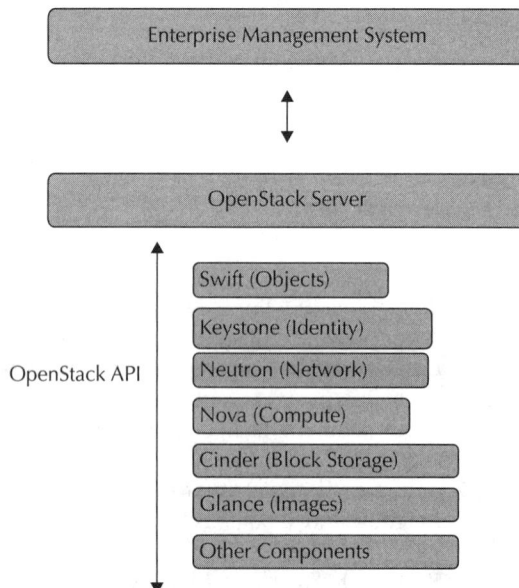

FIGURE 8-4. *OpenStack architecture*

- **Cinder**   Without block storage, most applications cannot run. Cinder provides the management framework for block storage. Modern storage arrays such as the ZS4 and FS1-2 are often used as the storage arrays.

- **Glance**   The repository of system images. Used to manage master copies of the system that can be used to clone to new instances, these are often called *golden images.*

In addition to the core components, there is an ever-growing collection of components that can enable management of technologies such as Trove (database), Zaqar (multitenant cloud messaging), Designate (DNS), and heat (orchestration services).

With Oracle VM, an Oracle Virtual Server (OVS) node can be managed by Nova, and for many environments this will meet the needs of the IT organization. However, because no single vendor owns the technology, administrators are often faced with complex issues when integrating different implementations of the framework.

> **NOTE**
> *OpenStack is written in multiple languages. Administrators need to understand Python to debug and troubleshoot most API issues. JavaScript and XML are the second most common languages used in OpenStack, but some more exotic components can use other languages.*

OpenStack is most commonly used by hosting companies and in DevOps environments, but it does not offer the rich blend of monitoring and provisioning features offered by Enterprise Manager 13*c*. With Enterprise Manager, a feature-rich private cloud can be up brought online by a single admin in a few days for managing IaaS, DBaaS, PaaS, and even the application tier. A comparable OpenStack deployment can often take weeks to months, as it is customized and technology conflicts are resolved.

Puppet and the Private Cloud

Puppet is a popular open-source configuration management tool that is included with Oracle Solaris 11.2 and is commonly installed on Oracle Linux servers. Using Puppet and its proprietary language, administrators can describe the system configuration they would like to apply to a system or a set of systems, thus helping to automate repetitive tasks. The system configuration can contain something as simple as a new DNS configuration, or as complex as an application installation. These capabilities are increasingly important in the cloud, as administrators need to manage more and more systems without adding additional staff. This information is stored in the Puppet *manifests,* which are files stored on the Puppet master containing the Puppet source code. Puppet then discovers the system information via a utility called Facter, which gathers system-specific details such as network settings, operating system, network configuration (including the IP and MAC addresses), Secure Shell (SSH) keys, and more. These facts are then made available in the Puppet manifests as variables, which can be used to compile the Puppet manifests with system-specific resources, which are then applied against the target systems. Any actions taken by Puppet are then reported back to the Puppet master.

Puppet is considered *model driven,* requiring some programming knowledge to use. As with any language, there is a learning curve. However, because the Puppet language is model driven, the time in minimal. Once the administrator has mastered the language, large-scale changes can

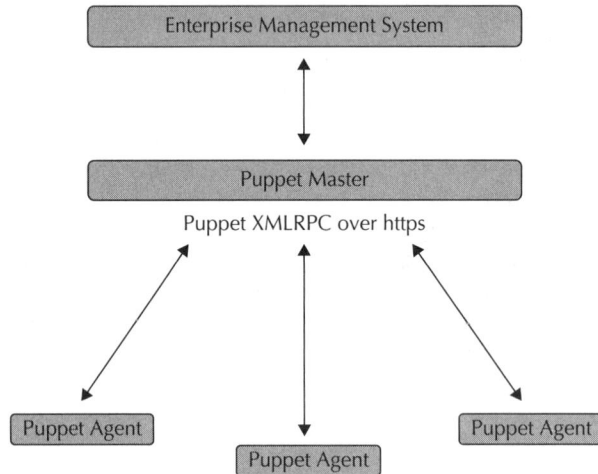

FIGURE 8-5. *Puppet architecture*

be automated in the data center. The administrator can also combine Puppet with the Oracle VM Manager command-line interface (CLI) to provision and destroy virtual machines.

NOTE
Starting in Oracle VM 3.2, the CLI utilities are installed when Oracle VM Manager is installed. Leveraging the CLI enables the administrator to integrate OVM to other systems.

As shown in Figure 8-5, Puppet is usually configured to use a client/server architecture where nodes (agents) periodically connect to a centralized server (Puppet master), retrieve configuration information, and then apply it.

The integration to an Enterprise Management system is up to the administrator. There currently is no web interface to Puppet, and the system provides only the change management functionality for a cloud. The billing, monitoring, and security are not included and must be developed by the cloud administrator. Because of this, Puppet is normally used to support existing deployments or is paired with a tool such as OpenStack, filling in one of the functional gaps missing when a fully integrated cloud management system such as Oracle Enterprise Manager is desired by the business.

Summary

This chapter addressed the management challenges faced when building private clouds. You learned how different tools can be used to provision and manage IaaS offerings while at the same time providing feedback to the users to show how their applications consume IT resources. You learned how Oracle Enterprise Manager, OpenStack, and Puppet can be used to build and manage a private cloud. Also, Oracle Enterprise Manager was explored in more detail. The next chapter covers how to configure Oracle Enterprise Manager 13c to manage an Oracle VM install.

PART
II

Installing and Configuring Oracle VM

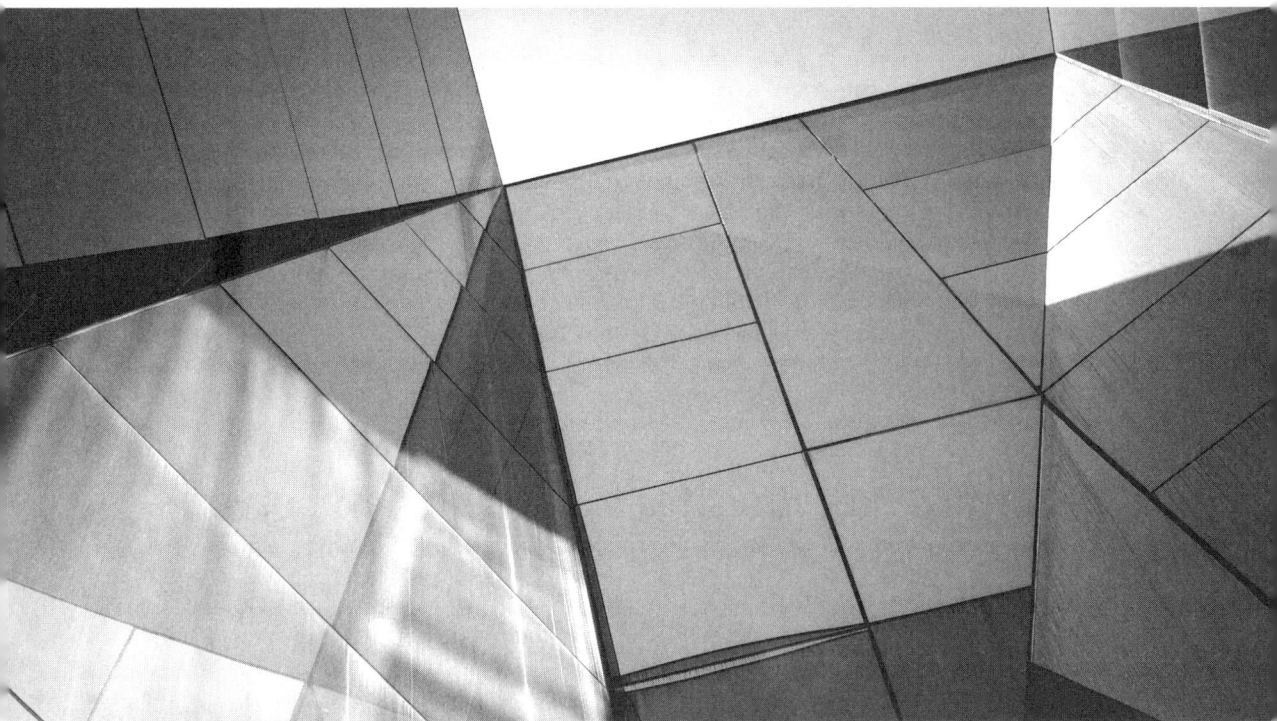

CHAPTER
9

Installing the
Oracle VM Server

I nstalling a VM server is a straightforward process, mostly because Oracle VM Server for x86 only supports the bare-metal installation method, which means Oracle VM is installed directly onto the hardware, just like you would install Linux or Windows. Unlike Oracle VM 2.*x*, Oracle VM 3.*x* is managed by both a command-line interface (CLI) and a web interface that runs on the Oracle VM Manager. Most of the initial configuration is performed using the web interface, which helps to simplify the configuration process. An additional advantage of the web interface is that it significantly reduces the learning curve for Oracle VM 3.*x*. This simplicity includes the discovery and configuration of Oracle VM Server (OVS). The idea is to install the Oracle VM Server system without very many options or customizations and then configure it later, with any customizations being performed and stored in the OVMM database. This architecture makes recovering from an OVS failure a simple task. In this chapter, we walk through the process of installing Oracle VM Server.

Hardware Prerequisites for Oracle VM Server

The hardware requirements for Oracle are minimal, although this will change rapidly as you size the system for your workloads. Oracle recommends that you have at least one dual-core, 64-bit, i686-class CPU and at least 2GB of RAM. In addition, 2GB of swap space and 4GB of disk space are required. As with most software vendors, the minimum requirements don't allow for any functionality, such as running actual virtual machines.

Because sizing was covered in a previous chapter, it won't be repeated here, except to remind you that it is important to perform a sizing exercise. The CPUs, RAM, and disk space must provide enough resources to support the virtual environment you want to create.

Oracle VM Server RAM Requirements

With the drop in disk storage costs, the primary constraint on modern servers becomes RAM. As such, you need a lot of RAM to support the applications on virtual machines. Table 9-1 lists a few examples of virtual machine sizes.

Oracle VM Server Local Disk Requirements

Although many installations of Oracle VM will use SAN or NAS storage, in some small configurations, local disks are used to host the virtual machines. If you are using local disks, a single virtual disk that is a mirrored boot disk is recommended, with a second virtual disk using RAID 5 or RAID 1+0

Virtual Machine	Estimated Disk Space
Basic Linux OS	1GB
Oracle Database on Linux	8GB + database memory target size
Application Server on Linux	4GB + application requirements
Windows 2012	4GB + application requirements
Total memory requirement:	17GB + application requirements

TABLE 9-1. *Virtual Machine RAM Requirements*

Virtual Machine Disk Space Requirements

Virtual Machine Type	Size	Number	Total Size
Basic Linux Server	1GB	10	10GB
Oracle Database on Linux	8GB + 4GB SGA	4	48GB
Application Server (Linux)	4GB + 12GB for WebLogic	4	64GB
Windows Server	4GB	5	20GB
Total:			142GB

TABLE 9-2. *Sample Sizing Worksheet*

for the data. The Oracle VM installer will slice up the boot disk for you during the installation. All you need is sufficient space to perform the installation. Adding resources later is not difficult, and that process will be covered later in this book.

The requirements shown in Table 9-1 are for a single virtual machine. A typical Oracle VM Server will support many virtual machines. To determine the total amount of disk space needed, multiply the requirements listed by the number of virtual machines of that type. You might create a worksheet similar to the one shown in Table 9-2.

Network Requirements

As networking becomes more complex, the requirements also require more planning prior to building an Oracle VM Server. OVS requires at least one static IPv4 address that does not change between server reboots. Although you can do static reservations with DHCP, it is recommended that you use static IP addresses. You will also need the network mask and the default gateway information, at a minimum, for installation.

Many actions performed within Oracle VM Manager (OVMM) require that OVS hostnames are properly resolved. It is highly recommended that you have at least one DNS server configured on your network and that the hostnames for each OVS can be resolved by all the systems within your Oracle VM environment. If you cannot set up a DNS infrastructure, you need to manually add host entries to the /etc/hosts file on each OVS and the OVMM server after you have finished your installation. Make sure you have your DNS server IPs and domain search information handy before installing the OVS.

Accurate time is also an important network function, and it is recommended that you also have a Network Time Protocol (NTP) infrastructure configured before installing any OVS. Using NTP will keep the time on all your hosts synchronized, which will help with troubleshooting and is considered a best practice for operational stability.

The number of network ports also can be a challenge. Although it is technically possible to run an OVS with a single network interface, you should plan to use more interfaces (usually at least two physical interfaces) connected to different switches for redundancy. You do not want your environment to stop working if one network interface fails, and a simple way to protect against that failure is to aggregate two interfaces in a bond interface. A *bond port,* as it is called in Oracle VM, can work in active-backup mode with no changes required on the network switch. Optionally, you can configure the network switch to enable an active-active aggregate, which will increase performance because it doubles the bandwidth. During the installation of each OVS, the management interface is configured. During discovery by OVMM, the server management interfaces are set as the default network for all functions. Because the management network is capable of providing all network functions in Oracle VM, including storage and virtual machine traffic, there is no functional need for additional networks. In a small production environment with basic network redundancy, a pair of interfaces is enough: the management network can be run on a VLAN and additional network connections can be made via VLAN interfaces configured on top of the single physical network interface. In larger environments, though, it is often ideal to physically separate the traffic across additional pairs of network interfaces.

The main reasons to opt for having multiple physical network interfaces are security and performance:

- **Security** In many environments, there is a requirement to physically separate internal and inter-server traffic onto different physical networks. Alternatively, you might need to guarantee that network traffic from different virtual environments, or different types of network traffic, are physically separated.

- **Performance** If you have multiple physical network interfaces, link aggregation is a good way to add bandwidth for a given network function. In addition, or as an alternative, you can create multiple physical networks and use them for dedicated functions (for example, a separate storage network or a network for virtual machine traffic only).

Installation Methods

You have several installation methods to choose from. The Oracle VM Server can be installed from a CD-ROM, hard drive, or network. The network option involves installing from a KickStart system. The CD-ROM option is the most common and perhaps easiest to perform because no additional configuration steps are required.

Basic Installation of the OVS from CD-ROM or ISO

With modern servers, the most common method of installing OVS is booting from an ISO image virtually mounted via the Lights Out Management interface. On Oracle X86 servers, the Lights Out Management interface is called the Integrated Lights Out Manager (ILOM). You still have the option of installing OVS from physical media on servers with optical drives. In either case, make sure that the ISO or CD-ROM image is mounted and that the BIOS is set to boot from the media. Next, power on the server. After POST (Power-On Self Test), the Oracle VM Server installer will appear. As mentioned before, the VM Server installer will install the hypervisor and dom0. Later, when you configure the VM Server, you'll decide whether it is a server pool master, utility server, or virtual machine server.

NOTE
Because of the large number of screens involved in installing the VM Server, only screenshots where action is required will be shown. Other screens will be described but not shown.

The POST screen is controlled by the hardware and performs operations such as testing memory and discovering and enabling devices at the hardware level. POST is an important part of the system boot process. The POST process performs operations that are crucial to the configuration and setup of devices. In addition, depending on the hardware installed, POST provides options for configuring devices by pressing a specific CTRL key series during device initialization. For example, during POST, the Fibre Channel host bus adapter (HBA) card might launch a configuration program when you press CTRL-Z or some other key combination. If necessary, configure any devices that require configuration at this stage. It is better to configure the hardware devices before any software is installed.

Once POST has completed, the OS installation process begins by booting the Oracle VM installer. During the startup of the Oracle VM installer, you will see additional device configuration steps. This process ends with the Oracle VM boot screen.

When OVS boots the first time, you can select to use the ISO to perform a physical-to-virtual conversion, or you can just install OVS, as shown here. Press ENTER to install OVS.

```
 -  Press the          key to begin the installation process.
 -  To perform a physical to virtual conversion type     and
    press the        key.
boot: _
```

This kicks off the installation process, as shown next.

```
[   1.603319] ACPI: bus type USB registered
[   1.603831] usbcore: registered new interface driver usbfs
[   1.604214] usbcore: registered new interface driver hub
[   1.604848] usbcore: registered new device driver usb
[   1.605524] PCI: Using ACPI for IRQ routing
[   1.606145] NetLabel: Initializing
[   1.606881] NetLabel:  domain hash size = 128
[   1.607356] NetLabel:  protocols = UNLABELED CIPSOv4
[   1.607949] NetLabel:  unlabeled traffic allowed by default
[   1.616582] Switched to clocksource xen
[   1.624355] pnp: PnP ACPI init
[   1.625256] pnp: PnP ACPI: found 2 devices
[   1.639352] PM-Timer failed consistency check  (0xffffff) - aborting.
[   1.640487] NET: Registered protocol family 2
[   1.640768] TCP established hash table entries: 16384 (order: 5, 131072 bytes
)
[   1.641653] TCP bind hash table entries: 16384 (order: 6, 262144 bytes)
[   1.642201] TCP: Hash tables configured (established 16384 bind 16384)
[   1.643339] UDP hash table entries: 1024 (order: 3, 32768 bytes)
[   1.643743] UDP-Lite hash table entries: 1024 (order: 3, 32768 bytes)
[   1.644297] NET: Registered protocol family 1
[   1.644814] pci 0000:00:00.0: Limiting direct PCI/PCI transfers
[   1.645353] pci 0000:00:01.0: Activating ISA DMA hang workarounds
[   1.647471] Trying to unpack rootfs image as initramfs...
```

Once the installer boots, you will be prompted to verify the boot media, as shown here. Normally, you will select Skip and proceed to the next step.

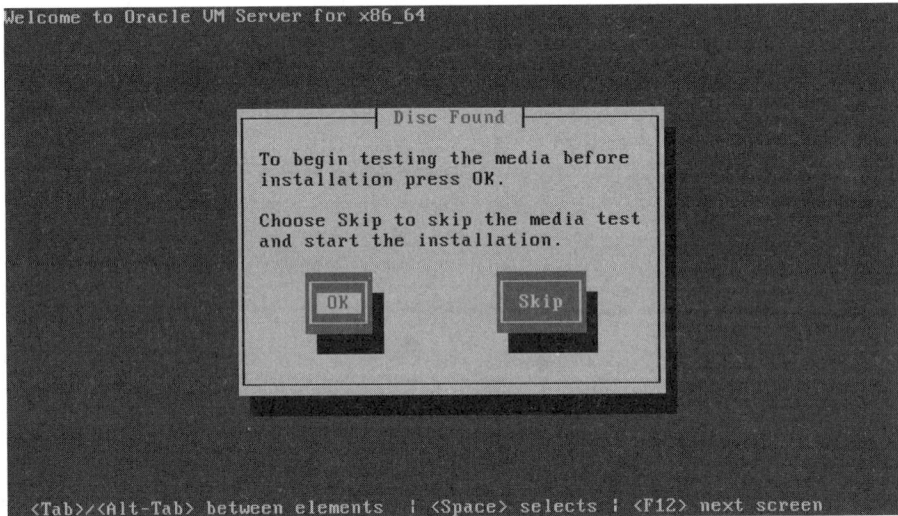

The ISO will now boot into the OVS installation mode, as shown here, and will present dialog boxes that ask you a few configuration questions, such as language, IP, name, and so on.

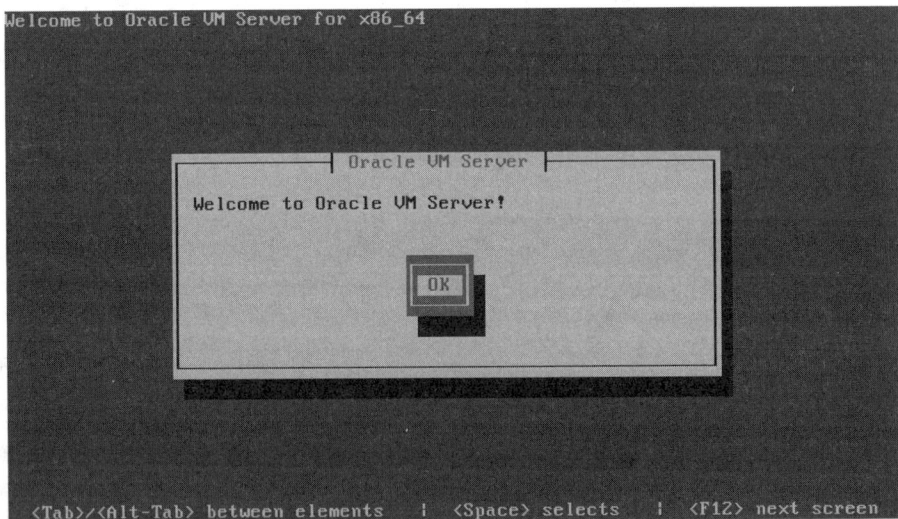

First, you will select the language, as shown here.

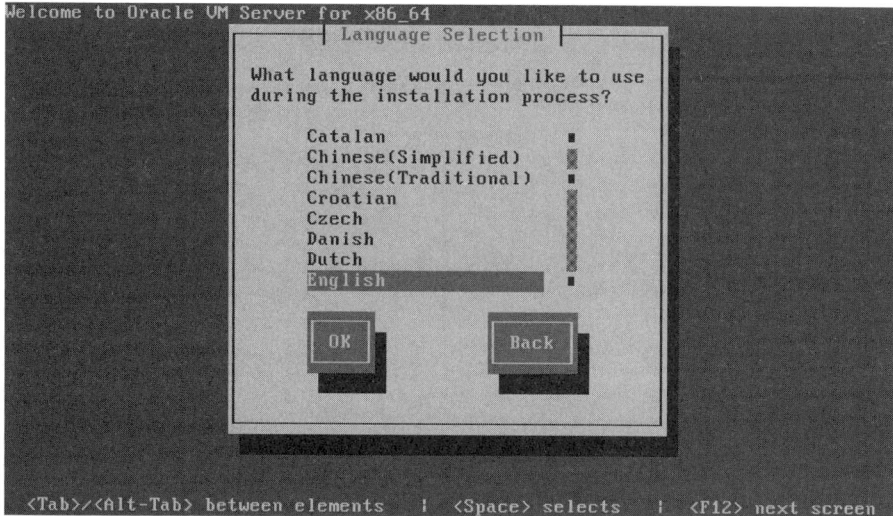

The reference install uses English, and here, a US keyboard is selected.

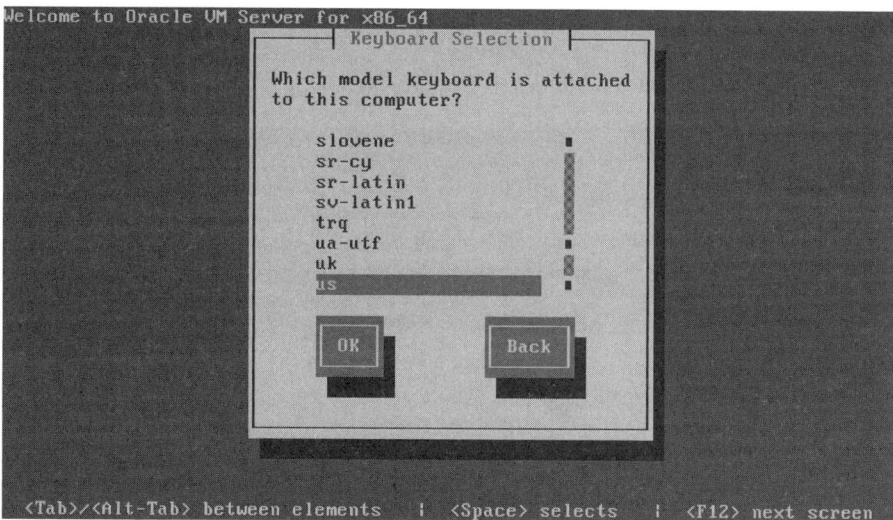

Next, you should read the OVS license agreement and accept the terms. You cannot continue without accepting Oracle's terms.

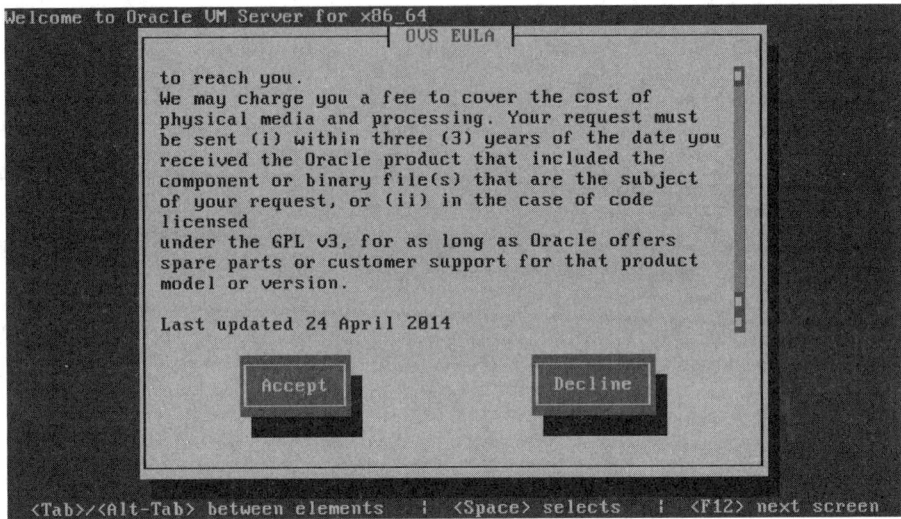

After you accept the EULA, the installer will run for a few seconds and probe for storage. If you have drives that are not initialized for OVM, the installer will prompt you to initialize the drives, as shown here. Note that if you select "Re-initialize all," any data on the drives will be lost. This includes LUNs and virtual drives that might have critical data you may not want destroyed.

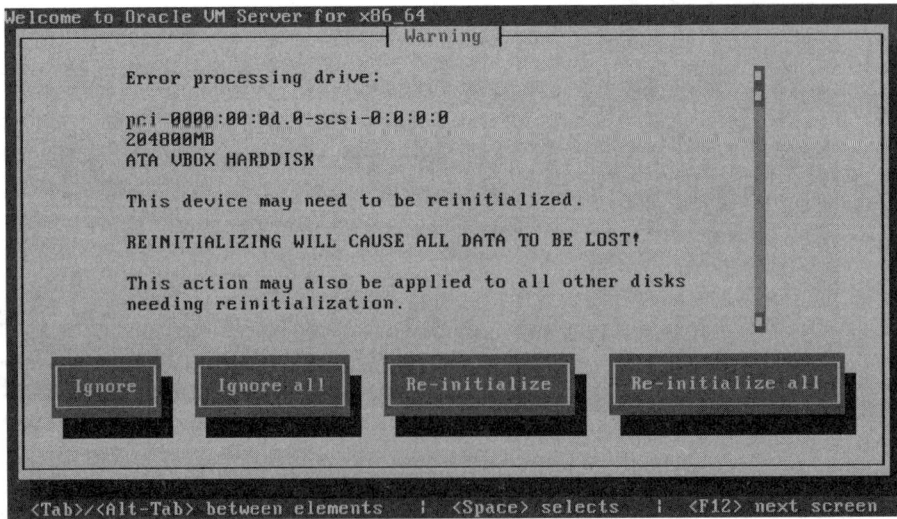

Once the drive is initialized, it is possible to create a custom partition table for the drive, or you can accept the default layout, as shown next.

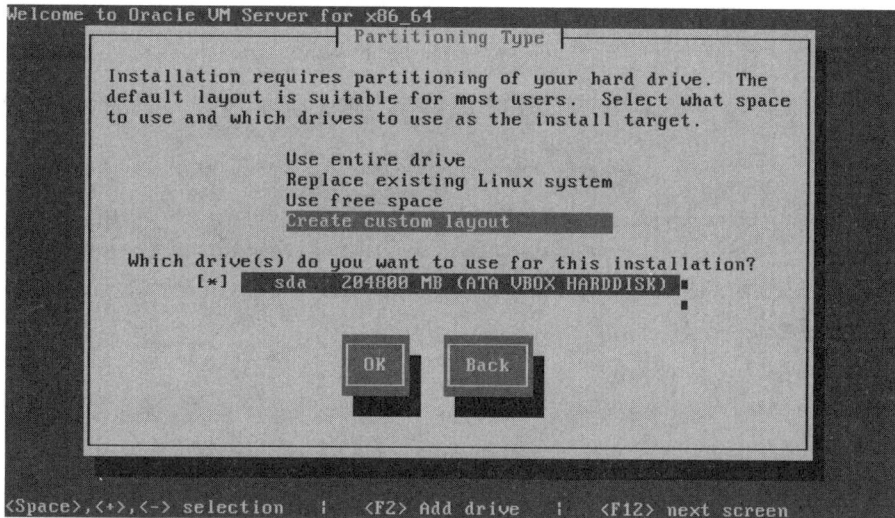

For this example, a custom partition is being created. As shown next, we have a 200GB drive available, and we will partition the drive as follows:

- 50GB for /
- 1GB for /boot
- 6GB for swap space
- 147GB unused

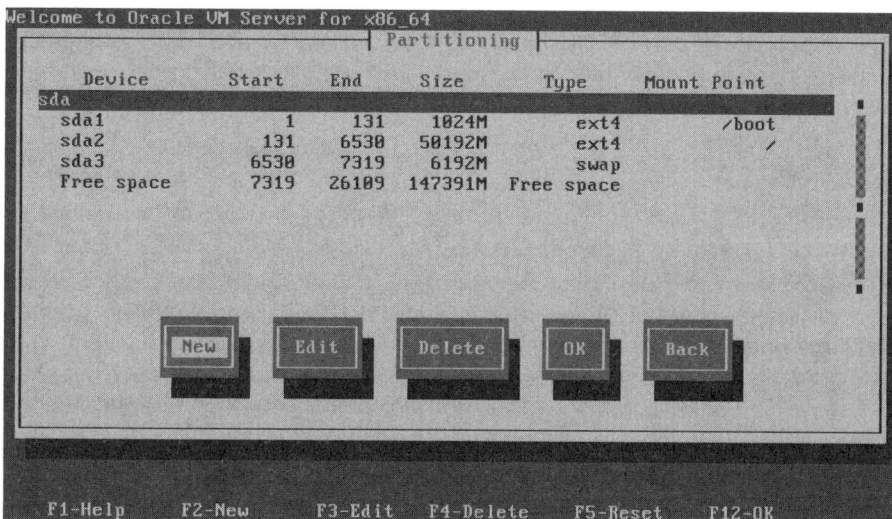

It is not required that you create a custom partition table, and the default installation will work well for most installations. Also, it is currently not possible to create a custom partition layout if you are installing in UEFI mode. If a partition is unused, it can later be used as a local repository for storing VM virtual disks, ISO images, templates etc.

Once the partitioning is finalized, do not forget to write the changes to disk, after selecting OK.

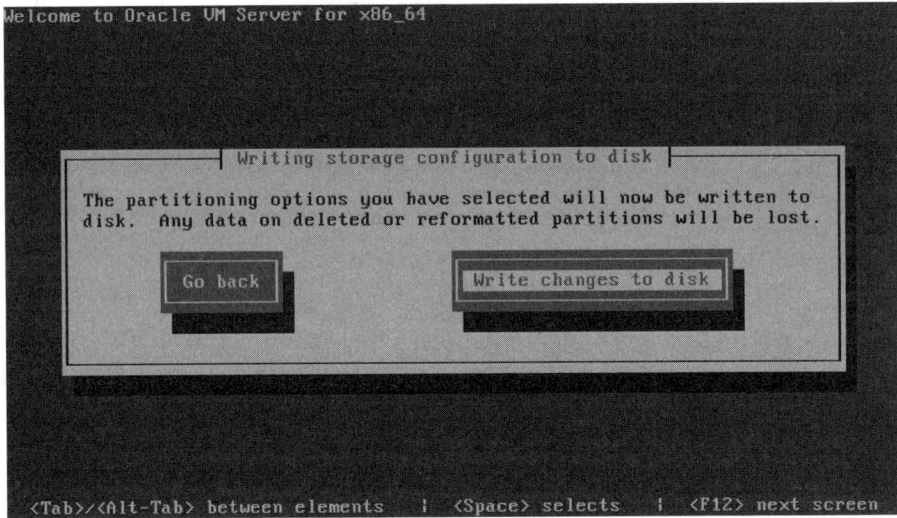

```
Welcome to Oracle VM Server for x86_64



              ┤ Writing storage configuration to disk ├

        The partitioning options you have selected will now be written to
        disk.  Any data on deleted or reformatted partitions will be lost.


                 Go back                    Write changes to disk




 <Tab>/<Alt-Tab> between elements   |   <Space> selects   |   <F12> next screen
```

The installer will now create the filesystems and configure the boot loader. In this example, the Master Boot Record is selected.

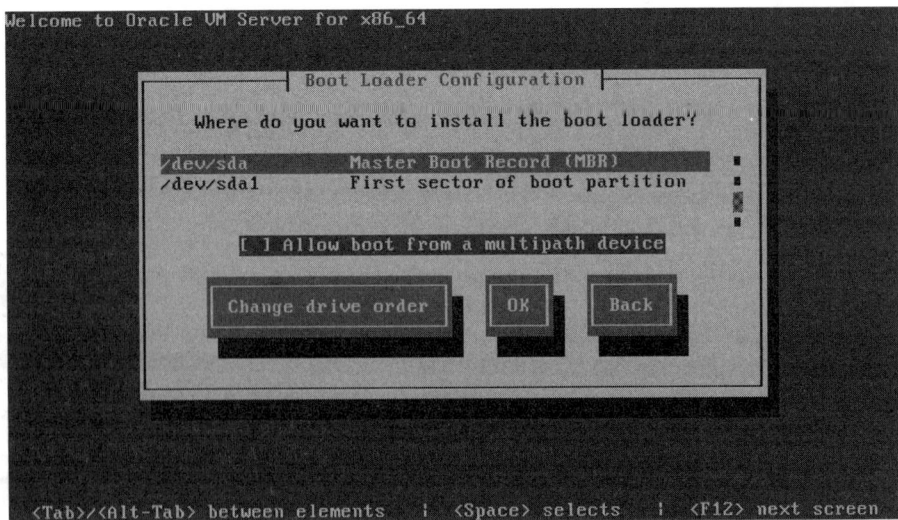

```
Welcome to Oracle VM Server for x86_64


                     ┤ Boot Loader Configuration ├

               Where do you want to install the boot loader?

        /dev/sda           Master Boot Record (MBR)
        /dev/sda1          First sector of boot partition



                [ ] Allow boot from a multipath device

           Change drive order        OK          Back




 <Tab>/<Alt-Tab> between elements   |   <Space> selects   |   <F12> next screen
```

Next is the option to enable a kernel crash dump. Kdump is a feature of the Linux kernel that will create a crash dump in the event of a kernel crash. When triggered, Kdump exports a memory image (also known as vmcore) that can be analyzed by support personnel for the purposes of debugging and determining the cause of the crash. Although helpful, Kdump does consume a little bit of RAM and is not supported on OVS when the server is using Non-Volatile Memory Express (NVME) or Fibre Channel over Ethernet (FCoE). As shown, Kdump will not be enabled in this example.

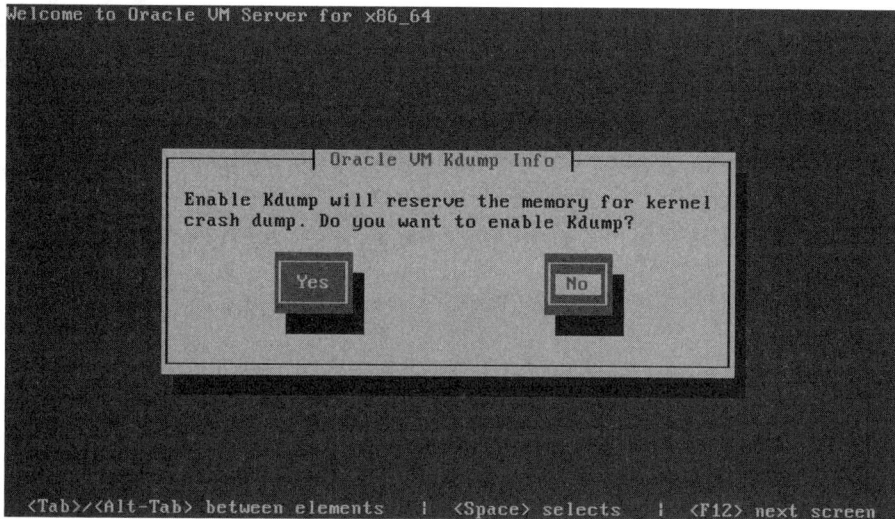

Next is the initial network configuration. In the reference OVS, no VLANs will be used, so eth0 is used as the primary management interface. After installation, VLANs and aggregates can be configured.

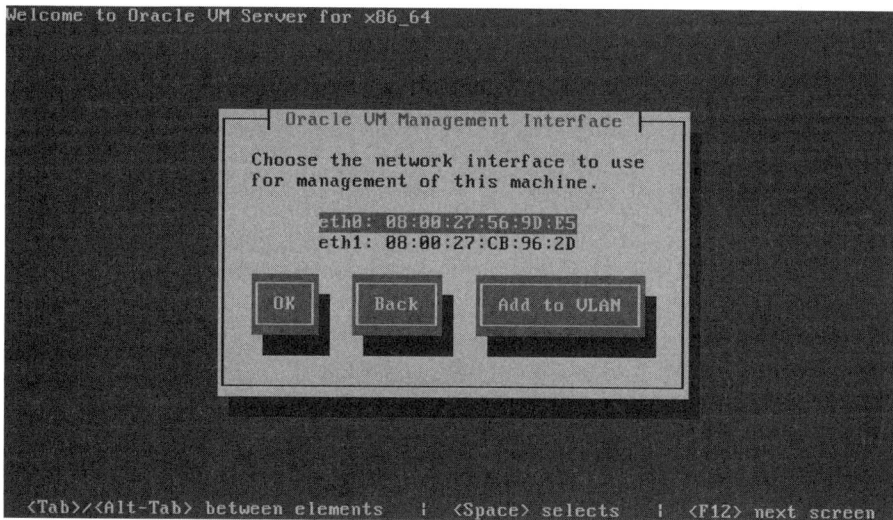

Once the network interface is selected, the static IP address and netmask will be assigned, as shown here. In newer versions of OVS, the netmask can be expressed in CIDR notation.

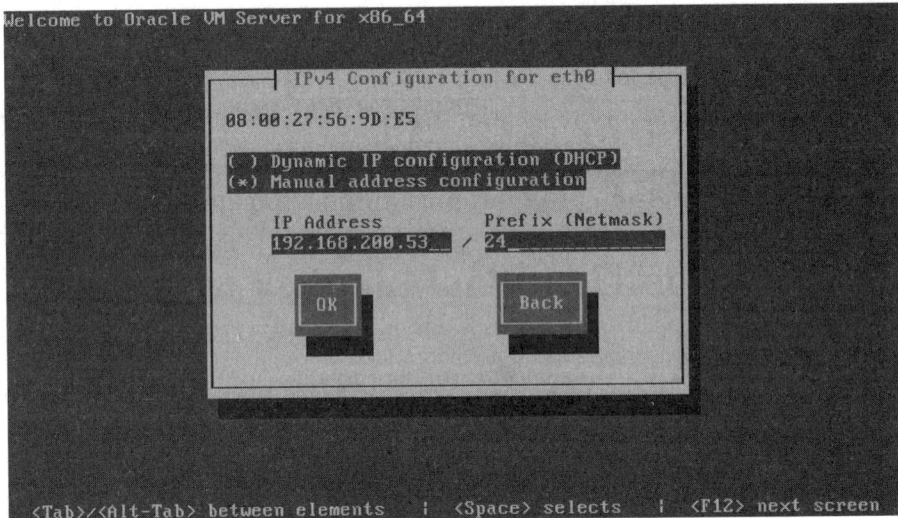

Installation of the OVS is almost complete. Next, the network settings for DNS and the IP default gateway are set.

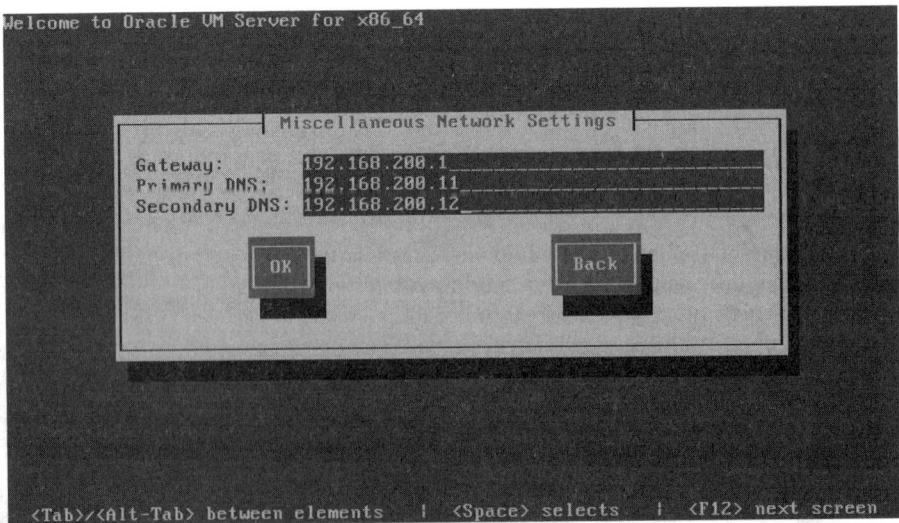

The next screen allows the DNS domain to be set. This is useful because, once set, the FQDN is not required to correctly resolve names in DNS.

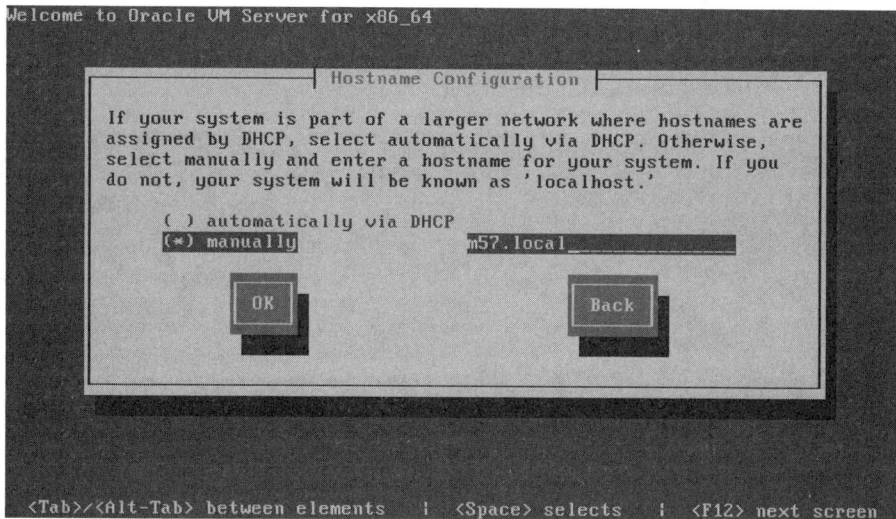

```
Welcome to Oracle VM Server for x86_64

                    ┤ Hostname Configuration ├

        If your system is part of a larger network where hostnames are
        assigned by DHCP, select automatically via DHCP. Otherwise,
        select manually and enter a hostname for your system. If you
        do not, your system will be known as 'localhost.'

            ( ) automatically via DHCP
            (*) manually              m57.local

                  OK                        Back




    <Tab>/<Alt-Tab> between elements  |  <Space> selects  |  <F12> next screen
```

The correct time on the system clock is important to a properly functioning installation. Verify that the system clock uses UTC, and select the operational time zone used for the server.

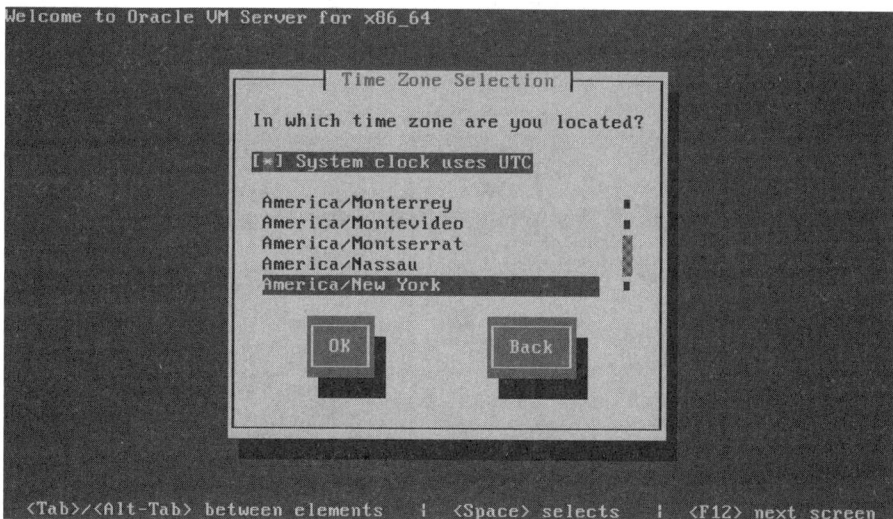

```
Welcome to Oracle VM Server for x86_64

                      ┤ Time Zone Selection ├

             In which time zone are you located?
            [*] System clock uses UTC

            America/Monterrey
            America/Montevideo
            America/Montserrat
            America/Nassau
            America/New York

                  OK                  Back



    <Tab>/<Alt-Tab> between elements  |  <Space> selects  |  <F12> next screen
```

Although many sites will use the local time zone, it is not uncommon in larger geographically diverse organizations for GMT to be used instead; this way, the timestamps in all log files will reflect the same time zone. The NTP settings are made via the OVMM interface later.

Setting the passwords is an important step that should not be done hastily. In OVS, two passwords are set during installation, the first being the OVM Agent password, as shown here. This is the password that OVMM uses to authenticate to OVS servers.

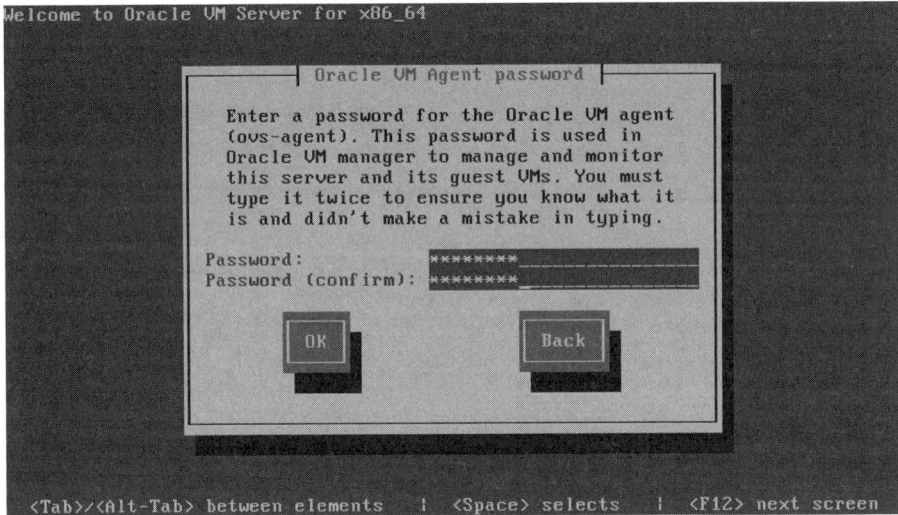

The second password is the root password for the OVS server, which is set in the screen shown here.

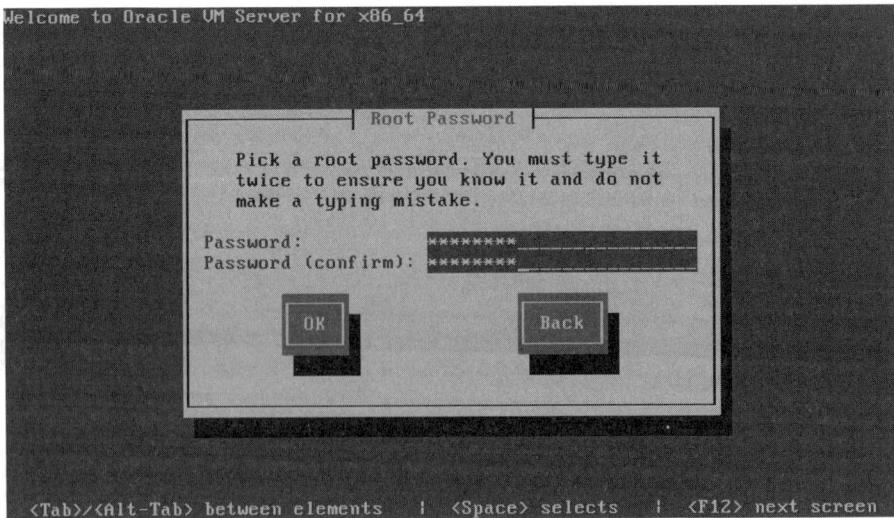

Next, the OVS system is installed, as shown here. This will take only a few minutes.

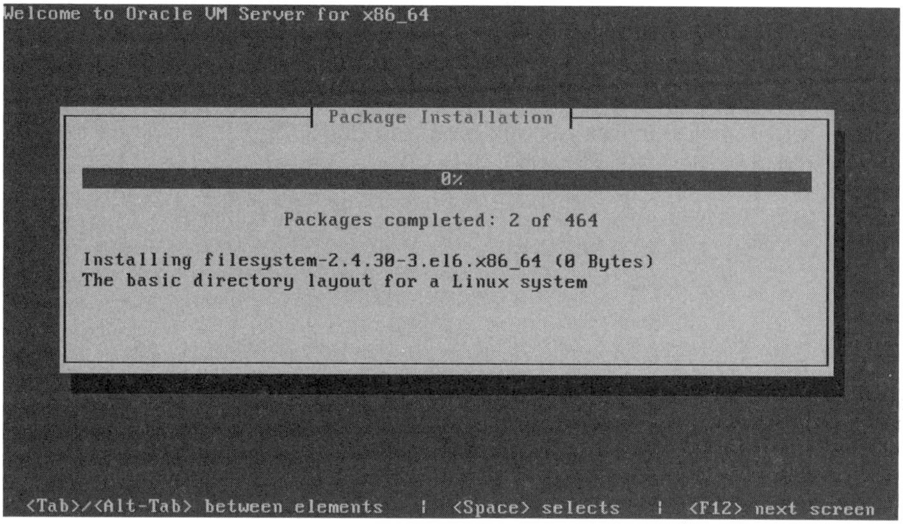

```
Welcome to Oracle VM Server for x86_64

                        ┤ Package Installation ├

                                      0%

                     Packages completed: 2 of 464

          Installing filesystem-2.4.30-3.el6.x86_64 (0 Bytes)
          The basic directory layout for a Linux system




     <Tab>/<Alt-Tab> between elements   |   <Space> selects   |   <F12> next screen
```

Once the installation is complete, the system will reboot. It is important to remove the media from the server before rebooting. If you're using ILOM, do not forget to "unpresent" the ISO file. If you're using physical media, be sure to remove the media from the optical drive.

Once the system is back up and running, you should see the OVS login screen, shown next. Unlike in older versions of OVS, you will not need to do anything else from the OVS server. All remaining configuration is performed from the OVMM.

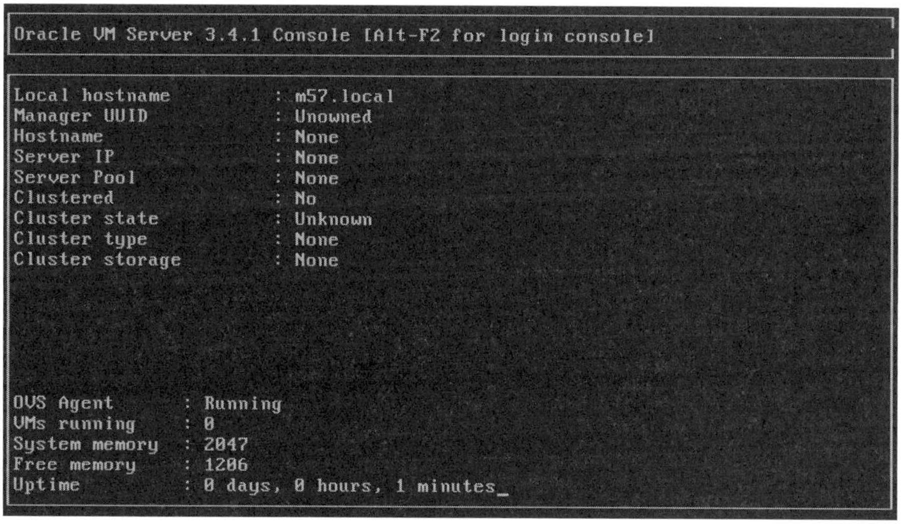

```
Oracle VM Server 3.4.1 Console [Alt-F2 for login console]

  Local hostname         : m57.local
  Manager UUID           : Unowned
  Hostname               : None
  Server IP              : None
  Server Pool            : None
  Clustered              : No
  Cluster state          : Unknown
  Cluster type           : None
  Cluster storage        : None




  OVS Agent     : Running
  VMs running   : 0
  System memory : 2047
  Free memory   : 1206
  Uptime        : 0 days, 0 hours, 1 minutes_
```

Summary

This chapter provided instructions on how to install the Oracle VM Server. There really isn't much work to installing the Oracle VM Server. Although you have several ways to do it, the installation process simply formats the disks and adds the software, including the VM Agent. Once the Oracle VM Server has been installed, you need to configure it as a server pool master, utility server, virtual machine server, or all of the above. Configuring the Oracle VM Server is where the real work begins, as discussed in the next few chapters.

CHAPTER
10

Oracle VM Concepts

Installing Oracle VM Manager (OVMM) only takes a few minutes. Oracle VM Manager can be installed on an Oracle Linux system, on either a physical server or a virtual machine. The installation can be a single non-clustered installation or a clustered installation using Oracle Clusterware. This chapter first describes how to install the Oracle VM Manager using the installation media and then discusses how to restore the Oracle VM Manager.

Hardware and Software Prerequisites for VM Manager

To install the Oracle VM Manager, you first need to allocate a host system and then install and configure the operating system (OS). The Oracle VM Manager runs on a 64-bit version of Linux— either Oracle Linux (OL) or Red Hat Enterprise Linux (RHEL) version 5.5 or higher. The Oracle VM Manager does not use an Oracle Database for its repository; therefore, not as many OS packages are required to support its installation.

> **NOTE**
> *If you are using a minimal installation of Oracle Linux, you will likely not have all the required packages installed. The OVMM runs additional checks for the required software packages. If a required package is missing, the installer might exit with a warning message, and the missing package will need to be installed. To install a missing package, run yum install -y followed by the package name to install it. The following example installs Perl:*

```
# yum install -y perl
```

The following components are installed with Oracle VM Manager:

- **Oracle MySQL**   Oracle MySQL 5.6 will be installed. If previous versions of MySQL are already installed, they should be removed before the Oracle VM Manager installation script is run. This includes the mariadb-libs package as well.

- **Oracle WebLogic 12c**   A limited-use licensed copy of WebLogic with the Application Development Framework (ADF) is installed. It is a limited-use license only for OVMM.

- **Oracle VM Tools**   The command-line interface (CLI) is now installed with OVMM as part of the standard installation.

- **ovmcore-console**   The software to support VM consoles is now automatically installed with OVMM.

Hardware Requirements for the Oracle VM Manager

The hardware requirements for the Oracle VM Manager are fairly straightforward. These are listed in Table 10-1.

The Oracle VM Manager system can be either a physical server or a virtual machine. A virtual machine is very capable of handling the workload of the Oracle VM Manager. In a fully virtualized environment, it seems like a waste to dedicate a server to just running the Oracle VM Manager. The contrary argument to using a virtual machine to host the Oracle VM Manager application,

Component	Minimum Required Value	Notes
CPU	2 × 1.8 GHz	Two cores are required. Additional CPUs may be needed, especially if features such as the RESTFul interface, Oracle Enterprise Manager Agent, and the CLI are used.
Memory	8GB	If the Oracle VM Manager is sharing the system with other applications, such as the HTTP Server required for a patch repository, then memory should be increased accordingly.
Hard disk space	9GB	To be safe, 50GB is recommended. As storage costs are minimal in most data centers, the larger sizes are highly recommended. The filesystem minimums are as follows: ■ 5.5GB in /u01; 20GB is recommended. ■ 3GB in /tmp; 10GB is recommended. ■ 400MB in /var; 10GB is recommended. ■ 300MB in /usr; 10GB is recommended. If running a patch repository on the OVMM server, you will need at least 50GB free in the filesystem being used for the repository. Over time, this filesystem will grow.
Swap space	2.1GB	If 2.1GB is not available, the installation will fail. During normal operations, if swapping occurs, you need to add memory.

TABLE 10-1. *Hardware Requirements for the Oracle VM Manager*

however, is that one should never monitor a critical system from within that system. This idea applies not only to the VM Manager, but potentially to Oracle Enterprise Manager (OEM) Cloud Control as well. If an OEM Cloud Control system is used to manage the virtual environment, installing OEM Cloud Control on a separate host system that is not part of the Oracle VM environment makes sense.

Oracle recommends that Oracle VM Manager never run as a guest operating system from within the Oracle VM environment it is managing. For maximum uptime, install Oracle VM Manager on two separate physical systems, each running Oracle Clusterware. This allows for maximum uptime and reliability. Keep in mind that Oracle VM servers, guests, and High Availability features continue to function whether the Oracle VM Manager is running or not.

A common use case is to run Oracle VM Manager on a virtualized Oracle Database Appliance, along with Enterprise Manager 13c, as shown in Figure 10-1.

This architecture provides an easy-to-manage, highly available installation of OVMM. This has the advantage of providing an isolated environment for both Oracle VM Manager and Oracle Enterprise Manager Cloud Control, with all the storage, CPU, and memory requirements isolated outside of the workload being managed. In the example, there are six VMs on the ODA: dual oda_base VMs, which are used for all Oracle Database workloads for the Enterprise Manager instance, dual OMS VMs to run a highly available Enterprise Manager instance, a VM supporting a Linux patch repository, and finally the VM running Oracle VM Manager. High Availability for the OVMM and patchrepo VMs is provided by automatic failover. Additionally, there is enough capacity for a few other VMs. The same Enterprise Manager Cloud Control system can be used to manage all targets in the enterprise.

Regardless of the type of hardware—physical or virtual—the software requirements are identical.

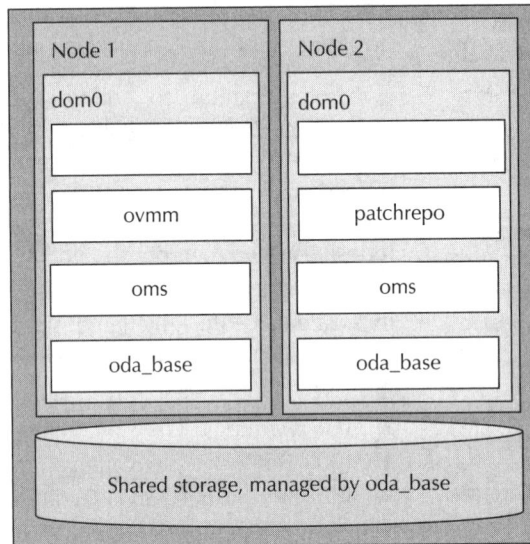

FIGURE 10-1. *Virtualized ODA architecture*

Virtual vs. Physical Host for the Oracle VM Manager

The Oracle VM Manager can very easily be hosted as a virtual machine. The hardware and software requirements are well within the parameters of what a virtual machine can provide. From a purely technical standpoint, running the Oracle VM Manager on a virtual machine makes a lot of sense. This argument holds true for small to medium OEM Cloud Control deployments as well. The most efficient way to host the most workloads is via a virtual machine.

The problem with hosting the Oracle VM Manager or Cloud Control on a virtual machine within the environment it is managing is that, in the event of a hardware issue, the Oracle VM Manager as well as the systems it is monitoring and managing are all unavailable. Even in a highly available environment, a power failure that disrupts power to the data center will most likely affect both systems.

An alternative is to host the Oracle VM Manager and/or Cloud Control on a physical system, preferably in another part of the data center. Another option is to host the Oracle VM Manager for one server pool in another server pool (hopefully, in a different part of the data center). The final option is to host the Oracle VM Manager in a different building from the VM servers. This option provides the most protection.

If absolute uptime is required for the Oracle VM Manager, install it on physical hardware running Oracle Clusterware. This will allow for failover to occur in the event of a system failure, and by not running Oracle VM Manager in a virtual environment, the loss of that environment will not affect it.

Software Requirements for the Oracle VM Manager

The software requirements for installing the Oracle VM Manager are very straightforward and direct. If you have installed MySQL or WebLogic, you are already familiar with all the requirements necessary to install those products. Compared to those installations, this process is very straightforward because the Oracle VM Manager installer checks for all the dependencies. Installation on top of a full install of the base OS is very simple.

The software prerequisites for installing the Oracle VM Manager are detailed in Table 10-2.

Modifying the Firewall Manually (If Necessary)

If a firewall is enabled on the host system, you must allow the Oracle VM Manager ports to be accessed. If you don't, browsers will not be able to access the Oracle VM Manager, nor will the Oracle VM Manager be able to access the Agents on the VM Server systems. Run the following **createOracle.sh** command found on the Oracle VM Manager installation media to automatically create the oracle user account and update the iptables configuration file with all required rules for service ports (this needs to be done before you execute the Oracle VM Manager installer):

```
# ./createOracle.sh
```

Although the createOracle.sh script can add the rules, many administrators prefer to manually add them, knowing some of the tools will help troubleshoot issues in the future. On Oracle Linux 6.*X*, modifying the firewall is accomplished by using the **chkconfig** and **iptables** commands. All of these commands should be run as the root user on your OVMM.

You can check to see if the firewall is on by looking at the output from the **iptables -L** command. If iptables is running, there will be several rules displayed. Rules are organized into *chains,* each representing a specific type of data flow. The INPUT chain represents traffic coming into the server. The OUTPUT chain represents traffic leaving the server. The third chain, FORWARD, is where packets are routed to another interface on a server, commonly used for network address translation (NAT) rules. On a default installation, all INPUT traffic is rejected, other than TCP port 22 (ssh) and ICMP requests (ping). All OUTPUT traffic is allowed, and there are no FORWARD rules. This is seen in the following example:

```
[root@ol6 ~]# iptables -L
Chain INPUT (policy ACCEPT)
target     prot opt source               destination
ACCEPT     all  --  anywhere             anywhere            state RELATED,ESTABLISHED
ACCEPT     icmp --  anywhere             anywhere
ACCEPT     all  --  anywhere             anywhere
ACCEPT     tcp  --  anywhere             anywhere            state NEW tcp dpt:ssh
REJECT     all  --  anywhere             anywhere            reject-with icmp-host-prohibited

Chain FORWARD (policy ACCEPT)
target     prot opt source               destination
REJECT     all  --  anywhere             anywhere            reject-with icmp-host-prohibited

Chain OUTPUT (policy ACCEPT)
target     prot opt source                  destination
```

Component	Notes
Oracle Enterprise Linux 5.5 or Red Hat Linux 5.5, 64-bit	As with most modern software, a 64-bit Linux kernel is required. The default installation is suggested. If this system will be used for other purposes, such as a HTTP server, check the documentation for required packages.
Hostname	Verify that the hostname is in the /etc/hosts file.

SELinux	It is recommended that you disable SELinux. This is done by editing the file /etc/selinuc/config and setting the SELINUX parameter to disabled. It should look similar to this:
	
	`# This file controls the state of SELinux on the system.`
	`# SELINUX= can take one of these three values:`
	`#     enforcing - SELinux security policy is enforced.`
	`#     permissive - SELinux prints warnings instead of enforcing.`
	`#     disabled - No SELinux policy is loaded.`
	`SELINUX=disabled`
	`# SELINUXTYPE= can take one of these two values:`
	`#     targeted - Targeted processes are protected,`
	`#     mls - Multi Level Security protection.`
	`SELINUXTYPE=targeted`

Network: OVMM to OVS	**TCP/6900-xxxx** SSL Secured VNC connections to the VNC consoles. One port is needed for each session. **TCP/8899** HTTPS connection to the Oracle VM Agent. **TCP/10000-xxxx** SSL secured port for serial connections for VMs using a serial console.
Network: OVS to OVMM	**TCP/7002** HTTPS connections from the OVS Agent to the OVMM core WSAPI. **UDP/123** NTP requests to an NTP server running on the OVMM.
Network: OVS to OVS	**TCP/7777** - OCFS2/DLM heartbeat communication for clustered server pools. **TCP/8002 (x86 only)** Non-encrypted live migrations. **TCP/8003 (x86 only)** SSL-encrypted live migrations. **TCP/8101 (SPARC only)** SSL-encrypted live migrations. **TCP/6482 (SPARC only)** LDoms Manager port used to initiate live migrations
Network: Management tools to OVMM	**TCP/7002** HTTPS to access the Web Services API. This is only required if the Web Services API will be used by external management tools.
Network: Management clients to OVMM	**TCP/7002** HTTPS connection from web browser to Oracle VM Manager web user interface, or WSAPI. **TCP/10000** SSH connection from SSH client to Oracle VM Manager CLI. **TCP/22** SSH connection to Oracle VM Manager host for administrative work.
Network: Shell access to OVS	**TCP/22** SSH connection to dom0 on each Oracle VM Server.

TABLE 10-2. *Oracle VM Manager Software Prerequisites*

If the firewall is not running, the output will look like this:

```
[root@ol6 ~]# iptables -L
Chain INPUT (policy ACCEPT)
target     prot opt source               destination

Chain FORWARD (policy ACCEPT)
target     prot opt source               destination

Chain OUTPUT (policy ACCEPT)
target     prot opt source               destination
```

To disable the firewall, you can stop it using the command **service stop iptables**:

```
[root@ol6 ~]# service iptables stop
iptables: Setting chains to policy ACCEPT: filter        [  OK  ]
iptables: Flushing firewall rules:                       [  OK  ]
iptables: Unloading modules:                             [  OK  ]
[root@ol6 ~]#
```

While this stops the firewall, at reboot the firewall will automatically restart. In Linux 6, you can use the command **chkconfig $SERVICE_NAME –list** to see the run state that each service runs:

```
[root@ol6 ~]# chkconfig iptables --list
iptables        0:off   1:off   2:on   3:on   4:on   5:on   6:off
[root@ol6 ~]#
```

In this example, you can see the iptables will run when the server is in run states 2, 3, 4, and 5. To disable a service from starting at boot, you can use the command **chkconfig $SERVICE_NAME off**. The following commands illustrate how the iptables service is disabled (**chkconfig iptables off**) and verify that at reboot the service will not start (**chkconfig iptables –list**):

```
[root@ol6 ~]# chkconfig iptables off
[root@ol6 ~]# chkconfig iptables --list
iptables        0:off   1:off   2:off   3:off   4:off   5:off   6:off
[root@ol6 ~]#
```

Not all environments will allow the Linux firewall to be disabled. In this case, you will need to add the required ports into the OVMM. This is done using the **iptables** command to add in new rules that accept requests on specific ports. On a standard installation, you will need to add ports 7002, 123, and 10000.

First, let's add the ports to the existing iptables chain:

```
# iptables -A INPUT -m state --state NEW -m tcp -p tcp --dport 7002 -j ACCEPT
# iptables -A INPUT -m state --state NEW -m udp -p udp --dport 123 -j ACCEPT
# iptables -A INPUT -m state --state NEW -m tcp -p tcp --dport 10000 -j ACCEPT
```

Once the rules are added, they will not be reenabled on reboot, unless they are saved. This is done by using the **service** command to save the configuration:

```
[root@ol6 ~]# service iptables save
iptables: Saving firewall rules to /etc/sysconfig/iptables:[  OK  ]
[root@ol6 ~]#
```

Installing VM Manager

Installing the Oracle VM Manager is not a difficult process. Once the system has been properly configured for the installation, the installation itself is fairly straightforward. Only when you get to the stage where you are configuring Oracle VM does the complexity begin.

Installing and Configuring the OS for the Oracle VM Manager

Oracle recommends a minimal (default) Linux installation be used for the Oracle VM Manager. Install Oracle Linux (OL) or Red Hat Enterprise Linux with the default packages. In addition, allocate hardware resources as shown earlier in this chapter. If you did not create a /u01 filesystem with your initial installation, you should create that now, allocating at least 20GB. Next, transfer the OVMM ISO file you downloaded from Oracle to the OVMM. In this example, the 3.4.2 build 1384 is being installed from the source ISO file ovmm-3.4.2-installer-OracleLinux-b1384.iso. Although future versions will have a different filename, the core process is the same. You can download the OVMM ISO from the Oracle Technology Network site: https://www.oracle.com/virtualization/vm-server-for-x86/index.html.

Mounting the OVMM ISO

The next step is to mount the image as a virtual CD-ROM. This allows the image to be accessed as if it were a CD-ROM. Linux allows an ISO file to be directly mounted on the system without generating a physical CD from the ISO. Before you mount the ISO, verify that the mount point is created. By default, most administrators use the /mnt directory.

An ISO image can be mounted directly on the system using the following syntax:

```
mount -o loop,ro <image> <mount point>
```

The **loop** option specifies that is a special loopback mount, and the **ro** option mounts the ISO as read-only. This method is used for our example:

```
#  mount -o loop,ro /root/ovmm-3.4.2-installer-OracleLinux-b1384.iso /mnt
```

Once mounted, the ISO will show up in a **df** command:

```
[root@ovmm ~]# df -k /mnt
Filesystem              1K-blocks    Used Available Use% Mounted on
/root/ovmm-3.4.2-installer-OracleLinux-b1384.iso
                        2759916 2759916         0 100% /mnt
```

Once the ISO image has been mounted, change directory to the mount point. You will run the installation from here.

Preparing to Install the Oracle VM Manager

From the mount point where the image has been mounted, you need to prepare the operating system for the software. Oracle has automated this with the command **createOracle.sh**. As root, run the command. This command will not stop on minor issues, such as the oracle user already being created or firewall rules already being in place. Although the command sets up an oracle user, you will need to manually set the password for the user.

```
[root@ovmm mnt]# ./createOracle.sh
Adding group 'oinstall' with gid '54323' ...
```

```
groupadd: group 'oinstall' already exists
Adding group 'dba'
groupadd: group 'dba' already exists
Adding user 'oracle' with user id '54322', initial login group 'dba',
supplementary group 'oinstall'
and  home directory '/home/oracle' ...
User 'oracle' already exists ...
uid=54321(oracle) gid=54321(oinstall) groups=54321(oinstall),54322(dba)
Creating user 'oracle' succeeded ...
For security reasons, no default password was set for user 'oracle'.
If you wish to login as the 'oracle' user, you will need to set
a password for this account.
Verifying user 'oracle' OS prerequisites for Oracle VM Manager ...
oracle  soft    nofile       8192
oracle  hard    nofile       65536
oracle  soft    nproc        2048
oracle  hard    nproc        16384
oracle  soft    stack        10240
oracle  hard    stack        32768
oracle  soft    core         unlimited
oracle  hard    core         unlimited
Setting  user 'oracle' OS limits for Oracle VM Manager ...
Altered file /etc/security/limits.conf
Original file backed up at /etc/security/limits.conf.orabackup
Verifying & setting of user limits succeeded ...
Changing '/u01' permission to 755 ...
Modifying iptables for OVM
Adding rules to enable access to:
    7002  : Oracle VM Manager https
      123 : NTP
    10000 : Oracle VM Manager CLI Tool
service iptables status: stop
iptables: Applying firewall rules:                              [ OK ]
iptables: Saving firewall rules to /etc/sysconfig/iptables:     [ OK ]
iptables: Setting chains to policy ACCEPT: filter               [ OK ]
iptables: Flushing firewall rules:                              [ OK ]
iptables: Unloading modules:                                    [ OK ]
iptables: Applying firewall rules:                              [ OK ]
iptables: Setting chains to policy ACCEPT: filter               [ OK ]
iptables: Flushing firewall rules:                              [ OK ]
iptables: Unloading modules:                                    [ OK ]
Rules added.
```

Installing the Oracle VM Manager

Once the environment is configured, you will next install the Oracle VM Manager. Run the installer script **runInstaller.sh**:

```
[root@ovmm mnt]# ./runInstaller.sh

Oracle VM Manager Release 3.4.2 Installer
```

```
Oracle VM Manager Installer log file:
/var/log/ovmm/ovm-manager-3-install-2016-12-23-172008.log

Please select an installation type:
    1: Install
    2: Upgrade
    3: Uninstall
    4: Help

    Select Number (1-4):
```

You now have four options: Install, Upgrade, Uninstall, and Help. Select **1** to continue with the installation:

```
    Select Number (1-4): 1

Verifying installation prerequisites ...

Starting production with local database installation ...

One password is used for all users created and used during the installation.
Enter a password for all logins used during the installation:
Enter a password for all logins used during the installation (confirm):
```

The password will enforce some basic security. It must be between 8 and 16 characters, have at least one uppercase letter and one lowercase letter, and contain one numeric or special character. For example, **Welcome!** will work, but **welcome1** will not.

```
Please enter your fully qualified domain name, e.g. ovs123.us.oracle.com, (or IP address) of
your management server for SSL certification generation, more than one IP address are
detected: 10.0.2.15 192.168.56.20 [ovmm]:

Verifying configuration ...

Start installing Oracle VM Manager:
    1: Continue
    2: Abort
```

Enter **1** to continue the installation. Depending on the speed of your system, it will take anywhere from 10 to 45 minutes to complete the seven steps. This is a good time to save the password you set. This password will be used for all components of the Oracle VM Manager, including the WebLogic admin password.

```
Select Number (1-2): 1

Step 1 of 7 : Database Software ...
Installing Database Software...
Retrieving MySQL Database 5.6 ...
Unzipping MySQL RPM File ...
Installing MySQL 5.6 RPM package ...
Configuring MySQL Database 5.6 ...
Installing MySQL backup RPM package ...
```

```
Step 2 of 7 : Java ...
Installing Java ...

Step 3 of 7 : WebLogic and ADF ...
Retrieving Oracle WebLogic Server 12c and ADF ...
Installing Oracle WebLogic Server 12c and ADF ...
Applying patches to Weblogic ...
Applying patch to ADF ...

Step 4 of 7 : Oracle VM ...
Installing Oracle VM Manager Core ...
Retrieving Oracle VM Manager Application ...
Extracting Oracle VM Manager Application ...

Retrieving Oracle VM Manager Upgrade tool ...
Extracting Oracle VM Manager Upgrade tool ...
Installing Oracle VM Manager Upgrade tool ...

Retrieving Oracle VM Manager CLI tool ...
Extracting Oracle VM Manager CLI tool...
Installing Oracle VM Manager CLI tool ...
Installing Oracle VM Manager WLST Scripts ...

Step 5 of 7 : Domain creation ...
Creating domain ...

Step 6 of 7 : Oracle VM Tools ...

Retrieving Oracle VM Manager Shell & API ...
Extracting Oracle VM Manager Shell & API ...
Installing Oracle VM Manager Shell & API ...

Retrieving Oracle VM Manager Wsh tool ...
Extracting Oracle VM Manager Wsh tool ...
Installing Oracle VM Manager Wsh tool ...

Retrieving Oracle VM Manager Tools ...
Extracting Oracle VM Manager Tools ...
Installing Oracle VM Manager Tools ...

Retrieving ovmcore-console ...
Installing ovmcore-console RPM package ...
Copying Oracle VM Manager shell to '/usr/bin/ovm_shell.sh' ...
Installing ovm_admin.sh in '/u01/app/oracle/ovm-manager-3/bin' ...
Installing ovm_upgrade.sh in '/u01/app/oracle/ovm-manager-3/bin' ...

Step 7 of 7 : Start OVM Manager ...
Enabling Oracle VM Manager service ...
Shutting down Oracle VM Manager instance ...
Starting Oracle VM Manager instance ...

Please wait while WebLogic configures the applications...
Trying to connect to core via ovmwsh (attempt 1 of 20) ...
Trying to connect to core via ovmwsh (attempt 2 of 20) ...
Trying to connect to core via ovm_shell (attempt 1 of 5)...
Oracle VM Manager installed.
```

```
Installation Summary
--------------------
Database configuration:
  Database type              : MySQL
  Database host name         : localhost
  Database name              : ovs
  Database listener port     : 49500
  Database user              : ovs

Weblogic Server configuration:
  Administration username    : weblogic

Oracle VM Manager configuration:
  Username                   : admin
  Core management port       : 54321
  UUID                       : 0004fb0000010000e48a2ccbc5ac498e


Passwords:
There are no default passwords for any users. The passwords to use for Oracle VM Manager,
Database, and Oracle WebLogic Server have been set by you during this installation. In
case of a default install, all passwords are the same.

Oracle VM Manager UI:
  https://ovmm:7002/ovm/console
Log in with the user 'admin', and the password you set during the installation.

For more information about Oracle Virtualization, please visit:
  http://www.oracle.com/virtualization/

Oracle VM Manager installation complete.

Please remove configuration file /tmp/ovm_configWTzc2s.
[root@ovmm mnt]#
```

If your installation has any issues, several logs will be available to help you resolve any issues. The first log to check is the Oracle VM Manager installation log file. Usually, this log can be found in /var/log/ovmm/ovm-manager-3-install-date.log. However, if the installer is unable to create this directory and file for some reason, such as inadequate permissions, the install file will be located in /tmp/ovm-manager-3-install-date.log. During installation, the installer self-extracts into the /tmp directory; if the installer does not exit properly, you may also find an installation log in this location: /tmp/ovmm-installer.selfextract_id/ovm-manager-3-install-date.log.

There is not a lot of management to do on the Oracle VM Manager system. The regular, required maintenance is minimal and mainly requires some effort to monitor the automatic backups of the MySQL database.

Managing the Oracle VM Manager Operating System

Managing a virtual or physical Oracle VM management server is the same as managing any Linux server. Make regular backups of the system, and especially of files that regularly change, including the Oracle VM Manager database repository located under /u01. As with any physical system, normal maintenance routines, such as performance monitoring and error log monitoring, should be performed. All in all, there really isn't much required maintenance.

Managing the Oracle VM Manager

The Oracle VM Manager is made up of the MySQL database, the OVM CLI, and the Oracle VM Manager application. If necessary, you can start and stop each of these components using scripts installed in /etc/init.d:

- **/etc/initi.d/ovmm_mysql**   Manages the MySQL instance used by Oracle VM Manager
- **/etc/initi.d/ovmm**   Manages the Oracle VM Manager application and related WLS instance
- **/etc/initi.d/ovmcli**   Manages the Oracle VM Manager CLI

Using these commands, you can stop, start, restart, and check the status of each service. In order to affect service, pass the option you wish to use—either **start**, **stop**, **restart**, or **status**. The following example stops and then starts the OVM CLI, followed by checking the status:

```
[root@ovmm init.d]# /etc/init.d/ovmcli stop
Stopping Oracle VM Manager CLI                          [  OK  ]
[root@ovmm init.d]# /etc/init.d/ovmcli start
Starting Oracle VM Manager CLI                          [  OK  ]
[root@ovmm init.d]# /etc/init.d/ovmcli status
Oracle VM Manager CLI is running...
```

Because they are part of the Linux services, they are started and stopped automatically with the system. You can control this using the **chkconfig** command, just as you would with the network service.

Oracle VM Configuration Files

When Oracle VM is installed, a new configuration file is added to the operating system. The file will remain on the server even if Oracle VM Manager is uninstalled. This is helpful when recovering the universally unique identifier (UUID) of the installation. This file (/etc/sysconfig/ovmm) also contains several other key items:

```
[root@ovmm init.d]# more /etc/sysconfig/ovmm
JVM_MEMORY_MAX=4096m
JVM_MAX_PERM=512m
RUN_OVMM=YES
DBBACKUP=/u01/app/oracle/mysql/dbbackup
DBBACKUP_CMD=/opt/mysql/meb-3.12/bin/mysqlbackup
UUID=0004fb0000010000e48a2ccbc5ac498e
```

These parameters control the automatic backups and the Java virtual machine (JVM), as described in Table 10-3.

Oracle VM will also create a second configuration file located in /u01/app/oracle/ovm-manager-3/.config:

```
[root@ovmm init.d]# more /u01/app/oracle/ovm-manager-3/.config
DBTYPE=MySQL
DBHOST=localhost
SID=ovs
LSNR=49500
OVSSCHEMA=ovs
```

```
APEX=8080
WLSADMIN=weblogic
OVSADMIN=admin
COREPORT=54321
UUID=0004fb0000010000e48a2ccbc5ac498e
BUILDID=3.4.2.1384
```

This file is deleted if Oracle VM Manager is uninstalled. It contains the database connection information, version information, and the UUID, with the options described in Table 10-4.

Normally, you will not need to edit this file, unless you are changing the UUID of the installation. When backing up your Oracle VM Manager system, you need to make sure that both configuration files are backed up.

Backing Up the Oracle VM Manager Database

As of Oracle VM Manager Release 3.2.1, backups of the integrated MySQL database are performed automatically, with the schedule being set through the web interface. By default, the backups run every 1440 minutes, with 21 generations of backups kept. These parameters can be set in the VM Manager under Reports and Resources | Preferences, as seen in Figure 10-2.

Backups are stored within /u01/app/oracle/mysql/dbbackup by default and are rotated regularly so that only the most recent backups are stored at any point in time. Although you can use the default location, it is possible to set the backup location to an NFS mount point, providing automatic off-server backups. This is often done with the backups living on a NAS device.

Manual backups are also available, and most often performed before an upgrade. The command **/u01/app/oracle/ovm-manager-3/ovm_tools/bin/BackupDatabase -w** is used to perform a

Parameter	Description
JVM_MEMORY_MAX	This sets the Java heap for the WebLogic server. If you are managing more than 80 virtual machines, set it to 8192.
JVM_MAX_PERM	The permanent space is where the classes, methods, internalized strings, and similar objects used by the VM are stored and never deallocated. Do not adjust this unless directed to by Oracle Support.
RUN_OVMM	If this parameter is set to NO, /etc/init.d/ovmm will not start OVMM.
DBBACKUP	This sets the location of the automatic database backups.
DBBACKUP_CMD	This is the command used to run automatic database backups.
UUID	This is the unique ID. Each Oracle VM server receives a UUID that is used as the OVMM manages OVS and storage. Normally, you will not change this, except in a disaster recovery scenario where you are keeping the same UUID at your primary site and the disaster site.

TABLE 10-3. *OVMM Configuration File Parameters*

Variable	Description
DBTYPE	Database type. This is a legacy configuration property used with older versions of OVMM. On new installations, the value is always MySQL.
DBHOST	Hostname of database server. This is a legacy configuration property. The value is always localhost.
SID	Oracle system ID (SID). The default value is ovs.
LSNR	Database listener port number. The default value is 49500.
OVSSCHEMA	Oracle VM Manager database name. The default value is ovs.
APEX	This is a legacy configuration property. The default value is None.
WLSADMIN	Oracle WebLogic Server administrator username. The default value is weblogic.
OVSADMIN	Oracle VM Manager administrator username. The default value is admin.
COREPORT	Oracle VM Manager core port number. The default value is 54321.
UUID	Oracle VM Manager universally unique identifier; it should match the value found in /etc/sysconfig/ovmm.
BUILDID	Oracle VM Manager version and build number.

TABLE 10-4.   *OVMM Configuration File Parameters*

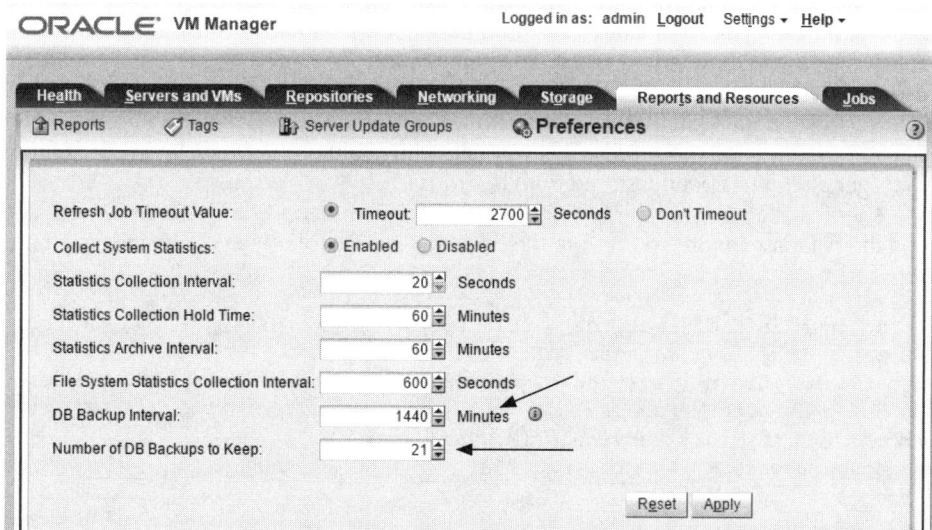

FIGURE 10-2.   *OVMM preferences*

manual backup. When running the command, you will need to provide the OVM Manager admin login credentials:

```
[root@ovmm init.d]# /u01/app/oracle/ovm-manager-3/ovm_tools/bin/BackupDatabase -w
Enter your OVM Manager username: admin
Enter your OVM Manager password:

INFO:  Backup job starting with destination:
       /u01/app/oracle/mysql/dbbackup/ManualBackup-20161224_143651

       Job Id   = 'Start Backup to: ManualBackup(1482608211883) Uri:
https://localhost:7002/ovm/core/wsapi/rest/Job/1482608211883'
       Job Name = 'Start Backup to: ManualBackup'

INFO:  Backup job finished

[root@ovmm init.d]#
```

Restoring the Complete Oracle VM Manager

When choosing to restore the entire Oracle VM Manager, you have several points to consider. If the MySQL database is corrupted, it is possible to just restore the database from one of the automatic backups. It is also possible to reinstall a fresh Oracle VM Manager, and simply take over the existing server pool and rediscover the system. The final option is to do a fresh installation of the Oracle VM Manager and then restore the database.

Reinstalling the Oracle VM Manager is not a difficult task. It is often done with a cold disaster recovery site. The steps are fairly straightforward: First, if you need to reinstall the Oracle VM Manager, use the Oracle VM Manager installation media to perform an install. The one change, however, is that when running the **runInstaller.sh** command, you will pass the UUID of your installation using the **runInstaller.sh --uuid uuid** command and provide the UUID from the /etc/sysconfig/ovmm file. Alternatively, if the configuration file is present, the installer will automatically use the UUID in the file.

Next, when the Oracle VM Manager installer prompts for installation information, reuse the same usernames and passwords. This will help you avoid problems restarting the Oracle VM Manager after it has been restored from backup.

After installation, stop the Oracle VM Manager command-line interface, Oracle VM Manager, and the database before you restore the backup. Run the following commands to stop all the services:

```
[root@ovmm init.d]# service ovmcli stop
Stopping Oracle VM Manager CLI                            [  OK  ]
[root@ovmm init.d]# service ovmm stop
Stopping Oracle VM Manager                                [  OK  ]
[root@ovmm init.d]# service ovmm_mysql stop
Shutting down OVMM MySQL.. SUCCESS!
[root@ovmm init.d]#
```

To restore the database as the oracle user, use the **RestoreDatabase** command located in /u01/app/oracle/ovm-manager-3/ovm_tools/bin. Here's an example:

```
[oracle@ovmm ~]$ /u01/app/oracle/ovm-manager-3/ovm_tools/bin/RestoreDatabase.sh \
ManualBackup-20161222_143651

Before the database can be restored, the following database directories/file
must be deleted:
appfw ibdata1 ib_logfile0 ib_logfile1 mysql ovs performance_schema

Are you sure it is safe to delete these directories/files now? [y,n] y
Deleting /u01/app/oracle/mysql/data/appfw
Deleting /u01/app/oracle/mysql/data/ibdata1
Deleting /u01/app/oracle/mysql/data/ib_logfile0
Deleting /u01/app/oracle/mysql/data/ib_logfile1
Deleting /u01/app/oracle/mysql/data/mysql
Deleting /u01/app/oracle/mysql/data/ovs
Deleting /u01/app/oracle/mysql/data/performance_schema
INFO: Expanding the backup image...
INFO: Applying logs to the backup snapshot...
INFO: Restoring the backup...
INFO: Restoring OVM keystores and certificates
INFO: Success - Done!
INFO: Log of operations performed is available
at: /u01/app/oracle/mysql/dbbackup/ManualBackup-20161222_143651/Restore.log


IMPORTANT:

    As 'root', please start the OVM Manager database and application using:
        service ovmm_mysql start; service ovmm start; service ovmcli start''
```

The **RestoreDatabase** script expects the name of the directory for a particular backup directory, as seen in the /etc/sysconfig/ovmm configuration file. You do not need to specify the full path to the backup directory because this is already specified in the **DBBACKUP** variable.

The **RestoreDatabase** script performs a version check to ensure that the database version matches the version of the database from which the backup was created. If there is a version mismatch, the script exits with a warning because this action may render Oracle VM Manager unusable. It is possible to override this version check by using the **--skipversionchecks** option when invoking the script. This option should be used with care, as version mismatches may have undesirable consequences for Oracle VM Manager.

Restart the database, the Oracle VM Manager, and the Oracle VM Manager CLI:

```
[root@ovmm init.d]# service ovmm_mysql  start
Starting OVMM MySQL. SUCCESS!
[root@ovmm init.d]# service ovmm start
Starting Oracle VM Manager                             [  OK  ]
[root@ovmm init.d]# service ovmcli start
Starting Oracle VM Manager CLI                   [  OK  ]
[root@ovmm init.d]#
```

Because the certificates required to authenticate various components, such as the Oracle VM Manager Web Interface and Oracle VM Manager CLI, are regenerated during the new installation and the mappings for these are overwritten by the database restore, it is necessary to reconfigure the certificates used to authenticate these components.

Run the following commands to reconfigure the Oracle WebLogic Server (remember that the weblogic user password is the same password used when performing the initial installation):

```
# export MW_HOME=/u01/app/oracle/Middleware
# /u01/app/oracle/ovm-manager-3/ovm_upgrade/bin/ovmkeytool.sh setupWebLogic
Dec 22, 2016 2:57:41 PM oracle.security.jps.JpsStartup start
INFO: Jps initializing.
Dec 22, 2016 2:57:43 PM oracle.security.jps.JpsStartup start
INFO: Jps started.
Updating keystore information in WebLogic
Oracle MiddleWare Home (MW_HOME): [/u01/app/oracle/Middleware]
WebLogic domain directory: [/u01/app/oracle/ovm-manager-3/domains/ovm_domain]
WebLogic server name: [AdminServer]
WebLogic username: [weblogic]
WebLogic password: [********]
WLST session logged at: /tmp/wlst-session562351056132953717.log
```

If you moved Oracle VM Manager to a new host, you must generate a new SSL key, as follows:

```
/u01/app/oracle/ovm-manager-3/ovm_upgrade/bin/ovmkeytool.sh gensslkey
```

```
#  /u01/app/oracle/ovm-manager-3/ovm_upgrade/bin/ovmkeytool.sh gensslkey
Dec 22, 2016 2:59:44 PM oracle.security.jps.JpsStartup start
INFO: Jps initializing.
Dec 22, 2016 2:59:46 PM oracle.security.jps.JpsStartup start
INFO: Jps started.
Path for SSL keystore:
 [/u01/app/oracle/ovm-manager-3/domains/ovm_domain/security/ovmssl.jks]
A file already exists at the path
/u01/app/oracle/ovm-manager-3/domains/ovm_domain/security/ovmssl.jks
Is it ok to ovewrite this file with your new keystore? [no] yes
The hostname should be the fully qualified hostname of the system
(this is the hostname you'd use to access this system from outside the
local domain).  Depending on your machine setup the value below may not be
correct.
Fully qualified hostname: [ovmm]
Key distinguished name is "CN=ovmm, OU=Oracle VM Manager,
O=Oracle Corporation, L=Redwood City, ST=California, C=US".
 Use these values? [yes]
Alternate hostnames (separated by commas): [ovmm]
You may either specify passwords or use random passwords.
If you choose to use a random password, only WebLogic, the Oracle VM Manager,
and this application will have access to the information stored in this
keystore.
Use random passwords? [yes]
Generating SSL key and certificate and persisting them to the keystore...
```

```
Updating keystore information in WebLogic
Oracle MiddleWare Home (MW_HOME): [/u01/app/oracle/Middleware]
WebLogic domain directory: [/u01/app/oracle/ovm-manager-3/domains/ovm_domain]
WebLogic server name: [AdminServer]
WebLogic username: [weblogic]
WebLogic password: [********]
WLST session logged at: /tmp/wlst-session6811063229241288206.log
```

Restart Oracle VM Manager and then run the client certificate configuration script, as follows:

```
[root@ovmm init.d]# service ovmm restart
Stopping Oracle VM Manager                            [  OK  ]
Starting Oracle VM Manager                            [  OK  ]
[root@ovmm init.d]#
```

Next, you will need to reconfigure the OVMM WebLogic instance with the correct certificate. This is already scripted with /u01/app/oracle/ovm-manager-3/bin/configure_client_cert_login.sh. Run the script as follows:

```
]# /u01/app/oracle/ovm-manager-3/bin/configure_client_cert_login.sh

Initializing WebLogic Scripting Tool (WLST) ...

Welcome to WebLogic Server Administration Scripting Shell

Type help() for help on available commands

2016-12-22 15:04:00,104 [main] INFO  ovm.wlst.commands –
Connecting using URL t3://localhost:7001

2016-12-22 15:04:01,931 [main] INFO  ovm.wlst.commands - Undeploying ovm_console
Undeploying application ovm_console ...
<Dec 22, 2016 3:04:02 PM EST> <Info> <J2EE Deployment SPI>
 <BEA-260121> <Initiating undeploy operation for application,
 ovm_console [archive: null], to AdminServer .>
.Completed the undeployment of Application with status completed
Current Status of your Deployment:
Deployment command type: undeploy
Deployment State : completed
Deployment Message : no message
2016-12-22 15:04:16,794 [main] INFO  ovm.wlst.commands - Undeploying ovm_core
Undeploying application ovm_core ...
<Dec 22, 2016 3:04:16 PM EST> <Info> <J2EE Deployment SPI>
 <BEA-260121> <Initiating undeploy operation for application,
ovm_core [archive: null], to AdminServer .>
....Completed the undeployment of Application with status completed
Current Status of your Deployment:
Deployment command type: undeploy
Deployment State : completed
Deployment Message : no message
2016-12-22 15:04:29,134 [main] INFO  ovm.wlst.domainbuilder.Domain
- Stopping AdminServer...
Stopping Weblogic Server...
```

```
Initializing WebLogic Scripting Tool (WLST) ...

Welcome to WebLogic Server Administration Scripting Shell

Type help() for help on available commands

Connecting to t3://localhost:7001 with userid weblogic ...
Successfully connected to Admin Server "AdminServer" that belongs
to domain "ovm_domain".

Warning: An insecure protocol was used to connect to the
server. To ensure on-the-wire security, the SSL port or
Admin port should be used instead.

Shutting down the server AdminServer with force=false while connected
to AdminServer ...
Disconnected from weblogic server: AdminServer


Exiting WebLogic Scripting Tool.

Done
Stopping Derby Server...
Derby server stopped.
WLST lost connection to the WebLogic Server that you were
connected to, this may happen if the server was shutdown or
partitioned. You will have to re-connect to the server once the
server is available.
Disconnected from weblogic server: AdminServer
2016-12-22 15:08:11,311 [main] INFO  ovm.wlst.domainbuilder.Domain
 - Starting AdminServer...
2016-12-22 15:08:11,314 [main] INFO  ovm.wlst.domainbuilder.Domain
 - Trying to connect to t3://localhost:7001...
2016-12-22 15:08:21,884 [main] INFO  ovm.wlst.domainbuilder.Domain
 - Trying to connect to t3://localhost:7001...
2016-12-22 15:08:33,470 [main] INFO  ovm.wlst.domainbuilder.Domain
 - Trying to connect to t3://localhost:7001...
2016-12-22 15:08:44,499 [main] INFO  ovm.wlst.domainbuilder.Domain
 - Trying to connect to t3://localhost:7001...


2016-12-22 15:08:45,336 [main] INFO  ovm.wlst.domainbuilder.Domain
 - Connected.
2016-12-22 15:08:45,363 [main] INFO  ovm.wlst.domainbuilder.Domain
 - AdminServer state is RUNNING
2016-12-22 15:08:45,364 [main] INFO  ovm.wlst.commands - Deploying ovm_core
Deploying application from
 /u01/app/oracle/ovm-manager-3/ovm_wlst/deploy/ovm_core/app/
ovm_core_3.4.2.1384.ear to targets AdminServer (upload=false) ...
<Dec 22, 2016 3:08:45 PM EST> <Info> <J2EE Deployment SPI>
 <BEA-260121> <Initiating deploy operation for application, ovm_core
[archive: /u01/app/oracle/ovm-manager-3/ovm_wlst/deploy/ovm_core
/app/ovm_core_3.4.2.1384.ear], to AdminServer .>
...Completed the deployment of Application with status completed
Current Status of your Deployment:
Deployment command type: deploy
```

Deployment State : completed
Deployment Message : no message
Already in Domain Config Tree

Already in Domain Config Tree

2016-12-22 15:08:55,368 [main] INFO ovm.wlst.domainbuilder.Domain –
Created a user named appframework
SLF4J: Class path contains multiple SLF4J bindings.
SLF4J: Found binding in
[jar:file:/u01/app/oracle/ovm-manager-3
/ovm_cli/lib/slf4j-log4j12.jar!/org/slf4j/impl/StaticLoggerBinder.class]
SLF4J: Found binding in
[jar:file:/u01/app/oracle/Middleware/wlserver/modules/features
/weblogic.server.merged.jar!/org/slf4j/impl/StaticLoggerBinder.class]
SLF4J: See http://www.slf4j.org/codes.html#multiple_bindings for an explanation.
Dec 22, 2016 3:08:55 PM oracle.security.jps.JpsStartup start
INFO: Jps initializing.
Dec 22, 2016 3:08:57 PM oracle.security.jps.JpsStartup start
INFO: Jps started.
2016-12-22 15:10:07,281 [main]
 INFO com.oracle.appfw.ovm.ws.client.KeytoolHelper - Writing cacert.pem
2016-12-22 15:10:07,282 [main]
 INFO com.oracle.appfw.ovm.ws.client.KeytoolHelper - Importing cacert.pem with
alias ovmca
2016-12-22 15:10:07,542 [main]
INFO com.oracle.appfw.ovm.ws.client.KeytoolHelper - Generating key pair for
appframework in /u01/app/oracle/ovm-manager-3/domains/ovm_domain/security/ovmclient.jks
2016-12-22 15:10:09,130 [main]
 INFO com.oracle.appfw.ovm.ws.client.KeytoolHelper - Exporting clientcert.pem
from /u01/app/oracle/ovm-manager-3/domains/ovm_domain/security/ovmclient.jks
2016-12-22 15:10:09,257 [main]
 INFO com.oracle.appfw.ovm.ws.client.KeytoolHelper - Reading clientcert.pem
2016-12-22 15:10:09,257 [main]
 INFO com.oracle.appfw.ovm.ws.client.SSLClientUtil - Signing certificate
2016-12-22 15:10:09,407 [main]
 INFO com.oracle.appfw.ovm.ws.client.KeytoolHelper - Writing clientcert.pem
2016-12-22 15:10:09,408 [main]
INFO com.oracle.appfw.ovm.ws.client.KeytoolHelper - Importing clientcert.pem with alias
appframework
2016-12-22 15:10:09,816 [main]
 INFO com.oracle.appfw.ovm.ws.client.SSLClientUtil - Deleting cacert.pem
2016-12-22 15:10:09,816 [main]
INFO com.oracle.appfw.ovm.ws.client.SSLClientUtil - Deleting clientcert.pem
2016-12-22 15:10:09,827 [main] INFO ovm.wlst.commands - Deploying ovm_console
Deploying application from
 /u01/app/oracle/ovm-manager-3/ovm_wlst/deploy/ovm_console/app/
ovm_console_3.4.2.1384.ear to targets AdminServer (upload=false) ...
<Dec 22, 2016 3:10:09 PM EST> <Info> <J2EE Deployment SPI>
 <BEA-260121> <Initiating deploy operation for application, ovm_console
 [archive: /u01/app/oracle/ovm-manager-3/ovm_wlst/deploy/ovm_console
/app/ovm_console_3.4.2.1384.ear], to AdminServer .>
.........Completed the deployment of Application with status completed
Current Status of your Deployment:

```
Deployment command type: deploy
Deployment State : completed
Deployment Message : no message
<Dec 22, 2016 3:10:40 PM EST> <Warning> <JNDI> <BEA-050001>
 <WLContext.close() was called in a different thread than the
one in which it was created.>

Client certificate login configuration complete
```

Optionally, you can append a path to the certificate. This is helpful when you've used a CA other than the default Oracle VM Manager CA to sign the SSL certificate.

The script requires that Oracle VM Manager is running, and it prompts you for the administrator username and password that should be used to access Oracle VM Manager. The script makes changes that may require Oracle VM Manager to be restarted:

```
[root@ovmm init.d]# service ovmm restart
Stopping Oracle VM Manager                         [  OK  ]
Starting Oracle VM Manager                         [  OK  ]
[root@ovmm init.d]#
```

Once Oracle VM Manager is running, you will need to go to the Servers and VMs tab and perform a Refresh All on your existing server pools. This is covered in Chapter 14.

Summary

This chapter covered the tasks necessary to configure a Linux system to prepare for installing the Oracle VM Manager. This is often the preferred method for installing the Oracle VM Manager. In addition, the chapter covered how to manually stop and start the Manager and its components.

This chapter also covered the tasks necessary to perform regular maintenance on the Oracle VM Manager, including how the automatic database backups can be modified and how to restore the Oracle VM Manager. The bulk of the work in setting up the Oracle VM Manager environment is in the configuration of the Oracle VM Manager itself, which is a topic covered in later chapters.

CHAPTER
11

Installing and Configuring the Oracle VM CLI

One of the best features of Oracle VM is the ability to script management operations using the Oracle VM CLI (command-line interface). The OVM CLI allows you to run Oracle VM commands directly from the command line without having to access the graphical user interface (GUI). The biggest advantage of this is the ability to script repetitive operations—that is, operations that should be run over and over again. Scripts can be developed in any number of scripting languages, including shell, Perl, and Python.

Introduction to OVM CLI

The OVM CLI provides a command-line interface to the OVM Manager. The function of the OVM CLI is similar to that of the OVM Manager, but it does not require the graphical interface and therefore does not need to be run from a browser. This means you can use the OVM CLI where you might not have browser access. This also allows you to manage the OVM via scripts, which means repetitive tasks can be done easily and with greater consistency. For example, you can create and automate reports.

The CLI does not include all the checks that are provided within the GUI, which allows you to perform some tasks that cannot be done via the CLI, but also requires more care and more understanding of the relationships between objects. The CLI is very powerful and can provide great benefits for your OVM installation. In this chapter, we discuss the uses of the CLI and provide many examples of beneficial uses.

Managing the OVM CLI

The CLI is installed as part of the OVM Manager and exists by default on the OVM Manager system. This does not mean that all of your maintenance tasks have to be run on the OVM Manager system. As you will see, the CLI is run through an SSH interface, thus allowing connectivity from other systems within the network. I often create shell, Perl, and Python scripts that run CLI commands via SSH in order to run maintenance tasks on a system separate from the OVM Manager. The CLI is maintained on the OVM management server.

Starting and Stopping the CLI

The CLI is managed as a Linux service on the OVM Manager system. As a Linux service, it is started, stopped, and queried via the **service** command or directly by the **/sbin/service** command. The commands to manage the CLI are shown in the following table:

Task	Command
Start the CLI	`/sbin/service ovmcli start` `service ovmcli start`
Stop the CLI	`/sbin/service ovmcli stop` `service ovmcli stop`
Restart the CLI	`/sbin/service ovmcli restart` `service ovmcli restart`
Get status of the CLI	`/sbin/service ovmcli status` `service ovmcli status`

Again, you can use either the **/sbin/service** command or the **service** command. An example is shown here:

```
[root@OVMManager ~]# service ovmcli stop
Stopping Oracle VM Manager CLI                          [  OK  ]
[root@OVMManager ~]# service ovmcli start
Starting Oracle VM Manager CLI                          [  OK  ]
[root@OVMManager ~]# service ovmcli status
Oracle VM Manager CLI is running...
[root@OVMManager ~]# service ovmcli restart
Stopping Oracle VM Manager CLI                          [  OK  ]
Starting Oracle VM Manager CLI                          [  OK  ]
```

Starting and stopping the CLI is done on the OVM Manager itself. As you will see in the next section, running CLI commands can be done from anywhere.

Using OVM CLI

The OVM CLI works by connecting to the OVM Manager through the core API. The interface that is used to connect to the CLI from your system is SSH. In the next few sections, you will learn how to connect to the CLI, how to use the CLI, and how to connect to the CLI via scripts.

Connecting to the CLI

The CLI is accessed via an SSH interface on port 10000. You can access it directly using **ssh** by specifying the port and user ID. SSH takes various options for specifying the user ID:

```
ssh -l admin ovmmanager -p 10000
ssh admin@ovmmanager -p 10000
```

If you are performing multiple commands, you can use the SSH keepalive option, as shown here:

```
ssh admin@ovmmanager -p 10000 -o ServerAliveInterval=60
```

Alternatively, you can set the keepalive in the ~/.ssh/config file. The ~/.ssh/config file can be useful for many different parameters, including the hostname, port, and user commands. A sample ~/.ssh/config file is shown here:

```
Host ovmcli
    Hostname ovmmanager
    Port 10000
    User etwhalen
    ServerAliveInterval 40
```

In this file, I have configured the ovmcli entry as an alias for my ovmmanager system and included the port and username for the OVM Manager user. I also included the keepalive. The ~/.ssh/config file is a very useful option. Here is an example of one:

```
[root@ptc01 .ssh]# ssh ovmcli
etwhalen@ovmmanager's password:
OVM>
```

In order to enable password-less connectivity to the OVM Manager, you can use SSH keys for connectivity. This creates a connection without using a password, and it takes advantage of the keepalive feature.

NOTE
Whenever the CLI or Manager is restarted, you must pass in the OVM Manager password again. Therefore, you cannot rely on this for connectivity every time.

In order to set up key-based connections, follow these steps:

1. Set up the ~/.ssh/config file as shown previously.

2. Using **ssh-keygen**, create an SSH key, like so:

```
$ ssh-keygen -t rsa -f ~/.ssh/ovmcli
[etwhalen@ptc01 .ssh]$ ssh-keygen -t rsa -f ~/.ssh/ovmcli
Generating public/private rsa key pair.
Enter passphrase (empty for no passphrase):
Enter same passphrase again:
Your identification has been saved in /home/etwhalen/.ssh/ovmcli.
Your public key has been saved in /home/etwhalen/.ssh/ovmcli.pub.
The key fingerprint is:
e1:f1:54:8b:c9:37:48:15:60:10:3c:aa:fc:0c:d1:11 etwhalen@ptc01.perftuning.com
The key's randomart image is:
+--[ RSA 2048]----+
|     Eooo+o+.    |
|     . o+ = .    |
|     . oo.* +    |
|     . o. = . .  |
|     . o  S .    |
|       +         |
|        +        |
|         o       |
|                 |
+-----------------+
```

3. Add the private key to the authentication agent:

```
$ ssh-add ~/.ssh/ovmcli

[etwhalen@ptc01 .ssh]$ ssh-add ~/.ssh/ovmcli
Enter passphrase for /home/etwhalen/.ssh/ovmcli:
Identity added: /home/etwhalen/.ssh/ovmcli (/home/etwhalen/.ssh/ovmcli)
```

4. Copy the public key to the ovmmanager system:

```
scp ~/.ssh/ovmcli.pub oracle@hostname:/home/oracle/.ssh/
[etwhalen@ptc01 .ssh]$ scp ~/.ssh/ovmcli.pub oracle@ovmmanager:.ssh/
The authenticity of host 'ovmmanager (192.168.50.4)' can't be established.
RSA key fingerprint is 44:d1:3d:3c:dc:ed:cd:f5:52:1d:0d:9a:fc:a7:7c:31.
Are you sure you want to continue connecting (yes/no)? yes
```

```
Warning: Permanently added 'ovmmanager,192.168.50.4' (RSA) to the list of known
hosts.
oracle@ovmmanager's password:
ovmcli.pub                                    100%   411     0.4KB/s   00:00
```

5. Add the ovmcli.pub contents to authorized_keys on the OVM Manager server:

```
$ ssh oracle@ovmmanager
$ cd /home/oracle/.ssh
$ cat [etwhalen@ptc01 ~]$ ssh oracle@ovmmanager

oracle@ovmmanager's password:
Last login: Tue Mar  8 15:16:58 2016 from ptc01.perftuning.com
[oracle@OVMManager ~]$ cd .ssh
[oracle@OVMManager .ssh]$ cat ovmcli.pub >> ovmcli_authorized_keys
[oracle@OVMManager .ssh]$ cat ovmcli_authorized_keys
[oracle@OVMManager .ssh]$ exit
```

6. Test your setup:

```
$ ssh -l etwhalen ovmmanager -p 10000
```

or

```
$ ssh ovmcli (if using config file)
```

Once you have set up the SSH keys correctly, you can make connections without the use of a password:

```
[etwhalen@ptc01 ~]$ ssh -l etwhalen ovmmanager -p 10000
OVM>
```

or

```
[etwhalen@ptc01 ~]$ ssh etwhalen@ovmmanager -p 10000
OVM>
```

You can also use the config file:

```
[etwhalen@ptc01 ~]$ ssh ovmcli
OVM>
```

Once you have connected to the CLI, you can begin running commands. Commands can be included with the **ssh** command itself. An example of running **list vm** via the CLI is shown here:

```
[root@ptc01 ovm-scripts]# ssh ovmcli "list vm"
OVM> list vm
Command: list vm
Status: Success
Time: 2016-08-11 20:01:49,260 CDT
Data:
  id:0004fb000006000010093bddfdadd79f  name:win-template.0
  id:0004fb0000060000a348701155142bac  name:gg20b
  id:0004fb00000600005739434bdae95cda  name:pv-with-net.0
  id:0004fb0000060000aef75cb552b3b943  name:pv-template.0
```

```
id:0004fb0000060000762ccd44ca399a35    name:ol66-template.0
id:0004fb0000060000f55c08712aa9f71a    name:gg20a
id:0004fb00000600006d56b5c461cb97a4    name:ptc03
id:0004fb0000060000a19f4591caebe908    name:ggwin20a
id:0004fb000006000024d3177c02221978    name:ggwin20b
id:0004fb0000060000c28fa306d48e7690    name:rac20b
id:0004fb0000060000ae96f283873dd6b5    name:mysql00
id:0004fb000006000067f61e3ce78624d5    name:cc03
id:0004fb00000600003e3ef12544af3fd9    name:win00
id:0004fb0000060000c8804e2dbcc72544    name:gg21c
id:0004fb000006000026979008  37ee12fb    name:odi00
id:0004fb0000060000c9fe407a85f2087e    name:ggwin21a
id:0004fb00000600001b620e2f106d4f42    name:gg21a
id:0004fb0000060000e79a7e1357fcbdd9    name:rac20a
id:0004fb0000060000ca6b4e5a62df6d2c    name:gg21b
id:0004fb0000060000e5c84bf3773d23e2    name:ora10ga
id:0004fb0000060000765744ad10ba1f05    name:veridata01
```

Exiting the VM CLI is done via the **exit** command:

```
OVM> exit
Connection to ovmmanager closed.
```

In the next sections, you will see how to run basic commands via the CLI and how to script commands to run in the CLI.

Basic Commands

A number of commands can be used with the CLI that allow you to perform almost all the functions you can do within the OVM Manager—and in some cases, the CLI allows for much more flexibility and functionality. In addition to the functions these commands provide, they also allow you to get help with the CLI. Let's look at the help functions of the CLI before we discuss the informational commands and functional commands.

Help Commands

You have a few ways to get help and information about the commands available within the CLI. For example, the **help** command provides information about the commands themselves:

```
OVM> help
For Most Object Types:
    create <objectType> [(attribute1)="value1"] ... [on <objectType> <instance>]
    delete <objectType> <instance>
    edit <objectType> <instance>   (attribute1)="value1" ...
    list <objectType>
    show <objectType> <instance>
For Most Object Types with Children:
    add <objectType> <instance> to <objectType> <instance>
    remove <objectType> <instance> from <objectType> <instance>
Client Session Commands:
    set alphabetizeAttributes=[Yes|No]
    set commandMode=[Asynchronous|Synchronous]
```

```
    set commandTimeout=[1-43200]
    set endLineChars=[CRLF,CR,LF]
    set outputMode=[Verbose,XML,Sparse]
    showclisession
Other Commands:
    exit
    showallcustomcmds
    showcustomcmds <objectType>
    showobjtypes
    showversion
```

This gives you an idea of the commands available. In order to get detailed information about these commands, you can use the **?** command. An example is shown here:

```
OVM> ?
        add
        create
        delete
        edit
        embeddedcreate
        embeddeddelete
        embeddededit
        exit
        help
        list
        remove
        set
        show
        showallcustomcmds
        showclisession
        showcustomcmds
        showobjtypes
        showversion
```

Using the **?** command, you can get detailed information about the commands listed. For example, to get additional information on the **list** command, use **list ?**, as shown next. (Note that because of the number of options, the complete list is not shown.)

```
OVM> list ?
            AccessGroup
            AntiAffinityGroup
            Assembly
            AssemblyVirtualDisk
            AssemblyVm
            . . . . .
            VirtualCdrom
            VirtualDisk
            VlanInterface
            Vm
            VmCloneCustomizer
            VmCloneNetworkMapping
```

```
VmCloneStorageMapping
VmDiskMapping
Vnic
VolumeGroup
```

In the next section, you will see how to use some of these commands to get information about the OVM system. The two most important CLI commands you need to know are **help** and **?**.

Informational Commands

The informational commands are **list** and **show**. The **list** command is used to display a list of all of the objects of a particular type. The **show** command provides detailed information on a specific object. For example, **list server** lists all of the servers:

```
OVM> list server
Command: list server
Status: Success
Time: 2016-08-11 22:15:39,810 CDT
Data:
  id:4c:4c:45:44:00:4d:53:10:80:52:ca:c0:4f:39:4b:31  name:ovm03
  id:4c:4c:45:44:00:4d:53:10:80:52:c7:c0:4f:39:4b:31  name:ovm02
  id:4c:4c:45:44:00:4c:43:10:80:36:c6:c0:4f:39:4b:31  name:ovm01
```

To get detailed information on a particular server, use **show server name=<name>** or **show server id=<id>**, as shown here (note that only the first 25 lines are provided):

```
OVM> show server name=ovm01
Command: show server name=ovm01
Status: Success
Time: 2016-08-11 22:18:00,593 CDT
Data:
  Status = Running
  Role 1 = Vm
  Role 2 = Utility
  Ip Address = 172.17.50.11
  Maintenance Mode = Off
  Inbound Migration Locked = No
  Agent Login = oracle
  Statistic Interval = 20
  NTP Server 1 = 192.168.50.4
  BIOS Vendor = Dell Inc.
  BIOS Version = 6.4.0
  BIOS Release Date = 07/23/2013
  Processor Type = x86-64b
  Processor Speed (GHz) = 2.93
  Processor Sockets Populated = 2
  Threads per Core = 1
  Cores per Processor Socket = 6
  Processors = 12
  Enabled Processor Cores = 12
  Memory (MB) = 122867
  Usable Memory (MB) = 77317
```

The **list** and **show** commands can be run followed by the **?** qualifier in order to see all of the objects they can operate on. These and a few other commands provide information on the state and configuration of Oracle VM. The other commands are used to actually configure Oracle VM.

Functional Commands

The functional commands let you perform tasks in OVM such as shut down, start up, create, and so on. The basic functional commands include **add**, **create**, **delete**, **edit**, **set** and **remove**. These commands allow you to perform functions on the OVM Manager that affect objects in the OVM server pool. Let's look at some of these commands.

Add   The **add** command is used to add resources to an object. For example, the following can be used to add an NFS filesystem to a server:

```
OVM>    add FIleSystem name=nfs01:/u01/repo01 to NfsAccessGroup name=NfsAccess01
```

The difference between **add** and **create** is that the **add** command takes an object that already exists and assigns it to another entity, whereas the **create** command is used to create an object from scratch.

Objects that can be added include the following:

BondPort	StorageInitiator
FileSystem	Tag
PhysicalDisk	VlanInterface
Port	Vm
Server	Vnic
ServerPool	

For help on these objects, use the command **add <item> ?**. For further information on the available options, continue to use the commands provided from the previous command using **?**. Here's an example:

```
OVM> add ?
          BondPort
          FileSystem
          PhysicalDisk
          Port
          Server
          ServerPool
          StorageInitiator
          Tag
          VlanInterface
          Vm
          Vnic
OVM> add filesystem ?
                    id=<object identifier> OR
                    name=<object name>
OVM> add filesystem name=ed ?
                         to
```

```
OVM> add filesystem name=ed to ?
                              AccessGroup
OVM> add filesystem name=ed to AccessGroup ?
                                      id=<parent object identifier> OR
                                      name=<parent object name>
```

In addition, you can find very good documentation on the OVM CLI.

Create   The **create** command is used to create new objects in OVM. The **create** command can take a few or many options, depending on what you are trying to create. For example, **create vm** takes (but is not limited to) the following parameters:

```
*domainType
*name
*repository
cpuCount
memory
server
```

* denotes a required parameter.
   Therefore, creating a VM using the CLI would look something like this:

```
OVM> create vm domainType=XEN_PVM name=test01 repository=Repo01 cpuCount=4
memory=4092
  memoryLimit=8192 server=ovm01 on ServerPool name=OVM
```

NOTE
This command should appear all on one line. If you need to use multiple lines, use \ as the line-continuation character.

Here are the objects that can be created:

AccessGroup	ServerUpdateGroup
AntiAffinityGroup	ServerUpdateRepository
BondPort	StorageArray
CpuCompatibilityGroup	Tag
FileServer	VirtualDisk
FileSystem	VlanInterface
Network	Vm
PhysicalDisk	VmCloneCustomizer
Repository	VmCloneNetworkMapping
RepositoryExport	VmCloneStorageMapping
ServerController	VmDiskMapping
ServerPool	Vnic
ServerPoolNetworkPolicy	

For help on these objects, use the command **add <object> ?**.

Delete   The **delete** command is used to delete existing objects in OVM. The **delete** command varies based on the object that is being deleted. Here's an example:

```
Delete vm takes either a name or an id
OVM> delete vm name=test01
Command: delete vm name=test01
Status: Success
Time: 2016-08-21 04:40:43,227 CDT
JobId: 1471772441533
```

This example deletes the virtual machine created in the previous example. The following are the objects that can be deleted:

AccessGroup	ServerUpdateGroup
AntiAffinityGroup	ServerUpdateRepository
Assembly	StorageArray
BondPort	Tag
CpuCompatibilityGroup	VirtualAppliance
FileServer	VirtualCdrom
FileSystem	VirtualDisk
Network	VlanInterface
PhysicalDisk	Vm
Repository	VmCloneCustomizer
RepositoryExport	VmCloneNetworkMapping
Server	VmCloneStorageMapping
ServerController	VmDiskMapping
ServerPool	Vnic
ServerPoolNetworkPolicy	

For help on these objects, use the command **delete <object> ?**.

Edit   The **edit** command is used to modify existing objects in OVM. More objects can be operated on with the **edit** command than with **create** or **delete**. The **edit** command takes a variety of options, depending on the type of object being edited. Here is an example using **edit vm**:

```
OVM> edit vm name=test01 memory=4096
Command: edit vm name=test01 memory=4096
Status: Success
Time: 2016-08-21 04:52:51,363 CDT
JobId: 1471773170977
```

The **edit** commands provide many different options for configuring and using OVM. The preceding example shows how to change the memory allocated to the VM.

Here's a list of the objects that can be edited:

AccessGroup	ServerPool
AntiAffinityGroup	ServerPoolNetworkPolicy
Assembly	ServerUpdateGroup
AssemblyVirtualDisk	ServerUpdateRepository
AssemblyVm	StorageArray
BondPort	StorageArrayPlugin
ControlDomain	Tag
Cpu	VirtualAppliance
CpuCompatibilityGroup	VirtualApplianceVirtualDisk
FileServer	VirtualApplianceVm
FileServerPlugin	VirtualCdrom
FileSystem	VirtualDisk
Manager	VlanInterface
Network	Vm
PeriodicTask	VmCloneCustomizer
PhysicalDisk	VmCloneNetworkMapping
Port	VmCloneStorageMapping
Repository	VmDiskMapping
RepositoryExport	Vnic
Server	VolumeGroup
ServerController	

For help with these objects, use the command **edit <object> ?**.

Remove   The **remove** command corresponds to the **add** command. It removes an object from another object, whereas the **delete** command actually destroys the object. The **remove** command takes a variety of options, depending on the type of object being removed. Here is an example using **remove filesystem**:

```
OVM>    remove FIleSystem name=nfs01:/u01/repo01 from NfsAccessGroup
name=NfsAccess01
```

The **remove** command provides many different options for configuring and using OVM. Here's a list of the objects that can be removed:

BondPort	StorageInitiator
FileSystem	Tag
PhysicalDisk	VlanInterface
Port	Vm
Server	Vnic
ServerPool	

For help with these objects, use the command **remove <object> ?**.

Migrate   The **migrate** command is used to migrate a virtual machine to a new server or server pool. Here is the syntax of the **migrate vm** command:

```
migrate vm { id=<id> or name=<name> } { destServer=<server> or
destServerPool=<server pool> }
```

This command migrates the named virtual machine to the server or server pool you specify.

Clone   The **clone** parameter is used to clone a virtual machine. Here is the syntax of the **clone vm** command:

```
clone vm {name=<name> or id=<id>} destType= { Vm or VmTemplate }
[ destName=<name> ] serverPool=<server pool> [ cloneCustomizer=<value>]
[targetRepository=<value>]
```

An example of the **clone vm** command is shown here:

```
OVM> clone vm name=ora10ga destType=vmTemplate destName=ora10g-template
serverPool=OVM targetRepository=Repo02
Command: clone vm name=ora10ga destType=vmTemplate destName=ora10g-template
serverPool=OVM targetRepository=Repo02
Status: Success
Time: 2016-08-21 21:22:04,688 CDT
JobId: 1471832523488
Data:
  id:0004fb000006000083ce8d11976daef6  name:ora10g-template
```

This command clones the named virtual machine to the server or server pool you specify.

Scripting with OVMCLI

The OVM CLI is useful for running commands that can provide information about the OVM environment as well as commands to create, modify, and delete objects in OVM. These commands are very useful, but the real power comes when they are put together into programs used to provide useful functions. Programs can be written using a number of different languages, including the following:

- **Shell**   Bash, ksh, and sh can be used to create useful scripts.
- **Perl**   The Perl language is very popular for developing OVM CLI scripts.
- **Python**   Python is one of the most popular languages used with OVM. It also works with ovmwsh (not covered here).
- **Other**   Java and other languages can also be used for OVM scripting.

Scripts enable you to use variables, conditionals, and looping in order to automate repetitive tasks. In order to use a script, it is often best to contain the CLI within a single-line command. This is done by appending the **cli** command to the end of the connection screen. Here's an example:

```
[etwhalen@ptc01 ovm]$ ssh ovmmanager -p 10000 "list vm"
```

This has the effect of listing the VMs.

> **NOTE**
> *ssh ovmcli uses the definition in the .ssh/config file. It is the equivalent of **ssh -l etwhalen ovmmanager** with a slightly shorter syntax.*

You can add onto this by passing the output of the **ovmcli** command to filters in order to pass this to other commands:

```
vms=`ssh ovmcli "list vm" | cut -d: -f3 | grep -v template | grep -v pv`

for vm in $vms
do
    ssh ovmcli "show vm name=$vm"
done
```

You are probably getting the idea now of how to start using the OVM CLI in scripts.

> **NOTE**
> *Whitespace and special characters can sometimes be a problem when scripting in bash or shell. The \ character can be used to delimit a special character. Here is an example:*
>
> ```
> "name=\'Unmanaged FibreChannel Storage Array\'"
> ```
>
> *With the single quotes, the spaces are maintained and processed as part of the name.*

CLI Useful Examples

The uses of OVM's command-line interface are unlimited. You can use it to create VMs, delete VMs, and manage and monitor VMs. Here are two examples of the same function using different languages.

Status of VMs Using Shell

The first is a script to display the status of the VMs in the server pool using standard shell scripting:

```
#
# List a vm
#

vms=`ssh ovmcli "list vm" | grep id | cut -d: -f2 | cut -d" " -f1`

i=0
for target in $vms
do

  name=$(ssh ovmcli "show vm name=$target" | grep "Name =" | tr -d '\n' |
tr -d '\r')
  status=$(ssh ovmcli "show vm name=$target" | grep "Status =" | tr -d '\n' |
tr -d '\r')
```

```
  procs=$(ssh ovmcli "show vm name=$target" | grep "Processors" | grep -v Max |
tr -d '\n' | tr -d '\r')
  memory=$(ssh ovmcli "show vm name=$target" | grep "Memory" | grep -v Max |
tr -d '\n' | tr -d '\r')
  echo "${name}          ${status}        ${procs}          ${memory}"

i=$i++
done
```

Here is the abbreviated output of this script:

```
Name = gg20b      Status = Running      Processors = 1      Memory (MB) = 8192
Name = gg20a      Status = Running      Processors = 1      Memory (MB) = 8192
Name = ptc03      Status = Running      Processors = 2      Memory (MB) = 4096
Name = pv00       Status = Running      Processors = 1      Memory (MB) = 4096
```

NOTE
*I am using the same shortcut from my .ssh/config file. The **ssh ovmcli**
command is equivalent to **ssh etwhalen@ovmmanager -p 10000**. SSH
keys are used in lieu of passwords.*

Scripting with shell is easy and very standard.

Status of VMs Using Python
Performing the same function in Python is a little more complicated and involves more coding,
but it offers more flexibility:

```python
#!/usr/bin/python

import os

vms = os.popen('ssh ovmcli "list vm" | grep id | grep -v template |
cut -d: -f3 | cut -d" " -f1').read()

templates = os.popen('ssh ovmcli "list vm" | grep id | grep template |
cut -d: -f3 | cut -d" " -f1').read()

vms = vms.splitlines()
vms.sort()

#print vms

for vm in vms:
    command = "ssh ovmcli show vm name=" + vm
    out = os.popen(command).read()
#    print "out:", out
    ind = out.find("Name =")
    name = out[ind+6:]
    ind = name.find("\n")
    name = name[:ind]
```

```
    ind = out.find("Status =")
    status = out[ind+8:]
    ind = status.find("\n")
    status = status[:ind]

    ind = out.find("Processors =")
    processors = out[ind+12:]
    ind = processors.find("\n")
    processors = processors[:ind]

    ind = out.find("Memory")
    memory = out[ind+14:]
    ind = memory.find("\n")
    memory = memory[:ind]

    print "Name:", name, "\tStatus: ", status, "\tProcessors: ", processors,
"\tMemory: ", memory, " (MB)"

templates = templates.splitlines()
templates.sort()

for vm in templates:
    command = "ssh ovmcli show vm name=" + vm
    out = os.popen(command).read()
#    print "out:", out
    ind = out.find("Name =")
    name = out[ind+6:]
    ind = name.find("\n")
    name = name[:ind]

    ind = out.find("Status =")
    status = out[ind+8:]
    ind = status.find("\n")
    status = status[:ind]

    ind = out.find("Processors =")
    processors = out[ind+12:]
    ind = processors.find("\n")
    processors = processors[:ind]

    ind = out.find("Memory")
    memory = out[ind+14:]
    ind = memory.find("\n")
    memory = memory[:ind]

    print "Name:", name, "\tStatus: ", status, "\tProcessors: ", processors,
"\tMemory: ", memory, " (MB)"
```

NOTE
*I am using the same shortcut from my .ssh/config file. The **ssh ovmcli**
command is equivalent to **ssh etwhalen@ovmmanager -p 10000**. SSH
keys are used in lieu of passwords.*

The output of the Python script is essentially the same, with some cosmetic differences:

```
Name:  cc03    Status:  Running    Processors:  4    Memory:  16384  (MB)
Name:  gg20a   Status:  Running    Processors:  1    Memory:  8192   (MB)
Name:  gg20b   Status:  Running    Processors:  1    Memory:  8192   (MB)
Name:  gg21a   Status:  Running    Processors:  2    Memory:  8192   (MB)
Name:  gg21b   Status:  Running    Processors:  2    Memory:  8192   (MB)
Name:  gg21c   Status:  Running    Processors:  2    Memory:  8192   (MB)
```

Cloning VMs

Cloning one or more VMs is easy with the OVM CLI. Simply put the new VM names in a loop, as shown here:

```
#
# Clone a source vm to multiple target vms
#

#source=ol66-template.0
#target="linux03 linux04"

source=pv-template.0
target="gg20a gg20b"

ssh ovmcli "list vm"

for t in $target
do
  echo "Cloning $source to $t"

  ssh ovmcli "clone vm name=$source destName=$t destType=Vm
serverPool=\"x86 Server Pool\""

done

ssh ovmcli "list vm"
```

You can see how straightforward it is to clone with the CLI.

Other Scripts

In addition to the scripts we have covered thus far, you can create other scripts for stopping, starting, listing, and cloning VMs as well as specific components. You can even write scripts for creating RAC clusters by adding shared disks to newly cloned VMs. What you do with CLI scripting is totally up to your imagination.

Summary

In this chapter, you have seen how to use the OVM CLI and some basic commands to create scripts that serve useful functions. We looked at examples for scripts written in shell as well as scripts written in more sophisticated languages such as Python. The chapter not only provided examples but also illustrated the power of command-line processing in OVM.

CHAPTER
12

Configuring the Oracle VM Server Network

The two most important components of the Oracle VM server that are most likely to be modified on a regular basis are network and storage. The network configuration tends to change as the requirements for network bandwidth and subnets change. Also, within most environments, the need for storage always grows and never shrinks. Network requirements typically change at the virtual machine level, but the Oracle VM Server network does not need to change very often, except as needed to support new virtual LANs (VLANs). The configuration and functionality of the network are important because the network is the foundation for accessing virtual machines. By making sure that network capacity has not been exceeded, you can optimize the performance of the virtual machines.

This chapter covers the Oracle VM Server network—how it is configured and how it is managed. Once it is configured and working properly, making significant changes is often unnecessary. The VM Server network configuration requirements are simple to manage once you understand the basics of networking technologies—mainly bonds and VLANs.

NOTE
The most common addition to an Oracle VM Server network is VLANs. VLANs are used at the hardware switch layer, however, and do not normally affect the physical configuration of the Oracle VM servers.

What Makes Up a Network?

Virtual machines can share and use the networks configured on the host Oracle VM server; therefore, for multiple networks to be used with virtual machines, each virtual network must be created for the Oracle VM server.

Although the physical configuration is simple (just a few Ethernet wires), the logical configuration can be far more complex, as shown in Figure 12-1. The basic building block of the network is the

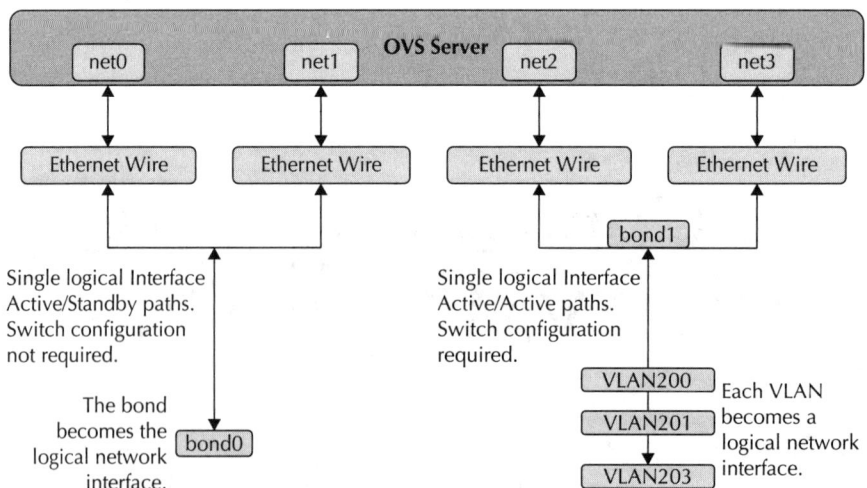

FIGURE 12-1. *Sample network topology*

Ethernet port. It is not uncommon to have multiple physical ports bonded into a single logical port. The new logical port can then have multiple VLANs stacked on top of the "port," with bonds, VLANs, and then finally virtual interfaces layered on top. Although the logical configuration may initially seem daunting, once you understand the building blocks involved, it rapidly becomes simple to understand and design.

All configuration is performed through the Oracle VM Manager (OVMM)—from the initial configuration of network on each OVM server, to the assignment of virtual network interfaces to the Oracle VM guests. To set up networking, perform the following steps:

1. Configure the initial networks on the Oracle VM server (OVS).

    a. Set the OVS for switched or bridged network management.

    b. Configure bonds for failover (recommended).

    c. Configure the maximum transmission unit (MTU) as needed.

    d. Add in optional IP addresses for troubleshooting.

2. Configure the networks in OVMM.

    a. Select what ports will be used on each OVS.

    b. Assign predefined network uses.

    c. Create and assign VLAN interfaces (optional).

Configuring the Oracle VM network is not extremely complicated. However, to understand how the Oracle VM network works, you need to understand networking, bonding, and VLANs.

Oracle VM Networking

The networks used by virtual machines are run through Xen bridges or switches. The Xen interface is the connection between the virtual world (virtual machines) and the physical world (your company network). You can configure Xen bridges in a number of different ways, including bridged, NAT, and routed. Although you can configure all these network types and they will work, only a bridged or switched network is supported by Oracle. Routed and NAT networks are usually found in smaller, home network environments, due to most enterprise environments providing these services as dedicated devices such as firewalls and routers. The bridged network is most commonly found in server environments. Because Oracle VM is designed for the data center, bridged networking is typically the network type of choice, with the switched configuration being popular in more security conscious environments. There are four key network concepts to understand:

■ **Bridged networking**   Bridged networks allow the virtual machine network to reside on the same network as the Xen bridge. In order to be seen by other systems on the network, the virtual machine network adapter must be configured so that it's on the same subnet as the dom0 xen bridge (xenbr) adapter. Bridged networks allow you to easily add new virtual machines to the virtual machine farm that are accessible from other systems on the network. The downside of using a bridge is that all VMs on the bridge can sniff the network traffic of other nodes.

■ **Switched networking**   Switched networks perform the same functionality as the default bridged configuration. The main difference is that the ability of one VM to sniff the traffic of another VM is limited.

- **NAT networking** A Network Address Translation (NAT) network takes the IP address of the Oracle VM server and allows multiple virtual machines to appear to both themselves and other virtual machines as if they have their own IP addresses. However, to the outside world, it appears as if there is only the Oracle VM server's IP address. This is similar to how your home router works. With NAT networks, connecting outside systems to the NAT system is difficult.

- **Routed networking** With routed networking, traffic is routed through the dom0 (Oracle VM Server) system to a private subnet that is accessible by one or more virtual machines. Routed networks must be set up manually and are more difficult to maintain, but they provide functionality that might be useful in some cases.

Network Bonding

A degree of redundancy at the network level is often desirable. With redundancy, the Oracle VM Server system continues to operate even in the event of a single network failure. Common practice is to use network teaming, or *bonding*, to provide this extra bit of protection. *Network teaming* and *network bonding* are just different terms for the same thing: network redundancy. For the sake of this chapter, the term *network bonding* is used to describe this function.

If you use active switching, you can use network interface controller (NIC) bonding to increase the throughput of a VM network. For instance, if you have many virtual machines, a single 1GbE network connection might not provide enough throughput. By increasing the number of NICs in the bond, you increase the throughput. Although having multiple 1GbE ports sounds like a good idea, each communication path between a VM and another system on the network is still limited to a 1GbE connection, even if the aggregate is more than a single 1GbE pipe. This is one of the reasons why 10GbE networks have become so popular. One advantage with Oracle servers is that almost all models have four built-in 10GbE ports.

Is Network Bonding Necessary?

Depending on your particular point of view, network bonding may or may not be necessary. If reliable hardware (both server and network) is used and redundant components are not available, then network bonding will result in extra effort without benefit. For example, using multiple network cards in the server system that are both plugged into the same network switch provides some degree of redundancy, but doing this does not eliminate all single points of failure because the loss of the entire switch would still cause a complete network loss.

Network Bonding Hardware Support In order for some types of bonding to work, such as load balancing and trunking, all network hardware must support the same IEEE specifications; otherwise, they will not work reliably. In other words, support must be "end to end." Certain NAS vendors will not support your network unless this condition is met.

In addition to the physical interfaces in the network stack, each physical interface can be combined in what is called a *bond*. When you install an OVS, bond0 is automatically created on it, with the management IP already allocated. As shown in Figure 12-2, you can see the same bond0 on a newly installed server. You can navigate to this page by clicking the Servers and VMs tab and then selecting the physical server. From there, select Bond Ports from the Perspective drop-down. In this example, the server ovs3.m57.local was assigned an IP address of 192.168.200.26.

Although a bond with a single port works, adding a second port to the bond will provide several advantages. To understand these advantages, we first have to look at the type of bonds available:

- **Active/Backup** This is the default bond type, and it provides an automatic failover between the ports in the bond. Its major advantage is that it is simple to configure because nothing special has to be done of the switch side. This bond type is recommended for all types of traffic, including VLANs.

- **Link Aggregation** This bond type not only provides the highest level of uptime for the connection but can also improve network performance because multiple physical ports are combined into a single logical interface. The downside is that the switch ports must be configured correctly, using the IEEE 802.3ad Dynamic Link Aggregation standard (also known as LACP). This complexity also imposes some physical limitations because most switches require that all Ethernet ports in an LACP bind be connected to the same physical switch. This solution also works well with VLANs but is not recommended for the management bond.

- **Load Balanced** This technology is a hybrid of Active/Backup and Link Aggregation. It can provide some load balancing between the physical ports in the bond (VLAN technology is notoriously unreliable). Its main advantage is that no switch configuration is required to support the technology. It is often used for management bonds, especially when live migration traffic traverses the same bond. This bond mode does not work at all with Xen bridges that are associated with a VLAN device, so it cannot be used as an interface for NetFront devices on Oracle VM guests.

To modify bond0 to a Load Balanced configuration, highlight bond0 from the Bond Ports perspective view and then click the edit icon, as shown in Figure 12-3.

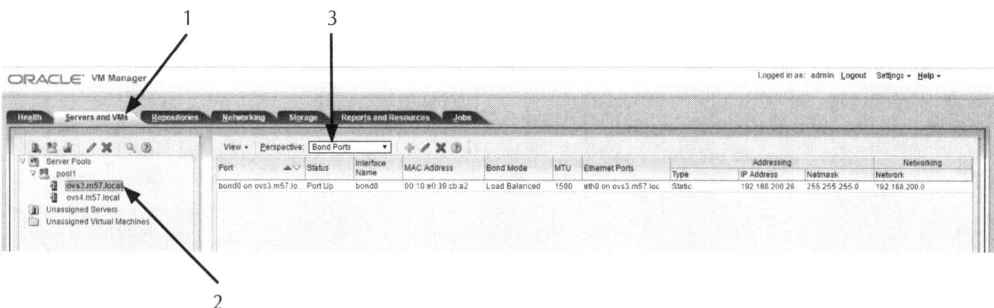

FIGURE 12-2. *Default bond*

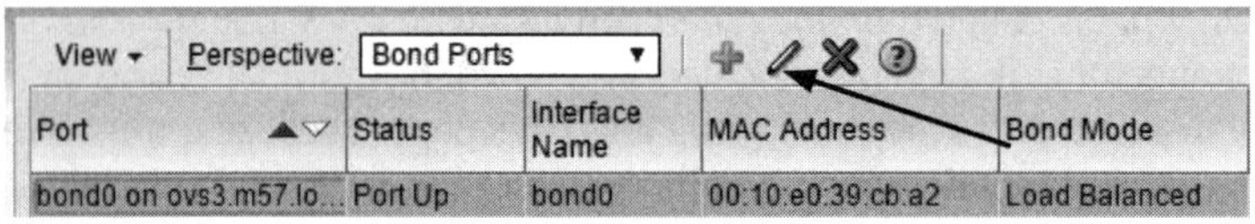

Port		Status	Interface Name	MAC Address	Bond Mode
bond0 on ovs3.m57.lo...		Port Up	bond0	00:10:e0:39:cb:a2	Load Balanced

View ▾ | Perspective: Bond Ports ▼ | ✚ ✎ ✖ ⑦

FIGURE 12-3. *Selecting a bond to edit*

Next, you will see a dialog (shown in Figure 12-4) that details how the bond is configured. This dialog includes the following information:

- **Bonding** The bonding method used.
- **Addressing** Static, Dynamic (DHCP), or None.
- **IP Address** If configured for a static IP address.
- **Netmask** If configured for a static IP address.
- **MTU** The maximum transmission unit defines the largest block of data that can be sent in a single network packet. This is set to 1500 by default, but is often set to a larger value on 10GbE networks. *All* servers on the network must have the same MTU setting.
- **Available Ports** What ports are available to be added to the bond.
- **Selected Ports** What ports are currently in the bond.

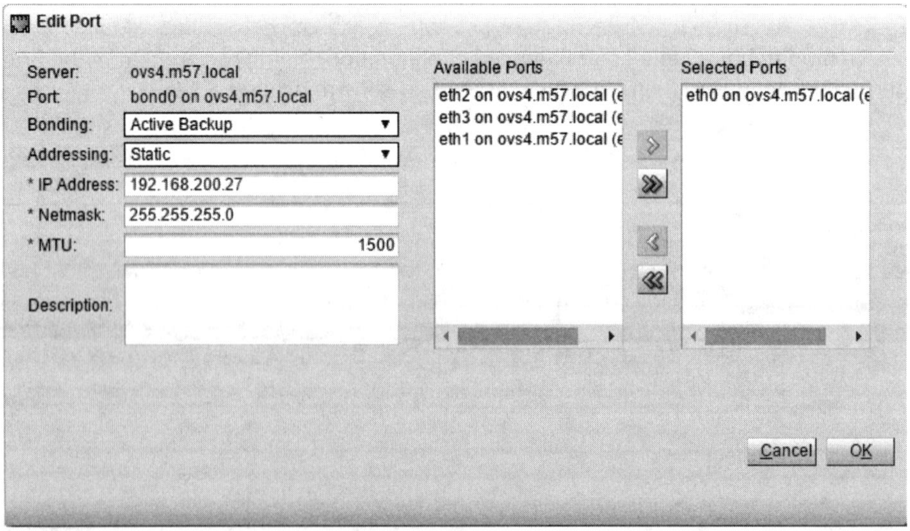

Edit Port

		Available Ports	Selected Ports
Server:	ovs4.m57.local	eth2 on ovs4.m57.local (e	eth0 on ovs4.m57.local (e
Port:	bond0 on ovs4.m57.local	eth3 on ovs4.m57.local (e	
Bonding:	Active Backup ▼	eth1 on ovs4.m57.local (e	
Addressing:	Static ▼		
* IP Address:	192.168.200.27		
* Netmask:	255.255.255.0		
* MTU:	1500		
Description:			

Cancel   OK

FIGURE 12-4. *Bond configuration dialog*

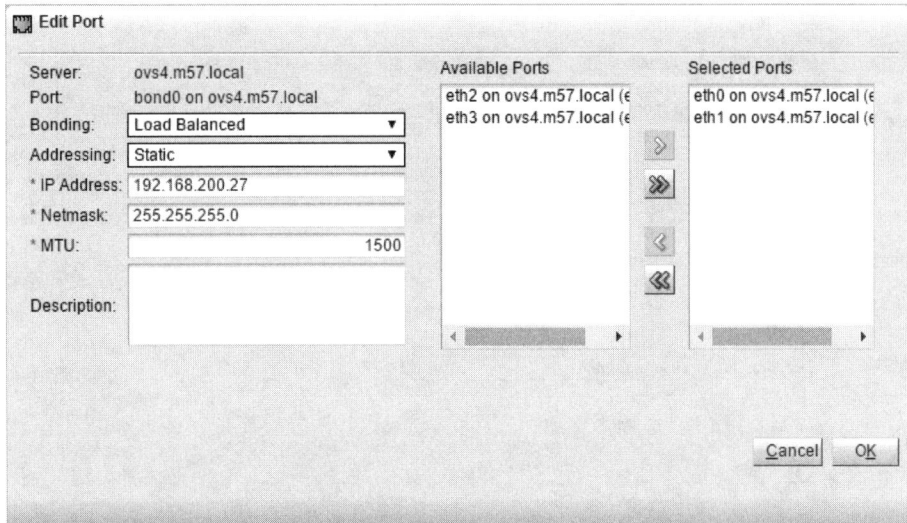

FIGURE 12-5. *Reconfiguring the management bond*

To add a port, simply double-click it. In the example shown in Figure 12-5, we see eth1 being added to the ports and Bonding being set to Load Balanced.

Additional bonds can be created. In this example, bond1 will be created on two Oracle VM servers, using both Link Aggregation and VLANs. Prior to the bond being configured, the switch was configured and wired to ovs3.m57.local and ovs4.m57.local, with ports net2 and net3 on the switch side being configured into a single bond per pair. In addition, VLANs 200–210 were configured to work on the aggregates.

NOTE
Although Oracle VM calls this a "bond," the method can go by a variety of names, including trunk, link aggregation, NIC teaming, and EtherChannel. The end result is basically the same when several physical interfaces are combined into a single logical interface.

The next bond device, bond1, will be created on both OVS3 and OVS4, with link aggregation being used for the bond mode, and the VLANs riding on top of the new bond1 device. On both servers, bond1 will be created. You do this by going back into the Bond Ports perspective on both nodes and using the "+" icon to add a bond. Because VLANs will be used, no IP address is added to the bond. When this is completed, the dialog should look like Figure 12-6.

After bond1 is added, it should show in the list of bond ports, and if the switch is configured correctly, it should have a status of "up," as you can see in Figure 12-7.

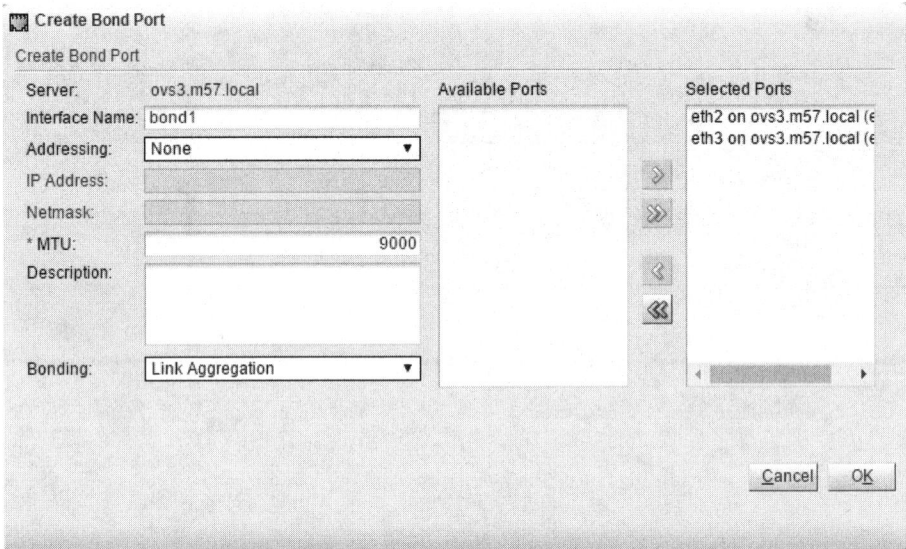

FIGURE 12-6. *Creating a bond port*

FIGURE 12-7. *Bond port status*

Network VLANs

Often, when building large or complex private clouds, the number of networks that virtual machines need access to will exceed the number of physical ports of the Oracle VM Server. In order to support this, the network industry created a standard (IEEE 802.1Q) that allows for multiple virtual local area networks (VLAN) to share the same physical cable. These VLANs also can share a bonded connection, just as created in the previous section.

The next step will be to create the initial VLANs. VLANs allow multiple networks to use the same physical connection. This enables efficient use of the network ports. To enable VLANs on the OVS systems, go to the Network tab in OVMM and select the VLAN Interfaces option. Initially, Oracle VM will not create any VLANs, so the system should show empty, as you can see in Figure 12-8.

To create the VLANs, select the green "+" symbol, which will start a guided process for creating them. First, we need to identify the ports the VLANs will use. In this example, we select bond1, as shown in Figure 12-9.

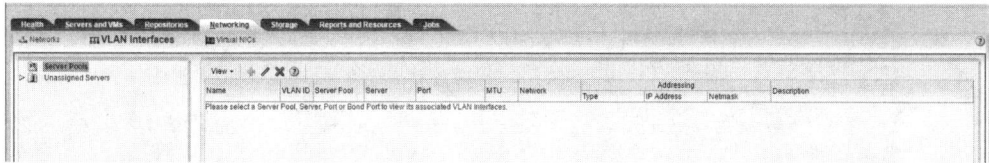

FIGURE 12-8. *Initial VLAN configuration*

Next, the VLANs will need to be created. A VLAN is identified with a number between 1 and 4094. The network administrator will know the VLAN numbers and should inform the OVM administrator what numbers to use. In our example, we will create VLANs 200–210 in bulk by entering in the numbers and clicking the Add button. Figure 12-10 shows the dialog after these VLANs have been added.

The final part of the process allows each VLAN to have an IP address set for each server, as well as a unique MTU set. Having an IP address on the OVS makes troubleshooting VLAN configurations much simpler, so this is highly recommended. If you are working with a large number of VLANs, it is recommended that you only add a few at a time, because the complexity can quickly become difficult to manage, as seen in Figure 12-11.

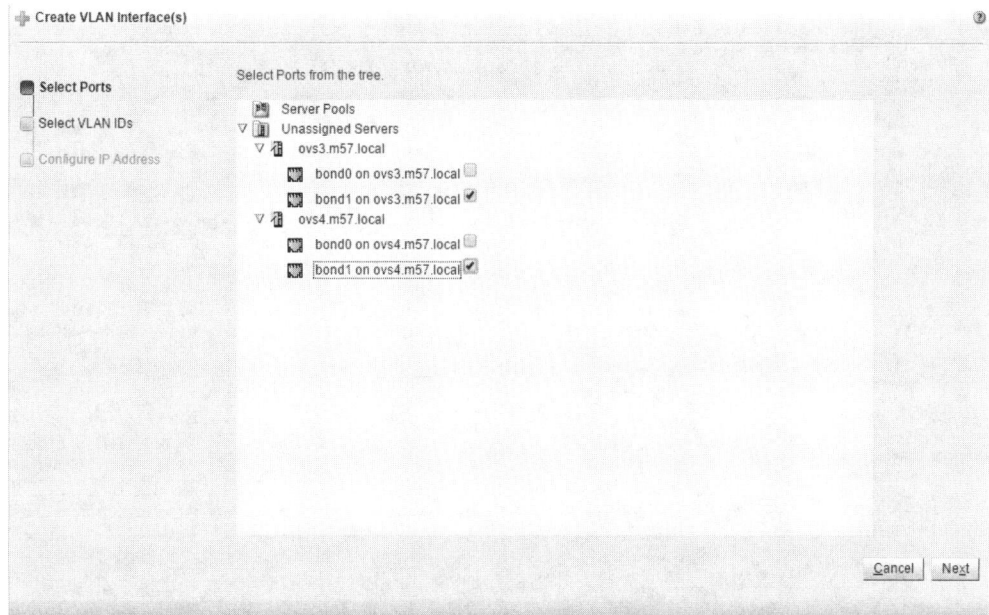

FIGURE 12-9. *VLAN port selection*

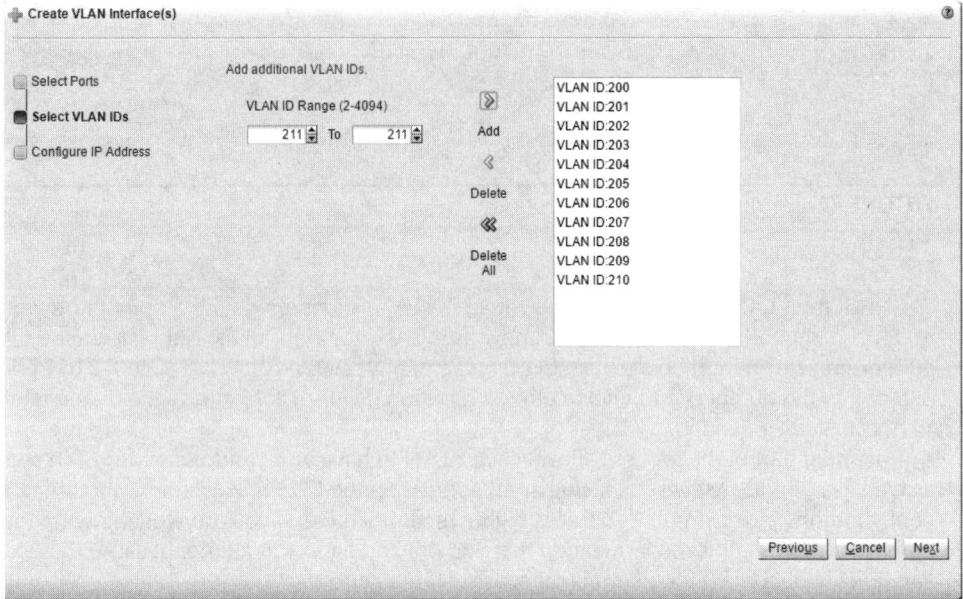

FIGURE 12-10. *VLAN numbers*

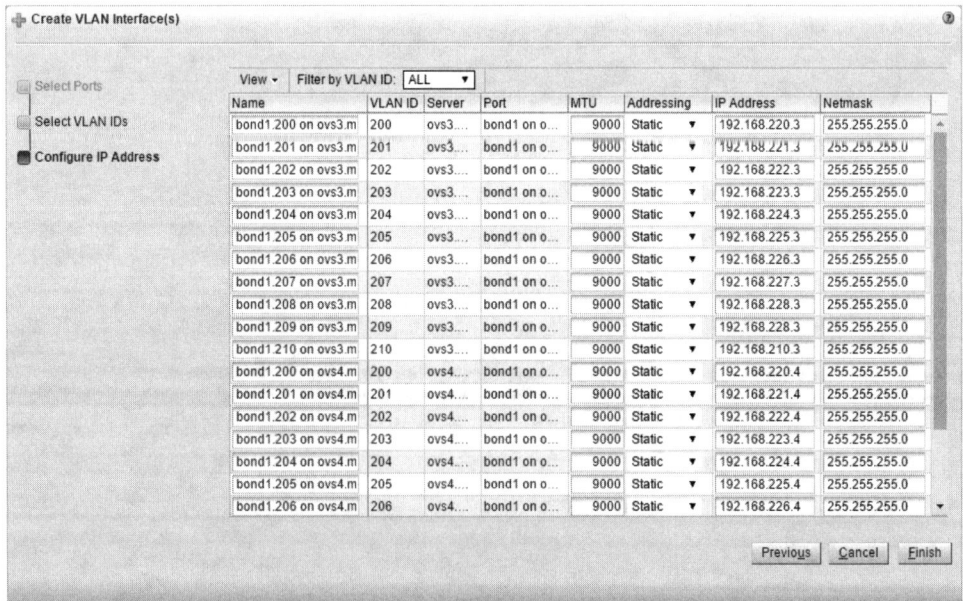

FIGURE 12-11. *VLAN IPs*

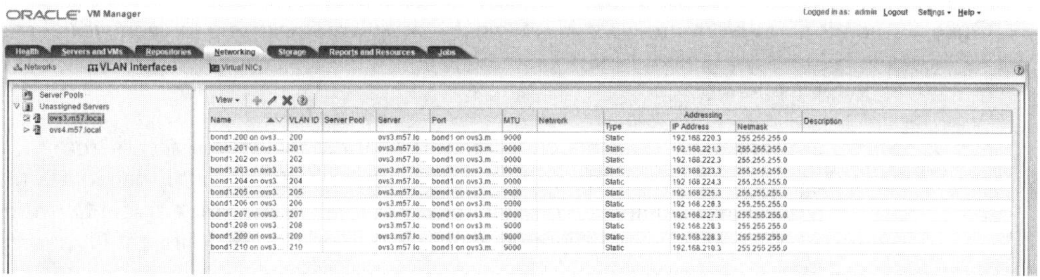

FIGURE 12-12. *VLAN summary*

Once you click Finish, an OVM job will run, adding the VLANs to all the Oracle VM servers that were selected. Depending on the number of VLANs added, this can take several minutes. Once the job completes, the VLAN Interfaces screen will list all the available VLANs, as shown in Figure 12-12.

NOTE
As mentioned earlier, Oracle VM is designed as an enterprise server virtualization product. Bridged networks (the default network type) and switched networks are the only supported network types in Oracle VM. Other networking types such as NAT and routed are really intended more for the home or personal network. Although NAT and bridged networks can be configured manually in Oracle VM, they are not recommended or supported and therefore will not be covered in this book.

Configuring the Network Adapters

The first step in setting up networking is to set up the adapters and bonds on each OVS. This is all performed from the Oracle VM Manager. Once you have set up the OVS network, you'll define the networks in OVM, allocating how each network is used.

The primary network adapter is configured during the installation process and is created as a bond with an Active/Standby configuration. The IP address and type of address assignment are determined during the initial installation setup. Using static networking is recommended instead of using DHCP-assigned IP addresses.

Static Configuration vs. DHCP
Although DHCP networking is possible, it is not recommended for Oracle VM Server systems. For small, home networks, you can use DHCP, but for server systems meant for multiple users, DHCP networking can be difficult to manage. However, if the Oracle VM server uses DHCP for networking, the virtual machines should use DHCP as well.

Configuring Networks

Once the bonds and VLANs are created, the next task is to assign a role to each virtual network. As shown in Figure 12-13, each network can be used for the following five predefined roles (under "Network Channels"):

- **Server Management**   This network role is used for management access from the OVMM to the OVS systems. The traffic should be routed (NAT access to this network is not supported). Only a single network can have this functionality on a single OVM server; however, you can have different management networks across different OVM servers.

- **Cluster Heartbeat**   This network role is used by the OVS systems to communicate via TCP packets. The cluster is sensitive to network stability and should not be shared with roles that can cause spikes in network traffic, such as Live Migrate and Storage. The network with the heartbeat should have some redundancy. Usually this is the same network used for Oracle VM Server management. This cannot be changed once the server pool has been created.

- **Live Migrate**   The Live Migrate network role is used to migrate virtual machines from one OVS to another in a server pool without a VM outage. In most environments, live migration should not be occurring frequently because it could cause interruption to other services, particularly the cluster heartbeat. As a result, configuring a separate network for this purpose can improve the performance and availability of the VMs and also prevent cluster heartbeat timeouts due to heavy network traffic.

- **Storage**   Although the storage network role has no specific functionality, it allows the administrator to quickly identify what networks are used to connect to storage.

- **Virtual Machine**   Network with this functionality allows VMs to have access to it. This is the most commonly used role for networks. Enabling this role on a network will automatically create a Xen bridge for the network.

Adding a new network is a straightforward task. Click the green "+" icon from the Networks screen to start the guided process, as shown in Figure 12-14.

ORACLE VM Manager

| Health | Servers and VMs | Repositories | Networking | Storage | Reports and Resources | Jobs |

🔹 Networks   🔹 VLAN Interfaces   🔹 Virtual NICs

View ▾ + ✏ ✖ ⑦

| Name | ID | Intra-Network Server | Network Channels | | | | | Description |
			Server Management	Cluster Heartbeat	Live Migrate	Storage	Virtual Machine	
192.168.200.0	c0a8c800		√	√	√			
VLAN201	108c460526						√	
VLAN202	1034d62c4f						√	

FIGURE 12-13.   *Network roles*

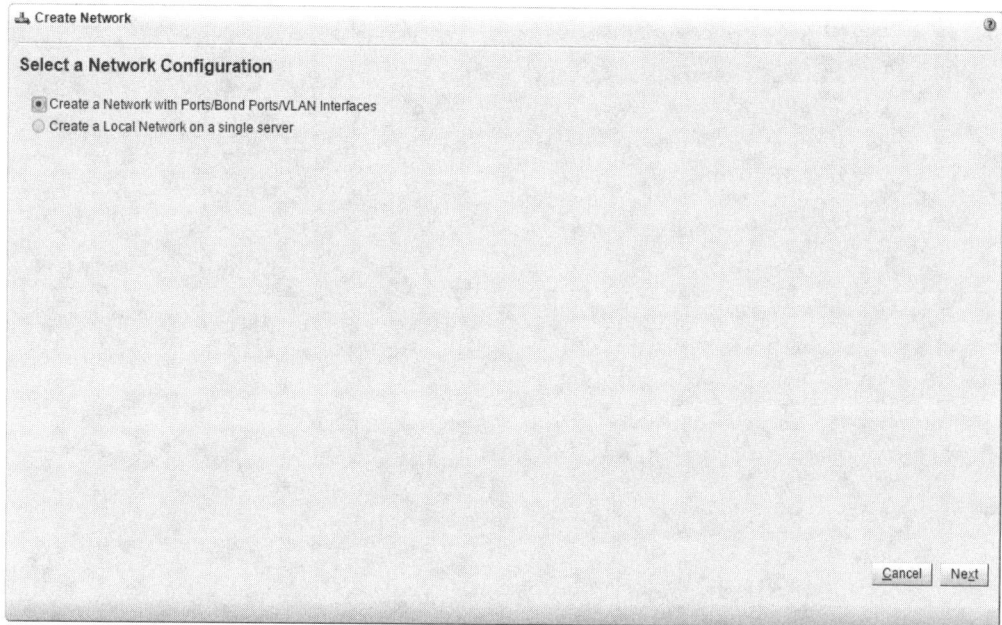

FIGURE 12-14.   *Adding a network, step 1*

You have two paths you can take here. The first path is to add a network using physical ports on multiple OVM servers (either physical ports or bonds). The second path is just for single servers. You can enable a local network that allows VMs to communicate between themselves only on that server and no other systems. For our example, we will add a new VLAN, so the default (first) option will be chosen. VLAN 200 will be the name, and it will be configured for VMs and flagged for storage as well. This is shown in Figure 12-15.

If physical ports are being used, they can be added in the next screen. In most cases, though, the network team will use VLANs, so this step will remain empty, as shown in Figure 12-16.

Next, click the green "+" button and select the physical server that will have access to the VLANs. You must highlight the server to see the VLANs available to it. In the example shown in Figure 12-17, the server ovs3.m57.local is selected and the VLAN200 bond is checked.

This single VLAN/server combination will now be added. This same process needs to be repeated for all Oracle VM servers that will be hosting VMs using this network. In the example shown in Figure 12-18, both ovs3.m57.local and ovs4.m57.local have been added.

Click Finish. The Network tab will now list network VLAN200, as shown in Figure 12-19, with both storage and virtual machine access.

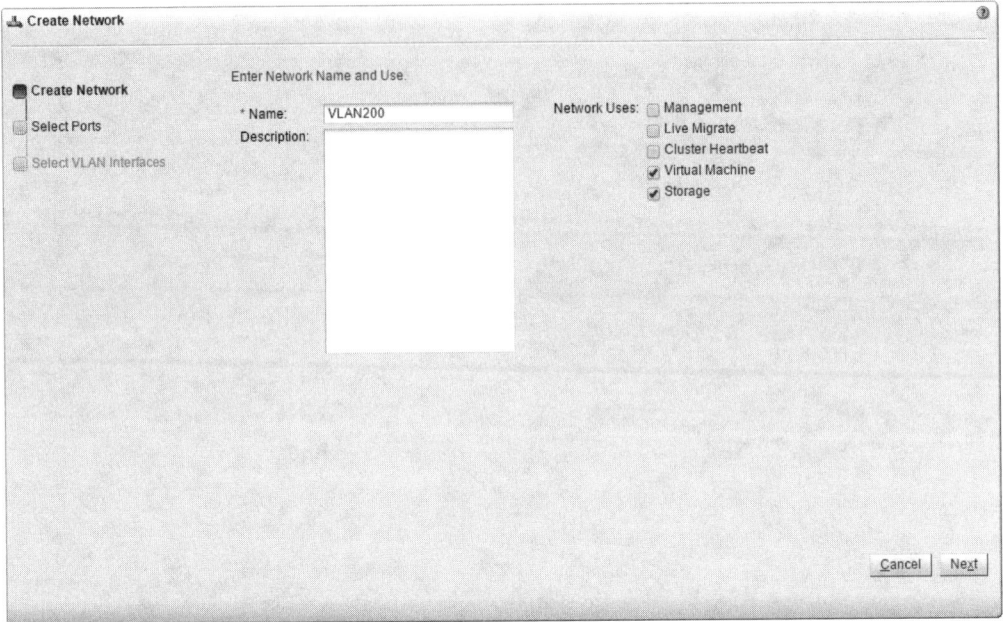

FIGURE 12-15. *Adding a network, step 2*

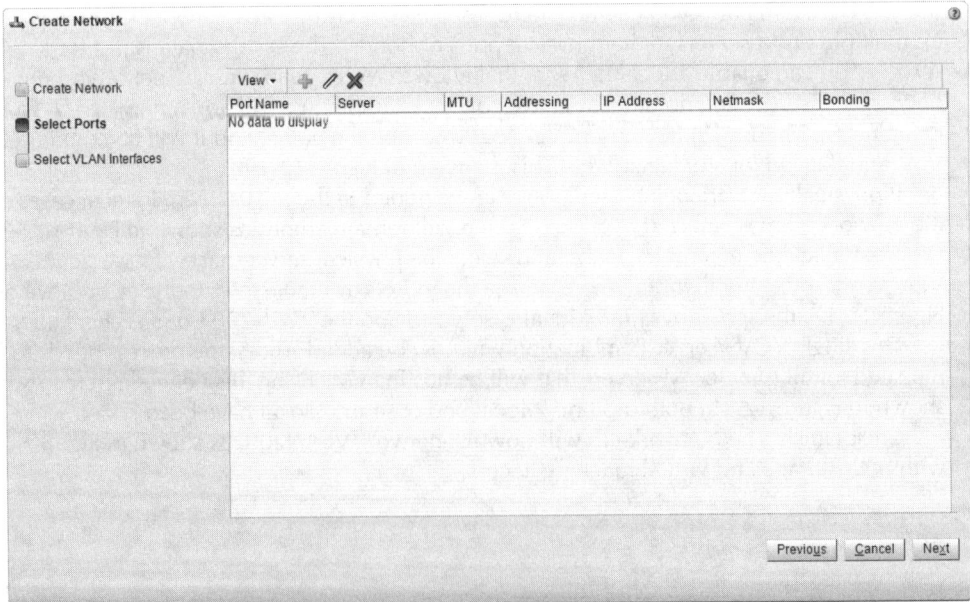

FIGURE 12-16. *Adding a network, step 3*

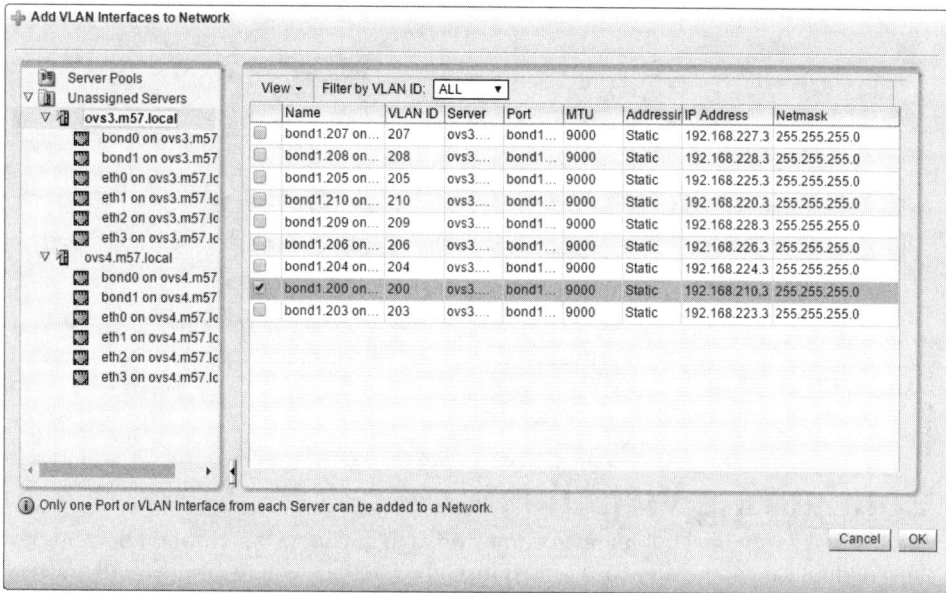

FIGURE 12-17. *Adding a network, step 4*

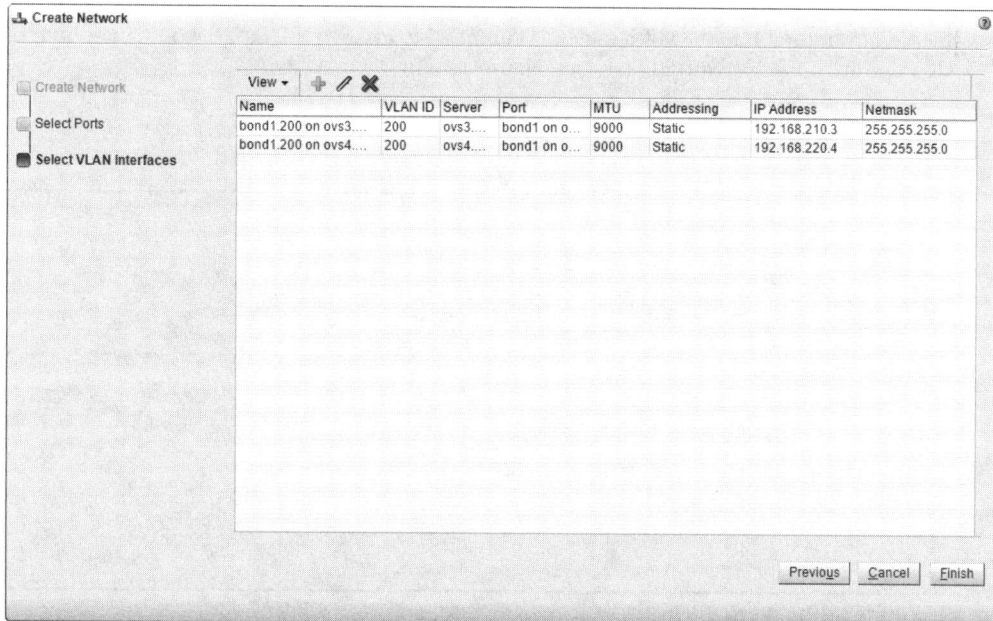

FIGURE 12-18. *Adding a network, step 5*

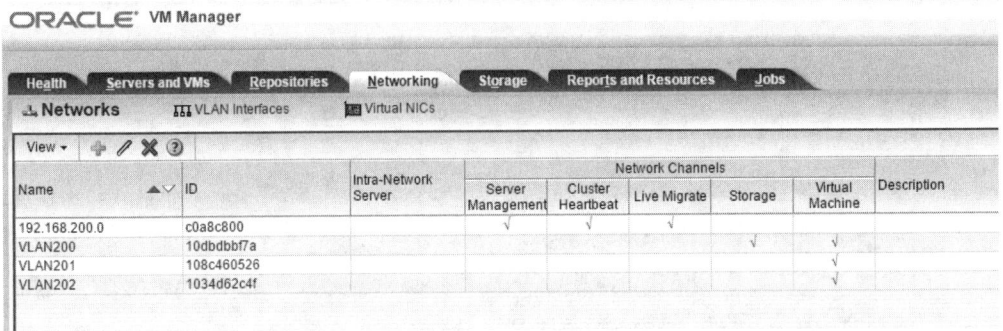

FIGURE 12-19. *Network added*

Configuring Virtual NICs

This last task is optional but highly recommended in any large organization because it will
prevent duplicate addresses. Each virtual machine interface will receive a Media Access Control
(MAC) address, which is a unique identifier assigned to a network interface. Outside of a few
special cases, all network interfaces on a network should have a unique MAC. The IEEE manages
ranges of MAC addresses and can assign ranges to vendors and companies that request them.
Oracle has many ranges, and Oracle VM by default will start with 00:21:F6:0:0:0 for new interfaces.
In many large organizations, this is broken down into a smaller subset, with some organizations
even owning their own range of addresses. When an interface is created, a new MAC is automatically
reserved from the Oracle VM Manager. If you need to change the range, you can go to the Virtual
NICs option in the Networking tab (see Figure 12-20).

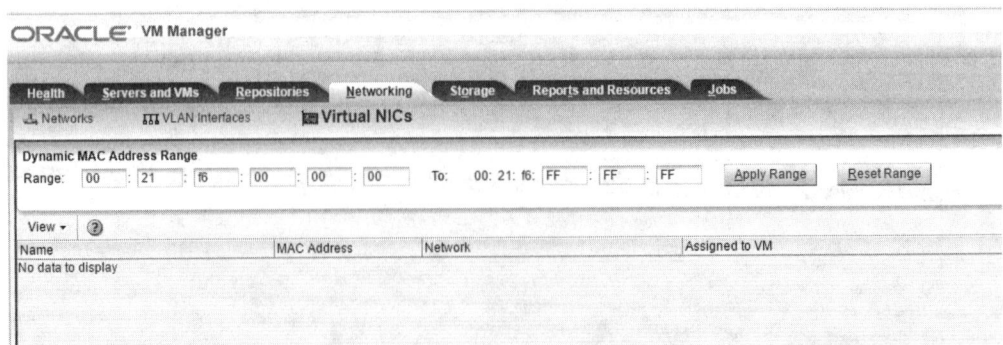

FIGURE 12-20. *Virtual NICs*

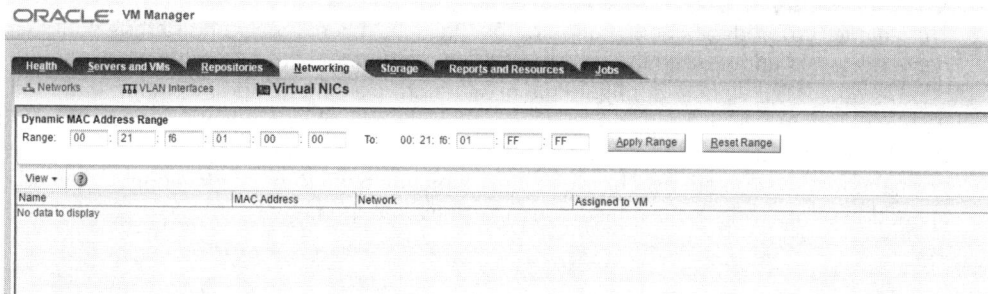

FIGURE 12-21. *MAC range*

Here, the range can be edited. Be careful making changes outside of the 00:21:f6 range, because it is possible to accidently create a duplicate MAC address. The most common use case is to reduce the available range within the existing range—usually one subset per each Oracle VM instance in the enterprise (see Figure 12-21).

In this example, the range has been limited to 00:21:f6:01:00:00 to 00:21:f6:01:ff:ff. Once MAC addresses have been assigned, the same page will show each MAC address as well as the network and VM using it, as shown in Figure 12-22.

CAUTION
Having a duplicate MAC address is very bad and will cause all sorts of difficult-to-resolve issues on a network. Be very careful when randomly selecting a MAC address range.

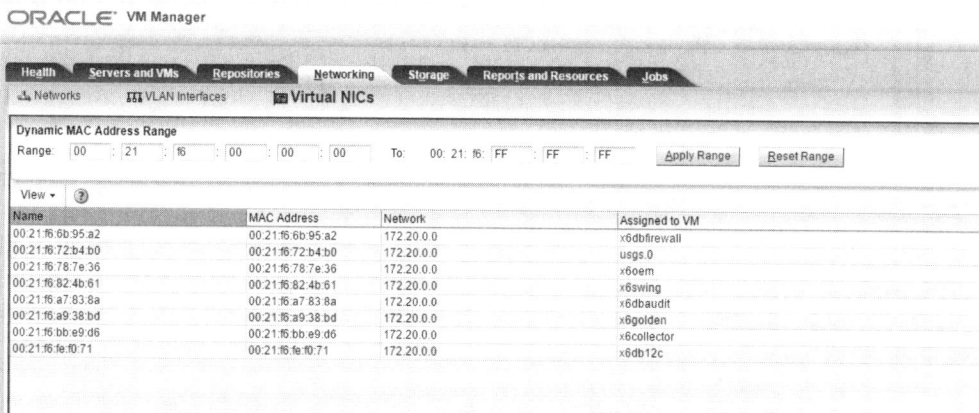

FIGURE 12-22. *Allocated MAC addresses*

Summary

This chapter covered the configuration of the Oracle VM Server network, starting with Xen networking and ending with the configuration of additional virtual network adapters. You do not need to do a lot of work to configure the network, from a general administration standpoint. As mentioned in this chapter, you configure only the first network adapter as part of the initial installation and then configure other adapters after the Oracle VM server is running. During the normal course of operations, changes do not typically need to be made—only if new adapters are added or networks are changed due to business requirements.

CHAPTER
13

Configuring the
VM Server Storage

Although data cannot move without the network, there is no data without storage, which is arguably the heart of a cloud. To support this, Oracle VM has one of the most powerful storage systems available, enabling flexibility in a virtualized environment and performance almost equal to bare metal. The administrator has a choice of many storage options, as shown in Figure 13-1. These range from Network File System (NFS) shares mounted from a Network Attached Storage (NAS) system, to local storage on an OVS, cluster filesystems using block storage logical unit numbers (LUNs) from a Storage Area Network (SAN), and iSCSI and LUNs directly allocated to a virtual machine to bypass the overhead of the filesystem.

Each option has its own advantages and disadvantages, but the flexibility of the Oracle VM storage system allows the administrator to use each of the options as best fits the needs of the data. NFS solutions present a filesystem from the Network Attached Storage (NAS) device that allow the NAS to manage the filesystem that the Oracle VM cluster sees. NFS-based solutions are the easiest to configure, yet traditionally have less than optional performance. Block storage, using Internet Small Computer System Interface (iSCSI) or SAN technologies, uses a cluster filesystem that can improve on the performance seen with NFS, but it has some additional complexity due to managing the LUNs. Local storage is simple to use, but it limits the virtual machines to a single host. Finally, directly allocated storage has the best performance, but it increases the complexity of the configuration. As with any resource, often the user will need more allocated—and this most often occurs with disk resources. When the time comes, adding more resources is necessary. This chapter explains the storage options and how to manage them.

The administrator will also use storage to configure an Oracle VM server pool by creating a filesystem, usually on shared storage that's either NFS or block-based storage. This can be done using local storage on an Oracle VM server (OVS); however; if you plan on enabling High Availability (HA) by creating a VM cluster and a shared storage system is not configured, you need to actually migrate to a shared storage solution. This is the reason why most deployments use shared storage, with a mix of NFS and block-based storage.

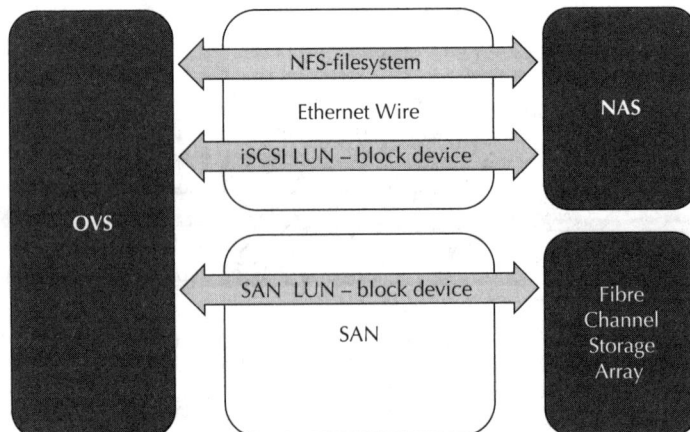

FIGURE 13-1. *Storage options*

In addition to HA, shared storage using a Storage Area Network (SAN) or Network Attached Storage (NAS) offers additional benefits such as Enterprise Storage Management, which provides the ability to add more storage easily, as well as redundancy, backup/restore features, and other enterprise storage features. When planning the storage for the Enterprise VM farm, carefully consider the additional features available with SAN and NAS storage.

Shared Storage vs. Non-Shared Storage

Shared storage refers to storage that can be equally accessed by all VM Server systems in the server pool. This means that all the servers can both read from and write to this storage. Several types of storage can be shared, including SAN, iSCSI shares, and NAS systems using NFS.

Non-shared storage refers to storage local to the Oracle VM Servers. This storage is comprised of disks installed internally to the Oracle VM Server that cannot be shared with other servers in a server pool.

SAN storage uses a network that is designed specifically for storage and does not allow normal network traffic. SAN systems typically include extensive redundancy and performance features. Because of that, SAN systems are usually fairly expensive. In the author's opinion, SAN systems are usually worth the cost. For SAN storage to be shared, you must configure it such that all the nodes in the server pool can access the storage, and you must configure it with a shared filesystem. Fortunately, Oracle VM comes with Oracle Cluster File System (OCFS2) built in. OCFS2 is a high-performance cluster filesystem that was originally developed for Oracle Real Application Clusters (RAC).

NAS storage can also include many of the same redundancy and performance features as SAN storage, but because it uses off-the-shelf network hardware, it usually comes at a lower price. Both SAN and NAS storage are suitable for Oracle VM and, depending on the brand and model, offer a high level of performance. NAS storage arrays often support two different varieties: iSCSI and NFS. The iSCSI protocol (technically a block technology) provides network storage for the Oracle VM server that looks like a disk drive and must be configured with OCFS2 in order to be clustered. A Network File System (NFS) is inherently shared because the storage is presented to the Oracle VM system with the filesystem being managed at the storage system, not the host.

If a shared server pool (cluster) is desired, all storage used for virtual machines must be shared. Without shared storage, a cluster cannot pass the virtual machines between the different nodes. This is crucial for both HA and live migrations. In addition, the Oracle VM servers must be configured as a server pool with shared storage.

Server Pools Using Non-Shared Storage

A server pool does not need to use shared storage; however, if shared storage is not used, some of the HA and load-balancing tools will not be available to the server pool. The clustered server pool is defined as a set of VM servers that use the same shared storage. The shared storage is required for HA and is used for both HA and load balancing. You might define a server pool cluster as a server pool that has more than one server using shared storage. The server pool cluster uses a quorum to keep track of the cluster's state. This chapter focuses on the most common deployment using clustered storage. Unless otherwise mentioned, the term *server pool* refers to both a clustered and non-clustered server pool.

Configuring the Hardware for Storage

Before you can configure the storage in Oracle VM, you must first configure it properly on the VM Server system. That is, the storage must be visible to the dom0 layer before you can add it to the VM server and/or cluster. The method employed to configure and verify the storage system depends on the type of storage and the amount and type of redundancy used by that storage. This process can be fairly simple, as with NFS storage, or fairly complicated, as with multipath storage.

The next few sections cover connecting to storage based on the type of storage and the amount of redundancy required. To review, several types of storage are supported by Oracle VM: directly attached disks, SAN storage, iSCSI storage, and NAS storage with NFS support. When using local storage, SAN, or NAS with iSCSI, you configure the storage using the OCFS2 filesystem. Local storage can also be created using an unused partition on a local disk drive. When you're using a NAS with NFS, the filesystem that's used is determined by the backend storage. To the Oracle VM system, it is considered NFS storage.

How the storage is configured at the hardware level does not vary based on whether it is used in a cluster. It does vary, however, when the VM Server configuration layer is in a High Availability cluster, because all of the storage must be visible by all Oracle VM servers. The next sections cover hardware connectivity using multipath storage.

Connecting and Configuring the Storage

How you connect the storage varies based on the type of storage you're using. With SAN storage, setup typically involves adding and configuring one or more Host Bus Adapters (HBAs). These HBAs are typically designed for SAN storage and generally use fiber-optic connections, and may also require array-specific additions to the /etc/multipath.conf file on the OVS to support multipathing. Check with your storage vendor and Oracle support to see if changes are required to this file.

Storage can involve either the built-in Ethernet connections or the addition of an HBA for Fibre Channel block storage. If an iSCSI HBA is used, a device driver might be required. If a recent version of Oracle VM was installed, the device driver might be up to date, although often a new driver is recommended. Again, follow the hardware vendor's instructions for installing and updating the device driver.

Redundant Storage
Redundant storage is designed to be highly available because it avoids a single point of failure. It accomplishes this by having at least two of each component, including the path between the storage array and the OVS system. This way, even if a single component fails, access to storage is retained. Redundancy is accomplished in a number of different ways— through multiple paths to storage, Redundant Array of Inexpensive Disks (RAID) disk storage, and multiple power supplies.

Most of these components are transparent to the installer; however, creating redundant paths to storage requires intervention by the storage administrator. Multipath storage requires both hardware and software configuration on the VM Server system itself.

NOTE

In order to support High Availability and live migration, the storage must be visible by all the VM servers in the cluster, which involves both hardware and software configuration, which is detailed in these next sections.

Depending on the type of storage, the configuration differs slightly. The various configurations are covered in the next sections.

Configuring NFS Storage

NFS storage is fairly easy to configure for Oracle VM. All configuration is performed from the Oracle VM Manager. Generic NAS devices are managed as "file servers" and are easily discovered. Before discovering a new NAS device, make sure that you have already created the NFS share, that all OVS systems have read/write access to the share, and that the root user is not squashed. It is also important that the NFS server returns the list of exported filesystems. This can be tested using the **showmount** command. If the NFS server does not return a list of filesystems, Oracle VM cannot discover the mounts.

WARNING

The NFS root squash parameter must be disabled on each share used by Oracle VM. This is a security feature that will disable root access to the share.

Also, verify that each OVS system can ping the NAS device. A simple ping test, **ping $NAS**, is all that is required, as shown here:

```
[root@ovs4 etc]# ping nas
PING nas.m57.local (192.168.200.10) 56(84) bytes of data.
64 bytes from nas.m57.local (192.168.200.10): icmp_seq=1 ttl=64 time=0.170 ms
64 bytes from nas.m57.local (192.168.200.10): icmp_seq=2 ttl=64 time=0.161 ms
64 bytes from nas.m57.local (192.168.200.10): icmp_seq=3 ttl=64 time=0.160 ms
64 bytes from nas.m57.local (192.168.200.10): icmp_seq=4 ttl=64 time=0.173 ms
64 bytes from nas.m57.local (192.168.200.10): icmp_seq=5 ttl=64 time=0.163 ms
64 bytes from nas.m57.local (192.168.200.10): icmp_seq=6 ttl=64 time=0.155 ms
64 bytes from nas.m57.local (192.168.200.10): icmp_seq=7 ttl=64 time=0.155 ms
^C
--- nas.m57.local ping statistics ---
7 packets transmitted, 7 received, 0% packet loss, time 6478ms
rtt min/avg/max/mdev = 0.155/0.162/0.173/0.013 ms
[root@ovs4 etc]#
```

Oracle VM does not need to use all the mounts exported from the NFS server. You can also verify what NFS shares are visible from the OVS by using the **showmount -e $NAS** command, where $NAS is the name of the NAS device:

```
[root@ovs4 etc]# showmount -e nas
Export list for nas:
/shared
/qnap_vms
```

```
/photos
/ovmm_repo0
/ovmm_pool0
/old_nas
/iso
/homes
/esx1
/Web
/Recordings
/Public
/Multimedia
/MPS3
/Download
```

> **CAUTION**
> *If the **showmount** command does not display the exported filesystems,*
> *the NFS mount cannot be used by Oracle VM. With some arrays,*
> *iSCSI may need to be used when the array is not capable of displaying*
> *exported mounts.*

Next, you will need to discover a new NAS device (see Figure 13-2). From the Oracle VM manager, access the Storage tab and then highlight the File Servers option. Click the folder icon with the green + sign to add a new NAS.

This displays the dialog where you can select the storage plug-in. For NAS devices, use the Oracle Generic Network Filesystem plug-in. For the example shown in Figure 13-3, the array name is *Generic NAS* and the hostname is *nas10g.m57.local.*

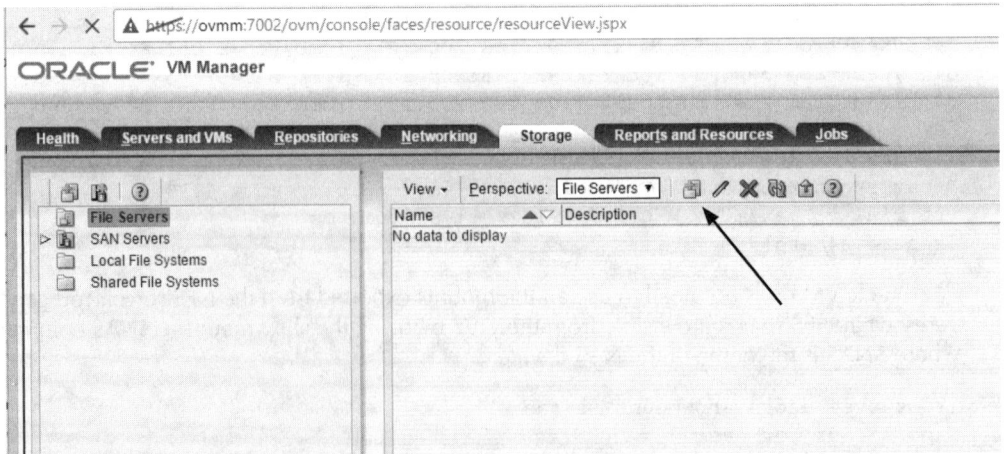

FIGURE 13-2. *Discover NAS*

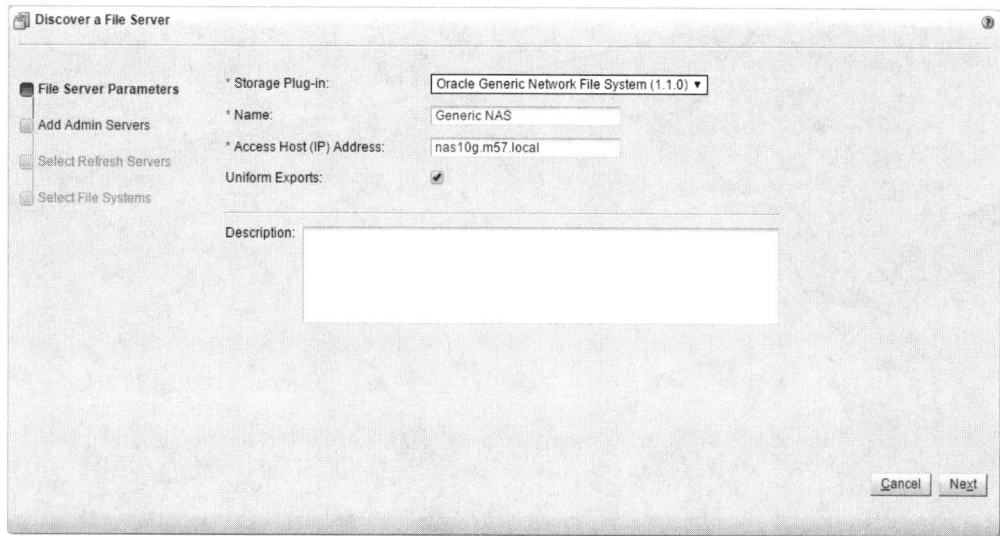

FIGURE 13-3. *Generic NAS*

NOTE
Although the generic plug-in will work for block storage, using the vendor-supplied plug-in (if available) will provide additional automation and features such as snapshots, LUN creation, cloning, and more. At the time of this writing, plug-ins are available from Oracle for the Oracle ZFS Storage Appliances. Additionally, plug-ins are also available from EMC, Fujitsu, and Hitachi. Contact your storage vendor for assistance obtaining the plug-in for your array.

The system will use uniform exports because all OVS systems, regardless of pool membership, will use the same export from the NAS to the OVS. If different server pools will use different NFS exports, then the Uniform Exports box should be unchecked, and access groups will need to be configured after new NFS filesystems are discovered for the first time. This is most often done when a production pool uses a different network than a non-production pool.

Next, you will need to select the admin servers for the generic storage (see Figure 13-4). The admin servers define what systems can access the storage array to perform maintenance on the shares. For an NFS server, the admin servers are used to validate the file server and also perform file server refreshes.

The last step is to select what filesystems from the NAS will be used by Oracle VM (see Figure 13-5). Because not all filesystems from a NAS could be used for virtual machines, you should select only the filesystems to be used by Oracle VM. There is also a handy option for filtering on specific patterns seen in the name of the filesystem.

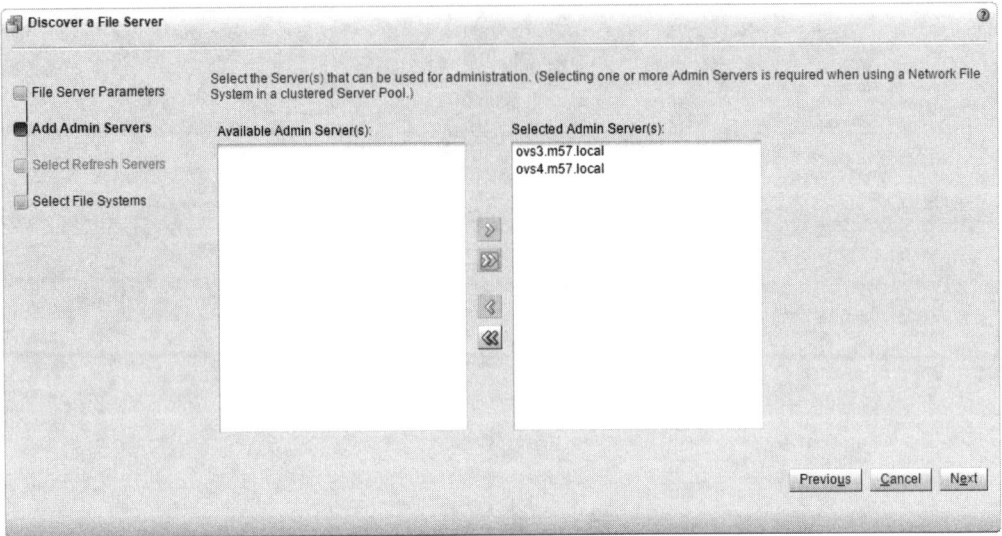

FIGURE 13-4. *Adding admin servers*

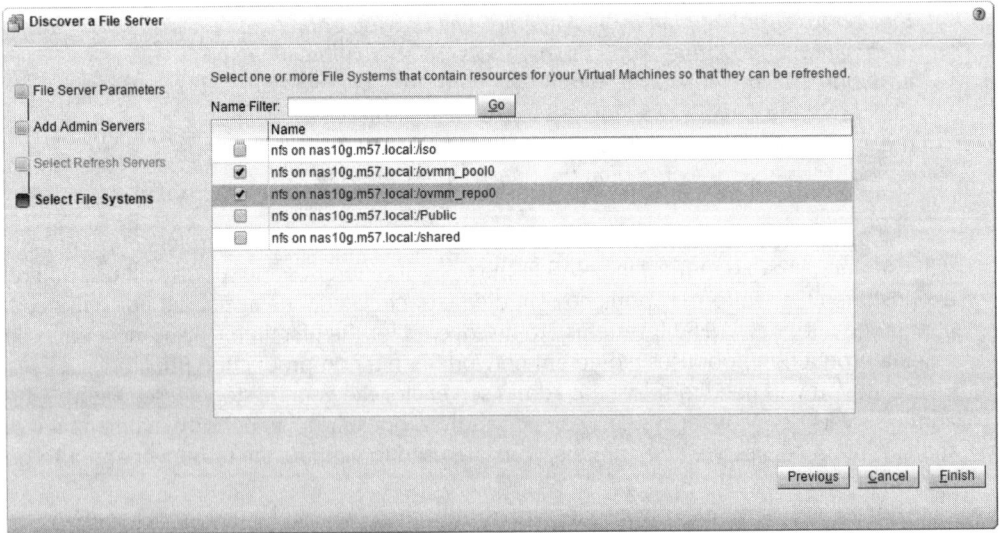

FIGURE 13-5. *Selecting filesystems*

If non-uniform exports are used, an additional step is required to assign refresh servers. The more refresh servers assigned, the longer your NFS file server discovery and subsequent refreshes will take. The best practice is to assign only a single refresh server, to improve the performance of discoveries and refreshes. If the single refresh server is unavailable, a new refresh server can be assigned. If the assigned refresh server is down, then no filesystem or NFS server refreshes will be possible.

The selected filesystems will then be refreshed by Oracle VM (see Figure 13-6). The refresh process scans the filesystem to detect what changes may have been made outside the control of Oracle VM Manager.

Normally, if all operations are performed via Oracle VM Manager, it is unlikely that this information will become inconsistent; however, manual updates or modifications may result in an inconsistency within Oracle VM Manager. For instance, if files are manually copied into a repository via the filesystem where the repository is located, then Oracle VM Manager is unaware of the changes within the repository and is also unaware of the changes to the amount of available and used space on the filesystem where the repository is located. When the repository is refreshed, Oracle VM will discover the changes made, including any new ISO files, templates, or VMs added manually outside of the normal process. This discovery is also useful when performing disaster recovery operations, because the repository can be replicated and then discovered at the disaster recovery site.

Once the NAS filesystem is refreshed, it can be used for a storage location by Oracle VM. This includes use as a valid location for the server pool metadata and for storage repositories.

Configuring iSCSI and Fibre Channel Storage

Configuring iSCSI storage requires a few more manual steps. iSCSI at its heart is a block-level data transport that can leverage an Ethernet network to share storage LUNs by encapsulating the SCSI commands into TCP/IP packets. How it works is functionally similar to a normal SAN, other than it can share the same network that is used for VM traffic. From a performance standpoint, an iSCSI LUN is better than file-based storage like NFS; however, traditional SAN technologies usually perform better than iSCSI. Because iSCSI storage is attached from a remote server, it is perfectly suited for a clustered *server pool* configuration where the high availability of storage and the possibility to use a live migration of virtual machines are important factors. It also works well for database workloads, especially when a LUN is directly assigned to a VM, thus bypassing the storage repository. It does add in some additional layers that need to be configured, mainly concerning the concepts of initiators and targets. The *initiator* is the storage client, whereas the *target* is the provider of the storage. With Oracle VM, all network interfaces have iSCSI initiators

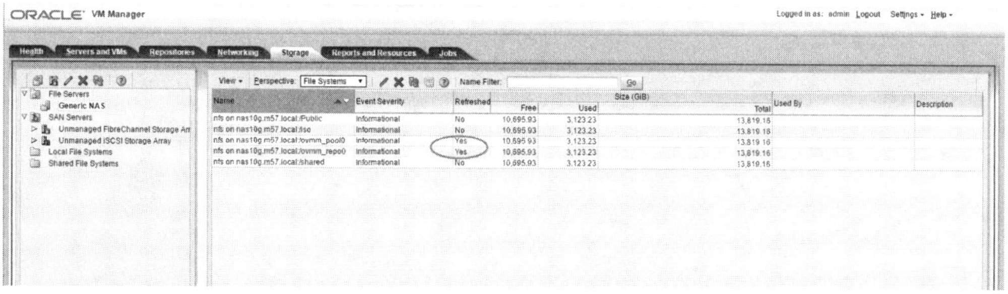

FIGURE 13-6.   *Refreshed filesystems*

configured by default; it is the role of the Oracle VM admin to make sure that storage network traffic and other network traffic do not conflict. See Chapter 12 for more information on this.

NOTE
Although, in general, iSCSI performs better than NFS, there is one notable exception using a technology called Direct NFS (dNFS). If you are running a database with a NAS device, using dNFS for your database mounts should perform better than iSCSI. The exception occurs when dNFS is used in combination with Hybrid Columnar Compression (HCC). HCC over NFS or dNFS is only supported with Oracle ZFS storage arrays.

The generic iSCSI Oracle VM Storage Connect plug-in allows Oracle VM to use virtually all iSCSI storage providers. As with NFS arrays, the vendor-specific Oracle VM Storage Connect plug-ins exist for several iSCSI-enabled arrays, allowing Oracle VM Manager to manage additional functionality such as creating and deleting LUNs, snapshots, clones, and so on. Check with your storage array vendor if an Oracle VM Storage Connect plug-in is available.

The process of discovering a generic iSCSI array is similar to that of an NFS array. From the Oracle VM Manager, access the Storage tab and then highlight the Unmanaged iSCSI Storage Array option. Click the storage icon with the green + sign to add a new array (see Figure 13-7).

Next, name the new target device and then select the storage type and plug-in to be used. In the example shown in Figure 13-8, the generic iSCSI storage plug-in will be used for the iSCSI storage.

The process for adding a regular unmanaged SAN, or an unmanaged SAN array, is practically identical, with the exception that the iSCSI array requires some access additional information. iSCSI normally uses the Challenge Handshake Authentication Protocol (CHAP) to authenticate initiators to providers. When configuring the storage on the array, you'll need the CHAP username and password. To add the CHAP access information, select the green + icon shown in Figure 13-9.

This will give you the option to set up the access host and port for the iSCSI array. The access host should be the name or IP of the network interface used to access the storage. In the example shown in Figure 13-10, although nas.m57.local is a valid interface, storage is accessed over a 10 gigabit network (10G) using the hostname nas10g.m57.local. The CHAP username and password have also been added.

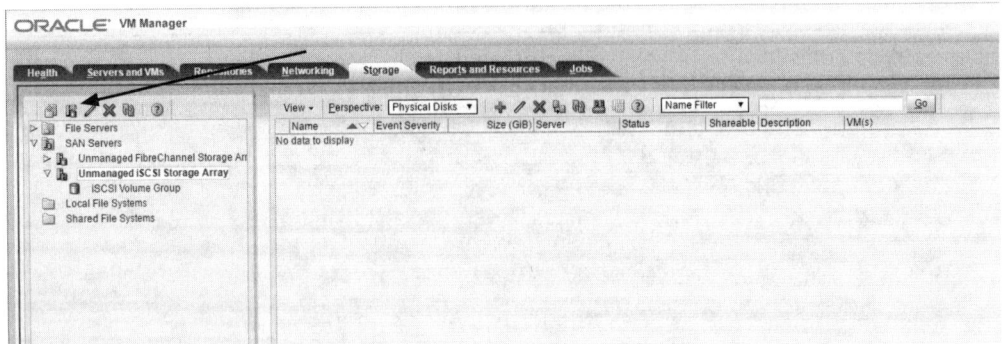

FIGURE 13-7. *Unmanaged iSCSI discovery*

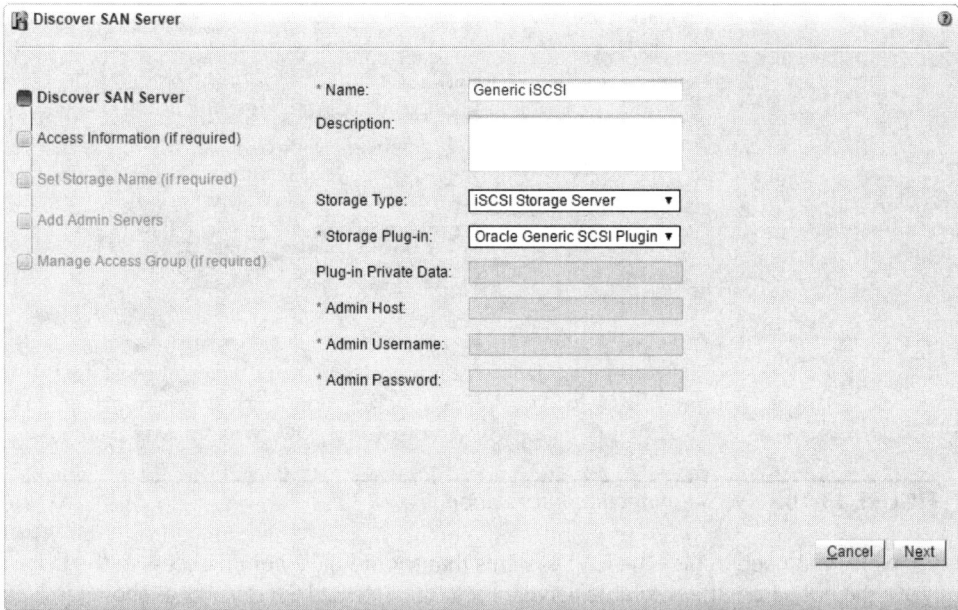

FIGURE 13-8.   *Adding an iSCSI array*

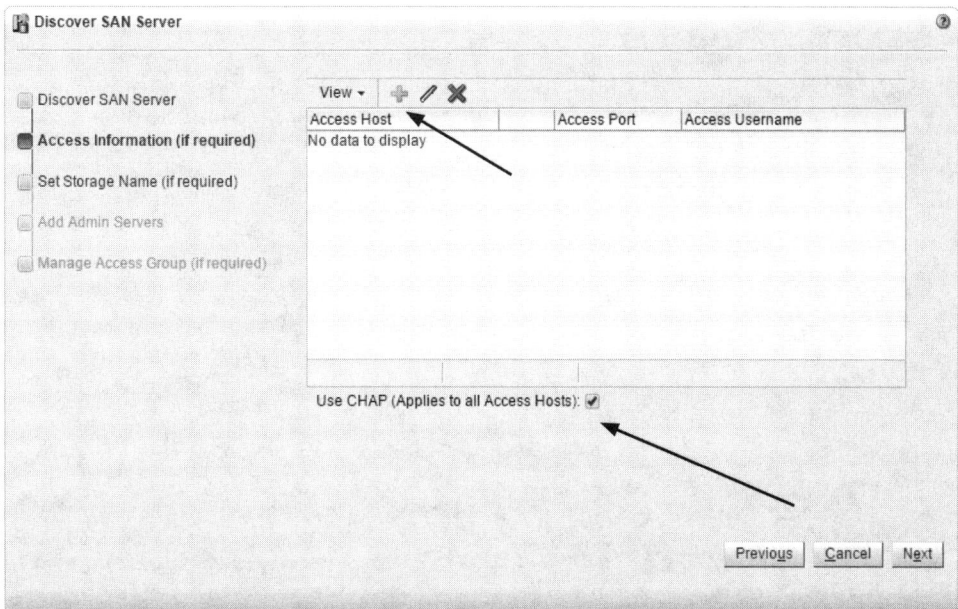

FIGURE 13-9.   *Adding access information*

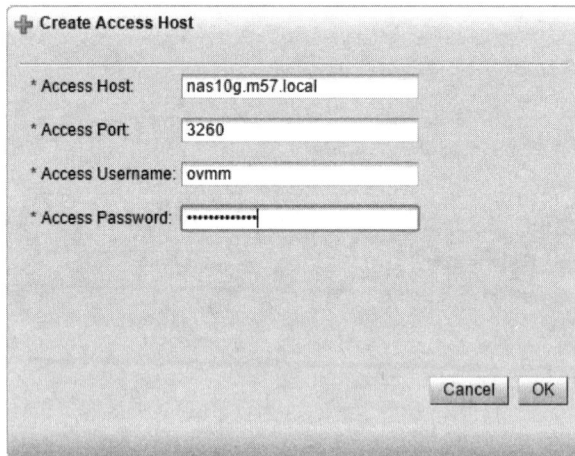

FIGURE 13-10. *iSCSI connection information*

Next, you need to pick the OVS systems that should have admin access to the LUN. Simply move the hosts from the Available Servers list to the Selected Servers list, as shown in Figure 13-11. This is the same role as admin servers for NFS. When new LUNs are added, you'll need to refresh the array. These admin servers are used to perform the refresh.

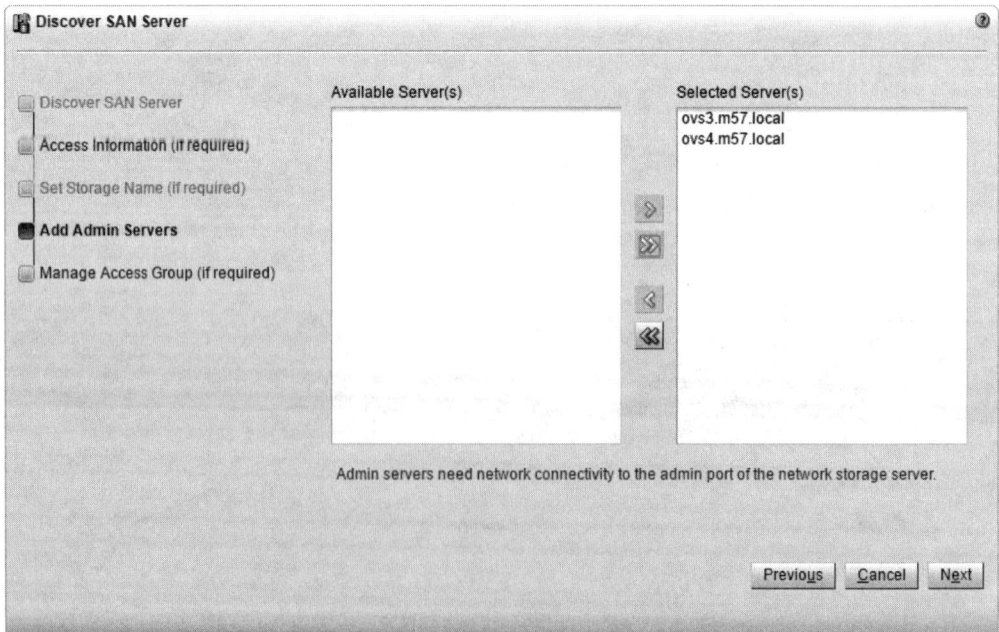

FIGURE 13-11. *Admin servers*

Next, you need to define what servers will see the LUN. This is done by using an access group. SAN access groups define which storage initiators can be used to access the LUNs on the SAN. This is the same for both iSCSI and Fibre Channel LUNs. SAN access group functionality is defined by the Oracle VM Storage Connect plug-in being used for the array. By default, the generic iSCSI plug-in creates a single group that manages all available storage initiators and is added at the time of discovery. Other plug-ins can provide more specific control and support multiple access groups that limit access to particular LUNs. Select the edit icon while the access group is highlighted, as shown in Figure 13-12.

The next part of the process shows the access group in one tab and the storage initiators in a second tab. Select the second tab and then move the host initiators from the Available Storage Initiators list to the Selected Storage Initiators list, as shown in Figure 13-13.

The process is almost done. Once you click OK in the Edit Access Group screen, the final screen requires you to click Finish to kick off the job to refresh the array and add the available LUNs to the hosts (see Figure 13-14).

The entire process can be followed using the Job Summary window in the Oracle VM Manager (see Figure 13-15). Monitoring the jobs as the work is performed is helpful because a problem can be detected if a job fails.

Once the job completes, the new LUN and its array will appear in the Storage tab, under SAN Servers (see Figure 13-16). The initial name of the LUN will consist of the brand of the array and a sequential number. The size of the LUN is also displayed, as are the OVS hosts that see the LUN, the status of the LUN (online, offline), the VMs using the LUN (if it's directly allocated to a VM),

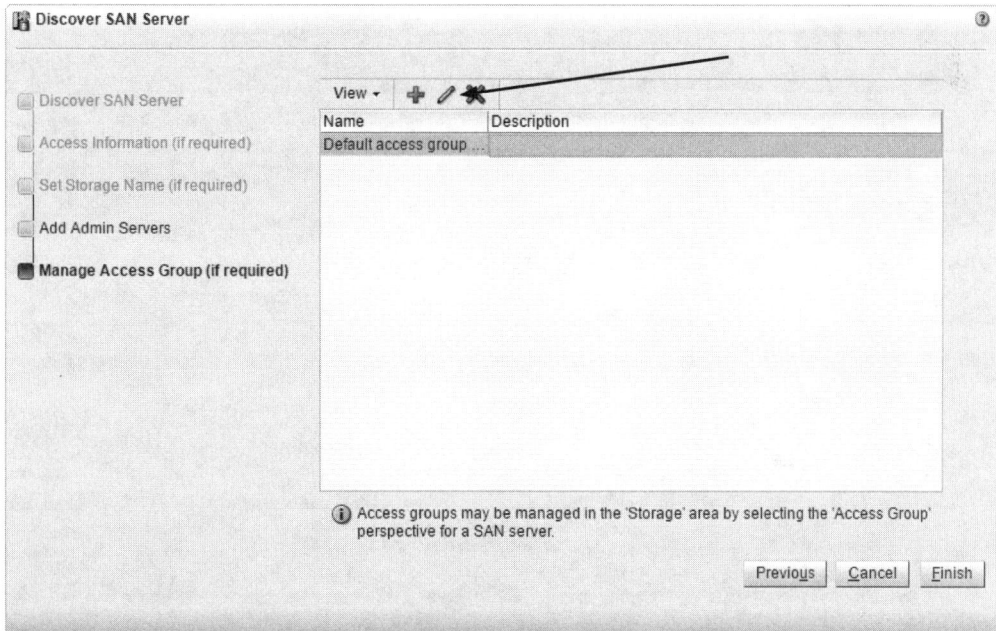

FIGURE 13-12. *Adding hosts*

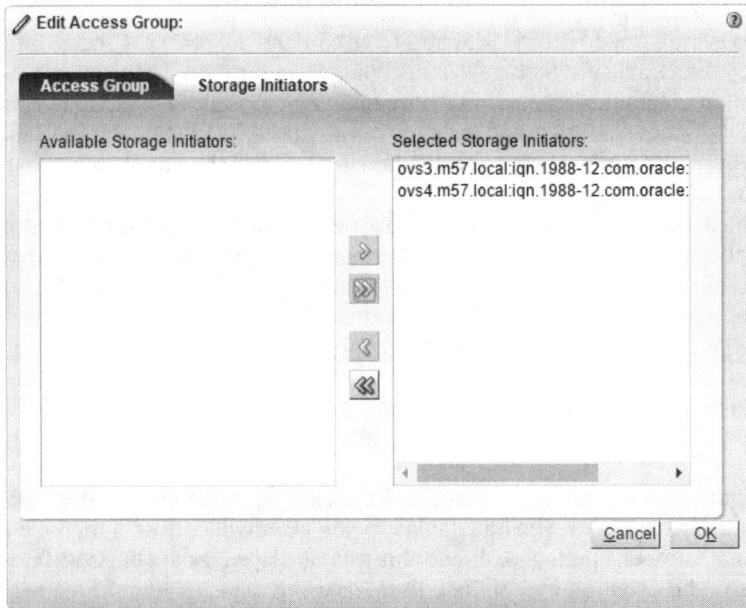

FIGURE 13-13. *Host initiators*

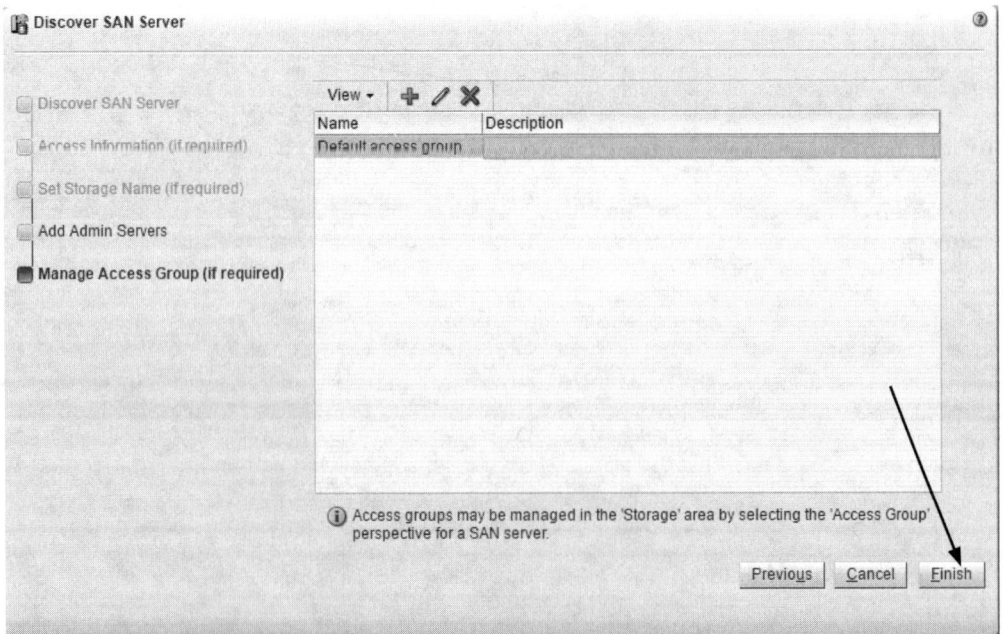

FIGURE 13-14. *Wrapping up*

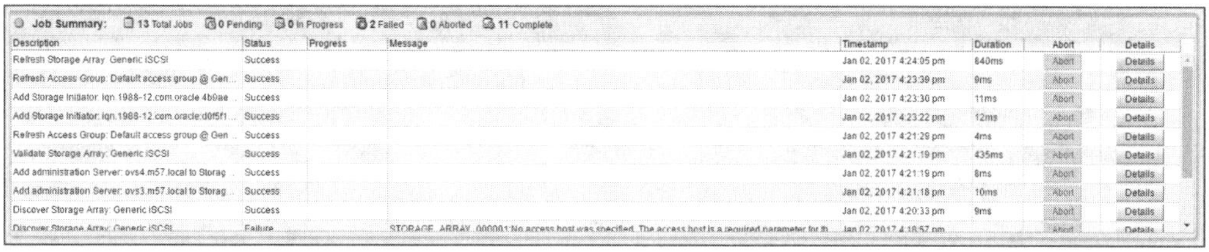

FIGURE 13-15. *Job Summary window*

as well as whether the LUN is marked as shareable. A shareable LUN is a LUN that can be bused by multiple VMs at the same time, but this feature should not be used with LUNs that support pool filesystems or storage repositories. Shared LUNs are required for RAC clusters, ASM clustered filesystems (ACFSs), and other clustered storage technologies.

WARNING
Shared LUNs are a powerful tool, but you need to be careful because not all filesystems and volume managers support them. The Linux lvm volume manager and ext4 filesystems are examples of technologies that do not work well with shared storage. In most cases, the boot disk will not be shared; only data LUNs are shared.

To change the LUN name or the Shareable flag, highlight the LUN and select the edit icon, as shown in Figure 13-17.

Configuring SAN Storage
How you configure SAN storage varies based on the brand and type of SAN storage. In general, SAN storage uses an HBA that comes with a specific device driver; however, many of the most popular HBA drivers are now built into the Linux distribution. If multipath storage is available and desired, configure it using the instructions provided by the hardware vendor.

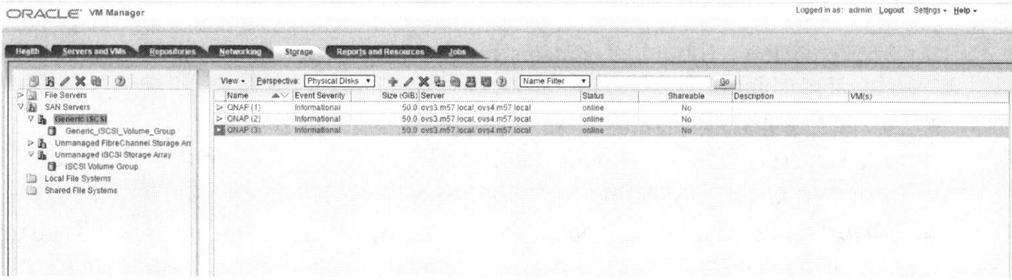

FIGURE 13-16. *Available LUNs*

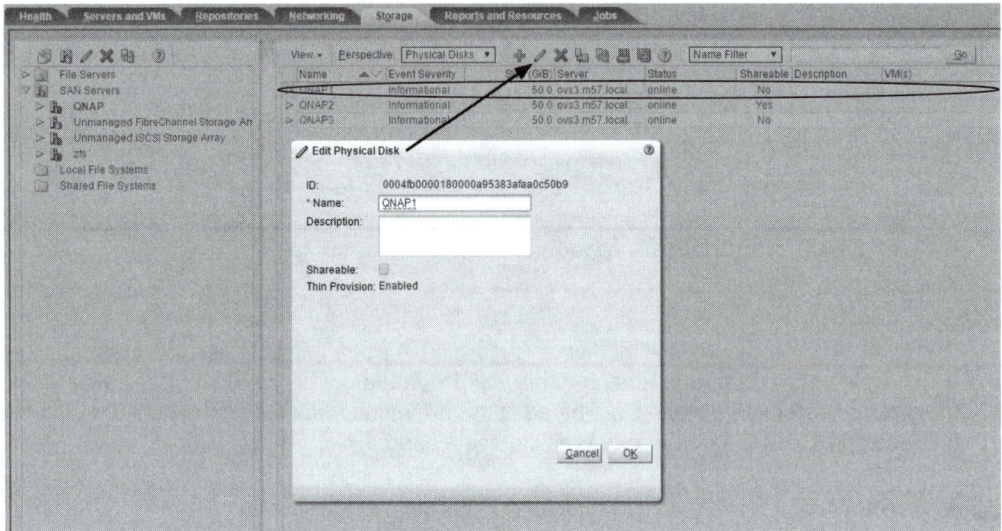

FIGURE 13-17. *Editing a LUN*

As mentioned earlier, the storage must be configured with OCFS2 and shared in order to use it in a cluster. This process happens automatically with Oracle VM 3.*x*.

Creating a Repository

Disk storage for the virtual environment is referred to as the *storage repository*. The storage repository is the home for the virtual machines, the ISO images, virtual machine templates, shared virtual disks, and so on. The top-level directory for the storage repository is the storage repository name (see Figure 13-18).

Underneath the top-level directory are the following folders:

■ **ISOs** This folder contains ISO files that can be mounted in virtual machines or used to install new virtual machines.

■ **VM Files** This folder contains the configuration data for virtual machines—specifically the vm.cfg file for each VM.

■ **VM Templates** This folder contains virtual machine templates, which can be used to clone virtual machines.

■ **Virtual Appliances** Virtual appliances contain of a set of preconfigured virtual machines that can contain an entire application stack. An example would be a virtual appliance for E-Business, which contains the database tier and application tier in a single deployment.

■ **Virtual Disks** This folder contains virtual disks, which can be either dedicated to a virtual machine or shared by multiple virtual machines. Virtual disks are different from dedicated LUNS, in that multiple virtual disks can live in a single repository.

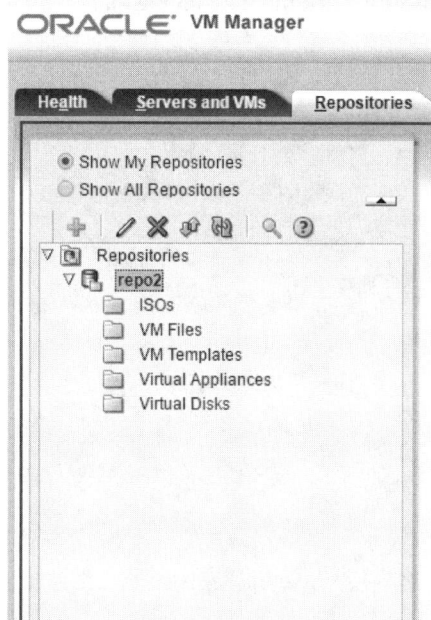

FIGURE 13-18.   *Repository layout*

Whether a single repository or multiple repositories are used, the rule is that if a VM cluster is going to be used, all storage must be shared. In an all-in-one (non-clustered) configuration, either shared or non-shared storage can be used, but in a cluster, all storage must be clustered. This clustered storage can be either NFS or block devices; however, a repository can only use a single LUN, which limits the ability to grow the repository. This makes NFS shares a more popular choice.

To create a repository, navigate to the Repositories tab in Oracle VM Manager and select the green + icon, shown next.

Next, the repository will need a name. On the following screen, you can select the type of storage. For an NFS repository, click the magnifying glass icon to select the NFS share.

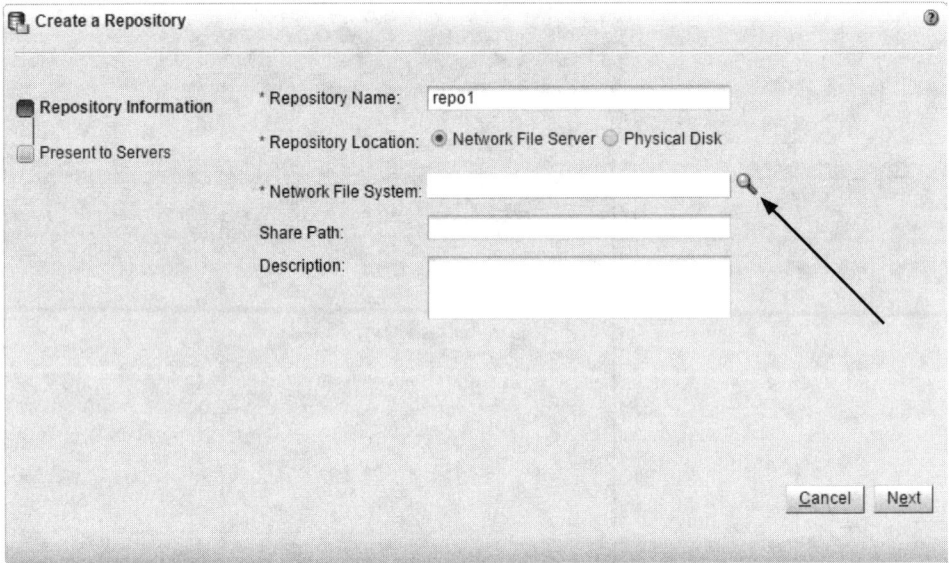

A list of unused NFS shares should be displayed, as shown next. Highlight the share that will host this repository.

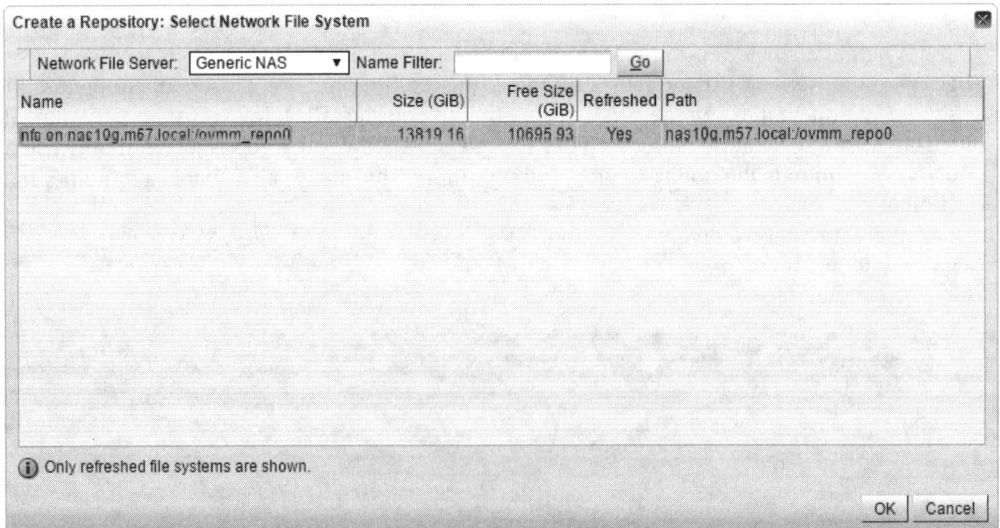

If a LUN-based repository is being created, you will need to select a LUN from a server pool. Select the LUN by clicking the magnifying glass icon. The following shows what a selected LUN will look like.

Next, verify the information and make any changes as necessary. If an NFS share is used, as shown in here, the option Share Path allows you to select a subdirectory of the NFS share to use for the repository. Click Next to continue.

Next, you need to select which OVSs will have access to the repository. As shown next, you simply move the servers to the Present to Servers list and click Finish.

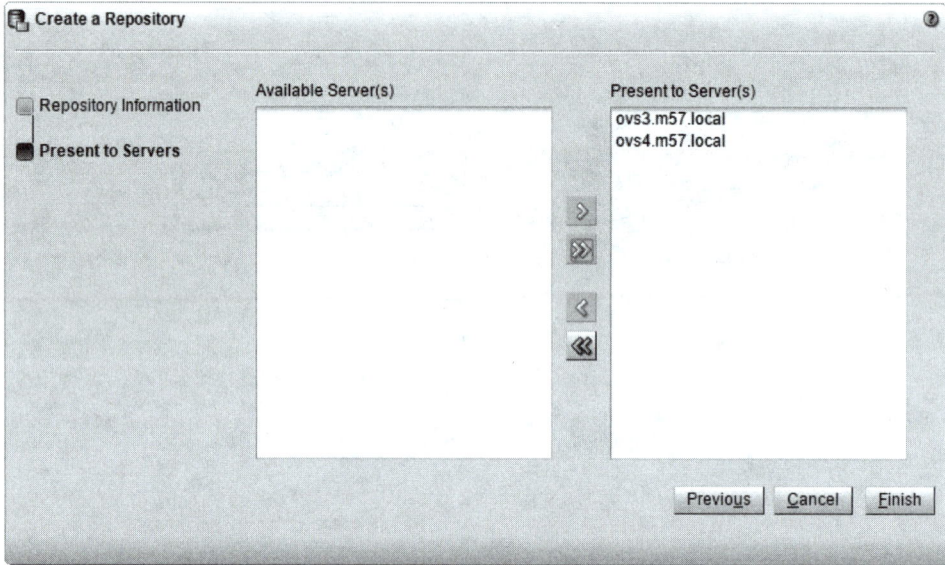

The repository is now created, and the Repositories tab will show the available repositories (see Figure 13-19). Also, storage consumption information will be displayed for each repository.

Storage Plug-Ins

As previously discussed, the ability to integrate Oracle VM with the storage array is provided using a Storage Connect plug-in specific to the storage array used. The plug-in leverages an API framework that provides for storage management from the Oracle VM Manager. This can include storage discovery, provisioning, and management features. It enables administrators to provision and manage storage platforms through Oracle VM Manager, thus simplifying cloud storage management. The plug-in provides a layer of abstraction, so cloud administrators do not need to

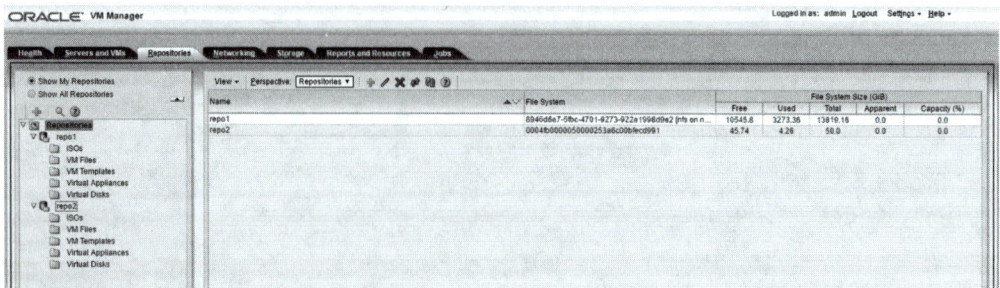

FIGURE 13-19. *Created repositories*

know the specific management interface of each storage array used by the cloud built with Oracle VM, and they are able to perform most common operations as a natural part of Oracle VM management. An important note is that the plug-in is written by the storage vendor to take advantage of the features already built into its array. For the following example, the array used is an Oracle ZFS array. To prepare for this, the following tasks need to be completed:

1. Download the Oracle VM Storage Connect plug-in for the Oracle ZFS Storage Appliance.

2. On the ZFS array to be managed, create an admin user for Oracle VM. In the example, the user ovmm is created with the following admin privileges:

   - changeAccessProps
   - changeGeneralProps
   - changeProtocolProps
   - changeSpaceProps
   - changeUserQuota
   - clearLocks
   - clone
   - createProject
   - createShare
   - destroy
   - promote
   - rename
   - rollback
   - rrsource
   - rrtarget
   - scheduleSnap
   - scrub
   - shadowMigration

3. Grant takeSnapCreate target and target group's privileges:

   - For iSCSI, create an OVM target group and OVM target. Keep note of the OVM target group name because it will be needed during discovery.
   - For Fibre Channel, create an OVM target group. Keep note of the OVM target group name because it will be needed during discovery.

Installing the Plug-in on the OVS

The storage plug-in needs to be installed on each OVS that will be leveraging the ability of the plug-in. To do this, copy the appropriate plug-in to the OVS. The plug-in is version specific, with OVM 3.2.*x* using one version and OVM 3.3.*x* and OVM 3.4.*x* using a different version. The reason for this is that the API changed significantly between OVM 3.2 and OVM 3.3.

Before installing the RPM Package Manager (RPM) file, verify that an older version of the RPM is not already installed:

```
[root@ovs3 storage-connect]# rpm -qa | grep -i s7k
```

If a version exists, remove it using the command **rpm -ev osc-oracle-s7k**.

Next, install the plug-in with RPM; the warning messages can be safely ignored:

```
[root@ovs3 storage-connect]# rpm -ivh /root/osc-oracle-s7k-2.1.1.el6.noarch.rpm
warning: /root/osc-oracle-s7k-2.1.1.el6.noarch.rpm: Header V3 RSA/SHA256
Signature, key ID ec551f03: NOKEY
Preparing...                ########################################### [100%]
   1:osc-oracle-s7k          ########################################### [100%]
[root@ovs3 storage-connect]#
```

Now that the plug-in is installed, the ZFS can be discovered and managed by the OVMM. This is started the same way you would add any SAN storage array, but when you pick the plug-in, you would select Oracle ZFS (see Figure 13-20).

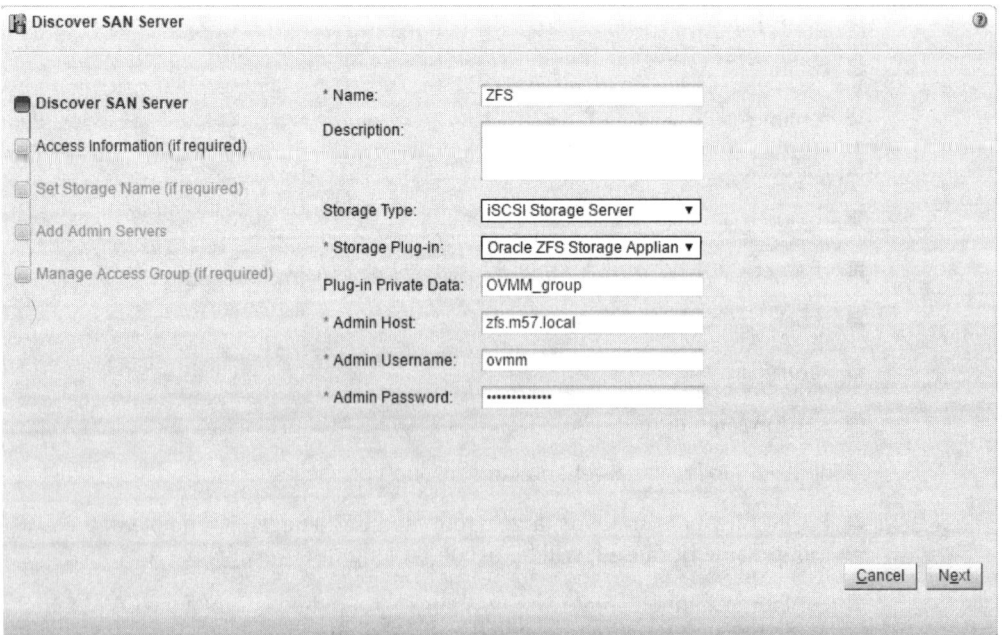

FIGURE 13-20. *ZFS array discovery*

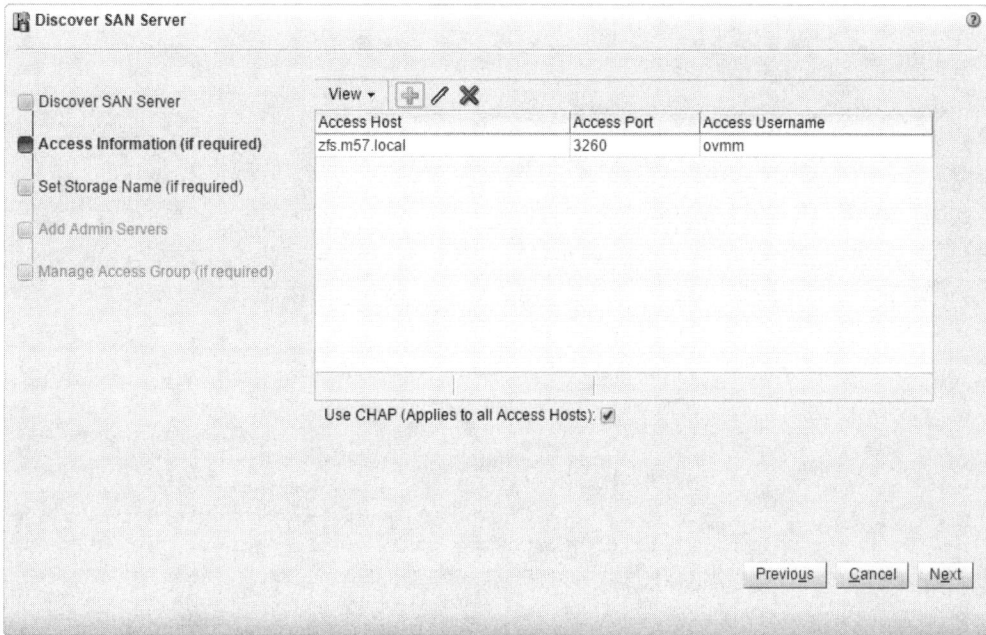

FIGURE 13-21.   *ZFS access information*

When using the ZFS plug-in, you have several new options. The first is the Plug-in Private Data field, which should be the OVM target group that was configured on the array as part of the preparation work. The second is the Admin Host field, which should be the admin IP for the array being used.

Next, you need to add the access information, which is identical to what you did when using the Storage Connect plug-in for the generic array, but instead you use the ZFS user for authentication (see Figure 13-21).

The remaining steps are the same: you add the admin servers, finish with the validation, and refresh the jobs. Once this discovery is complete, you can add LUNs directly from the OVMM, without the need to create them first on the storage array. Other features, such as replication, snaps, and clones, may be supported, depending on how the vendor wrote the plug-in.

Summary

This chapter covered storage management in an Oracle VM environment. Storage configuration is a very straightforward process without much complexity. The real complexity comes with configuring the hardware. Some storage vendors require additional device drivers and multipathing software. These should be configured according to the storage vendor's instructions.

Once you have configured the storage at the Oracle VM Server level, you can further modify and assign storage to virtual machines. This part of the process is done when the virtual machines are created or modified, and will be covered in later chapters in this book.

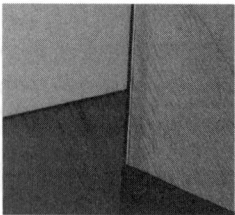

PART

III

Managing Oracle VM

CHAPTER
14

Swimming in Server Pools

The Oracle server pool is truly the first bridge between real-world hardware and the ethereal world of virtualization. The hardware of each Oracle VM server (OVS) is positioned and combined with other Oracle VM servers to form server pools where guest VMs are created and interoperate with each other, oblivious to the dom0 features and functions of the virtual machine server. Within the Oracle VM server pool, an Oracle VM server can operate independently or share the responsibility of providing availability to the guest VMs by participating in a cluster. This cluster management is afforded through the use of the Oracle Cluster File System (OCFS2).

In this chapter, we cover the concept of the server pool as well its capacity considerations and performance requirements. Oracle VM servers are organized into pools in order to provide the processor, memory, and storage needed by the guest VMs while maintaining live migration capability. Although there are some limits to live migration, beginning with version 3.4, some of those limits (such as use of VM server local storage) have been overcome.

Getting Wet: Introducing the Server Pool

Think about what it is like to jump into a body of water for the first time. A number of questions run through the mind: How deep is the water? Is it cold? Are there any hidden dangers? Similarly, questions arise when creating a server pool for the first time: Jump right in and just create the server pool? Or begin by defining all the various configurable items, features, and components of the server pool? This chapter will discuss a simple pool and its basic features and then gradually dive into a complex scenario ripe with functionality.

The most basic consideration when creating a server pool is whether or not to make it a clustered server pool. This decision cannot be changed after the pool is created. In other words, once the server pool is created as a non-clustered pool, it cannot be made into a clustered pool. Instead, the pool must be created as a clustered pool. The converse is also true. Once a pool is created as a clustered pool, it cannot be changed to a non-clustered pool. The difference between clustered and non-clustered pools is the underlying constructs put in place to maintain the cluster. The Oracle Cluster File System (OCFS2) is the key component that maintains the server participation in a cluster, and it's the heartbeat used to indicate the overall availability of the servers in a cluster. Figure 14-1 shows the Create a Server Pool Wizard, which contains the option used to designate whether to create a clustered server pool.

The Create a Server Pool Wizard provides the following key parameters:

- **Server Pool Name** This is the unique name used to identify the pool within the VM environment.

- **Virtual IP Address for the Pool** This parameter is for backward compatibility and is not required for Oracle VM 3.4; it is only required if all the servers in the server pool are Oracle VM 3.3.

- **VM Start Policy** This parameter establishes the default VM server qualifier that will be used to start the guest VMs, and it can be overwritten at the guest VM level. The following options are available:

  - **Best Server** The VM server used to start guest virtual machines will be determined based on resource policy metrics (distributed resource scheduling and power management). These metrics are set in the Edit Server Pool Wizard and can be seen in the "Policies" perspective. Note that this option may move the Oracle VM guest to a different server from where you attempted to start the virtual machine.

- ■ **Current Server**   Indicates that the VM server specified in the definition of the guest virtual machine will be used to start the guest VM. Unlike the Best Server option, this choice leaves the Oracle VM guest running on the server that started the virtual machine.

■ **Secure VM Migrate**   Indicates that during a migration, virtual machine configuration information will be encrypted. This choice significantly increases the time it takes for an Oracle VM agent to complete a live migration.

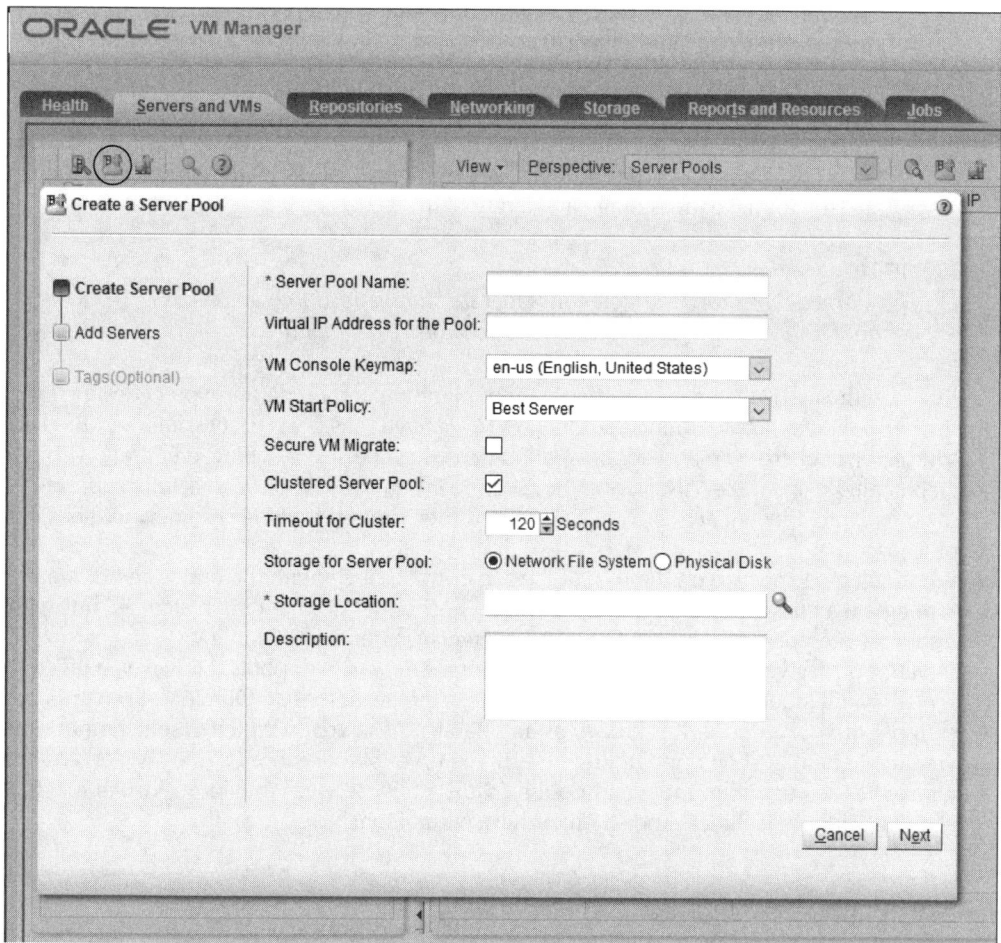

FIGURE 14-1.   *The Create a Server Pool Wizard*

- **Clustered Server Pool**   Required to support the live migration of guest virtual machines. If selected, this option will create and format the pool file system with OCFS2. This option cannot be changed except by re-creating the server pool.

- **Timeout for Cluster**   Indicates the amount of time (in seconds) that OCFS2 on each Oracle VM server will wait before fencing itself if it loses access to other Oracle VM servers in the pool over the cluster heartbeat network. An Oracle VM server will reboot itself if this timeout threshold is exceeded. The default is 120 seconds, and the maximum value is 300 seconds. Keep in mind that a two-node server pool will behave in a counterintuitive manner: a pool with an even number of servers will always favor the server with the lowest OCFS2 node number. This means the Oracle VM server with an OCFS2 node number of zero will always remain running even if it is the server that lost network connectivity. Therefore, always design server pools with odd numbers of servers to avoid this peculiar behavior.

- **Storage for Server Pool**   Indicates the type of storage used for the server pool filesystem. The server pool filesystem only needs to be 12GB in size, and it can be NFS, iSCSI, or Fibre Channel. The pool filesystem will never exceed 12GB, even with the maximum number of pools, servers, and virtual machines allowed by the product, so there is no reason to make this storage any larger than 12GB.

NOTE
The storage repository is a uniquely separate storage resource and cannot be shared with any other server pool or virtual machine.

As with any IT-related task, a modicum of planning and preparation precedes the task of server pool creation. Assuming the Oracle VM Manager has been successfully installed, Oracle VM server pool creation and administration can be successfully achieved entirely within the graphical web interface. Also, using the GUI means any required triage is fully supported—that is, of course, provided an active Oracle CSI (Customer Support Identifier) somewhere has been purchased.

To get a perspective on the role of the server pool, begin with the end in mind: the objective is to create a guest Oracle VM. The virtualized host under normal circumstances runs within the resources presented to it by the Oracle VM server. One or more Oracle VM servers run within a server pool. A given environment may have one or more server pools. However, a given VM server is a member of zero or one server pool. In the event that an Oracle VM server is not a member of a server pool, it is known as an unassigned server, in which case it cannot run a guest virtual machine. A server pool therefore is made up of one or more Oracle VM servers, and each Oracle VM server within the server pool provides utility services (migrating virtual machines, copying, virtual machines, and so on) or hosts virtual machines (or both).

Server Pool IP Address

The server pool IP address is deprecated in version 3.4 and does not provide any functionality because the agent communicates directly with other servers in the pool and with the Oracle VM Manager. However, the IP address is required if version 3.3 servers are in the pool. As a rule of thumb, if there is any chance a version 3.3 server will be placed into the pool, it is a good idea to assign an IP address to server pool.

After the initial installation and configuration of the Oracle VM server is completed (as covered in Chapter 9), the OVS might be discovered and participate in an Oracle server pool and ultimately be a host of guest Oracle VMs. It is automatically designated as a utility server within the server pool and acts as the administrative focal point of utilities (VM migration, VM deletion, and so on); the role as utility server or virtual machine server can be unassigned at any time. More information on VM server roles is provided later in this chapter.

The process of adding a candidate OVS to the Oracle VM infrastructure (and ultimately a server pool) is known as *discovery*. However, although many tasks can be performed using the command-line interface (CLI) in order to maintain a strict sense of support, it is highly recommended that many (if not all) tasks be performed via the Oracle VM Manager, GUI web interface. The discovery process begins by selecting the Servers and VMs tab and clicking the first icon, which will bring up the Discover Servers Wizard (see Figure 14-2).

Figure 14-2 shows a password and a list of hostnames or IP addresses. In Figure 14-2, the process looks for any server in the given subnet whose last octet is 55 through (and including) 60. It should also be noted that the use of a hostname implies resolution to the hostname will be available any time this OVS is to be used in a pool. In other words, when in doubt, use the IP address when adding an OVS to the Oracle VM infrastructure. The password is used to access the agent on each server in order to execute utilities and perform various operations. The password is also required for agent administration. It is a best practice to use the same password for all the agents; otherwise, tasks that are required across multiple servers must be executed separately because different passwords need to be submitted.

NOTE
The password is stored and associated with each of the servers that are discovered and ultimately added to the unassigned servers list. Although it can be changed later, the password is required when performing operations on a given VM server (for instance, via a Telnet session).

Once the OVS is discovered, it should appear in under Unassigned Servers, as shown in Figure 14-3. Servers that have not yet been assigned to a server pool can be added to a server pool either during the server pool creation process or sometime later.

Agent Passwords

The agent password can be changed at any time without removing the servers from the pool, like so:

```
/usr/sbin/ovs-agent-passwd oracle
```

The password can be verified for correctness at any time, as follows:

```
ovs-agent-rpc -s :<your password>@localhost:8899/ echo "'Password
works'"
```

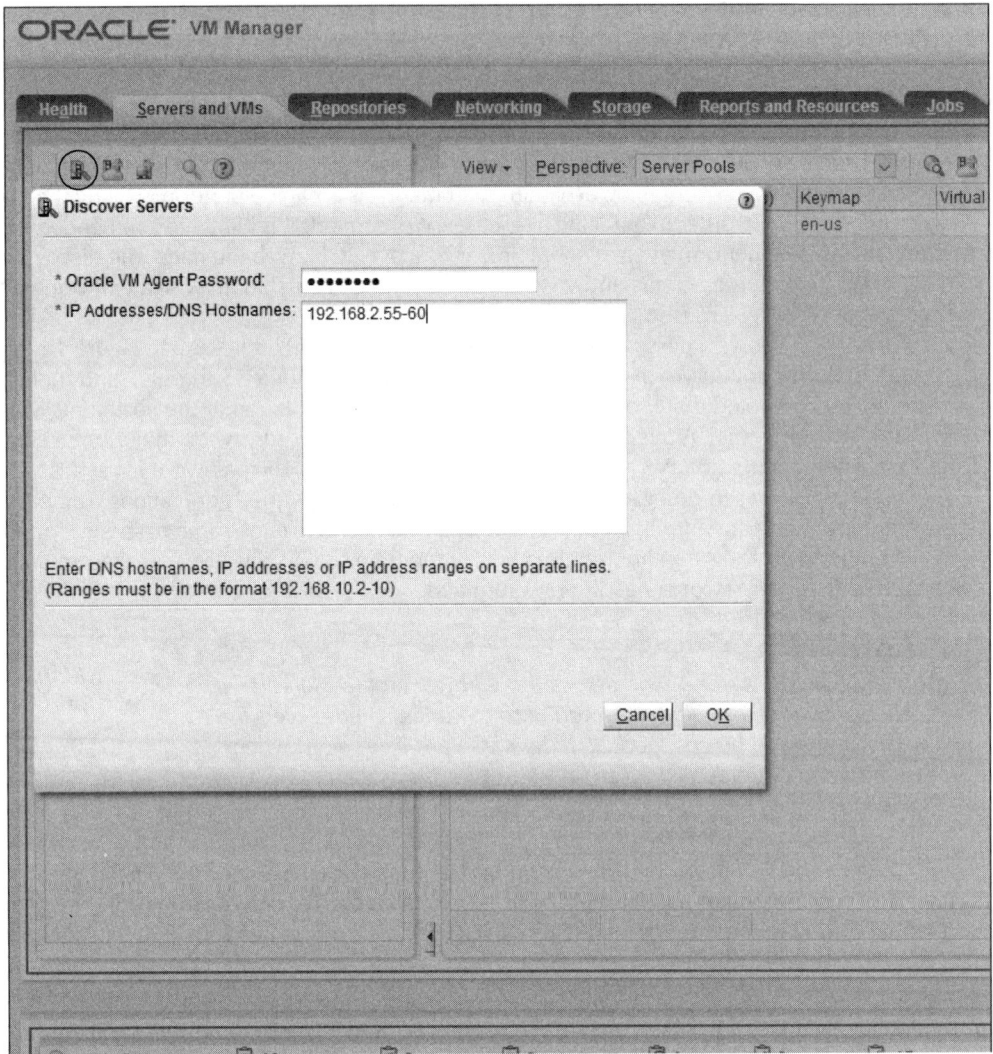

FIGURE 14-2. *Discover Servers Wizard*

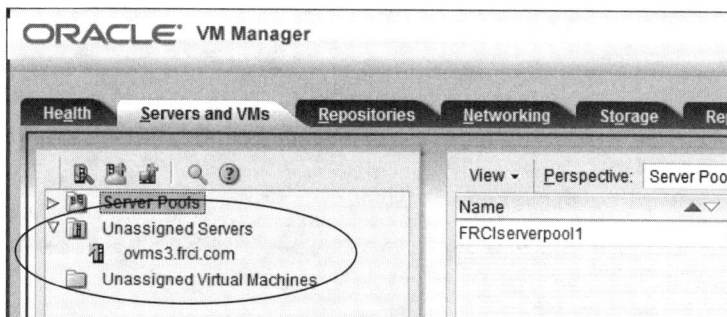

FIGURE 14-3. *Unassigned servers*

Skimming the Surface: A Simple, Shallow Pool

After the initial installation and configuration of the Oracle VM server have been completed (as covered in Chapter 9), the OVS may be added to the newly created server pool. In its most simple form, a clustered or non-clustered server pool may be created with just one VM server. As shown in Figure 14-3, a server pool has been created with a single VM server, and there is another server that has not yet been assigned to a server pool. Before a virtual machine can be added to an unassigned server, the unassigned server must be added to a server pool.

Urge to Show Off

Across the globe, administrators cringe at the idea of using a graphical user interface when a command-line interface exists. It is often believed that a task or group of tasks can be perform more easily and quickly at a command line rather than clicking options and entering details. However, this is not the case with the Oracle VM Manager graphical user interface. In fact, the command-line interface should only be used due to explicit instructions from Oracle Support and for processes such as CPU pinning that can only be accomplished with the CLI. As a general rule, do not use the CLI unless specifically directed to do so. The Oracle VM Manager GUI should be used if at all possible.

Resist the urge to show off CLI prowess and use the Oracle VM Manager graphical user interface instead.

As stated in the "Getting Started" section of the Oracle VM Manager documentation, prior to creating the server pool the OVS machines should have already been created and they should have been discovered. Also, the storage (for use by guest VMs and the storage pool repository) should also have been discovered. Finally, any virtual machine network should have been defined and configured in the Oracle VM Manager. These key components are required to have been installed, discovered, and configured prior to creating a server pool. Now, assuming the steps have been followed to discover servers and storage and to create the appropriate networks, the next logical step is to create the server pool.

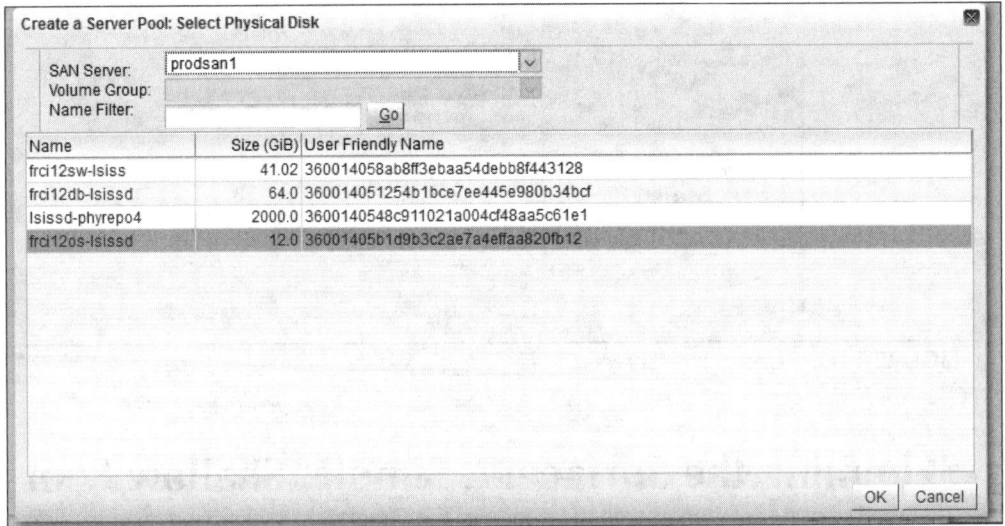

FIGURE 14-4. *Server pool physical disk assignment*

As stated earlier, a critical component for even the most simple server pool is the storage. This storage must be pre-allocated, and it is understood that this particular storage will be used in support of administration of a specific server pool as the server pool filesystem. In other words, the storage cannot be shared across server pools. Each server pool requires its own storage, and it can be storage from a NFS fileserver or a physical disk that is a logical unit number (LUN) carved out of SAN-based storage. This storage will never grow beyond the recommended 12GB of space. Figure 14-4 shows the physical disk assignment of the storage that will be used by the new server pool.

After specifying the server pool name and defining the storage (the other parameters will be explained in detail later), the next page in the wizard displays any servers that have been discovered but not yet assigned to a server pool.

Server Pool Management

Managing a server pool is not a full-time job—and it's barely a part-time job. Nearly all aspects of the server pool can be changed as requirements, performance, and capacity characteristics change over time. The most significant factor to consider is whether or not to enable cluster management at the time the server pool is created. This cannot be changed.

Realistically, the thing that will change the most is the VM server participation in the pool and the role a given VM server will be assigned. By default, all the VM servers added to a pool will be designated with both the utility server and VM server roles.

NOTE
*So little overhead is involved in being a utility server that it is not
worthwhile to even worry about assigning the utility server role to a
VM server. In other words, unless there is a particular alignment of the
planets requiring the separation of utility servers, it is okay to keep the
default settings of the server being assigned both the utility server and
VM server roles.*

Server Pool Anti-Affinity Groups

In some situations it may be desired (or even required) that certain virtual machines run separately
from other virtual machines, such as in the case of database Real Application Clusters (RAC)
configurations. Each node of the database cluster must specifically run on a separate machine
for obvious performance and systems-integration testing purposes. Naturally, in a production
environment, each node of the RAC database must be on a separate physical machine in support
of availability, in case one physical machine goes down. This requirement is afforded by the anti-
affinity group feature (see Figure 14-5), which identifies specific guest VMs that should never run

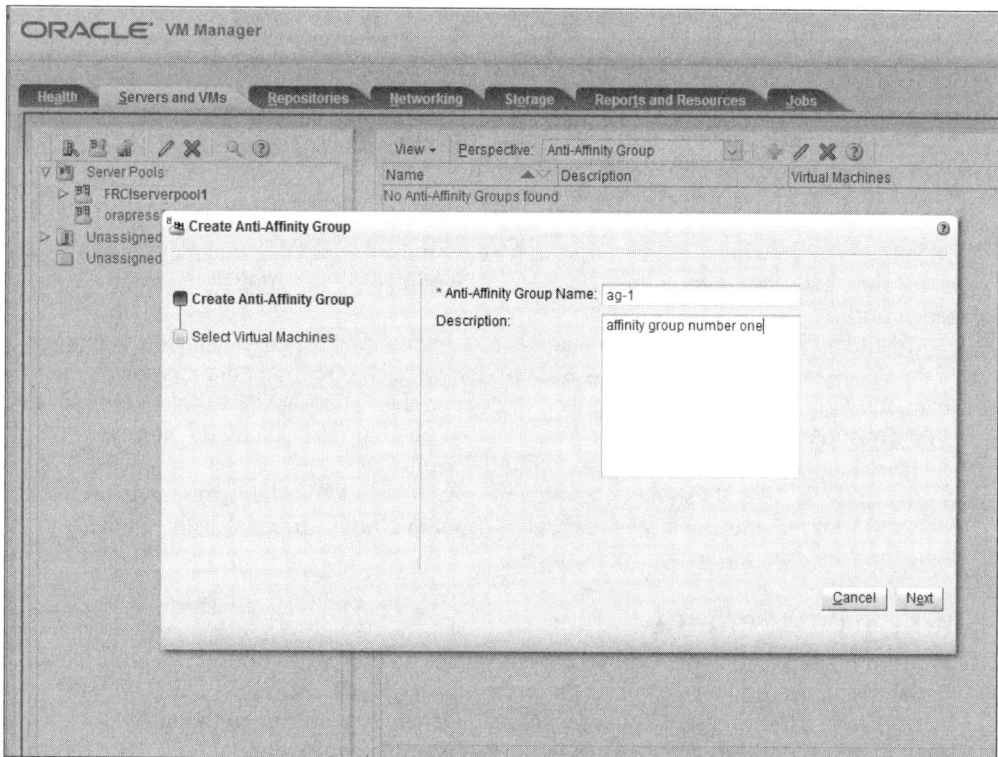

FIGURE 14-5. *Anti-affinity group creation*

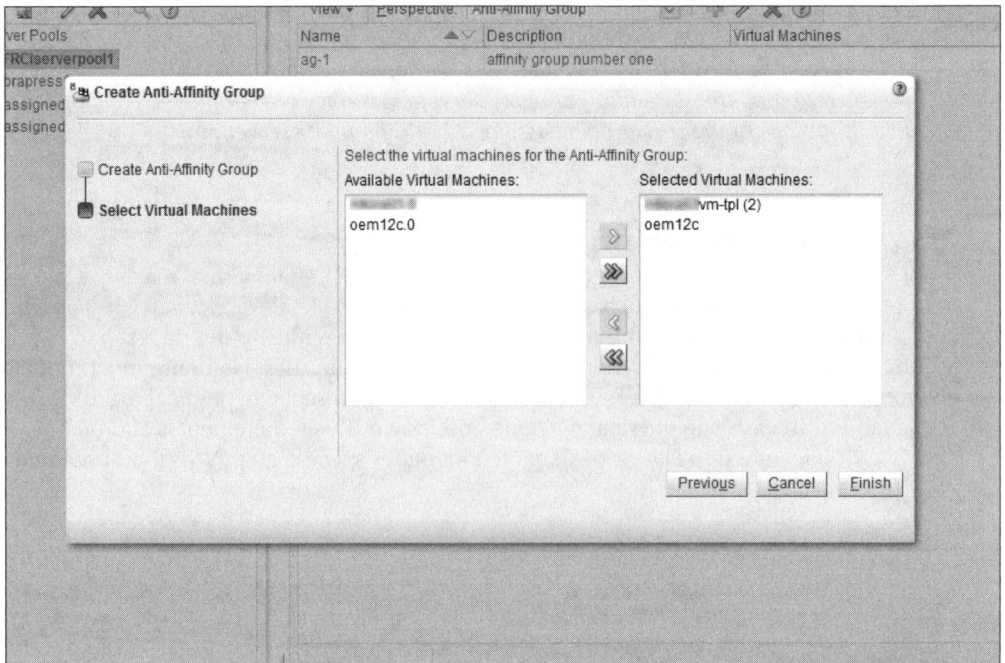

FIGURE 14-6. *Anti-affinity group guest VM membership*

on the same OVS within the server pool. An anti-affinity group can be created, edited, or deleted at any time after the server pool is created, but it can also be created at the same time as the server pool.

To add an anti-affinity group, navigate to the server pool in the navigation tree on the left side of the VM Manager pane. Figure 14-6 shows the wizard used to maintain guest VM membership in an anti-affinity group. Select the server pool and then choose Anti-Affinity Group from the drop-down perspectives and then click the green plus sign to add an anti-affinity group or click the pencil icon to edit an existing anti-affinity group.

The process of establishing an anti-affinity group begins by editing the server pool that contains the guest VMs that must operate separately. Each anti-affinity group is given a name, and then guest virtual machines in the server pool can be selected and added to the given anti-affinity group.

Role Management

As mentioned earlier, under normal circumstances, the OVS functions as the host to the guest virtual machines running on the server. In this scenario, the OVS is operating with the VM server role. However, in the case where specific management operations are required (such as during live migration of a running guest VM or during a template import operation), the tasks to support the operation are given to one of the OVS machines assigned with the utility server role. The OVS assigned with the utility server role may also be assigned the VM server role, but the OVS with the utility server role may not be the VM server where the guest VM (requiring migration) is running—which is a reason to have many (if not all) OVS machines assigned the utility server role. Figure 14-7 shows the wizard used for server role maintenance. The ability to perform utility services without the VM Manager is another example of Oracle's unique perspective on and achievement of abstraction; that is, a separate device outside the operation of the VM server and guest VMs is not required to perform utility services. In fact, the VM Manager, while serving as the user interface into the management of the Oracle VM infrastructure, is not even required to be up and running while these operations are taking place.

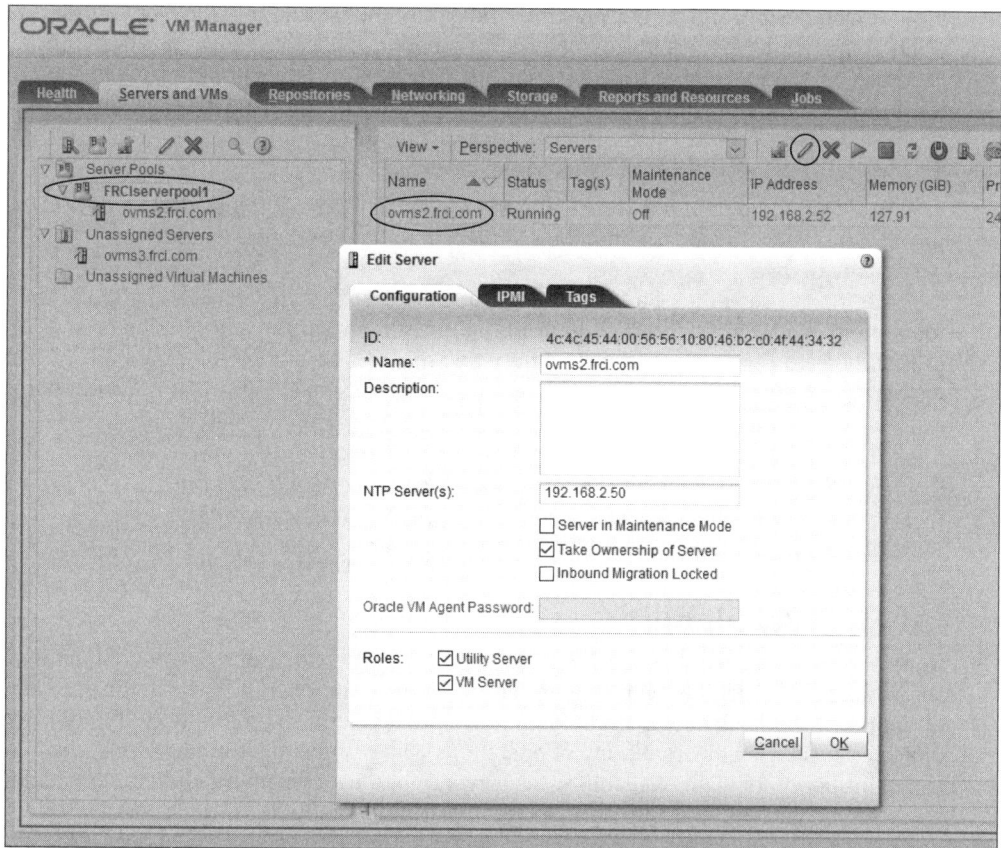

FIGURE 14-7. *Role assignment via the Edit Server Wizard*

VM server roles can be assigned during server pool creation when VM servers are being added to the pool. Alternatively, they can be assigned later after the server pool has been created and a VM server is being added and its role assigned, or when a VM server is currently assigned to a server pool and its role is to be changed. The guiding principles of role assignment are based on the VM server's capabilities and some estimation of the load during operations at different points of the VM server lifecycle. During times of heavy load, for example, it may not matter which VM server is assigned the additional role of utility server. However, at times when a given VM server does not have as high a load as the other VM servers in the server pool, it makes sense to assign that particular server (with the lower utilization requirement) the utility server role.

Server Pools and Availability

Several factors need to be considered relative to server pools. The server pool itself in support of virtual machine High Availability must be clustered and therefore is associated with an OCFS2-based storage device, and that storage must be part of the backup and recovery/disaster recovery (BR/DR) plan. However, this is only part of the equation. After the storage device is restored from backup, very little is required to recover the server pool. The server pool filesystem should just pick up where it left off with the execution of the following command on each server:

```
service restart ovs-agent
```

This will remount the pool filesystem, and the server pool is back in business. A new LUN/NFS share that has been created without the old filesystem on it will require additional steps, including the recovery of data.

In addition to server pool availability, the actual guest VMs may have a High Availability requirement (specified in the definition of the guest VM), but the actual failover and availability features are afforded by the clustering mechanism of the server pool (OCFS2) and the functionality of the OVS agent running on each of the OVS machines in the server pool cluster.

> **NOTE**
> *High Availability features are a function of the OVS agent and the pool filesystem, not the Oracle VM Manager. All High Availability features work regardless of whether the Oracle VM Manager is running.*

VM High Availability

A direct correlation exists between High Availability and server pool cluster configuration. There can be no High Availability with single-point-of-failure components. As such, the components that support virtual machine operations (storage, process, and so on) must also be replicated or duplicated to support the continuity of operations with respect to a running virtual machine. Hence, in support of High Availability, the server pool must contain multiple OVS machines and have been created with the Clustered Server Pool option enabled.

Ideally, server pools should always contain odd numbers of servers to allow OCFS2 fencing policies to behave in the most expected way. Having an even numbers of servers always forces the servers with node0 to win any battle around fencing/rebooting. In addition, as seen in Figure 14-8, the virtual machine must also be configured with the Enable High Availability option selected. This can be set either at creation or later by editing the guest VM configuration in the Oracle VM Manager.

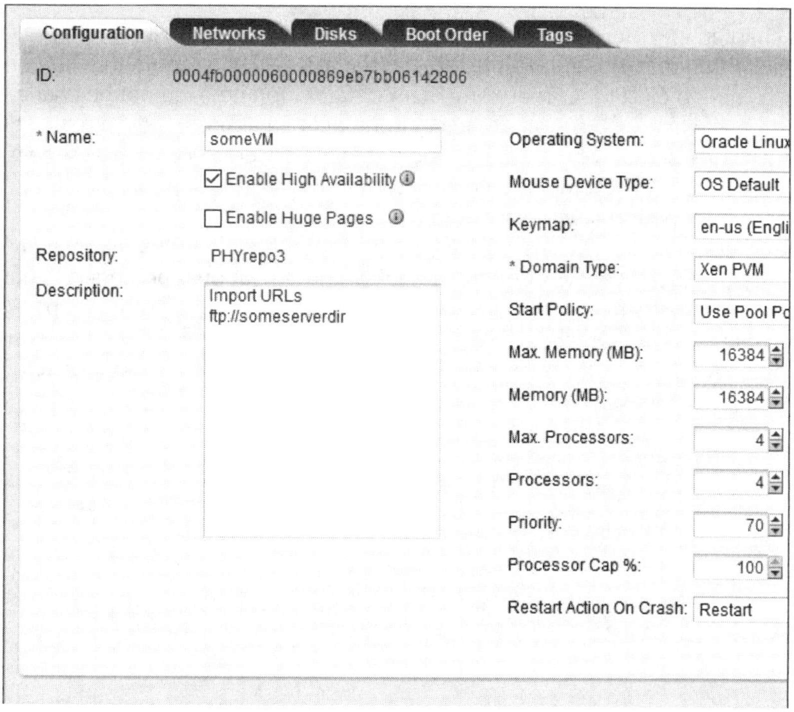

FIGURE 14-8. *Guest VM High Availability*

Also, storage High Availability considerations are usually maintained at the storage management layer of the storage provider (that is, RAID configurations and/or data duplication and replication methodologies). With that said, one of the new features as of version 3.4 is the ability to migrate guest machines that are using storage that's locally attached to the VM server. This was not supported (or even available) in previous versions.

In OVM 3.4, the "storage live migration" feature allows for the migration of local-to-local storage between servers in the same pool without needing to stop the VM. This feature is really ideal for non-clustered server pools that have no shared storage!

CAUTION
Do not be creative when using NFS storage repositories with non-clustered server pools. The lack of dynamic lock management allows the same VM to be started on multiple servers, which means bad things will happen, *including duplicate MACs, duplicate IPs, and corrupted virtual systems and boot disks!*

Summary

In this chapter, we discussed creating and managing an Oracle VM server pool. As stated earlier, this is not a full-time job. In fact, the most important decision required before creating a server pool is related to clustering. That particular configuration item cannot be changed and is only specified at the time of creation. If the environment can afford it, best practice dictates that two (or more) server pools—one clustered and one not—are created. The VM servers in the non-clustered pool can be equipped with enough local storage to support the virtual machines using local storage for performance reasons (or for RAC nodes).

In addition, Oracle VM server pools provide guest Oracle virtual machine High Availability capabilities through live migration functionality and operational processes to ensure virtual machines are physically separate from each other through anti-affinity groups. Also, through the use of server roles, an Oracle VM server can be assigned the role of utility server through which the Oracle VM agent performs required tasks in the background without Oracle VM guest configuration changes.

CHAPTER
15

Configuring Guest Resources

One of the major features of Oracle VM that distinguishes it from other virtualization products is the use of templates. Templates are used for creating "golden images" of a complete software stack. The Oracle VM templates are considered part of the guest resources. Oracle VM guest resources include the virtual appliances (formerly assemblies), ISOs, templates, virtual disks, and configuration files (vm.cfg files). Server resources include the use of the Oracle VM utilities to manage CPU partitioning, report on VM storage details, and gather Oracle VM Server (OVS) performance data for reporting to a VM.

This chapter covers managing Oracle VM Server resources. As you learned in the previous chapter, there are three different ways to configure guest resources: via the Oracle VM Manager, the OEM Grid Control, and the Oracle VM CLI. This chapter focuses on using Oracle VM Manager, with subsequent chapters covering Oracle Enterprise Manager 13c and the Oracle VM CLI.

Guest Resources

The guest resources are key features that give Oracle VM its functionality and ease of use. The guest resources consist of virtual machine templates, virtual appliances, and shared virtual disks. Virtual machine templates are used to install virtual machines. Shared virtual disks are used in clusters, such as Oracle Real Application Clusters, for shared disk usage. Configuring and administering these guest resources using the Oracle VM Manager are covered in this chapter.

Templates

Virtual machine templates are a core feature of Oracle VM. Virtual machine templates allow you to create virtual machines quickly and efficiently with less chance of making mistakes than if you had to build them from scratch. Here are some of the advantages of using VM templates:

- **Ease of use**   By using a template, you can quickly and easily deploy virtual machines. Because templates are preconfigured, you can use them to deploy many consistent copies of the same virtual machine, with each one customized for your environment.

- **Consistency**   Because creating a virtual machine from a template does not require extensive configuration changes, the virtual machines are very consistent. If the VM template is configured ready to install the Oracle Database, then all virtual machines created from this template will be able to install the Oracle Database consistently. If the VM template is configured with the Oracle Database preconfigured, then all virtual machines created from this template will include a consistently installed Oracle Database ready to go.

- **Provisioning efficiency**   Because templates are preconfigured and can be created or obtained with applications preinstalled, the time it takes to deploy these applications can be greatly reduced.

Using templates is the preferred method of configuring virtual machines. By using templates, you are guaranteed consistently configured virtual machines. In addition, Oracle offers a wide number of templates, not only for the basic operating systems, but also for applications such as E-Business Suite, Enterprise Manager 13c, JD Edwards, and more. These can be downloaded from the Oracle Technology Network.

In addition, you can create your own custom templates, preconfigured to fit the specific requirements in your data center. You can create a template from scratch, or you can create a template using any Oracle VM guest in your environment. This means you don't have to depend on just templates offered for download by Oracle; you can build your own custom templates that

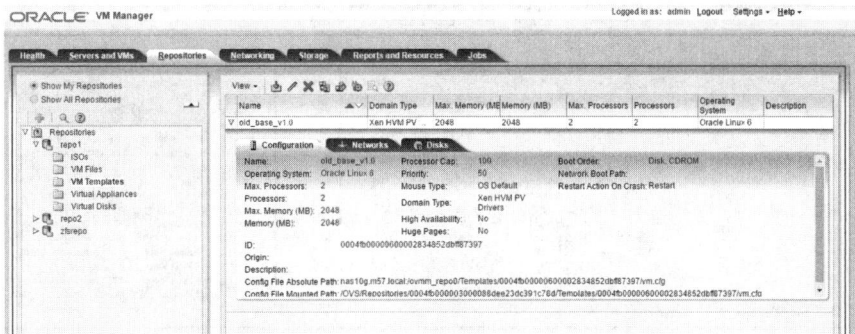

FIGURE 15-1. *Template details*

can include applications, databases, and other tools unique to your environment. This topic is covered in more detail in Chapter 18.

VM templates are stored in the repositories, under the VM Templates folder (see Figure 15-1 for an example). You can click a template to expand the selection to see the details, including the operating system, processors, memory, and more.

Virtual Appliances

Imagine the power of templates expanded to the entire application. Virtual appliances provide this by enabling entire application stacks to be consolidated into a single object. This enables the administrator to deploy complex systems, including multiple virtual machines to support each tier of the application, from the RAC cluster supporting the database to tomcat clusters supporting the middle tier. This technology is very helpful when deploying complex applications like Oracle E-Business Suite and SAP. Virtual appliances can also include virtual machines using third-party formats such as Open Virtualization Format (OVF) from VMware. This makes migration from VMware to OVM as simple as exporting the virtual machine from VMware to an OVF file and then importing it into Oracle VM. As with templates, Oracle VM stores the virtual appliances in the repositories, in a folder named "Virtual Appliances." Just click a virtual appliance to view what virtual machines are contained within it (see Figure 15-2).

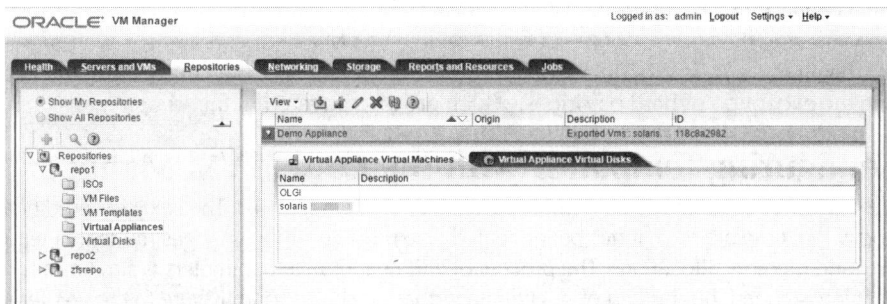

FIGURE 15-2. *Virtual Appliances*

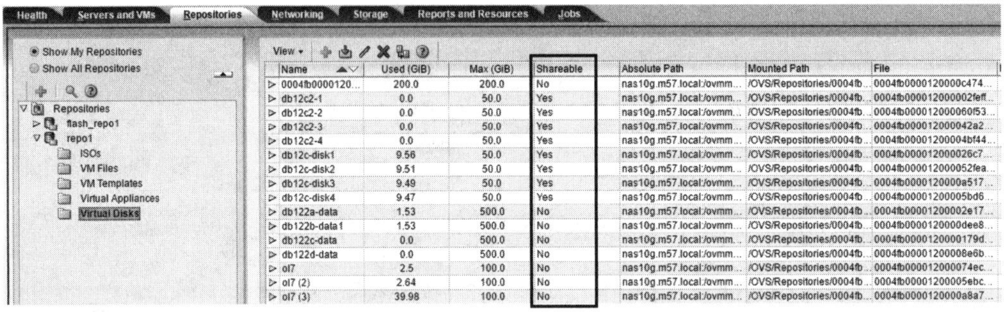

FIGURE 15-3. *Shareable virtual disks*

Shared Virtual Disks

Shared virtual disks are disks that are available to one or more virtual machines. These virtual disks are managed outside of the virtual machine because they are not tied to any specific virtual machine. The shared virtual disks are stored in the repositories, in the "Virtual Disks" folder, and if a disk is shareable, it is identified as such in the Shareable column (see Figure 15-3). Any disk can be flagged as shareable, which becomes a useful feature when you're migrating a local ASM group into a RAC cluster.

The next sections cover configuring and managing guest resources using the Oracle VM Manager. You can also use the Oracle VM CLI or Oracle Enterprise Manager 13c. Which method you use depends on your individual configuration and needs.

Configuring Guest Resources Using the Oracle VM Manager

The Oracle VM Manager is the most common tool for managing small to medium Oracle VM Server farms. It is easy to install and use. Larger installations that already have Oracle Enterprise Manager (OEM) Cloud Control often use this tool to manage the VM Server farm because it enables features such as user self-provisioning and chargeback of resources. Included with the installation of Oracle VM Manager is the Oracle VM CLI. This chapter covers the use of Oracle VM Manager, with EM13c usages being covered in Chapter 23 through Chapter 25 and the CLI being covered in Chapter 11.

Managing the guest resources via the Oracle VM Manager is done in a web browser, with the URL being https://$HOST:7002/ovm/console. From here, you can manage all of the guest resources, with the exception of hard partitions, which are also covered in this chapter.

Configuring Templates with the Oracle VM Manager

The process of creating custom templates is covered in Chapter 18. The steps covered here are used to modify the template once it has been created. The most common changes made to a template are the CPU and memory allocations. The process of editing template parameters is similar to how a virtual machine is edited, but instead of selecting a virtual machine, you navigate to the VM Templates folder in the repository and click the Edit button (highlighted in Figure 15-4) while the template is selected.

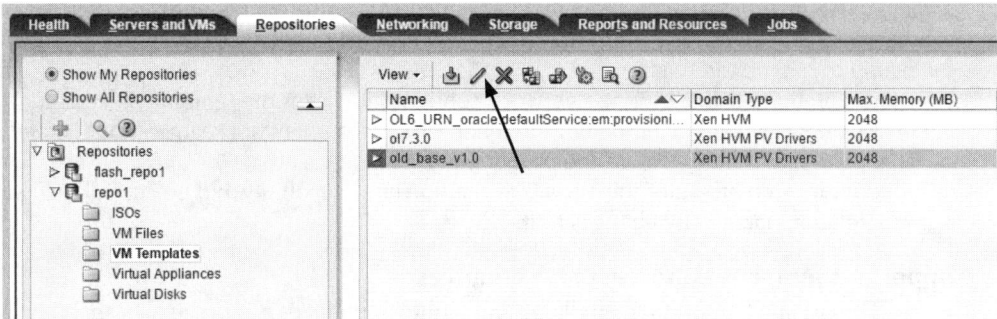

FIGURE 15-4. *Editing the template*

The two most common areas to be edited are the network configuration and the core configuration of the template. The core configuration, shown in Figure 15-5, is where the amount of CPU, RAM, and other parameters related to the system performance are set.

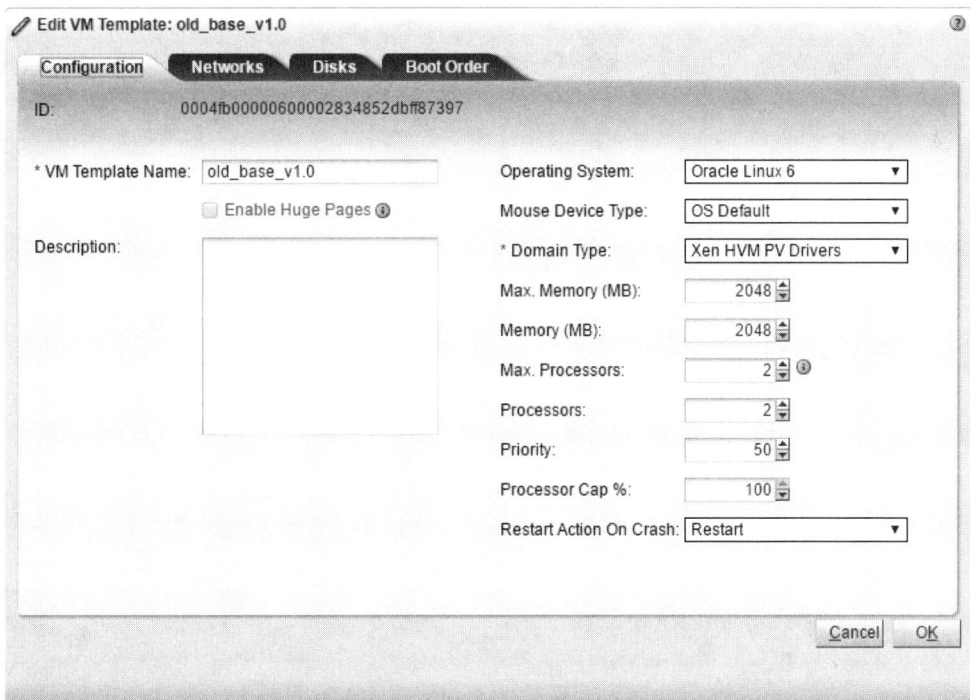

FIGURE 15-5. *Configuring the template*

These are the exact same parameters used when creating a virtual machine. An example of a change you might make after the template is created is adjusting the behavior of future virtual machines when they crash. Administration might not want to have them restart automatically, for example, but instead to stop.

More common is changing the network configuration after the template is created (see Figure 15-6). A template could be built in a non-production network segment, but copied to a new template and updated to use the production network.

Modifying templates after their creation is a powerful capability, but be careful to always test a template after making any changes to it.

Importing Templates and Virtual Appliances

As previously stated, importing templates and virtual appliances is a powerful capability. The importing process is easy but requires that the source file be copied to either a web server or an anonymous FTP site that can be accessed by the Oracle VM Manager. It is common for the yum path repository server to also serve as an HTTP server for importing templates and virtual appliances. When you're collocating other functions on the Oracle VM Manager, be careful not to place too much load on the server. Having the Oracle VM Manager also act as the HTTP server for importing templates is fine, but in larger environments, having the Oracle VM Manager server also act as a yum repository for hundreds of Linux servers will likely cause performance issues when you're managing the Oracle VM environment.

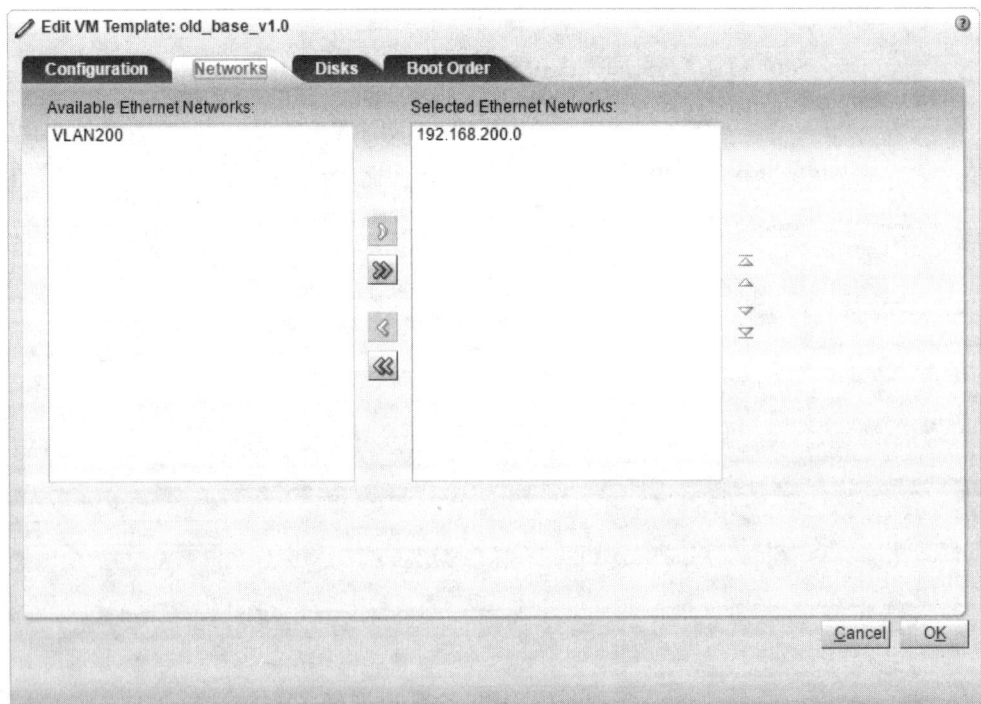

FIGURE 15-6. *Changing the network configuration*

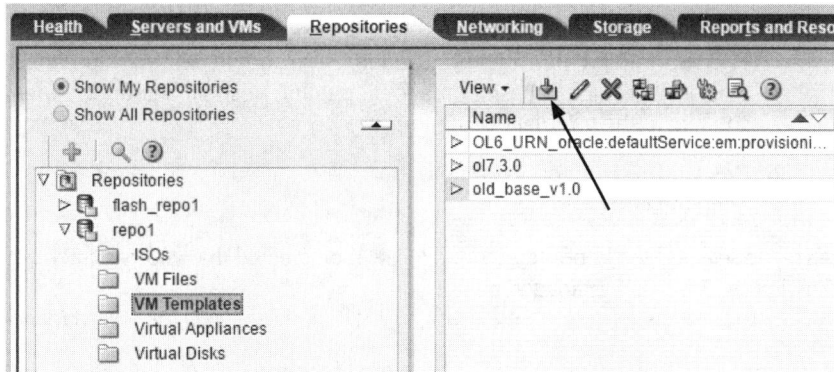

FIGURE 15-7.   *Importing a template*

NOTE
If you find yourself confusing templates and virtual appliances, keep in mind that a virtual appliance should have the extension .ova, whereas a template will often use .tgz or .ovf as its extension. If a template fails with the error "No VM configure file found," try importing it as a virtual appliance.

Follow these steps to import an existing template into the VM Manager:

1.   Templates are managed from the repository in which they reside. Navigate to the repository and select the VM Templates folder. From there, you'll see a list of all templates currently imported. From the VM Templates screen, click the Import button, highlighted in Figure 15-7.

2.   Clicking the Import button begins the template import process. On the first screen that appears, you define the source for the template import, as shown in Figure 15-8.

FIGURE 15-8.   *Template import parameters*

3. Select a method from the following two options:

- **VM Template URLs** This is the URL that points to the template. It can be an HTTP, HTTPS, or FTP URL. The URL used in this example is http://repo.m57.local/ol7_master.tgz, which is based on a local patch repository server. The filename will be specific to the template being imported.

- **Proxy** This is an optional field, but it is required if a proxy needs to access the VM template URL.

Once you've selected the import method, a job will be created that you can track in the Job Summary window in the Oracle VM Manager.

Follow these steps to import an existing virtual appliance into the VM Manager:

1. Virtual appliances are managed from the repository in which they reside. Navigate to the repository and select the Virtual Appliances folder. From there, you can see a list of all virtual appliances currently imported. From the Virtual Appliances screen, click the Import button, highlighted in Figure 15-9.

2. Clicking the Import button begins the virtual appliance import process. On the first screen that appears, you define the source for the virtual appliance import, as shown in Figure 15-10.

3. Select a method from the following four options:

- **Virtual appliance download location** This is the URL that points to the virtual appliance. It can be an HTTP, HTTPS, or FTP URL. Our example uses http://repo.m57.local/sol-11_3-ovm-x86.ova, which is the local patch repo. The filename will be specific to the virtual appliance being imported.

- **Proxy** This is an optional field, but it's required if a proxy needs to access the virtual appliance URL.

- **Create VM** This option creates a virtual appliance once the file is successfully imported.

- **Server Pool** If the Create VM box is checked, this drop-down is used to select the server pool where the VM(s) will be created. If multiple VMs are in the imported appliance, all of them will be created if this is checked.

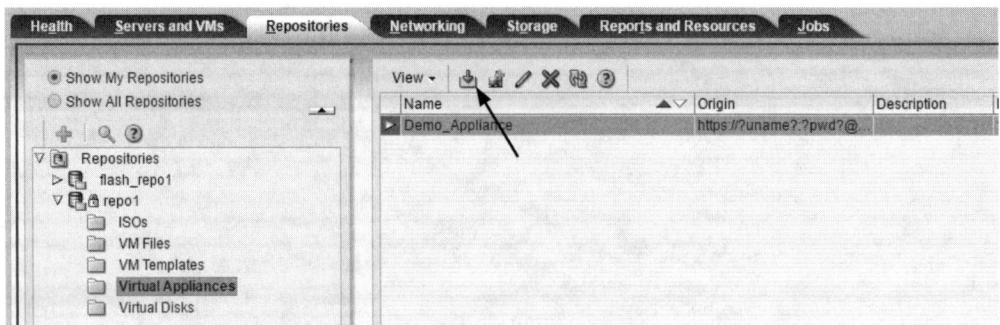

FIGURE 15-9. *Importing a virtual appliance*

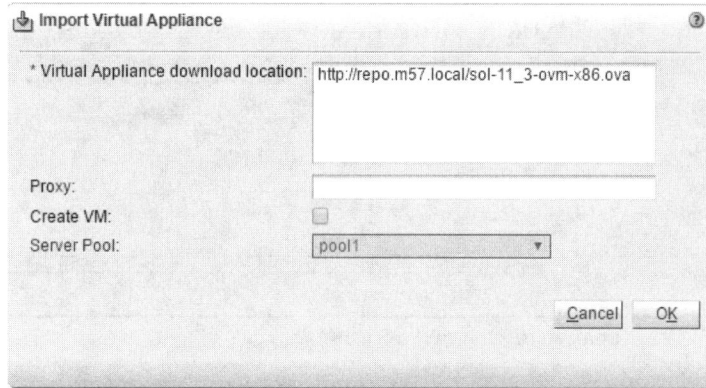

FIGURE 15-10. *Virtual appliance import parameters*

Once you've selected the import method, a job will be created that you can track in the Job Summary window in the Oracle VM Manager, as shown in Figure 15-11.

Manually Exporting a Template or Virtual Appliance

It is not uncommon for Oracle VM administrations to need to export a VM template to another system. Follow these steps to export an existing template into the VM Manager:

1. Templates consist of at least two files—one being vm.cfg, which contains all the configuration data for the VM, and the second being at least one disk .img file. In order to export the template, you will need to locate these two files and then combine them into a compressed .tar file. From the initial Oracle VM Manager screen, click the Resources tab. From the Resources tab, you can import a template by clicking the Import button.

2. To locate the vm.cfg file for the template, navigate to the VM Templates folder in the repository where the template is stored. As shown in Figure 15-12, the location of the vm.cfg file will be shown when the selection is expanded.

3. To identify the location of the disk file for the template, select the Disks tab in the details area for the VM template. This shows each of the disks used by the template (see Figure 15-13).

   Several columns are visible, but what is needed is the "mounted path" for the disk image, which, for our example, is

   ```
   /OVS/Repositories/0004fb000003000088dee23dc391c78d/VirtualDisks/0004fb0
   000120000f407a2456b889e50.img
   ```

FIGURE 15-11. *Completed import job*

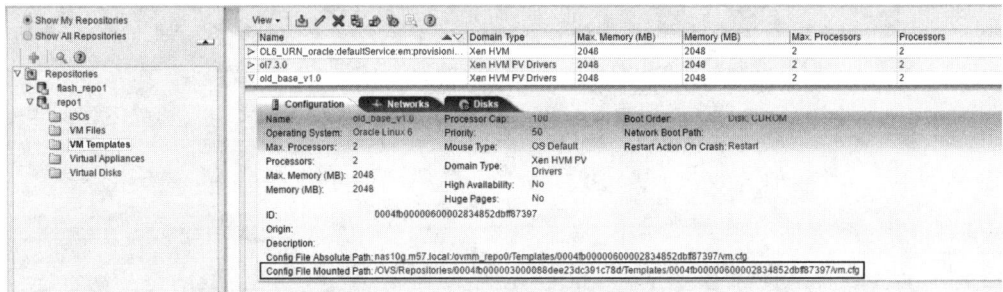

FIGURE 15-12. *Location of vm.cfg file*

4. The last step is actually fairly simple—if there is enough scratch space on one of the OVS systems. A single compressed .tar file will be created that contains both files. Use SSH to access the OVS, and then use tar to create the file. The format is **tar -cvfz $TEMPLATE_NAME.tgz $CFG_PATH $DISK_PATH**, as seen in the example:

```
[root@ovs3 ~]# tar cvfz /var/template.tgz /OVS/Repositories/0004fb00000
3000088dee23dc391c7
8d/Templates/0004fb00000600002834852dbff87397/vm.cfg
/OVS/Repositories/0004fb000003000088d
ee23dc391c78d/VirtualDisks/0004fb0000120000f407a2456b889e50.img
tar: Removing leading `/' from member names
/OVS/Repositories/0004fb000003000088dee23dc391c78d/Templates/
0004fb00000600002834852dbff87397/vm.cfg
/OVS/Repositories/0004fb000003000088dee23dc391c78d/VirtualDisks/
0004fb0000120000f407a2456b889e50.img
```

The file /var/template.tgz can now be copied to an HTTP server and then Imported Into a repository.

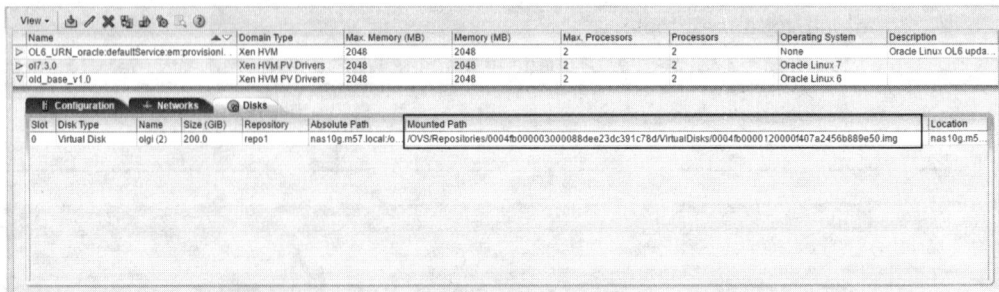

FIGURE 15-13. *Disk location*

CPU Pinning and the Oracle VM Utilities

Although the resource scheduler often works well in keeping one VM from impacting the performance of another VM, a problem often arises called *noisy neighbor*. A noisy neighbor is a common problem in virtualized environments and is caused when one VM monopolizes resources like CPU, network, and I/O bandwidth. This can cause performance issues for systems that use the same shared infrastructure. At times, more direct control is required, and Oracle VM has the ability to isolate a VM to a single group of cores on the physical OVS, essentially dedicating a physical CPU resource to a particular virtual CPU or a set of virtual CPUs. *CPU pinning* is also used to restrict a VM to a subset of physical cores for licensing needs. The optional Oracle VM Utilities package includes a program called **ovm_vmcontrol** that makes pinning a simple task. The Oracle VM Utilities package also includes several other advanced commands:

- **ovm_vmcontrol**   This command lets the administrator configure CPU pinning, also known as *hard partitioning,* on virtual machines.

- **ovm_vmdisks**   This script retrieves details about virtual disks. It includes the device path for physical disks as well as the NFS server name, mount point, and the filename and location for NFS-based disks.

- **ovm_vmhostd**   This command collects metrics about the Oracle VM Server host on which a virtual machine is running.

- **vm-dump-metrics**   This SAP-specific script gathers metrics about the Oracle VM Server host in XML format, which can be imported into an SAP application.

Installing the scripts is simple: after downloading the file from Oracle's Support site, you need to identify the version required, which is based on the version of Oracle VM Manager running in your environment, and then extract the scripts into a folder. The scripts do not need to be extracted or run from the Oracle VM management server. Oracle Support currently provides three ZIP files:

- **ovm_utils_1.0.2.zip**   For Oracle VM versions 3.0, 3.1, and 3.2
- **ovm_utils_2.0.1.zip**   For Oracle VM version 3.3
- **ovm_utils_2.1.0.zip**   For Oracle VM version 3.4

To pin cores on a VM, first check the current configuration. In this example, the OVMM server is ovmm.m57.local and the VM being managed is repo. The **-c** options are **setvcpu**, **getvcpu**, and **rmvcpu**.

```
[root@ovmm ovm-utils_2.1]# ./ovm_vmcontrol -u admin -h ovmm.m57.local \
 -v repo -c getvcpu
Setup OVM SDK libs for utilities ...
Setup OVM SDK libs for utilities completed.
Oracle VM VM Control utility 2.1.
Enter your OVM Manager password:
Connecting to OVM Manager using Web Service.
Connected.
OVM Manager version: 3.4.2.1384
Command : getvcpu
Getting pinned CPU list...
No CPU pinned for VM 'repo'
```

Next, lets pin CPU 6 and 7 to the VM.

```
[root@ovmm ovm-utils_2.1]# ./ovm_vmcontrol -u admin -h ovmm.m57.local -v repo -c
etvcpu -s 6,7
Oracle VM VM Control utility 2.1.
Enter your OVM Manager password:
Connecting to OVM Manager using Web Service.
Connected.
OVM Manager version: 3.4.2.1384
Command : setvcpu
Pinning vCPU '6,7' to VM 'repo'
Pin vCPU succeed.
[root@ovmm ovm-utils_2.1]#
```

Once configured, **getvcpu** will now show the cores that are pinned:

```
[root@ovmm ovm-utils_2.1]# ./ovm_vmcontrol -u admin -h ovmm.m57.local \
 -v repo -c getvcpu
Oracle VM VM Control utility 2.1.
Enter your OVM Manager password:
Connecting to OVM Manager using Web Service.
Connected.
OVM Manager version: 3.4.2.1384
Command : getvcpu
Getting pinned CPU list...
Current pinned CPU:6,7
[root@ovmm ovm-utils_2.1]#
```

The password is required each time the command is run. It can be set as an environmental variable, which enables scripting and simplifies access to the scripts when they are being used heavily. To set the password, run the command **export OVMUTIL_PASS=$PASSWORD**, where **PASSWORD** is the password being used. When the **OVMUTIL_PASS** environmental variable is set, add the option **-E** to the scripts, as shown in the following example:

```
[root@ovmm ovm-utils_2.1]# ./ovm_vmcontrol -u admin -E \
 -h ovmm.m57.local -v repo -c getvcpu
Oracle VM VM Control utility 2.1.
Connecting to OVM Manager using Web Service.
Connected.
OVM Manager version: 3.4.2.1384
Command : getvcpu
Getting pinned CPU list...
Current pinned CPU:6,7
[root@ovmm ovm-utils_2.1]#
```

The pinned CPUs can be removed using the **rmvcpu** option, but the VM will need to be shut down before this option can be run against the VM. Once the VM is offline, run the command, as shown here:

```
[root@ovmm ovm-utils_2.1]# ./ovm_vmcontrol -u admin\
 -h ovmm.m57.local -v repo -c rmvcpu -s 6,7
Oracle VM VM Control utility 2.1.
```

```
Enter your OVM Manager password:
Connecting to OVM Manager using Web Service.
Connected.
OVM Manager version: 3.4.2.1384
Command : rmvcpu
Removing vCPU setting...
Remove vCPU succeed.
```

The **ovm_vmdisks** script allows you to retrieve information about disks assigned to virtual machines. The script also identifies the name and location of the vm.cfg file. This is the same information required to manually export a template of a VM from one Oracle VM system.

```
[root@ovmm ovm-utils_2.1]# ./ovm_vmdisks -u admin  -E -h ovmm -v solaris11.3
Oracle VM Retrieve Disk utility 2.1.
Connecting to OVM Manager using Web Service.
Connected.
Virtual Machine : 'solaris11.3'
Assigned Server : ovs3.m57.local
Virtual Disk : 'sol11' size : 100GB
    repository='repo1'
    Mounted Path=/OVS/Repositories/0004fb000003000088dee23dc391c78d/
VirtualDisks/0004fb00001200008f97655c68e1afaf.img
    Absolute Path=nas10g.m57.local:/ovmm_repo0/VirtualDisks/


0004fb00001200008f97655c68e1afaf.img
Virtual Disk : 'Empty CDROM' size : 0GB
    Mounted path=N/A
    Absolute Path=N/A
    shareddisk=true
Physical Disk : 'QNAP3'
    device=/dev/mapper/36e843b69a5bda19d2d5bd43f3dbf01dd
Config File :
    Mounted Path=/OVS/Repositories/0004fb000003000088dee23dc391c78d/
VirtualMachines/0004fb0000060000e27d76cb83cb44bf/vm.cfg
    Absolute Path=nas10g.m57.local:/ovmm_repo0/VirtualMachines/
0004fb0000060000e27d76cb83cb44bf/vm.cfg
```

In this example, not only is a disk served from NFS (**Virtual Disk : 'sol11'**), but also a physical LUN is assigned to the VM:

```
Physical Disk : 'QNAP3'
    device=/dev/mapper/36e843b69a5bda19d2d5bd43f3dbf01dd
```

The command **ovm_vmhostd** collects metrics from the OVS and sends them to the VM specified in the options. The OVS will then send metrics about itself to the VM. These metrics can be recovered using the **vm-dump-metrics** script from the guest VM. The utility will run every 60 seconds until stopped with CTRL-C.

```
[root@ovmm ovm-utils_2.1]# ./ovm_vmhostd -u admin -E  -h ovmm.m57.local -v repo
Oracle VM Hostd 2.1.
Connecting to OVM Manager using Web Service.
```

```
Connected.
Processing VM : 'repo'

VM : 'repo' has status :   Running.
Message sent.
Sleeping 60 seconds.
Processing VM : 'repo'

VM : 'repo' has status :   Running.
Message sent.
Sleeping 60 seconds.
^C
[root@ovmm ovm-utils_2.1]#
```

While the **ovm_vmhostd** script is running, on the VM named in the script, run the **vm-dump_ metrics** command to collect the data. The output can be redirected to a text file for use by SAP or to custom-written processing scripts.

```
root@repo ovm-utils_2.1]# ./vm-dump-metrics > /tmp/data2.xml
[root@repo ovm-utils_2.1]#
```

An example of this file is as follows:

```
<metrics>
  <metric type='real64' context='host'>
    <name>TotalCPUTime</name>
    <value>426641.5</value>
  </metric>
  <metric type='uint64' context='host'>
    <name>PagedOutMemory</name>
    <value>0</value>
  </metric>
  <metric type='uint64' context='host'>
    <name>PagedInMemory</name>
    <value>0</value>
  </metric>
  <metric type='uint64' context='host'>
    <name>UsedVirtualMemory</name>
    <value>7690</value>
  </metric>
  <metric type='uint64' context='host'>
    <name>FreeVirtualMemory</name>
    <value>123324</value>
  </metric>
  <metric type='uint64' context='host'>
    <name>FreePhysicalMemory</name>
    <value>123324</value>
  </metric>
```

```
  <metric type='uint64' context='host'>
    <name>MemoryAllocatedToVirtualServers</name>
    <value>7690</value>
  </metric>
  <metric type='uint32' context='host'>
    <name>NumberOfPhysicalCPUs</name>
    <value>8</value>
  </metric>
  <metric type='string' context='host'>
    <name>HostSystemInfo</name>
    <value>ovs3.m57.local</value>
  </metric>
  <metric type='string' context='host'>
    <name>VirtProductInfo</name>
    <value>Oracle VM 3</value>
  </metric>
  <metric type='string' context='host'>
    <name>VirtualizationVendor</name>
    <value>Oracle Corporation</value>
  </metric>
  <metric type='uint64' context='host'>
    <name>Time</name>
    <value>1485064760537</value>
  </metric>
  <metric type='string' context='host'>
    <name>HostName</name>
    <value>ovs3.m57.local</value>
  </metric>
  <metric type='uint64' context='vm' id='0'
uuid='0004fb00-0006-0000-0da7-51aac2e82537'>
    <name>PhysicalMemoryAllocatedToVirtualSystem</name>
    <value>2051</value>
  </metric>
  <metric type='uint64' context='vm' id='0'
uuid='0004fb00-0006-0000-0da7-51aac2e82537'>
    <name>ResourceMemoryLimit</name>
    <value>2048</value>
  </metric>
  <metric type='uint32' context='vm' id='0'
uuid='0004fb00-0006-0000-0da7-51aac2e82537'>
    <name>ResourceProcessorLimit</name>
    <value>2</value>
  </metric>
  <metric type='real64' context='vm' id='0'
uuid='0004fb00-0006-0000-0da7-51aac2e82537'>
    <name>TotalCPUTime</name>
    <value>14.963504791259766</value>
  </metric>
</metrics>
```

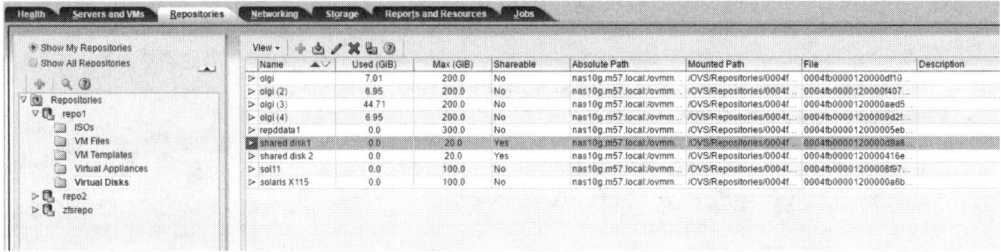

FIGURE 15-14. *Selecting a virtual disk to edit*

Configuring Shared Virtual Disks with the VM Manager

Shared disks are used to support applications that require a disk to be available (read and write simultaneously) from multiple Oracle VM guests, not Oracle VM servers. These applications include Oracle Real Application Clusters, Microsoft Cluster Services, and others. Because a shared virtual disk does not belong to any particular virtual system alone, it is part of the guest resources. You can convert any existing virtual disk to a shared disk by selecting the Shareable check box when editing the virtual disk. To edit a virtual disk, go to the "Virtual Disks" folder in the repository that holds the virtual disk, highlight the disk to be edited, and then click the Edit icon (see Figure 15-14).

This will bring up the Edit dialog for the virtual disk. To make the Virtual Disk shareable, simply check the Shareable box (shown in Figure 15-15). The virtual disk can now be allocated to multiple VMs.

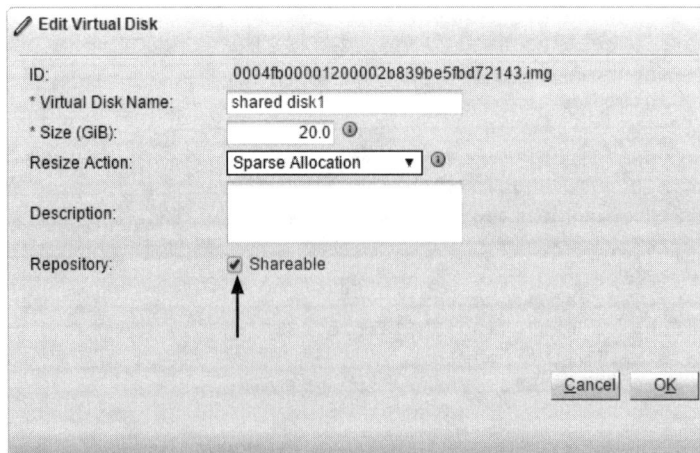

FIGURE 15-15. *Making a virtual disk shareable*

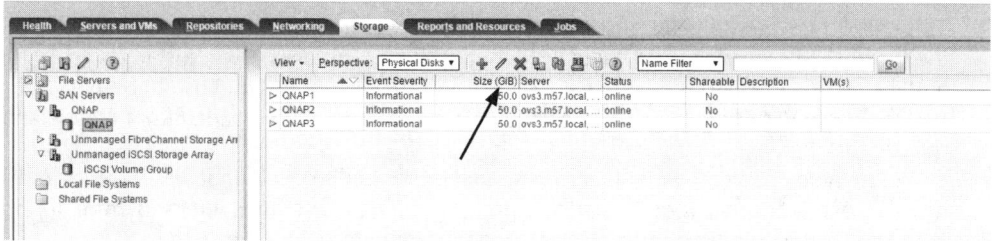

FIGURE 15-16.   *Editing a physical disk*

Configuring Shared Physical Devices

In addition to using file-based virtual disks as shared disks for Oracle RAC (or any application that requires a shared disk), Oracle VM allows the virtual machine to use physical devices as well. Physical devices offer performance advantages over virtual disks, but they do not have the flexibility that virtual disks offer. Physical devices can be shared by all devices in the server pool. Sharing a physical disk is similar to sharing virtual disks, but the process is managed from the Storage tab. To share a physical disk, select the disk by accessing it from the Storage tab and then select the array the disk is being served from (see Figure 15-16).

This will bring up the Edit dialog for the virtual disk. To make the virtual disk shareable, simply check the Shareable box (see Figure 15-17). The virtual disk can now be allocated to multiple VMs.

Once you've completed these steps, you can use the physical device as a shared device.

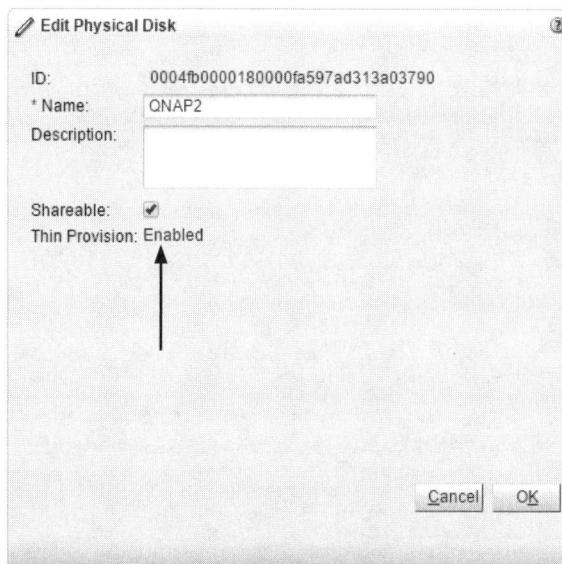

FIGURE 15-17.   *Making a physical disk shareable*

Summary

This chapter covered several server resource management tasks and how to administer them via the Oracle VM Manager and Oracle VM Utilities. Both tools are easy to install and easy to use, and they work together (for example, Oracle VM Utilities requires and uses the OVM CLI installed on the Oracle VM Manager). The VM Utilities can be readily downloaded from Oracle and can be quickly installed and configured.

In the next chapter, you will learn how to monitor and tune an Oracle VM server. A poorly tuned or overloaded server will lead to virtual machine performance issues. By monitoring the load on your VM servers, you can often head off problems before they occur.

CHAPTER
16

Monitoring and Tuning
Oracle VM Servers

O nce the virtual machine environment has been configured and deployed, it should be monitored and managed to provide an efficient and well-performing system. An overloaded Oracle VM server and I/O subsystem result in a poorly performing virtual environment, which in turn results in unhappy customers and users. There are two parts to tuning and monitoring the virtual environment: monitoring and tuning Oracle VM servers and monitoring and tuning the virtual machines themselves. This chapter covers monitoring and tuning Oracle VM servers.

Performance Monitoring

Performance monitoring can be done via Oracle Enterprise Manager Cloud Control and several tools that are available within the Oracle VM system. Remember, the domain-0 (dom0) system is not a normal virtual machine, though it has some of the properties of a virtual machine. For example, running top, sar, or vmstat (Linux monitoring utilities) in dom0 only provides statistics for dom0 itself. To determine what is happening on the entire Oracle VM server, you must use other utilities. Let's look at a couple examples.

Running top (Display Top Linux Tasks) in dom0 gives you information on the dom0 system only. You can see this in Figure 16-1. In this figure, top shows a system with 12 CPU cores and 3214404k (3GB) of total system memory. The VM server used in this example actually has 120GB of RAM and 12 CPU cores. What Figure 16-1 reveals is the performance and resources that have been allocated to dom0.

```
root@ovm01:~                                                         —  □  ✕

top - 06:29:16 up 22 days, 13:53,  1 user,  load average: 0.02, 0.07, 0.07
Tasks: 446 total,  1 running, 443 sleeping,  0 stopped,  2 zombie
Cpu(s):  0.1%us,  0.2%sy,  0.0%ni, 99.7%id,  0.0%wa,  0.0%hi,  0.0%si,  0.0%st
Mem:    3214404k total,  3013240k used,   201164k free,   427612k buffers
Swap:   4194300k total,        0k used,  4194300k free,  2028596k cached

  PID USER      PR  NI  VIRT  RES  SHR S %CPU %MEM    TIME+  COMMAND
12760 root      20   0 15360 2316 1724 R  0.7  0.1  0:00.03 top c
 1998 root       0 -20     0    0    0 S  0.3  0.0  5:05.73 [kworker/9:1H]
 3602 root      20   0     0    0    0 S  0.3  0.0  0:36.67 [jbd2/dm-6-617]
 7428 root      20   0  106m 3060 1824 S  0.3  0.1  0:05.33 /bin/bash /usr/sbin/OSWatche
16085 root       0 -20     0    0    0 S  0.3  0.0 21:56.45 [loop17]
16295 root       0 -20     0    0    0 S  0.3  0.0  0:36.61 [loop22]
18089 root      20   0     0    0    0 S  0.3  0.0  0:02.95 [kworker/u24:3]
    1 root      20   0 19292 2280 1992 S  0.0  0.1  0:00.91 /sbin/init
    2 root      20   0     0    0    0 S  0.0  0.0  0:00.08 [kthreadd]
    3 root      20   0     0    0    0 S  0.0  0.0  0:04.43 [ksoftirqd/0]
    5 root       0 -20     0    0    0 S  0.0  0.0  0:00.00 [kworker/0:0H]
    7 root      20   0     0    0    0 S  0.0  0.0 13:04.26 [rcu_sched]
    8 root      20   0     0    0    0 S  0.0  0.0  0:00.00 [rcu_bh]
    9 root      20   0     0    0    0 S  0.0  0.0  4:04.56 [rcuos/0]
   10 root      20   0     0    0    0 S  0.0  0.0  0:00.00 [rcuob/0]
   11 root      RT   0     0    0    0 S  0.0  0.0  0:05.01 [migration/0]
   12 root      RT   0     0    0    0 S  0.0  0.0  0:05.73 [watchdog/0]
   13 root      RT   0     0    0    0 S  0.0  0.0  0:05.66 [watchdog/1]
   14 root      RT   0     0    0    0 S  0.0  0.0  0:04.85 [migration/1]
   15 root      20   0     0    0    0 S  0.0  0.0  0:01.81 [ksoftirqd/1]
   17 root       0 -20     0    0    0 S  0.0  0.0  0:00.00 [kworker/1:0H]
```

FIGURE 16-1. *Example of running top in dom0*

By using **xm top** (a Xen command), you can gather information from the hypervisor and display it within dom0. The information from **xm top** in Figure 16-2 shows five domains: dom0 and four virtual machines. In addition, the summary information at the top of the display gives configuration information for the entire Oracle VM server with 120GB of RAM and 12 CPUs. The **xm top** command is one of several **xm** commands that provide performance and configuration information.

You can use most of the **xm** commands to manage the Oracle VM server, but there are several that you can use to monitor the Oracle VM guests, including the following:

- **xm list**   Lists the virtual machines.
- **xm top**   Displays performance usage of virtual machines.
- **xm uptime**   Displays the uptime of all the virtual machines on the Oracle VM server.

In addition to the **xm** commands used for monitoring, a number of **xm** commands provide specific information about devices and resources, including the following:

- **xm vcpu-list**   Lists the virtual CPUs (VCPUs) for domains.
- **xm info**   Provides information on the Oracle VM Server system (not dom0). This command provides information about the resources available to dom0 and the hypervisor. (**xm info** output is shown later in this section.)

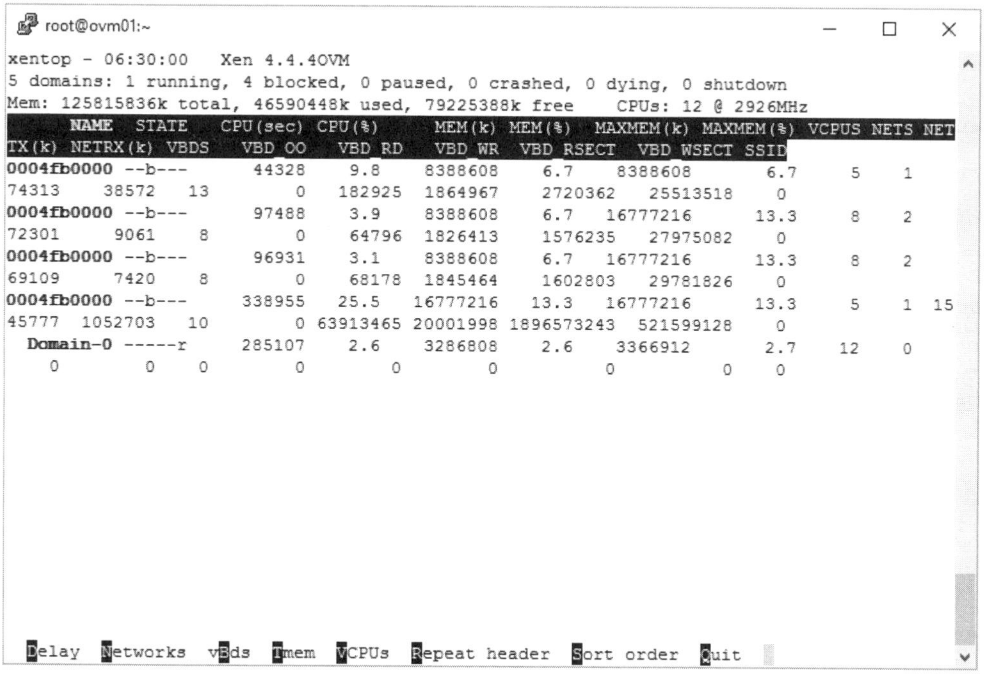

```
root@ovm01:~                                                    —   □   ×
xentop - 06:30:00    Xen 4.4.4OVM
5 domains: 1 running, 4 blocked, 0 paused, 0 crashed, 0 dying, 0 shutdown
Mem: 125815836k total, 46590448k used, 79225388k free     CPUs: 12 @ 2926MHz
      NAME   STATE   CPU(sec) CPU(%)     MEM(k) MEM(%)  MAXMEM(k) MAXMEM(%) VCPUS NETS NET
TX(k) NETRX(k) VBDS   VBD_OO    VBD_RD    VBD_WR  VBD_RSECT  VBD_WSECT SSID
0004fb0000 --b---       44328    9.8    8388608    6.7    8388608       6.7     5    1
74313    38572    13        0   182925  1864967    2720362   25513518      0
0004fb0000 --b---       97488    3.9    8388608    6.7   16777216      13.3     8    2
72301     9061     8        0    64796  1826413    1576235   27975082      0
0004fb0000 --b---       96931    3.1    8388608    6.7   16777216      13.3     8    2
69109     7420     8        0    68178  1845464    1602803   29781826      0
0004fb0000 --b---      338955   25.5   16777216   13.3   16777216      13.3     5    1   15
45777  1052703    10        0 63913465 20001998 1896573243  521599128      0
  Domain-0 -----r      285107    2.6    3286808    2.6    3366912       2.7    12    0
     0         0    0        0        0        0          0          0      0


Delay   Networks   vBds   mem   VCPUs   Repeat header   Sort order   Quit
```

FIGURE 16-2.   *Running the xm top command in dom0*

- **xm log**   Prints the Xen error log.
- **xm block-list**   Lists the block devices for the virtual machines.
- **xm network-list**   Lists the virtual machine networks and their MAC addresses.

Examples from some of the commands are provided in the upcoming sections. These commands are useful for monitoring the Oracle VM server and the virtual machines. In addition to these commands, you can also monitor from within the virtual environment, but monitoring within the virtual machine only gives you performance and resource utilization from the perspective of the virtual machine itself and does not provide information on the entire environment.

CAUTION
Statistics gathered from a virtual machine itself (including dom0) are, by their very nature, not accurate because a virtual machine is only allocating a part of the actual resources. For example, within the virtual machine, it might appear that the CPU is 100 percent busy, but that 100 percent might be physically only 50 percent of the CPU. Therefore, be skeptical of any statistics gathered from within the virtual machine itself.

The xm top Command

As mentioned earlier in this chapter, the **xm top** command shows a different perspective. In the upper part of the screen, the resources for the entire Oracle VM server are listed, as shown in Figure 16-2. You can see the number of domains (including dom0) and what state they are in, as shown here. In addition, the memory and CPU information reflects the entire VM server, not just dom0.

```
xentop - 06:49:34   Xen 4.4.4OVM
5 domains: 1 running, 4 blocked, 0 paused, 0 crashed, 0 dying, 0 shutdown
Mem: 125815836k total, 46590448k used, 79225388k free    CPUs: 12 @ 2926MHz
```

Below the information about the Oracle VM server, you'll see information on each of the virtual machines, including information on how much activity is happening in that particular domain. Note that this information includes dom0 as one of the domains.

```
     NAME    STATE   CPU(sec) CPU(%)   MEM(k)   MEM(%)  MAXMEM(k) MAXMEM(%) VCPUS NETS   NET TX(k) NETRX(k)
VBDS  VBD_OO   VBD_RD     VBD_WR    VBD_RSECT    VBD_WSECT   SSID
0004fb0000 --b---   44449   27.1   8388608    6.7   8388608      6.7      5    1      74466    38650
3      0     183173   1868905    2721722     25565582     0
0004fb0000 --b---   97575    3.7   8388608    6.7  16777216     13.3      8    2      72352     9064
8      0      64796   1828054    1576235     27999122     0
0004fb0000 --b---   97017    3.7   8388608    6.7  16777216     13.3      8    2      69160     7423
8      0      68178   1847123    1602803     29807826     0
0004fb0000 -----r  339245   15.6  16777216   13.3  16777216     13.3      5    1    1546186  1053253
10     0   63958873 20009831 1897884834    521738836     0
Domain-0   -----r  285277   22.8   3286808    2.6   3366912      2.7     12    0          0        0
0      0         0        0          0           0        0
```

The **xm top** command is very useful for finding out which domains are the busiest and contributing the most to the Oracle VM server's load.

Unfortunately, the domain name is truncated; therefore, all of the virtual machines appear to have the same name. You might be able to correlate by using the NET field and **xm list**.

Also note that although Domain-0 is allocated all of the CPUs, it is only allocated a small amount of memory.

The xm list Command

The **xm list** command lists the virtual machines that are currently running, how much memory they are allocated to use, the number of virtual CPUs, the state, and the length of time that they have been running. This output is shown here:

```
[root@ovm01 ~]# xm list
Name                                        ID    Mem VCPUs      State   Time(s)
0004fb00000600001b620e2f106d4f42             5   8192     2      -b----   44460.8
0004fb0000060000c28fa306d48e7690             4   8192     5      -b----   97584.9
0004fb0000060000e79a7e1357fcbdd9             3   8192     4      -b----   97025.7
0004fb0000060000f55c08712aa9f71a             2  16384     1      -b---- 339277.9
Domain-0                                     0   3209    12      r----- 285293.6
```

The **xm list** command does not show significant information about system performance, but it does provide a quick way to determine which virtual machines are running and how many resources have been allocated to each.

The ID is important when coordinating with other **xm** commands, because the name may or may not be truncated in those outputs. Also take note of the number of virtual CPUs as well as the amount of memory allocated to the VM. Domain-0 has access to all the CPUs, but as a virtual machine it's not allocated very much memory. Oracle has carefully given Domain-0 what it needs to do the job optimally.

The xm uptime Command

The **xm uptime** command does not provide significant information and is redundant with **xm list**, but with less information. The **xm uptime** command basically lists how long each virtual machine has been running, as shown here:

```
[root@ovm01 ~]# xm uptime
Name                                ID Uptime
0004fb00000600001b620e2f106d4f42     5  6 days, 19:09:52
0004fb0000060000c28fa306d48e7690     4 15 days, 19:00:23
0004fb0000060000e79a7e1357fcbdd9     3 15 days, 19:00:41
0004fb0000060000f55c08712aa9f71a     2 21 days, 16:25:11
Domain-0                             0 22 days, 14:17:40
```

As you can see, this command only provides minimal information.

The xm info Command

The **xm info** command provides a great deal of information about the Oracle VM server:

```
[root@ovm01 ~]# xm info
host                   : ovm01
release                : 4.1.12-32.1.3.el6uek.x86_64
version                : #2 SMP Fri Jan 29 21:07:58 PST 2016
machine                : x86_64
nr_cpus                : 12
nr_nodes               : 2
cores_per_socket       : 6
threads_per_core       : 1
cpu_mhz                : 2926
hw_caps                :
bfebfbff:2c100800:00000000:00003f00:029ee3ff:00000000:00000001:00000000
virt_caps              : hvm
total_memory           : 122867
free_memory            : 77368
free_cpus              : 0
xen_major              : 4
xen_minor              : 4
xen_extra              : .4OVM
xen_caps               : xen-3.0-x86_64 xen-3.0-x86_32p hvm-3.0-x86_32
hvm-3.0-x86_32p hvm-3.0-x86_64
xen_scheduler          : credit
xen_pagesize           : 4096
platform_params        : virt_start=0xffff800000000000
xen_changeset          :
xen_commandline        : placeholder dom0_mem=max:3288M allowsuperpage
cc_compiler            : gcc (GCC) 4.4.7 20120313 (Red Hat 4.4.7-3)
cc_compile_by          : mockbuild
cc_compile_domain      : us.oracle.com
cc_compile_date        : Thu Feb 11 14:09:59 PST 2016
xend_config_format     : 4
```

This command does not provide specific performance information, but it can be used to provide significant information about the resources used by the system as well as about the system's configuration.

The xm vcpu-list Command

The **xm vcpu-list** command provides information about CPU allocation and affinity, which can be useful in determining which physical CPUs a virtual CPU is running on. This command will be shown in further detail later on in this chapter in the section "Tuning Virtual Machines." The **xm vcpu-list** command is shown here:

```
[root@ovm01 ~]# xm vcpu-list
Name                              ID   VCPU    CPU  State   Time(s)  CPU Affinity
0004fb0000060000c28fa306d48e7690   4     0      3    -b-    19907.3  any cpu
0004fb0000060000c28fa306d48e7690   4     1     10    -b-    18377.4  any cpu
0004fb0000060000c28fa306d48e7690   4     2      0    -b-    18856.2  any cpu
```

```
0004fb0000060000c28fa306d48e7690    4    3    8    -b-    20590.2 any cpu
0004fb0000060000c28fa306d48e7690    4    4    4    -b-    19877.7 any cpu
0004fb0000060000c28fa306d48e7690    4    5    -    --p        0.0 any cpu
0004fb0000060000c28fa306d48e7690    4    6    -    --p        0.0 any cpu
0004fb0000060000c28fa306d48e7690    4    7    -    --p        0.0 any cpu
0004fb0000060000e79a7e1357fcbdd9    3    0    3    -b-    23998.2 any cpu
0004fb0000060000e79a7e1357fcbdd9    3    1    5    -b-    25175.3 any cpu
0004fb0000060000e79a7e1357fcbdd9    3    2    5    -b-    24304.4 any cpu
0004fb0000060000e79a7e1357fcbdd9    3    3    6    -b-    23571.5 any cpu
0004fb0000060000e79a7e1357fcbdd9    3    4    -    --p        0.0 any cpu
0004fb0000060000e79a7e1357fcbdd9    3    5    -    --p        0.0 any cpu
0004fb0000060000e79a7e1357fcbdd9    3    6    -    --p        0.0 any cpu
0004fb0000060000e79a7e1357fcbdd9    3    7    -    --p        0.0 any cpu
0004fb0000060000f55c08712aa9f71a    2    0    7    -b-   339359.1 6-11
0004fb0000060000f55c08712aa9f71a    2    1    -    --p        0.0 6-11
0004fb0000060000f55c08712aa9f71a    2    2    -    --p        0.0 6-11
0004fb0000060000f55c08712aa9f71a    2    3    -    --p        0.0 6-11
0004fb0000060000f55c08712aa9f71a    2    4    -    --p        0.0 6-11
Domain-0                            0    0    9    -b-    22183.6 any cpu
Domain-0                            0    1    6    -b-    18860.3 any cpu
Domain-0                            0    2   11    -b-    20189.2 any cpu
Domain-0                            0    3    2    r--    21049.2 any cpu
Domain-0                            0    4    6    -b-    18674.3 any cpu
Domain-0                            0    5    1    -b-    23896.1 any cpu
Domain-0                            0    6    5    -b-    36949.8 any cpu
Domain-0                            0    7    8    -b-    24468.5 any cpu
Domain-0                            0    8    0    -b-    21791.9 any cpu
Domain-0                            0    9    3    -b-    25217.5 any cpu
Domain-0                            0   10    2    -b-    19726.1 any cpu
Domain-0                            0   11    0    -b-    32334.4 any cpu
0004fb00000600001b620e2f106d4f42    5    0    1    -b-    23054.6 0-5
0004fb00000600001b620e2f106d4f42    5    1    4    -b-    21439.7 0-5
0004fb00000600001b620e2f106d4f42    5    2    -    --p        0.0 0-5
0004fb00000600001b620e2f106d4f42    5    3    -    --p        0.0 0-5
0004fb00000600001b620e2f106d4f42    5    4    -    --p        0.0 0-5
```

This command also gives the CPU time accumulated by the virtual machine, not the clock time that the virtual machine has been running. This is an especially important view when considering CPU pinning, also known as hard partitioning. In this example, you can see where the virtual CPUs from each of the VMs share the same physical CPUs in some cases, and in other cases they might be alone on a physical CPU. Note that CPU Affinity shows that the virtual CPUs can run on any physical CPU. If CPU pinning or hard partitioning were used, you would see virtual CPUs locked down to specific CPUs. This is shown later in the chapter.

The xm log Command

The **xm log** command is simply a shortcut to the Oracle VM server console log. Running this command prints the Xend log (/var/log/ovm-consoled.log) to the screen. Beware: the log can be quite long. This command prints out /var/log/ovm-consoled.log, but really the more important log is going to be /var/log/ovs-agent.log. There is not a command to print out this log.

The xm block-list Command

The **xm block-list** command lists the virtual block devices that have been allocated to a domain. The **xm block-list** command requires a domain name to be passed to it. This domain name is a long, hexadecimal name that was generated by OVM.

Find the domain number using **xm list**. Then run **xm block-list 1**, for example. Domain names can get long and confusing in Oracle VM 3 because it sets each domain name to a unique number rather than a name, as was done in previous versions.

```
[root@ovm01 ~]# xm list
Name                                    ID   Mem VCPUs      State   Time(s)
0004fb00000600001b620e2f106d4f42         5  8192     2    -b----   44540.4
0004fb0000060000c28fa306d48e7690         4  8192     5    -b----   97642.8
0004fb0000060000e79a7e1357fcbdd9         3  8192     4    -b----   97082.8
0004fb0000060000f55c08712aa9f71a         2 16384     1    -b----  339472.9
Domain-0                                 0  3209    12    r-----  285404.4
[root@ovm01 ~]# xm block-list 0004fb0000060000c28fa306d48e7690
Vdev   BE handle  state evt-ch ring-ref  BE-path
51712  0     0      4     41      9      /local/domain/0/backend/vbd/4/51712
51728  0     0      4     42      10     /local/domain/0/backend/vbd/4/51728
51744  0     0      4     43      11     /local/domain/0/backend/vbd/4/51744
51760  0     0      4     44      12     /local/domain/0/backend/vbd/4/51760
51776  0     0      4     45      14     /local/domain/0/backend/vbd/4/51776
51792  0     0      4     46      15     /local/domain/0/backend/vbd/4/51792
51808  0     0      4     47      17     /local/domain/0/backend/vbd/4/51808
51824  0     0      4     48      18     /local/domain/0/backend/vbd/4/51824
```

The **xm block-list** command provides some information but is usually not that helpful to the OVM administrator.

The xm network-list Command

The **xm network-list** command lists the virtual network devices that have been allocated to a virtual machine, including the MAC address of the virtual adapter, as shown next. This command can be very useful for troubleshooting network problems, configuring DHCP, and so on. It also uses the OVM-generated name of the virtual machine.

```
[root@ovm01 ~]# xm network-list 0004fb0000060000c28fa306d48e7690
Idx BE   MAC Addr.     handle state evt-ch tx-/rx-ring-ref BE-path
0   0  00:21:f6:de:5a:e7  0     4    -1      1280/1281     /local/domain/0/backend/vif/4/0
1   0  00:21:f6:26:3c:25  1     4    -1      1282/1283     /local/domain/0/backend/vif/4/1
```

Most of these commands provide information only and not performance data; however, some of this information can be useful when tuning the system. You might find more information by using the **brctl** command, as will become evident in the next sections.

Tuning the Oracle VM Server System

There really isn't a lot that you have to tune in the Oracle VM Server system. In fact, as you will see, tuning the Oracle VM Server system actually involves monitoring and adjusting the resources rather than tweaking parameters and settings. The Oracle VM Server system is based on Xen, with Oracle enhancements, and as such is set up and ready to go when installed. Dom0 is based on a stripped-down version of Linux that Oracle calls a "Just enough OS" (JeOS). The next few sections provide tips on tuning the OS, network, and I/O subsystem. In this case, OS tuning includes not only software (Linux and Oracle VM tuning) but also hardware. The out-of-the-box OVM system is typically tuned well enough. It is unusual that you will need to make any changes.

Tuning the OS and CPUs

From a software perspective, there really aren't any OS tuning changes that can be made. In fact, making changes to the OS should only be done after careful consideration because it could cause more harm than good. Hardware tuning at the OS layer consists of CPU and memory. As shown earlier in this chapter, you can monitor memory and CPU utilization via several Xen commands, such as **xm top**. If additional memory and/or CPUs are needed, you can add them (depending on your current hardware configuration).

You can do a few things at the virtual machine level to tune the CPUs. Virtual CPUs can run on one or more physical CPUs. The physical CPUs are the actual hardware running on the Oracle VM server, whereas the virtual CPUs are the CPUs that are seen by the virtual machine. The virtual machine's virtual CPUs can run on one or more physical CPUs. Oracle VM allows virtual CPUs to be pinned to physical CPUs. This gives you a lot of control over how the system resources are used. This topic is covered in the Oracle whitepaper "Hard Partitioning with Oracle VM Server for x86," which can be found at http://www.oracle.com/technetwork/server-storage/vm/ovm-hardpart-168217.pdf.

When you're configuring a VM to use multiple CPUs, it is important that the CPU core or thread that is being allocated to the virtual machine resides on the same CPU socket (if possible). The CPU socket is the actual CPU chip. A *core* is a CPU within the CPU, and a *thread* is a portion of a core. The more you can keep things together, the better.

In order to determine which CPU thread is on which core and which CPU (and node if using non-uniform memory access, or *NUMA*), you can run **xenpm get-cpu-topology**. This will provide information on the core, socket, and node for each CPU. An example is shown here:

```
[root@ovm01 ~]# xenpm get-cpu-topology
CPU      core    socket   node
CPU0     0        1        0
CPU1     1        1        0
CPU2     2        1        0
CPU3     8        1        0
CPU4     9        1        0
CPU5     10       1        0
CPU6     0        0        1
CPU7     1        0        1
CPU8     2        0        1
CPU9     8        0        1
CPU10    9        0        1
CPU11    10       0        1
```

As you can see, there are two sockets with six cores each. Note that hyperthreading is not turned on. Here is an example with hyperthreading enabled. Notice that there are two CPUs per core (not all rows are shown).

```
[root@ovm02 ~]# xenpm get-cpu-topology
CPU     core    socket  node
CPU0    0       1       0
CPU1    0       1       0
CPU2    1       1       0
CPU3    1       1       0
...
CPU20   9       0       1
CPU21   9       0       1
CPU22   10      0       1
CPU23   10      0       1
```

You have a few ways to allocate CPU resources: by using the **xm vcpu** command, by configuring the vm.cfg file, and by using ovm_vmcontrol (part of the OVM Utilities). Each of these methods is described in this section, but using ovm_vmcontrol is the preferred method. Remember that only the vm.cfg file and ovm_vmcontrol utility methods are permanent. If the Oracle VM server were to restart, all changes made with **xm** commands will be lost.

NOTE
Only ovm_vmcontrol is supported for CPU pinning. It is covered here as well as in Chapter 15. Also note that live migration is not supported with hard partitioning unless you are using an Oracle Private Cloud Appliance (PCA).

Pinning CPUs Using xm vcpu Commands

Three commands are used to configure CPU affinity on a live system. These commands are **xm vcpu-list**, **xm vcpu-pin**, and **xm vcpu-set**. Each command serves a slightly different purpose. These commands for pinning vCPUs have been replaced by the use of the OVM Utilities, which is the preferred way of managing hard partitioning.

NOTE
*Any changes made using the **xm cpu** commands are lost when the virtual machine is restarted.*

The **xm vcpu-list** command lists the virtual machines (domains) and their current CPU settings. This command takes the domain ID as an optional qualifier. If the domain or set of domains is not provided, all of the domains on the system will be displayed, as shown here:

```
[root@ovm01 ~]# xm vcpu-list
Name                                    ID   VCPU  CPU State   Time(s)  CPU Affinity
0004fb0000060000c28fa306d48e7690        4    0     5   r--     19919.1  any cpu
0004fb0000060000c28fa306d48e7690        4    1     7   -b-     18387.1  any cpu
0004fb0000060000c28fa306d48e7690        4    2     6   -b-     18863.1  any cpu
0004fb0000060000c28fa306d48e7690        4    3     3   r--     20608.7  any cpu
```

```
0004fb0000060000c28fa306d48e7690    4    4   10   r--    19893.7 any cpu
0004fb0000060000c28fa306d48e7690    4    5    -   --p        0.0 any cpu
0004fb0000060000c28fa306d48e7690    4    6    -   --p        0.0 any cpu
0004fb0000060000c28fa306d48e7690    4    7    -   --p        0.0 any cpu
0004fb0000060000e79a7e1357fcbdd9    3    0    4   -b-    24013.8 any cpu
0004fb0000060000e79a7e1357fcbdd9    3    1   10   -b-    25189.2 any cpu
0004fb0000060000e79a7e1357fcbdd9    3    2    4   -b-    24320.4 any cpu
0004fb0000060000e79a7e1357fcbdd9    3    3   11   -b-    23588.3 any cpu
0004fb0000060000e79a7e1357fcbdd9    3    4    -   --p        0.0 any cpu
0004fb0000060000e79a7e1357fcbdd9    3    5    -   --p        0.0 any cpu
0004fb0000060000e79a7e1357fcbdd9    3    6    -   --p        0.0 any cpu
0004fb0000060000e79a7e1357fcbdd9    3    7    -   --p        0.0 any cpu
0004fb0000060000f55c08712aa9f71a    2    0    8   -b-   339568.6 6-11
0004fb0000060000f55c08712aa9f71a    2    1    -   --p        0.0 6-11
0004fb0000060000f55c08712aa9f71a    2    2    -   --p        0.0 6-11
0004fb0000060000f55c08712aa9f71a    2    3    -   --p        0.0 6-11
0004fb0000060000f55c08712aa9f71a    2    4    -   --p        0.0 6-11
Domain-0                            0    0    7   -b-    22193.9 any cpu
Domain-0                            0    1    5   -b-    18868.0 any cpu
Domain-0                            0    2    2   -b-    20196.7 any cpu
Domain-0                            0    3    1   -b-    21056.0 any cpu
Domain-0                            0    4    7   -b-    18681.2 any cpu
Domain-0                            0    5    9   -b-    23903.5 any cpu
Domain-0                            0    6    9   -b-    36963.0 any cpu
Domain-0                            0    7    0   -b-    24481.5 any cpu
Domain-0                            0    8    2   -b-    21802.0 any cpu
Domain-0                            0    9    4   -b-    25228.3 any cpu
Domain-0                            0   10    4   r--    19736.1 any cpu
Domain-0                            0   11    2   -b-    32349.3 any cpu
0004fb00000600001b620e2f106d4f42    5    0    1   -b-    23099.7 0-5
0004fb00000600001b620e2f106d4f42    5    1    0   -b-    21480.3 0-5
0004fb00000600001b620e2f106d4f42    5    2    -   --p        0.0 0-5
0004fb00000600001b620e2f106d4f42    5    3    -   --p        0.0 0-5
0004fb00000600001b620e2f106d4f42    5    4    -   --p        0.0 0-5
```

Optionally, you can provide a domain ID as a qualifier. In this case, the **xm vcpu-list** command provides only CPU information about the requested domain. This command as well as others can be qualified by either the name or the ID of the virtual machine. Each provides an equivalent output.

```
[root@ovm01 ~]# xm vcpu-list 4
[root@ovm01 ~]# xm vcpu-list 0004fb0000060000c28fa306d48e7690
Name                               ID  VCPU  CPU State   Time(s) CPU Affinity
0004fb0000060000c28fa306d48e7690    4    0    9   -b-    19920.2 any cpu
0004fb0000060000c28fa306d48e7690    4    1    7   -b-    18387.9 any cpu
0004fb0000060000c28fa306d48e7690    4    2   10   -b-    18863.7 any cpu
0004fb0000060000c28fa306d48e7690    4    3    2   -b-    20609.7 any cpu
0004fb0000060000c28fa306d48e7690    4    4    3   -b-    19895.4 any cpu
0004fb0000060000c28fa306d48e7690    4    5    -   --p        0.0 any cpu
0004fb0000060000c28fa306d48e7690    4    6    -   --p        0.0 any cpu
0004fb0000060000c28fa306d48e7690    4    7    -   --p        0.0 any cpu
```

Notice in this example that the four virtual CPUs allocated to the domain named 4590_pvtest2 are configured to run on any of the physical CPUs in the system.

To pin a virtual CPU to a physical CPU, use the **xm vcpu-pin** command. The syntax is as follows:

```
xm vcpu-pin <domain> <VCPU> <CPU>
```

For example, to pin the four virtual CPUs just shown on physical CPUs 2, 3, 7, 9, and 10, you would use the following commands:

```
[root@ovm01 ~]# xm vcpu-pin 0004fb0000060000c28fa306d48e7690 0 9
[root@ovm01 ~]# xm vcpu-pin 0004fb0000060000c28fa306d48e7690 1 7
[root@ovm01 ~]# xm vcpu-pin 0004fb0000060000c28fa306d48e7690 2 10
[root@ovm01 ~]# xm vcpu-pin 0004fb0000060000c28fa306d48e7690 3 2
[root@ovm01 ~]# xm vcpu-pin 0004fb0000060000c28fa306d48e7690 4 3
[root@ovm01 ~]# xm vcpu-list 0004fb0000060000c28fa306d48e7690
```

Name	ID	VCPU	CPU	State	Time(s)	CPU Affinity
0004fb0000060000c28fa306d48e7690	4	0	9	-b-	19925.5	9
0004fb0000060000c28fa306d48e7690	4	1	7	-b-	18392.2	7
0004fb0000060000c28fa306d48e7690	4	2	10	-b-	18867.9	10
0004fb0000060000c28fa306d48e7690	4	3	2	-b-	20615.2	2
0004fb0000060000c28fa306d48e7690	4	4	3	-b-	19905.7	3
0004fb0000060000c28fa306d48e7690	4	5	-	--p	0.0	any cpu
0004fb0000060000c28fa306d48e7690	4	6	-	--p	0.0	any cpu
0004fb0000060000c28fa306d48e7690	4	7	-	--p	0.0	any cpu

NOTE
You would want to pin all *CPUs, not just a few, as was done in this example.*

Use the **xm vcpu-set** command to limit (set) the number of virtual CPUs that a domain can see. The number of VCPUs can be decreased from the limit that's originally set, but it cannot be increased above that number.

```
[root@ovm01 ~]# xm vcpu-list 0004fb0000060000c28fa306d48e7690
```

Name	ID	VCPU	CPU	State	Time(s)	CPU Affinity
0004fb0000060000c28fa306d48e7690	4	0	9	-b-	19927.7	9
0004fb0000060000c28fa306d48e7690	4	1	7	-b-	18393.8	7
0004fb0000060000c28fa306d48e7690	4	2	10	-b-	18868.9	10
0004fb0000060000c28fa306d48e7690	4	3	2	-b-	20616.1	2
0004fb0000060000c28fa306d48e7690	4	4	3	-b-	19908.2	3
0004fb0000060000c28fa306d48e7690	4	5	-	--p	0.0	any cpu
0004fb0000060000c28fa306d48e7690	4	6	-	--p	0.0	any cpu
0004fb0000060000c28fa306d48e7690	4	7	-	--p	0.0	any cpu

```
[root@ovm01 ~]# xm vcpu-set 0004fb0000060000c28fa306d48e7690 2
[root@ovm01 ~]# xm vcpu-list 0004fb0000060000c28fa306d48e7690
```

Name	ID	VCPU	CPU	State	Time(s)	CPU Affinity
0004fb0000060000c28fa306d48e7690	4	0	9	-b-	19927.8	9
0004fb0000060000c28fa306d48e7690	4	1	7	-b-	18393.9	7

```
0004fb0000060000c28fa306d48e7690    4    2    -    --p    18868.9 10
0004fb0000060000c28fa306d48e7690    4    3    -    --p    20616.1 2
0004fb0000060000c28fa306d48e7690    4    4    -    --p    19908.3 3
0004fb0000060000c28fa306d48e7690    4    5    -    --p        0.0 any cpu
0004fb0000060000c28fa306d48e7690    4    6    -    --p        0.0 any cpu
0004fb0000060000c28fa306d48e7690    4    7    -    --p        0.0 any cpu
```

You can then re-enable the virtual machine by using the **xm vcpu-set** command again, but this time with the number of CPUs set to 4:

```
[root@ovm01 ~]# xm vcpu-set 0004fb0000060000c28fa306d48e7690 4
[root@ovm01 ~]# xm vcpu-list 0004fb0000060000c28fa306d48e7690
Name                                 ID  VCPU   CPU State  Time(s) CPU Affinity
0004fb0000060000c28fa306d48e7690    4    0     9   -b-    19931.0 9
0004fb0000060000c28fa306d48e7690    4    1     7   -b-    18396.9 7
0004fb0000060000c28fa306d48e7690    4    2    10   -b-    18868.9 10
0004fb0000060000c28fa306d48e7690    4    3     2   -b-    20616.2 2
0004fb0000060000c28fa306d48e7690    4    4     -   --p    19908.3 3
0004fb0000060000c28fa306d48e7690    4    5     -   --p        0.0 any cpu
0004fb0000060000c28fa306d48e7690    4    6     -   --p        0.0 any cpu
0004fb0000060000c28fa306d48e7690    4    7     -   --p        0.0 any cpu
```

Using CPU affinity can be a good way to prioritize specific virtual machines. Note that it is possible (and likely) to have two virtual CPUs sharing the same physical CPU. In fact, with **xm vcpu-pin**, you can set all of the VCPUs to the same physical CPU.

NOTE
The State field in **xm vcpu-list** *can have one of several values:*
r *running*
b *blocked*
p *paused*
s *shutdown*
c *crashed*
d *dying*
The virtual CPUs must exist in one of these states.

In addition to the **xm** commands. CPUs can be configured in the **vm.cfg** file as well.

Pinning CPUs Using the vm.cfg File

In addition to using the **xm** commands, you can configure the number of CPUs and their affinity within the vm.cfg file. The vm.cfg file has two pertinent parameters. The **vcpus** parameter specifies the number of CPUs used by the VM. In addition, an optional **cpu** parameter can be added, specifying the physical CPUs that the virtual CPUs can run on. This parameter takes single quotes, as shown here:

```
vcpus = 5
cpu = '2,4,6,8'
```

A vm.cfg file generated by the VM Manager only has the **vcpus** parameter specified. Setting the **cpu** parameter, as shown here, locks the virtual CPUs to physical CPUs 2, 4, 6, and 8. If you want to set a specific order, put it in the **cpu** variable, as shown here:

```
cpu = '9,7,10,2'
```

The resulting configuration locks the CPUs, as shown here:

```
[root@ovm01 0004fb0000060000c28fa306d48e7690]# xm vcpu-list 0004fb0000060000c28fa306d48e7690
Name                                ID  VCPU   CPU State   Time(s) CPU Affinity
0004fb0000060000c28fa306d48e7690     6    0     2   -b-     5.0 2,7,9-10
0004fb0000060000c28fa306d48e7690     6    1     2   -b-     2.8 2,7,9-10
0004fb0000060000c28fa306d48e7690     6    2     7   -b-     3.6 2,7,9-10
0004fb0000060000c28fa306d48e7690     6    3    10   -b-     4.9 2,7,9-10
0004fb0000060000c28fa306d48e7690     6    4     7   -b-     2.3 2,7,9-10
0004fb0000060000c28fa306d48e7690     6    5     -   --p     0.1 2,7,9-10
0004fb0000060000c28fa306d48e7690     6    6     -   --p     0.2 2,7,9-10
0004fb0000060000c28fa306d48e7690     6    7     -   --p     0.2 2,7,9-10
```

As mentioned earlier, you can also lock one or more virtual CPUs to the same physical CPUs. The **cpu** variable will take either a specific set of CPUs that are comma separated or a set of CPUs with a range. The result differs based on the configuration, for example:

- Specifying a range of CPUs, as in **cpu = '1-2'**, locks the four virtual CPUs to physical CPUs 1 and 2; however, they will be able to move between those CPUs.

- Specifying a single CPU, as in **cpu = '1'**, locks all four virtual CPUs to the same physical CPU.

- Specifying a specific list of CPUs that has the same number of CPUs as specified in the **vcpus** parameter locks each virtual CPU to a physical CPU, as shown previously.

CPU affinity is presented in this chapter because it is not just a tool for tuning the virtual machine; it is also a tool for tuning the Oracle VM server as well by specifying the load on the Oracle VM server's CPUs.

Pinning CPUs Using ovm_vmcontrol

One of the new features of OVM 3 is the OVM Utilities, which can be downloaded from Oracle Support as patch number 13602094. The OVM Utilities comes with a number of OVM command-line utilities, including ovm_vmcontrol, ovm_reporestore, ovm_vmdisks, ovm_vmhostd, and vm-dump-metrics. In order to pin CPUs, we will be using vm_vmcontrol.

The ovm_vmcontrol utility can be used to display and configure CPU pinning. In order to view any pinned CPUs, use ovm_vmcontrol with the **getvcpu** parameter, as shown here:

```
[root@OVMManager ovm-utils_2.1]# ./ovm_vmcontrol -u admin -E -h ovmmanager -v
gg20a -c getvcpu
Oracle VM VM Control utility 2.1.
Connecting to OVM Manager using Web Service.
Connected.
OVM Manager version: 3.4.2.1384
Command : getvcpu
Getting pinned CPU list...
No CPU pinned for VM 'gg20a'
```

NOTE
*The **-E** option uses the environment variable OVMUTIL_PASS to store the OVM Manager password so it does not show up in the command.*

Unlike the **xm** commands, because this command is going through the OVM Manager, you will use the name that was provided when you created the VM, rather than the OVM-assigned hexadecimal value.

To pin CPUs (also known as hard partitioning), use ovm_vmcontrol with the **setcpu** and **cpulist** parameters, as shown here:

```
[root@OVMManager ovm-utils_2.1]# ./ovm_vmcontrol -u admin -E -h ovmmanager -v
gg20a
-c setvcpu -s 2,4,6,8
Oracle VM VM Control utility 2.1.
Connecting to OVM Manager using Web Service.
Connected.
OVM Manager version: 3.4.2.1384
Command : setvcpu
Pinning vCPU '2,4,6,8' to VM 'gg20a'
Pin vCPU succeed.
```

Once you have pinned the CPUs, you must stop and start the virtual machine in order for the change to take effect. A restart is not effective for pinning CPUs, it must be a stop and start. After starting the VM, you can verify by running **getvcpu** again:

```
[root@OVMManager ovm-utils_2.1]# ./ovm_vmcontrol -u admin -E -h ovmmanager -v
gg20a -c getvcpu
Oracle VM VM Control utility 2.1.
Connecting to OVM Manager using Web Service.
Connected.
OVM Manager version: 3.4.2.1384
Command : getvcpu
Getting pinned CPU list...
Current pinned CPU:2,4,6,8
```

The ovm_vmcontrol utility easily allows you to pin and unpin VCPUs.

Whether you pin via the **xm** commands or via ovm_vmcontrol, the outcome is the same: VCPUs will be pinned to physical CPUs.

Tuning the Network

As with the OS, from a software standpoint, there really isn't much to tune in the Oracle VM Server. The network is tuned via what I like to refer to as "hardware tuning." Hardware tuning involves properly allocating the hardware resources to take advantage of these resources and to not overload them. Because the network devices are physically limited to a specific speed (for example, Gigabit), the only way to improve network performance is to add more network interfaces. Fortunately, Oracle VM is perfectly suited for that.

NOTE
*See the Oracle whitepaper "Oracle VM 3: 10GbE Network
Performance Tuning" for more information on tuning the 10GbE
network with OVM 3.4 on NUMA systems. This whitepaper is
available at http://www.oracle.com/technetwork/server-storage/vm/
ovm3-10gbe-perf-1900032.pdf.*

The network can be configured for Jumbo Frames using a 9000-byte maximum transmission
unit (MTU). This works well for large payloads, but care must be taken that the MTU for both
guests and dom0 are set the same.

You can monitor the network using the built-in Linux command **sar**. In addition, the OVM
server comes with the iperf utility, which allows for testing the bandwidth between any two
servers. Both methods are described here.

Monitoring the Network with sar

You can monitor network utilization via the **sar** command. The **sar –n DEV** command presents
information on the utilization of each network device. The **sar** command takes two parameters
that specify the time interval and the count of the results. For example **sar –n DEV 10 100** displays
results every 10 seconds, 100 times. This is shown here:

```
[root@ovm01 0004fb0000060000c28fa306d48e7690]# sar -n DEV 10 100
Linux 4.1.12-32.1.3.el6uek.x86_64 (ovm01)     03/03/2017    _x86_64_     (12 CPU)

08:29:29 AM      IFACE    rxpck/s   txpck/s   rxkB/s    txkB/s   rxcmp/s   txcmp/s  rxmcst/s
08:29:39 AM      vif6.0     0.00      0.60     0.00      0.04     0.00      0.00      0.00
08:29:39 AM    ac113200     8.12      8.52     0.71      9.61     0.00      0.00      0.00
08:29:39 AM      vif6.1     0.00      0.00     0.00      0.00     0.00      0.00      0.00
08:29:39 AM       bond0    14.23     19.54     1.76     10.86     0.00      0.00      0.50
08:29:39 AM         em2   410.02    215.53   499.18    114.25     0.00      0.00      0.00
08:29:39 AM         em4     0.00      0.00     0.00      0.00     0.00      0.00      0.00
08:29:39 AM      vif2.0     3.91      4.21     0.56      0.51     0.00      0.00      0.00
08:29:39 AM  10338370ab     0.00      0.00     0.00      0.00     0.00      0.00      0.00
08:29:39 AM      vif3.0     0.00      0.60     0.00      0.04     0.00      0.00      0.00
08:29:39 AM          lo     0.00      0.00     0.00      0.00     0.00      0.00      0.00
08:29:39 AM      vif3.1     0.00      0.00     0.00      0.00     0.00      0.00      0.00
08:29:39 AM         em1    14.23     19.54     1.76     10.86     0.00      0.00      0.50
08:29:39 AM      vif5.0     1.40      1.70     0.22      0.33     0.00      0.00      0.00
08:29:39 AM         em3     0.00      0.00     0.00      0.00     0.00      0.00      0.00
```

This information is very useful for determining whether a specific network adapter is saturated.
However, you cannot take this information at face value. A 1GB adapter can become saturated at
less than 1GB of traffic if the packets are small. If you see the receive and transmit packets per
second getting close to 80 percent of the limit, it is time to get concerned. In this case, some of
the load (some of the virtual machines on that adapter) should be shifted to another adapter.

Bits and Bytes
Unfortunately, most of the performance monitors display results in kilobytes or KB/sec, whereas the throughput of a network device is in bits. Thus, a Gigabit network interface has a theoretical maximum performance of 125 megabytes (MB) per second because there are 8 bits in a byte.

Testing the Network with iperf

If you think you are having a network problem or if you just want to test the performance of your network, you can use the iperf utility, which is included with Oracle VM Server. The iperf utility allows you to test the performance of the network and to see if any errors show up under load. In order to run iperf, you must first set up a listener server.

To run the listener on one of the systems to be tested, run **iperf -s**, as shown here:

```
[root@ovm02 ~]# iperf -s
------------------------------------------------------------
Server listening on TCP port 5001
TCP window size: 85.3 KByte (default)
```

Once the listener is running, run **iperf -c <host>** to invoke iperf. By default, iperf will run for 10 seconds, but that is configurable via the command-line options. You should see something similar to this on the source system:

```
[root@ovm01 ~]# iperf -c ovm02
------------------------------------------------------------
Client connecting to ovm02, TCP port 5001
TCP window size: 85.0 KByte (default)
------------------------------------------------------------
[  3] local 172.17.50.11 port 39241 connected with 172.17.50.12 port 5001
[ ID] Interval       Transfer     Bandwidth
[  3]  0.0-10.0 sec  1.10 GBytes   942 Mbits/sec
```

You will see this on the target system where you are running **iperf -s**. In order to check for network errors, you can run ifconfig, which will show you all the network controllers and any errors that might have occurred on those network controllers.

```
[root@ovm02 ~]# iperf -s
------------------------------------------------------------
Server listening on TCP port 5001
TCP window size: 85.3 KByte (default)
------------------------------------------------------------
[  4] local 172.17.50.12 port 5001 connected with 172.17.50.11 port 39241
[ ID] Interval       Transfer     Bandwidth
[  4]  0.0-10.0 sec  1.10 GBytes   941 Mbits/sec
```

The iperf utility provides the ability to check the network between any two systems, thus not only testing performance, but checking for errors as well.

I/O Performance

I/O performance is limited by the performance of the disk drive itself. In disk arrays, more disk drives mean more I/O performance because the performance of the array is the sum of the performance of the individual disk drives. When purchasing an I/O subsystem, make sure you have a sufficient number of disk drives, a large cache, and a high-performing bus. A slow I/O subsystem slows down I/O performance and subsequently the performance of the virtual machines.

Tuning the I/O Subsystem

As with the other components mentioned in this chapter, the I/O subsystem cannot be tuned per se. Rather, you tune it by spreading out the load or by using "out-of-the-box" solutions for solving this problem. I/O performance is probably the most common performance problem associated with virtual machines. The most common solution to this problem is to create the system with sufficient I/O performance to handle the load of multiple virtual machines. In existing systems, you might need to add more I/O storage to improve I/O performance to an acceptable level.

In addition to the more traditional storage systems, newer technologies can be used to vastly improve the I/O performance of virtual machines. These include solid-state disks (SSDs) and other more powerful solutions such as the IODrive by FusionIO. These memory-based solutions provide much higher throughput and response time. Because I/O is such a critical resource in a virtualized environment, it is well worth the investment.

Testing the I/O subsystem is important if you think you are having an I/O problem. Tools available to do this include ioperf and vdbench. Both can help you determine the performance of your I/O subsystem. However, neither dd nor scp is a good tool for measuring I/O performance.

Tuning Virtual Machines

Within the virtual machine, you tune the OS like any other Linux or Windows system. You can modify the parameters and configure the system as necessary to support the application being run on that server. As mentioned earlier in this chapter, you can manage the number of VCPUs and their placement on physical CPUs at the Oracle VM server. In addition, you can configure the priority of the virtual CPUs as well.

When you're configuring the virtual machine, it is very important to provide sufficient memory. A virtual machine with insufficient memory configured will perform poorly. Memory has become less expensive and is more readily available, so don't skimp on it.

In general, there is not much to tune at the OS level. Most of the tuning efforts are geared toward proper sizing and planning of the system. Most of the tuning changes that must be made to the OS are to support applications such as Oracle, so that large amounts of shared memory can be allocated, and to support large numbers of semaphores and such. Other configuration changes in the OS are to support the addition of new hardware.

As mentioned at the beginning of this chapter, it is a good idea to monitor each of your virtual machines using Oracle Enterprise Manager Cloud Control. Treat each virtual machine as if it were a standalone machine running on actual hardware. Monitor the OS as well as the applications. If you see excessive paging or memory issues, it is time to add more memory to the virtual machine or reduce the amount of memory being used.

In addition to monitoring the virtual machine OS, it is also important to monitor the applications running within the virtual machine. This is especially true of databases and application servers. Oracle Enterprise Manager Cloud Control is an excellent way to monitor the entire stack.

Summary

This chapter covered the steps and tools necessary to monitor the Oracle VM server itself. Because the Oracle VM Server OS that is visible from a user's prospective is actually dom0, traditional methods of monitoring, such as using sar, top, and vmstat, don't work. This chapter covered some of the utilities that can be used to monitor the hypervisor and VM server as a whole, such as the **xm** tools. Tuning the actual I/O subsystem and network involve what I refer to as "hardware tuning," which involves allocating the right resources to the right need.

In the following chapters, the focus changes from the Oracle VM Server system to the virtual machines themselves. The next chapter starts by showing the process of creating templates that can then be used to create virtual machines.

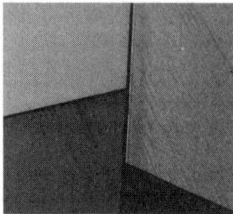

PART

IV

Installing and Configuring the VM Guest Additions

CHAPTER
17

Oracle VM Templates

 One of the primary advantages Oracle VM provides is the capability to create templates. Templates are preconfigured appliances that can range from a simple operating system installation to a complex application installation such as Oracle E-Business Suite. Not only can you easily create your own templates, but you can download many preconfigured and working Oracle VM templates from Oracle. These templates range from OS-only templates to entire E-Business Suite environments. The virtual machine templates allow for efficient and quick deployment of virtualized environments in a repeatable, reliable manner. Templates enable rapid provisioning of virtual machines in a private cloud environment, with each virtual machine based on a standard template. This standardization not only provides for a more agile environment, it also helps reduce the time to troubleshoot problems by leveraging a common set of paths and packages for all systems. This chapter covers the primary way of creating a template in Oracle VM 3.*x*—namely, creating the template manually.

> **NOTE**
> *Oracle VM templates are used for deployments in many of the Engineered Systems from Oracle, including the Oracle Database Appliance and the Private Cloud Appliance.*

Oracle VM Guest Additions

Oracle VM 3 introduced a new API, called Oracle VM Guest Additions, that allows you to make changes to the Linux operating system via the Oracle VM Manager during the first boot of the virtual machine. This capability is helpful when combined with Enterprise Manager to provide end-user self-service provisioning of VMs. This not only enables communications to the VM, it also allows the VM to communicate back to the Oracle VM Manager, providing the ability to directly integrate the guest operating systems with the virtualization layer and allowing you to integrate complex multi-VM deployments into your private cloud.

In addition to allowing the Oracle VM Manager to send messages directly to a virtual machine, Oracle VM Guest Additions enables the Oracle VM Manager to query an Oracle virtual machine, gather information (such as the SELinux state or the current IP address), and use the template configuration facility to automatically configure virtual machines as they are first started. This capability is the key to providing the automation expected in cloud architectures.

The Oracle VM Guest Additions API is available for Oracle Linux 5, Oracle Linux 6, Oracle Linux 7, Windows, and Solaris. Guest Additions for Solaris x86 is developed and supported by the Solaris team and does differ from the Linux implementation. For Linux systems, you can access Guest Additions from Oracle's public Yellowdog Updater Modified (yum) repository. To enable the Guest Additions add-ons, you need to edit the yum configuration file. Under an Oracle Linux 6 server using the public yum repository, this is managed by the file /etc/yum.repos.d/public-yum-ol6.repo. You need to edit the file and enable the **[public_ol6_addons]** stanza. To do this, edit the file and change **enabled=0** to **enabled=1**, which should look similar to the following:

```
[public_ol6_addons]
name=Oracle Linux $releasever Add ons ($basearch)
baseurl=http://public-yum.oracle.com/repo/OracleLinux/OL6/addons/$basearch/
gpgkey=file:///etc/pki/rpm-gpg/RPM-GPG-KEY-oracle
gpgcheck=1
enabled=1
```

Oracle VM Guest Additions includes several key components:

- **ovmd**   The Linux daemon that handles communication to and from the Oracle VM Manager, as well as the configuration and reconfiguration events.

- **xenstoreprovider**   A library that acts as an information storage space, facilitating communications between the guest and dom0. It passes key-clause paired messages to and from ovmd.

- **python-simplejson**   A simple and fast JSON library for Python.

- **ovm-template-config**   A collection of Oracle VM scripts used to configure an Oracle VM template during its initial boot.

- **libovmapi**   An automatically installed library used to communicate to the ovmapi kernel infrastructure.

- **libovmapi-devel**   An optional package required when creating additional extensions to **ovmd**.

- **ovmapi kernel module**   This kernel module provides the ability to communicate messages back and forth between the Oracle VM Server and the VM—and as such, between the Oracle VM Manager and the VM. Since the Unbreakable Enterprise Kernel version 2 (UEK2) (2.6.39), this kernel module has shipped with the kernel.

A number of packages support the communication between ovmd and the guest operating system. Each enables a specific family of supported capabilities. For many administrations, installing all the packages is recommended, but in some secure environments, only the needed packages can be installed.

A summary of these packages and their corresponding features is provided in Table 17-1.

Package	Oracle VM Configuration Family
ovm-template-config-authentication	Authentication management
ovm-template-config-datetime	Date-time configuration
ovm-template-config-firewall	Firewall configuration
ovm-template-config-network	Network configuration and discovery
ovm-template-config-selinux	SELinux management
ovm-template-config-ssh	SSH configuration and key management
ovm-template-config-system	System configuration, including hostname discovery
ovm-template-config-user	User Management API

TABLE 17-1.   *Packages for Configuring the Guest VM*

Creating Templates Manually

Creating a template manually is a very straightforward operation. You can start from the previously created VM, named *master*. This VM is based on Oracle Linux 6, but the steps are similar for Oracle Linux 5 and 7.

NOTE
Changes made to the template are performed in the VM and not directly against the OVMM or OVS.

First, install the Oracle VM Guest Additions by configuring yum to point to the public_ol6_addons repository hosted by Oracle. Edit the file /etc/yum.repos.d/public-yum-ol6.repo, edit the stanza called **[public_ol6_addons]**, and set the **enabled** flag to **1**. When you're finished, the stanza should look like this:

```
name=Oracle Linux $releasever Add ons ($basearch)
baseurl=http://public-yum.oracle.com/repo/OracleLinux/OL6/addons/$basearch/
gpgkey=file:///etc/pki/rpm-gpg/RPM-GPG-KEY-oracle
gpgcheck=1
enabled=0
```

Next, use yum to install the required packages with the following command:

```
yum -y  install ovmd xenstoreprovider python-simplejson ovm-template-config
```

This installs the packages and any missing dependencies. The command and its output should look similar to the following:

```
[root@master yum.repos.d]# yum -y  install ovmd xenstoreprovider python-simplejson
ovm-template-config
Loaded plugins: security
Setting up Install Process
public_ol6_UEKR3_latest                          | 1.2 kB     00:00
public_ol6_UEKR3_latest/primary                  |  19 MB     00:01
public_ol6_UEKR3_latest                                     505/505
public_ol6_addons                                | 1.2 kB     00:00
public_ol6_addons/primary                        | 104 kB     00:00
public_ol6_addons                                           348/348
public_ol6_latest                                | 1.4 kB     00:00
public_ol6_latest/primary                        |  53 MB     00:17
public_ol6_latest                                       32641/32641
Resolving Dependencies
--> Running transaction check
---> Package ovm-template-config.noarch 0:3.0-75.el6 will be installed
---> Package ovmd.x86_64 0:3.0-41.el6 will be installed
--> Processing Dependency: libovmapi >= 3.0 for package: ovmd-3.0-41.el6.x86_64
--> Processing Dependency: libovmapi.so()(64bit) for package:
      ovmd-3.0-41.el6.x86_64
---> Package python-simplejson.x86_64 0:2.0.9-3.1.el6 will be installed
---> Package xenstoreprovider.x86_64 0:3.0-11.el6 will be installed
--> Running transaction check
```

```
---> Package libovmapi.x86_64 0:3.0-6.el6 will be installed
--> Finished Dependency Resolution

Dependencies Resolved

================================================================================
Package                 Arch        Version            Repository        Size
================================================================================
Installing:
 ovm-template-config     noarch      3.0-75.el6         public_ol6_addons  62 k
 ovmd                    x86_64      3.0-41.el6         public_ol6_addons  32 k
 python-simplejson       x86_64      2.0.9-3.1.el6      public_ol6_latest 126 k
 xenstoreprovider        x86_64      3.0-11.el6         public_ol6_addons  24 k
Installing for dependencies:
 libovmapi               x86_64      3.0-6.el6          public_ol6_addons  19 k

Transaction Summary
================================================================================
Install       5 Package(s)

Total download size: 263 k
Installed size: 748 k
Downloading Packages:
(1/5): libovmapi-3.0-6.el6.x86_64.rpm                        |  19 kB      00:00
(2/5): ovm-template-config-3.0-75.el6.noarch.rpm             |  62 kB      00:00
(3/5): ovmd-3.0-41.el6.x86_64.rpm                            |  32 kB      00:00
(4/5): python-simplejson-2.0.9-3.1.el6.x86_64.rpm            | 126 kB      00:00
(5/5): xenstoreprovider-3.0-11.el6.x86_64.rpm                |  24 kB      00:00
--------------------------------------------------------------------------------
Total                                       224 kB/s | 263 kB     00:01
warning: rpmts_HdrFromFdno: Header V3 RSA/SHA256 Signature, key ID ec551f03: NOKEY
Retrieving key from file:///etc/pki/rpm-gpg/RPM-GPG-KEY-oracle
Importing GPG key 0xEC551F03:
 Userid : Oracle OSS group (Open Source Software group) <build@oss.oracle.com>
 Package: 6:oraclelinux-release-6Server-6.0.2.x86_64
     (@anaconda-OracleLinuxServer-201507280245.x86_64/6.6)
 From   : /etc/pki/rpm-gpg/RPM-GPG-KEY-oracle
Running rpm_check_debug
Running Transaction Test
Transaction Test Succeeded
Running Transaction
  Installing : libovmapi-3.0-6.el6.x86_64                            1/5
  Installing : ovm-template-config-3.0-75.el6.noarch                 2/5
  Installing : ovmd-3.0-41.el6.x86_64                                3/5
  Installing : xenstoreprovider-3.0-11.el6.x86_64                    4/5
  Installing : python-simplejson-2.0.9-3.1.el6.x86_64                5/5
  Verifying  : ovmd-3.0-41.el6.x86_64                                1/5
  Verifying  : python-simplejson-2.0.9-3.1.el6.x86_64                2/5
  Verifying  : ovm-template-config-3.0-75.el6.noarch                 3/5
  Verifying  : libovmapi-3.0-6.el6.x86_64                            4/5
  Verifying  : xenstoreprovider-3.0-11.el6.x86_64                    5/5
```

```
Installed:
  ovm-template-config.noarch 0:3.0-75.el6  ovmd.x86_64 0:3.0-41.el6
  python-simplejson.x86_64 0:2.0.9-3.1.el6  xenstoreprovider.x86_64 0:3.0-11.el6

Dependency Installed:
  libovmapi.x86_64 0:3.0-6.el6

Complete!
```

Once you have installed the required packages, you can begin installing each of the optional packages. Installing all the packages is a simple process, and it gives you the option to leverage each add-on in the future without having to rebuild the template. To install all the add-ons, simply run yum again and use a wildcard to install all the ovm-template-config packages. The command and its results should look similar to the following:

```
[root@master yum.repos.d]# yum -y install ovm-template-config-*
Loaded plugins: security
Setting up Install Process
Package ovm-template-config-3.0-75.el6.noarch already installed and latest version
Resolving Dependencies
--> Running transaction check
---> Package ovm-template-config-authentication.noarch 0:3.0-75.el6 will be installed
---> Package ovm-template-config-datetime.noarch 0:3.0-75.el6 will be installed
---> Package ovm-template-config-firewall.noarch 0:3.0-75.el6 will be installed
---> Package ovm-template-config-network.noarch 0:3.0-75.el6 will be installed
---> Package ovm-template-config-selinux.noarch 0:3.0-75.el6 will be installed
---> Package ovm-template-config-ssh.noarch 0:3.0-75.el6 will be installed
---> Package ovm-template-config-system.noarch 0:3.0-75.el6 will be installed
---> Package ovm-template-config-user.noarch 0:3.0-75.el6 will be installed
--> Finished Dependency Resolution

Dependencies Resolved

================================================================================
 Package                    Arch      Version      Repository        Size
================================================================================
Installing:
 ovm-template-config-auth      noarch   3.0-75.el6   public_ol6_addons  7 k
 ovm-template-config-datetime  noarch   3.0-75.el6   public_ol6_addons  18 k
 ovm-template-config-firewall  noarch   3.0-75.el6   public_ol6_addons  17 k
 ovm-template-config-network   noarch   3.0-75.el6   public_ol6_addons  18 k
 ovm-template-config-selinux   noarch   3.0-75.el6   public_ol6_addons  17 k
 ovm-template-config-ssh       noarch   3.0-75.el6   public_ol6_addons  18 k
 ovm-template-config-system    noarch   3.0-75.el6   public_ol6_addons  17 k
 ovm-template-config-user      noarch   3.0-75.el6   public_ol6_addons  18 k

Transaction Summary
================================================================================
Install       8 Package(s)

Total download size: 140 k
Installed size: 38 k
Downloading Packages:
(1/8): ovm-template-config-authentication-3.0-75.el6.noarch.rpm |17 kB 00:00 (2/8):
```

```
           ovm-template-config-datetime-3.0-75.el6.noarch.rpm         |18 kB 00:00
(3/8):  ovm-template-config-firewall-3.0-75.el6.noarch.rpm           |17 kB 00:00
(4/8):  ovm-template-config-network-3.0-75.el6.noarch.rpm            |18 kB 00:00
(5/8):  ovm-template-config-selinux-3.0-75.el6.noarch.rpm            |17 kB 00:00
(6/8):  ovm-template-config-ssh-3.0-75.el6.noarch.rpm                |18 kB 00:00
(7/8):  ovm-template-config-system-3.0-75.el6.noarch.rpm             |17 kB 00:00
(8/8):  ovm-template-config-user-3.0-75.el6.noarch.rpm               |18 kB 00:00
-------------------------------------------------------------------------------
Total                                    65 kB/s | 140 kB      00:02
Running rpm_check_debug
Running Transaction Test
Transaction Test Succeeded
Running Transaction
  Installing : ovm-template-config-network-3.0-75.el6.noarch            1/8
  Installing : ovm-template-config-authentication-3.0-75.el6.noarch     2/8
  Installing : ovm-template-config-selinux-3.0-75.el6.noarch            3/8
  Installing : ovm-template-config-ssh-3.0-75.el6.noarch                4/8
  Installing : ovm-template-config-datetime-3.0-75.el6.noarch           5/8
  Installing : ovm-template-config-firewall-3.0-75.el6.noarch           6/8
  Installing : ovm-template-config-system-3.0-75.el6.noarch             7/8
  Installing : ovm-template-config-user-3.0-75.el6.noarch               8/8
  Verifying  : ovm-template-config-user-3.0-75.el6.noarch               1/8
  Verifying  : ovm-template-config-system-3.0-75.el6.noarch             2/8
  Verifying  : ovm-template-config-firewall-3.0-75.el6.noarch           3/8
  Verifying  : ovm-template-config-datetime-3.0-75.el6.noarch           4/8
  Verifying  : ovm-template-config-ssh-3.0-75.el6.noarch                5/8
  Verifying  : ovm-template-config-selinux-3.0-75.el6.noarch            6/8
  Verifying  : ovm-template-config-authentication-3.0-75.el6.noarch     7/8
  Verifying  : ovm-template-config-network-3.0-75.el6.noarch            8/8

Installed:
ovm-template-config-authentication.noarch 0:3.0-75.el6
ovm-template-config-datetime.noarch 0:3.0-75.el6
ovm-template-config-firewall.noarch 0:3.0-75.el6
ovm-template-config-network.noarch 0:3.0-75.el6
ovm-template-config-selinux.noarch 0:3.0-75.el6
ovm-template-config-ssh.noarch 0:3.0-75.el6
ovm-template-config-system.noarch 0:3.0-75.el6
ovm-template-config-user.noarch 0:3.0-75.el6

Complete!
```

Next, enable the ovmd daemon to start at boot. This is done with the **chkconfig** command, as shown next. If ovmd is not running at boot, the Oracle VM Manager will be unable to communicate with the virtual machine.

```
[root@master yum.repos.d]# chkconfig ovmd on
```

To verify when the daemon will start, using **chkconfig –level**. The **chkconfig** command shows the initial state for any service when the operating system changes to the target level. In this case, the ovmd daemon is set to run at the init states 2, 3, 4, and 5.

```
[root@master yum.repos.d]# chkconfig --list  ovmd
ovmd              0:off   1:off   2:on    3:on    4:on    5:on    6:off
```

Next, manually start the daemon and then check to verify that it is running using the command **/etc/init.d/ovmd status**. Often when new templates are not communicating with the Oracle VM Manager, it is because the ovmd is not set to start at reboot.

```
[root@master yum.repos.d]#  /etc/init.d/ovmd start
Starting OVM guest daemon:                          [  OK  ]
[root@master yum.repos.d]#  /etc/init.d/ovmd status
ovmd (pid  2204) is running...
```

Once the daemon is running, more information about the VM will be visible in Oracle VM Manager. To verify that the Oracle VM Manager is communicating with a virtual machine, look at the Networks tab in Oracle VM Manager to see the IP address for the VM, as shown in Figure 17-1. If an IP address is not visible, you need to verify that ovmd is running.

Before the VM can be cloned to a template, one critical task remains: the VM needs to be cleaned up in preparation for cloning. Because these commands will effectively wipe the network configuration, you must run them from the VM console.

CAUTION
It is recommended that you run the following commands from the console on the virtual machine. Part of the process will deconfigure the network, disabling remote access to the virtual machine.

The first command used, **ovmd –s cleanup**, will wipe the configuration:

```
[root@master ~]# ovmd -s cleanup
```

The next command enables ovmd to run the initialization scripts on the next boot:

```
[root@master ~]# service ovmd enable-initial-config
```

Finally, you need to shut down the VM before cloning it:

```
[root@master ~]# shutdown -h now
```

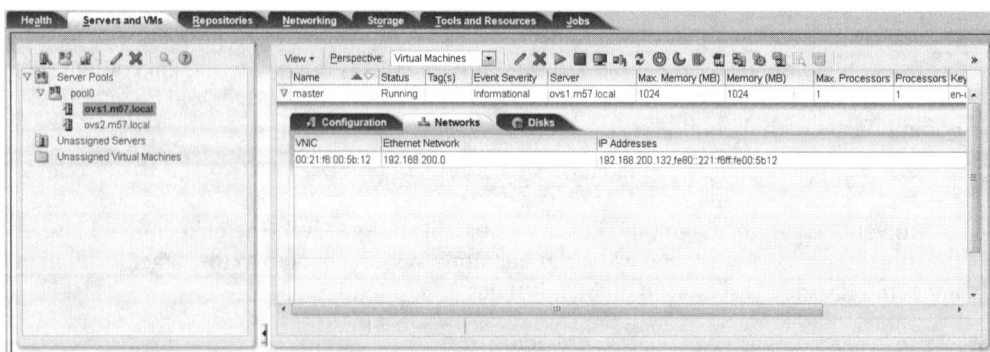

FIGURE 17-1. *VM network summary*

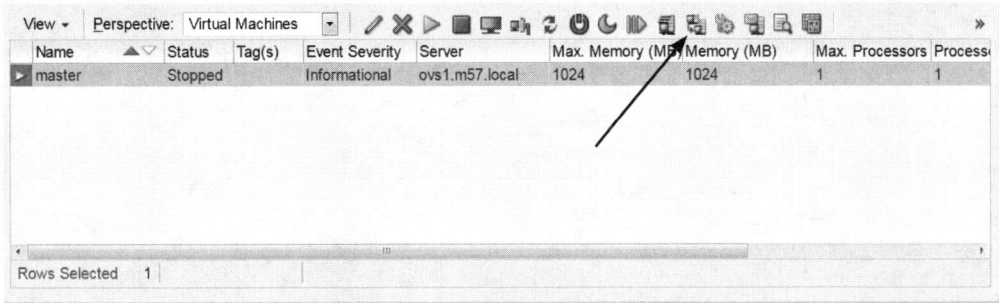

FIGURE 17-2.   *Clone VM*

Once the VM is down in Oracle VM Manager, it can be cloned to a template for reuse. To do this, log into the Oracle VM Manager. Then, under the Servers and VMs tab, drill down to the VM. While the VM is highlighted, click the Clone button to start the wizard, as shown in Figure 17-2.

When the wizard starts, several options are available. Not only can you clone a VM to a template, but you can also use the wizard to move the VM from one repository to another. In this case, we'll simply clone the VM to a template, as shown in Figure 17-3.

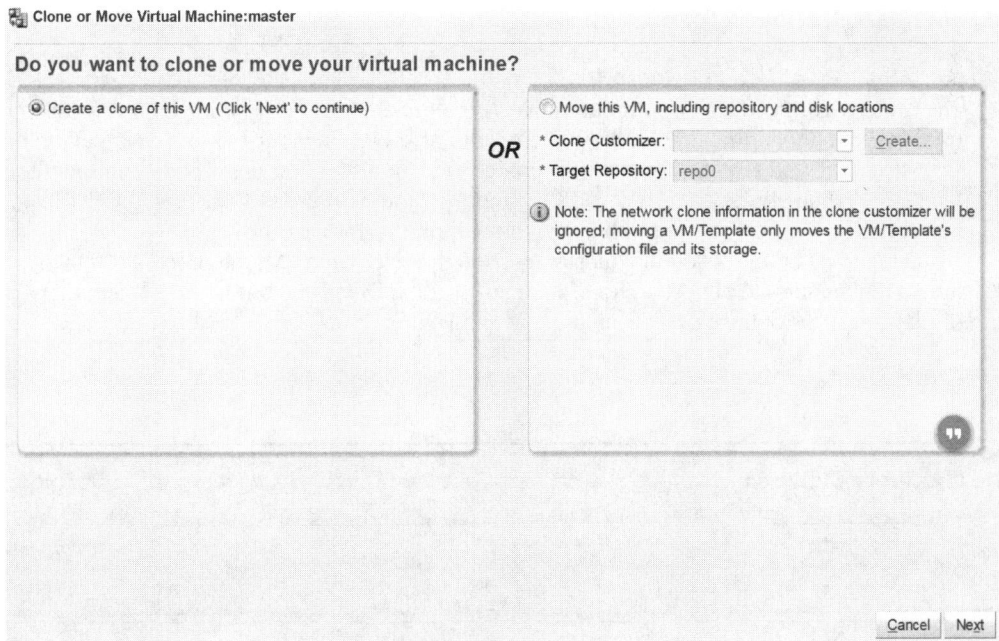

FIGURE 17-3.   *Clone VM—Step 1*

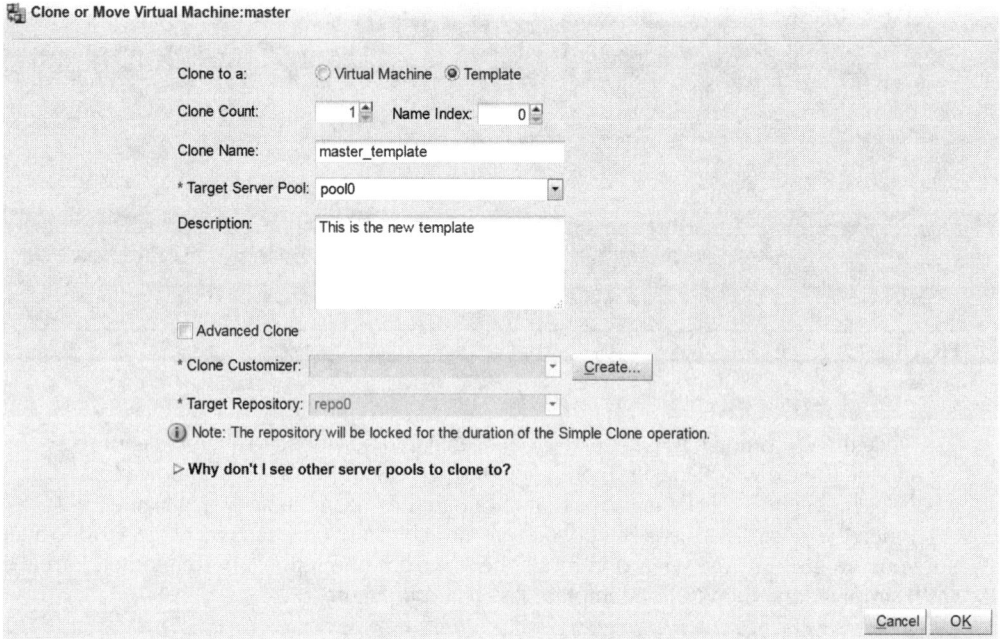

FIGURE 17-4. *Clone VM—Step 2*

The same wizard can also be used to move virtual machines to new storage. In this case, it will be used to clone the virtual machines to a template, as shown in Figure 17-4. Click Next to continue.

Make sure you select Clone to a Template. You can also add a descriptive comment for the template. When you're done, click OK to start the cloning process. The wizard will close, and you should now see a running job in the Job Summary panel, as shown in Figure 17-5.

Depending on the speed of your storage, and the size of the VM, the process can take anywhere from a few minutes to almost an hour. You can click the Details button in the Job Summary panel to display the status of the clone event, as shown in Figure 17-6.

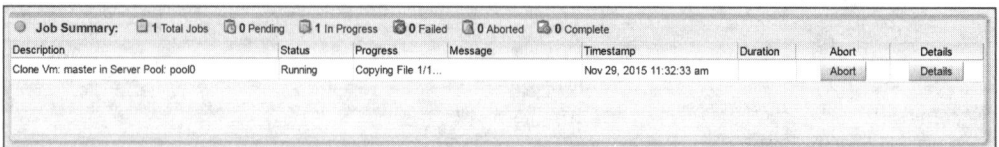

FIGURE 17-5. *Clone VM job*

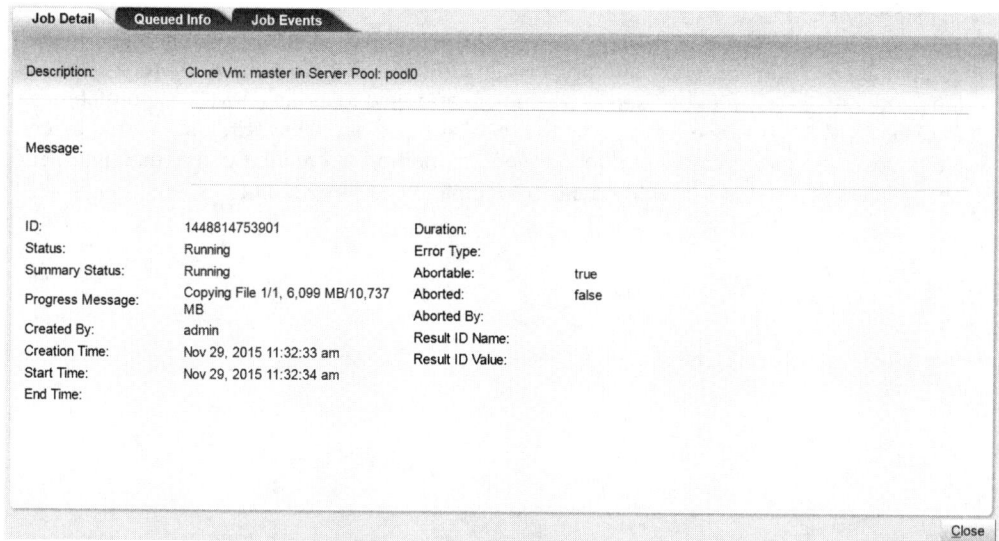

Job Detail Queued Info Job Events

Description: Clone Vm: master in Server Pool: pool0

Message:

ID:	1448814753901	Duration:	
Status:	Running	Error Type:	
Summary Status:	Running	Abortable:	true
Progress Message:	Copying File 1/1, 6,099 MB/10,737 MB	Aborted:	false
Created By:	admin	Aborted By:	
Creation Time:	Nov 29, 2015 11:32:33 am	Result ID Name:	
Start Time:	Nov 29, 2015 11:32:34 am	Result ID Value:	
End Time:			

Close

FIGURE 17-6.   *Clone VM job info*

Once the job is complete, move to the Repositories tab and drill down into the repository where the template was created to see that the template is now available for VMs, as shown in Figure 17-7.

NOTE
Once the template has been created, you can reuse it as many times as necessary, easily creating hundreds of identical virtual machines in just hours. The only limitation is the speed of the attached storage array.

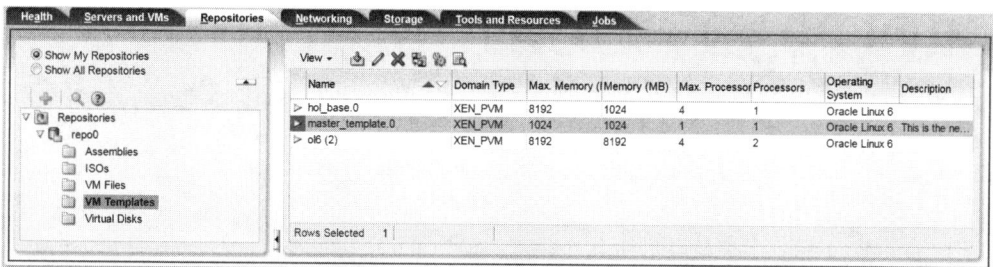

FIGURE 17-7.   *Clone VM success*

Summary

This chapter showed you how to create a template with OVMD, thus enabling automated configuration of the VM when building private clouds. You learned how to prepare the Oracle Linux operating system to be used as a template and how to clone a VM to a template. The process in Oracle VM 3 is a very effective way to create and use templates. Creating virtual machines from templates is the most reliable and recommended method of creating virtual machines. The next chapter covers just that—how to create virtual machines using templates.

CHAPTER
18

Creating Virtual Machines
Using Templates

N ow we come to the crux of cloud computing: the creation of the guest virtual machine. This is the process through which the target host operating system will run using resources that have been defined and presented to the Oracle VM infrastructure and application systems, databases, and any program that would otherwise execute on bare-metal but is now executing in the virtual machine. With rare exception, anything that runs in the bare-metal machine environment can run without modifications in the virtual machine environment.

The following sections present the process of creating a virtual machine in the Oracle VM infrastructure. Other sections of this book covered processes where the necessary resources are configured and presented, including network and storage resources. As a prerequisite to creating virtual machines, the network and storage resources must be available and understood.

The process of importing templates is slightly different from importing appliances. Most notable are the "undefined networks" imported along with templates. This can be addressed as follows:

1. Remove any undefined networks from the templates.

2. Associate the correct networks with the templates.

The "undefined network" needs to be deleted from the Networking section of Oracle VM Manager. With respect to importing and preparing Oracle VM appliances, this is the newer and now preferred construct for using pre-built virtual machines. The process differs slightly from templates because these will not come based on OVM 2 xenbrX bridge names.

Oracle VM Template or Appliance as a VM Source

The Oracle VM creation process is the same whether it's done from an imported template or an imported appliance. The most common (and overall simplest) method of creating a virtual machine is to use a template or virtual appliance. Oracle Corporation provides numerous Oracle VM templates and appliances that can be downloaded from the eDelivery site edelivery.oracle.com. A template can also be generated from an existing virtual machine using the Oracle VM Manager GUI. Alternatively, a virtual machine can be created manually by cloning another virtual machine or by installing the target operating system from an ISO using the same process as if you were installing the operating system on a bare-metal machine. The manual process of creating a virtual machine is covered in the next chapter.

The process of creating a virtual machine from a template can be summarized as follows:

1. Import the template into a storage repository (this process is detailed later in this chapter in "Importing a Template").

2. Present the necessary storage LUN(s) if using physical disks for the virtual machine boot disk.

3. Add one or more networks (the process of creating Oracle VM networks is detailed in the "Network Management" section of this chapter).

4. Create the template clone customizer. The clone customizer is particularly useful to ensure that the storage components associated with the Oracle VM (the ISOs, templates, appliances, vm.cfg, and virtual disks) are kept is the same place, especially since NFS-based repositories can be shared across server pools.

5. Clone the template to a virtual machine.

Understanding the Resources

The Oracle VM Manager operations can be performed using the web-based graphical user interface (GUI) or the command-line interface (CLI), which can be launched from any machine with SSH connectivity to the machine running the VM manager software. For more information about the Oracle CLI-based operations, refer to the VM manager CLI documentation. The process of creating a virtual machine is presented in this document through the use of the web-based GUI.

Network Management

The Oracle VM network environment supports detailed Layer 2 and Layer 3 switching and routing and advanced configurations, and it's fully virtualized. This includes VLAN definitions and support as well as other advanced network concepts. Figure 18-1 shows the Networking tab of the Oracle VM Manager GUI and reflects various networks defined for the network channels used by the Oracle VM operations. Note that any detailed network administration tasks will be discussed in a separate section and/or will reference Oracle VM networking documentation. Also, although a single virtual machine network may be defined and assigned to the Oracle VM for virtual machine communications, the best practice recommendation is to dedicate network processes based on the following specific types of traffic (that is, each of the following should be on a physically separate and dedicated network).

- **Cluster Heartbeat** The heartbeat network is required for clustered VM servers in the server pool and is used as the "interconnect" between the servers. It should have extremely low latency and near-zero dropped packets. Heartbeat operations have an extremely low tolerance. Virtually any degradation to the communications over the heartbeat network will cause VM server eviction or fencing, resulting in unplanned guest VM migrations to the remaining operating VM servers.

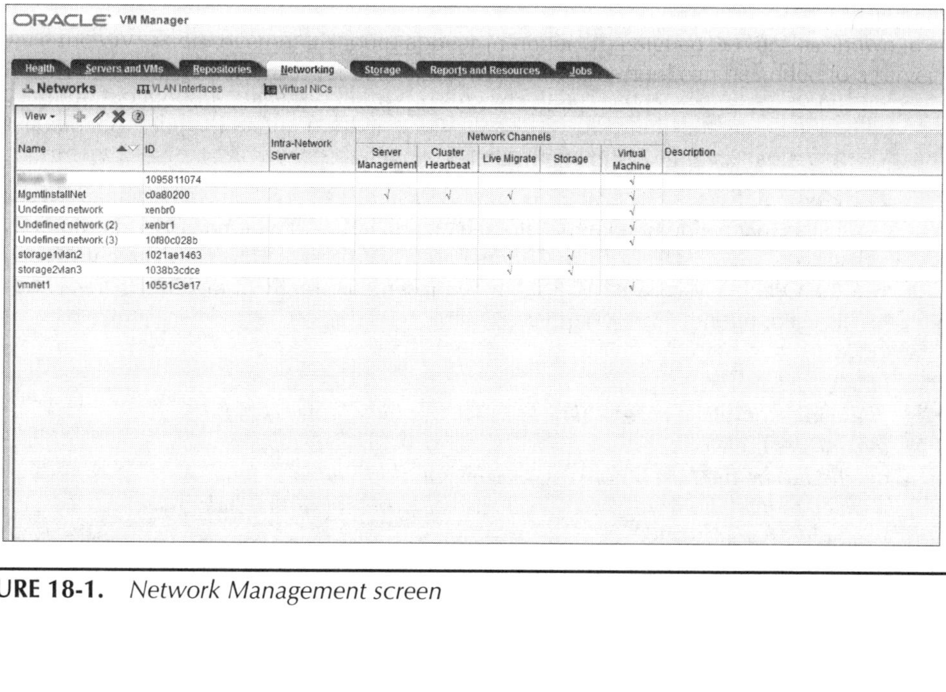

ORACLE VM Manager

Health | Servers and VMs | Repositories | Networking | Storage | Reports and Resources | Jobs

Networks | VLAN Interfaces | Virtual NICs

View ▾

Name	ID	Intra-Network Server	Network Channels					Description
			Server Management	Cluster Heartbeat	Live Migrate	Storage	Virtual Machine	
	1095811074						√	
MgmtInstallNet	c0a80200		√	√	√		√	
Undefined network	xenbr0						√	
Undefined network (2)	xenbr1						√	
Undefined network (3)	10f80c028b						√	
storage1vlan2	1021ae1463				√	√		
storage2vlan3	1038b3cdce				√	√		
vmnet1	10551c3e17						√	

FIGURE 18-1. *Network Management screen*

■ **Virtual Machine** The guest VM network is used for normal network communications between guest VMs, whether running on a given VM server or across VM servers, either in the same server pool or across server pools. The Virtual Machine checkbox also instructs OVM to create a Xen bridge on the OVM servers to allow VMs to connect to the rest of the world through the network. This virtual network is what the guest VMs will use for their access to resources in the Oracle VM infrastructure, resources across the enterprise, or Internet-based resources.

■ **Server Management, Live Migrate, and Storage** These network services are described in detail in the Oracle documentation, but it suffices to say the recommended best practice is to dedicate a physical network for each of these, depending on the level of activity required across the enterprise. If the resources are available, each physical network should be configured to use a bonded interface of two or more network interface cards.

Combining Server Management and Heartbeat Networks
Both server management and cluster heartbeat network channels are very lightweight and are frequently combined without problem. Additionally, the server management and cluster heartbeat network channels can be assigned to a different VLAN/subnet for each server pool in cases where more than two or three different server pools are going to be controlled by a single OVM Manager.

Storage Management

As with network operations, details of storage management can be found in the Oracle documentation. Here, we discuss the tasks related to guest VMs that are deployed from templates or used as the source to create a template. In general, two types of disks are associated with guest virtual machines and templates:

■ **Virtual disks** Virtual disks are sparse files that are contained in Oracle VM storage repositories for use by Oracle VM guests. Virtual disks are optional but pretty common; they are created and used by Oracle VM guests to contain the guest operating system or any other data the VM owner requires.

■ **Physical disks** Physical disks can be local disks found on each Oracle VM server or LUNs that reside on external storage arrays. LUNs can be presented to the Oracle VM servers using iSCSI or Fibre Channel and then presented to the Oracle VM guests through the Oracle VM servers. LUNs can be presented directly to the Oracle VM guests if iSCSI is used, but not Fibre Channel.

NOTE
The choice of which type of disk to use and which protocol is best depends entirely on requirements. The "best" storage is what is deemed to be the best fit for your needs; you don't need to limit yourself to just one storage protocol—use all protocols if that helps you achieve your goals.

Repository-Based Storage

To be supported in a production capacity, virtual machines must be deployed using physical disk definitions for disks used by database management systems to contain data. Virtual disks used to contain the guest operating system are fully supported in production. With that said, virtual disk definitions provide more rapid deployment of guest virtual machines because the disks do not need to be pre-allocated and can be used from storage assigned to the repository "on the fly." Naturally, care must be taken to ensure that storage is available for the virtual machine to be deployed from the template, and this can be determined by examining the template storage requirement on the Disk tab of the expanded template or the expanded source guest VM from which the template was created.

Figure 18-2 shows the information screen of an Oracle VM repository where the information of available storage for use by virtual disks can be quickly gleaned.

Oracle VM Repository

The Oracle VM repository is based on storage allocated on a file server or a storage area network (SAN). In either case, repository-based storage is used for housing guest VMs, configuration files, ISO files, templates, and so on. Virtual disk storage is also carved out of the storage allocated to the repository.

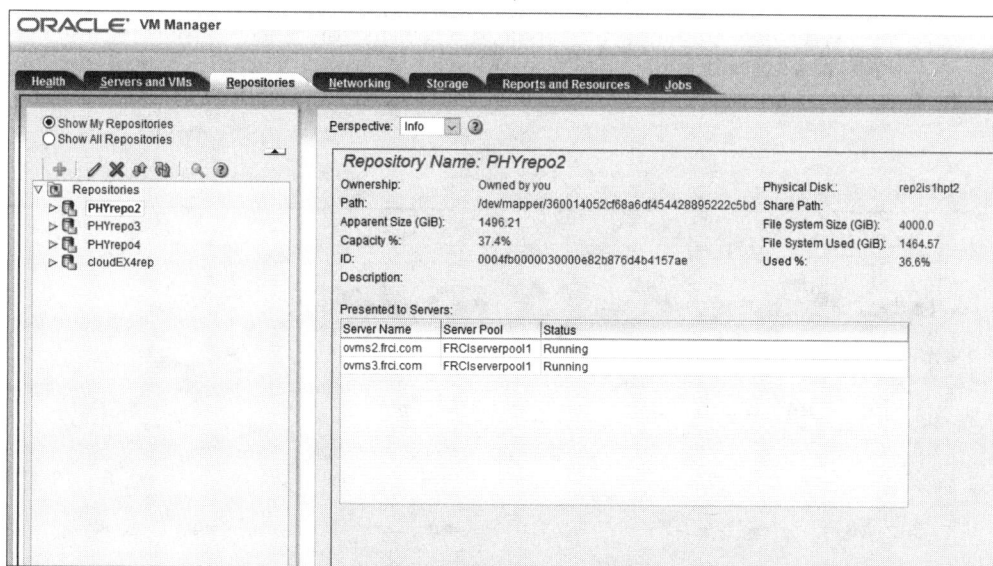

FIGURE 18-2. *Repository management screen*

Physical Disk-Based Storage

Even though the name implies a physical disk allocation, the physical disk definition merely indicates a disk allocation with a definition that is closer to an actual physical allocation with physical beginning and ending points (that is, the LUN beginning and ending blocks, which are defined at the hardware layer of the storage source). Care is taken here not to refer to the storage source as network-attached storage because the storage source may be locally attached disks that are local to the VM server running the guest VMs. Note, however, that if local storage (that is, local to the VM server) is used for a particular VM, then it follows that guest VMs cannot run on any other VM server and must always execute on the VM server where the local storage is defined. This means that in the event of any migrations, the guest VM will not be able to run except on the VM server where the storage physically resides.

Figure 18-3 shows the storage management screen with a SAN logical volume that has been allocated for use by a repository. Similarly, a file server could have been used to allocate file system–based files for use by the repository. In either case, the storage allocated for the repository is destined to contain the same types of files—ISO files, guest VM virtual disks, assemblies, and so on.

Oracle VM Server Resources

This section provides an overview of the VM server resources used by guest virtual machines.

Processors

The number of processors available to guest virtual machines can theoretically exceed the number of processors (or processor cores) available on the VM server. However, if the actual number of processors required by the guest virtual machines is larger than the number of physical processors available on the VM server hosting the virtual machines, there is a risk the virtual machines will cause the VM server to crash or at the very least be evicted (or "fenced") from the cluster or server pool where the VM server is running. In the event a VM server is fenced, all virtual machines (even the ones that are not currently running) will be migrated to the remaining VM servers.

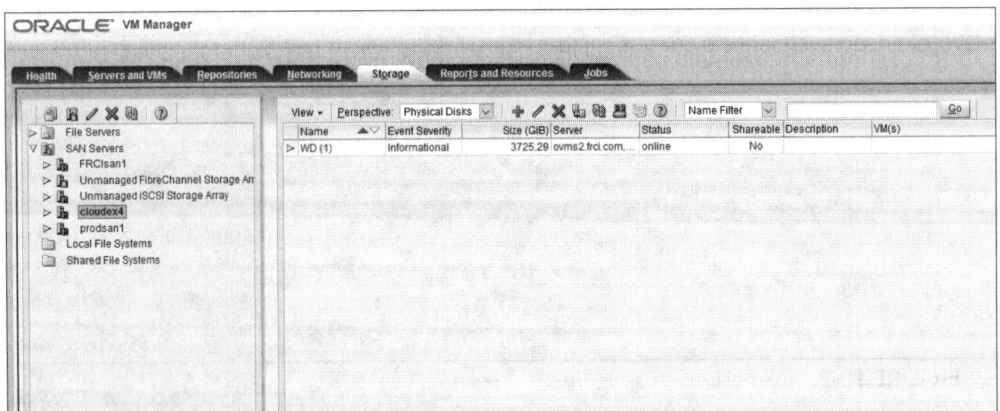

FIGURE 18-3. *Storage management screen*

Memory

Just like the number of processors available to guest virtual machines, the amount of memory allocated to guest virtual machines can theoretically exceed the amount of memory available on a given VM server. But again, as with processor availability, if the amount of memory required by active guest virtual machines exceeds the physical memory available on a VM server, node eviction/fencing can occur. With processor and memory limits in mind, as a general rule, the number of processors and the amount of memory allocated to the virtual machines should be lower than the actual physical number of processors and the physical amount of memory available. Even though this may seem to be a commonsense statement, it is often misunderstood that virtualization does not magically allow processor or memory requirements to exceed physical availability.

VM Server Storage

VM server-based storage is a very tricky thing. It can be used for virtual disk or physical disk definitions used by templates, repositories, and/or virtual machines; however, it restricts the associated operations of the virtual machines to be limited to working only on the VM server that owns the storage. In the past, this was a crippling limitation. With the release of OVM 3.4, a very important feature has been included called "live migration." OVM 3.4 incorporates *storage live migration,* which allows for the live migration of VMs and their storage from the local disk on one OVM server to the local disk on another OVM server. For the purposes of this chapter, all references to storage allocated to virtual or physical disks will be with respect to shared network-based storage—whether it's storage area network, network attached storage, network file systems, or file servers—and this shared storage is available to all the VM servers in the server pool where the virtual machines will be operating.

Using a Template or Appliance to Create an Oracle VM

Although the template and appliance creation processes are outside the scope of this chapter, for reference purposes, the steps are listed here. Depending on the source of the template or appliance, it is a good idea to become familiar with the configuration items within its definition. Figure 18-4 shows an example of an expanded template in the repository management screen. Each of the primary candidate configuration items can be selected from the Network and Disk tabs. To edit a templates configuration, highlight the template and select the Edit icon (the pencil in the menu bar), as shown in Figure 18-5.

There are two methods for creating a template: you can clone a virtual machine to a template or you can clone a template to another template. In either case, you must complete the previous steps to allocate storage and configure a network for each template. The template customizer is a construct that is used during the cloning process to specify the specific storage and network components that will be incorporated into the template. The customizer is also used when deploying a virtual machine from a template and/or migrating templates, virtual machines, and so on, from one repository to another and the general processes are described here.

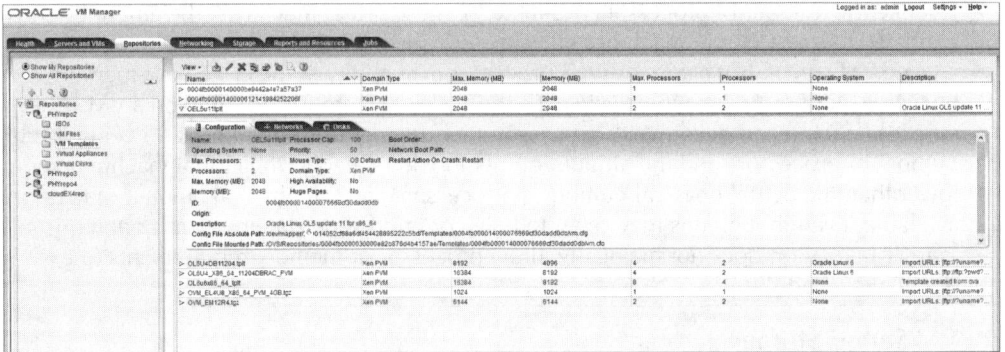

FIGURE 18-4. *Repository-based source template*

Importing a Template

The following process describes template creation using a .tar file as the source:

1. Place the .tar file in a directory accessible to the HTTP or FTP service.

   a. Determine the stub or parent directory structure for the HTTP or FTP service.

   b. Create a dedicated directory where the .tar file will reside (at least one directory name must be specified during the import operation).

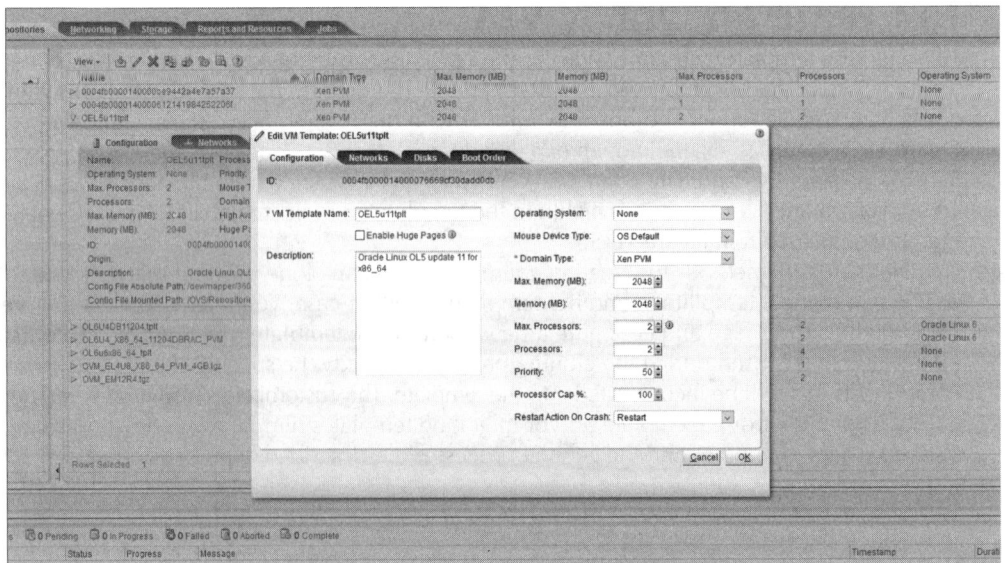

FIGURE 18-5. *Template edit screen*

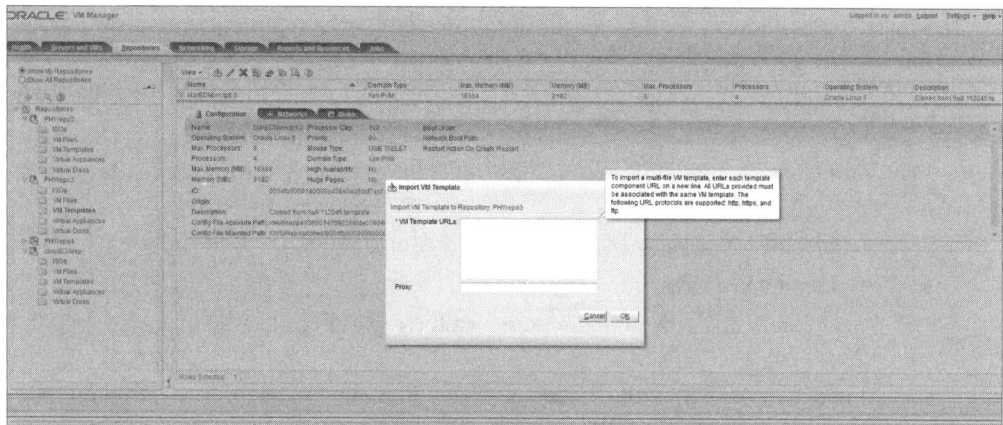

FIGURE 18-6. *Template import dialog*

2. Verify the target repository has sufficient resources to support the import operation.

   a. Increase the storage for the repository or create a new repository.

   b. Present the repository to the administration VM server.

   c. Designate the refresh VM server.

   d. Refresh the Oracle VM storage and repository.

3. Begin the import operation using the HTTP or FTP service. The command will look similar to the following (Figure 18-6 shows an example of the dialog used to input this information):

```
ftp://uname:pwd@192.168.2.61/tplts/OVM_MADB_1of2.tgz,
ftp://uname:pwd@192.168.2.61/tplts/OVM_MADB_2of2.tgz
```

where:

   ■ **uname:pwd** is the username and password of an account that has access to the .tar file.

   ■ **@192.168.2.61** is the IP address or fully qualified server name where the HTTP or FTP service is running and the file is located.

   ■ **/tplts/OVM_MADB_1of2.tgz** is the path to the .tar file that is a directory subordinate to the HTTP or FTP default service directory. (Note that the parent folders /var/http/www and /var/ftp/pub are not specified.)

Exporting an Oracle VM to an Appliance

The process of exporting an Oracle VM appliance is slightly different from that of an Oracle VM template with respect to the use of the appliance: Oracle VMs that are exported to an appliance may be *directly used in other VirtualBox and VMware environments!* This is an important topic because it allows customers to export images for use in those environments without any intervening steps.

Exporting an Oracle VM to an appliance is also the recommended and preferred practice.

Exporting a Template

The following process describes .tar file creation using a VM template as the source. Although this process is not required in order to create a virtual machine from a template, the steps are provided here in support of moving a template from one Oracle VM infrastructure installation to another.

1. Verify that the target file system has sufficient resources to support the .tar file creation operation.

   a. Identify VM physical disk storage and configuration file size.

   b. Identify VM virtual disk storage size.

2. Locate the virtual machine directories in the repository file system shared with the VM servers.

   The location of the virtual machine–related files can be determined based on the repository file system where the virtual machine definition is located. For more information about the file system structure, refer to the Oracle VM Manager Administration Guide.

3. Use the UNIX tar command create the .tar file using compression. The contents of the .tar file will include the following:

   ■ All virtual machine virtual disks

   ■ All virtual machine physical disks

   ■ The virtual machine configuration file

   ■ Any other files stored in the virtual machine repository directory

The file size maximum needed for a file transfer can be determined using one or more of the following criteria:

   ■ File transfer across the Internet
   ■ File transfer across the local network
   ■ File transfer during the import process

If the virtual machine being exported exceeds the predetermined amount, the exported .tar file may need to be broken up into two or more files.

Oracle Corporation recently released additional information regarding the creation of template files. This information is captured in the backup and recovery strategy of an Oracle VM infrastructure. Specifically, the .tar file can be created by using the repository export feature and a shell script that is passed the unique identifier of the VM guest. For more information, refer to the Oracle documentation regarding repository exports.

Creating a Virtual Machine from a Template

The following describes the virtual machine creation process using a template that was imported as described in the "Importing a Template" section of this chapter:

1. Import the template as described in the "Importing a Template" section of this chapter.

2. Identify the resource requirements (storage and network).

3. Allocate and configure resources as required.

4. Create a virtual machine clone customizer using the resource requirements identified and allocated. Figures 18-7 through 18-10 show the basic progression within the VM Manager GUI when a clone customizer is created for a given template that is about to be used to generate a guest VM. To add a clone customizer to a given template, highlight the template, select the Manage Customizers icon from the menu bar, and then click the Add Customizer icon (the big green plus sign) from the Manage Clone Customizers for VM dialog.

   Note that in the storage management clone customizer screen, after you select the target storage type (virtual or physical disk), the search icon (the magnifying glass) will reveal only available storage objects (that is, predefined storage) available for use.

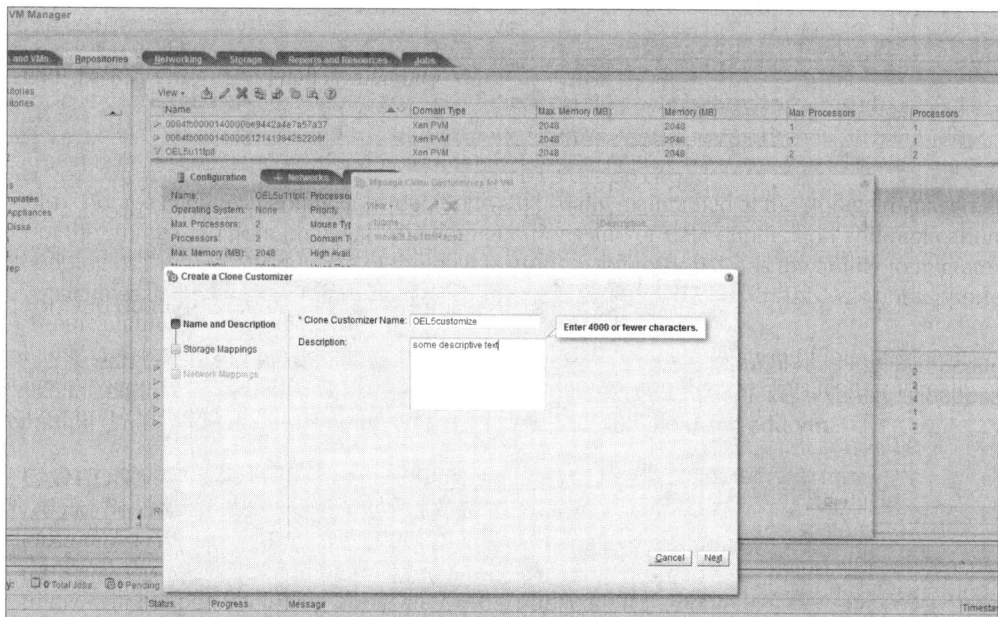

FIGURE 18-7. *Initial clone customizer screen*

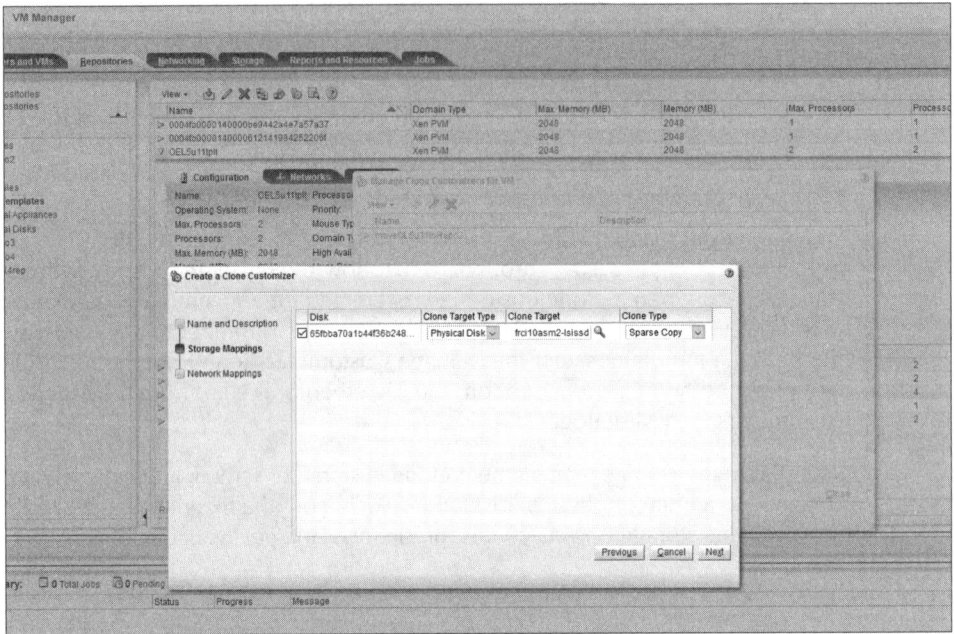

FIGURE 18-8. *Storage Mappings clone customizer screen*

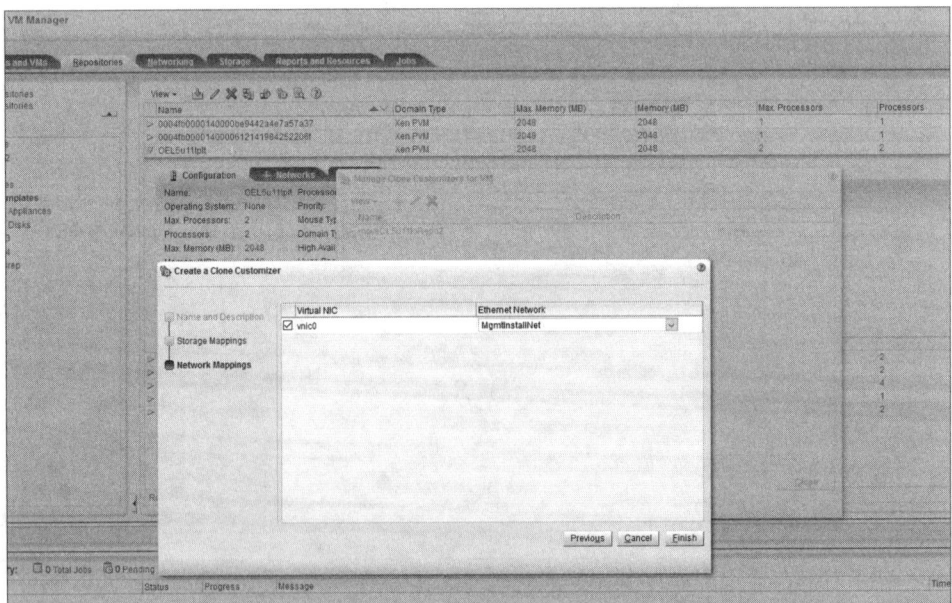

FIGURE 18-9. *Network Mappings clone customizer screen*

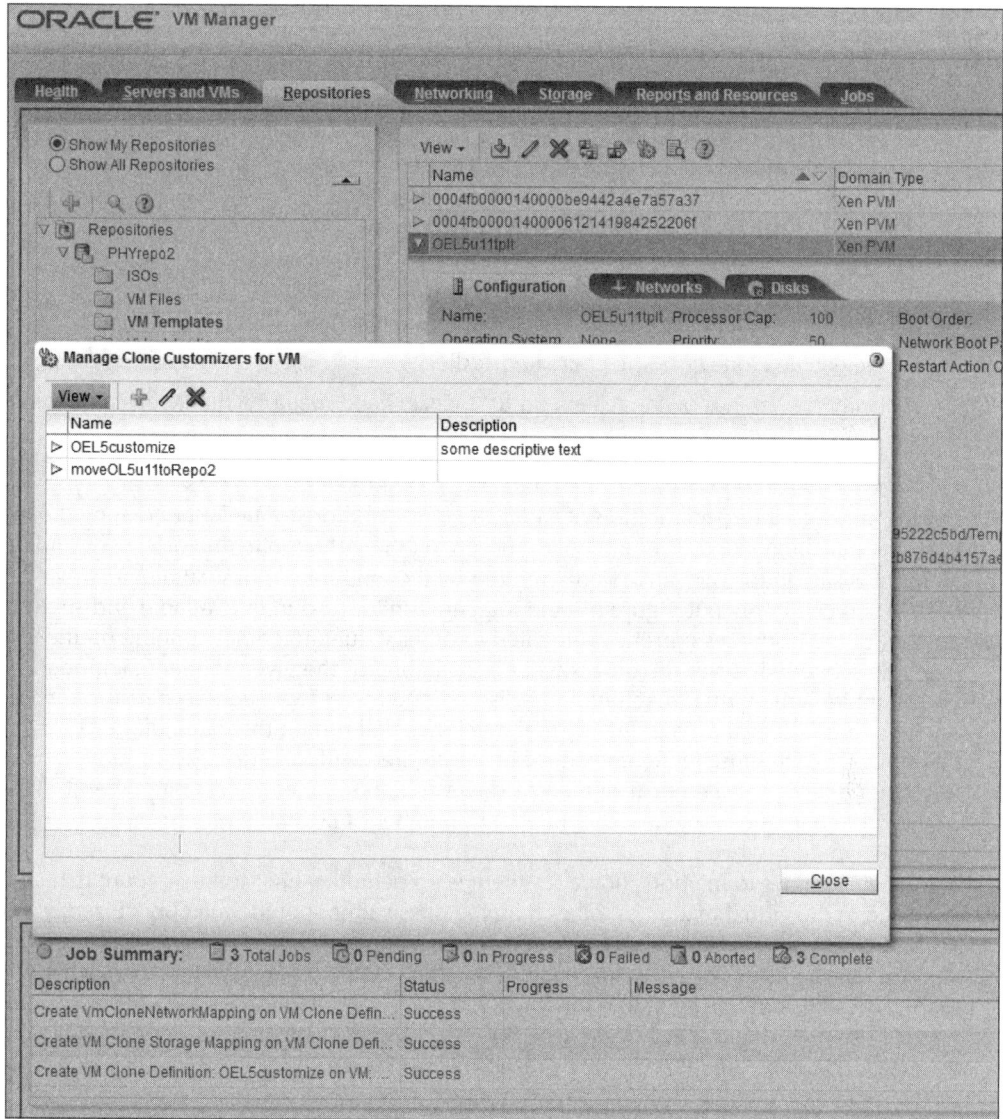

FIGURE 18-10.   *Final clone customizer screen*

> **NOTE**
> *After you complete the Network Mappings dialog and click the Finish button, the VM Manager will kick off the jobs to create the clone customizer, which includes the processes associated with network and storage mappings and the clone customizer definition being added to the template in the repository. These jobs can be seen executing in the status window at the bottom of the VM Manager GUI. If they are successful, the Manage Clone Customizer window is displayed showing the newly added clone customizer to the list of customizers available for the given template.*

5. Select the template to be cloned to the virtual machine.
6. Select the clone customizer created earlier.
7. After the VM has been created, adjust the CPU and memory allocations accordingly.

Adding Resources to the New Virtual Machine

Modifications to the configuration of CPUs, memory, and/or storage after creating the virtual machine may be needed. The process of modifying the virtual machine processor and/or memory is straightforward and is only limited by the amount of physical memory available on the VM server. Simply put, figure out the total amount of resources available and subtract the amount of the resources currently allocated to other virtual machines running on the virtual machine server; whatever remains is what is available for the given virtual machine in question. For example, if the virtual machine server is equipped with two quad-core processors, a total of eight cores are available. If four virtual machines will run on this particular VM server, then theoretically each virtual machine could be configured with two processors each. However, this is not a best practice because the VM server requires some processing power for its own background operations. Hence, the maximum number of available processor cores in this example would be seven.

When it comes to memory, however, there is no definitive limit to the amount that can be allocated to the virtual machines, other than the physical limit of the memory currently available. With that said, service requests have been opened related to virtual machines causing VM server eviction from a cluster when the active virtual machine memory requirements approach 100 percent of the available memory. Keep in mind that the memory requirements of the VM server background operations are not significantly large. The 80/20 rule is very likely the safest ratio of allocated memory to available memory.

Oracle VM Assemblies

Creating guest virtual machines from a template is performed as a "single result" set of operations (that is, the guest virtual machine is the single result of the overall set of tasks). There are other, more advanced ways to deploy a set of virtual machines, including some specific interoperability configuration items that can be controlled during the deployment of multiple machines that are tightly integrated; this construct is known as an assembly. Deploying an assembly is a one-shot process, which results in multiple virtual machines based on multiple templates. However, deploying a set of templates in a "one-shot" stream of processes requires the use of Oracle Enterprise Manager 12c or 13c. It should be noted that the exact same process can be done without using Enterprise

Manager. However, the process is done one virtual machine at a time and is still based on a template for each virtual machine.

With the release of Oracle VM 3.4, assemblies are no longer part of the Oracle VM Manager GUI and are, in fact, managed only through Oracle Enterprise Manager. An assembly is a tightly coupled set of virtual machines with complex deployment requirements, which are part of the assembly definition and are managed during the deployment process. One such example is the Oracle eBusiness Suite Oracle VM Assembly, which can be downloaded from the eDelivery site. After successfully importing the assembly into the OEM software library and after deploying the Oracle VMs inside the assembly using the template import and deployment processes described in this chapter, an entire eBusiness suite set of virtual machines will be running. This suite includes a multi-node RAC database, a highly available and load-balanced middle tier, and a fully populated and production-ready vision database with a network-file-system-capable management layer, which is also production ready. All these components make up a single assembly, which is composed of several template or appliance files (close to 30 files). After applying the underlying principles of this chapter, you will have multiple Oracle virtual machines in a tightly integrated configuration, deployed from an assembly that is constructed and subsequently deconstructed using Oracle VM Manager.

Summary

Creating an Oracle guest virtual machine using templates is the most common method and the basic foundation of deploying complex, loosely coupled machines in a virtualized infrastructure. A more advanced method of integrating templates is through the use of an assembly, which is basically a collection of templates with specific deployment characteristics that, when combined with the basic deployment of a guest from a template, can be used to deploy tightly coupled guest virtual machines. For example, Oracle Corporation has made assemblies available that include all the pieces and parts of a complete E-business Suite infrastructure, including the database machines and databases (in RAC and stand-alone configurations) and the middle-tier application servers, including the SOA infrastructure and WebLogic hosts.

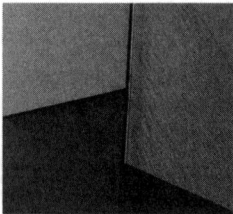

CHAPTER
19

Creating Virtual
Machines Manually

The counterpart to the process of creating a guest VM using a template is the process of creating a guest VM manually. Consider this: the only difference between creating a host machine running a choice-flavored operating system on a bare-metal host versus a guest virtual machine host is the preparation before installing and configuring the host operating system software. If you are creating a host machine on bare metal, your preparation includes installing the CPU, memory, and storage on a motherboard with a power supply, a fan, and a beverage-cooled chassis. By contrast, if creating the host machine in an Oracle VM infrastructure, preparation involves allocating the storage from the SAN and/or file server, choosing the number of processors to assign, and deciding how much memory to use of what's available. Other than that, the guest VM will be created from an ISO file or from a PXE server (named Tinkerbell) or cloned from another machine (physical or virtual). In short, there literally is no difference between operating system installation steps after the environment has been prepared.

Creating a Virtual Machine Manually: Process Overview

The process of creating a virtual machine manually in an Oracle VM environment is basically the same as installing an operating system on a bare-metal host machine. Assuming the operating system installation source is available (for example, the ISO file has been staged in the repository of the target Oracle VM environment or the PXE server has been configured on the network with the machine image source and so on), then the virtualization configuration items associated appear in the first few screens of the process. Namely, the boot source is specified (as being either an ISO file or the network location of the PXE server) and then the virtual machine is started while watching the Tiger VMC terminal, much like the process of inserting a disk in a machine (in the bare-metal "real-world" example) and watching the monitor while the machine is "powered up" and engaging in the dance of keystroke combinations to force boot-up from a CD or thumb drive device. In fact, in the event the VM guest to be manually created is one of an ancient operating system such as Microsoft Windows 98, then be prepared to recall the fond memory of pressing F6 during the boot process—which only further illustrates the point that manual creation of the guest VM is very similar to manual creation of a bare-metal host.

The following summarizes the manual creation process (note many of these steps are also covered in the previous chapter where we discussed creating guest virtual machines using templates):

1. Determine the basic resource requirements.

   - **Storage** If the machine to be generated is to be used for production support of an Oracle RAC database, the storage must be defined as physical (if the disks are used for the ASM grid infrastructure of a RAC database usage). Otherwise, the storage may be defined with virtual disks carved out of the repository storage.

     - Allocate at least one disk device for the root file system. Production considerations should include separate disks for performance engineering and capacity planning excellence (that is, temp storage, home storage, or software-specific storage such as the Oracle home and so on). Again, just like in the real world, it is much easier to segregate these specific file systems onto separate disks at the time of machine creation rather than go through the painful process of separating the storage later.

- Allocate additional disk devices if the requirements are known; otherwise, disk devices can be added later at any time.

- **Network**   In most cases, the virtual machine network has already been defined, and generating a new vNIC will not cause problems. However, in the event 254 virtual network interface cards have already been defined, an additional virtual machine network may be required (but again, it is highly unlikely). This limitation is platform specific.

2. Estimate the initial CPU and memory requirements.

3. Import the installation ISO into an Oracle VM storage repository.

4. Start the create virtual machine process.

5. Enter details and add storage and networking.

6. Launch the terminal console and start the guest VM.

7. Execute the installation process normally.

8. Remove the installation media from the guest VM.

Creating a Virtual Machine Manually: Process Details

Regardless of the source media, you must allocate and assign the resources for the guest VM prior to starting it, although it is possible to create a guest VM with no target resources allocated. Just like when using a template, however, you must allocate a network and storage to the target guest virtual machine.

Storage Management

Prior to starting the new guest VM, allocate and configure the storage for use. The details of storage management are found elsewhere in this book, but for the purposes of this chapter, just know that the storage management process is the same regardless of the guest VM source media.

As shown in Figure 19-1, the resources for the target guest virtual machine have been allocated and configured.

Beginning with the storage management screen, the target storage in this example has been allocated as a physical disk. Recall that only physical disk-based storage is supported for production virtual machines. Although virtual disks may be carved out of repository-based storage, physical disk definitions are based on LUNs carved out of network-attached storage or a storage area network (SAN) resource.

The storage device needs to be refreshed so that the storage can be detected. The naming convention, by default, is cryptic and will be based on the SAN device if a physical disk is used as the system or boot disk. It is a best practice to edit the physical device and change the simple name of the target storage to something appropriate for the guest virtual machine and to include a brief description.

Figures 19-2, 19-3, and 19-4 show the process before and after modifying the name and including a brief description.

It is a good idea to include some meaningful information about the guest virtual machine and the storage device for quick reference, especially during triage and performance-tuning exercises.

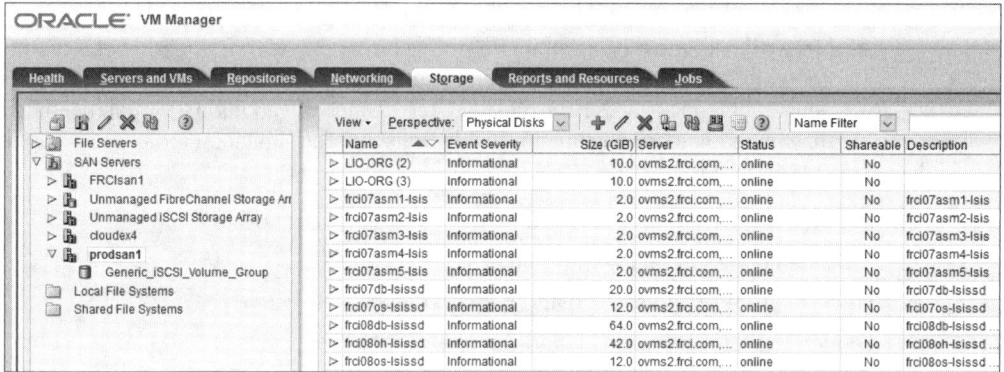

FIGURE 19-1. *Storage management screen*

Critical to the process of manually creating a guest VM is staging the media that will be used for creating the guest VM. In this example, a Microsoft Windows Server 2012 guest VM will be created. The source ISO, shown in Figure 19-5, must have been imported to an accessible repository. Details of this process are found throughout this book and include staging the ISO media and using the import facility of the VM Manager repository.

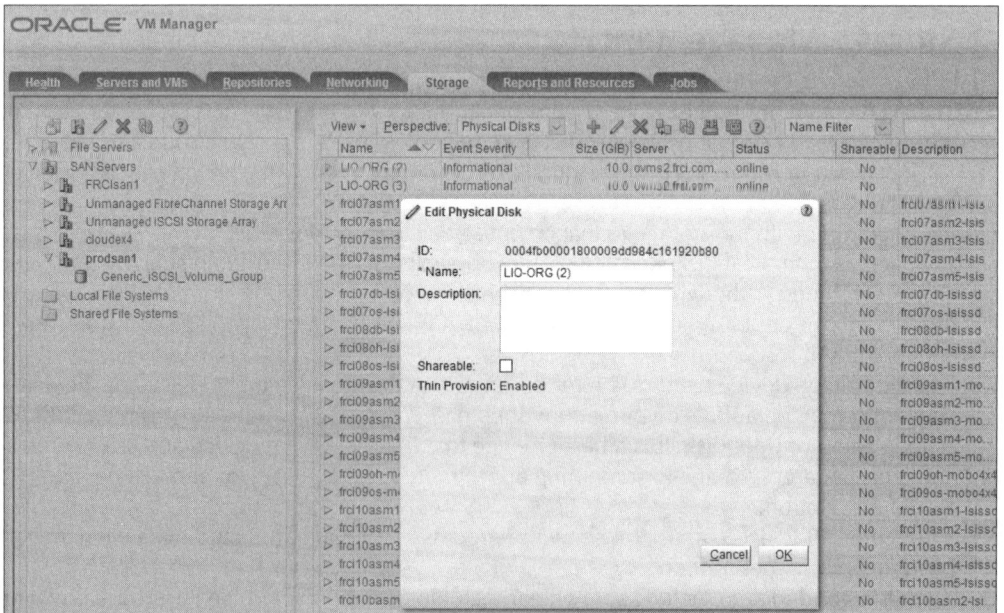

FIGURE 19-2. *The Edit Physical Disk dialog*

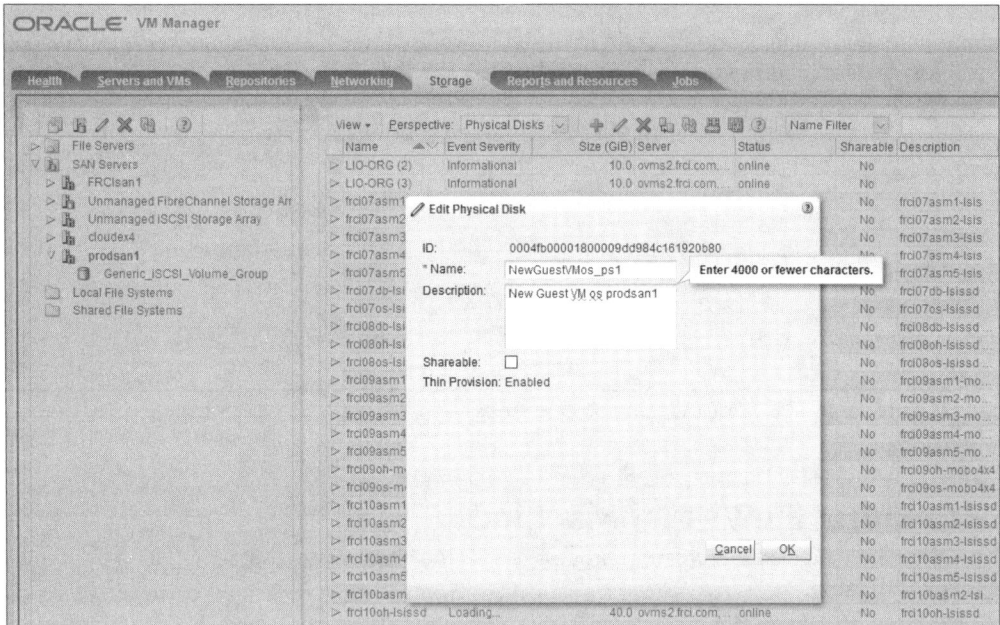

FIGURE 19-3.   *The Edit Physical Disk dialog modified*

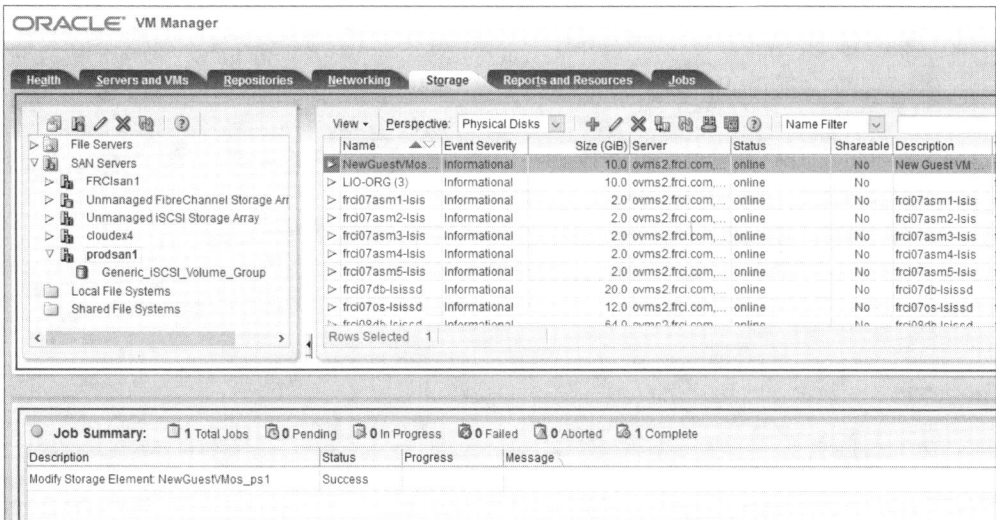

FIGURE 19-4.   *Physical disk screen showing the naming modification*

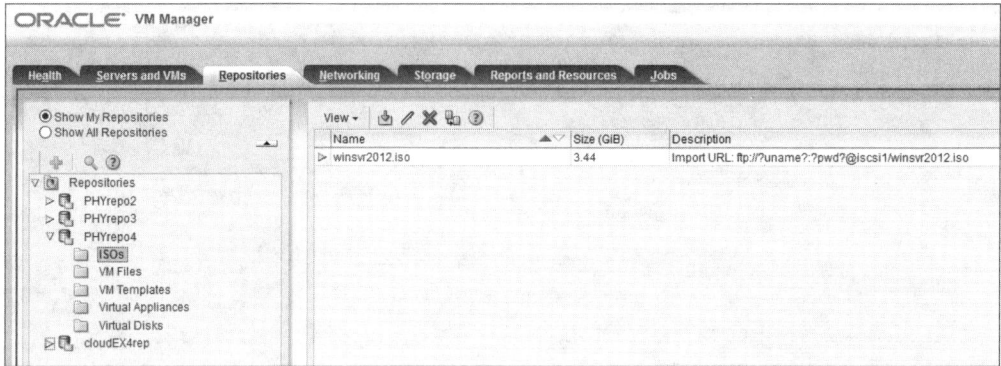

FIGURE 19-5. *Repository-based ISO screen*

Creating the Virtual Machine

To initiate the guest VM creation process, select the Create Virtual Machine icon from the Servers and VMs tab.

Manually Building the Oracle VM

The first screen of the process presents the choices related to "how" the Oracle VM is to be built (see Figure 19-6). Depending on the choices, the source must have been staged or configured, as is the case with a PXE server-based installation.

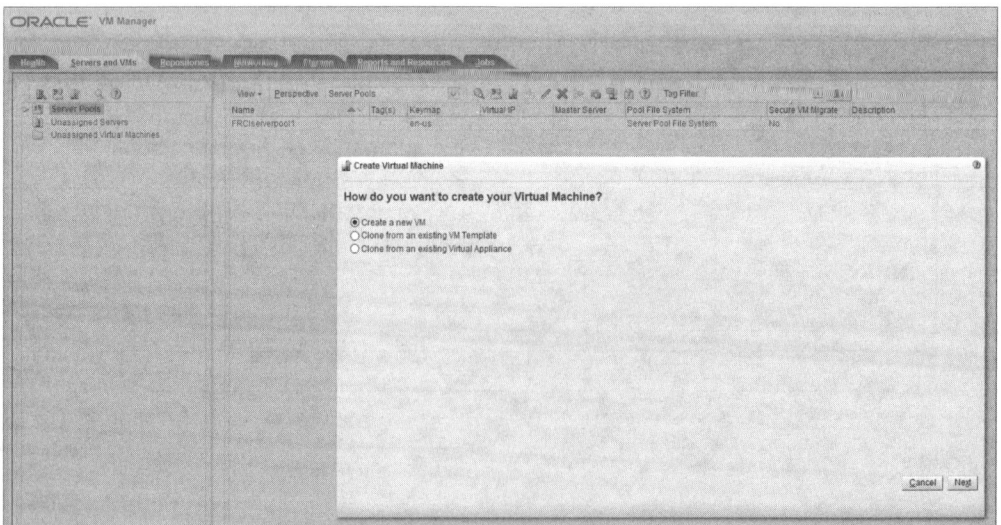

FIGURE 19-6. *The first screen of the Create Virtual Machine dialog*

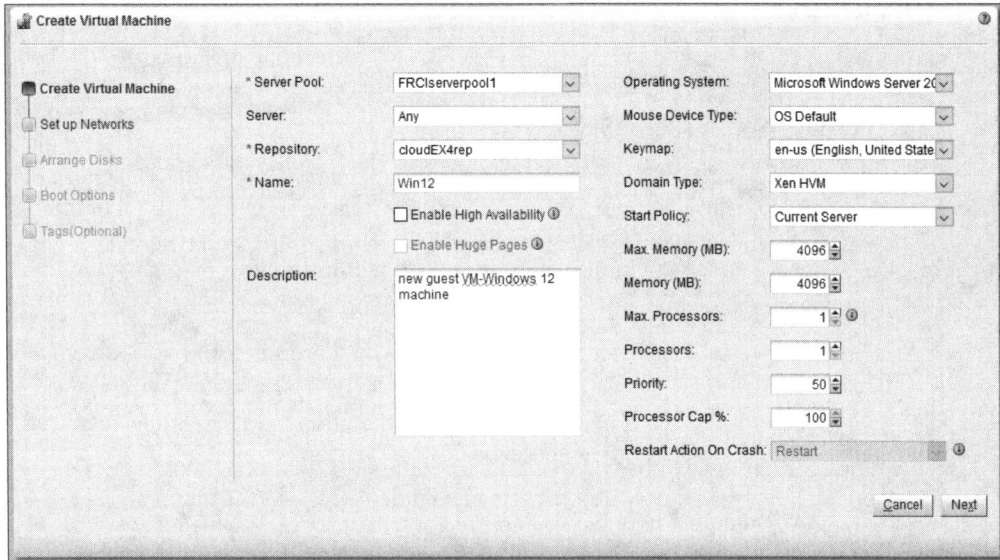

FIGURE 19-7. *General info dialog*

Selecting the Create a New Virtual Machine option displays a general information dialog for the VM (see Figure 19-7). Although some of the information is optional (for example, the operating system type), during the creation process it is extremely helpful to populate these fields with meaningful information. This comes in handy later when scanning multiple virtual machines in the Servers and VMs tab.

After entering the needed information and clicking Next, the Set Up Networks dialog is displayed (see Figure 19-8).

Choose a network and add the virtual network interface card by clicking the Add button. Multiple network interface cards may be added, or this task can be deferred until a later time. Figure 19-9 shows an example of this screen with a virtual machine network (defined in the Network Channels section of the Oracle VM Manager GUI).

After the appropriate networks are added, the Arrange Disks dialog appears. This is where the boot media and installation target storage are added to the target guest VM. Figures 19-10 through 19-13 show the process of adding the boot media as well as the target storage for the operating system.

It should be noted here that choosing the CD-ROM as the first disk is optional. If the target CD-ROM is listed second or later, then by default it will not be selected as the boot device. However, just as with a bare-metal installation, the BIOS may be used to indicate which disk to use as the boot device. There may be an order to the boot device used to start the machine based on the presence of an operating system. In other words, if the physical disk is selected first and the CD-ROM is selected second, then the boot process will look to the physical disk for an operating system. If no OS is found, the boot process will automatically look to the CD-ROM. Hence, it is equally important during the configuration of a target guest VM to indicate the proper boot device order.

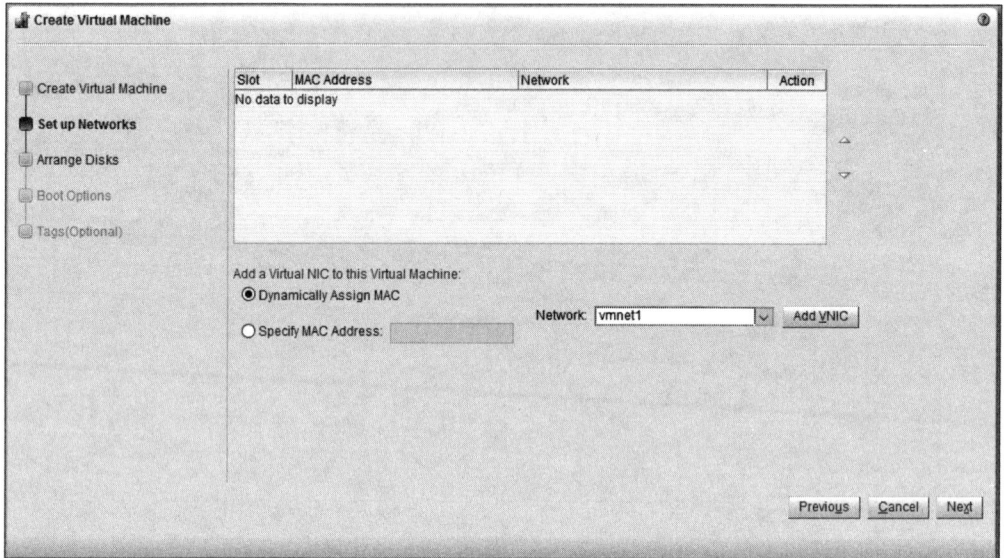

FIGURE 19-8. *Set Up Networks dialog*

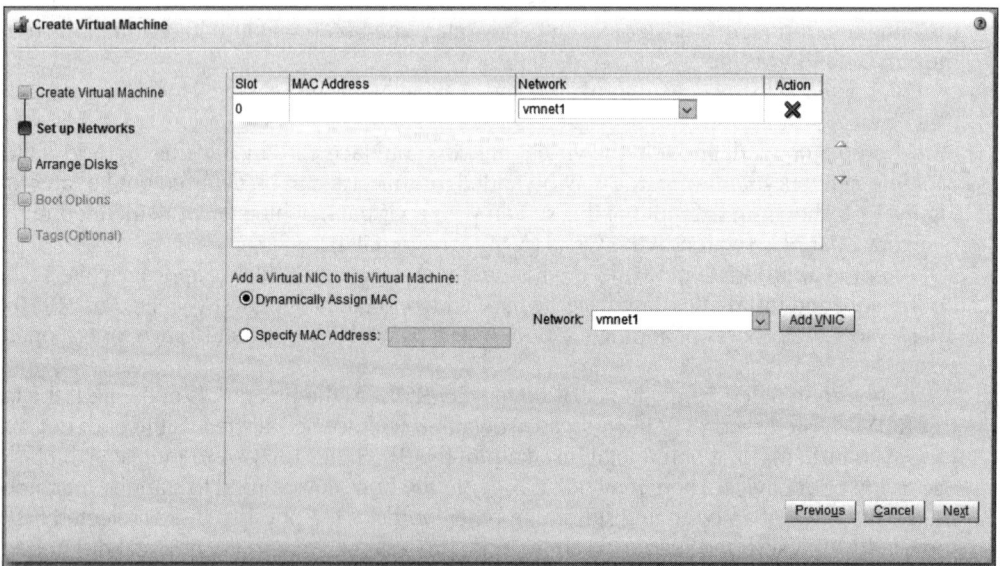

FIGURE 19-9. *Set Up Networks dialog modified*

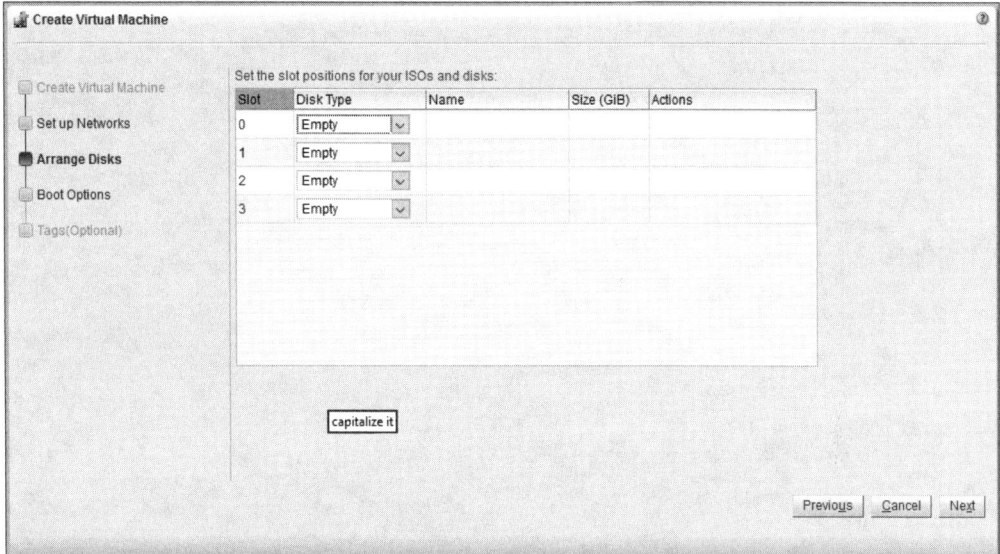

FIGURE 19-10.   *Arrange Disks dialog*

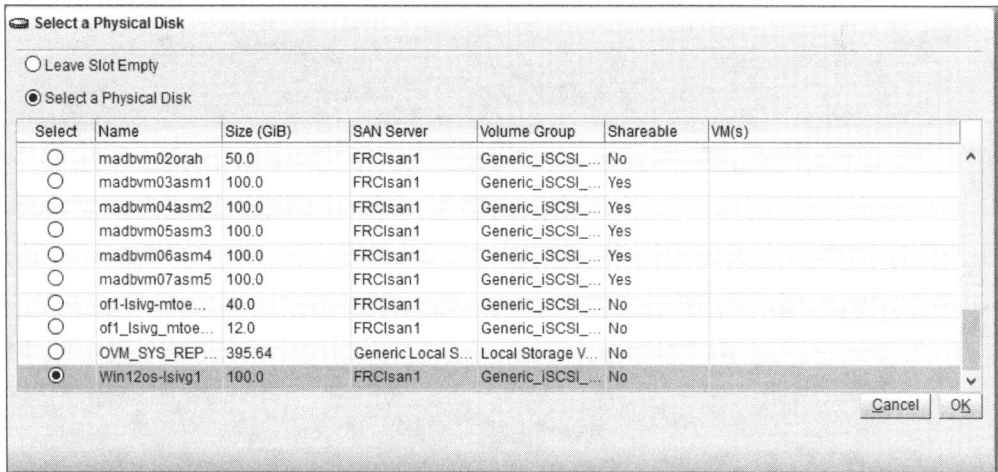

FIGURE 19-11.   *Select a Physical Disk dialog*

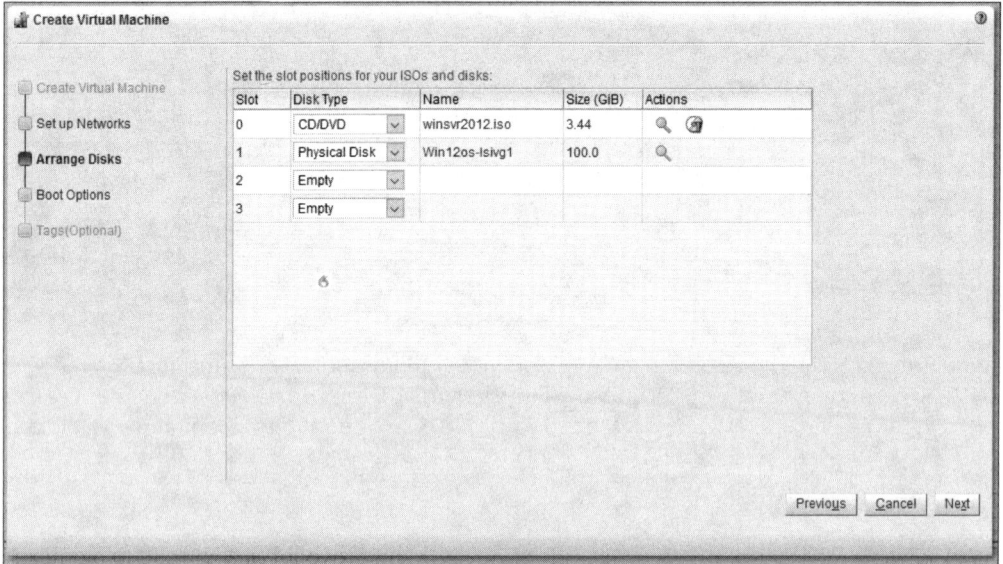

FIGURE 19-12. *Choosing the CD and guest VM OS disks*

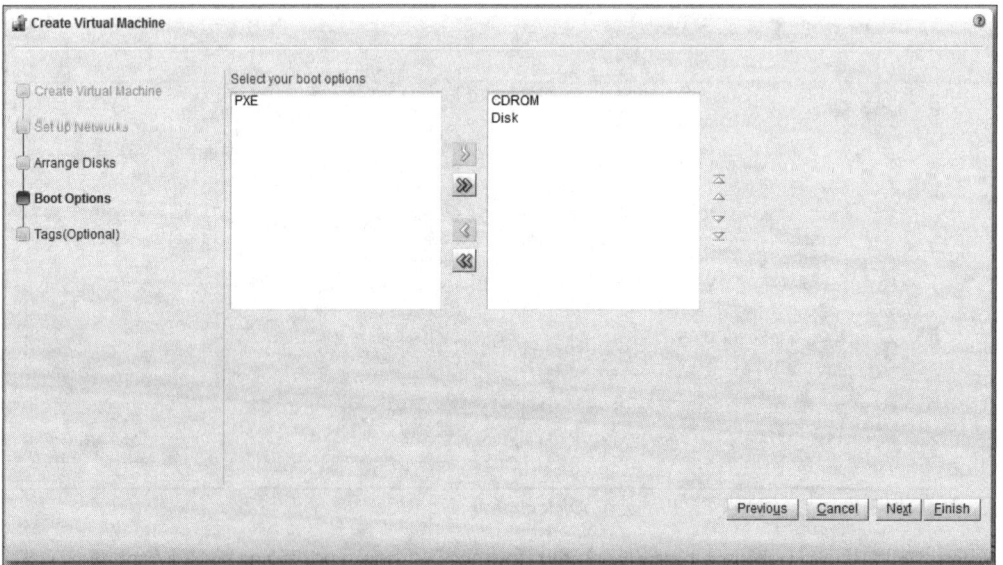

FIGURE 19-13. *Choosing the boot disk*

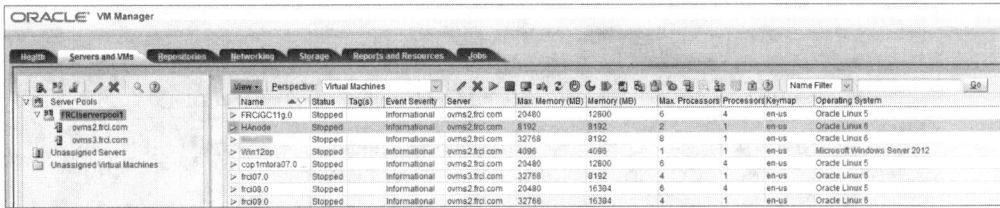

FIGURE 19-14.   *New guest VM Win12op*

The order of the disks will determine the boot device if the boot order is not specifically defined in the Boot Options dialog. If this is left blank, the boot device order will be determined by the order of the disks in the Arrange Disks dialog. Regardless of the position of the CD, after the guest VM is installed, the virtualized boot order will behave just like the BIOS on a bare-metal platform.

As stated, regardless of the order of the disks, a boot device may be selected. Be careful, though, because slot order is significant. Most OS systems administrators expect /dev/xvda to be the boot disk. The device name is based on which slot each device is allocated to. Although any disk may be selected as the boot device, the slots will be used by Oracle VM to name the devices in the OS being deployed. In the example shown in Figure 19-14, the target OS being deployed is a Windows 2012 Server.

Starting the New Guest VM

After you have gone through the set of screens in the Create Virtual Machine dialog, the new virtual machine resource assignments are made, but the creation process has not yet been started. To start the virtual machine creation process, select the virtual machine and click the Start icon in the menu. However, because the actual operating system has not yet been installed, a virtual console must be launched to manually participate in the installation and configuration process of the target operating system. Figures 19-15 and 19-16 show an example of launching the virtual terminal console.

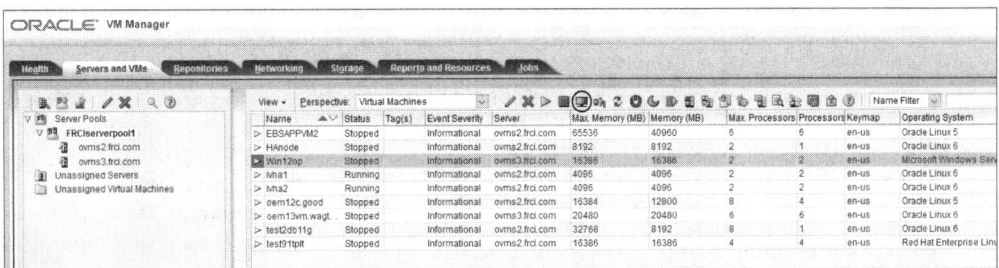

FIGURE 19-15.   *Launching the terminal console*

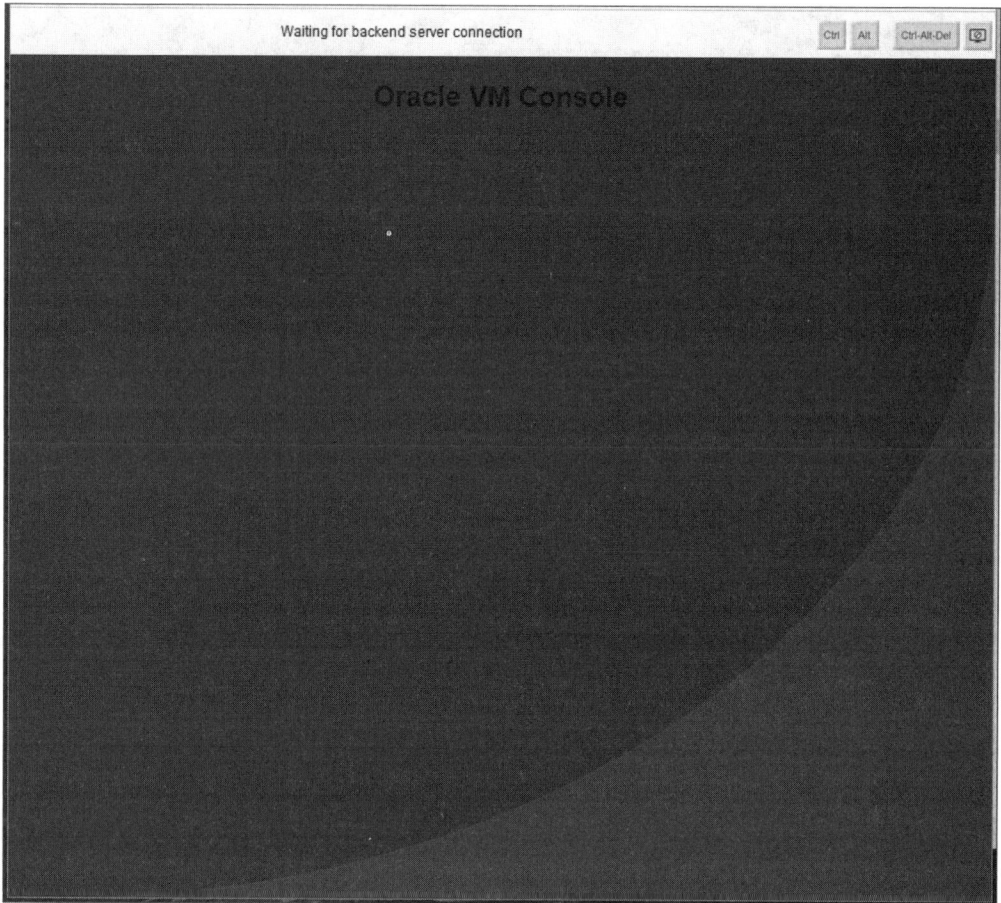

FIGURE 19-16. *Terminal console view*

After selecting the virtual machine and launching the terminal console, start the virtual machine by selecting the Start icon, as shown in Figure 19-17. The terminal console view presents a dialog for configuration tasks. The manual interaction process is illustrated in Figure 19-17.

After you start the virtual machine for the first time, the boot device will be accessed based on the boot device configuration or the order of the disks in the Arrange Disks dialog. You can also monitoring the OS installation process through the virtual console, as shown in Figure 19-18, and the level of detail and amount of information is dependent on the OS vendor.

Just as if you were sitting in front of the terminal connected to a bare-metal machine, the virtual terminal console will display the installation process from the boot installation media. Figure 19-19 shows an example of this interaction. Proceed with the dialog as normal when installing the target guest operating system.

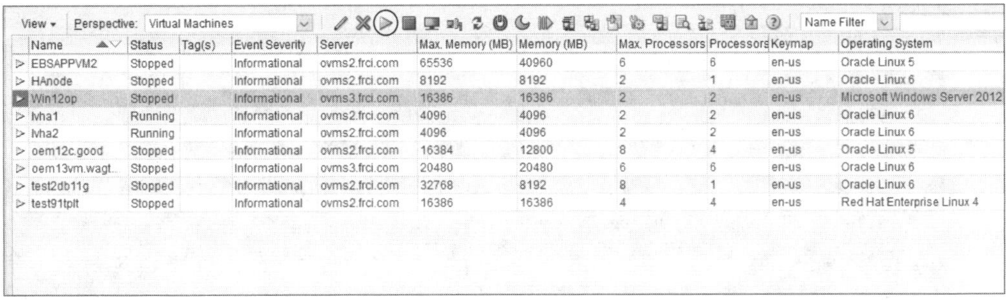

FIGURE 19-17.   *Starting a guest VM*

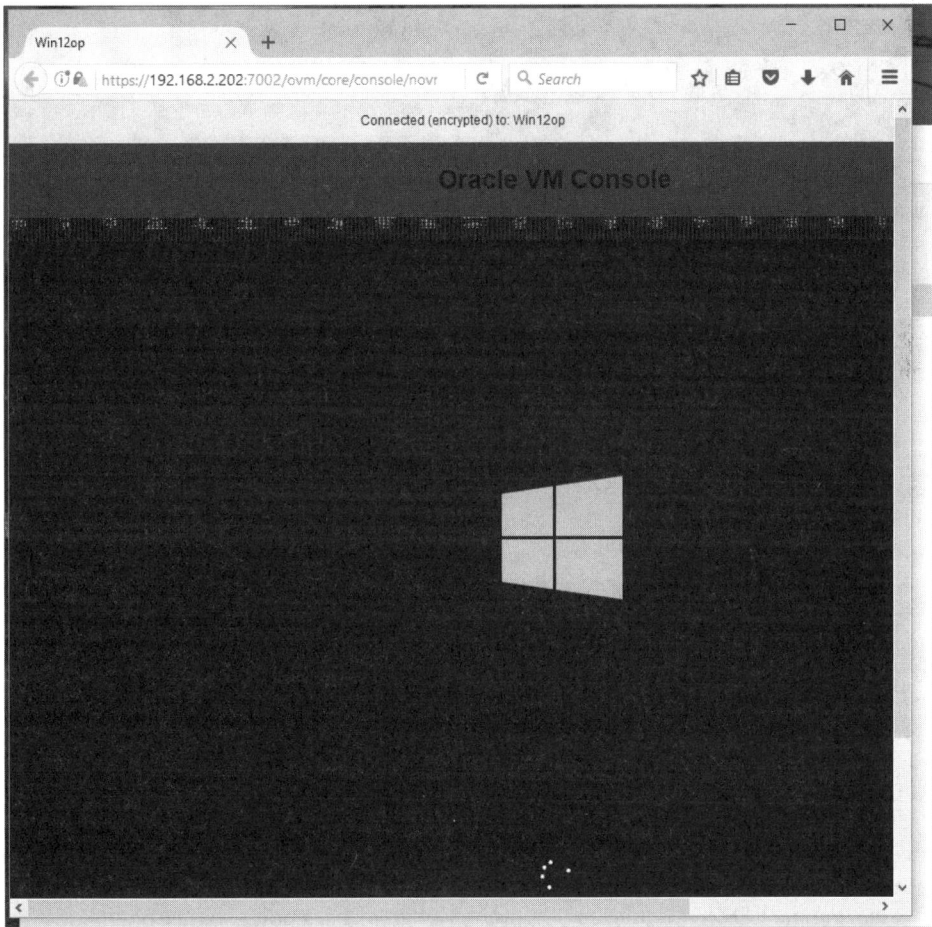

FIGURE 19-18.   *Monitoring the guest VM in the console*

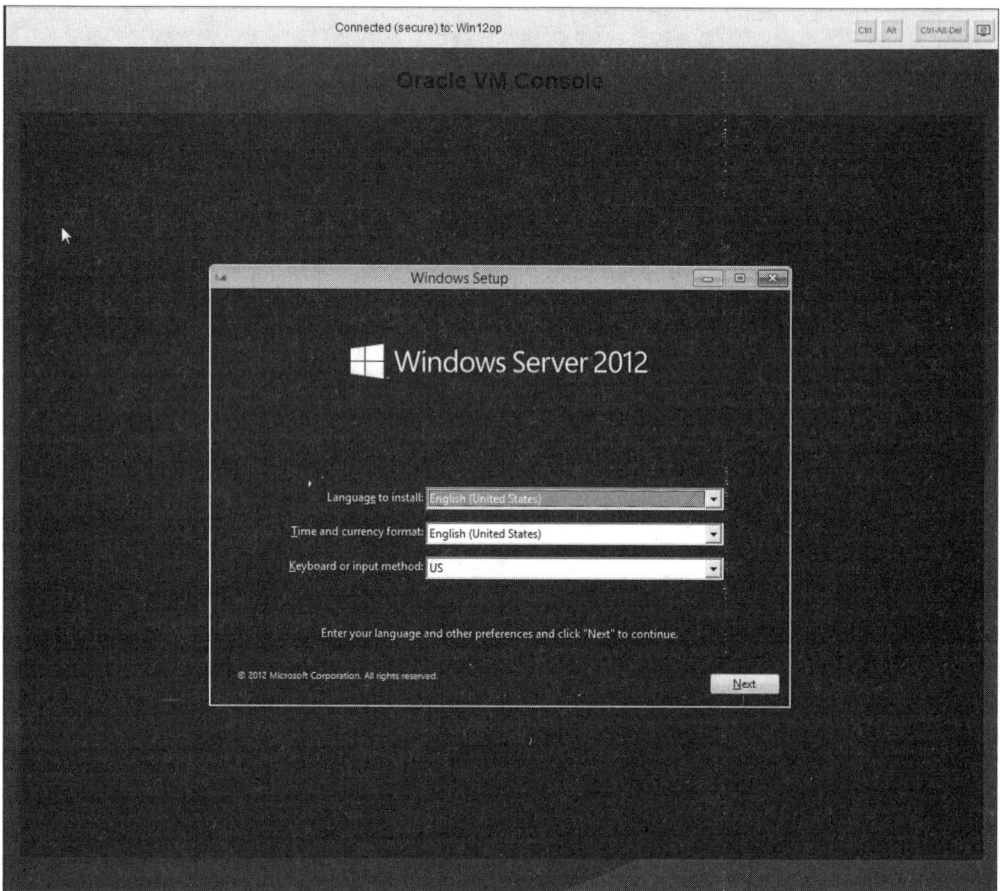

FIGURE 19-19. *Initial OS installation screen*

Post–Guest VM Creation

After you have installed the guest operating system, either the installation media used as the boot device will need to be removed or the boot device (for subsequent machine startup) will need to be specified in the Oracle VM configuration (in case the target operating system was not specified as the first disk). If, however, the first disk was specified as the operating system disk and the boot device screen was left blank, then the new guest virtual machine will boot from the operating system disk.

Figures 19-20, 19-21, and 19-22 illustrate the process of editing the guest VM and removing the installation ISO. As can be seen in Figure 19-21, removing the installation media can be accomplished by either removing the CD-ROM drive altogether or by simply ejecting the media but leaving the CD-ROM drive as part of the VM. It is your choice; either operation achieves the desired result.

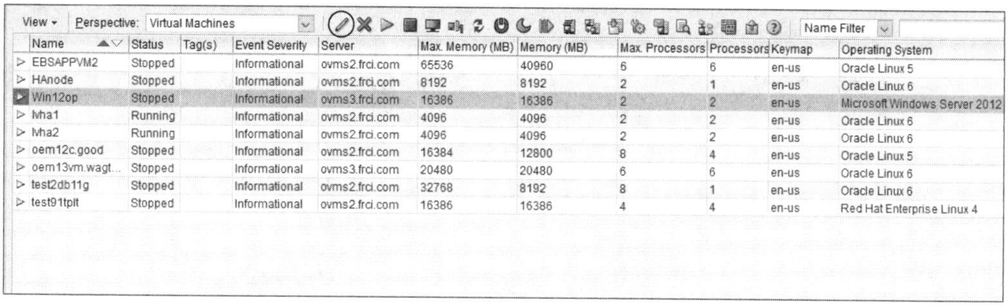

FIGURE 19-20. *Editing the guest VM*

Assuming the installation source media was based on a CD-ROM, and the guest Oracle VM used the ISO via a virtual CD-ROM device, the virtual device may be removed after the Oracle VM has been created. An example of removing the CD-ROM device altogether is shown in Figure 19-22.

Adding Resources to the New Virtual Machine

Just as with creating a guest virtual machine from a template, you may need to modify the configuration of the CPUs, memory, and/or storage after creating the virtual machine manually. The process of adding or changing resources is identical to what's found in Chapter 18.

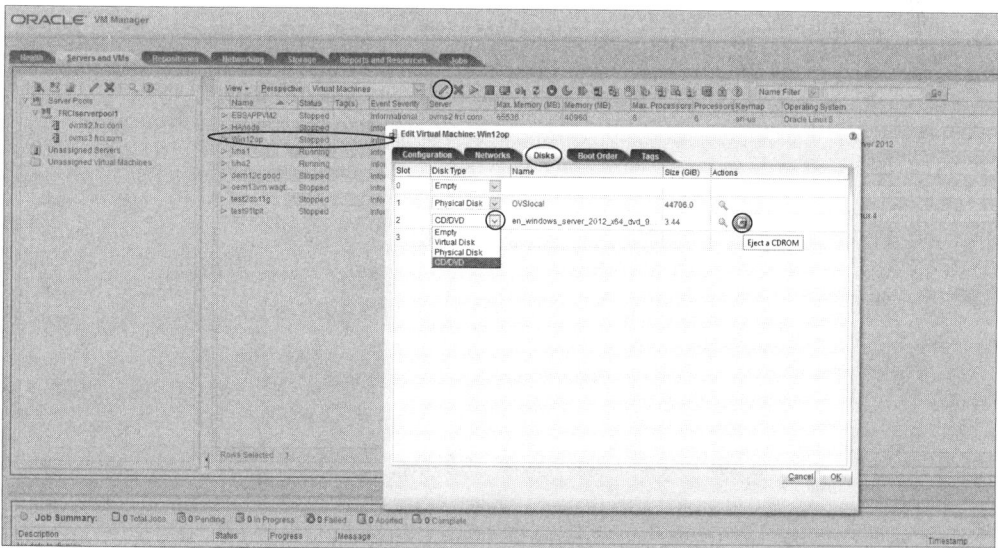

FIGURE 19-21. *Removing the guest VM installation ISO*

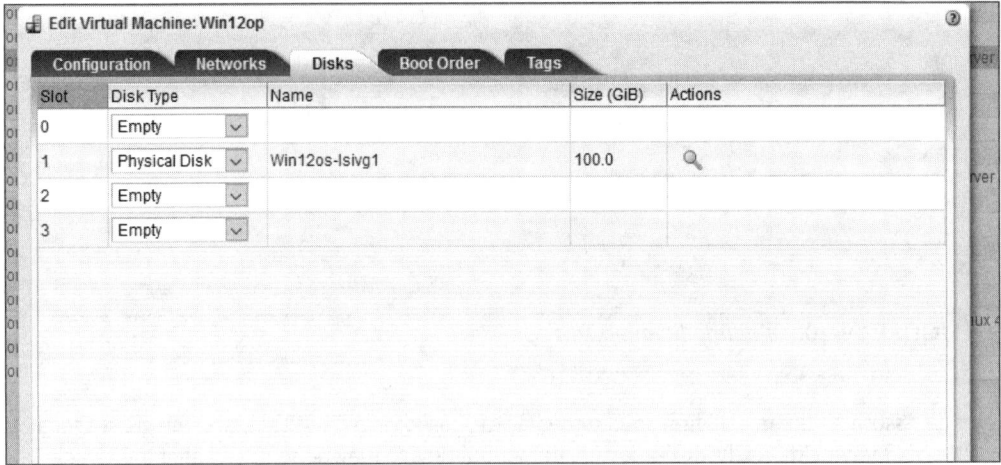

FIGURE 19-22. *Removing the guest VM CD drive*

Summary

Creating an Oracle guest virtual machine manually is an extremely forgiving process in that the guest VM structure can be created prior to your allocating any resources. The guest VM creation process is based on a "source," which may be a template, a pixie server (PXE), or another guest VM. In actual practice, you can create a guest "object" while managing a given object. In other words, while managing a current guest VM, you can request a "clone," in which case that is simply another entry point into the guest VM manual creation process.

CHAPTER
20

Managing the VM Environment and Virtual Machines

Throughout this book, you have seen how to configure the Oracle VM Server farm and Oracle VM guests. This chapter focuses on some of the day-to-day operations that the VM administrator will perform, including state management and configuring options that might change regularly, such as memory, network, and disks. As with most operations, you have several ways to perform these tasks: the Oracle VM Manager, OEM Cloud Control, Oracle VM CLI, and Xen **xm** commands.

Whereas day-to-day one-off operations such as monitoring and viewing the VM farm work great with the Oracle VM Manager and OEM, anything that is repetitive and complicated will benefit from using the Oracle VM CLI.

NOTE
*The OEM Cloud Control 13c method of managing virtual machines is not covered in this chapter because it is covered in detail later in the book in Chapters 23–25. This chapter covers managing virtual machines via OVM Manager, OVM CLI, and **xm** commands.*

Managing the State of Virtual Machines

As you learned in Chapter 4, the virtual machine can exist in many states. The current state of the virtual machine determines what states the virtual machine can transition into. This section covers the available state transition commands. Some of these commands were covered in earlier chapters, but are provided here for the sake of completeness. Almost every task can be done in the Oracle VM Manager, OEM Cloud Control 13c, the OVM CLI, and via Xen **xm** commands.

Determining the Status of Virtual Machines

Knowing the status of virtual machines is very useful to the VM administrator and can be accomplished through several methods. In order to demonstrate the different methods, the first part of this chapter uses tables to show the same task performed in the Oracle VM Manager, In the OVM CLI, and via **xm** commands. How to get the current status of virtual machines is shown here:

Management Application	Description
Oracle VM Manager	Browse to the server pool in the Navigation pane. From the Management pane, select Virtual Machines. You should see the virtual machines and their status in the Management pane.
Oracle VM CLI	Use the command **ssh -l admin -p 10000 ovmmanager "show vm name=<virtual machine>"** to get the status of a virtual machine.
Xen Tools	Using the Xen **xm** command, you can show the status of virtual machines from the VM Server with the following syntax: **xm list**. Note that only running virtual machines will be shown.

Using the CLI for Monitoring

Listing the status of the virtual machines is an excellent example of when to use a shell script with the OVM CLI, as shown here:

```
#
# List Virtual Machine Statuses
#

vms=`ssh -l admin -p 10000 ovmmanager "list vm"
| grep id | cut -d: -f2 | cut -d" " -f1`

i=0
for target in $vms
do
  name=$(ssh admin@ovmmanager -p 10000 "show vm name=$target"
| grep "Name =" | tr -d '\n' | tr -d '\r')
  status=$(ssh admin@ovmmanager -p 10000 "show vm name=$target"
| grep "Status =" | tr -d '\n' | tr -d '\r')
  procs=$(ssh admin@ovmmanager -p 10000 "show vm name=$target"
| grep "Processors" | grep -v Max | tr -d '\n' | tr -d '\r')
  memory=$(ssh admin@ovmmanager -p 10000 "show vm name=$target"
| grep "Memory" | grep -v Max | tr -d '\n' | tr -d '\r')
  echo "${name}    ${status}    ${procs}    ${memory}"

i=$i++
done
```

Here is the output:

```
[root@ptc03 ovm-scripts]# status-vms
  Name = cc03-template    Status = Template    Processors = 4    Memory (MB) = 16384
  Name = ora10ga      Status = Stopped      Processors = 1    Memory (MB) = 4096
  Name = ol66-template.0    Status = Template  Processors = 2    Memory (MB) = 2048
  Name = win00      Status = Stopped    Processors = 2    Memory (MB) = 4096
  Name = udb00      Status = Stopped    Processors = 1    Memory (MB) = 4096
  Name = gg21a      Status = Running    Processors = 2    Memory (MB) = 8192
  Name = rac20b      Status = Running    Processors = 5    Memory (MB) = 8192
  Name = rac20a      Status = Running    Processors = 4    Memory (MB) = 8192
  Name = cc03      Status = Running    Processors = 4    Memory (MB) = 16384
  Name = gg20b      Status = Running    Processors = 1    Memory (MB) = 16384
  Name = pv00-template.0    Status = Template    Processors = 1    Memory (MB) = 4096
  Name = gg20a      Status = Running    Processors = 1    Memory (MB) = 16384
  Name = gg21b          Processors = 2    Memory (MB) = 8192
  Name = ggwin20a      Status = Stopped      Processors = 2    Memory (MB) = 4096
  Name = ptc03      Status = Running    Processors = 2    Memory (MB) = 4096
  Name = studio00      Status = Stopped      Processors = 2    Memory (MB) = 8192
  Name = pv00      Status = Stopped    Processors = 1    Memory (MB) = 4096
  Name = veridata01    Status = Stopped      Processors = 2    Memory (MB) = 12288
  Name = ora10g-template    Status = Template    Processors = 1    Memory (MB) = 4096
  Name = ggwin20b      Status = Stopped      Processors = 2    Memory (MB) = 4096
  Name = gg21c      Status = Running    Processors = 2    Memory (MB) = 8192
  Name = mysql02      Status = Running    Processors = 1    Memory (MB) = 4096
  Name = odi00      Status = Running    Processors = 2    Memory (MB) = 4096
```

```
   Name = dis00      Status = Running     Processors = 1      Memory (MB) = 8192
   Name = BigDataLite450    Status = Running   Processors = 2    Memory (MB) = 5200
   Name = mysql00      Status = Running    Processors = 1    Memory (MB) = 4096
   Name = mysql01      Status = Running    Processors = 1    Memory (MB) = 4096
   Name = pv-template.0    Status = Template   Processors = 1    Memory (MB) = 4096
key_verify failed for server_host_key
   Name = pv-with-net.0    Status = Template    Processors = 1
   Name = win-template.0    Status = Template   Processors = 2   Memory (MB) = 2048
```

Getting info on virtual machines is a critical part of managing the virtual environment.

Starting Virtual Machines

The most basic of the virtual machine commands is to start the virtual machine. How to perform this function is detailed in the following table:

Management Application	Description
Oracle VM Manager	Select the virtual machine by clicking it in the Virtual Machines window to highlight it and then click the Start button. The status of the virtual machine will change to Running.
Oracle VM CLI	Use the command **ssh -l admin -p 10000 ovmmanager** "**start vm name=<virtual machine>**" to start the desired virtual machine.
Xen Tools	Using the Xen **xm** command, you can start a virtual machine from the VM Server with the following syntax: **xm create <Config File Path>**. Here's an example: xm create /OVS/Repositories /0004fb00000300001c9bd84feea35191/VirtualMachines /0004fb00000600002697900837ee12fb/vm.cfg

You can determine the status of the virtual machine in a number of ways, including **xm list** (on the VM Server), **ovm list vm**, and, of course, using the GUI tools.

Stopping Virtual Machines

Stopping the virtual machine is another important command. How to perform this function is detailed in the following table:

Management Application	Description
Oracle VM Manager	Select the virtual machine by clicking it in the Virtual Machines window to highlight it and then click the Stop button. The status of the virtual machine will change to Stopped.
Oracle VM CLI	Use the command **ssh -l admin -p 10000 ovmmanager** "**stop vm name=<virtual machine>** to stop the desired virtual machine.

Management Application	Description
Xen Tools	Using the Xen **xm shutdown** command, you can stop a virtual machine from the VM Server with the following syntax: **xm shutdown <DomainName>**. Here's an example: xm shutdown 0004fb00000600001b620e2f106d4f42 Note: In an emergency, use **xm destroy**. The **xm destroy** command powers off the guest immediately. This should only be used when **xm shutdown** doesn't work. The **xm shutdown** command performs an orderly shutdown.

Again, you can determine the status of the virtual machine in a number of ways, including **xm list** (on the VM server), **ovm list vm**, and, of course, using the GUI tools.

Suspending/Resuming Virtual Machines

Suspending a virtual machine causes the virtual machine to stop executing, and the state is written out to disk and removed from memory. If the VM Server is rebooted, the virtual machine is still available and can be restored to its previous state. A suspended virtual machine can be resumed to restart execution. How to perform this function is explained in the following table:

Management Application	Description
Oracle VM Manager	Select the virtual machine by clicking it in the Virtual Machines window to highlight it and then click the Suspend button. The status of the virtual machine will change to Stopping and then to Suspended. In order to resume the virtual machine, select it by clicking it in the Virtual Machines window to highlight it and then click the Resume button. The status of the virtual machine will change to Starting and then to Running.
Oracle VM CLI	Use the command **ssh -l admin -p 10000 ovmmanager "suspend vm name=<virtual machine>** to suspend the virtual machine. Use the command **ssh -l admin -p 10000 ovmmanager "resume vm name=<virtual machine>** to resume the virtual machine.
Xen Tools	Using the Xen **xm** command, you can suspend or resume a virtual machine from the VM Server with the following syntax: **xm suspend <DomainName>** or **xm resume <DomainName>**. With the Xen **xm** commands, you can also pause and unpause a domain; however, the pause/unpause functionality is not supported from the Oracle VM Manager or CLI.

Migrating Virtual Machines

Migrating a virtual machine can be done live, with only a very small interruption in service. This interruption in service is rarely even noticed by users. Migrating virtual machines can be performed via several different methods, including using the GUI tools as well as the command-line tools detailed in the following table:

Management Application	Description
Oracle VM Manager	Select the virtual machine by clicking it in the Virtual Machines window to highlight it and then click the Migrate or Move button. This will bring up the Migrate or Move Virtual Machine pop-up box.
	In the Migrate or Move Virtual Machine pop-up, you are presented with radio buttons for selecting from the following options:
	■ Migrate a running VM to a different Server within the same Server Pool.
	■ Migrate a running VM, and migrate its local storage, to a different Server within the same Server Pool. (This is also known as storage live migration and only works when Oracle VM guest resources such as virtual disks reside on a local storage repository. It does not currently work with shared storage repositories.)
	■ Move this VM to a different Repository.
Oracle VM CLI	Migrate the virtual machine to another VM Server by using the OVM **migrate** command.
	Use the command **ssh -l admin -p 10000 ovmmanager "migrate vm name=<virtual machine> destServer=<Destination>** to migrate the virtual machine.
Xen Tools	Utilize the Xen Tools to migrate a virtual machine using the following **xm migrate** command: **xm migrate <Domain> <Host>**.

Changing the Configuration of Virtual Machines

From time to time, it is necessary to make changes to both the environment and the virtual machines themselves. Oracle VM is very adaptable and can be configured as needed. You can add hardware and make changes to storage and the network as necessary. Changes fall into two categories: changes to the virtual machines and changes to the VM servers.

Modifying Virtual Machines

On occasion you must modify a virtual machine. A number of different commands can be used to change the configuration and/or attributes of the virtual machines, as detailed in the following table:

Management Application	Description
Oracle VM Manager	Select the virtual machine by clicking it in the Virtual Machines window to highlight it and then click the Edit button. This will bring up the configuration pop-up.
Oracle VM CLI	The Oracle VM CLI has a number of specific commands for changing specific attributes, including **edit cpuCount**, **edit memory**, **edit osType**, **edit startPolicy**, and others.
	Use the command **ssh -l admin -p 10000 ovmmanager "edit vm name=<virtual machine> cpuCount=<# of CPUs>** to edit the virtual machine.

Management Application	Description
Xen Tools	There are no **xm** tools for configuring the virtual machines per se. The virtual machines are configured by editing their individual vm.cfg files. Some dynamic changes such as pinning VCPUs can be performed using **xm** commands; however, dynamic changes will not survive a reboot or migration. Therefore, pinning VCPUs using **xm** commands does not meet Oracle's definition of "pinned CPUs."

Modifying the virtual machines should be done with care because changing the configuration might also require changes within the virtual machines themselves.

Configuring Virtual Machine Networks

Virtual machines networks are easy to modify. They can be configured graphically via the Oracle VM Manager or the OEM Cloud Control. Networks can also be modified via the Oracle VM CLI. Once you have added the virtual network adapter to the virtual machine, you will need to configure the adapter in the virtual machine itself. The first step is to add the network adapter to the virtual machine. The second step is to reboot the virtual machine and configure the network during the startup process as normal. Configuring the network is covered in detail in Chapter 12.

Configuring Storage on Virtual Machines

Multiple methods are available for configuring storage on the virtual machines. Several methods can be used to add storage to a virtual machine. The primary storage method is a virtual disk, which is created by Oracle VM and assigned to the virtual machine, but other methods exist as well. Storage is covered in detail in Chapter 13.

Using Virtual Storage

The primary method of adding storage to an Oracle VM is as a virtual disk. You can easily add a virtual disk to a virtual machine via the Oracle VM Manager, the OEM Cloud Control, or the Oracle VM CLI. Depending on the underlying operating system, a reboot of the virtual machine may or may not be required.

Using iSCSI Storage

Because the virtual machine has a network, any network storage that is supported on the guest OS is supported on the virtual machine. If the guest OS supports iSCSI, then this is a good choice for network storage. No additional configuration steps are needed because it is a virtual machine. You simply follow the normal iSCSI setup steps.

Using NFS Storage

Just as with iSCSI, because the virtual machine has a network, any network storage that is supported on the guest OS is supported on the virtual machine. NFS is a good choice for network storage because of its ease of use and built-in support. As with iSCSI, no additional configuration steps are needed because it is a virtual machine.

NOTE
The network on a paravirtualized guest is faster than the network on an HVM guest. If the intent is to use network storage, keep this in mind. The HVM accelerations speed up memory access, so it is a trade-off among I/O, network (paravirtualized), and memory (HVM).

Changing the Configuration of VM Servers

From time to time, it is necessary to make changes to both the environment and the virtual machines themselves. Oracle VM is very adaptable and can be configured as needed. You can add hardware and make changes to storage and the network as necessary. Changes fall into two categories: changes to the virtual machines and changes to the Oracle VM servers. Making changes to the Oracle VM servers is covered in Chapter 9 and throughout Part II of the book.

Creating and Cloning Virtual Machines

Creating and cloning virtual machines gives you the ability to create a new virtual machine and copy virtual machines. *Creating* a virtual machine allows you construct a new virtual machine. *Cloning* a virtual machine allows you to create one or more copies of a virtual machine. Creating and cloning are very similar; in fact, cloning has really made the deploying process obsolete because you can start with an already configured virtual machine.

Creating a Virtual Machine

The deployment process allows you to create a new virtual machine, either from scratch or using a template. Using a template you have created from another virtual machine allows you to preconfigure the virtual machine and then deploy it at will. As with other tasks, there are several ways to deploy a virtual machine.

Creating Virtual Machines with the Oracle VM Manager

You can create virtual machines in the Oracle VM Manager by selecting the server pool and then clicking the Create Virtual Machine icon or selecting Create Virtual Machine from the drop-down menu. Both methods result in the Create Virtual Machine window shown in Figure 20-1.

From the Create Virtual Machine window, you can select to create a virtual machine from an Oracle VM template or a Virtual Appliance, or you can create an entirely new VM from scratch using installation media such as Kickstart, Jumpstart, or any other network-installation method supported by the guest OS. If you select to create a new VM, you will see the Create Virtual Machine window shown in Figure 20-2.

Here, you have many options for creating the virtual machine, including the number of CPUs, amount of RAM, and using HVM versus paravirtual. Some of the choices such as RAM, Processors, and Priority, can be changed dynamically. Other choices such as the Domain Type and Operating System cannot be changed while the VM is running.

> **NOTE**
> *Newer versions of Linux will dynamically pick up some changes while the VM is active.*

Once you have filled out the main screen, you have several other tabs of options you can configure, including Networks, Disks, Boot Order, and Tags. Once you have filled out all the screens and have appropriately set up an ISO image and boot order, you can start the VM and install from the installation ISO.

Creating Virtual Machines with the OVM CLI

Virtual machines can be created in the Oracle VM Manager via the OVM CLI **create vm** command. The **create vm** command can be used to create a new virtual machine on a specific

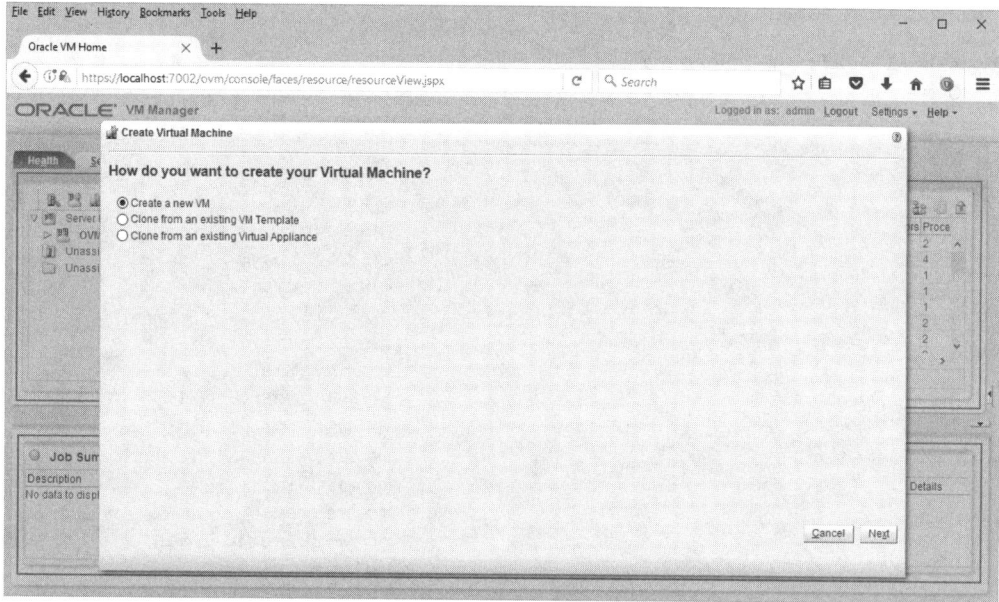

FIGURE 20-1. *The Create Virtual Machine window*

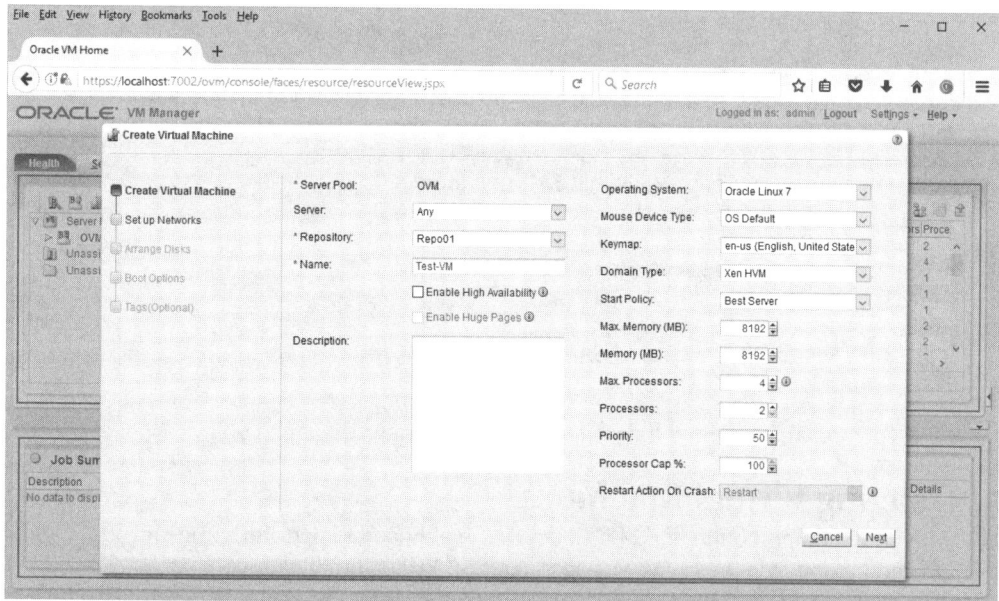

FIGURE 20-2. *Options for creating a VM*

repository. In order to view the options for additional parameters, you can use the CLI help function. Here is an example:

```
ssh -l admin -p 10000 ovmmanager
OVM> create vm name=ed domainType=XEN_PVM -?
                                        *domainType
                                        *name
                                        *repository
                                        bootOrder
                                        cpuCount
                                        cpuCountLimit
                                        cpuPriority
                                        cpuUtilizationCap
                                        description
                                        highAvailability
                                        hugePagesEnabled
                                        keymapName
                                        memory
                                        memoryLimit
                                        mouseType
                                        networkInstallPath
                                        osType
                                        restartActionOnCrash
                                        server
                                        startPolicy
                                        *on
```

Once you have chosen all the options you want to use, you can create the VM. Here is a complete example:

```
OVM> create vm name=ed domainType=XEN_PVM
repository=Repo01 CPUCountLimit=4 CPUCount=2 MemoryLimit=8192
Memory=4096 on ServerPool name=OVM
Command: create vm name=ed domainType=XEN_PVM
repository=Repo01 CPUCountLimit=4 CPUCount=2 MemoryLimit=8192
Memory=4096 on ServerPool name=OVM
Status: Success
Time: 2016-12-11 11:14:34,020 CST
JobId: 1481476472008
Data:
   id:0004fb0000060000df30be6931c5565f  name:ed
OVM>
```

If you are creating more than one VM, the CLI is a great way to do it.

Deleting Virtual Machines

When a VM comes to the end of its lifecycle, you'll need to perform some cleanup. Deleting a VM can be done via the OVM Manager, the OVM CLI, and the **xm** commands.

Deleting Virtual Machines with the Oracle VM Manager

In order to delete a virtual machine using the Oracle VM Manager or OVM CLI, you must first stop the virtual machine, as detailed earlier in this chapter. In the Oracle VM Manager, navigate to the Servers and VMS tab in the Management pane and highlight the virtual machine you want to delete. Highlight the stopped virtual machine and click the Delete icon or select Delete from the context menu.

Once you have clicked Delete, you will be prompted to verify the deletion and select the virtual disks to be deleted that are assigned to this virtual machine. If you do not delete all of the disks, they will remain in the repository unassigned. This is shown in Figure 20-3.

Once you verify the delete operation, the virtual machine and selected disks will be deleted.

Deleting Virtual Machines with the OVM CLI

Virtual machines can be deleted via the OVM CLI **delete vm** command. The **delete vm** command can be used to delete a virtual machine using either the VM's name or ID. Unfortunately, the **delete vm** command does not remove the associated virtual disks. That must be done manually or via a script. Here is an example:

```
ssh -1 admin -p 10000 ovmmanager
OVM> delete vm name=ed
```

If you are deleting more than one VM, the CLI is a great way to do it.

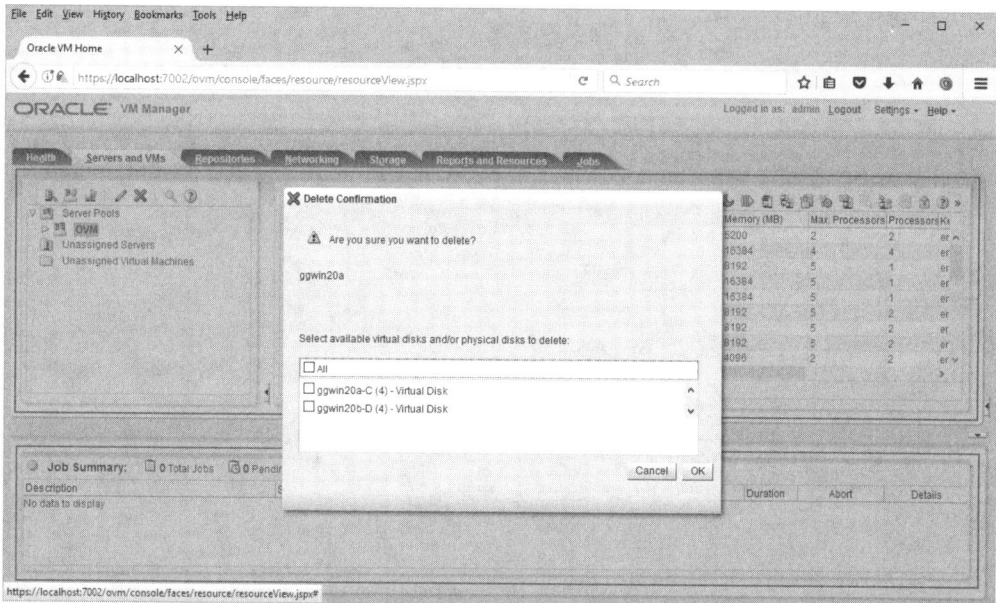

FIGURE 20-3. *Select the virtual disks to delete.*

Cloning Virtual Machines

The cloning process is only slightly different from the deployment process. Cloning allows you to create several copies of the same virtual machine. These copies are then placed in the same or a different storage repository.

Cloning Virtual Machines with the Oracle VM Manager

With the Oracle VM Manager, cloning begins with selecting the virtual machine to be cloned by highlighting it in the Oracle VM Manager and then selecting Clone… from the context menu or clicking the Clone button in the toolbar. You will be provided with a pop-up where you can fill in the details of the clone, as shown in Figure 20-4.

You can select to clone to a VM or template. Input the virtual machine name index and number of copies and then select the server pool name from the drop-down list. Once you are satisfied with your selections, click OK to start the cloning process. There is no confirmation screen for this task. Once you have clicked OK, cloning begins and control returns to the Virtual Machines screen, where you can watch the progress of the cloning operation.

Cloning Virtual Machines with the Oracle VM CLI

To clone a virtual machine from within the Oracle VM CLI, use the OVM CLI **clone vm** command. This command takes the options listed here:

- destName
- destType

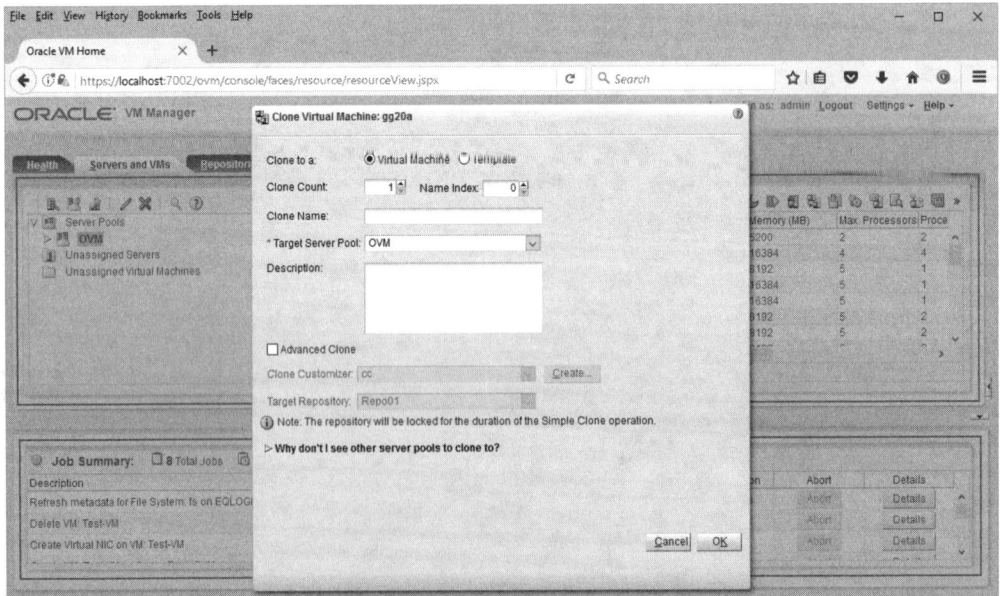

FIGURE 20-4. *The Clone Virtual Machine pop-up*

- serverPool
- cloneCustomizer
- targetRepository

Here is an example of cloning a virtual machine via the Oracle VM CLI:

```
OVM> clone vm name=gg20b destName=gg20b-template destType=VmTemplate
serverPool=OVM
Command: clone vm name=gg20b destName=gg20b-template
destType=VmTemplate serverPool=OVM
Status: Success
Time: 2016-12-13 20:45:19,583 CST
JobId: 1481683517944
Data:
   id:0004fb000006000051f7daa45de3c2d9  name:gg20b-template
```

Once the cloning process has completed, the new systems are ready for use, as shown here:

```
OVM> show vm name=cc03-template
Command: show vm name=cc03-template
Status: Success
Time: 2016-12-14 15:11:56,984 CST
Data:
   Status = Template
   Memory (MB) = 16384
   Max. Memory (MB) = 16384
   Processors = 4
   Max. Processors = 4
   Priority = 50
   Processor Cap = 100
   High Availability = No
   Operating System = Oracle Linux 6
   Mouse Type = USB TABLET
   Domain Type = Xen HVM PV Drivers
   Keymap = en-us
   Start Policy = Current Server
   Boot Order 1 = Disk
   Boot Order 2 = CDROM
   Disk Limit = 107
   Huge Pages Enabled = No
   Config File Absolute Path = /dev/mapper/36090a048b07935f5074105cf3e01f09b/
Templates/0004fb0000060000b92e0eca3a10b581/vm.cfg
   Config File Mounted Path = /OVS/Repositories/0004fb00000300001c9bd84feea35191/
Templates/0004fb0000060000b92e0eca3a10b581/vm.cfg
   Repository = 0004fb00000300001c9bd84feea35191   [Repo01]
   Vnic 1 = 0004fb00000700004b07872a5cab4f9e   [Template Vnic]
   VmDiskMapping 1 = 0004fb00001300003d22b031a7ecc3b0
[Mapping for disk Id (0004fb000012000083ddad8615d7097a.img)]
   VmDiskMapping 2 = 0004fb0000130000b7b74b0c95224a67
[Mapping for disk Id (EMPTY_CDROM)]
   VmDiskMapping 3 = 0004fb000013000059c28646ee5ce169
```

```
[Mapping for disk Id (0004fb0000120000fbebf7df3e944a1e.img)]
  VmDiskMapping 4 = 0004fb00001300005c0b30ff46407748
[Mapping for disk Id (0004fb00001200006f838b8764270ee6.img)]
  VmDiskMapping 5 = 0004fb000013000082e9268051f59a71
[Mapping for disk Id (0004fb00001200002cb8f1ef356006bc.img)]
  VmDiskMapping 6 = 0004fb00001300008af1edebac11a372
[Mapping for disk Id (0004fb0000120000c0c257e7aabc355c.img)]
  VmDiskMapping 7 = 0004fb000013000037c6012dca5778c8
[Mapping for disk Id (0004fb0000120000ba62e156ae55b3f3.img)]
  VmDiskMapping 8 = 0004fb00001300008e3bd5664144ada4
[Mapping for disk Id (0004fb0000120000441abd9be93025f6.img)]
0c5ef74683a37c825  [Mapping for disk Id (0004fb0000120000f5e26d8816fc962e.img)]
  VmDiskMapping 10 = 0004fb00001300007b499bdff6e10d2d
[Mapping for disk Id (0004fb00001200007fc40430edec10e2.img)]
  VmDiskMapping 11 = 0004fb00001300000a14e002c757aa8a
[Mapping for disk Id (0004fb000012000090cc1f586822e66a.img)]
  VmDiskMapping 12 = 0004fb000013000052f7b79f9d460e82
[Mapping for disk Id (0004fb000012000042c35d4369fb0b15.img)]
  VmDiskMapping 13 = 0004fb000013000068bb0fbddace46b9
[Mapping for disk Id (0004fb0000120000e46f82b4907bb33f.img)]
  VmDiskMapping 14 = 0004fb000013000050cbfceebfbb8fca
[Mapping for disk Id (0004fb0000120000df2a75f7d5e1b11a.img)]
  VmDiskMapping 15 = 0004fb0000130000307420188ba2404
[Mapping for disk Id (0004fb0000120000c2de1da41f31c784.img)]
  VmDiskMapping 16 = 0004fb000013000014e9b0e63c0e822c
[Mapping for disk Id (0004fb00001200004d4e7a0b90d9d16a.img)]
  VmDiskMapping 17 = 0004fb00001300003a00b892efee053b
[Mapping for disk Id (0004fb0000120000e5c986691e57c63f.img)]
  VmDiskMapping 18 = 0004fb000013000082d5da448149d43c
[Mapping for disk Id (0004fb0000120000224ef9089aca24be.img)]
  Restart Action On Crash = Restart
  Id = 0004fb0000060000b92e0eca3a10b581  [cc03-template]
  Name = cc03-template
  Locked = false
  DeprecatedAttrs = [Huge Pages Enabled (Deprecated for PV guest)]
```

The cloning process addresses the MAC address issue we used to have with creating templates in earlier versions of Oracle VM. When you create a new VM from this template, a new MAC address will be assigned.

Summary

This chapter covered some of the different options for managing the state of Oracle VM virtual machines, including the starting and stopping of virtual machines, the suspending and resuming of virtual machines, as well as the older deployment process and the cloning process. Managing the state of the virtual machines is really the most important task an administrator has to take on—in addition to making sure everything is properly backed up.

Chapter 21 covers physical to virtual migration.

CHAPTER
21

Physical-to-Virtual Migration and Virtual-to-Virtual Migration

I n previous chapters, you learned how to create virtual machines by hand and via templates and assemblies. In addition to these methods, it is also possible to create a virtual machine in Oracle VM from an existing physical machine. This opens up many possibilities for both testing and upgrading without putting your production system at risk. It also provides the ability to quickly move a legacy system on old hardware to a more stable and robust virtual machine. Uses of the physical-to-virtual migration include the following:

- **Migration**   Migrating physical servers on old hardware to a newer, faster virtual machine.

- **Upgrade testing**   It is unwise to upgrade the operating system on a production server to a newer version without testing. Here, you can convert the physical machine to a virtual machine and test the upgrade process several times until you are comfortable with the outcome.

- **Application upgrades**   You can easily take a copy of the production server and create a virtual machine for application upgrade testing.

- **Problem resolution**   If you are experiencing a production issue, a virtual machine can be created in order to perform testing in order to determine what the problem is without affecting production users.

As you can see, there are multiple reasons why performing a physical-to-virtual (P2V) migration is useful. In addition, if hardware virtualization is being used, there is no reason why this technique cannot be used to migrate from another vendor's virtualization product to OVM.

Migrating a Physical Server to OVM

The migration process of moving a physical server to OVM is fairly straightforward. In order to migrate a physical machine to a virtual machine, the physical machine must be shut down. Therefore, some downtime is required.

In order to convert a physical machine to a virtual machine, you must boot the OVM 3 Server CD-ROM. The boot screen will appear. Click Enter to install OVM on this system (you don't want to do that for this example) or type **p2v** at the boot prompt and press ENTER. This is shown in Figure 21-1.

From here, the system will boot into the OVM installer by booting the Linux operating system (OS). Once it has completed the boot process, you will see the Disk Found screen. Here, you can choose to test the CD-ROM or press TAB to move the focus to Skip and then press ENTER, as shown in Figure 21-2.

The installation process will begin to discover the hard disk of the physical system and will eventually end up at the "Select the disks to include in the image" dialog. From here, you should select all the disks you intend to migrate. The sample system in the figures has only one disk associated with it. Highlight all the disks to be included by using the arrow keys and SPACEBAR to select the disks. Once you have selected all the disks you want to include, tab to OK and proceed by pressing ENTER. This screen is shown in Figure 21-3.

At this point, you will be prompted to provide some additional information about the virtual machine to be created. The information requested includes the name of the VM, the memory to be allocated, the number of virtual CPUs, and the console password. This is shown in Figure 21-4. When you have filled in all of the blanks, tab to OK and press ENTER.

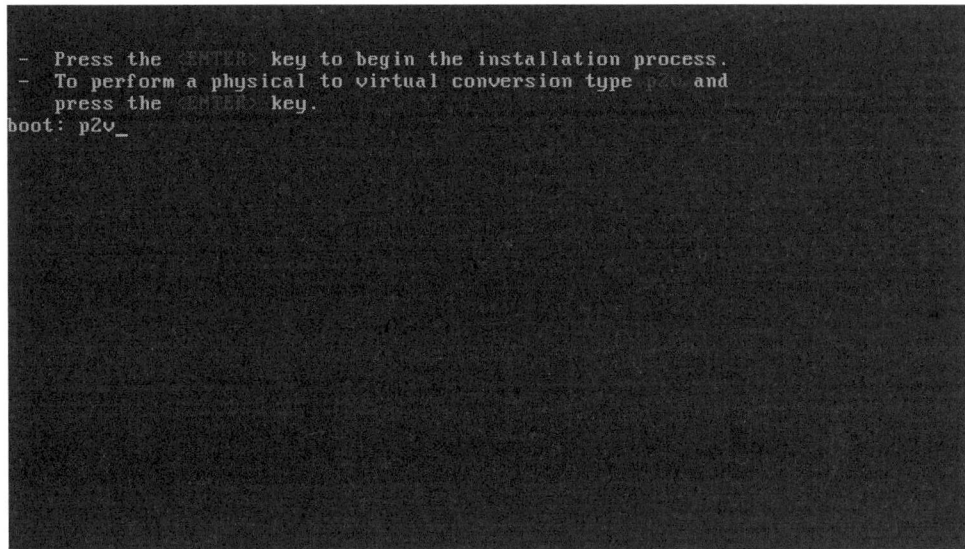

FIGURE 21-1. *The OVM Server boot screen*

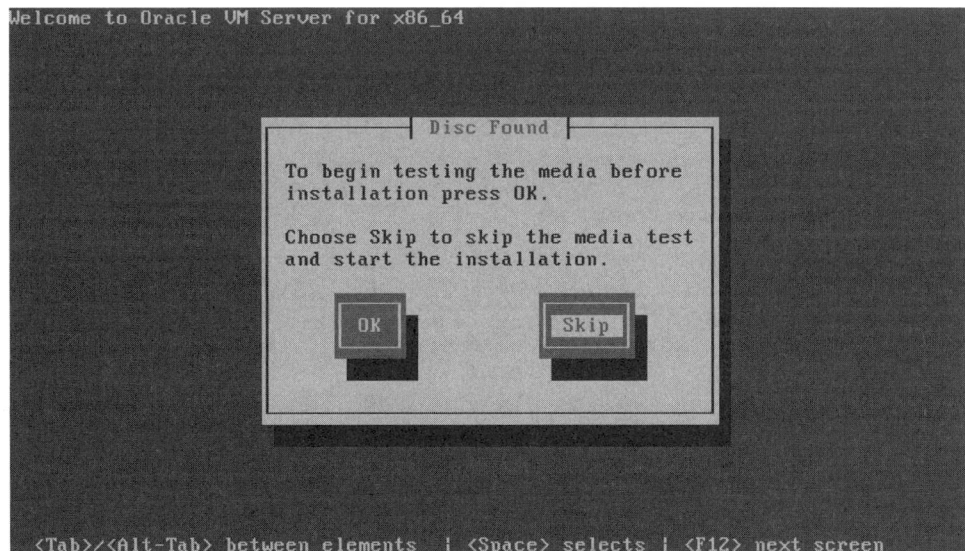

FIGURE 21-2. *The Disk Found dialog*

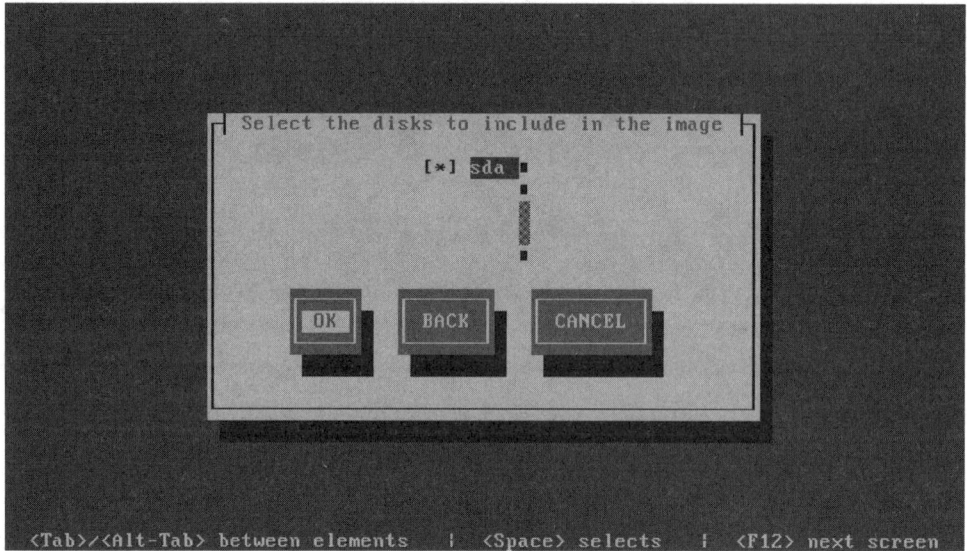

FIGURE 21-3. *The "Select the disks to include in the image" dialog*

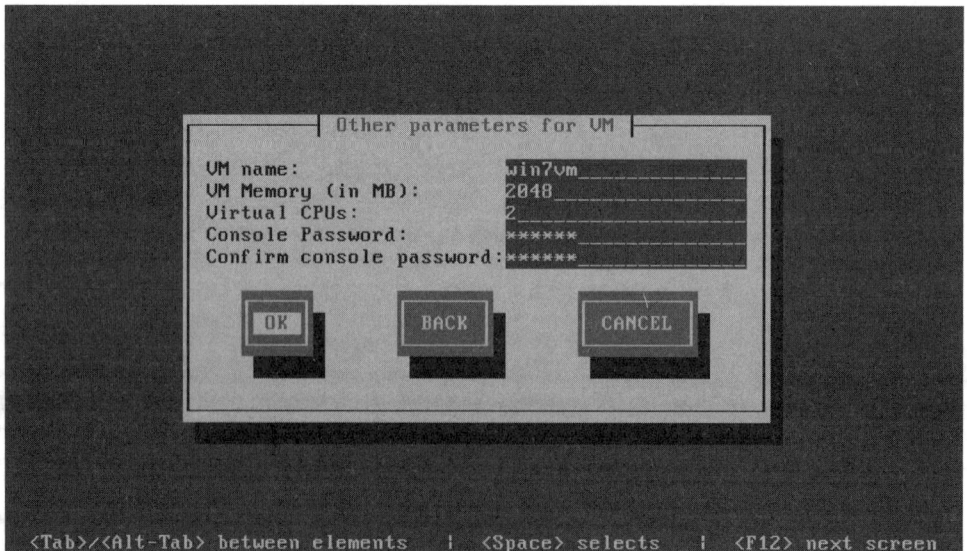

FIGURE 21-4. *The "Other parameters for VM" dialog*

```
Starting web server
HTTPS web server is running on 192.168.1.77 port 443...
Interrupt with control-C
```

FIGURE 21-5. *The web server URL*

Once you click ENTER, you will see a message at the bottom of the screen informing you of a web server that has been started. The URL of the web server is the IP address that has been provided here, as shown in Figure 21-5. You will use this URL in the next stage.

Open the URL (IP address) in a browser using HTTPS. This will open a web page showing you a list of files that are available for download. This is shown in Figure 21-6.

Take note of the files that have been displayed. You will need the vm.cfg and virtual disk image System-sda.img in the next step.

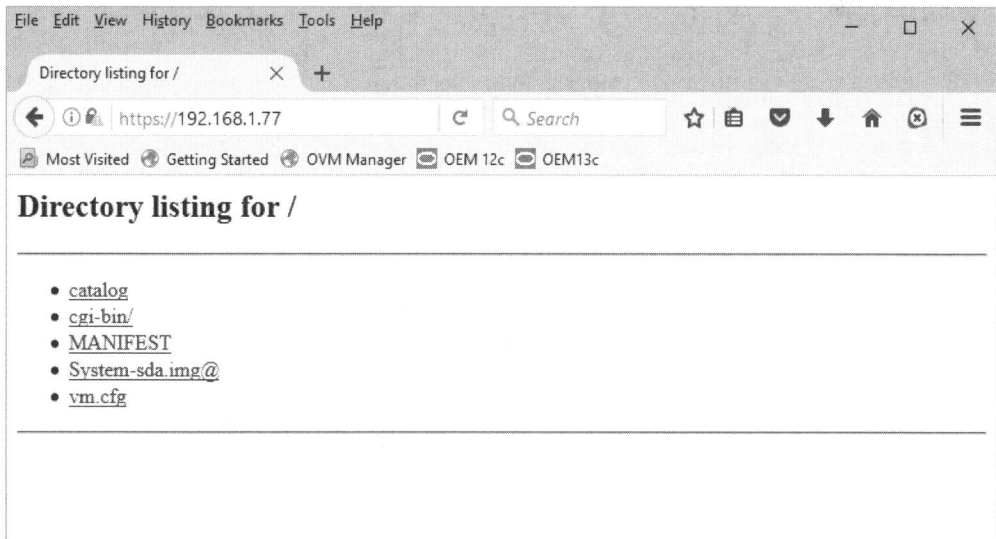

FIGURE 21-6. *The web server URL page*

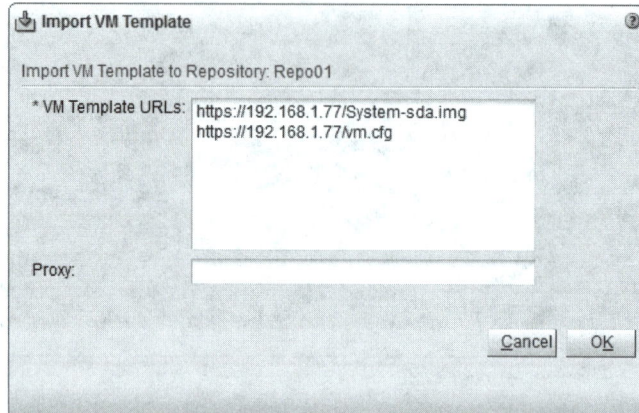

FIGURE 21-7. *The Import VM Template dialog*

Now that you have the URL of the images, you will import them into OVM via the OVM Manager. In the OVM Manager repositories screen, select the repository to be used and navigate to templates. Once you are in the templates screen, you can select Import Template. Fill in the URL for the virtual disks and vm.cfg file that you noted in the previous screen. The Import VM Templates dialog is shown in Figure 21-7.

Once the template has been imported, you will create a virtual machine using the methods described in this book to create a virtual machine from a template.

Migrating Another Vendor's VM to OVM

It is often necessary to move a virtual machine from another vendor to OVM. This other vendor might be VMware or Microsoft Hyper-V. In this section we will take a look at moving a VMware virtual machine to OVM. In earlier versions of OVM you would use the same P2V process that you used in the previous section. This does not work with the current version of OVM. In order to migrate from VMware to OVM you must take the VMware images and convert them directly into an OVM virtual appliance.

Migrating from VMware

In order to migrate a virtual machine from VMware to OVM, you must first export the VM in VMware and then import it into OVM. In order to export a virtual machine in VMware, the virtual machine must be stopped. Highlight the virtual machine in the VMware vSphere client. From the File menu, select Export | Export OVF Template. This will invoke the Export OVF Template dialog shown in Figure 21-8.

Fill in the path to the local directory where you want the OVF template to be exported to. This will be a directory on the system from which you are running, not on the Oracle VM server. Once you have completed this, you will see the progress in the Exporting dialog, as shown in Figure 21-9.

Depending on the size of the virtual machine, this could take a while. Once it has completed, you will see the Export Complete dialog (not shown). The next step moves from the VMware vSphere client to the Oracle VM Manager.

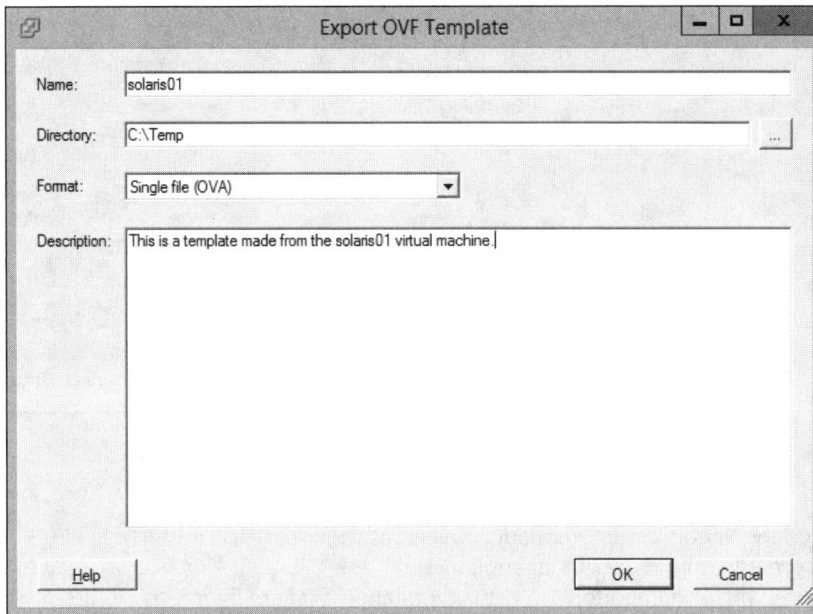

FIGURE 21-8.   *The Export OVF Template dialog*

In order to import an OVA image into Oracle VM, you must use a web server to download the file. However you decide to do this, you must move the OVA file that you just created to a web server that is accessible from OVM. Once you have uploaded the file to a web server, you will be able to import using the Oracle VM Manager.

From the Oracle VM Manager, select the repository into which you want to import the OVA image. Select the Virtual Appliances folder within the repository that you want to use and then choose the Import Virtual Appliance icon from the toolbar in the management pane. This will

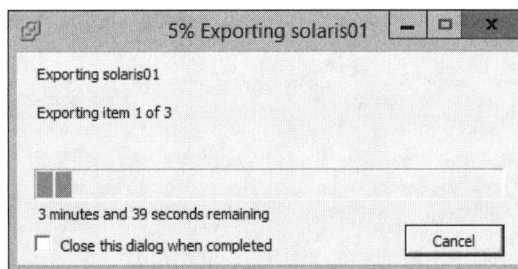

FIGURE 21-9.   *The Exporting dialog*

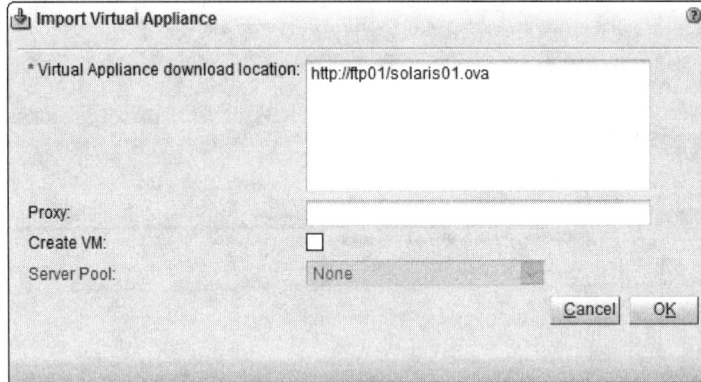

FIGURE 21-10. *The Import Virtual Appliance dialog*

bring up the Import Virtual Appliance dialog, as shown in Figure 21-10. Fill in the URL and click OK in order to import the virtual appliance.

Once you have imported the virtual appliance, you are then ready to use it. Select Create Virtual Machine (available from several menus) and select Clone from an Existing Virtual Appliance, as shown in Figure 21-11.

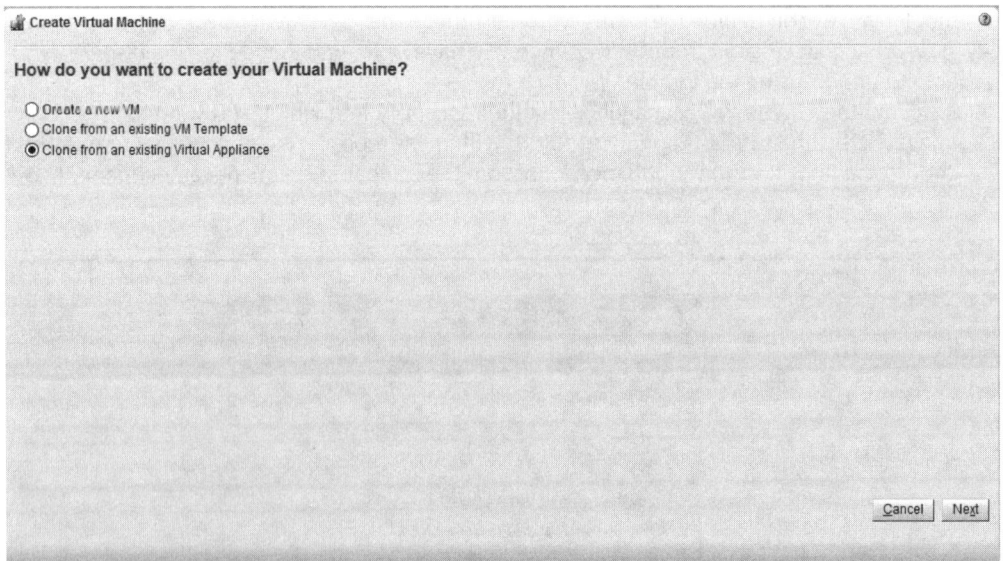

FIGURE 21-11. *The Create Virtual Machine dialog*

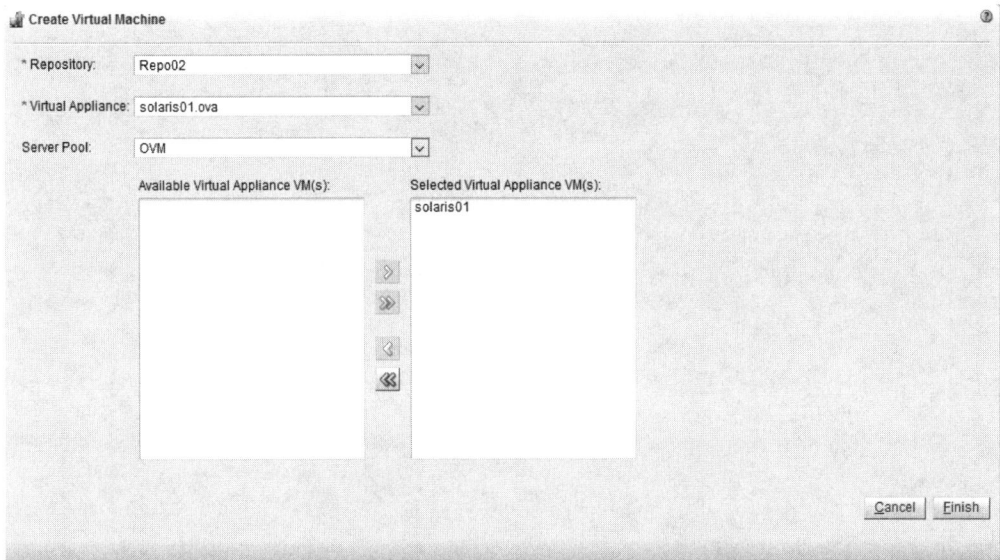

FIGURE 21-12. *Select the repository, virtual appliance, and server pool.*

Once you have selected to create from a virtual appliance, you will be asked what the repository is, what the virtual appliance is, and which server pool to install it in. This is shown in Figure 21-12.

Once you have clicked Finish, the virtual machine will be created. This will complete the conversion from VMware to Oracle VM.

Before starting the virtual machine, you should edit it and make sure the network and disk are set up correctly. Once you have completed this step, you can start the VM.

Summary

As you can see from this chapter, it isn't very difficult to create a virtual machine from either a physical system or from a VMware virtual machine. Each process is different, but both are very straightforward and easy to do. Both also require the virtual or physical machine to be down during the process.

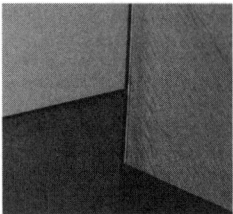

CHAPTER
22

Virtualization Summary
and Best Practices

This chapter summarizes the key concepts and tasks presented in this book relating to the Oracle virtualization platform. This chapter uses two approaches: the minimalist approach (sometimes confused with "least expensive") and the realist approach, whereby benefits of virtualization are realized using recommended best-practice methods without breaking the bank. For example, although it is true only one virtual machine server is required to deploy guest VMs, and although such a configuration may be deemed acceptable for demonstration or discussion purposes, a single-VM-server configuration cannot realistically meet even the most basic availability and performance requirements. In addition, a single Oracle VM Server configuration is also limited to the scaling capability of just that machine (that is, the number of CPU sockets, memory slots, expansion slots, and so on). Meanwhile, a recommended best practice is to have three or more virtual machine servers. Again, depending on the objective, three, five, seven, or nine OVS machines may be required in the long run, but the initial deployment requirements are satisfied with five servers.

Each approach (minimalist or realist) will be followed by a summary of post-deployment, management, and operations best practices. These include the concepts and tasks in support of backup and recovery, monitoring and tuning, and capacity planning, which will primarily focus on storage volume, network traffic, and process performance, including virtualization administrative tasks such as VM migrations and patching.

Oracle VM Resource Basics

The importance of planning could be emphasized at the beginning of every section of every chapter and it would still not be emphasized enough. The following sections summarize the key concepts when standing up a new Oracle VM environment. Each section is based on the primary computing environment resource—namely, storage, networking, memory, and CPU.

Storage

The source of storage from the perspective of the guest VM is either storage presented by the repository, storage presented directly to the guest VM by a SAN or a file server, or storage residing locally on an Oracle VM server. Generally speaking, all storage in an Oracle VM environment is based on SAN storage, file server storage, or storage residing locally on an Oracle VM server. The main difference is whether or not additional maintenance and operations are required when you're growing the storage used by the guest virtual machine. Regardless of the source (SAN, NFS, or disk attached locally to the Oracle VM server), if the guest VM is using storage presented through a repository, and the repository has available space, then the guest VM storage can grow dynamically without additional SAN, NFS, or VM server local disk administration. If, however, the guest VM is using storage presented directly from the SAN, NFS, or local disk (as opposed to presented through a repository), then additional administration is required to grow the LUN.

Repository-Based Storage

The storage used by an Oracle VM storage repository is based on SAN storage, file server storage, or storage residing locally on an Oracle VM server. Although there are performance implications between using network-based storage versus locally attached storage, it is more important to understand the maintenance and operational issues when you're considering using either storage method. Figure 22-1 shows information about physical storage that is locally attached to the Oracle VM server. In this case, the storage is a 44TB array defined as a single LUN. The Oracle VM server detects the storage and lists it as available. This storage can be used when you're defining the repository.

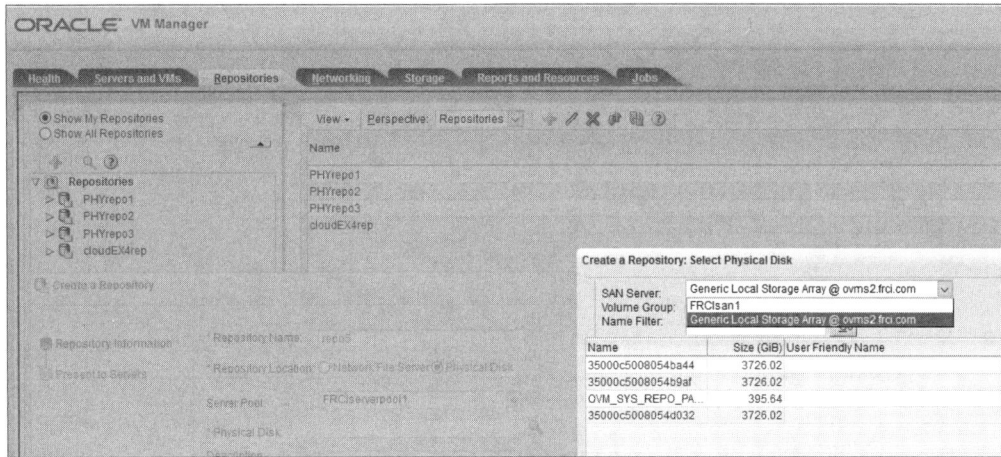

FIGURE 22-1. *Repository using locally attached storage*

Using locally attached storage, however, limits the VM migration capabilities regardless of the way the storage is presented to the guest VM (that is, through a repository or directly) and restricts any VM using the locally attached storage to operate strictly on the VM server where the locally attached storage resides. This limitation is somewhat resolved with the release of Oracle VM 3.4; however, there are still some limitations that have an impact on live migration and are covered in greater detail in the release notes.

The key point is that guest VMs using repository-based storage have the flexibility to grow the storage allocated to them dynamically from storage available in the storage repository VM without having to allocate additional storage LUNs from the SAN or grow a file system. Repository-based storage is therefore a general best practice to use as a source of storage for guest VMs.

Network-Based Shared Storage

Network-based shared storage presented to the Oracle VM servers either is a storage area network (SAN) using the iSCSI protocol or is based on file server sharing (NAS) using NFS exports/shares. In either case, a virtual disk used by a guest VM is defined at the storage layer with a specific size, and it requires manual intervention to grow if additional space is needed. Figure 22-2 shows the Storage tab of the VM manager GUI, which lists a 2TB LUN that was created in the SAN server "prodsan1" and is currently being used by the repository "PHYrepo1."

This LUN could have instead been presented directly to a guest VM, but that would have been a 2TB dedication. Because the LUN has been presented to the repository PHYrepo1, the 2TB is available to any VM and the storage can be allocated based on the VM's need. For example, if an Oracle Linux guest VM (OLVM1) were to be created and needed two disks (for example, 20GB for the root file system and 80GB for everything else), that guest virtual machine (once created) would use a total of 100GB out of the 2TB allocated to the repository, and the repository would still have 1.9TB available for other virtual machines. Meanwhile, if the storage requirements of OLVM1 were to increase, then the disks of that guest virtual machine could be increased to whatever size is necessary (provided it's less than 1.9TB), and no other administration would be

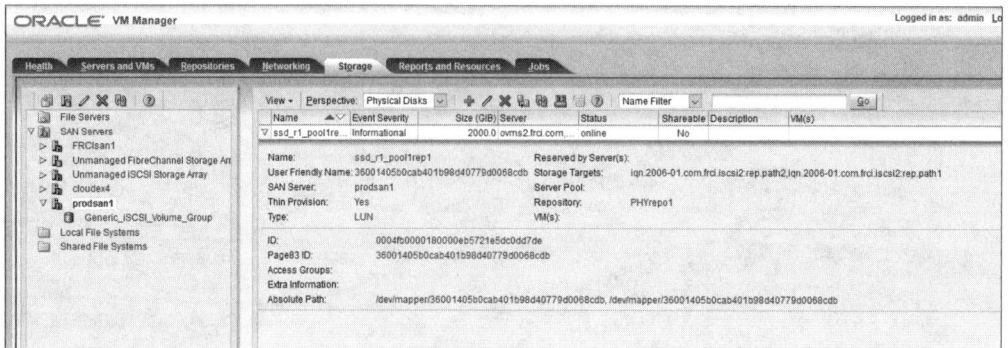

FIGURE 22-2. *Storage tab showing SAN storage*

required because the storage is available in the storage repository. If the two discs created in this example were allocated as individual LUNs, then a system administrator would be required to grow each of the LUNs at the operating system before the disks could be grown in the guest virtual machine.

There may also be performance benefits between using physical LUNs versus virtual disks out of a storage repository. However, each environment and situation should be tested to determine whether the performance benefits outweigh the additional administration required to manage the shared storage as opposed to using repository-based storage.

Locally Attached Storage

A given VM server may have storage that is locally attached and is therefore only available to processes running on that server. With the release of Oracle VM version 3.4, locally attached storage can be migrated, but other limitations generally prohibit the use of locally attached storage. For these reasons, use of locally attached storage is discouraged. However, with that said, locally attached storage does work well for the minimalist approach because with that approach the Oracle VM architecture very likely has only one VM server, so live migration activities are very likely not an issue. Figure 22-3 shows locally attached storage for VM usage.

Networking

Generally speaking, there are two primary considerations in the Oracle VM network environment: the physical network components and the virtual network components, also known as *network channels.* Figure 22-4 shows the Networking tab in the Oracle VM Manager GUI. From the minimalist perspective, there will be one physical network interface card (NIC) per machine, and all Oracle VM network channels use the single NIC. This is an acceptable configuration from the perspective of an operational environment. However, even from a minimalist perspective, in production there should be at least two physical NIC adapters per network path, and these should be bonded to provide at least a minimum sense of availability (in most cases, this provides performance benefits as well).

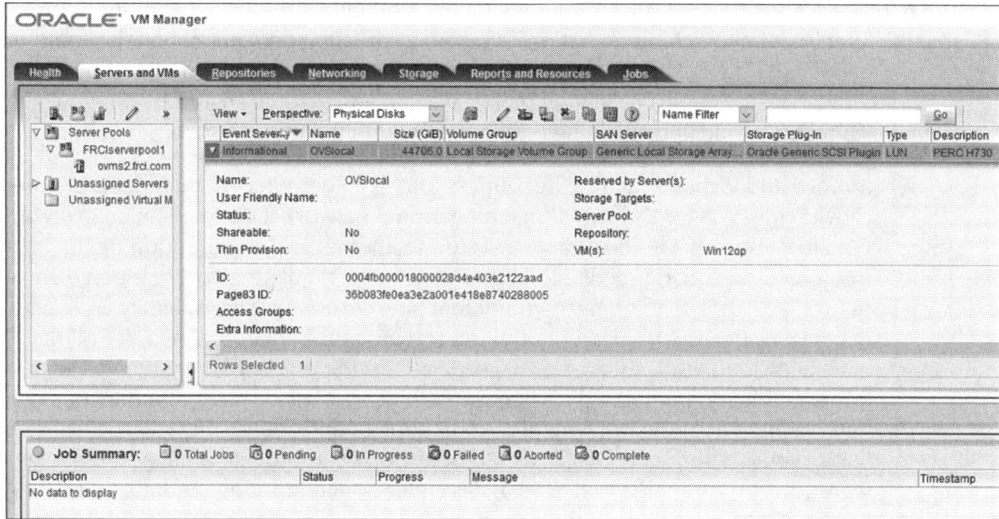

FIGURE 22-3. *Locally attached storage for VM usage*

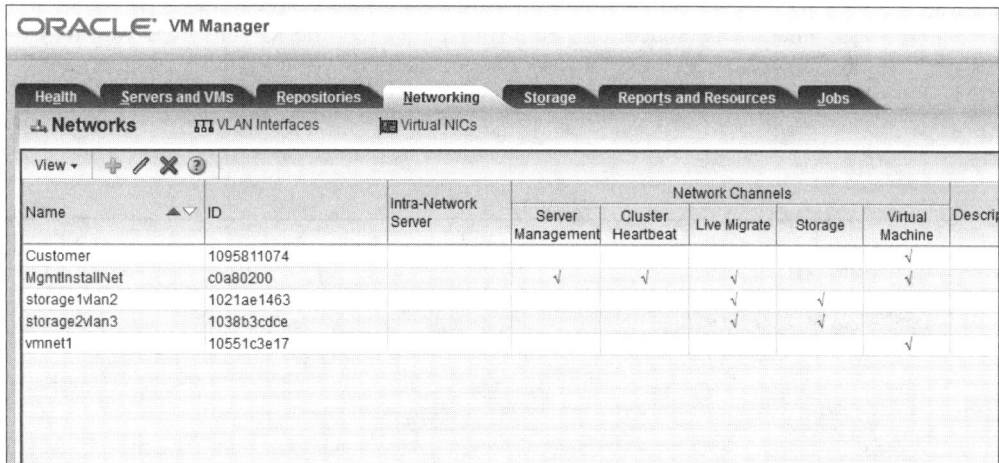

FIGURE 22-4. *Networking tab*

Oracle VM Network Channels

The purpose of the Oracle VM network channel is to provide a dedicated path in support of specific Oracle VM networking operations. Ideally, each of the network channels would have one or more dedicated physical NIC network connections. Whereas the minimalist approach may have only one NIC (or at least a bonded pair of NIC adapters) to be shared by all network channels, a realist would approach the configuration with the following considerations:

- **Storage and Virtual Machine network channels** These network channels are used to provide the path for the virtual machine virtual network (communications between Oracle VMs and from the Oracle VMs to the Internet and resources on the local network). It is a recommended practice to define VLAN virtual adapters for the storage and network, as well as to manage virtual machine communications. Figure 22-5 shows an example of the VLAN adapter definition screen. In this example, two VLAN interfaces have been defined. They are on two separate bond ports of two Oracle VM servers. In this example, no addressing was chosen for the VLAN interfaces, but they could've easily been defined as Static or Dynamic. An IP address and subnet mask would be required if Static were chosen, and DHCP would be expected to provide an IP address if Dynamic were chosen. Ultimately, CIDR (classless inter-domain routing) addressing may be used for the VLAN adapter definitions to manage traffic and access to specific address ranges, as well as to provide additional security.

- **Server Management and cluster heartbeat network channels** These two network channels may be combined, given the notion that the cluster heartbeat is a high-priority virtual network, and the traffic on this network should not (if at all possible) ever be degraded or impeded because the cluster heartbeat is used to monitor the overall health of a given Oracle VM server. If a problem is detected for a given Oracle VM server on the cluster heartbeat network, that particular Oracle VM server may be "fenced" and the associated virtual machines will be migrated to another Oracle VM server in the cluster. The Server Management network channel is used by the agents running on the Oracle VM servers.

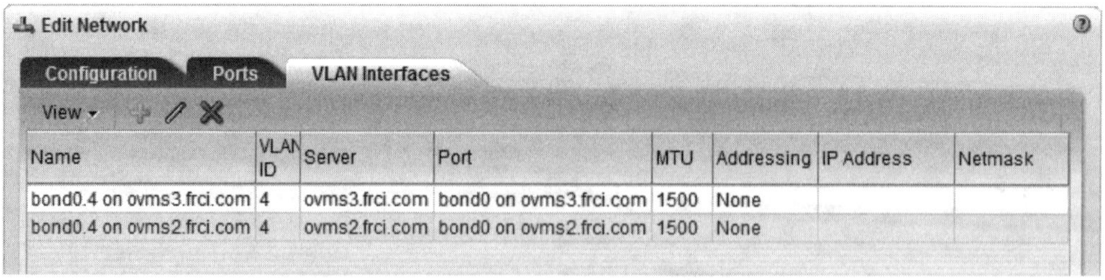

FIGURE 22-5. *VLAN adapter definition*

- **Live Migrate network channel** As the name implies, this network channel is used during Oracle guest VM migration operations. Migration operations occur manually or indirectly. During live migration, the memory semaphores of an Oracle guest VM are moved from one VM server to another. This operation may also be performed for a stopped guest virtual machine, in which case there are no memory semaphores to move because the guest VM is not currently running. Indirectly, however, if the agent running on an Oracle VM server detects unacceptable latency or an outage of the heartbeat, then the agent spawns the request to migrate running guest VMs to another VM server in the cluster. It is therefore a recommended best practice to dedicate a physical network path to live migration operations.

Memory and CPU

The minimalist approach to memory is simple: pack the Oracle VM server with enough memory to support the guest VMs, plus a little more for the hypervisor. This is not far from reality. Although it is not required to have the same amount of memory on each of the VM servers, it is recommended that all the servers in a given cluster are of the same "family" in terms of CPU, and any given VM server should conceivably be able to handle the load of all guest VMs. Realistically, this should never be expected, especially for some larger implementations. However, there are no rules to the size and speed of memory, save one: more is better.

Again, although it is true no given Oracle VM server should be expected to run all Oracle VMs simultaneously, the consideration must be made that in the event of a failure of one or more Oracle VM servers, the remaining Oracle VM servers should be able to sustain the operations of the guest virtual machines currently running. At best, there should be sufficient memory in a single Oracle VM server to run the mission-critical guest VMs. This is the minimalist approach. Realistically, however, a given Oracle VM server or several Oracle VM servers in a cluster should have sufficient memory to support the mission-critical guest virtual machines as well as a few additional servers, for example, servers used for administration and maintenance (Oracle Enterprise Manager RMAN catalog database, etc.) Also keep in mind that the memory resources are not "shared" across the Oracle VM servers (which would really be nice).

Understanding VLANs and CIDR Addressing

Oracle VM uses VLANs that have been defined on network switches. Oracle VM does not create VLANs; it only accesses existing VLANs that have been created by network administrators on network switches. Network administrators must provide information about VLANs such as VLAN ID, subnet, netmask, and default gateway in order for the Oracle VM network to use the VLAN.

As VLANs are created, CIDR addressing can be used to enhance security and limit traffic on the VLAN. The CIDR addressing is specified in the VLAN adapter definition. The CIDR addressing technique can be applied to any VLAN or another Oracle VM NIC adapter definition.

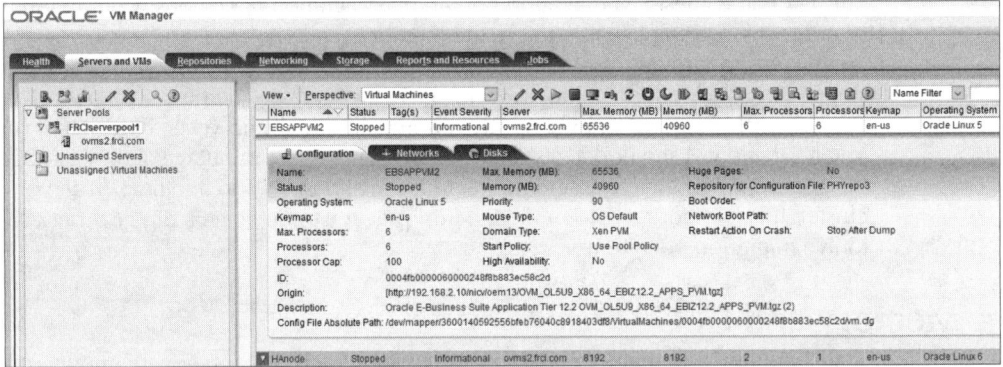

FIGURE 22-6. *VM server-based guest VMs showing memory and CPU cores*

Finally, the amount of memory on a given VM server needs to be sufficient to run not only the guest VMs, but also to support the requirements of the dom0 hypervisor. Figure 22-6 is an example of a guest VM showing memory and CPU cores. Rule of thumb: add up the memory required by each guest VM and then add another 4 to 8GB.

With respect to CPU requirements, as with memory, the number of available CPU cores on a given Oracle VM server should be based on the number of CPU cores required by the virtual machines, plus one or two CPU cores for the hypervisor dom0. For example, if there are 10 guest machines, and each guest VM requires two virtual CPUs, then the VM server should have a minimum of 22 cores available: (two cores per guest VM × 10 guest VMs) + two cores for the hypervisor dom0. Again, this is the minimalist approach. Realistically, because there should be at least three Oracle VM servers, and the load should be spread more or less equally across the VM servers, then each Oracle VM server should have approximately eight CPU cores. Keep in mind this does not mean 12 sockets. In today's world, a 24-core equipped machine may fit on just three CPU sockets.

In short, both the minimalist and realist approaches to CPU and memory are basically the same: more is better (that is, more available physical resources), and ultimately the virtual requirement must be equal to or less than the physical resources available. The difference between the two approaches (minimalist and realist) with respect to CPU and memory resources is a factor of capacity rather than performance; in other words, regardless of the CPU core "speed" (in terms of hertz) or the cores-to-socket ratio, the minimum number of CPUs "to go into the plan" should be equal to or greater than the number of virtual machines. Similarly, for the memory, the total physical memory should be equal to or greater than the maximum that will be allocated (or allowed) to the respective guest virtual machines. Again, a resource's speed is not the limiting factor.

Oracle VM and Resource Virtualization

The discussion of computer system virtualization is often framed from a data center and hosted operating system perspective with concepts and components related to "*X* as a Service."

When presenting a recipe, the chef first discusses or explains the ingredients needed. In the case of virtualization, the ingredients equate to the resources defined, configured, integrated, and finally deployed and managed in support of virtualizing the application and database systems. These resources are then presented as a service to the cloud customers. These ingredients, or resources, include storage, networking, memory, and CPU.

- **Storage**   Shared storage that is defined for the Oracle VM repository is a general best practice. An NFS-mounted file system can be used for the repository and may be easier to manage than a LUN carved out of SAN storage, but the SAN storage may perform better. Ultimately, the guest VM use of storage from the repository is easier to manage because the storage is served out of the repository and managed by Oracle VM. Storage that is carved out of a SAN LUN must be manually adjusted in the SAN to accommodate an increase in storage requirements. If space from a storage repository were used, then the same requirement increase can be handled within Oracle VM alone, without a change in the SAN—the difference being that the storage repository must have been defined with the extra storage to start with.

- **Networking**   The minimalist approach is to run all network channels out of a single NIC or a single bonded pair. However, the realist approach is to dedicate physical resources to a logical grouping of the network channels such that the cluster heartbeat is the most volatile for a clustered server pool configuration, and each of the remaining network channels should be configured with VLANs. CIDR addressing (at the VLAN adapter) may also be used based on the deployment requirements. It should be noted that although the Oracle VM networking facilities provide virtual switching and networking capabilities, the physical network must also be configured with the appropriate VLAN characteristics required by the Oracle VM network.

- **Memory and CPU**   Simply put, more is better. There should be one or two more CPU cores than required by the sum of all guest VMs running at a given point in time. Regarding memory, there should be 4 to 8GB more memory than required by the sum of all guest VMs running at a given point in time.

The Oracle VM Start to Finish

This section covers a hypothetical deployment of an Oracle VM technology stack. After the Oracle VM Manager, Oracle VM server, guest Oracle VM templates, and the requisite Oracle Linux software have been acquired, the concepts and tasks for deploying an Oracle VM installation begin with planning the configuration, with the objective of sustaining some basic guest VMs.

The source of the installation and upgrade software should be the Oracle eDelivery site "Oracle Software Delivery Cloud" whenever possible. Although there are many other sources of software, including the Oracle Technology Network, only the eDelivery site is guaranteed to contain production-ready bundles. The URL for this site is https://edelivery.oracle.com, and it contains the Oracle VM software and templates required for most deployments. Figure 22-7 shows a partial Oracle software-delivery site listing of Oracle VM Server software. If the term "template" would have been included in the search, the result would have included 38 products, each of which require further refinement to drill down to the specific required template.

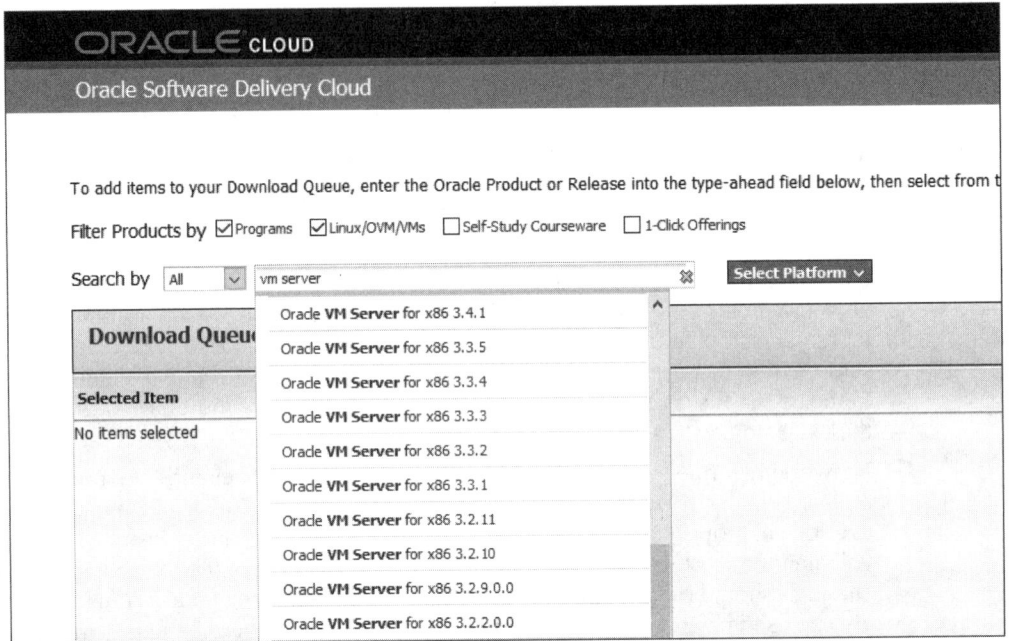

FIGURE 22-7. *Oracle software-delivery site listing VM software*

In preparation for our hypothetical Oracle VM environment deployment, the following software should be downloaded:

- Oracle VM Manager
- Oracle VM Server
- Oracle Linux template (optional)
- Oracle Linux server software (optional)
- Other operating system(s), such as Windows, CentOS, and so on

Storage, Pools, Servers, and Repositories

The downloaded software will be used to establish the environment. As discussed previously in this book, it is a good practice (if not a best practice) to establish a local yum repository. Although it is not required, the local yum repository can be used to store the entire set of Oracle VM software. It is mentioned here purely as a suggestion, but it is not required. In fact, there is no "yum install" command to deploy the Oracle VM Manager or VM Server software. The best practice is to install the VM Manager into a supported bare-metal-based operating system using the process documented in this book, along with the Oracle VM documentation. The yum repository is an option for storing and deploying subsequent patches as they become available. Oracle VM patches can be downloaded and deployed into the local yum repository so that the software is available not only to the Oracle

VM Manager and Oracle VM Server machines running the Oracle VM environment, but also to the guest VMs deployed into the Oracle VM environment.

Deploying Oracle VM

The deployment of Oracle VM begins with planning. The Oracle VM Manager is the first major component to deploy. As such, the following serves to clarify some points:

- OVM Manager should not be installed on the same server as Enterprise Manager. The OVM Manager installation *cannot* use the WebLogic server that is installed with Oracle Enterprise Manager. The OVM Manager installation requires its own technology stack.

- Oracle VM Manager is an application that is installed on a normal Linux operating system such as Oracle Linux or Redhat Linux 5.8+ (including 6 and 7), and it can be a physical or virtual machine. (However, you should learn the process first before complicating it with virtualizing the virtualization management tools.)

- The Oracle VM Manager doesn't need anything special for networking. It just needs enough network to allow connectivity; nothing else is needed.

- The Oracle VM Manager does not need access to SAN or NAS storage used by the OVM servers (this is an especially misunderstood aspect of storage).

- The Oracle VM Manager GUI is the best place to manage the Oracle VM environment. Very few operations (by design) are performed from the command line outside the Oracle VM Manager. Unless directed specifically by Oracle Support, you should perform all Oracle VM management operations from within the Oracle VM Manager environment.

Assuming enough thought and planning have been given to the storage and networking, a typical deployment will have storage served to three or more Oracle VM servers through multiple repositories. It is advisable, if not a best practice, to group the Oracle VM guest virtual machines of a similar type, business system, or role into a given repository or group of repositories, which makes backing up the guest VMs and their associated data much simpler and more logical. In other words, you should create each repository with the intent of putting logically grouped VMs into it. This practice applies not only to repositories, but also to the server pools and network-creation tasks. Figure 22-8 shows an example of logically grouped VM repositories, where there are multiple repositories for guest virtual machines based on physical disks and another repository for guest VMs targeted for cloud deployment.

With respect to the planning of the server pools, the most important restriction to remember is that the clustering is only available at creation time. A nonclustered, stand-alone server pool cannot be dynamically "clustered." It must be re-created as a clustered server pool. The converse is also true: that is, a clustered server pool cannot be made into a nonclustered, stand-alone server pool but rather must be dropped and re-created. The main difference between clustered and nonclustered server pools is the OCFS2 file system used to support the clustered server pool. The crux of the biscuit: it is perfectly acceptable (and is a recommended best practice) to create the server pool as a clustered server pool with only one server and then add servers down the road as the Oracle VM environment grows.

The first major task is to install the Oracle VM Manager on a machine. Again, generally speaking, it is this author's opinion that you should run Oracle products in and around other Oracle products. In other words, it is a recommended best practice to deploy Oracle Fusion middleware, for example, within an Oracle Linux environment, and if you're virtualizing the environment, to do so with Oracle

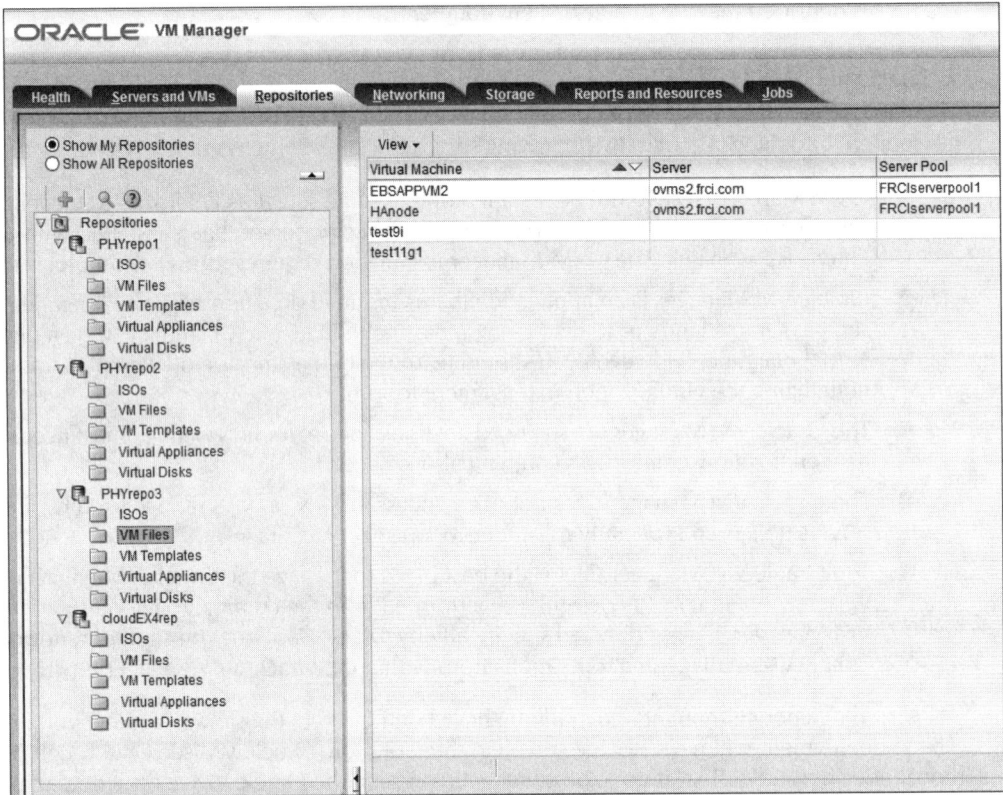

FIGURE 22-8. *Logically grouped VM repositories*

virtualization products. This may be the most obvious of general best practices, but it is also no doubt the most difficult to address, especially if the given environment is running another flavor of virtualization product.

Clustered server pools are defined at the time of server pool creation. A server pool is created using one or more Oracle VM servers; the recommended number of Oracle VM servers is three (or more), but it should also be an odd number of Oracle VM servers (three, five, seven, and so on). In a larger environment, it is also a best practice to logically group the Oracle VM components. Logical groupings include the following:

- **Logically grouped VMs within a repository** Having multiple repositories is a common best practice. Each repository is a related collection of VMs and the related storage and associated components (ISOs, templates, and assemblies).

- **VM servers within a server pool** Some large deployments will have 13 or more VM servers; grouping the Oracle VM servers and running specific guest VMs in a given server pool is akin to separating hardware environments in a data center.

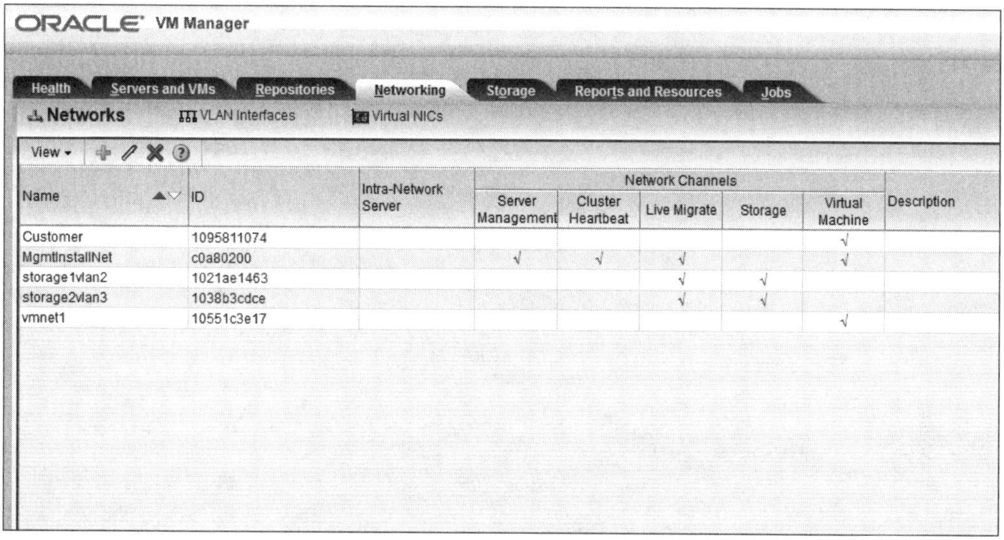

FIGURE 22-9. *Networking tab showing multiple channels for storage, virtual machines, and Live Migrate*

- **Guest VM networks**   Having multiple guest VM networks helps to isolate traffic based on the processing requirements and system's objective. Figure 22-9 displays an example of multiple VM machine and storage networks. Separating networks also provides additional security by isolating guest VM communications in one group from the communications of another group of guest VMs. In the example, the "Customer" network supports the guest VMs of a "customer" group of VM guests, whereas the "vmnet" network supports a network for development activities, including functional/systems integration testing, QA (quality assurance), and training.

Summary

This chapter summarized the most important basic best practices of the Oracle VM environment. Namely, you should logically group guest virtual machines into repositories that can be placed into a backup strategy whereby the repository backups capture the logical grouping of guest VMs, including the guest VM, the configuration, and the data presented through the repository. Additionally, repository-based storage is presented in comparison to storage offered by the SAN or file server directly to the guest VM.

With respect to networking, a similar concept prevails as a best practice: to logically group the traffic used by the guest virtual machines into VLANs and furthermore to control the grouping of the traffic (while adding a layer of security) through CIDR addressing schemes.

This chapter also showed that some of the best practices allow for a minimalist approach as a proof of concept, while leaving open the opportunity to grow into a more realistic deployment using Oracle VM software for virtualizing the data center in the cloud.

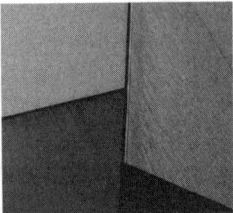

PART

V

Installing and Configuring Enterprise Manager Cloud Control for IaaS

CHAPTER
23

Basic Cloud Control
Installation

Although the default management interface for Oracle VM provides a feature-rich interface for administrators, it does not enable some key parts required for a true self-service Infrastructure as a Service (IaaS) platform. To enable an enterprise-grade IaaS private cloud system, Enterprise Manager Cloud Control 13c is required. As discussed in previous chapters, Enterprise Manager Cloud Control can enable more than just IaaS: it also is the foundation for almost any XaaS feature, including Database as a Service (DBaaS) and Middleware as a Service (MWaaS), which both fall under Platform as a Service (PaaS). This chapter covers how to connect an Enterprise Manager 13c system to Oracle VM Manager, covering steps 1 and 2 of the workflow for setting up a cloud infrastructure (see Figure 23-1). Chapter 25 will cover Steps 3–6 as part of setting up the IaaS self-service portal.

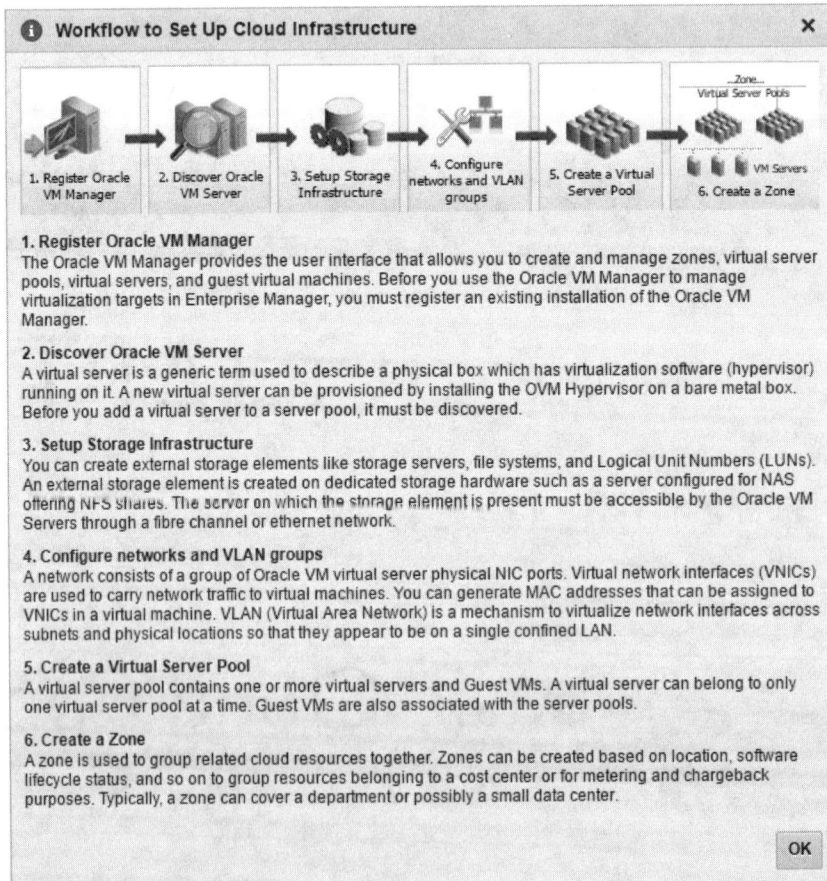

ⓘ Workflow to Set Up Cloud Infrastructure ✕

1. Register Oracle VM Manager → 2. Discover Oracle VM Server → 3. Setup Storage Infrastructure → 4. Configure networks and VLAN groups → 5. Create a Virtual Server Pool → 6. Create a Zone

1. Register Oracle VM Manager
The Oracle VM Manager provides the user interface that allows you to create and manage zones, virtual server pools, virtual servers, and guest virtual machines. Before you use the Oracle VM Manager to manage virtualization targets in Enterprise Manager, you must register an existing installation of the Oracle VM Manager.

2. Discover Oracle VM Server
A virtual server is a generic term used to describe a physical box which has virtualization software (hypervisor) running on it. A new virtual server can be provisioned by installing the OVM Hypervisor on a bare metal box. Before you add a virtual server to a server pool, it must be discovered.

3. Setup Storage Infrastructure
You can create external storage elements like storage servers, file systems, and Logical Unit Numbers (LUNs). An external storage element is created on dedicated storage hardware such as a server configured for NAS offering NFS shares. The server on which the storage element is present must be accessible by the Oracle VM Servers through a fibre channel or ethernet network.

4. Configure networks and VLAN groups
A network consists of a group of Oracle VM virtual server physical NIC ports. Virtual network interfaces (VNICs) are used to carry network traffic to virtual machines. You can generate MAC addresses that can be assigned to VNICs in a virtual machine. VLAN (Virtual Area Network) is a mechanism to virtualize network interfaces across subnets and physical locations so that they appear to be on a single confined LAN.

5. Create a Virtual Server Pool
A virtual server pool contains one or more virtual servers and Guest VMs. A virtual server can belong to only one virtual server pool at a time. Guest VMs are also associated with the server pools.

6. Create a Zone
A zone is used to group related cloud resources together. Zones can be created based on location, software lifecycle status, and so on to group resources belonging to a cost center or for metering and chargeback purposes. Typically, a zone can cover a department or possibly a small data center.

OK

FIGURE 23-1. *EM13c IaaS workflow*

Enterprise Manager IaaS Best Practices

Although this chapter will not cover how to install Enterprise Manager 13c, we need to discuss a few points that should be covered to better prepare the Enterprise Manager 13c environment:

■ **Software Library** When you're using Enterprise Manager 13c to manage private clouds, the Software Library can grow quite large. If possible, locate the Software Library on a NAS device, such as a ZFS storage array to simplify growing the filesystem in the future. Oracle VM virtual appliances allow the cloud administrator to model an entire application platform, define all dependencies and deployment constraints, and deliver the entire multitier software stack in a single file. This file can then be stored in the Software Library and be made available to users as a cloud service. For example, administrators may offer an application service that includes a VM with a Database 12.2 instance, a VM with WebLogic 12c, a web server running Apache, and a Windows server running a .NET component. Therefore, virtual appliances can by their very nature take a considerable amount of disk space. As a note, although images are stored in the Software Library, a copy is also stored in the Oracle VM repository when the image is made available to that server pool.

■ **Target counts** When sizing Enterprise Manager 13c, do not forget to include the IaaS VMs as targets. When sizing an Enterprise Manager Cloud Control implementation, pay attention to the number of targets, as that will impact the CPU and memory requirements as well as how the system is tuned. For more information, see the Cloud Control Administrators Guide at http://docs.oracle.com.

■ **OMS heap size** When large numbers of users utilize Enterprise Manager, the Enterprise Manager administrator might need to increase the Java virtual machine (JVM) heap size for the Oracle Management Server (OMS).

Enterprise Manager Required Plug-Ins

Enterprise Manager 13c functionality is enhanced using plug-ins. These plug-ins extend the functionality of Enterprise Manager 13c and are managed by the Enterprise Manager 13c administrator. The features that collectively comprise the Enterprise Manager 13c IaaS solution are provided via several plug-ins, which must be deployed to the Enterprise Manager 13c Oracle Management Server. By default, a new Enterprise Manager 13c installation includes the following plug-ins:

■ Oracle Database
■ Oracle Fusion Middleware
■ Oracle Cloud Framework

Additional plug-ins are required to support managing IaaS. The following plug-ins must be installed (in order) prior to your configuring the Enterprise Manager 13c IaaS service:

1. Oracle Virtualization plug-in
2. Oracle Cloud Application plug-in
3. Oracle Virtual Infrastructure plug-in
4. Oracle Consolidation Planning and Chargeback plug-in

When you are upgrading the plug-ins, use the following order; upgrading them in the incorrect order could potentially cause problems with the system. Each plug-in has several internal dependencies.

1. Oracle Cloud Framework plug-in
2. Oracle Database plug-in
3. Oracle Fusion Middleware plug-in
4. Oracle Virtualization plug-in
5. Oracle Cloud Application plug-in

Deploying the Enterprise Manager Agent to Oracle VM Manager 3.4

Before the Oracle VM Manager (OVMM) system can be discovered as the manager for an Oracle VM system, the OM13c agent must be deployed to the server. This uses the normal process to push an agent to a server. In addition, if the system is running on OVMM 3.4 or later, then Oracle Virtualization plug-in version 13.2.1.0 or later must be deployed on both Oracle Enterprise Manager Server and the management agent running on the OVMM. If you are deploying against a version of Oracle VM prior to 3.4, you should follow a different process, as detailed in the documentation specific to the version of Oracle VM, which can be found at http://docs.oracle.com.

Once the agent is deployed, you need to make a change to add in the SSL key from OVMM to the agent. This allows the Enterprise Manager 13c agent to talk to OVMM using a secure method.

The first step is to show the current SSL keystore location using the command **/u01/app/ oracle/ovm-manager-3/ovm_upgrade/bin/ovmkeytool.sh show**. The location of the WebLogic installation is also needed, which by default is /u01/app/oracle/ovm-manager-3/domains/ovm_ domain for Oracle VM 3.4. The WebLogic user password is required as well. By default, it is the same password as the admin user in OVMM. When running the command, enter in the WebLogic domain directory when prompted, and use the WebLogic server name and username. The following is an example of running the command:

```
[oracle@ovmm ~]$ /u01/app/oracle/ovm-manager-3/ovm_upgrade/bin/ovmkeytool.sh show
Feb 04, 2017 6:11:07 PM oracle.security.jps.JpsStartup start
INFO: Jps initializing.
Feb 04, 2017 6:11:08 PM oracle.security.jps.JpsStartup start
INFO: Jps started.
```

```
CA Keystore File: /u01/app/oracle/ovm-manager-3/domains/ovm_domain/security/ovmca.jks
CA Key Alias: ca
Certificate details:
  Algorithm: SHA256withRSA
  Subject: CN=OVM CA ovmm, OU=Oracle VM Manager, O=Oracle Corporation,
 L=Redwood City, ST=California, C=US
  Issuer: CN=OVM CA ovmm, OU=Oracle VM Manager, O=Oracle Corporation,
 L=Redwood City, ST=California, C=US
  Serial number: 76205959255788491065660470031292826674014114650
  Valid from Thu Dec 22 17:33:06 EST 2016 to Wed Dec 23 17:33:06 EST 2026
  SHA256 Fingerprint: ca:b8:b4:46:84:1a:95:62:c4:26:6e:f6:0b:78:f3:6e:
93:a4:72:46:23:70:f0:84:73:da:01:ec:51:bd:3c:b6
  This is a valid Certificate to be used as a CA.
Full Certificate:
-----BEGIN CERTIFICATE-----
```
MIIDwzCCAqugAwIBAgIUDVkxgoKrq0MFt5NIBcp68bg601owDQYJKoZIhvcNAQEL
BQAwgYgxCzAJBgNVBAYTAlVTMRMwEQYDVQQIEwpDYWxpZm9ybmlhMRUwEwYDVQQH
EwxSZWR3b29kIENpdHkxGzAZBgNVBAoTEk9yYWNsZSBDb3Jwb3JhdGlvbjEaMBgG
A1UECxMRT3JhY2xlIFZNIE1hbmFnZXIxFDASBgNVBAMTC09WTSBDQSBvdm1tMB4X
DTE2MTIyMjIyMzMwNloXDTI2MTIyMzIyMzMwNlowgYgxCzAJBgNVBAYTAlVTMRMw
EQYDVQQIEwpDYWxpZm9ybmlhMRUwEwYDVQQHEwxSZWR3b29kIENpdHkxGzAZBgNV
BAoTEk9yYWNsZSBDb3Jwb3JhdGlvbjEaMBgGA1UECxMRT3JhY2xlIFZNIE1hbmFn
ZXIxFDASBgNVBAMTC09WTSBDQSBvdm1tMIIBIjANBgkqhkiG9w0BAQEFAAOCAQ8A
MIIBCgKCAQEApHW8jxUA5U6rnZDyMag4RcEp+QUutVGfCpDSDU83NELK5T9e9Xcz
5t28LZpckT2pS+66vIWe4m/dtSm6GEETcUHkaUC+STnmpVEoBnv4Aw9Bk4CCxSk1
BlOruHf934qwzSAnpM6ER0qi0vKhJqnEJKJzxKUZCJS/MekdFdKL21JZ85Ld3QC1
VoSa26qUvTMo6nkqmL52QVDPQURJQY96Hr0hXitXJuHvt6ZcHFmmrY1NEt6JBcz5
kt7a17r0QOeCzuDqV6ZoEJdzxUuxgwSfpf4RC0FHxvu1RpHv8OIT4lPxPb95RqyE
pXTIvs4H09r1mbBaKpafYa5YjE7vzAmxTwIDAQABoyMwITAPBgNVHRMBAf8EBTAD
AQH/MA4GA1UdDwEB/wQEAwIABTANBgkqhkiG9w0BAQsFAAOCAQEAfd2RiYWUdBI+
L6prY4MQ+V5y7TQrJUMsdDZtBI5iOMjBq9V375fiGjMB415JkmMgPgCblDFz3ob3
KnRrc7uZtVKJVoHysYzas7+HbLeUNk7pnrXSXmrh68ZNH0BtUThF1VEvTpSVJVfV
iY9EtuyT6m/gxGCX2JJgKQ4ycCtwVrgjM4kWqznxrkg8D9O0O9+QsmH/6rQ2y3PC
fvjEwj6XJSlOjDYDig2kIflSQGYSHdsvrI9REM3OdoTib+sAD+aX/1U11+ap8RV+
67fQ6Tv7APrXHcF8VsBMoHOIJMHdoxMe+HJo/DEvdvzjTAduI19uMQ+/MV1089eQ
SMikFlgmMw==
-----END CERTIFICATE-----

```
SSL Keystore File: /u01/app/oracle/ovm-manager-3/domains/ovm_domain/security/ovmssl.jks
SSL Key Alias: ovmcore
Certificate details:
  Algorithm: SHA256withRSA
  Subject: CN=ovmm, OU=Oracle VM Manager, O=Oracle Corporation, L=Redwood City,
 ST=California, C=US Issuer: CN=OVM CA ovmm, OU=Oracle VM Manager, O=Oracle Corporation,
 L=Redwood City, ST=California, C=US
  Serial number: 132344000442480412687535399332622122660336824107
  Valid from Fri Dec 23 15:00:18 EST 2016 to Thu Dec 24 15:00:18 EST 2026
  SHA256 Fingerprint: 6e:59:28:50:37:e2:ab:4d:3d:d9:34:2f:40:89:af:dc:de:1f:fd:ef:1c:4d:
a0:18:b1:14:91:97:46:1b:c7:a2
  Subject Alternative Names:
    Hostnames:
      ovmm
Full Certificate:
```

```
-----BEGIN CERTIFICATE-----
MIIDrTCCApWgAwIBAgIVAOfRGi4iSp5LTnk4rXJpHsOhmVewMA0GCSqGSIb3DQEB
CwUAMIGIMQswCQYDVQQGEwJVUzETMBEGA1UECBMKQ2FsaWZvcm5pYTEVMBMGA1UE
BxMMUmVkd29vZCBDaXR5MRswGQYDVQQKExJPcmFjbGUgQ29ycG9yYXRpb24xGjAY
BgNVBAsTEU9yYWNsZSBWTSBNYW5hZ2VyMRQwEgYDVQQDEwtPVk0gQ0Egb3ZtbTAe
Fw0xNjEyMjMyMDAwMThaFw0yNjEyMjQyMDAwMThaMIGBMQswCQYDVQQGEwJVUzET
MBEGA1UECBMKQ2FsaWZvcm5pYTEVMBMGA1UEBxMMUmVkd29vZCBDaXR5MRswGQYD
VQQKExJPcmFjbGUgQ29ycG9yYXRpb24xGjAYBgNVBAsTEU9yYWNsZSBWTSBNYW5h
Z2VyMQ0wCwYDVQQDEwRvdm1tMIIBIjANBgkqhkiG9w0BAQEFAAOCAQ8AMIIBCgKC
AQEA0TWtq+DmukmJa+u6E3xzNpMzUJ88EpC4X0EvR7pG9zjEvDWD7kp1D56jMpKS
f1sR3x1MfMDOB++qlzRGcXBW3RxNCcm21LZDZOqbQYKbdbYQmpSib4MZJaY2azoz
zSAqTqQcyRSXzK/3V+ExjgBfQGtLaH1dzWZv1hhD4k6YbF7mqgBuF5r7j5ZLa4E2
BGMJDYx6czxzk8fKeyNmHLvkK2o6AZ5ehBJ6/B8BpuAopWUD3XYc2ef/DyUnsHJK
v5Jpdy5UuVPOP29c3yPX1ZeD5crIhqF9c5C2GaSRKfGeRCgZ5Bj3sa2Frc4FJF1z
8VyNB3dlhveoMXxhYF+zdNTfRwIDAQABoxMwETAPBgNVHREECDAGggRvdm1tMA0G
CSqGSIb3DQEBCwUAA4IBAQA6i5Vlae3OeW+ybHc7c3+j1s5iVimHSsQnAY2me1+v
sY98SwNq5BKErN2bKSzcCML0iknypc/IXeTgGYE+ZauTAczNvqExvqKn20Nqsyxh
D1SncDe/pXaQ9BhYVjsMm7Rc/1OmerktVZAXaj4qtFXsDJojzfNpUawfDnwH+2Bi
iGKPseLhtGKbQhGpwsf0+DNqp2AwF01v8CMf0Dhsnmrtb/TKx6ouZBhxb3O1JGwq
MUTO8oeAuUC9ABRnc4ZvhGWFciODdhqyrwK8hgCyvFE5urlr4pga9K5/T8LDIKYj
6roWU1z/eiH1D+yV4rAmoF0fxn9PGtW6jmW1PwZUh3In
-----END CERTIFICATE-----
```

```
SSL Trust Keystore File: /u01/app/oracle/ovm-manager-3/domains/ovm_domain/security/
ovmtrust.jks
Trusted certificates:
  CN=OVM CA ovmm, OU=Oracle VM Manager, O=Oracle Corporation,
L=Redwood City, ST=California, C=US
CA certificiate found in SSL Trust-Store

Oracle MiddleWare Home (MW_HOME): /u01/app/oracle/ovm-manager-3/domains/ovm_domain
WebLogic domain directory: [/u01/app/oracle/ovm-manager-3/domains/ovm_domain]
WebLogic server name: [AdminServer]
WebLogic username: [weblogic]
WebLogic password: [********]
WLST session logged at: /tmp/wlst-session8101806755105371642.log

WebLogic SSL Keystore File:
/u01/app/oracle/ovm-manager-3/domains/ovm_domain/security/ovmssl.jks
WebLogic SSL Key Alias: ovmcore
WebLogic SSL Trust Keystore File:
/u01/app/oracle/ovm-manager-3/domains/ovm_domain/security/ovmtrust.jks
[oracle@ovmm ~]$
```

Save the output from the command because the entire SSL certificate section (in bold in the example) will need to be imported into the Enterprise Manager 13*c* agent. Note that there are two different keystore files:

■ **The CA keystore** /u01/app/oracle/ovm-manager-3/domains/ovm_domain/security/ ovmca.jks)

■ **The WebLogic keystore** /u01/app/oracle/ovm-manager-3/domains/ovm_domain/ security/ovmssl.jks

Therefore, two certificates will be shown.

It is important to only use the certificate from the ovmssl.jks file. Copy the lines from

-----BEGIN CERTIFICATE-----

to

-----END CERTIFICATE-----

and place them into a temporary file. In the example, /tmp/ovmm_ssl.txt is used and will look like this:

```
[oracle@ovmm ~]$ cat /tmp/ovmm_ssl
-----BEGIN CERTIFICATE-----
MIIDrTCCApWgAwIBAgIVAOfRGi4iSp5LTnk4rXJpHsOhmVewMA0GCSqGSIb3DQEB
CwUAMIGIMQswCQYDVQQGEwJVUzETMBEGA1UECBMKQ2FsaWZvcm5pYTEVMBMGA1UE
BxMMUmVkd29vZCBDaXR5MRswGQYDVQQKExJPcmFjbGUgQ29ycG9yYXRpb24xGjAY
BgNVBAsTEU9yYWNsZSBWTSBNYW5hZ2VyMRQwEgYDVQQDEwtPVk0gQ0Egb3ZtbTAe
Fw0xNjEyMjMyMDAwMThaFw0yNjEyMjQyMDAwMThaMIGBMQswCQYDVQQGEwJVUzET
MBEGA1UECBMKQ2FsaWZvcm5pYTEVMBMGA1UEBxMMUmVkd29vZCBDaXR5MRswGQYD
VQQKExJPcmFjbGUgQ29ycG9yYXRpb24xGjAYBgNVBAsTEU9yYWNsZSBWTSBNYW5h
Z2VyMQ0wCwYDVQQDEwRvdm1tMIIBIjANBgkqhkiG9w0BAQEFAAOCAQ8AMIIBCgKC
AQEA0TWtq+DmukmJa+u6E3xzNpMzUJ88EpC4X0EvR7pG9zjEvDWD7kp1D56jMpKS
f1sR3x1MfMDOB++qlzRGcXBW3RxNCcm21LZDZOqbQYKbdbYQmpSib4MZJaY2azoz
zSAqTqQcyRSXzK/3V+ExjgBfQGtLaH1dzWZv1hhD4k6YbF7mqgBuF5r7j5ZLa4E2
BGMJDYx6czxzk8fKeyNmHLvkK2o6AZ5ehBJ6/B8BpuAopWUD3XYc2ef/DyUnsHJK
v5Jpdy5UuVPOP29c3yPXlZeD5crIhqF9c5C2GaSRKfGeRCgZ5Bj3sa2Frc4FJFlz
8VyNB3dlhveoMXxhYF+zdNTfRwIDAQABoxMwETAPBgNVHREECDAGggRvdm1tMA0G
CSqGSIb3DQEBCwUAA4IBAQA6i5Vlae3OeW+ybHc7c3+j1s5iVimHSsQnAY2me1+v
sY98SwNq5BKErN2bKSzcCML0iknypc/IXeTgGYE+ZauTAczNvqExvqKn20Nqsyxh
D1SncDe/pXaQ9BhYVjsMm7Rc/1OmerktVZAXaj4qtFXsDJojzfNpUawfDnwH+2Bi
iGKPseLhtGKbQhGpwsf0+DNqp2AwF01v8CMf0Dhsnmrtb/TKx6ouZBhxb3OlJGwq
MUTO8oeAuUC9ABRnc4ZvhGWFciODdhqyrwK8hgCyvFE5urlr4pga9K5/T8LDIKYj
6roWU1z/eiHlD+yV4rAmoF0fxn9PGtW6jmW1PwZUh3In
-----END CERTIFICATE-----
```

Next, this SSL key will need to be imported into the Enterprise Manager 13*c* agent. When prompted for a password, use "welcome" (the default password for the keystore).

```
[oracle@ovmm ~]$ /u01/oem/agent/agent_inst/bin/emctl secure add_trust_cert_to_jks \
-trust_certs_loc /tmp/ovmm_ssl -alias ovmm
Oracle Enterprise Manager Cloud Control 13c Release 2
Copyright (c) 1996, 2016 Oracle Corporation.  All rights reserved.
Password:

Message  :  Certificate was added to keystore
ExitStatus: SUCCESS
```

Once the key is successfully imported into the keystore, the OVMM can be discovered in Enterprise Manager 13*c*.

Discovering the OVMM in Enterprise Manager 13c

Discovery in Enterprise Manager 13c is a straightforward task: log into Enterprise Manager 13c and navigate to Enterprise | Cloud | Oracle VM Infrastructure Home, as shown in Figure 23-2.

This will show the Infrastructure Cloud home page, which will be fairly sparse of information until the OVMM is registered. To register the OVMM, select the menu option Register OVM Manager under Infrastructure Cloud, as shown in Figure 23-3.

This will start the registration process, where you will input the following information:

- **Name**   This is the name you give to this OVMM system.

- **Monitoring Agent**   Use the magnifying glass icon to select the Enterprise Manager 13c agent deployed on the OVMM.

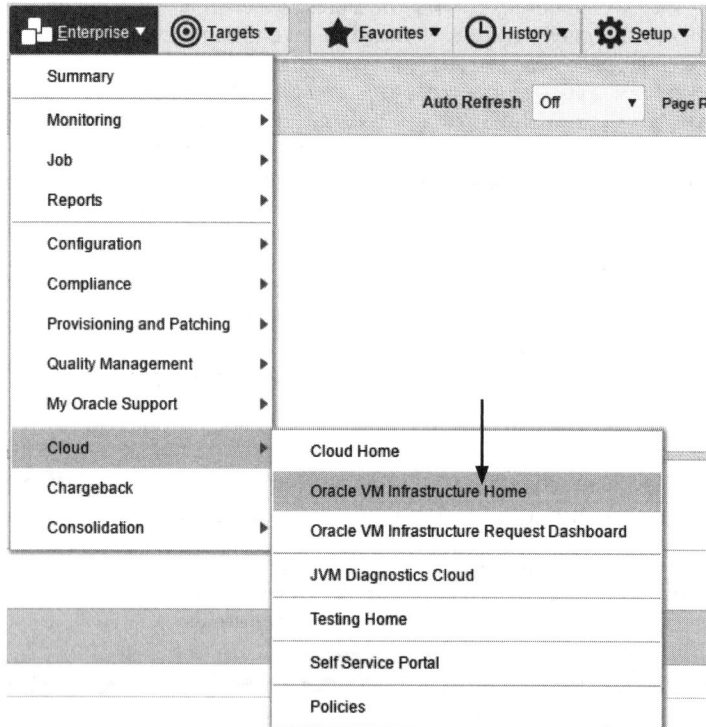

FIGURE 23-2.   *Navigating in Enterprise Manager 13c to the infrastructure home*

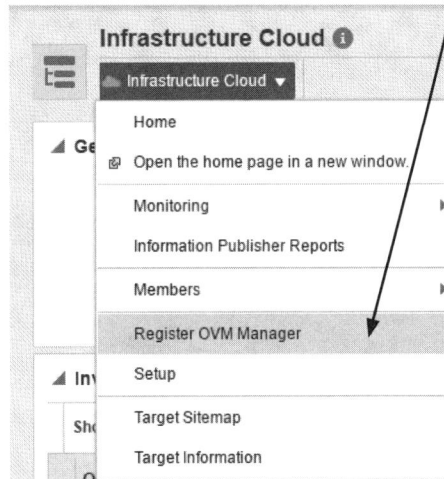

FIGURE 23-3.   *Starting OVMM registration*

- **Oracle VM Manager URL**   This is the secure TCP URL for the OVM Manager core (in the example, tcps://ovmm.m57.local:54322 is used).

- **Oracle VM Manager Console URL**   This is the management URL for the OVMM (in the example, https://ovmm.m57.local:7002 is used). Depending on the Oracle VM version, the tcps setup is not required.

- **Monitoring Credentials**   Use the admin user and password for logging into the OVMM web interface.

- **Administration Credentials**   Nothing is required here, unless a second account was created in OVMM.

- **Automatic Synchronization with Oracle VM Manager**   Check this to keep Enterprise Manager 13c in sync with the OVMM.

A completed example is shown in Figure 23-4.

Once everything is filled out, click Submit, and an Enterprise Manager 13c job will be submitted to register the OVMM. Once registration is complete, navigate back to the Infrastructure Cloud home page. Initially, there will not be much information, as shown in Figure 23-5. If there are existing VMs in the Oracle VM pool, you can expect to see several new targets in the Target Flux section. Enterprise Manager 13c will report these as new when they are first discovered.

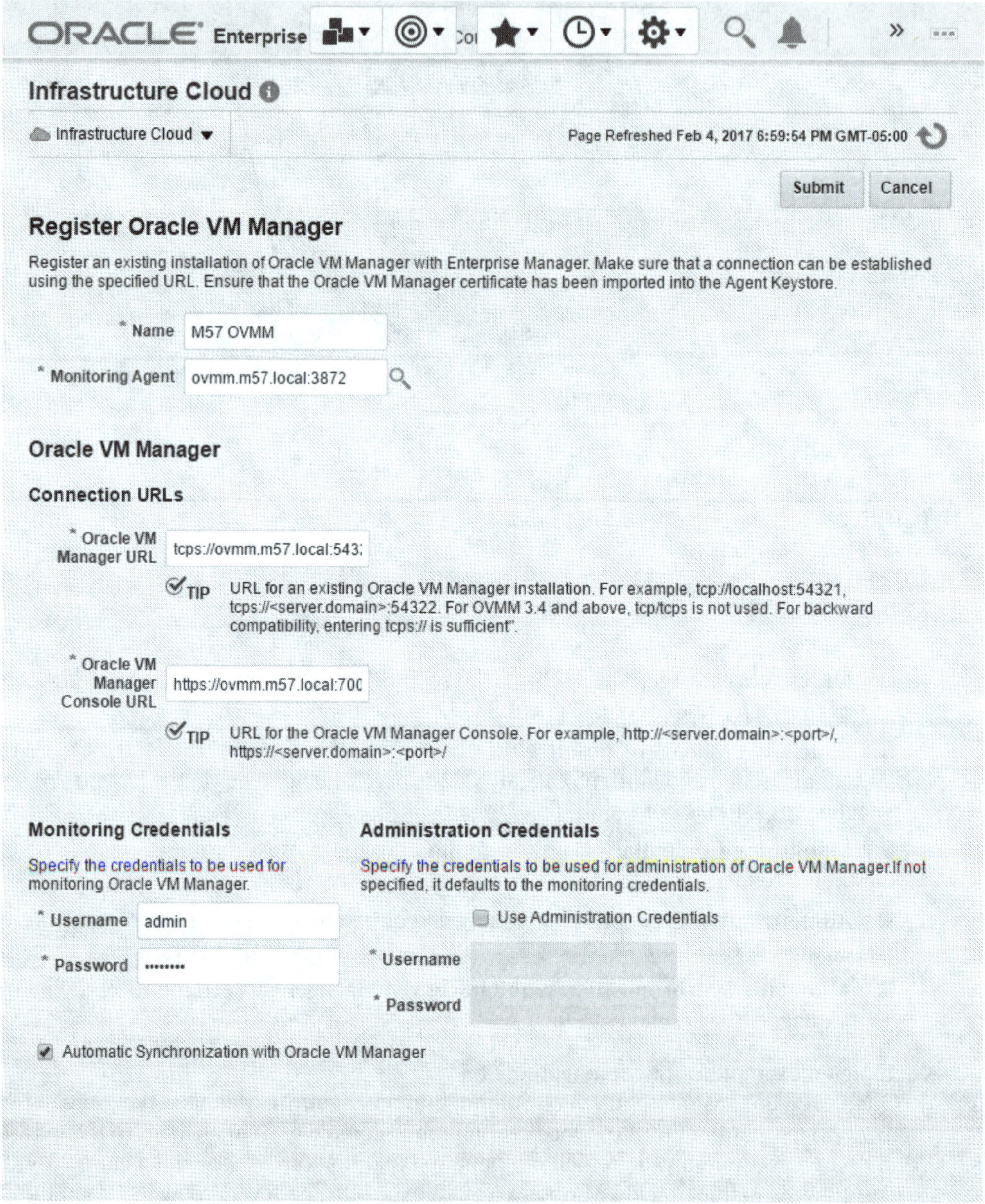

FIGURE 23-4. *OVMM registration*

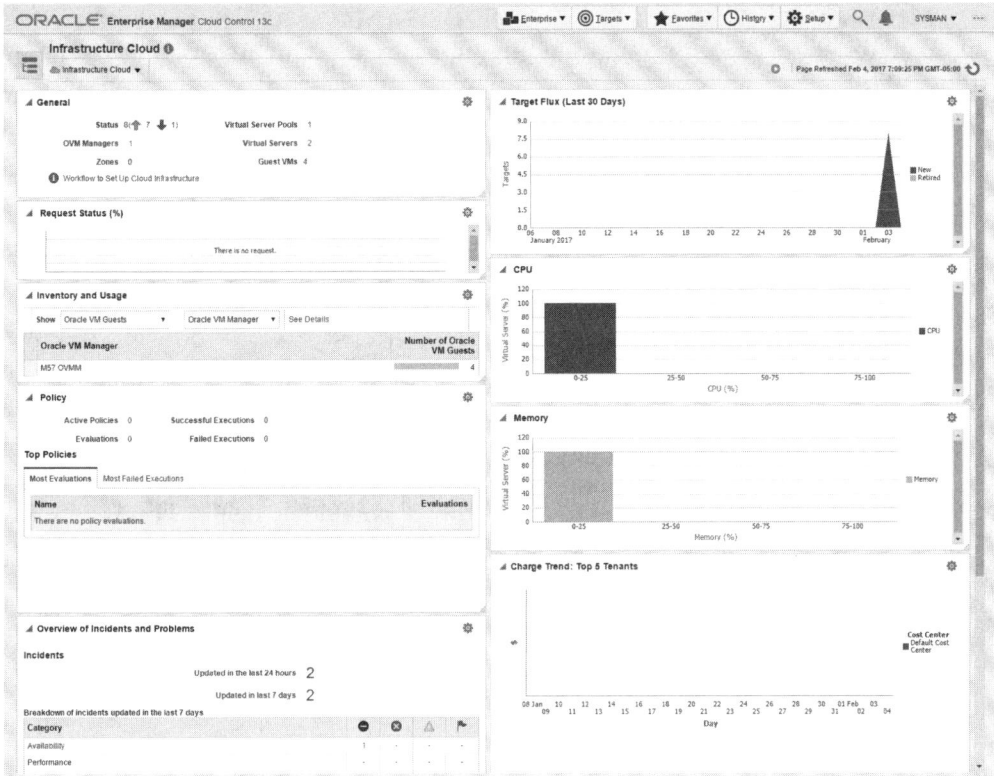

FIGURE 23-5.   *New Infrastructure Cloud page*

Over time, though, the page will show more historical information, as shown in Figure 23-6, including Charge Trend if the Chargeback feature is configured. Target Flux will also show retired VMs, which are VMs that have been deleted.

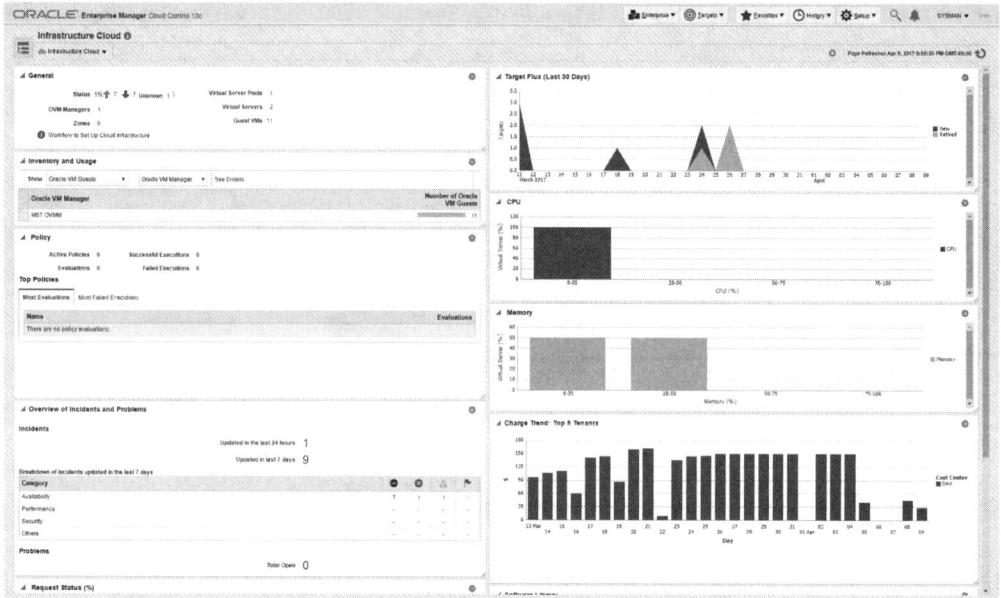

FIGURE 23-6. *Infrastructure Cloud page with historial information*

Summary

This chapter covered how to prepare the OVMM to be discovered by an Enterprise Manager 13*c* system. We discussed how to export the SSL key from OVMM and import it into the Enterprise Manager 13*c* agent. In addition, we covered the discovery process of the OVMM, and you learned how to add the OVMM system to Enterprise Manager 13*c*. In the next chapter, you will learn how to use Enterprise Manager 13*c* to perform several common tasks on the OVMM system.

CHAPTER
24

Using Cloud Control

Once Enterprise Manager 13c is linked to the Oracle VM Manager, an entirely new set of private cloud features are enabled in Enterprise Manager. Many of these features provide better security and automation for the administrator of Infrastructure as a Service (IaaS) with Oracle VM. Cloud security is enhanced because Enterprise Manager 13c allows granular control of resources in the private cloud. With Oracle VM Manager, only one user is created (admin) and that user has full access to all resources. With the Enterprise Manager 13c security subsystem, administrative access to targets can now be controlled. In addition, administrators can monitor and report on resource consumption, and even assign a cost to each resource with the Chargeback feature. What's more, most administrative tasks can be performed from Enterprise Manager, including building VMs from templates and destroying VMs. The common administrative tasks are covered in the "Common Tasks Using Cloud Control" section of this chapter.

User Access Control

Although a cloud can be built using the SYSMAN superuser, it is generally considered best practice to use specific users, each with a limited amount of functionality. In Enterprise Manager, user security is broken down into two areas: administrators and roles. An *administrator* is a user who can log into Enterprise Manager. A *role* is a grouping of privileges, for both targets and resources, that can be granted to administrators—or even to other roles. Roles can be as simple as read-only access to all features, or as complex as full administrative access for just VMs used by a specific application. When Enterprise Manager is installed, the SYSMAN user account (the super administrator) is created. Use this account to create new roles and administrators for your organization. Although the security model can be very complex, that topic is outside the scope of the chapter. What will be shown here is how to create a read-only administrator as well as an administrator with limited access to a pair of VMs.

Creating Cloud Control Users

Creating administrators in Oracle Enterprise Manager Cloud Control is not a difficult task. First, log into Cloud Control as the SYSMAN user, and then navigate to Setup | Security | Administrators, as shown in Figure 24-1.

Initially you will see the list of all administrators in Cloud Control. By default, only two users exist: SYSMAN (the superuser) and CLOUD_SWLIB_USER (an internal user for managing the software library). One of two options can be used to create a new user: Create or Create Like. The Create button is used to create a new administrator from scratch, with each role selected manually. For our example, we'll create a new user called "pellipox" who has full admin privileges on a single VM and read-only access on other VMs.

To create this user, click the Create button, as shown in Figure 24-2.

NOTE
You cannot clone the SYSMAN administrator using the Create Like button, but you can create future administrators this way.

In the next screen, shown in Figure 24-3, you set the login name (in the Name field) and the initial password. These are required fields. Optionally, you can set the other fields, including E-mail Address, Location, Department, and Cost Center. You can also require the user to change his or her password upon the initial login by selecting the Expire Password Now checkbox.

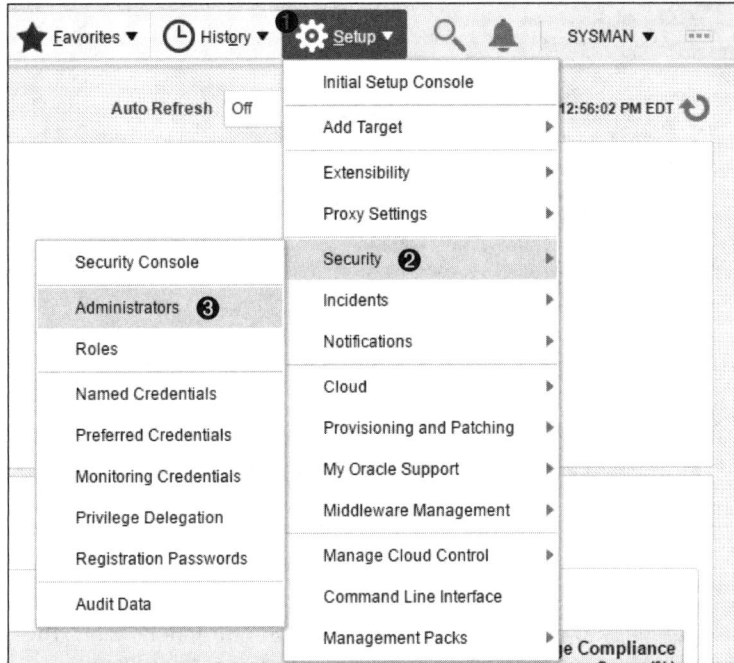

FIGURE 24-1. *Navigating Cloud Control to add an administrator*

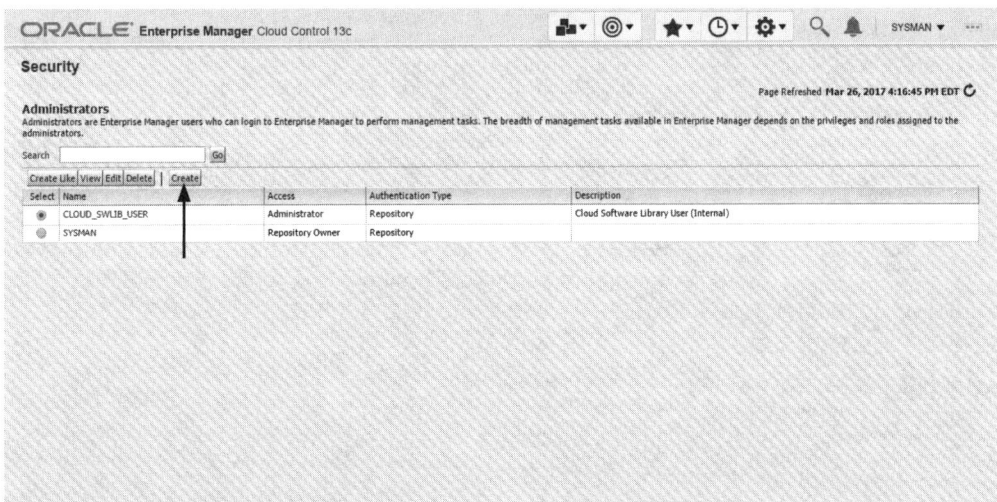

FIGURE 24-2. *Creating a new administrator*

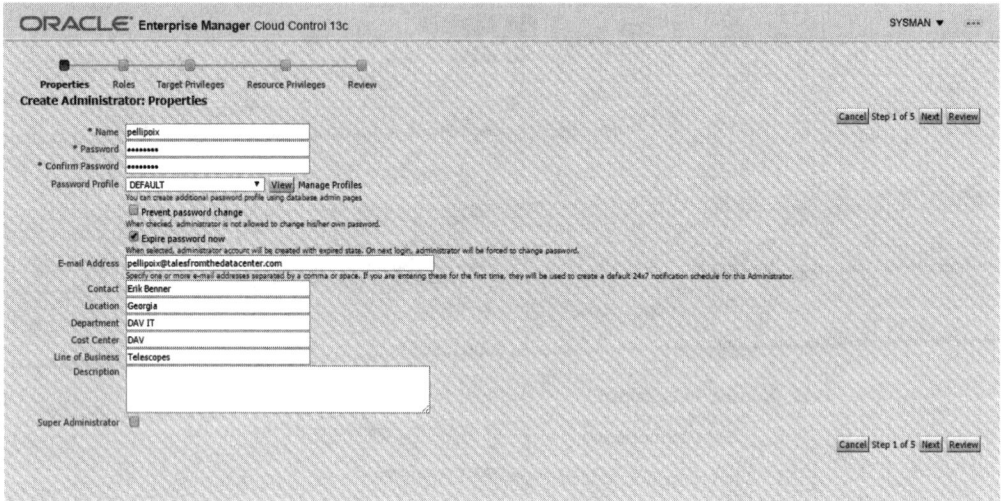

FIGURE 24-3. *Administrator properties*

The next screen, shown in Figure 24-4, sets the administrator's roles. These roles can be preset by the Enterprise Manager administrator and customized for the specific requirements for your site.

For our example, we'll only assign the role EM_CLOUD_ADMINISTRATOR, granting this administrator Enterprise Manager administrator access for setting up and managing the infrastructure cloud. This role is ideally set for the staff responsible for deploying the cloud infrastructure

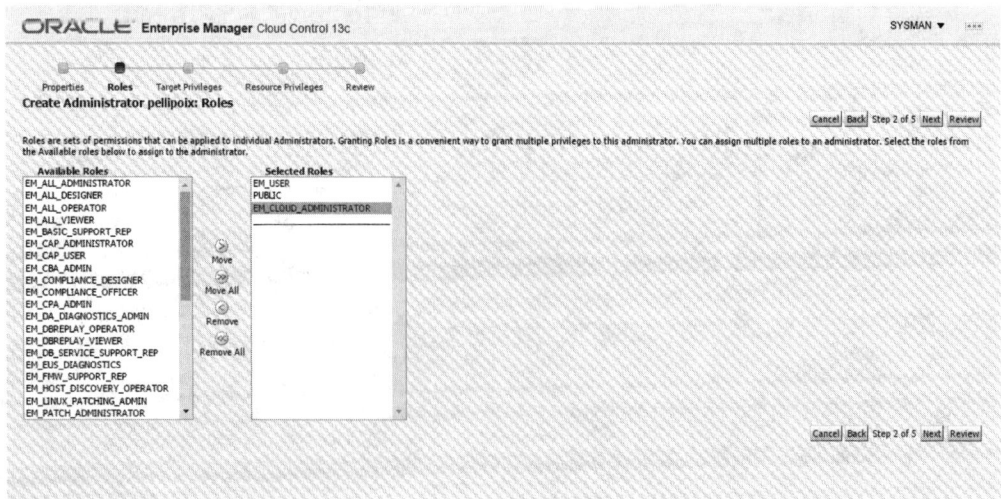

FIGURE 24-4. *Administrator roles*

(servers, pools, and zones) and the infrastructure cloud operations for performance and configuration management. For more information on the other roles, refer to Section 4 of "Oracle Manager Cloud Administration Guide," and Appendix A in "Enterprise Manager Cloud Control Security Guide," which can both be found at docs.oracle.com under Enterprise Manager | Oracle Enterprise Manager Cloud Control Documentation 13.2.

The next screen, shown in Figure 24-5, is where you set what targets the administrator has access to. If a user is given the EM_CLOUD_ADMINISTRATOR role, he or she gets the role

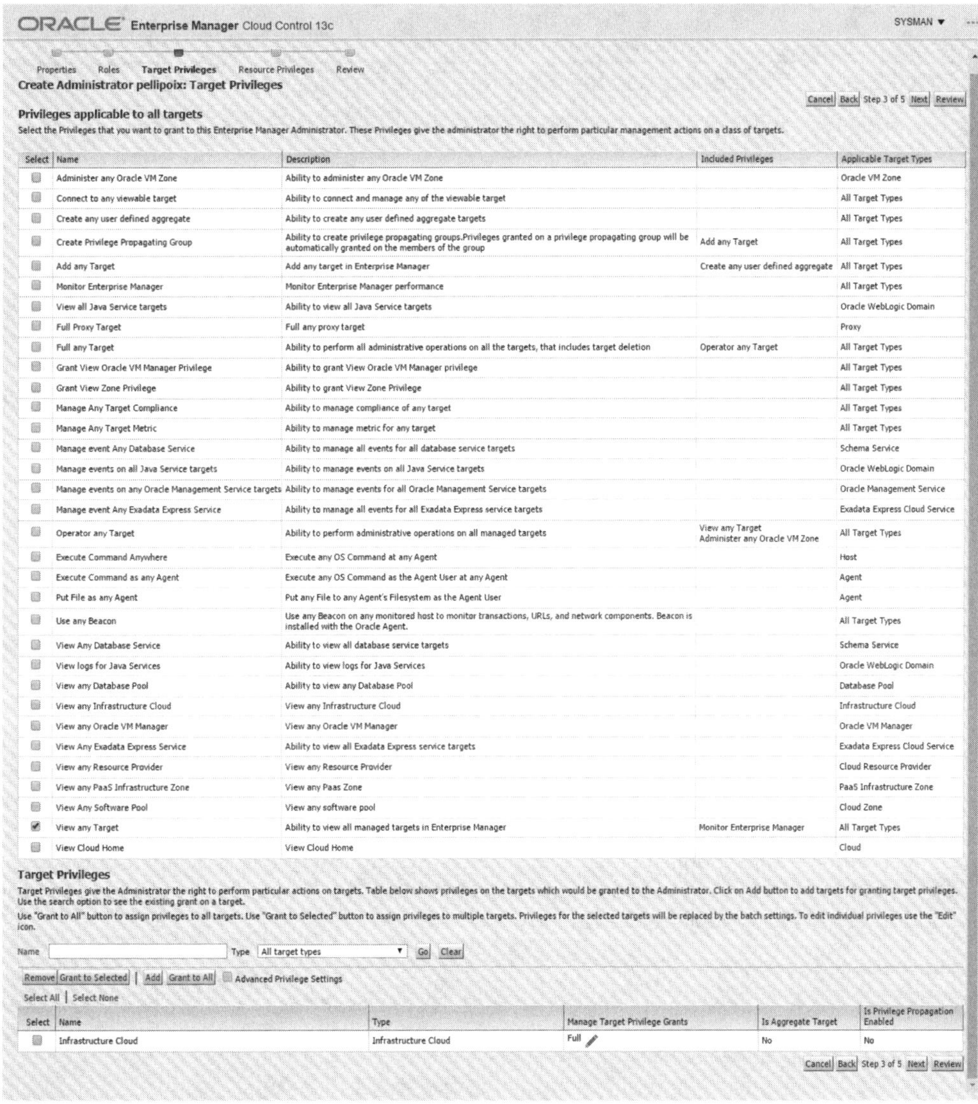

FIGURE 24-5. *Administrator target privileges*

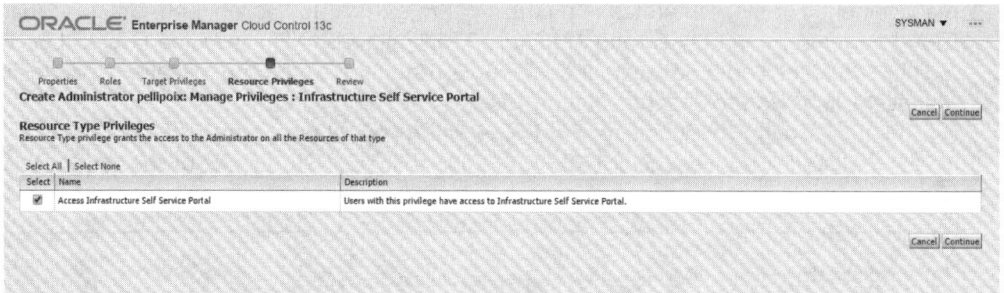

FIGURE 24-6. *Enable access to the Infrastructure Self Service Portal.*

EM_SSA_ADMINISTRATOR by default, which covers the setup of the Self Service Portal. The EM_CLOUD_ADMIN role can add any target and view any Oracle VM Manager.

Several privileges are available that apply to *all* targets, and these are often used to create read-only access to all targets with the View Any Target option. In addition, access to specific targets can be granted, such as full access to all Infrastructure Cloud targets.

The next screen is used to enable Enterprise Manager resource privileges for the administrator. To enable the Self Service Portal for an administrator, make sure to edit the line "Infrastructure Self Service Portal" and select the privilege "Access Infrastructure Self Service Portal," as shown in Figure 24-6.

The last step in the process is a review of all roles and privileges assigned to the new administrator, as shown in Figure 24-7.

Enterprise Manager Security

The ability to control user access is a critical function when building private clouds. Having end users with full administrative access violates most security best practices. User access is best done using a method called *separation of duties,* where each user is limited to only the functions needed for his or her specific jobs. Enterprise manager allows for the separation of duties, leveraging not only access control for a specific user but also more generic roles, allowing groups of users to have the same access to Enterprise Manager. While access can be manually configured using Enterprise Manager's internal database, optimally Enterprise Manager can be connected to an LDAP system or Active Directory infrastructure to automatically assign roles and privileges based on an administrator's groups in the access control system. All of this is detailed in the online documentation located at docs.oracle.com under Enterprise Manager | Oracle Enterprise Manager Cloud Control Documentation 13.2.

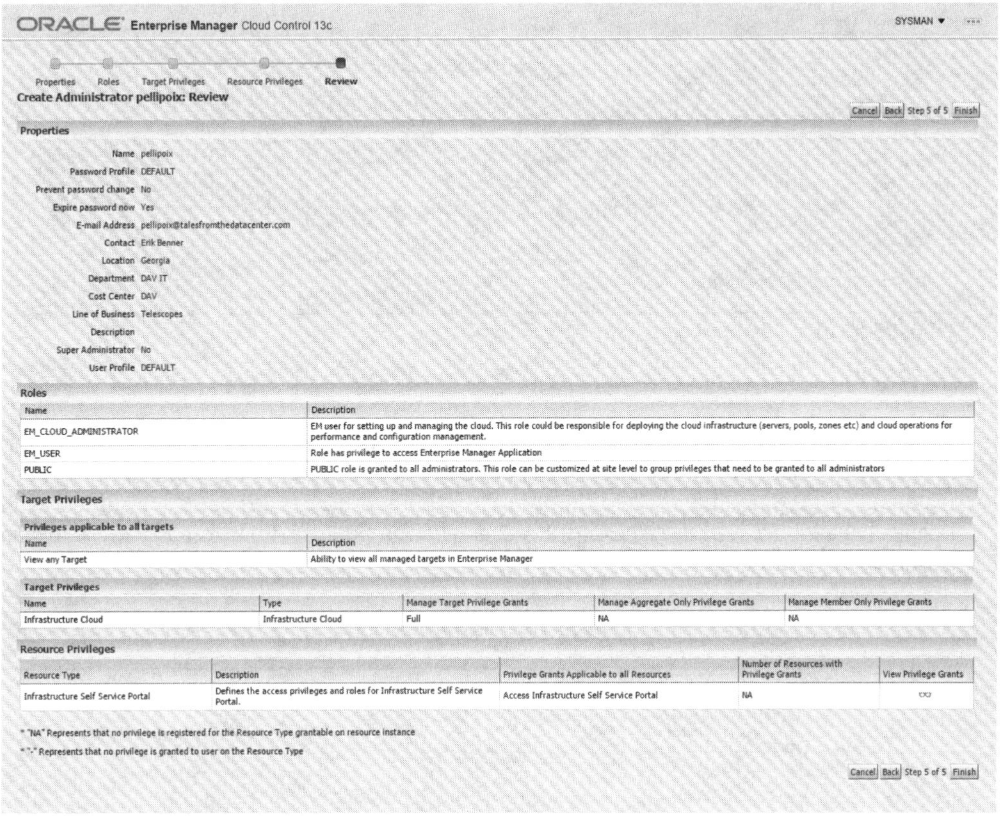

ORACLE' Enterprise Manager Cloud Control 13c   SYSMAN ▼   ...

Properties   Roles   Target Privileges   Resource Privileges   **Review**
Create Administrator pellipoix: Review

Cancel Back Step 5 of 5 Finish

Properties

Name	pellipoix
Password Profile	DEFAULT
Prevent password change	No
Expire password now	Yes
E-mail Address	pellipoix@talesfromthedatacenter.com
Contact	Erik Benner
Location	Georgia
Department	DAV IT
Cost Center	DAV
Line of Business	Telescopes
Description	
Super Administrator	No
User Profile	DEFAULT

Roles

Name	Description
EM_CLOUD_ADMINISTRATOR	EM user for setting up and managing the cloud. This role could be responsible for deploying the cloud infrastructure (servers, pools, zones etc) and cloud operations for performance and configuration management.
EM_USER	Role has privilege to access Enterprise Manager Application
PUBLIC	PUBLIC role is granted to all administrators. This role can be customized at site level to group privileges that need to be granted to all administrators

Target Privileges

Privileges applicable to all targets

Name	Description
View any Target	Ability to view all managed targets in Enterprise Manager

Target Privileges

Name	Type	Manage Target Privilege Grants	Manage Aggregate Only Privilege Grants	Manage Member Only Privilege Grants
Infrastructure Cloud	Infrastructure Cloud	Full	NA	NA

Resource Privileges

Resource Type	Description	Privilege Grants Applicable to all Resources	Number of Resources with Privilege Grants	View Privilege Grants
Infrastructure Self Service Portal	Defines the access privileges and roles for Infrastructure Self Service Portal.	Access Infrastructure Self Service Portal	NA	(X)

* "NA" Represents that no privilege is registered for the Resource Type grantable on resource instance

* "-" Represents that no privilege is granted to user on the Resource Type

Cancel Back Step 5 of 5 Finish

FIGURE 24-7. *Administrator review*

Configuring Showback/Chargeback

One challenge an enterprise experiences with building and managing private clouds is monitoring the resources consumed by applications and infrastructure systems. Monitoring is an important aspect of a cloud, and although not obvious, it's a critical component to a successful cloud deployment. Monitoring is done by Enterprise Manager using the Chargeback feature. The Chargeback feature can be used to assign a financial amount to many different types of resources, including CPU, storage consumption, memory consumption, and more. Note that many of these features are licenses under the database, middleware, and other management packs. This section focuses on the infrastructure capabilities included when using Oracle VM. The overall process for configuring this follows a simple path, as illustrated in Figure 24-8: first define the cost centers and charge plans and then assign the targets to a specific charge plan and cost center.

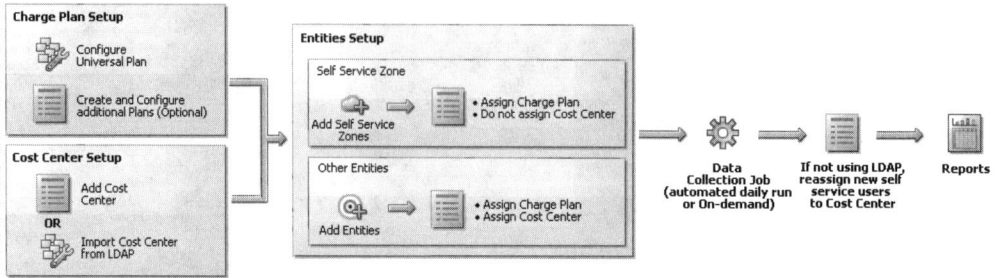

FIGURE 24-8. *Chargeback workflow*

Once this process is complete, reports can be generated as the systems are used. Although it is possible for the tool to provide very accurate financial reports to the application owners, this feature is most commonly used to simply show where resources are being consumed, which is frequently called *Showback*. Accessing the Chargeback module is done from Enterprise | Chargeback, as shown in Figure 24-9.

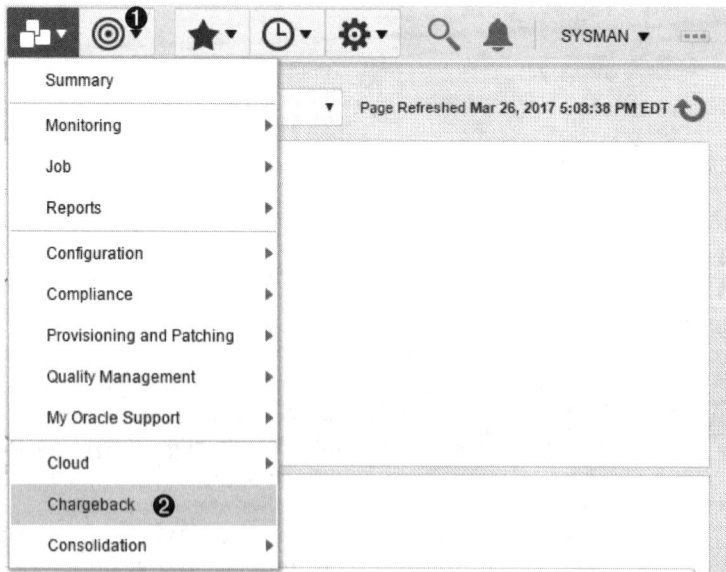

FIGURE 24-9. *Accessing Chargeback*

Charge Plans

The rate that is used to charge a cost center is set in the charge plan. By default, a universal charge plan is installed by default. This will only track CPU, storage, and memory consumption. Additional extended charge plans can be generated that track many different resource types and allow for more flexible models that can account for different license expenses, hardware costs, and even the expense difference between business hour support and full 24/7/365 tech support. An example of how this might work is that an OVS leveraging a high-core-speed CPU has higher acquisition and power costs than an OVS system running a slower speed and more efficient CPU. The charge plans can account for this cost difference. The same can be done for the storage expense, where all solid-state storage is significantly more expensive than storage that leverages a tiered approach, such as the Oracle FS1-2 array. To manage the charge plans, select the Charge Plans tab from the main Chargeback menu, as shown here.

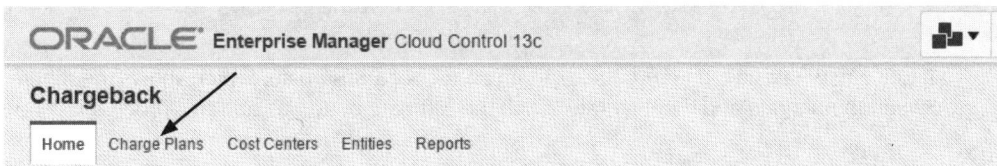

As previously stated, by default only a universal charge plan is created. This assigns a zero cost to CPU, memory, and storage allocations. The initial universal charge plan will be based on the installation date of the Chargeback plug-in. To edit the universal charge plan, you need to create a new plan revision that applies to all future charges. To do this, highlight the existing universal charge plan and click Create | Revision, as shown next.

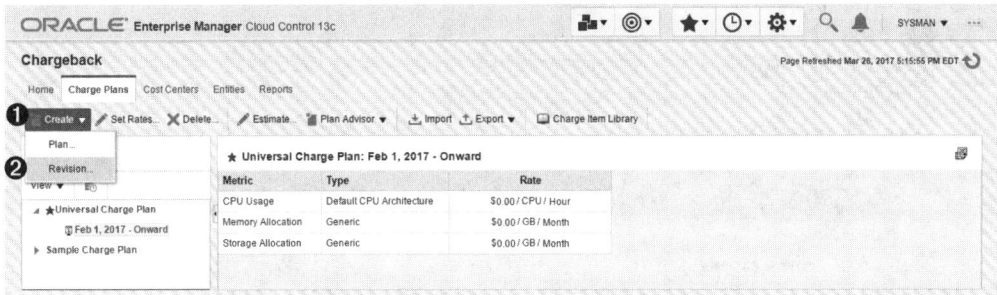

When creating the revised plan, you are first asked when the new effective date is and the name of the plan being copied, as shown here.

Next, you can place new rates into the charge plan. Because this is a universal charge plan, as shown next, only CPU, memory, and storage can be set. Different terms can be used for each rate; for example, you can bill storage on a monthly rate but CPU and memory on a different rate. Currently, the periods are hourly, daily, weekly, monthly, quarterly, and annually.

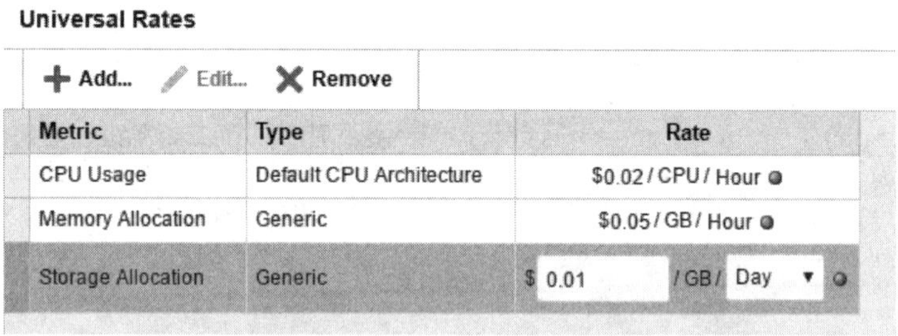
Universal Rates
Add...
Edit...
Remove
Metric
Type
Rate
CPU Usage
Default CPU Architecture
$0.02 / CPU / Hour
Memory Allocation
Generic
$0.05 / GB / Hour
Storage Allocation
Generic
$ 0.01 / GB / Day

Once new rates are entered, the system can model an estimate, which shows the difference between the old rate and the new rate. Click the Estimate button to start this process, as shown here.

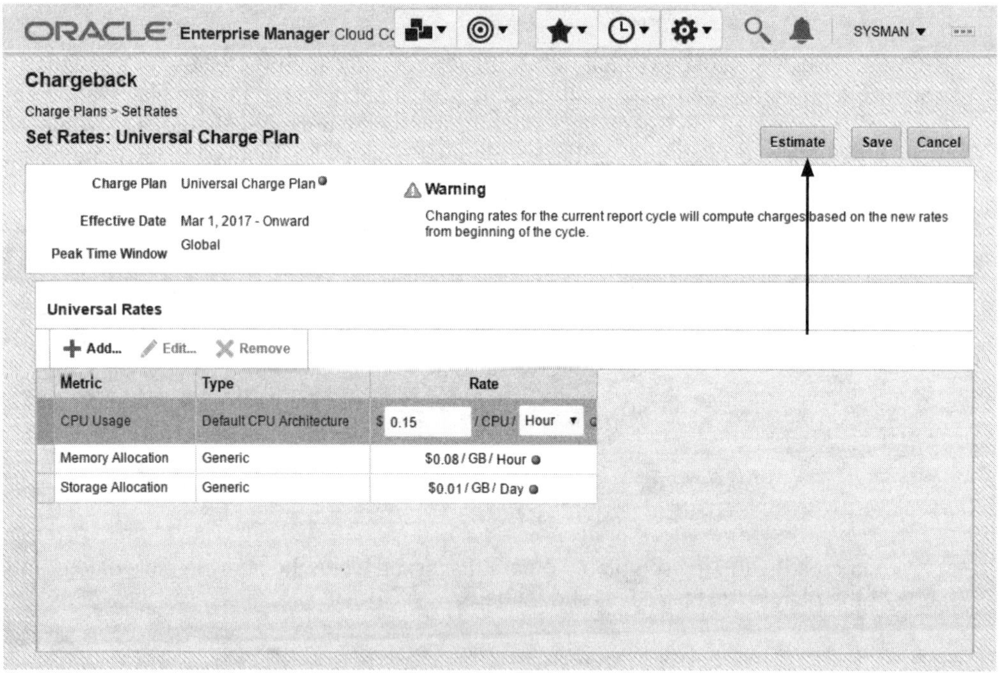
ORACLE Enterprise Manager Cloud Cc
SYSMAN
Chargeback
Charge Plans > Set Rates
Set Rates: Universal Charge Plan
Estimate
Save
Cancel
Charge Plan Universal Charge Plan
Effective Date Mar 1, 2017 - Onward
Peak Time Window Global
Warning
Changing rates for the current report cycle will compute charges based on the new rates from beginning of the cycle.
Universal Rates
Add...
Edit...
Remove
Metric
Type
Rate
CPU Usage
Default CPU Architecture
$ 0.15 / CPU / Hour
Memory Allocation
Generic
$0.08 / GB / Hour
Storage Allocation
Generic
$0.01 / GB / Day

Next, select the targets that will be used to generate the estimate. Click the Add button, and then the Entities option, shown next, will enable you to pick the sample systems. With a new installation, no entities/targets are assigned to the universal charge plan, so they will need to be manually selected for the first time.

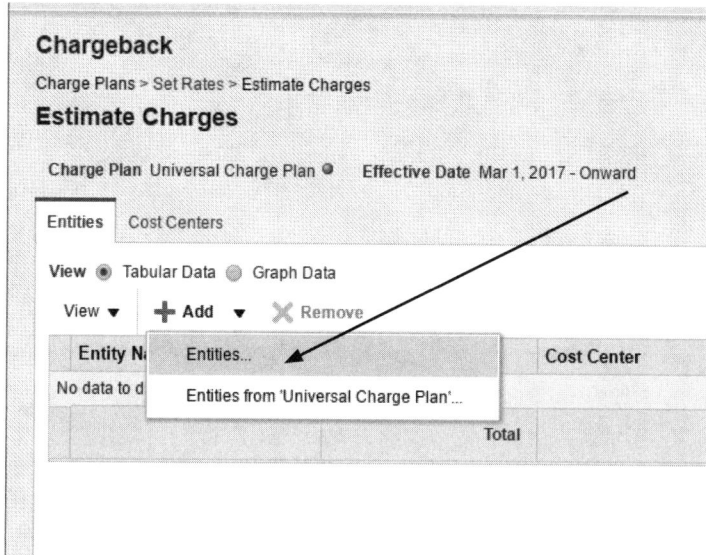

Next, select the entities from the list presented. Because this is only being used for VMs hosted by Oracle VM, select Oracle VM Guest from the Target Type drop-down. Then, using the

CTRL key, group-select the VMs you want to use for the analysis, as shown here. Optionally, you can select by zone or server pool.

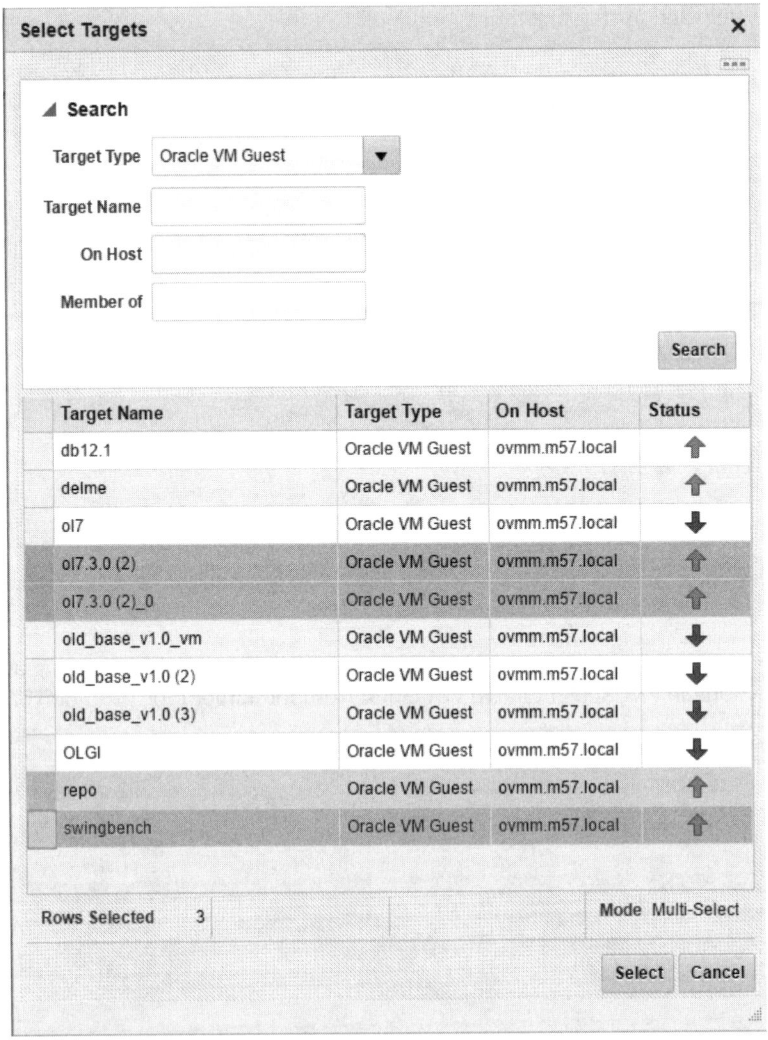

One you click the Select button, the system will calculate the estimated charges and the difference from the prior billing period, as shown next. Because this is a new system, the difference will be significant because the last period had no expenses allocated.

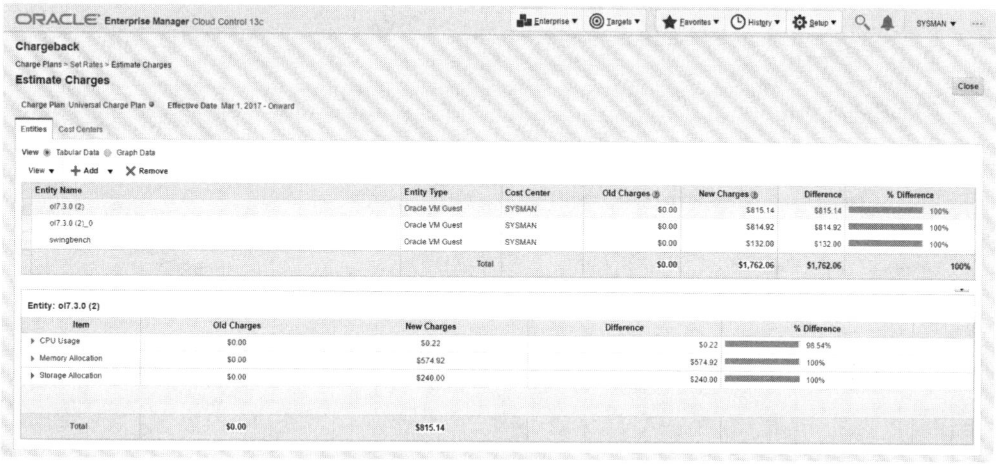

Once you are happy with the accuracy of the results, click Save to make this new universal charge plan active. Whereas the universal charge plan will provide a basic report on resource consumption, an extended charge plan can track more resource types. It can mix not only Oracle VM resources, as shown here, but also Database, WebLogic, Physical Host, Application, Java Virtual Machine resources—and more. You can see all the options using the Charge Item Library, which is found in the Charge Plan home screen.

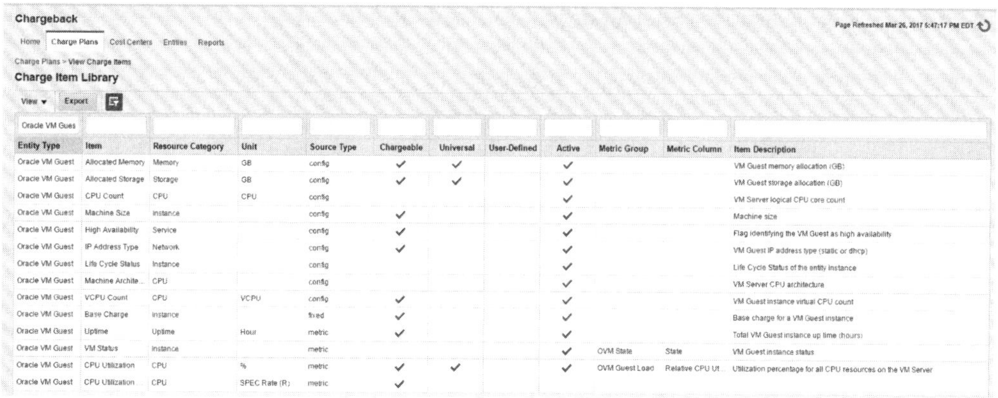

A new extended plan can be created by clicking Create | Plan from the Charge Plans home screen. The new plan (named "New Plan") will be empty, as shown here.

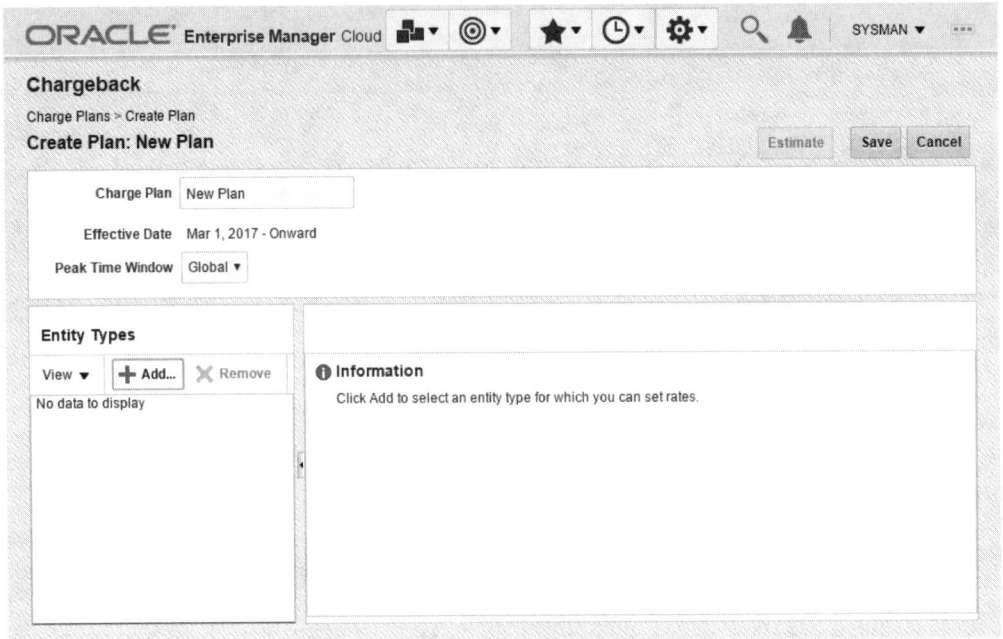

Adding new entity types is done using the Add button. This then prompts you for which types of resources are being added, as shown next. The example shows selecting a single VM, but you can also select by a zone or server pool.

The system will now start with the limited resources of the universal charge plan: CPU, memory, and storage. However, you can now add in other resource types by clicking the Add Item button, shown here.

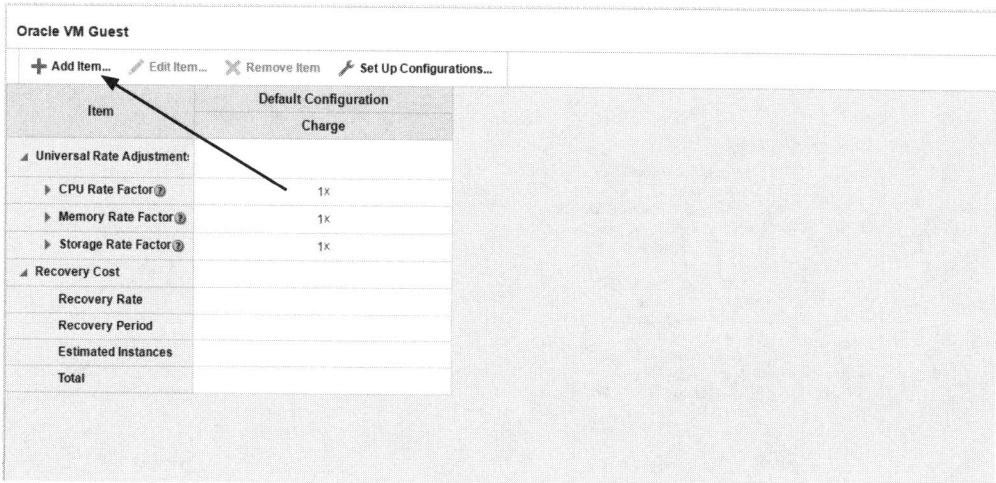

Oracle VM Guest

➕ Add Item...   ✏ Edit Item...   ✕ Remove Item   🔧 Set Up Configurations...

Item	Default Configuration Charge
◢ Universal Rate Adjustment	
▸ CPU Rate Factor ⓘ	1x
▸ Memory Rate Factor ⓘ	1x
▸ Storage Rate Factor ⓘ	1x
◢ Recovery Cost	
Recovery Rate	
Recovery Period	
Estimated Instances	
Total	

You are then presented with the Add Item dialog, shown next, where you can select the new item's name. In this case, High Availability is used to enable a higher cost of VMs that have the High Availability flag set.

Add Item   ✕

Item Name	High Availability ▾
Rate Formula Type	Standard
Charge Type	Flat ▾
Unit	Entity Instance
Type	○ Default (applies when no conditions match)
	● Use Condition
Condition Operator	Like ▾
Condition Value	Y 🔍

✔ Tip Condition value search works only when a Chargeback job has run recently.
✔ Tip Condition value is case sensitive and % can be used with search value

Add   Cancel

Once the item is added, you can add an uplift, an additional charge to the resource. In this example, because High Availability is the item, the CPU and memory will be charged at 1.5 times the normal price, as shown here, to account for the additional servers required to support the needed capacity. To change the rate, simply select the field and enter in new values.

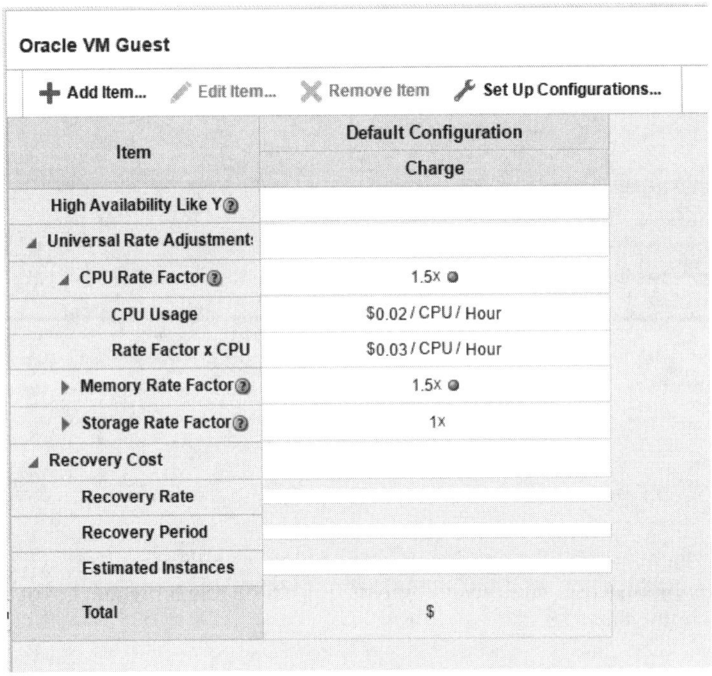

Oracle VM Guest	
+ Add Item... Edit Item... X Remove Item Set Up Configurations...	

Item	Default Configuration
	Charge
High Availability Like Y ⑦	
◢ Universal Rate Adjustment:	
◢ CPU Rate Factor ⑦	1.5x ⊘
CPU Usage	$0.02 / CPU / Hour
Rate Factor x CPU	$0.03 / CPU / Hour
▶ Memory Rate Factor ⑦	1.5x ⊘
▶ Storage Rate Factor ⑦	1x
◢ Recovery Cost	
Recovery Rate	
Recovery Period	
Estimated Instances	
Total	$

This is just a simple example of how to set up charge plans. More complex rules are possible to account for complex solutions.

Cost Centers

Once a charge plan is created, the next step is to set up the cost centers. The cost centers allow you to group targets to match your organization's structure. You can then match the resources to the cost centers and applications used by the organization. The example shown in Figure 24-10 uses the fake company Dummy Accounting Values (DAV), which has an IT department as well as an apps team that supports two different applications: APP1 and APP2.

The first step is to build this in Enterprise Manager. To access the cost center, from the Chargeback home screen click the Cost Centers tab. There is a default cost center, shown in Figure 24-11, that is a child of the root cost center.

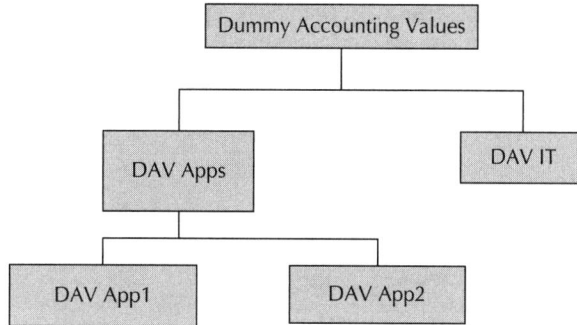

FIGURE 24-10.   *DAV org chart*

FIGURE 24-11.   *Cost centers*

To add a new cost center, highlight the root cost center and click the Add button. In the resulting dialog, you can enter the information for the new cost center. The Cost Center field shows the full name of the new cost center. The Display Name field is often the short name for the cost center.

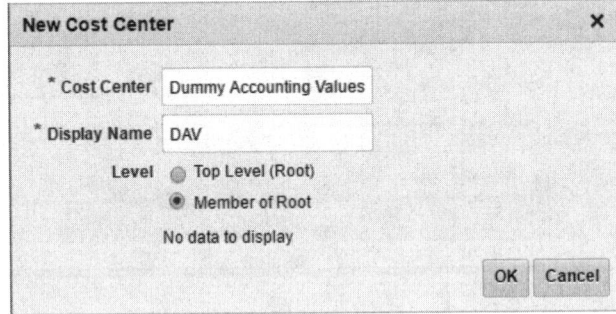

It is also possible to add cost centers underneath cost centers to match your organization's setup. Make sure that when you do this you select Member of $COSTCENTER instead of Top Level. When complete, the DAV dummy organization's cost centers look like what's shown in Figure 24-12.

At this stage, because no targets are assigned to the cost center, all charges are zero. The next step is to assign an entity/target to a cost center organization and a charge plan. You can make bulk entries from the Entities tab by selecting the Add button, as shown here.

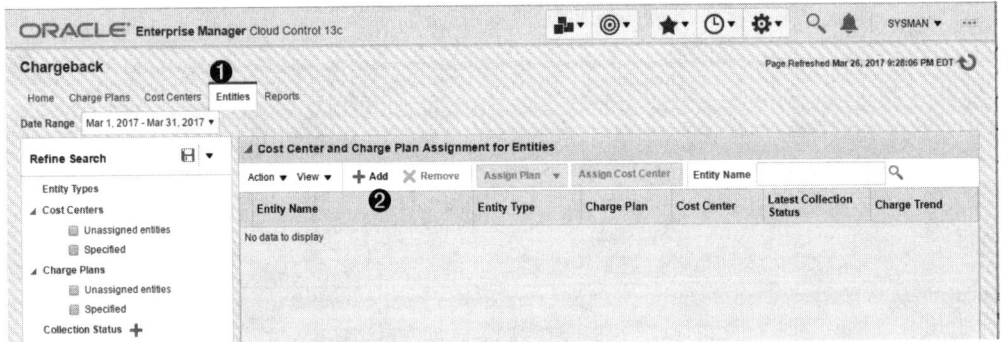

On the next screen, you can click Add to start adding targets for assignment. In the example shown in Figure 24-13, only Oracle VM guests are being assigned, and the CTRL key is used to multiselect all Oracle VM guests.

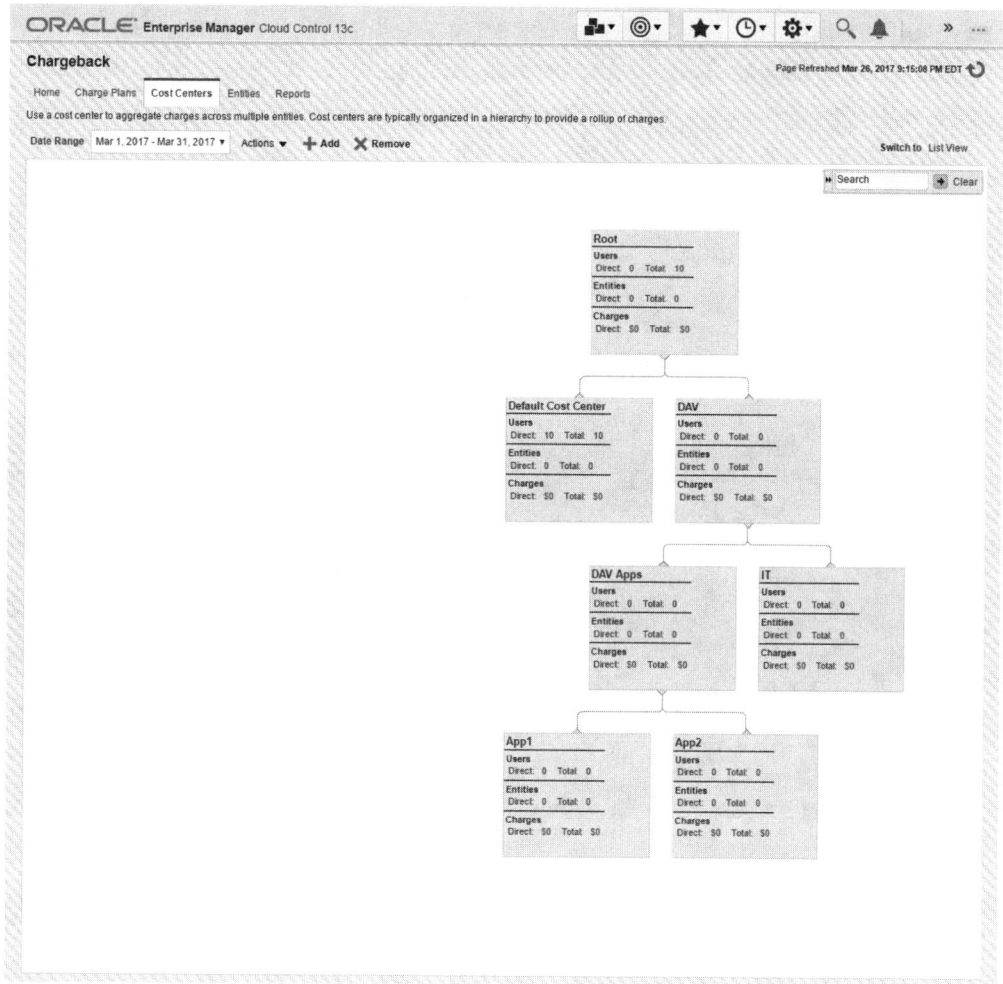

FIGURE 24-12. *Dummy organization*

Select Targets				×

◢ Search

Target Type   Oracle VM Guest ▼

Target Name

On Host

Member of

Search

Target Name	Target Type	On Host	Status
db12.1	Oracle VM Guest	ovmm.m57.local	⬆
delme	Oracle VM Guest	ovmm.m57.local	⬆
ol7	Oracle VM Guest	ovmm.m57.local	⬇
ol7.3.0 (2)	Oracle VM Guest	ovmm.m57.local	⬆
ol7.3.0 (2)_0	Oracle VM Guest	ovmm.m57.local	⬆
old_base_v1.0_vm	Oracle VM Guest	ovmm.m57.local	⬇
old_base_v1.0 (2)	Oracle VM Guest	ovmm.m57.local	⬇
old_base_v1.0 (3)	Oracle VM Guest	ovmm.m57.local	⬇
OLGI	Oracle VM Guest	ovmm.m57.local	⬇
repo	Oracle VM Guest	ovmm.m57.local	⬆
swingbench	Oracle VM Guest	ovmm.m57.local	⬆

Rows Selected   11   Mode   Multi-Select

Select   Cancel

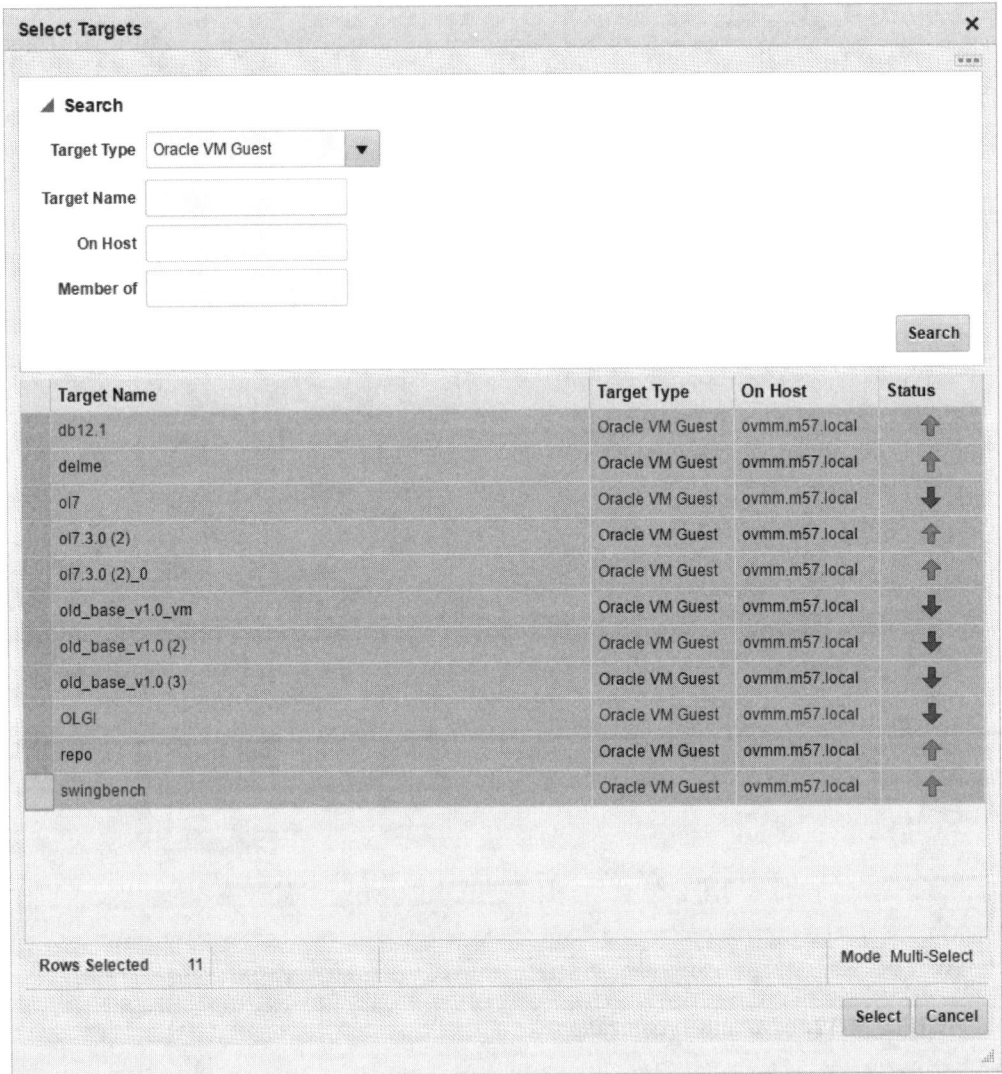

FIGURE 24-13. *Selecting Oracle VM guests*

Next, you should see all the systems selected in the Select Targets and Usage Modes screen, shown here. All targets of type Oracle VM Guests will use the Metered mode for usage.

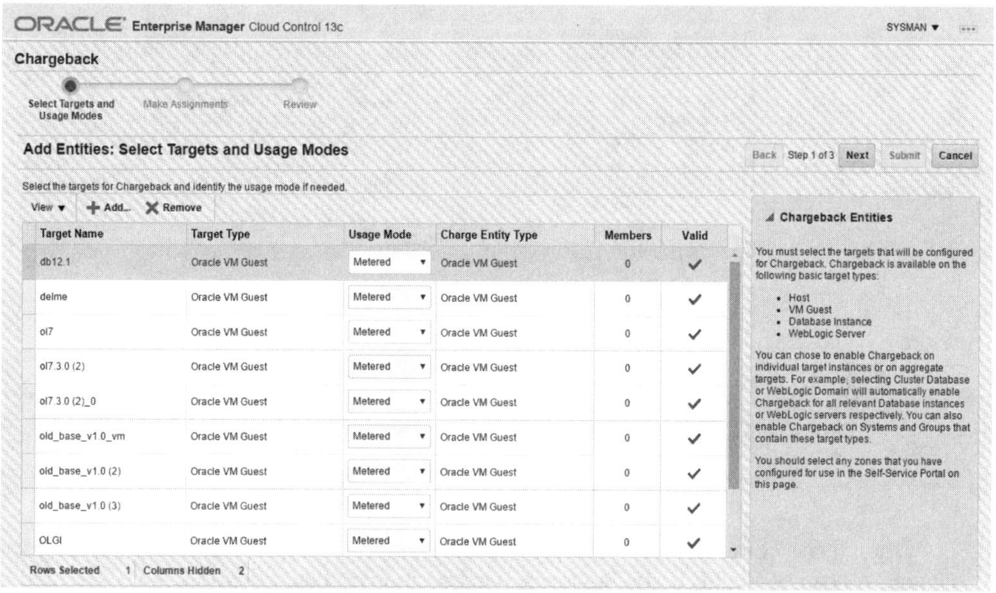

On the next screen, you can make assignments for both the charge plan and the cost center. To assign the charge plan, highlight the targets you want to assign the charge plan to and then click Assign Plan. You can then select the charge plan for the targets. The Action Type option allows you to control whether existing charge plans will be overridden or if only targets without an existing charge plan will have the selected plan propagated.

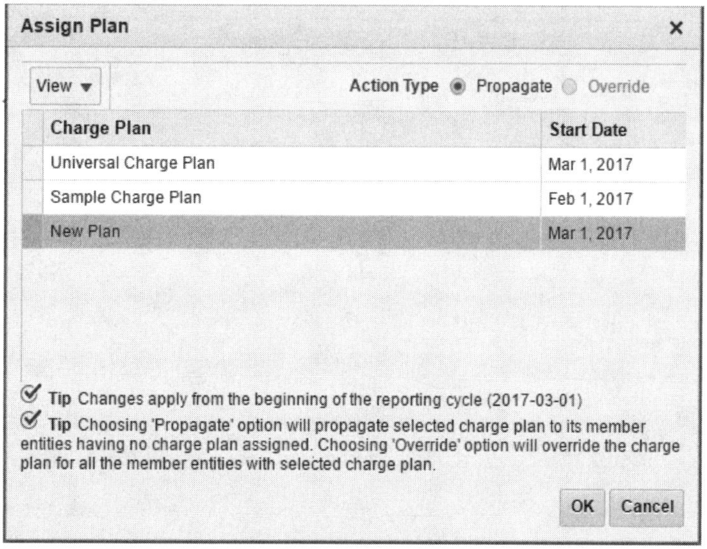

Next, you can assign a cost center to each target using the same basic selection method as with charge plans. When selecting the new cost center, you will need to drill down into your organization to select embedded cost centers, as shown next.

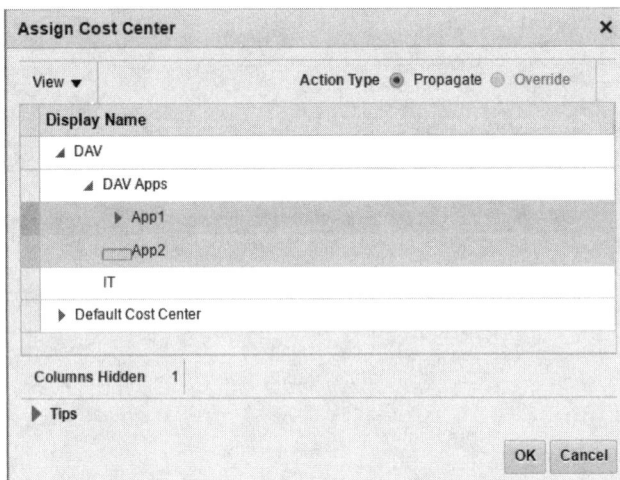

When this is complete, each entity name should now have an assigned charge plan and cost center. You can verify this in the Review screen, as shown in Figure 24-14.

Now that the Chargeback feature is configured, when creating new targets, you can select the charge plan and cost center as the target is created, thus simplifying the process.

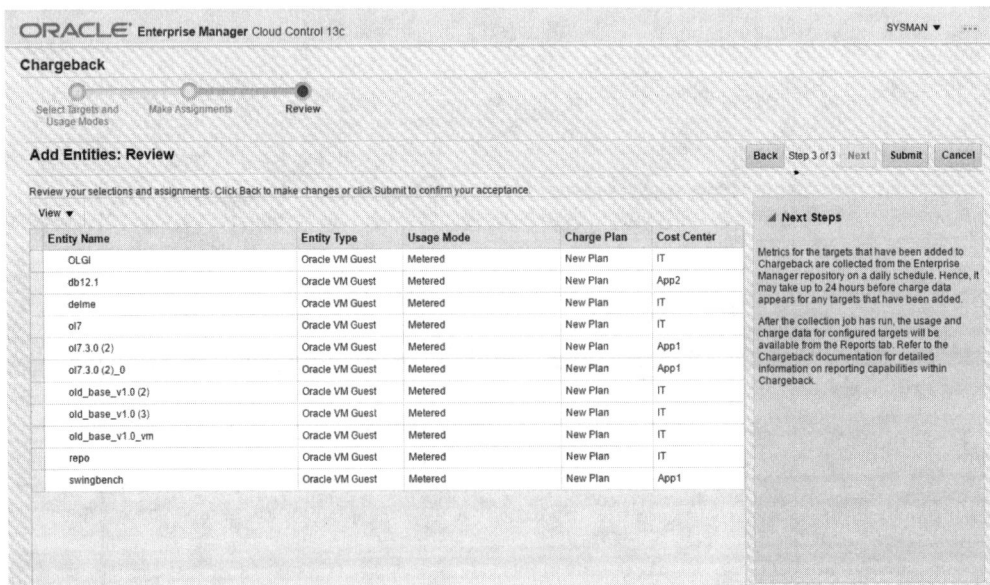

FIGURE 24-14. *Assignments completed*

Common Tasks Using Cloud Control

This section covers the following common management tasks that can be performed from Enterprise Manager:

- **Rapid navigation**   You can quickly navigate to a VM and its corresponding operating system.
- **Holistic topology maps**   These maps show the relationship between all the levels of the technology stack. This works best when running Oracle on Oracle/.
- **Monitoring an Oracle VM server**   You can monitor OVS resources in Enterprise Manager.
- **Resynchronizing Enterprise Manager to the Oracle VM Manager**   When targets are manually created in Oracle VM Manager, you can create the corresponding targets in Enterprise Manager.
- **Deploying templates**   You can create VMs using a template.

Navigating the Infrastructure Cloud

Navigating to targets within the Oracle VM Cloud is done from the Oracle VM Infrastructure home screen. Access this page from the Enterprise menu | Cloud | Oracle VM Infrastructure Home, as shown in Figure 24-15.

Once on the Oracle VM Infrastructure Home screen, shown in Figure 24-16, you can get a quick view of the health of the IaaS cloud, with specific blocks of information that give you critical information about the environment.

The General panel shows the overall status of all VMs in the environment, with the green arrow showing VMs that are online and the red arrow showing VMs that are offline. It is normal for some VMs to be offline, as they might not be needed. A common example is a VM used to create and maintain custom templates for the environment. There is also a count of all OVS servers, server pools, and zones. (Zones are covered in the next chapter.)

The Target Flux panel shows a history of the daily new and retired (deleted) VMs. This is helpful in agile environments to track overall activity. Environments with high levels of target flux (more than four to five a day) may need additional resources allocated to Enterprise Manager, and the OVS systems may need more RAM in dom0.

The CPU and Memory panels show the CPU and memory consumption, respectively, of all servers managed in the infrastructure cloud.

The Inventory and Usage panel shows summaries for virtual servers, guest virtual machines, and instances. You can select an option from the Show drop-down list to view the details in multiple dimensions. For example, for Oracle VM guests, you can view the number of virtual servers under each Oracle VM server.

The Policy panel shows the status of the policies that have been defined and executed for the infrastructure cloud. This panel reports on the number of corrective actions executed and whether they were successful. Corrective actions are an automation tool that enables Enterprise Manager to act on systems when an event is triggered. When combining corrective actions in an infrastructure cloud, you could automate starting new VMs to deal with a capacity issue, for example, or simply clean out a full file system.

The Incidents and Problems panel shows a count of incident and policy violations in the last 24 hours. Click the number of violations to drill down to see the details.

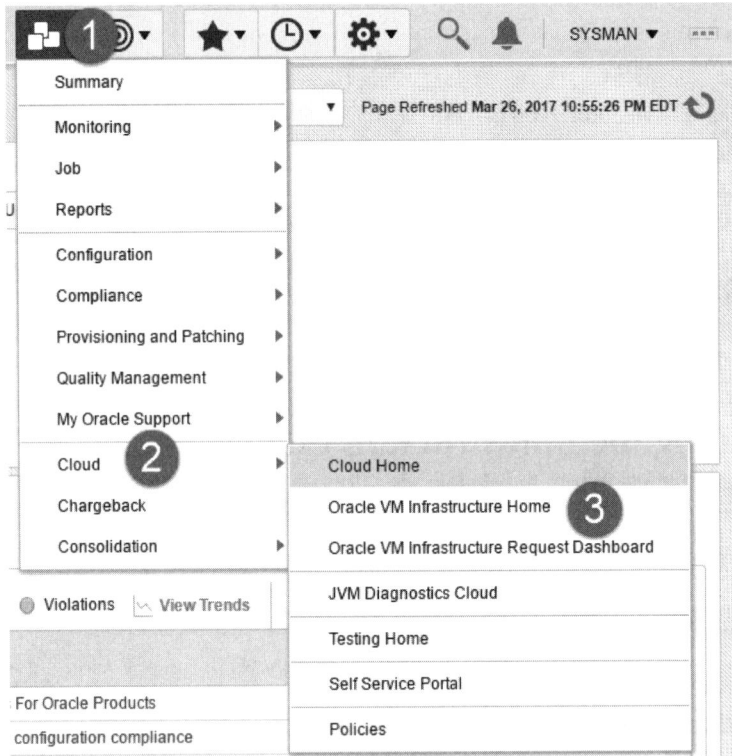

FIGURE 24-15. *Navigating to the Oracle VM Infrastructure Home page*

You can navigate the infrastructure cloud by expanding the Target Navigation icon in the top-left of the menu (see Figure 24-17). This allows you to directly select a component of the infrastructure cloud. You can also use the Expand and Collapse All options under the View menu to view all targets.

Using Topology Maps

One of the more attractive advantages of managing a cloud with Enterprise Manager 13c is the holistic monitoring that Enterprise Manager brings. Using Enterprise Manager, you can see up and down the entire technology stack that supports not only the cloud infrastructure, but also the

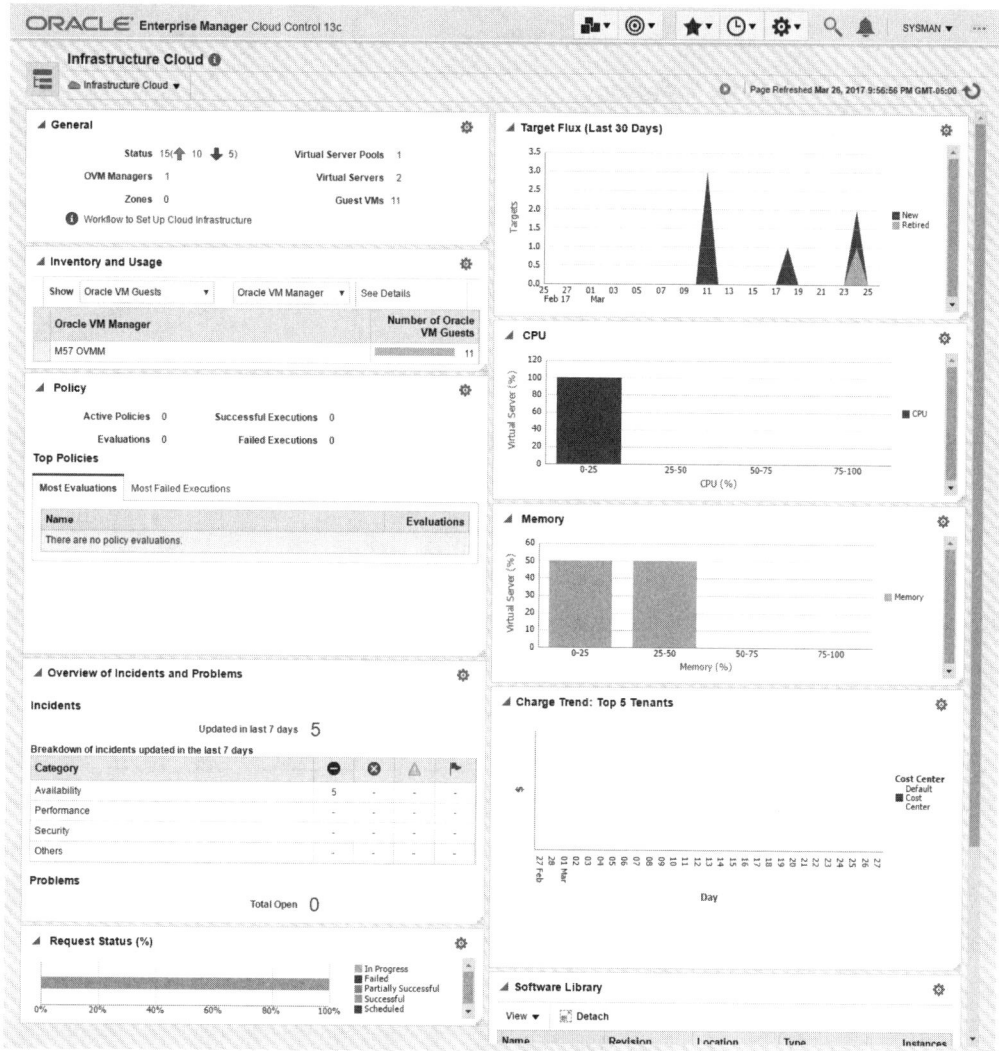

FIGURE 24-16. *Infrastructure Cloud home screen*

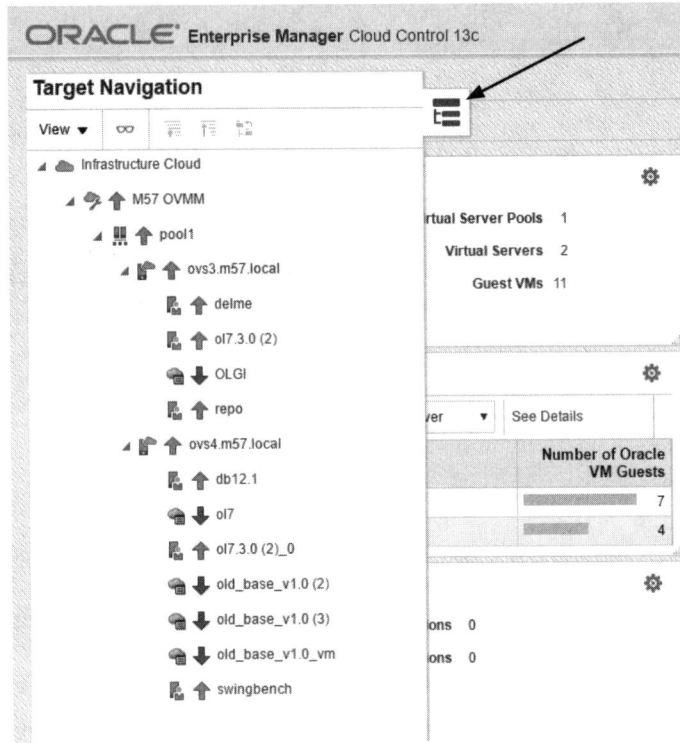

FIGURE 24-17. *Target navigation expanded*

database, middleware, and application tiers. This relationship can be graphically explored using the topology map available in any target, under the member's menu, as shown here.

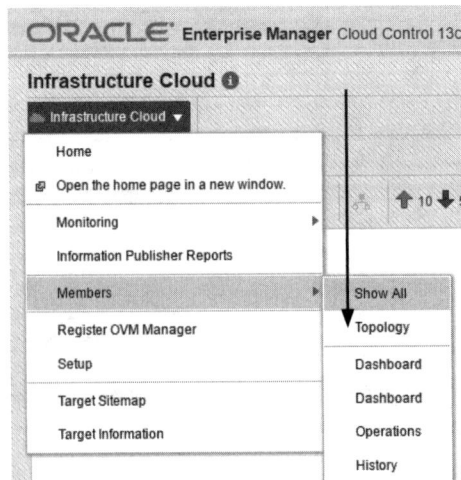

This starts a graphical tool that enables you to browse the relationships of all targets in Enterprise Manager. When called from the Infrastructure home screen, the view defaults to a "grouped" view that only shows the cloud, the OVMM server with any pools, and OVS nodes, if expanded.

By changing the view to Detailed from the View drop down, you expose all the relationships, as shown in Figure 24-18. This gives you the ability to quickly identify something as complex as what OVS, a deployed application in WebLogic, is running on, or what physical host a database listener is running on.

Hovering the mouse over any item will highlight the target as well as any direct relationships, as shown in Figure 24-19. From this view, you can navigate to individual targets directly by simply clicking the target name in the upper-left corner.

As you navigate to individual targets, the topology view will start to show a smaller view, thus aiding in the rapid drill-down of complex environments. The view can also be changed to a table view by selecting the Display option in the upper-left corner of the topology map and selecting Table instead of Graph, as shown in Figure 24-20.

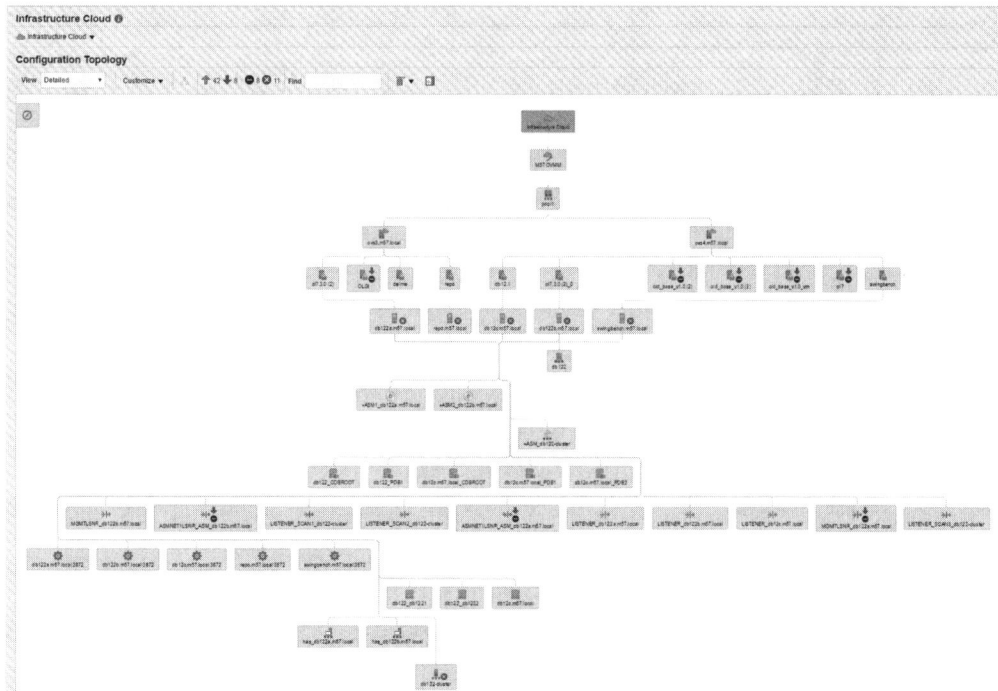

FIGURE 24-18. *Detailed topology view*

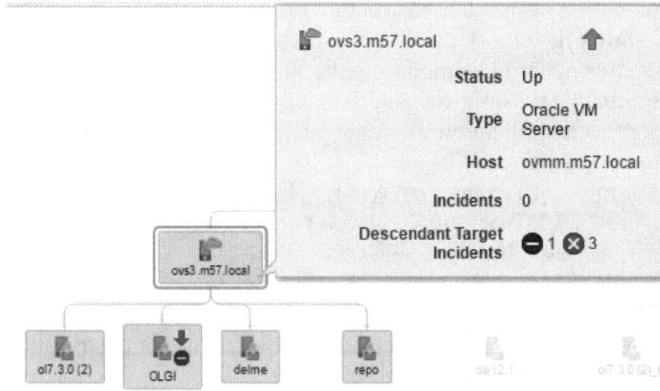

FIGURE 24-19. *Topology target drilldown*

FIGURE 24-20. *Topology table view*

Monitoring OVS

Monitoring the overall resource consumption of an Oracle VM server is simplified using Enterprise Manager. You can use the Target Navigation option from the Infrastructure home screen to navigate to any Oracle VM Server system. This will show the home screen for that host, as shown in Figure 24-21.

This summary screen not only shows the configuration details, but also the current and historical CPU, memory, disk, and network activity for the physical host. The default view of these sections show the last hour, but by selecting the magnifying glass icon to the left of the scroll bar, you can zoom in and out to show multiple days of history (see Figure 24-22). This is helpful in looking back in time to see how resources have been consumed by an Oracle VM Server, and it can help you decide whether to increase resources to the cloud systems.

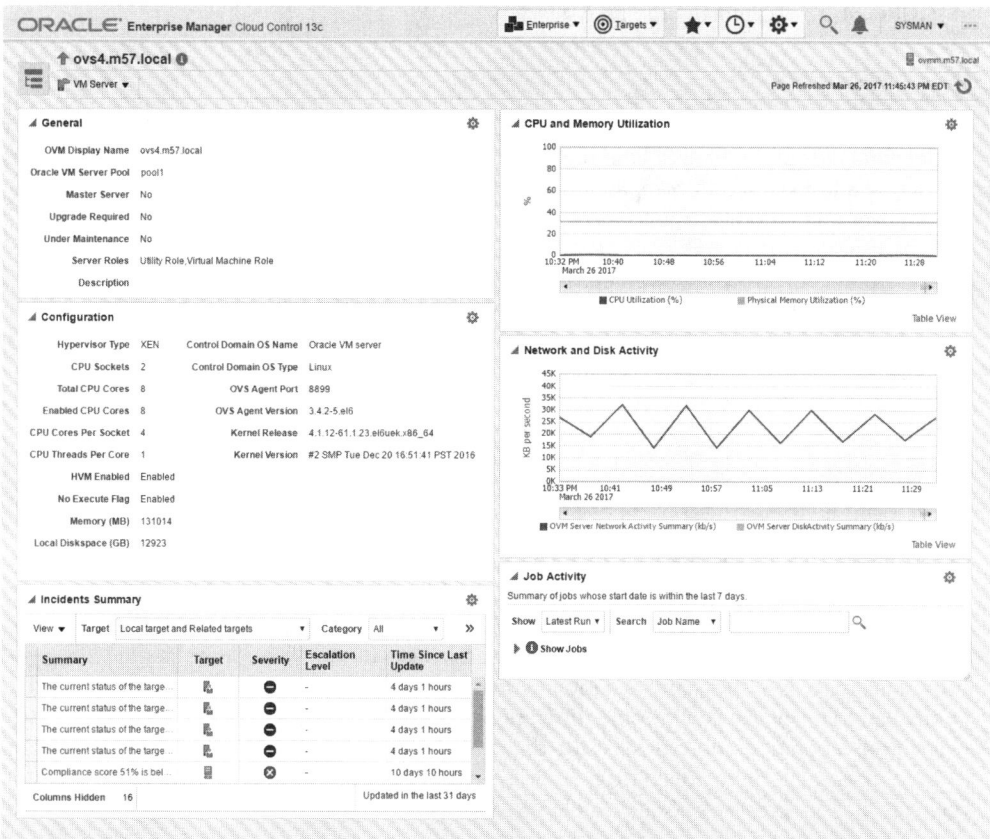

FIGURE 24-21. *Oracle VM Server home screen*

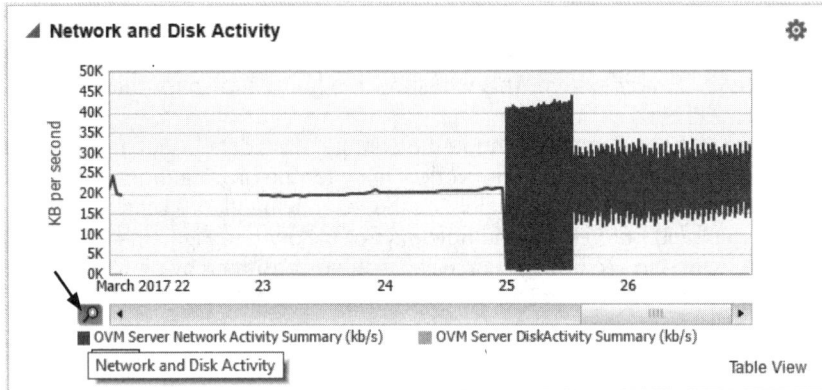

FIGURE 24-22.   *Changing the time window*

Monitoring the Oracle VM server configuration can also be tracked from this page via the Configuration option. Oracle Enterprise Manager gathers configuration data from every target and allows you to look at and compare configurations, not only between targets, but also for a single target over time. A quick way to see what has changed is to look at the VM Server | Configuration | History screen, shown in Figure 24-23.

From this screen, you can see past collections of configuration data as well as the details of what has changed, and you can select the highlighted number under the History Records column. This will display all the changes detected in that set of data, as shown in Figure 24-24. To see the details of the change, simply click the type of change on the line item you want to see more detail of. You can also track compliance of the VM server from the VM Server drop-down, which allows you to track against both security- and best-practice-based compliance templates.

Resynchronizing Enterprise Manager 13c to OVMM

Occasionally when you make changes on the Oracle VM Manager, Enterprise Manager will not show the change due to the time it takes to automatically refresh the server, which occurs every five minutes. Although just waiting a few minutes is one solution, it is sometimes easier to simply force Enterprise Manager to refresh its database against the running Oracle VM server. To do this, select the Oracle VM server from the Target Navigation menu. Then, from the VM Manager menu, select Synchronize. This submits a job in Enterprise Manager that refreshes the database. However, you need to be aware that no other operations on the Oracle VM Manager are possible while the synchronization operation runs. As the database is refreshed, targets that are not present in Oracle VM Manager will be removed from Enterprise Manager and new targets will be created for the objects that are present only in Oracle VM Manager. Configuration collection will be refreshed for all other targets.

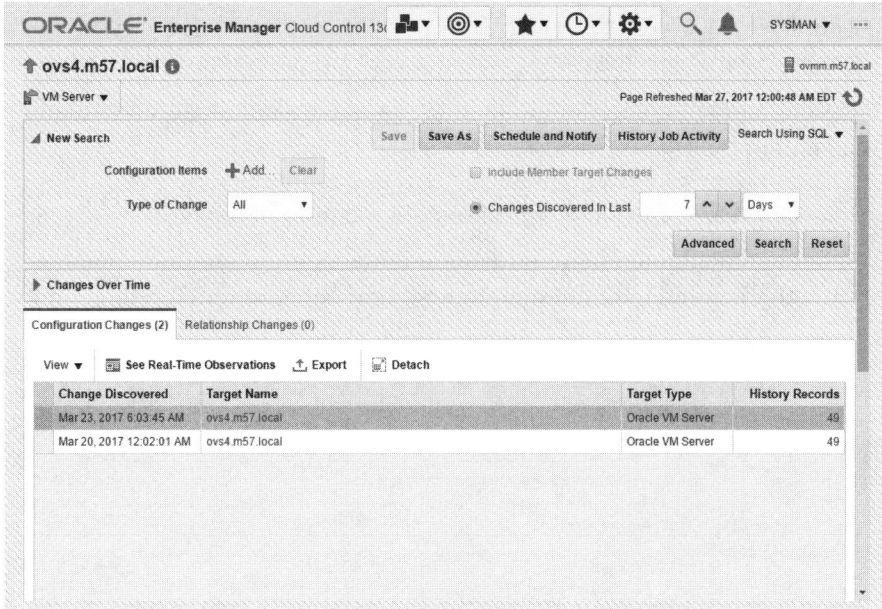

FIGURE 24-23. *VM server configuration history*

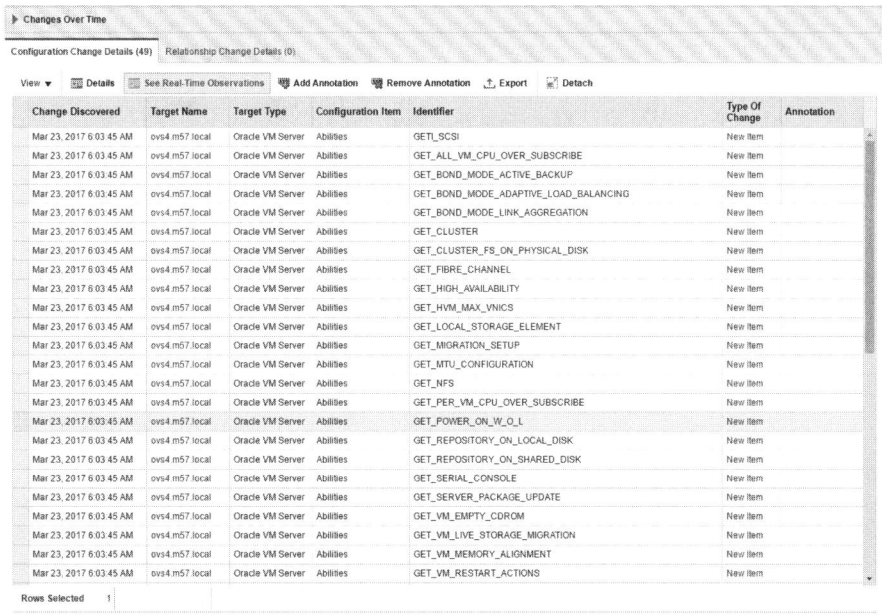

FIGURE 24-24. *List of changes detected*

Deploying Templates

Manually deploying a template as an Enterprise Manager administrator or power user is done from the Oracle VM Server home screen.

NOTE
End-user self-provisioning is covered in Chapter 25.

From the VM Server menu, select Deploy | Template, as shown next.

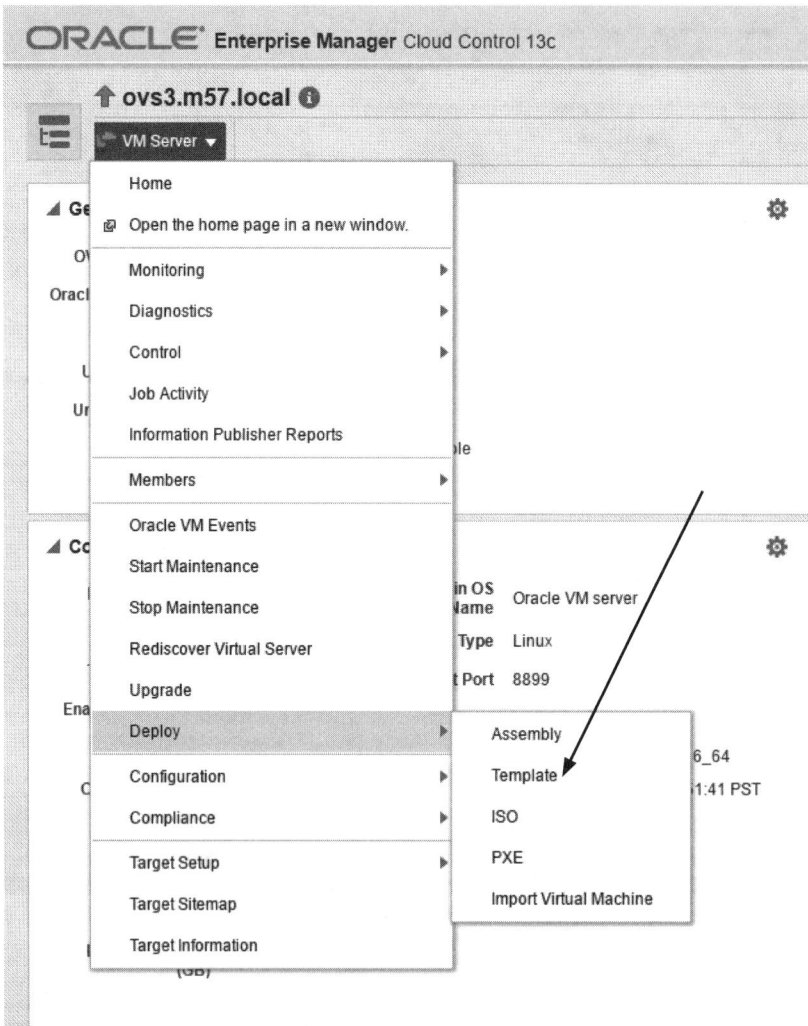

This starts a similar process to the one used directly from the Oracle VM Manager. The first screen, shown here, allows you to select the template to be used to create the VM. Enterprise Manager 13*c* can use templates that already exist in the Oracle VM repository.

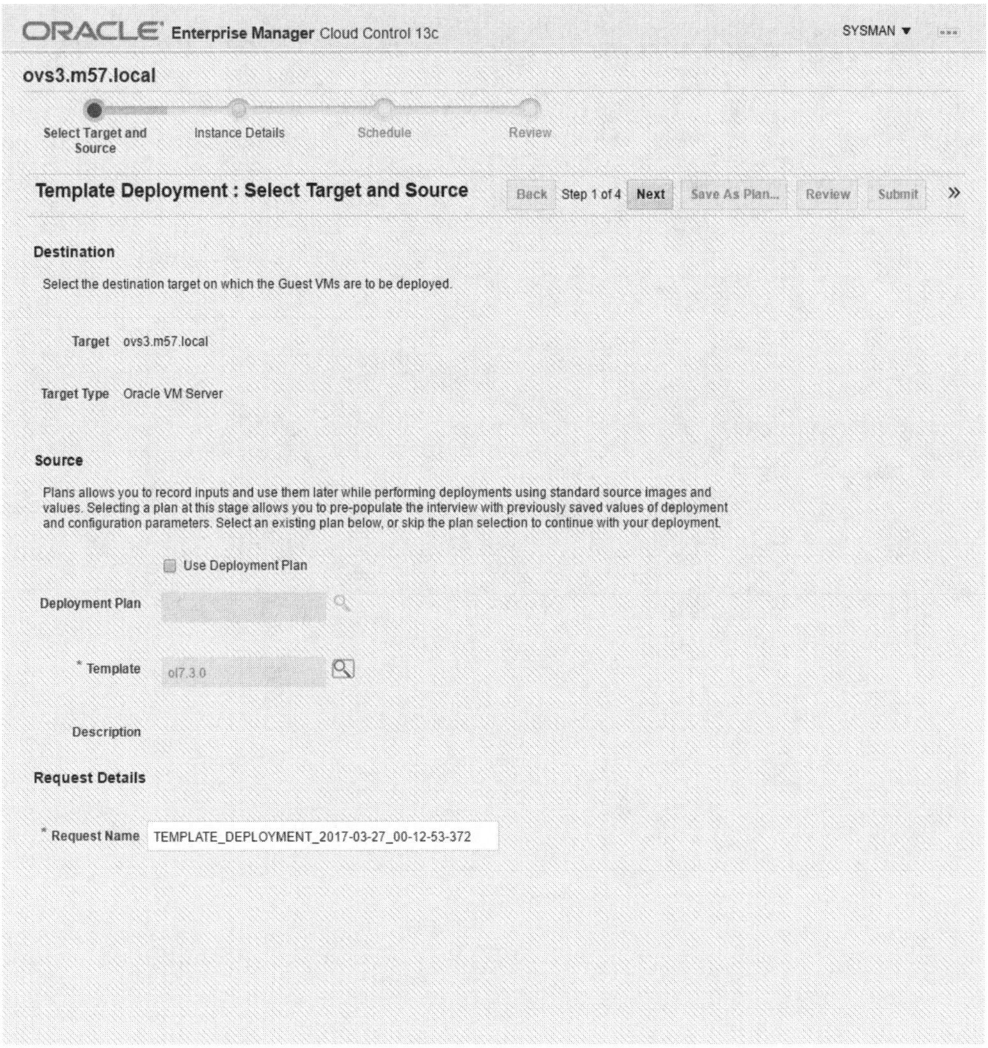

The next screen, shown here, allows you to specify the VM details, including the VM name, the CPU and memory to be allocated, the High Availability flag, and the CPU priority and scheduling cap. These are the same parameters used when you created the VM from Oracle VM Manager.

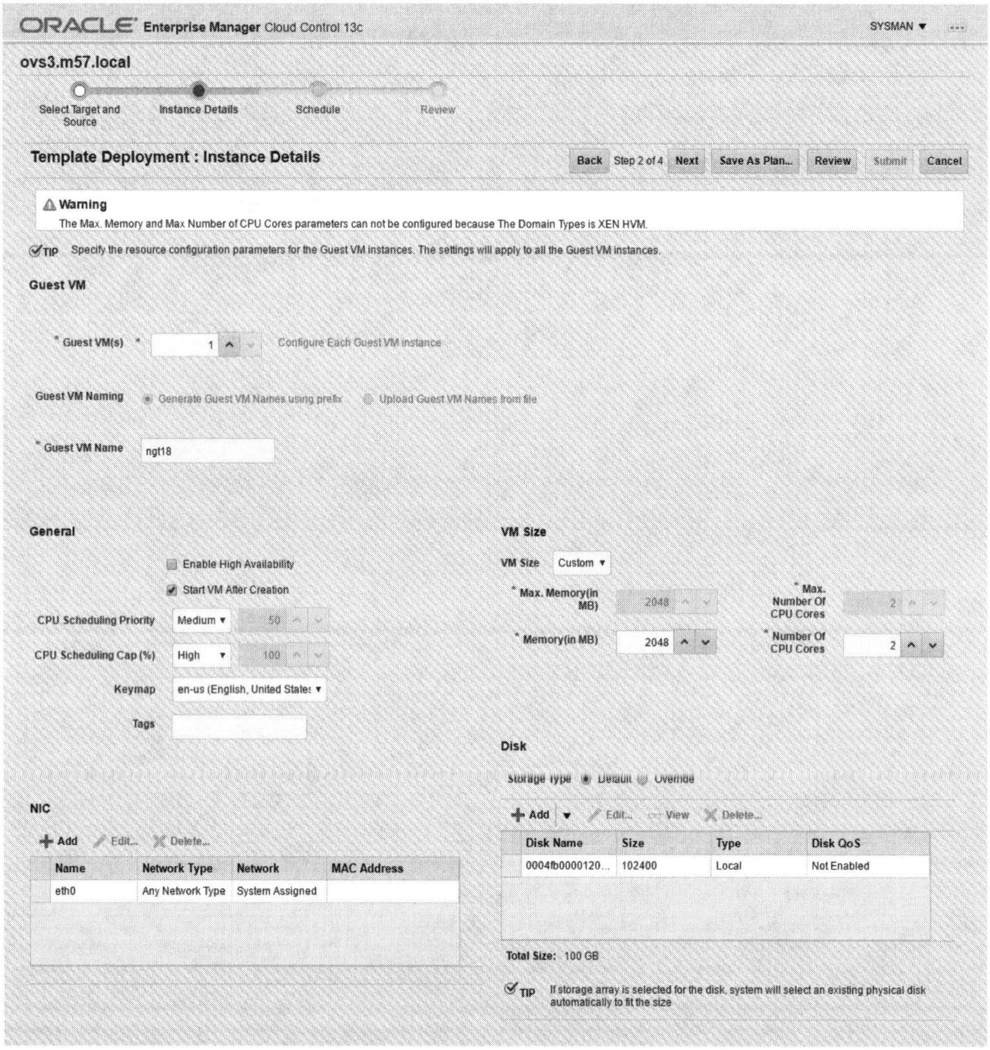

The third screen is the scheduling screen, which is where things start to become a little different from the Oracle VM Manager interface. Enterprise Manager allows you to schedule when the VM will be created. For example, you might schedule a large-scale deployment during an after-hours window. More importantly, you can schedule the end date of a VM, either by using the calendar to set a specific date and time or by setting a specific run length in minutes or hours. This is very helpful in environments where users commonly request VMs but forget to request for them to be decommissioned. Once the schedule is set, you can review the request and submit the job. Oracle Enterprise Manager will then provision and decommission the VM per the schedule and resources requested.

Summary

This chapter covered how to perform many of the common management tasks when building a cloud with Enterprise Manager, including how to create new administrators with limited privileges, how to configure the Showback/Chargeback feature, and several of the common day-to-day administrative tasks in Enterprise Manager 13c Cloud Control. The next chapter puts all this together and shows you how to build an end-user self-provisioning portal in Enterprise Manager 13c.

CHAPTER
25

Configuring Advanced Cloud Control and User Self-Provisioning

When you're building a private cloud, it all comes down to one simple feature: enabling the users to self-provision VMs on their own. In the previous chapters, all the perquisite components have been configured. The Oracle VM infrastructure, network, storage, and integration into Enterprise Manager Cloud Control 13c have all been covered. Although these components combined provide unique value, and the goal is for the users to be able to access a portal and provision their own VMs. This chapter covers the tasks of configuring and using the self-provisioning portal built into Enterprise Manager Could Control 13c.

Configuring IaaS Self Service

Enabling Enterprise Manager to provide the IaaS self-provisioning portal can be done in six steps (see Figure 25-1). The first five of these steps were completed in the previous chapters, when you learned how to configure an Oracle VM system. Once the final step is complete and the zone is created, the final task is to customize your IaaS cloud. Here's a review of the steps for configuring IaaS Self Service:

1. *Register Oracle VM Manager.* This step was covered in Chapter 23, when you registered Oracle VM Manager with Enterprise Manager. This enables Enterprise Manager to control the Oracle VM Manager system. This registration is a requirement for the common administrative tasks covered in Chapter 24. The administrator can also create and manage storage, the network, server pools, virtual servers, and guest virtual machines.

2. *Discover Oracle VM servers.* This step was also covered in Chapter 23. It automatically discovers any existing OVS systems, pools, storage servers and repositories, network configurations, and existing virtual machines. When new OVS machines are added, they can be discovered using Enterprise Manager or the OVMM system.

3. *Set up storage infrastructure.* In Chapter 13, we covered creating and managing storage servers, file systems, and logical unit numbers (LUNs). An external storage element is created on dedicated storage hardware such as a server configured for NAS offering NFS shares. We created a repository, which is where templates and assemblies are stored for deployment as VMs in a cloud. We also covered how custom templates can be created in Chapter 17.

4. *Configure networks and VLAN groups.* Chapter 12 covered the creation and configuration of networks in Oracle VM Manager. This included the configuration of the OVS physical NIC ports as well as expanded into how virtual network interfaces (vNICs) are used to carry network traffic across a VLAN—a mechanism used to virtualize network interfaces across subnets and physical locations so that they appear to be on a single confined LAN.

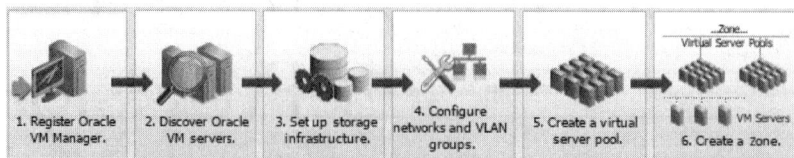

FIGURE 25-1.   *IaaS enablement workflow*

5. *Create a virtual server pool.* Chapter 14 covered the creation and management of a server pool, which groups one or more Oracle VM servers. The pool allows for a physical grouping of similar servers. As a reminder, a VM can only be "live migrated" within a pool.

6. *Create a zone.* A zone is an Enterprise Manager concept that's used to group related cloud resources together. Zones can be created based on location, software lifecycle status, and so on, to group resources belonging to a cost center or for metering and chargeback purposes. Typically, a zone can cover a department, project, or possibly even a data center. The cloud environment can be composed of one or more zones. Each zone has a set of metrics that show the aggregate utilization of the zone. A zone can contain multiple OVM server pools, but a OVMM pool can only be a member of a single zone. We cover the creation of zones in this chapter.

Once the initial configuration is complete, you need to configure the cloud environment itself, which you can do from the Infrastructure Cloud Setup menu. This includes configuring the following items:

- **Storage QoS** Storage QoS refers to the type or quality of storage used by a VM. This is defined at the storage server level. Setting up the storage QoS involves defining various storage properties. Before deploying a VM, you can define the storage QoS, map this QoS to a storage server, and then specify this QoS while deploying a guest virtual machine. Examples might include all flash storage for databases and low-cost archive storage for backups.

- **Network Types** You can define network types used by VMs. This can be defined to match your environment and may be something like Internet DMZ, RAC Interconnect, or Internally Routable. After the network type has been defined, you can map this to any network that is being created and assigned to a VM.

- **Machine Sizes** You can define the machine sizes that will be available to the self-service users when they deploy a VM. By default, three sizes are created: small, medium, and large.

- **Software Library User Configuration** With the storage repository, you can import VM templates, virtual appliances, and other software components into the storage repository. This makes it easier to share templates and virtual appliances across OVMM deployments.

- **Request Purging Policy** All deployment requests can be retained for review for a certain period of time and then purged. This section sets the number of days requests are archived in Enterprise Manager.

Creating a Zone

A *zone* is an Enterprise Manager concept used by database, Java, and infrastructure cloud management systems. It is used to group related cloud-delivery resources together. Zones can be created based on location, software lifecycle status, and so on, to group resources belonging to a cost center or for metering and chargeback purposes. Typically, a zone can cover a department, project, or possibly even a data center. The cloud environment can be composed of one or more zones. Each zone has a set of metrics that show its aggregate utilization. For an infrastructure zone, the members will be OVS pools previously defined in the OVMM. A zone can contain multiple OVM server pools, but a OVMM pool can only be a member of a single zone.

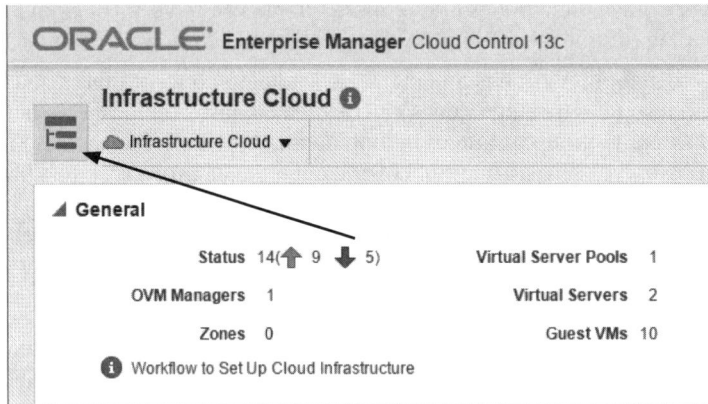

FIGURE 25-2. *Infrastructure Cloud target navigation*

To create a zone, navigate to the Infrastructure Cloud home screen and expand the Target Navigation option, as shown in Figure 25-2.

Next, right-click the OVMM server; this will present you with a variety of options for the OVMM server. To create a new zone, select Create Zone, as shown in Figure 25-3. The other options are described here:

- **Members** This option shows all members associated with the OVM Manager.

- **Edit** This option edits the connection registration information for the OVM Manager.

- **Synchronize** This option forces Enterprise Manager to synchronize its database with the configuration in the OVM Manager. This is useful when changes are made in the OVM Manager, and Enterprise Manager does not yet show them.

- **Deregister** This option deregisters the Oracle VM Manager from Enterprise Manager and removes all related targets from Enterprise Manager.

- **Create Zone** This option creates a new zone for IaaS.

- **Create Virtual Server Pool** This option creates an OVM server pool using Enterprise Manager instead of OVMM.

- **Discover Virtual Server** This option discovers a new OVS using Enterprise Manager instead of OVMM.

- **Manage Unowned Virtual Servers** This option allows OVMM to take control of unowned Oracle VM servers.

- **Manage Network** This option allows the Enterprise Manager admin to control the network configuration of the Oracle VM system, similar to how the same task can be performed using OVMM.

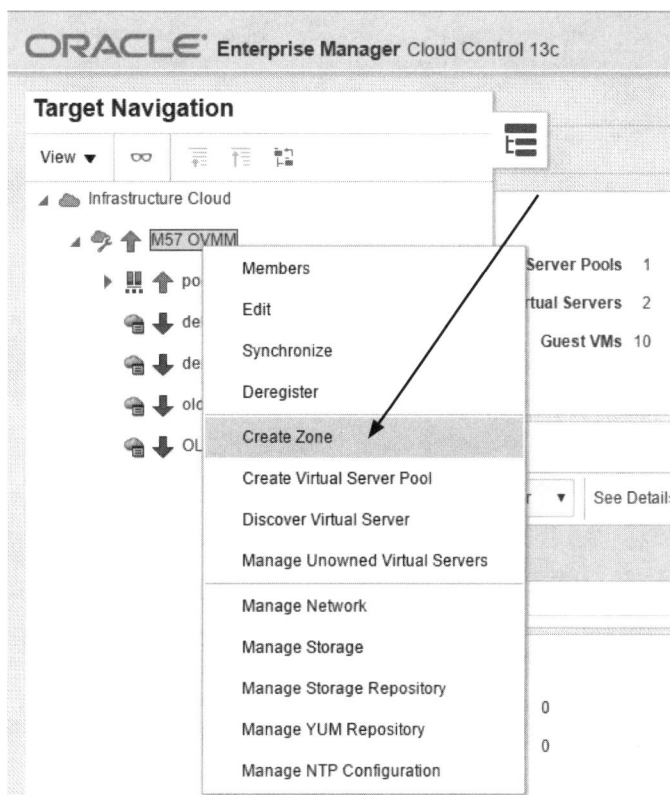

FIGURE 25-3.   *Creating a new zone*

- **Manage Storage**   This option allows the Enterprise Manager admin to control the storage configuration of the Oracle VM system, similar to how the same task can be performed using OVMM.

- **Manage Storage Repository**   This option allows the Enterprise Manager admin to control the storage repositories used by OVMM, similar to how the same task can be performed using OVMM.

- **Manage YUM Repository**   This option sets the YUM repository used for OVS patching.

- **Manage NTP Configuration**   This option allows the configuration of the NTP servers used by all OVS systems.

The next step is to name the zone, provide a description, and indicate whether the zone can be used by IaaS Self Service users. Use the Add button to select the server pools used by the zone. Although multiple pools can be place into a single zone, a pool can only be in one zone at a time.

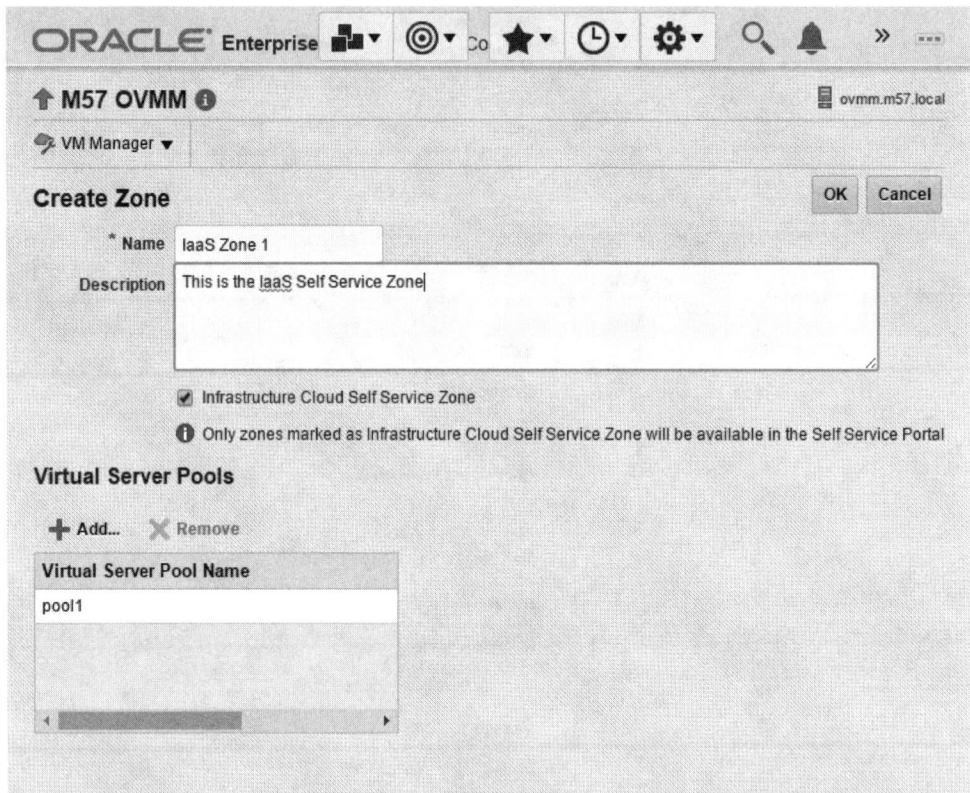

FIGURE 25-4. *IaaS zone configuration*

The final configuration should look similar to Figure 25-4. As a note, if the Infrastructure Cloud Self Service Zone option is not checked, the zone will not be available for Self Service users.

When the zone is created, an Enterprise Manager job will be created. When the job finishes, the zone should appear in the Target Navigation view, with the OVS pool and all its members showing underneath the zone, as shown in Figure 25-5.

It is worth noting that virtual machines not assigned to a pool will not show up in the hierarchy of the zone but instead will show as being peers of the pool. This is the case with the virtual machines delme, demo3.0, old_base_v1.0_vm, and OLGI in the example.

Once the zone is created, the next step is to customize the cloud for IaaS.

Configuring the Cloud for IaaS

Many of the settings in this phase will be unique to your specific environment. This step allows you to define the networks, storage types, and machine sizes available to Self Service users.

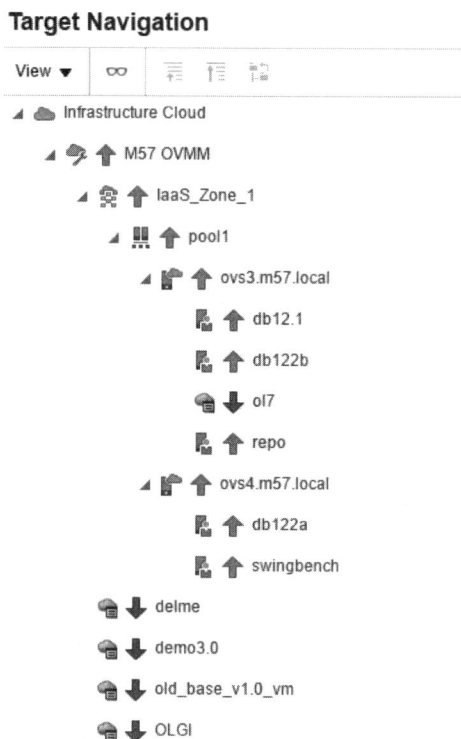

FIGURE 25-5. *Zone hierarchy*

These common settings are defined for the entire IaaS cloud. To start the setup process, from the Target Navigation menu, right-click Infrastructure Cloud and select Setup, as shown here.

From this screen, the global IaaS cloud settings can be defined and configured.

Storage QoS

The first setting defines the storage QoS available to Self Service users. Storage QoS refers to the type or quality of storage used by a VM. This is defined at the storage server level. Setting up the storage QoS involves defining various storage properties. Before deploying a VM, you can define the storage QoS, map this QoS to a storage server, and then specify this QoS while deploying a guest virtual machine. An example might be all flash storage for databases or low-cost archive storage for backups. These are basically tags, defined by the administrator, that can later be added to each storage repository. Follow these steps to add a new tag:

1. Select Storage QoS and click the Create button, as shown here.

2. Enter a name and description for the new tag. The name cannot contain any whitespace and should be descriptive, such as flash_storage, ebs_storage, and so on. An example is shown next.

When this is complete, the new Storage QoS option should show up in the list, as shown next.

3. You can now assign the storage QoS to the repositories previously created. To do this, navigate to the OVMM server using the Target Navigation menu and then right-click the OVM Manager and select Manage Storage, as shown here.

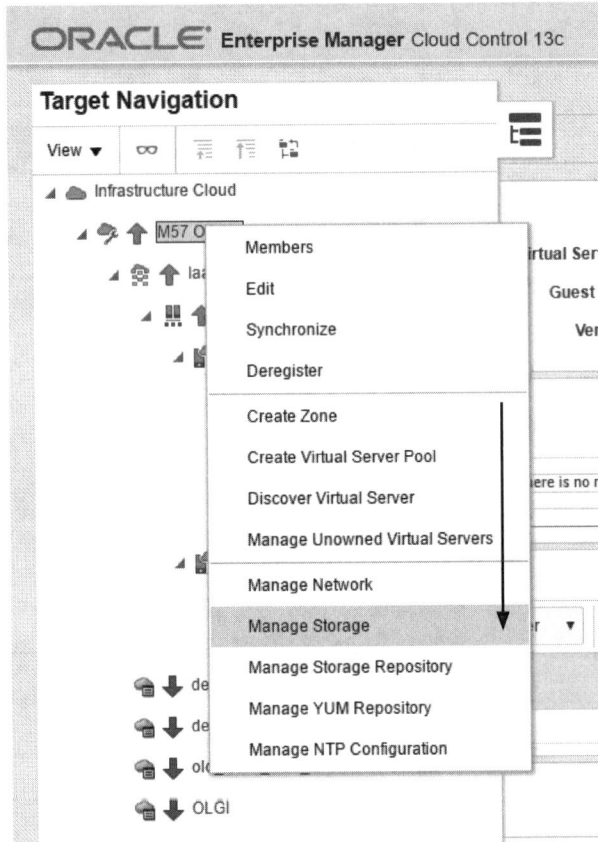

4. Select the file server that contains the share you want to assign the Storage tag to. In this
    example, Generic NAS will have a storage QoS assigned. Select Generic NAS, as shown here.

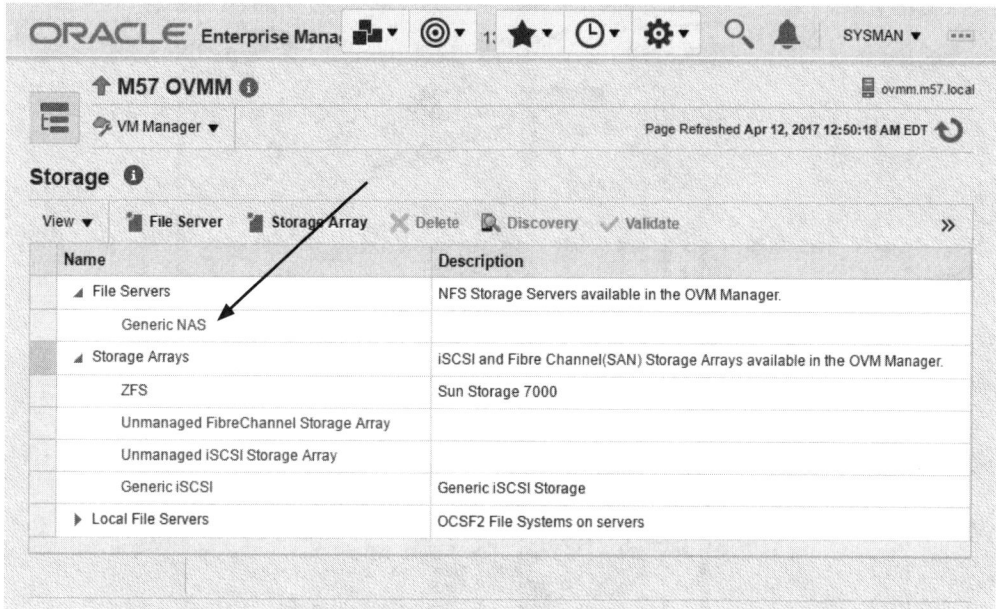

5. Scroll down until you see Storage QoS Mapping and click the Edit button, as shown here.

6. Click the Add button to assign a storage QoS to the array. Note that you can assign multiple storage QoS mappings to the same array.

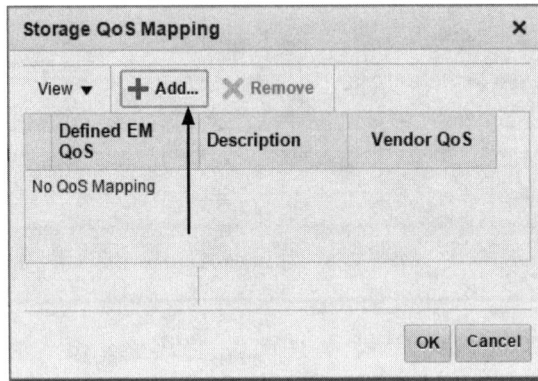

7. Choose the storage QoS selector that is to be added to the array.

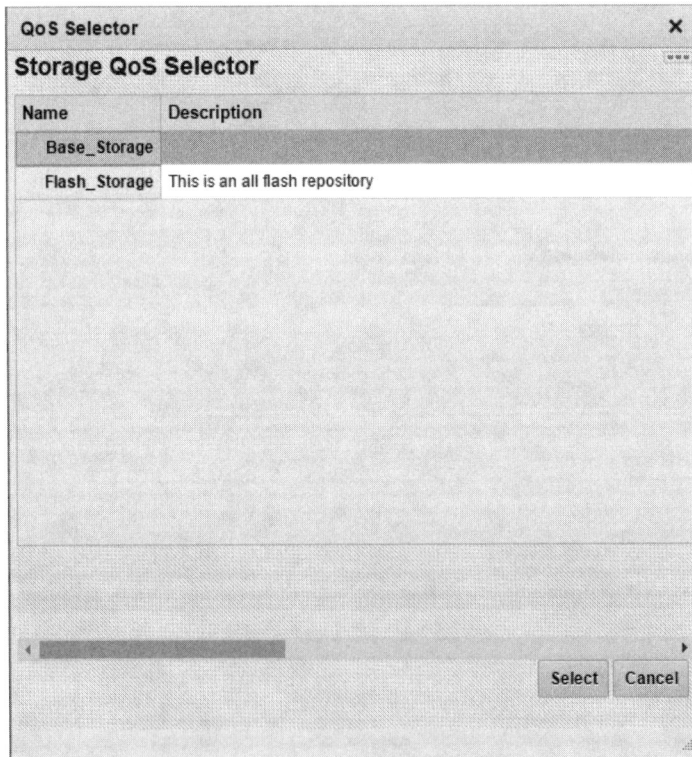

8. You should now see the new mapping, at which point you are ready to click the OK button to start the Enterprise Manager job that will assign the storage QoS mapping to the array.

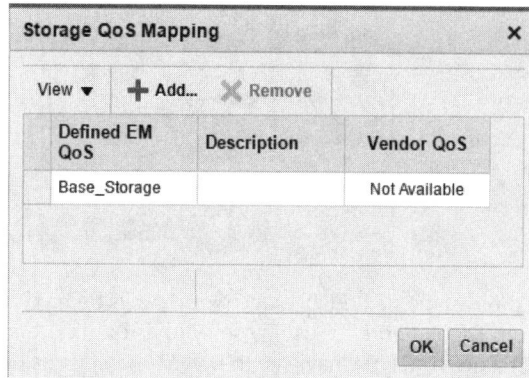

An Enterprise Manager job will now run, assigning the Storage QoS tag to the array.

Network Types

Just as with storage QoS, you can tag the networks used by Self Service users when they provision a VM. This can be defined to match your environment—perhaps something like Internet DMZ, RAC Interconnect, or Internally Routable. After the network type has been defined, you can map it to any network that is being created and assigned to a VM.

Although this may work for your cloud, it is easy to add additional network types. Start from the Infrastructure Cloud Setup screen used in Storage QoS and select the Network Types tab on the left. This will take you to the default configuration shown here.

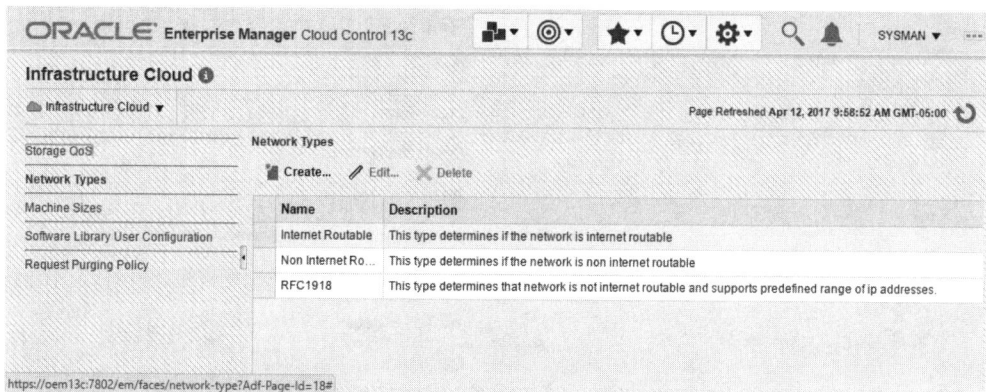

Initially, three network types are created when Enterprise Manager is installed:

■ **Internet Routable**   This type indicates the network is Internet routable.

■ **Non Internet Routable**   This type indicates the network is not Internet routable.

■ **RFC1918**   This type determines that the network is not Internet routable and supports a predefined range of IP addresses.

Although these network types may work for your cloud, it is easy to add additional ones. To do so, click the Create button. You will be prompted to provide the name for the new custom network type, as shown here.

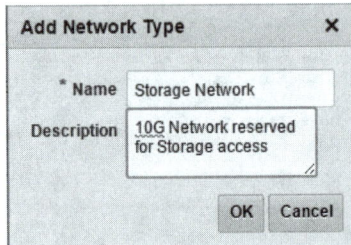

In this example, a new type named "Storage Network" is being defined so that the storage VLAN can be tagged as such. The network for use by self-provisioning users will then be tagged as well. To tag a network with a network type, navigate the OVM Manager using the Target Navigation menu, right-click the OVM Manager, and click the Manage Network option, as shown here.

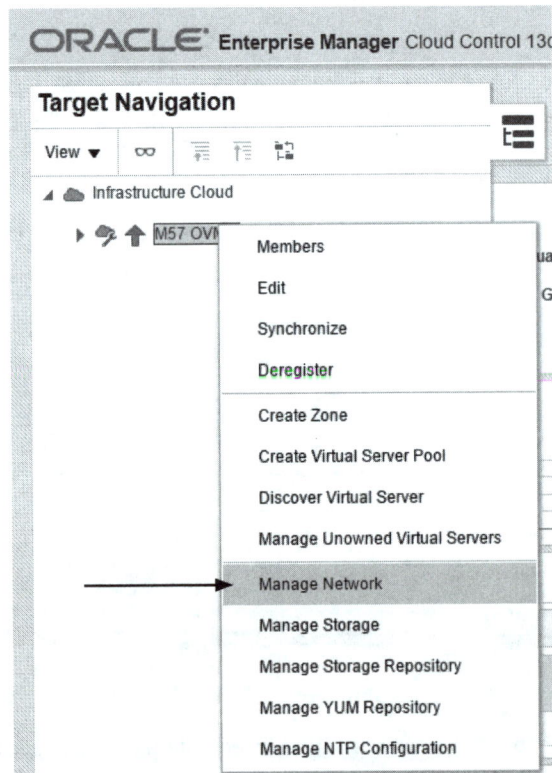

This takes you to the Network Management screen, which provides the same management capabilities as available using the Oracle VM Manager. To assign the network type to a network, make sure the Networks tab is selected and then click the space to the left of the network name to highlight the row you want to edit, as shown next. In this example, we assign a network type to the 192.168.200.0 network. Once the row is highlighted, click the Edit button.

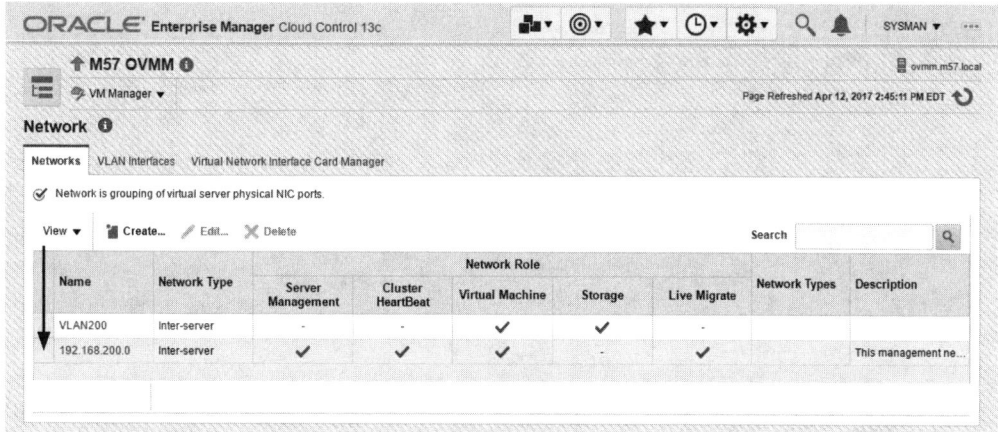

This takes you to a four-step process, shown next, where the network roles can be edited, the ports and VLAN interfaces changed, and the network profile updated. The last step is to review the changes before making them official.

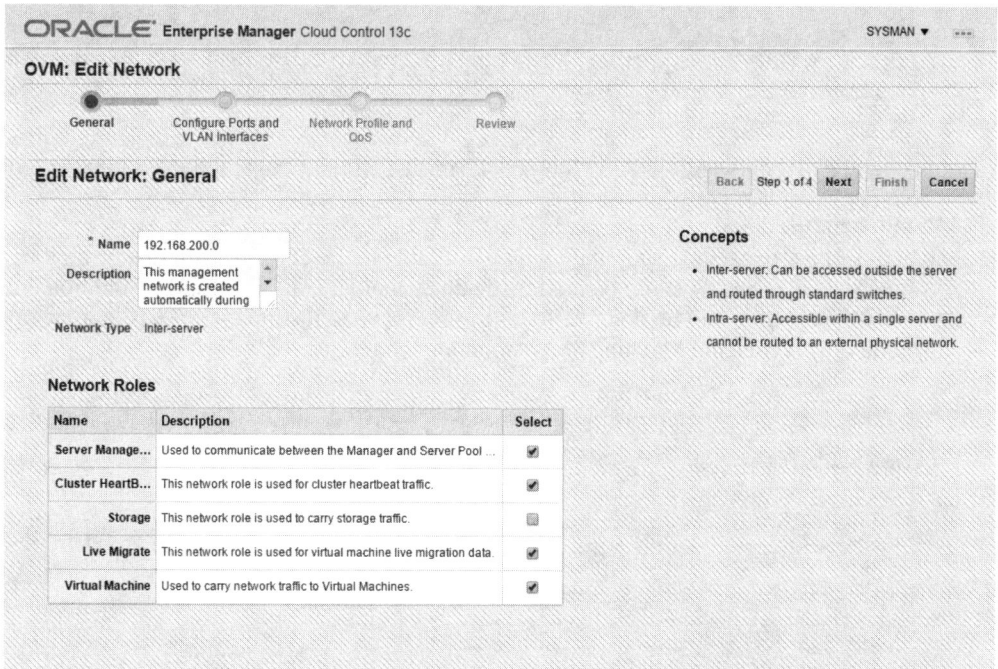

Click the Next button to get to the third step, where you can assign a network type by selecting the Target Search button to the left of the Select Network Type field and then selecting the type to tag this network with, as shown here.

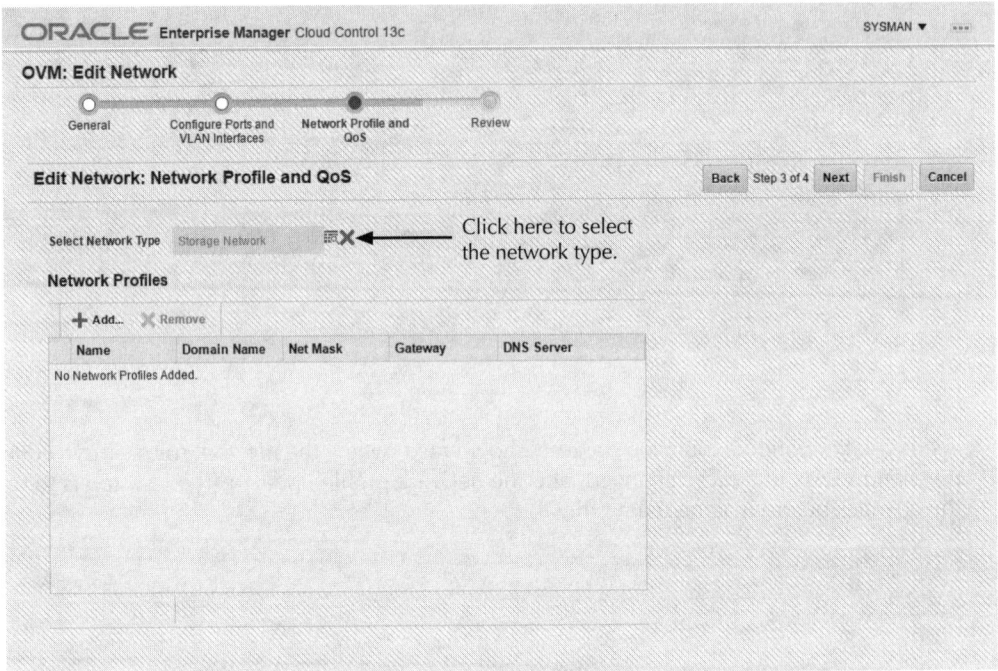

Continue to the review step and then click Finish to submit the Enterprise Manager job.

Machine Sizes

You can define the machine sizes that will be available to the Self Service users when they deploy a VM. By default, three sizes are created by default: small, medium and large. Additional sizes, also known as *shapes*, can be defined. To do this, navigate to the Infrastructure Cloud Setup screen, shown here, and click the Machine Sizes tab along the left side of the screen.

To create a new shape, click the Create button. From here, a dialog is presented where you can set the name of the shape and its parameters. In this example, a new size called Micro will be assigned.

NOTE
When hyperthreading is enabled on the server, a vCPU represents a single thread, not a whole core. To consume a full core, two vCPUs need to be assigned.

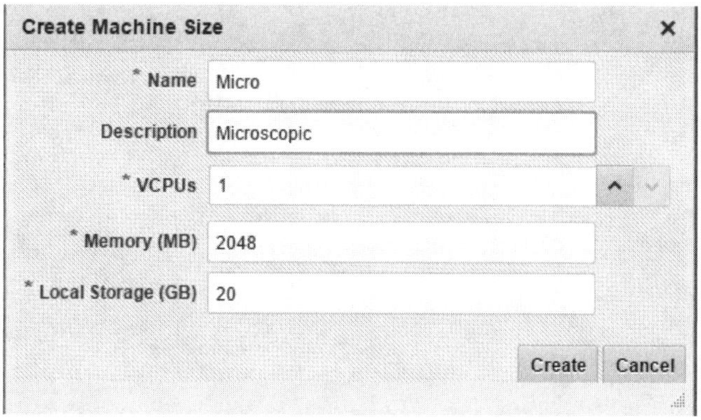

Software Library User Configuration

On the Software Library User Configuration screen, shown here, you can import VM templates, virtual appliances, and other software components and keep them in the storage repository. This makes it easier to share templates and virtual appliances across OVMM deployments. The user must have full access to the software library so that new templates can be imported, clones made, and so on. To set the password for the library, navigate to the Infrastructure Cloud Setup screen and click the Software Library User Configuration tab on the left side. This password must be specified when the user accesses the software library and downloads the required components.

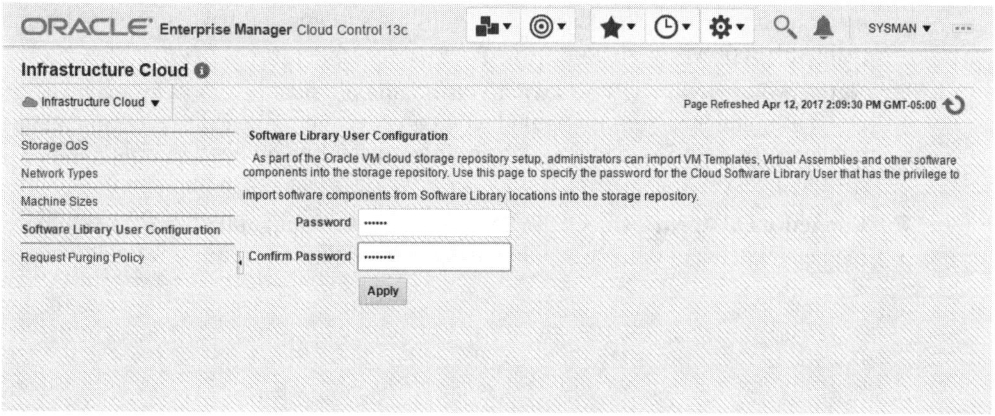

Enter the password and click Apply.

Request Purging Policy

All deployment requests can be retained for a certain period for review and then purged. This section sets the number of days requests are archived in Enterprise Manager. By default, Enterprise Manager will store the records for 30 days before purging them. If need be, you can adjust this time by setting the numbers of days and clicking Apply. If you do not want records purged, uncheck the Enable Purging box.

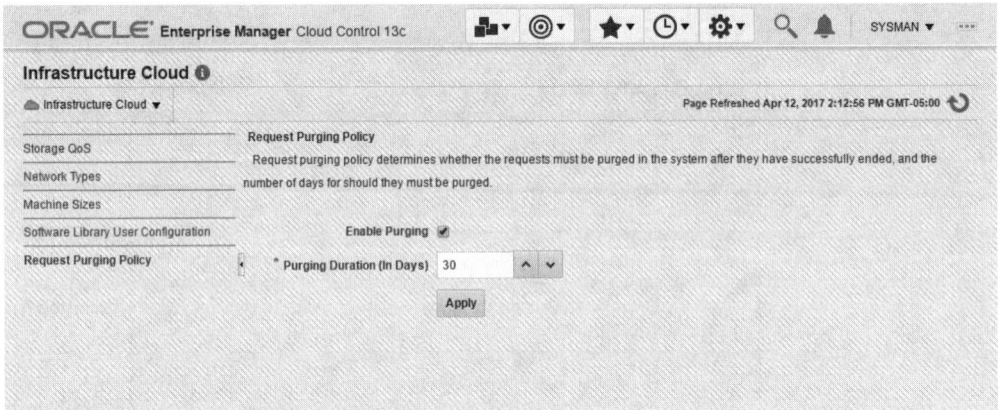

Configuring the Request Settings

The request settings establish the global settings that limit what users can request, in terms of networks, future provisioning, and so on. The settings are made in the Request Settings tab, under Infrastructure Cloud Self Service Setup (see Figure 25-6):

- **Future Reservation** Indicates how far in advance you can make a request. Although enabling the ability for a user to provision systems during idle periods can be helpful, enabling users to provision systems years in advance can cause issues.

- **Request Duration** The maximum duration for which requests should be made. This sets how long a VM will run before being automatically deprovisioned. This is very useful in environments where developers are requesting systems and have a habit of forgetting to manually deprovision them.

- **Network Restriction** Allows you to restrict the physical networks for each EM_SSA_ USER role. If this feature is enabled, you can navigate to the Roles page and assign networks for each EM_SSA_USER role. This is useful if you need to isolate a team to a specific network.

- **Configure EM Agent** Check the Enable EM Agent Configuration box to configure the management agent on servers while the Self Service user's request is being processed.

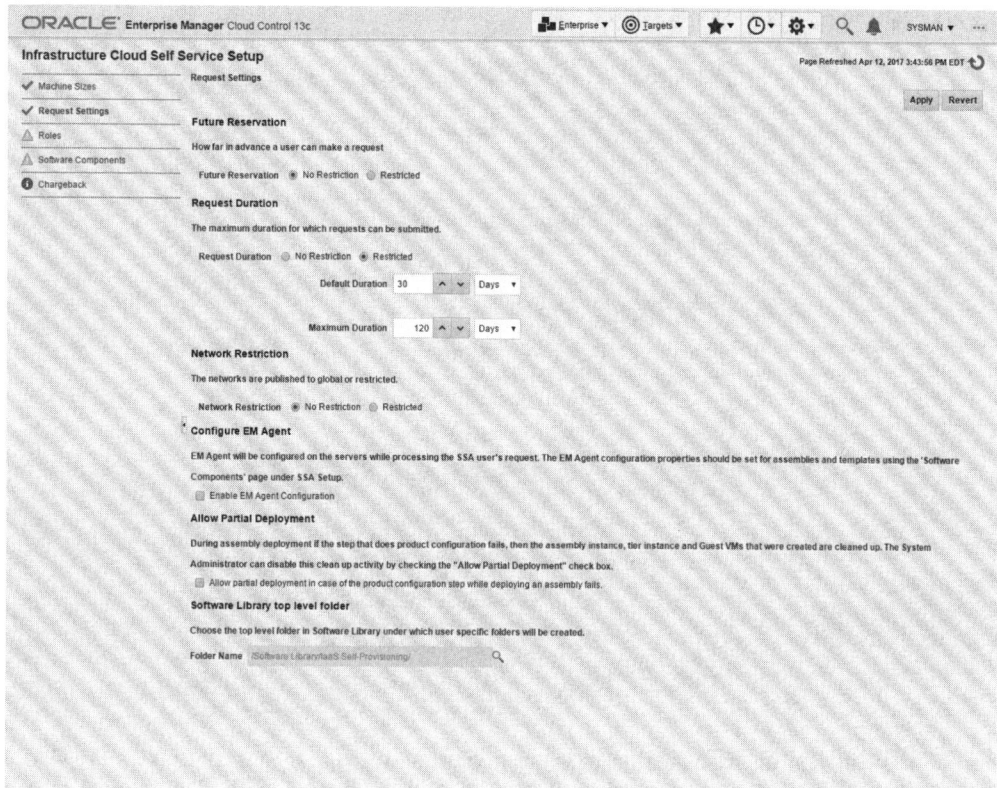

FIGURE 25-6.   *Request settings*

■ **Allow Partial Deployment**   Select this option to enable partial deployment. By default, when a deployment fails, the assembly instance, tier instance, and the guest VMs that have been created are automatically deleted. However, if partial deployment is enabled, this cleanup activity is disabled.

■ **Software Library Top Level Folder**   Select the top-level folder in the software library in which user-specific folders need to be created. This folder is used by the SSA users to store their assemblies, templates, and deployment plans. By default, this is not set but is required.

It is helpful to create a folder in the software library before assigning it. To do this, go to Navigate Setup | Provisioning and Patching | Software Library, as shown here.

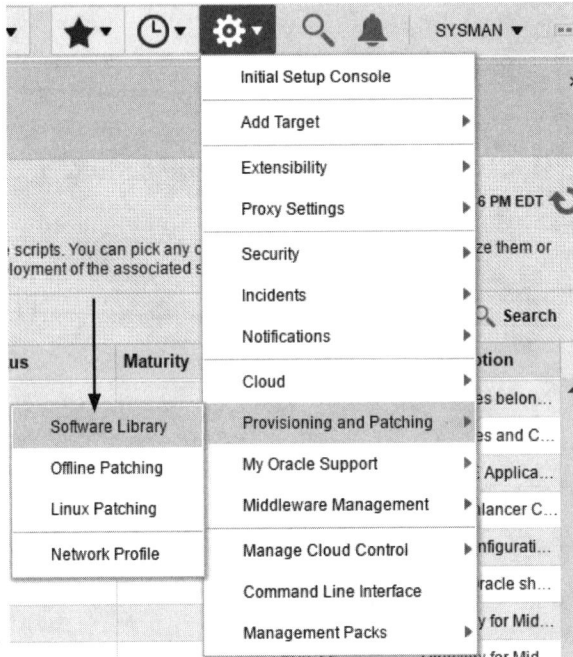

You will then see the available locations for the software library. Initially, only a single location exists; highlight the location and click the text "Software Library" in the line just under the heading "Software Library: Administration," as shown here.

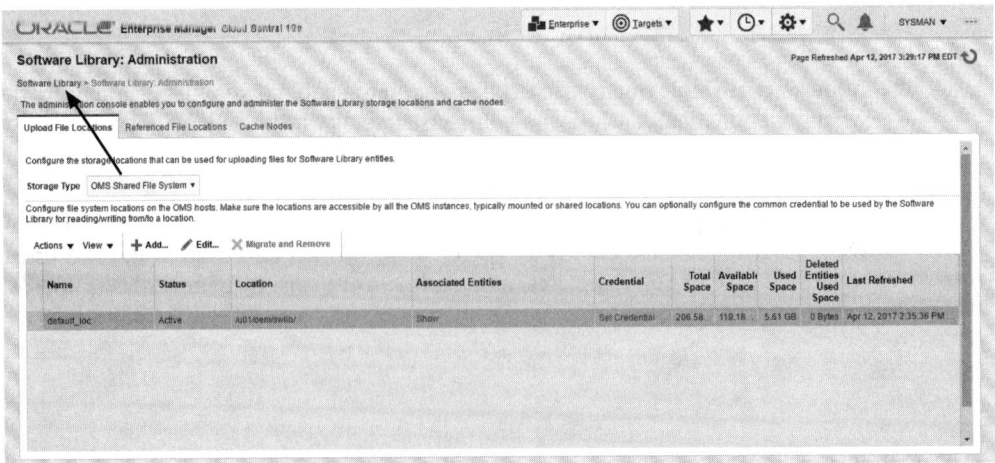

This shows all the folders in the software library. To add a folder, right-click Software Library and select Create Folder, as shown here.

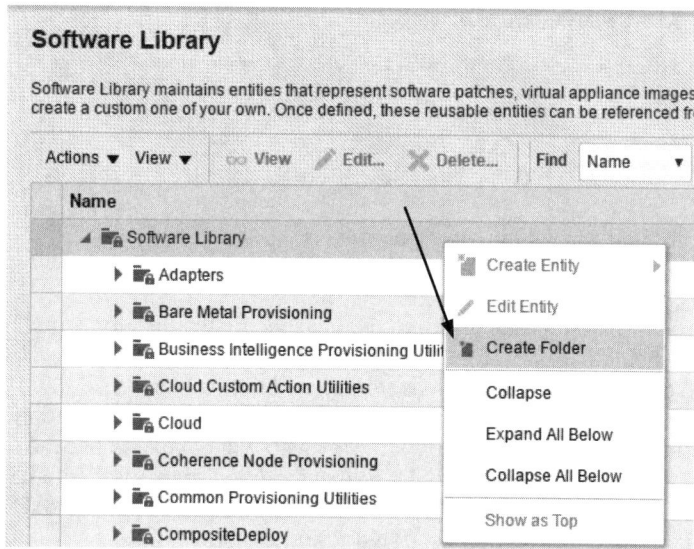

You will now be able to enter a folder (in this case, IaaS Self-Provisioning).

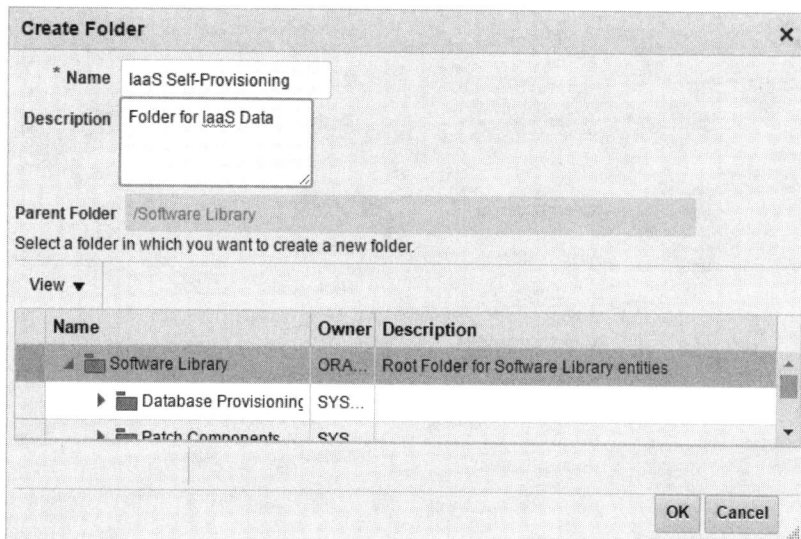

Click OK, and you will be returned to the list of software library folders. Scroll down to verify your new folder has been created. Now go back to the Request Settings screen and click the search icon next to Folder Name at the bottom of the page. Select the folder you just created and then click Apply.

Software Library top level folder

Choose the top level folder in Software Library under which user specific folders will be created.

Folder Name   /Software Library/IaaS Self-Provisioning/   🔍

Optionally, you can set the other parameters.

Configuring Roles

Roles are used in Enterprise Manager to enable specific features for users. The overall cloud administrator should have the EM_CLOUD_ADMINISTRATOR role assigned, as that role is required to set up the core components, such as storage and networking. In addition, the EM_SSA_ADMIN role can be used to isolate access to certain zones and for quota control. In Chapter 23, we created the Enterprise Manager user pellipoix. Any user who will be able to use the self-provisioning portal needs to be assigned the EM_SSA_USER role. In addition, if the user is to have access to manage the Self Service system, he or she should have the EM_SSA_ADMINISTRATOR role assigned. Users are managed under Setup | Security | Roles, as shown next.

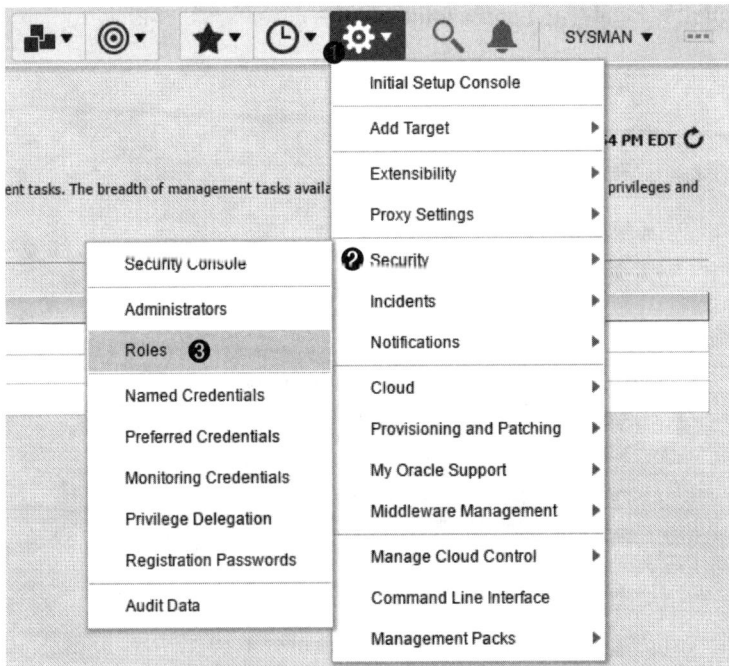

To edit the user, select the user and then click the Edit button, as shown next.

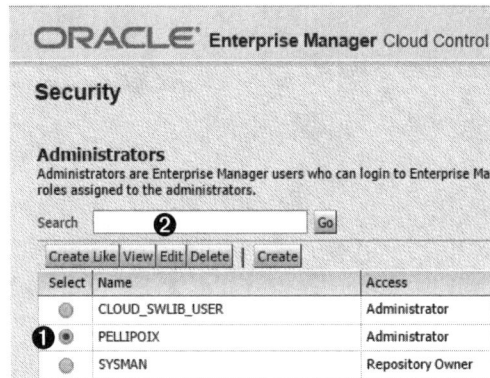

Click Roles and add the EM_SSA_USER role for end users and add the EM_SSA_ADMINISTRATOR role, shown here, for self-service administrators.

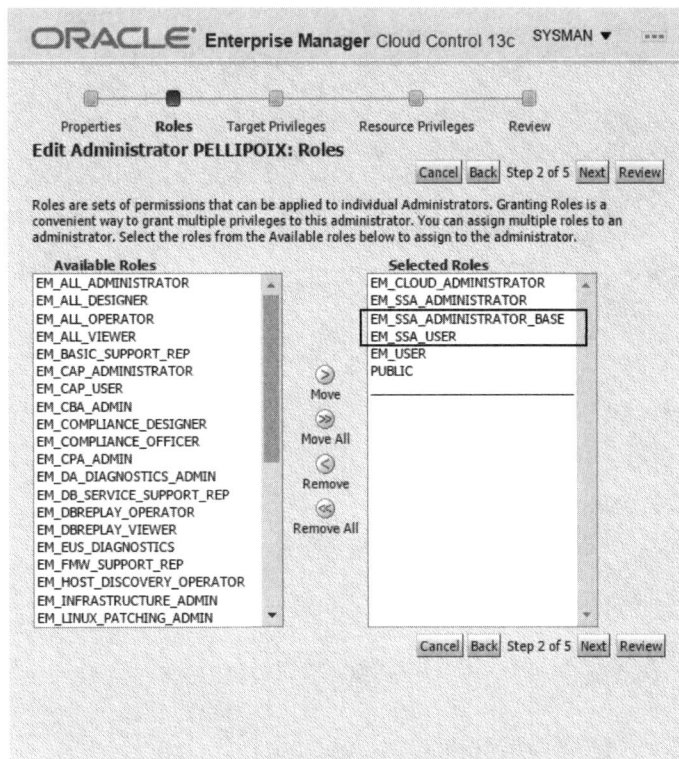

Once this has been reviewed, click Finish. You can now assign a quota to any user with that role. In addition, if you want to assign a quota to a group of users, you can clone the EM_SSA_USER role using a new name and then assign it to the user. Cloned roles can be assigned custom quotas in the next step. A new role, called "SSA_USER_DEFAULT," was cloned from the EM_SSA_USER roles and assigned to the pellipoix user.

To assign a quota to this custom role, access the Infrastructure Cloud Self Service Setup screen and click the Roles tab on the left. When you're performing the initial configuration, no roles are defined, as shown here.

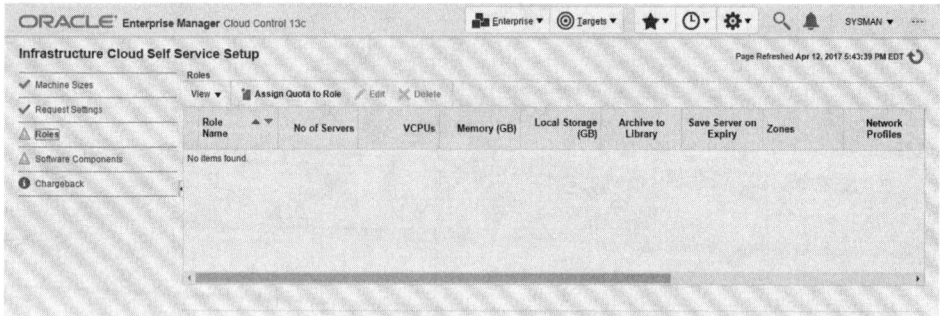

To create a new role, click the Assign Quota to Role button, which will open the dialog shown here for the quota settings.

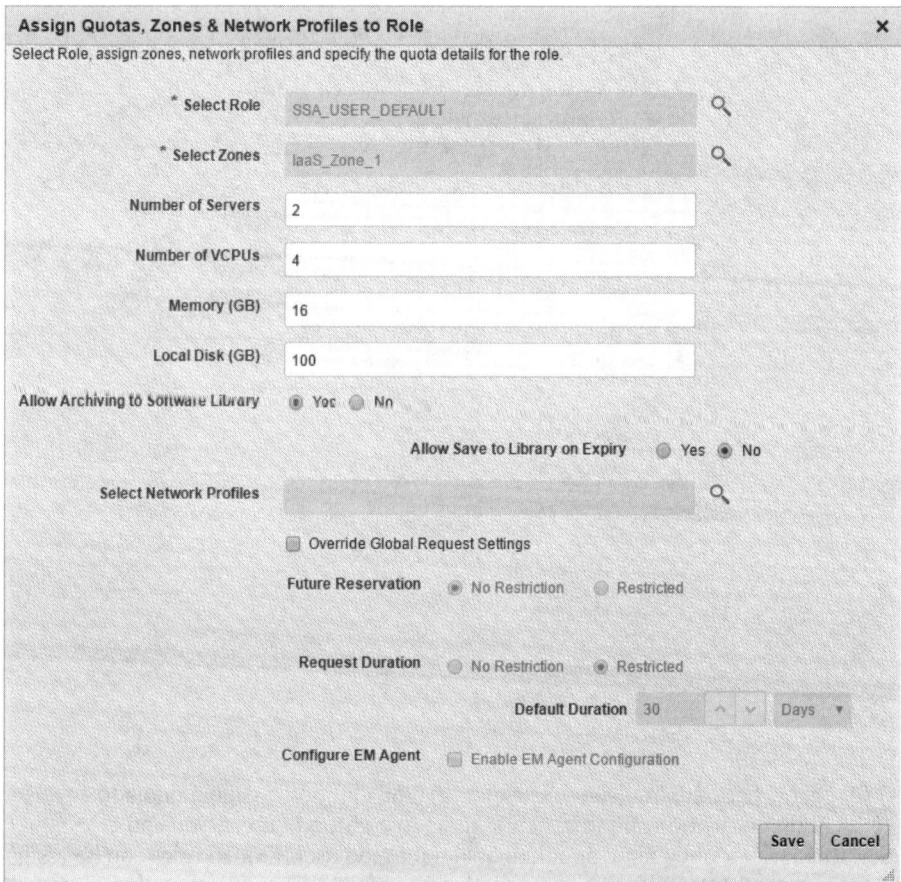

The fields are as follows:

- **Select Role**   Click the search icon to select a role for which the mapping is to be defined. The list of all the roles with Self Service access will appear. If no roles appear, double-check that you have a user with one of the SSA* roles assigned.

- **Select Zones**   Click the search icon. All zones defined under Infrastructure Cloud will be listed. Select a zone from the list and click OK.

- **Number of Servers**   This is the maximum number of VMs that can be reserved at any time across all zones.

- **Number of VCPUs**   This is the maximum number of VCPUs that can be allocated.

- **Memory**   This is the maximum amount of memory that can be allocated.

- **Local Disk**   This is the maximum amount of storage that can be allocated.

- **Allow Archiving to Software Library**   If this option is enabled, users can save machine images to the software library.

- **Select Networks**   This field is displayed only if Network Restriction has been enabled. This enables the admin to limit this group to specific networks.

- **Select Network Profiles**   Use the search icon to select any network profile to assign to the role. This will limit VMs to this network profile.

- **Override Global Request Settings**   Select this option to override the request settings for the role. You can modify the future reservation, the request duration, and configure the management agent.

Once these settings are complete, click the Save button.

Software Components

The Software Components tab is where access to predefined VM templates and virtual assemblies is granted. Before access can be granted, an image first needs to be uploaded to the software library.

This can be done by a Self Service administrator using the Self Service Portal. To access the Self Service Portal, go to Enterprise | Cloud | Self Service Portal, as shown next.

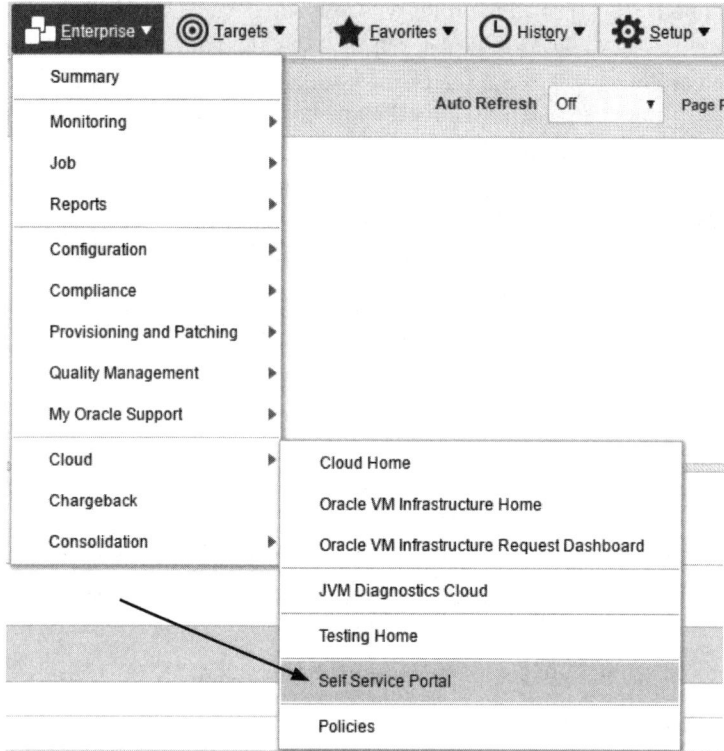

The initial view of the Self Service Portal reveals the Oracle Public Cloud features first, and under the list of additional service you will find the Infrastructure – Oracle VM Cloud Services option, shown next.

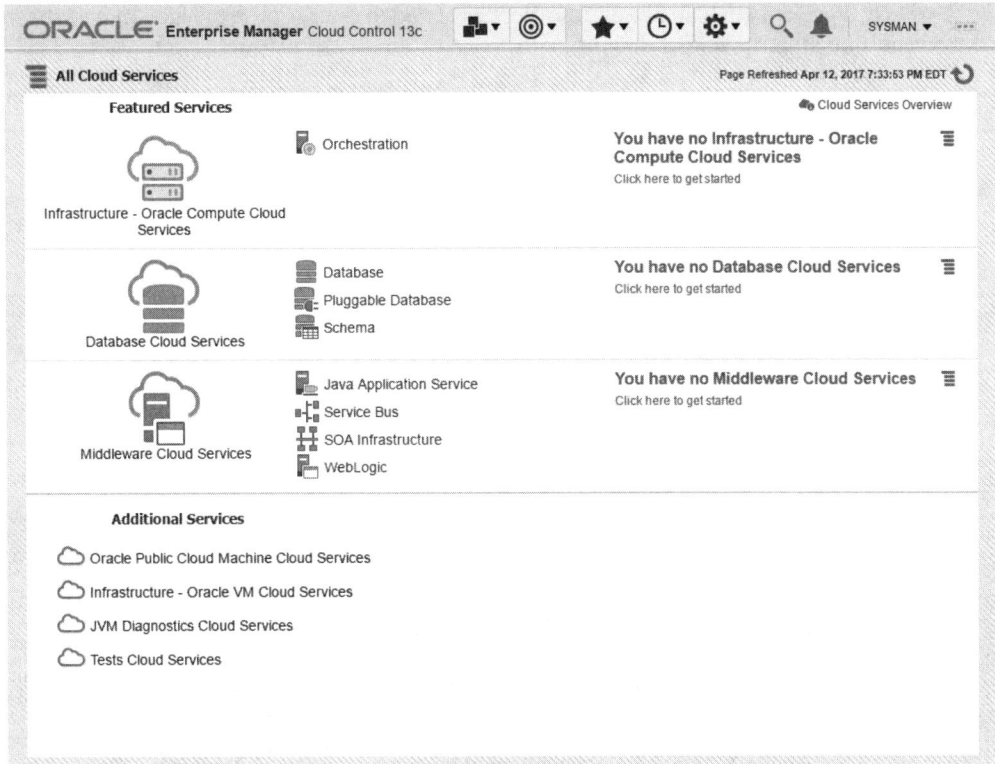

Click the Infrastructure – Oracle VM Cloud Services link to enter the Oracle VM IaaS Cloud screen.

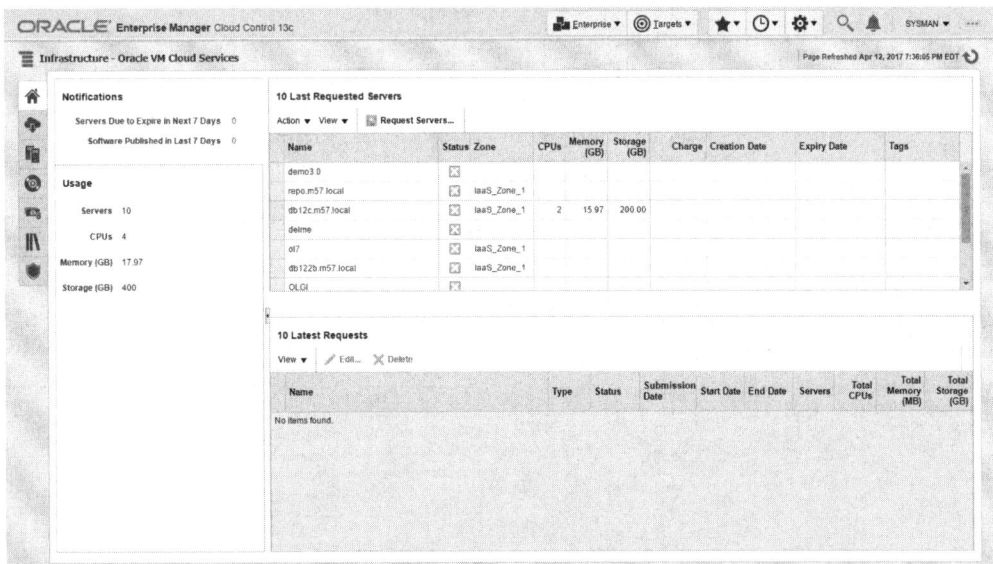

On this screen, you can see all resources assigned to your user. A navigation bar, shown here, appears along the left side.

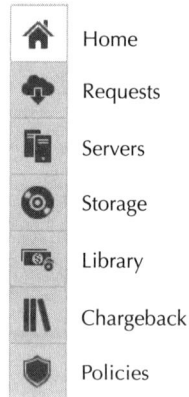

To upload an image to the software library, as an SSA admin, click the Library option and then the Upload button. Using the Choose File option, find the template exported in Chapter 15 and upload it to the library. Wait for the upload to report "Done" in the user interface, as shown here, before clicking the Upload button.

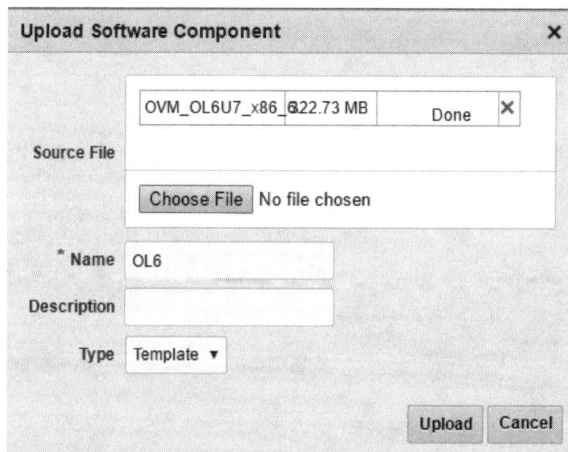

Once the file shows in the library, return to the Software Components screen. Click Add Components and then under Select Software Components click the Add button. From here, you can select the template from the library and then click Select. Make sure you select the correct type because an incorrect type will cause an issue importing the software into the zone in a future step. Some templates are actually virtual assemblies; you will need to read the documentation that comes with the template.

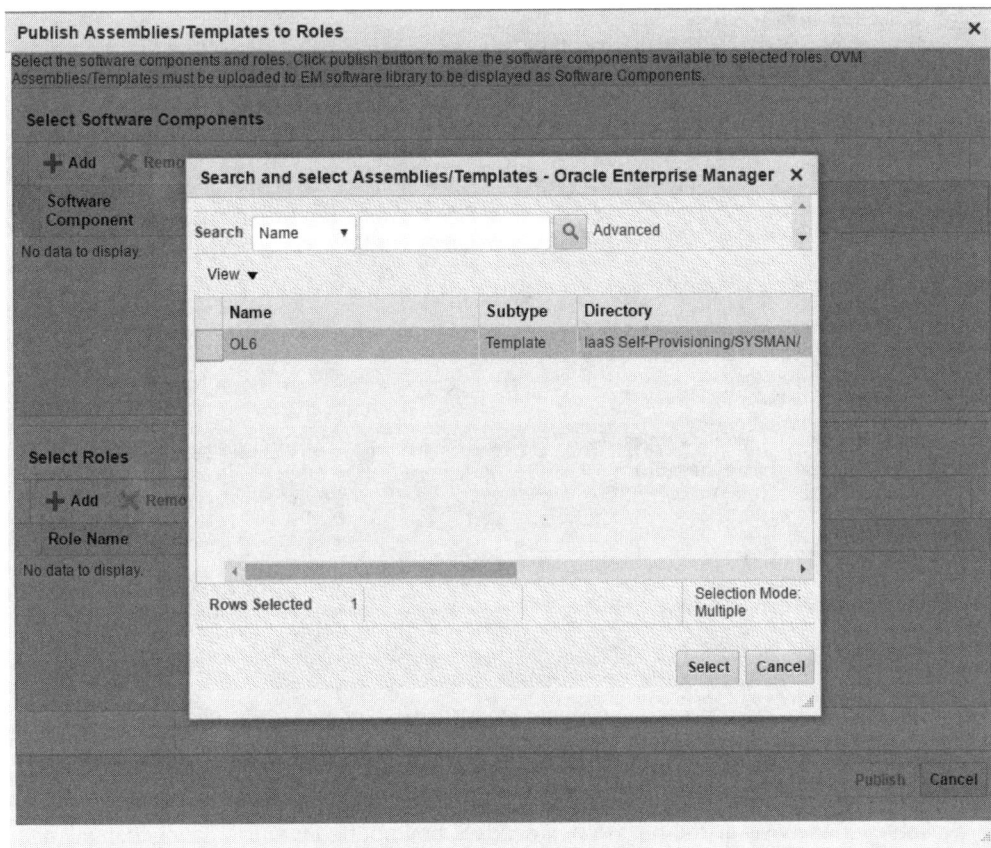

The same task is done for the role that will have access to the templates and assemblies in the list shown next. In this example, the OL6 template will be accessible to users with the SSA_USER_DEFAULT role.

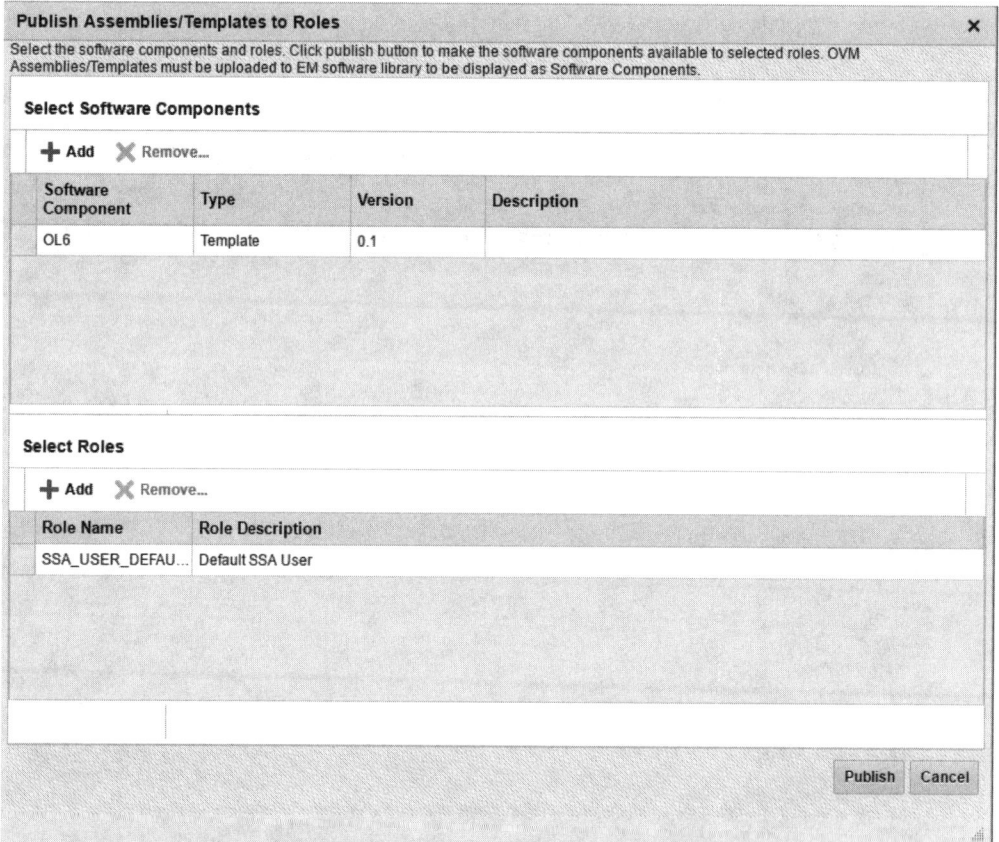

Publish Assemblies/Templates to Roles	✕

Select the software components and roles. Click publish button to make the software components available to selected roles. OVM Assemblies/Templates must be uploaded to EM software library to be displayed as Software Components.

Select Software Components

➕ Add   ✖ Remove...

Software Component	Type	Version	Description
OL6	Template	0.1	

Select Roles

➕ Add   ✖ Remove...

Role Name	Role Description
SSA_USER_DEFAU...	Default SSA User

Publish   Cancel

Once the template is published, you will see it in the list; however, the template is not yet available for any VMs. In the next step, it needs to be imported into each zone that will be using it.

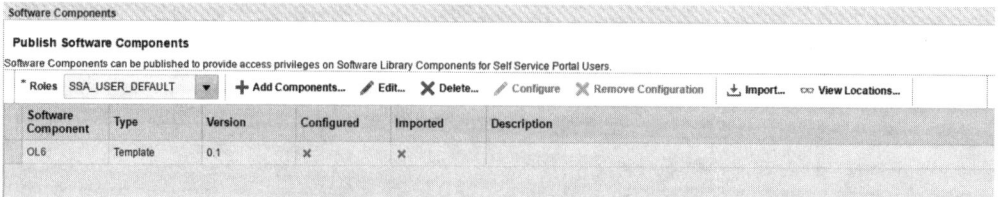

Software Components

Publish Software Components

Software Components can be published to provide access privileges on Software Library Components for Self Service Portal Users.

* Roles SSA_USER_DEFAULT ▼   ➕ Add Components...   ✏ Edit...   ✖ Delete...   ✏ Configure   ✖ Remove Configuration   ⬆ Import...   ∞ View Locations...

Software Component	Type	Version	Configured	Imported	Description
OL6	Template	0.1	✖	✖	

Click the Import button and select the zone to import the template to, as shown here.

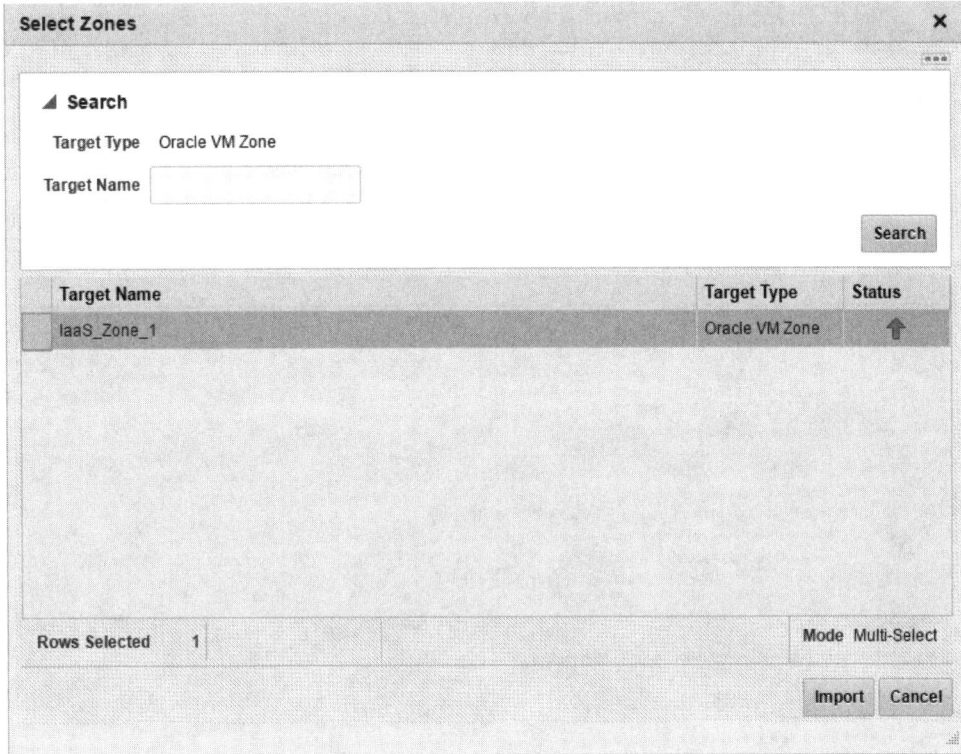

Select Zones			✕

◢ Search

Target Type   Oracle VM Zone

Target Name

Search

Target Name	Target Type	Status
IaaS_Zone_1	Oracle VM Zone	⬆

Rows Selected   1

Mode Multi-Select

Import   Cancel

This starts a job in Enterprise Manager that imports the template or virtual appliance into the zone. Once this is complete, the imported field should have a green checkmark. At this point, the software is ready to be deployed via a Self Service user.

Using IaaS

The final task is deploying a VM through the self-provisioning portal. In this example, log in as the pellipox user previously created.

NOTE
In the user's profile, a default root password for new VMs and the source template/assembly can be selected, but this example will assume these have not been set.

Once you are logged into Cloud Control, navigate to the self-provisioning portal. Because pellipox is a normal user, the screen (shown in Figure 25-7) will look slightly different.

The Usage section will now show how many resources are consumed and how many resources are available to be consumed. Because this user cannot provision any VMs yet, there is zero consumption, but the maximum resources match the quota settings previously configured. To provision a new server, click the Request Servers button.

The first screen, shown in Figure 25-8, allows the user to select the zone and source image to be used for the provisioning process. For this example, OL6 was selected as the image, and IaaS_Zone_1 for the zone.

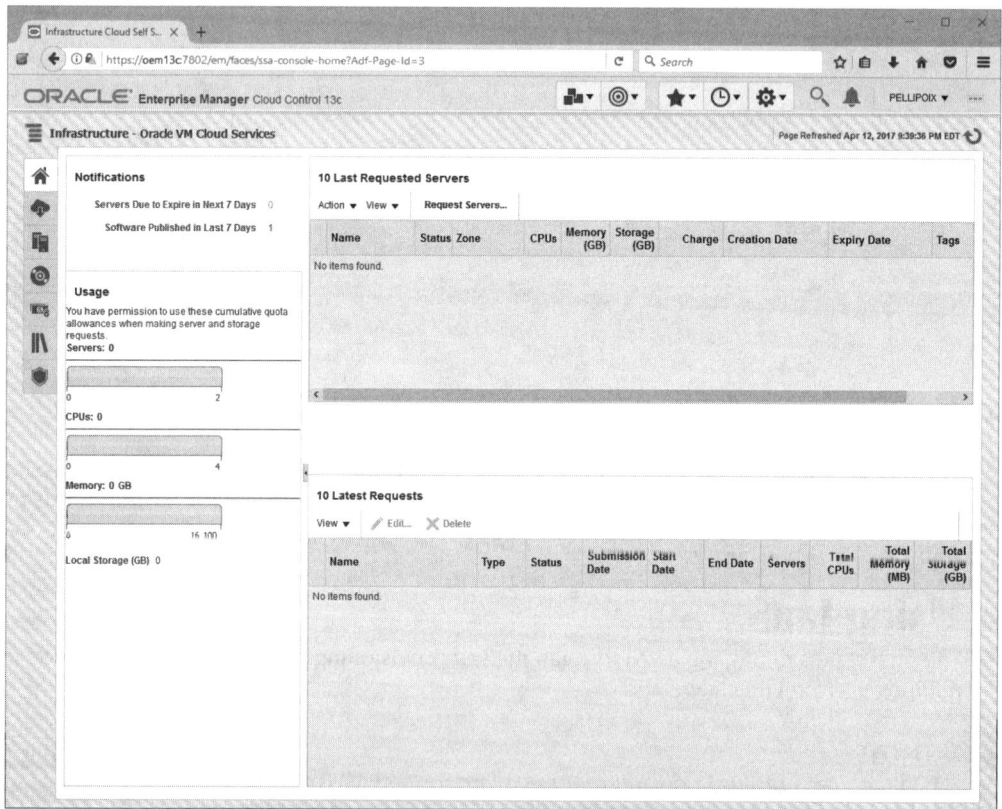

FIGURE 25-7. *IaaS user portal*

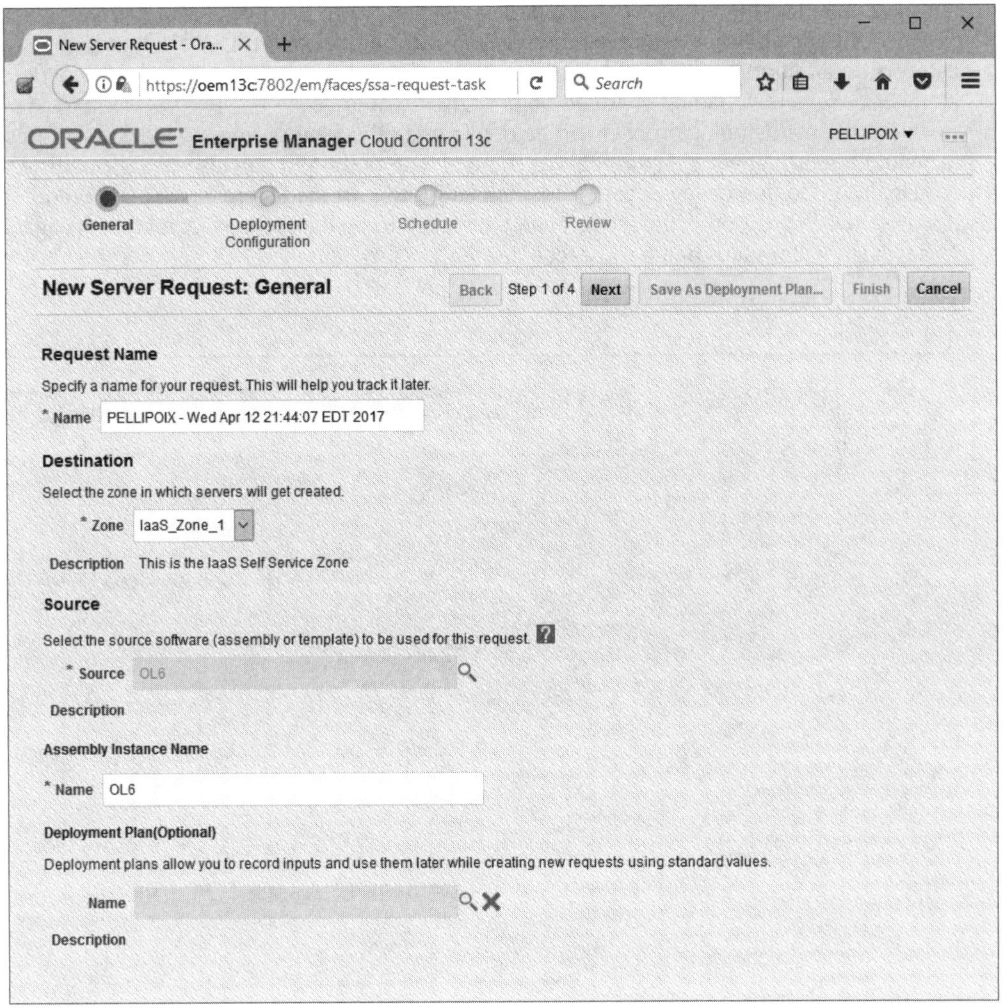

FIGURE 25-8. *The New Server Request: General screen*

The next screen is the Deployment Configuration screen, shown in Figure 25-9. This is where the server size and the initial root password are set, and additional networks and storage can be assigned. To add additional storage or network ports, simply click the Add button in the respective category. In addition, multiple VMs can be provisioned by simply increasing the Initial field under Number of Servers. Up to 64 VMs can be provisioned at once.

Next, the provisioning process can be deployed in the future using the New Server Request: Schedule screen, shown in Figure 25-10. The end date of the VM can also be set on this screen.

Finally, go to the Review screen and click Finish to start the Enterprise Manager request. With the self-provisioning portal, the request can be tracked using the Request icon in the navigation bar. This will show the status of the most recent requests (see Figure 25-11).

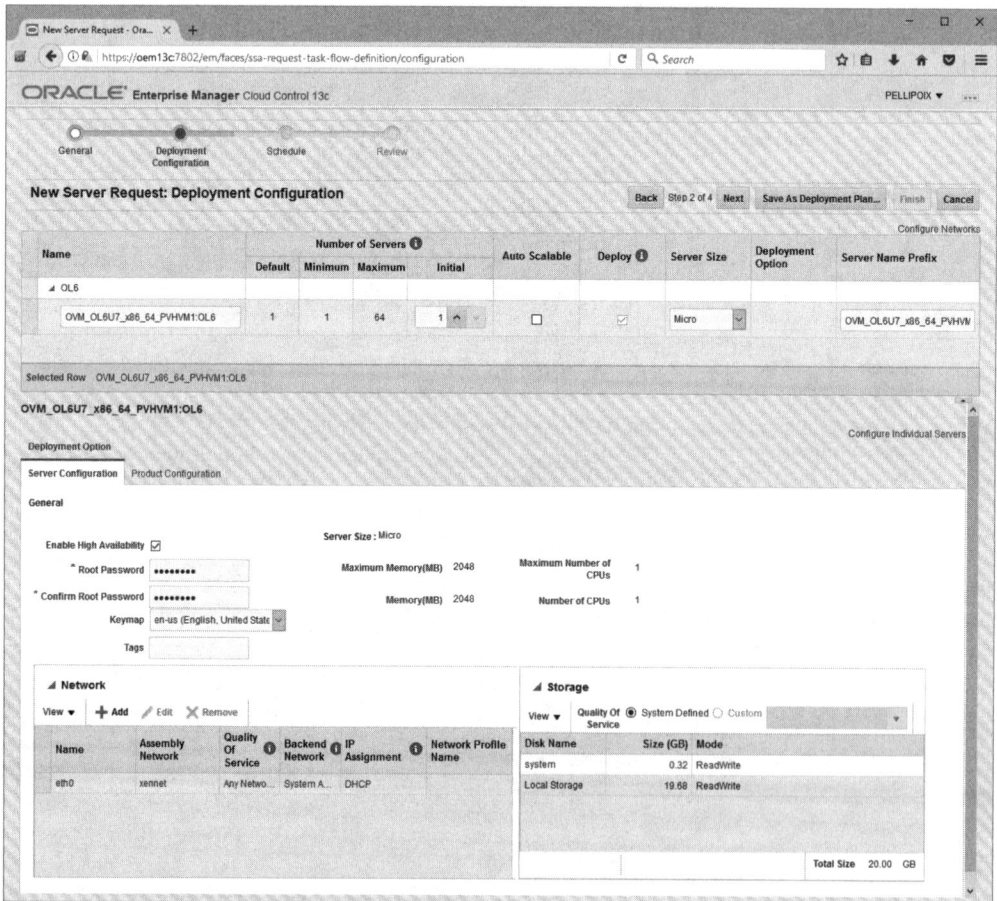

FIGURE 25-9. *The New Server Request: Deployment Configuration screen*

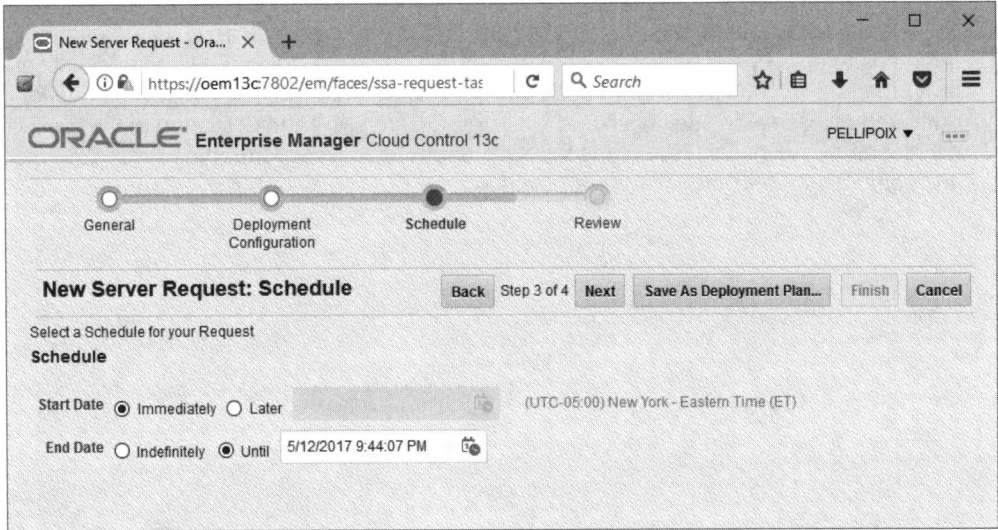

FIGURE 25-10. *The New Server Request: Schedule screen*

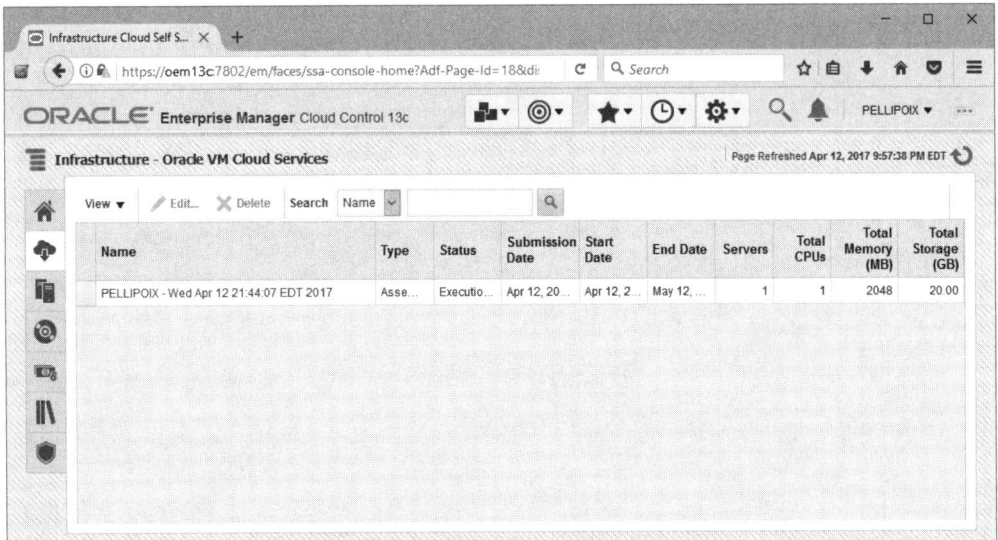

FIGURE 25-11. *Self Service requests*

Summary

This chapter covered how to configure the Self Service Portal for IaaS, as well as configuring quotas, importing templates and virtual assemblies, and the other tasks required to enable Self Service provisioning of VMs. This chapter builds on the previous chapters, bringing everything together to build and manage a private IaaS cloud based on Oracle VM. The last section of the book covers disaster recovery options, leveraging Site Guard for Oracle VM, performing system maintenance, and common troubleshooting tasks and features.

PART
VI

Disaster Recovery, Maintenance, and Troubleshooting

CHAPTER
26

Oracle VM
Disaster Recovery and
Oracle Site Guard

A ll computing environments, architectures, methods, and so on have one thing in common: the need for disaster recovery capabilities. Although a host of providers claim to have a solution, they rarely advertise the most salient and valuable point: the need to address the lack of understanding of the underlying pieces and parts that must be available in a recovery process and the manual steps needed to create the backups and ultimately achieve a recovery.

This chapter presents the following topics:

- A list of general Oracle VM–related parts included in a backup
- The manual steps to take to create a backup of the crucial Oracle VM components
- The manual steps to take to restore and recover an Oracle VM environment
- An overview of the flagship Oracle VM DR product Site Guard, which is recommended for use in the planning and execution of enterprise backup and recovery (BR) and disaster recovery (DR) of an Oracle VM environment

Management Challenges

The company's bottom line with respect to BR/DR is defined by two industry-standard concepts: recovery time objective (RTO) and recovery point objective (RPO). These two concepts, discussed next, have varying costs associated with them.

Recovery Time Objective

The RTO defines the amount of time required to restore application transaction functionality, beginning with the point in time an outage is identified and ending with the point in time when connectivity is restored and transaction processing may resume. Although it may be difficult to define an exact figure, the key indicators and contributing factors include potentially lost sales and the ever-present potential penalties (legal or otherwise) associated with the inability of the business to perform operations on its computer-based systems. The overall cost associated with RTO (along with its sibling RPO) must also take into account the labor and licensing costs associated with achieving an acceptable recovery time objective. On one end of the scale, synchronous parallel distributed transactions may reduce an RTO to a near-zero timeframe, but this also doubles or triples the cost of computer operations. On the other end of the scale, a single-point operational data center must be completely rebuilt and restored before computer operations can resume. And this does not take into account any transactions or data that must be reentered, nor does it account for the potentially lost transactions that could not be entered while the systems were unavailable.

Recovery Point Objective

The RPO represents the amount of acceptable loss in terms of transactions and data that will occur when the systems become operational after an outage. The RPO is usually defined by transactions or data that must be reentered. As with its sibling RTO, the recovery point objective may be reduced or eliminated based on redundant storage and distributed operations in support of synchronous commit points that capture committed data at a fraction of a second in support of the transactions and data being available immediately upon system recovery. Again, the cost of a near-zero RPO can be two or three times the normal operational cost of a single data center.

The RTO and RPO are typically defined in terms of hours and minutes. For example, a typical RTO and RPO would be one to three hours to become operational with a loss of no more than 15 minutes' worth of data. Depending on the transactions per second, an outage can be an extremely costly event.

Oracle VM BR/DR

Regardless of the BR/DR strategy, the RTO and RPO pose a critical management challenge that must be addressed. The RTO and RPO values (whether based on time or some sample of product and cost) will define and drive decisions in support of BR/DR objectives, planning, and operations. With a properly deployed Oracle Site Guard configuration, the RTO and RPO can be driven down to acceptable levels while minimizing the need for additional manpower and also minimizing the risks associated with loss of data and the inability to perform computer-based operations.

In the Beginning—Identifying Components for Backup and Recovery

Before we proceed with discussing automated BR/DR operations, it is important that you understand the concepts and components involved with the manual backup and recovery processes. This chapter assumes that an operational Oracle VM environment is already in place and is implemented using the best practices identified thus far in the book. For example, each repository should contain the unique Oracle VM configuration files for a particular group of virtual machines as well as the templates and assemblies (if any) used to build the initial virtual machines and the virtual disks being used by those virtual machines. In addition, the Oracle Enterprise Manager should be deployed and have access to the primary and target site Oracle VM–related resources that will be part of the backup, recovery, and failover processes.

Figures 26-1 through 26-4 illustrate how to identify a simple form of Oracle VM guest repository–based components: namely, the VM config file and the repository-based Oracle VM guest disks. Beginning with the repository where the Oracle VM guest resides, the configuration file is identified by expanding the Oracle VM in the VM Manager GUI, as shown in Figure 26-1. The information gleaned from the VM Manager GUI (namely, the VM ID and configuration file location) can be used within a putty session to access the files. Connect the putty session to a VM server in the server pool where the Oracle VM guest is running. Figure 26-2 shows a putty session connected to one of the Oracle VM servers in a very simple Oracle VM deployment. The **mount** command in the putty session displays the mounted filesystems, including the mounted OVS repository filesystems. In the example depicted in Figures 26-1 through 26-4, the Oracle VM guest ID is 0004fb000006000093831afe318b6496 and the OVS repository is in the mounted filesystem /OVS/Repositories/0004fb0000030000e33d20ebcb1e8a7b.

Next, the virtual disks used by Oracle VM guest can be found in a similar fashion: namely, after expanding the VM guest in the VM Manager GUI, you can use the Disks tab to list the disks used by the guest virtual machine. Figure 26-3 shows the Oracle VM Manager's virtual machine perspective expanded to show virtual disks used by the virtual machine in this example. Figure 26-4 shows the putty session listing the contents of the virtual disk directory within the OVS repository's mounted filesystem. This is a brute-force approach to identifying the files necessary to restore and/or recover an Oracle VM guest.

It is also important that you understand the difference between the backup and recovery process of a given guest Oracle virtual machine versus the failover process of an entire Oracle VM site.

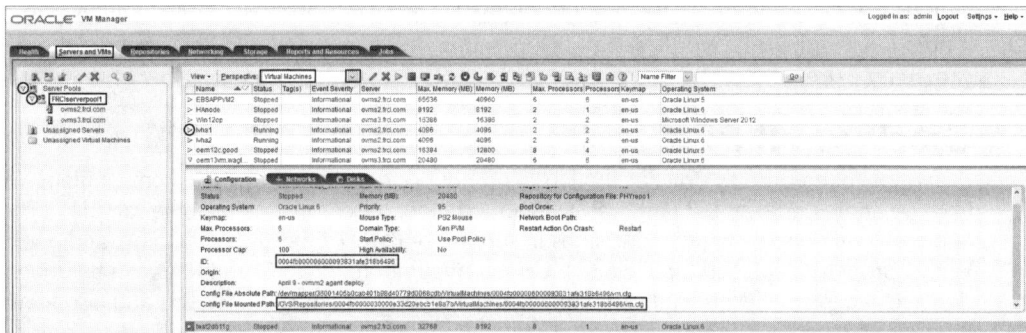

FIGURE 26-1. *Oracle VM guest configuration file and mounted path*

In the first case, consider a simple configuration of a single guest Oracle virtual machine in an Oracle VM environment with a single Oracle VM Server (OVS). The principal BR concepts include recovery of the VM configuration file and recovery of the repository database information (in particular, the various disks used by the Oracle VM guest).

However, when you're considering failover of a site, much of the Oracle VM environment configuration must already be in place. For disaster recovery, you can find the site preparation utility and tools at the Oracle Technology Network. At the time of this writing, the ovm-tools file can be found in the VM downloads area of Servers & Storage: http://www.oracle.com/technetwork/server-storage/vm/downloads/ovm-tools-3604795.html. You can download the tools along with supporting documentation. In general, the following setup is required:

■ The Oracle VM Manager is running at the primary and target sites (meaning a separate pool filesystem).

■ The required repository information is being replicated between the sites.

■ The network configuration is established at both sites and ready to go.

FIGURE 26-2. *Putty session showing the OVS repository mounted by an Oracle VM server*

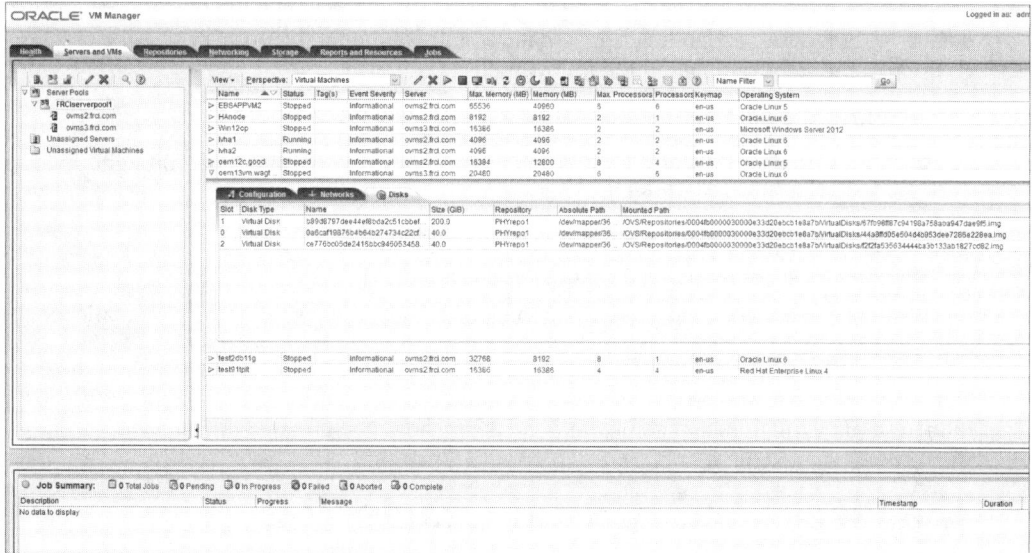

FIGURE 26-3. *Oracle VM Manager GUI expanded to show the guest VM's virtual disks*

FIGURE 26-4. *Putty session showing the virtual disks used by the Oracle VM guest*

If the primary site is running an Oracle database, then the Oracle Data Guard product should be configured and failover (or switchover) should be used to change the operational mode of the database. Otherwise, depending on the nature of the failure at the primary site, the target site will go through the steps outlined in the following list:

- The target site assumes ownership of the repository.
- Disks used by the guest Oracle VM must be updated or otherwise "brought up to speed" with recently committed transactions at the target site.
- The Oracle VM guest at the target site is started.
- The application on the guest Oracle VM is started.
- If necessary, the enterprise DNS configuration is updated with the target failover site.

A key difference between a failover process and a switchover process is that, in the event of a switchover (that is, the primary site is not taken offline), ownership of the repository must be relinquished by the primary site before ownership can be assumed at the target switchover site.

The Pieces and Parts of Oracle VM Backup and Recovery

When considering an Oracle VM backup and recovery or disaster recovery plan, it is important to remember that there are two categories of data: the data that is part of the backup and restoration process and the data that is local to each site and configured specifically for the given site. The key components to an Oracle VM switchover/failover strategy are the data that must be synchronized and the order in which the components must be started (and also the order in which the components must be shut down if the switchover/failover is a controlled process rather than an unexpected event). Note that switchover and failover are for distinctly different objectives and are detailed in the Oracle Database Administration documentation. Switchover is the process in which a switchback is also an objective. A failover is the process in which a switchback is *not* an option, even if the old primary site is recovered. A failover results in the separation of the original primary site from the Oracle Data Guard configuration. After a failover, the standby site becomes the new primary, and the old primary is henceforth considered "standalone" (if operational at all). Again, more information is available in the Oracle Database Administration documentation.

Site-Specific Local Data

Each site in an Oracle VM DR model contains data that is not part of the disaster recovery process and is otherwise configured to run at that particular site. Data that remains at each local site and is not part of the Oracle VM backup and recovery set includes the following:

- Oracle VM Manager (the VM Manager machine's operating system and the Oracle VM home).
- Oracle VM servers (operating system and storage that's local to the OVS and is not used by guest virtual machines that are part of failover operational requirements).
- Oracle Enterprise Manager (OEM High Availability data and operations are separate in the overall BR/DR operations).

- Data related to guest Oracle virtual machines that are not part of failover requirements.
- Oracle database software and data files (databases that are part of an Oracle VM BR/DR operational requirement should be configured with Oracle Data Guard).
- Pool filesystems are not copied for DR but are copied/backed up for BR.

Oracle VM BR/DR Data

The data that should be included in the replication model or backup set used to keep each site synchronized includes the following general categories.

- **Repositories**   Not all repositories need to be included in the backup or replication set for failover operations; rather, only the repositories that contain Oracle VM configuration files, virtual disks used by guest Oracle VM's targeted for failover, and their related templates and assemblies, if desired.
- **Storage**   This includes NFS, SAN, and local storage used by guest Oracle virtual machines targeted to be part of failover operations, as well as any of the Oracle VM guests' defined physical disks. These include Oracle VM guest operating system disks and Oracle VM application server disks.

Other Site-Specific Data and Configuration

In addition to the data and operating system storage, which must be replicated among the sites, the network configuration is critical to the pre- and post-recovery operations. Because the network configuration is virtualized within the Oracle VM environment, you must take care to ensure the virtual machine network IDs for the various virtual machine networks are identical between the primary and target switchover/failover sites. In other words, the switchover/failover operations described here assume the networks for the switchover/failover components are identical with respect to the networks servicing communications between virtual machines. However, this does not include the Oracle VM management networks (such as the server management, cluster heartbeat, or live migrate networks). The virtual machine network IDs are stored as part of the virtual machine configuration information. After the repositories are synchronized and virtual machine configuration information is owned by the target Oracle VM environment, the virtual machines that are started in the target environment will expect the networks (that is, the network IDs) to be present. The Oracle VM DR toolkit includes a tool named *chgnetid* that helps you change network IDs at one site or the other. The Oracle VM DR toolkit can be downloaded from Oracle Technology Network (OTN).

Site Preparation

As stated earlier, one of the assumptions made in this chapter is that each site has an Oracle VM technology stack running in an operational configuration. However, this does not mean identical configurations are necessary. In fact, each site may have a different number and capacity of Oracle VM servers. It does mean, however, that each site is configured to handle whatever operations and loads are required to sustain the Oracle virtual machines that are part of the switchover/failover

BR/DR operations. As such, during the installation and configuration of the Oracle VM manager at the target sites, each site will have its own UUID, pool filesystem, and Oracle VM manager database. In addition, each site maintains its own backup and recovery operation of the local site Oracle VM Manager. Each site will also have its own local storage and repositories. The primary site's Oracle VM Manager backup and unique ID are only mentioned here with respect to general BR/DR best practices for Oracle VM.

The important configuration items for target sites include the following:

- Network configuration
- File server and SAN server virtual disk and physical disk capacity
- Repository storage capacity
- CPU and memory

An important aspect of network configuration is how the enterprise domain name services (DNS) will be handled before, during, and after switchover/failover operations. In their simplest form, the network configuration changes required in support of switchover/failover operations are assumed here to be limited to the virtual machine network required to support only the communications between Oracle virtual machines within a given site. The complexities introduced in support of external communications (that is, communications from the outside world to virtual machines, and vice versa) are voluminous. Again, in their simplest form, these networking operations would include network address translation (NAT) and/or local DNS modification to allow routing to machines within the virtual machine network after virtual machines have been transitioned from one site to another.

Oracle VM BR/DR Component Shutdown/Startup Configuration
The data related to restore and recovery of the Oracle VM environment is critical to minimize the RTO and RPO defined by management. However, in order for the recovered environment to resume operations (and to be able to switch back in a controlled switchover operation), it is equally important that the configuration includes the correct and required shutdown and startup order and procedures. This is one of the main reasons why understanding the manual process is emphasized. Regardless of the switchover/failover operations (whether manual or automated), the order in which components are shut down and/or restarted can be directly related to successful operations—or in the worst case, data corruption. Hence, the proper order for system shutdown and startup should be well documented.

In the Middle—Establish Backup and Recovery Processes
After you have identified the data related to the restore and recovery of the Oracle VM environment, you need to implement the method by which the data is backed up, restored, and/or synchronized (that is, replicated). Having an environment equipped with an Oracle ZFS appliance is the recommended best practice. If, however, a different storage strategy is employed, the mechanism used for storage synchronization/replication will vary from vendor to vendor. In the event a replication

mechanism is not available, manual synchronization will be required. This means that during switchover/failover operations, you must pause the automated process at the step when the storage must be synchronized between the primary and target sites. Although this is fully supported, it is highly recommended that you put an automated replication mechanism in place, if at all possible, to allow full automation of the switchover/failover operation, from start to finish.

The controlled process to switch over from the primary site to the target site begins with shutting down the application processes and Oracle virtual machines of the primary site. The organized shutdown is followed by the primary site's server pool relinquishing ownership of the repositories that are part of the switchover/failover event. At this point, the requisite data from the primary site must be already replicated to the target site(s). Replication is an ongoing task; a final small synchronization is part of the switchover, which means the replication is ongoing and scheduled (or continuous or scheduled; the latter may be the preference to help avoid immediate propagation of corrupted data). Keep in mind that continuous replication on ZFS is not synchronous replication.

Replicated data should include the following:

■ Repository data (guest Oracle VM configuration files and repository-based virtual disks)

■ Shared storage data (physical disks that are defined by LUNs on SAN storage, and/or files on file server storage)

■ Local storage data (physical disks that are defined by LUNs and/or disks local to the OVS machines and provisioned to guest Oracle VMs that are defined to run on the OVS and are part of the switchover/failover site operations)

After the data has been synchronized to the target site, the switchover/failover operations resume with the target site taking ownership of the repository data. Once the target site owns the repositories, the guest Oracle virtual machines are started in the proper sequence. Again, this is why it is so important for you to understand and document the process! As each guest Oracle virtual machine is started at the target site, the correlated processes may be started, provided the associated processes have also been started, as necessary. For example, if an application server requires an Oracle database, that database must be started prior to the application server processes initiating. It is therefore critical that the application server not be started before the database server (and the associated database) is started. In the case of an Oracle database, Oracle Data Guard is the database availability mechanism that's used, in which case the database server would have already been operational and an Oracle database Data Guard switchover or failover process would have already been completed (Oracle Site Guard automates all the aforementioned tasks, including the Data Guard steps).

In the End—Testing Recovery and Switchover Processes

The final stage of the Oracle VM switchover/failover process involves the configuration changes required to establish the former primary site as a target site; then the new target site (used for the switchover/failover operation) needs to be established as the new primary site. This usually involves establishing storage replication changes and/or other adjustments to the former primary site. These adjustments include hardware and/or software upgrades, patching, and other operations. When the time is right, another switchover operation can take place, and the primary site can once again earn its place as the enterprise primary site for the given operational applications and databases.

Ultimately, the only difference between the before and after perspectives (with respect to switchover/failover operations) is the direction of storage replication. The real benefit to using Oracle Site Guard is realized during unintentional site failover rather than the controlled failover of just the Oracle virtual machines. And, for large complex sites, the value of Site Guard is the ability to trigger switchovers with the push of a single button for routine maintenance or temporarily rebalancing application workloads to other sites, not just "disaster recovery."

Preparing the OEM Environment

And now we get to the crux of the biscuit: the primary tool of the Oracle Site Guard solution is Oracle Enterprise Manager. As mentioned earlier, it is assumed the primary and target sites are configured and ready for site switchover and/or failover operations. If this is the case with the use of Oracle Enterprise Manager, then the following are assumed to be in place:

- The OEM 12c or 13c base product has been deployed as described in Part V of this book using a Level 3 or Level 4 MAA deployment. (Basically, OEM is needed at both sites or a third site; if OEM is only available at one site and that site goes down, the DR mechanism/engine is lost.)

- The primary and target sites' Oracle VM Managers have been discovered and configured as part of the cloud infrastructure, as described in Part V of this book.

- All the Oracle VM servers have been discovered and configured as part of the cloud infrastructure, as described in Part V of this book.

- All the guest Oracle virtual machines that are part of the sites participating in switchover/ failover operations have been discovered and the OEM management agents have been deployed.

These requisite configuration items are needed in order to proceed with configuring Oracle Site Guard in OEM. Figure 26-5 shows the Oracle VM Manager (in this example, named ovmmgr) that has been discovered and added into the cloud virtualization infrastructure of OEM 13c, ready for use in the creation of an Oracle Site Guard primary site.

Although the process for installing and configuring a complete OEM environment is well explained within the OEM 13c (13.2) documentation, it is briefly summarized here to correlate the manual steps previously listed with the automated failover described in the next section. Basically, the steps to configure OEM in support of Site Guard are as follows:

1. Create the cloud infrastructure.

2. Discover the targets and create administrators and credentials.

3. Create and refine the systems (both the primary and target).

4. Create and configure the software libraries (used for storage and management of additional custom scripts or software).

5. Refine the definition of the discovered sites.

The actual implementation of these steps can take several weeks to complete. However, the benefit is astounding! For example, traditionally, a controlled switchover of a Data Guard–configured database can take as little as 45 seconds, whereas the manual switchover or failover of an application and database within an Oracle VM–based data center can take many hours. Using OEM in the

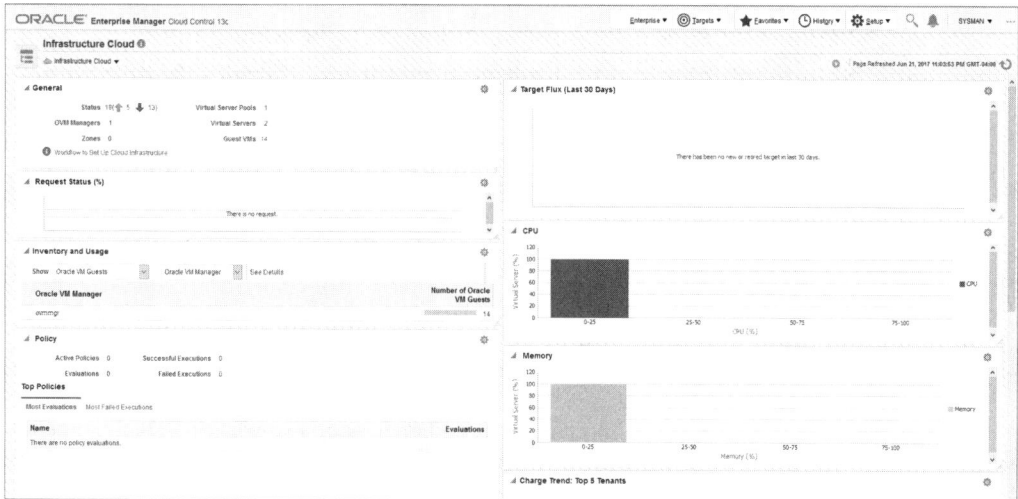

FIGURE 26-5. *Oracle VM Manager primary site in OEM 13c*

same manual failover with a properly defined set of primary and target sites can be accomplished in just a few minutes. Imagine what company management would say about the impact to the bottom line with an RTO and RPO of just a few minutes!

Automating Switchover/Failover

The processes and configurations needed in support of establishing an OEM-based controlled switchover are established by following these steps:

1. Define the cloud infrastructure.

2. Discover and configure Oracle VM Manager and Oracle VM Server within the cloud infrastructure.

3. Discover the Oracle virtual machine target (optional).

4. Create and define generic systems (sites).

5. Create and customize operation plans, which include the addition of scripts used for disaster recovery operations if you're using EMC, HDS, or something other than NetApp or ZFS.

6. Schedule operational plans and health checks and execute Oracle Site Guard operations.

7. Update site roles and define new operational plans for subsequent switchover/failover operations.

The workflow associated with an automated switchover/failover may take several weeks to complete. But again, the benefit is realized the first time the operation is required. These processes are detailed in the Oracle Enterprise Manager 13.2 documentation and demonstrated in the following Oracle-sanctioned videos and white papers.

Key white papers include the following:

- SN21001-6.1: "Oracle VM 3: Getting Started with Disaster Recovery"
- SN21305-1.0: "Oracle VM 3: Implementing Oracle VM Centric DR Using Site Guard"
- SN21705-0.4: "Oracle VM 3: Required Software for Oracle VM–Centric DR Using Site Guard"
- SN21810-0.1: "Oracle VM 3: Planning Network for Oracle VM–Centric DR Using Site Guard"
- SN21811-0.4: "Oracle VM 3: Planning Storage for Oracle VM–Centric DR Using Site Guard"
- SN21812-0.1: "Oracle VM 3: Planning the Site Guard Deployment for Oracle VM–Centric DR"
- SN21901-2.1: "Oracle VM 3: Implementing Networks for Disaster Recovery"
- SN21301-1.4: "Oracle VM 3: Oracle VM–Centric DR Validating Failover Process"

Also, the material covered in this chapter is documented in eye-watering detail in the following Oracle documentation and white papers:

- Oracle Enterprise Manager Cloud Control Online Documentation Library, Release 13.2 / Management: Site Guard Administrator's Guide
- Oracle VM Release 3.4 documentation
  - Repository Backup: Oracle VM Manager User's Guide for Release 3.4
  - VM Manager Backup and Recovery: Oracle VM Administration Guide for Release 3.4
- Oracle VM 3 Backup and Recovery Best Practices Guide (white paper)
- Oracle VM 3: Getting Started with Disaster Recovery Using Oracle Site Guard (Doc ID 1959182.1)

Finally, here are some helpful Oracle Site Guard videos:

- https://youtu.be/3mWuu-XRjDU
- https://www.youtube.com/watch?v=vz1GGxeqdOM
- https://www.youtube.com/watch?v=vz1GGxeqdOM&t=189s"&
- https://www.youtube.com/watch?v=vz1GGxeqdOM&t=189s"t=189s

Summary

Backup, restore, and recovery are not just "nice to have" practices. Like it or not, they are practices that are certain to be eventualities. Regardless of the tactical or strategic plans, it is inevitable that the manual steps, actual components, and the lifecycle of the processes become part of the overall enterprise solutions. In addition, the use of automation will speed up the processes and reduce or eliminate the errors inherent in manual steps. Although the two approaches (manual and automated) are not mutually exclusive (manual processes may be interjected during an automated Site Guard operation), the critical nature of disaster recovery merits having both well documented and understood by those who will be held responsible and accountable for the success of the operation.

CHAPTER
27

Oracle VM Maintenance

Proper maintenance of the Oracle VM system is important for its reliable operation. The Oracle VM servers can be easily updated (patched), which ensures that fixes to issues discovered in between errata releases get applied to the servers. The update process follows these simple steps:

1. Create the Yellowdog Updater Modified (yum) infrastructure. (Although this is done only once, periodic changes are required to maintain access to the latest version.)
   a. Create a yum infrastructure.
   b. Update the yum systems from the Oracle Unbreakable Linux Network (ULN).
   c. Configure settings for Server Update Groups in the Oracle VM Manager.
2. Periodically update or patch the Oracle VM servers.
   a. Upgrade to the latest version of Oracle VM Manager. You must always update the Oracle VM Manager before updating servers. This is a nonintrusive process and has no impact on running Oracle VM servers or guests.
   b. Update the Oracle VM servers using the Oracle VM Manager.

This chapter covers how to perform these steps. We'll start with the first step, which is creating the yum repository.

Creating a Repository

Patching an Oracle VM system requires the administrator to configure a yum repository. The yum repository is a warehouse of RPM package files, which allow for quick and easy software installation on Red Hat/Oracle Linux. YUM repositories hold several RPM package files and enable the downloading and installation of new software. YUM repositories normally share their files via an HTTP or HTTPS server, which is generally installed on the yum server. Oracle VM can update the Oracle VM servers in yum, providing for a simple way to maintain larger numbers of Oracle VM Server (OVS) systems. The same yum repository for Oracle VM can also serve as a yum repository for Oracle Linux. This is because each YUM server subscribes to distribution channels in the Unbreakable Linux Network. Although Oracle VM is free, the access to OLN is limited to customers who have a subscription. The good news is that a subscription is free for Oracle hardware under a valid support contract, and it comes at low cost for users running on non-Oracle systems.

YUM Repository Server Prerequisites

The onsite yum repository is created and managed on a physical server or virtual machine in your data center. Although it is not installed on any of the Oracle VM servers in your environment, you can use the same server where Oracle VM Manager was installed. Simply enable the HTTP server that is normally installed with Oracle Linux or Red Hat where you installed the Oracle VM Manager. Before you can create a local repository, you must have the following items:

- A server running Oracle Linux 6 or Oracle Linux 7. This can also be a virtual machine.
  - At least 2GB of RAM must be available, although 6GB is recommended.

- The available disk space varies, depending on the channels subscribed to. For just Oracle VM, at least 6GB is recommended. Some channels can consume over 80GB of data, so be sure to refer to https://linux.oracle.com for the requirements for each channel.

- The httpd RPM must be installed.

- An active Internet connection, either direct or through a proxy. This is required for the repository to update itself.

- A valid Oracle Support Identifier (SI, or often also called a CSI). This is included in an Oracle Support Contact for Oracle VM and is free with Oracle hardware support. An Oracle Support Contract for Oracle VM can be purchased through your preferred Oracle Partner.

- A valid Oracle Single Sign-On (SSO) account associated with the support identifier. For Enterprise deployments, the login e-mail is often a role e-mail, such as yumadmins@my.co.

ULN Registration

The following steps are performed on the yum repository server. To register the yum server, use the command **uln_register**. This will provide you with a few prompts for registering the server with the ULN. To start the process, run the command **uln_register** as root.

The first prompt, shown next, will ask you to verify that the network is connected and that an Oracle Single Sign-On account is available.

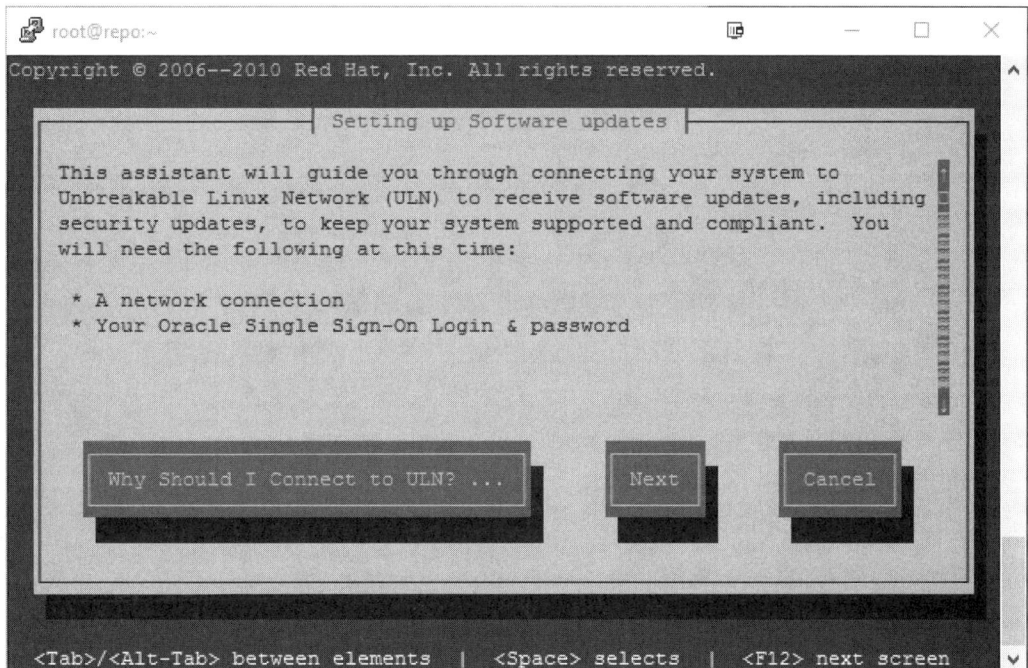

Next, enter in the e-mail address and password for the Oracle Single Sign-On account, along with the CSI that includes a subscription to the ULN, as shown next.

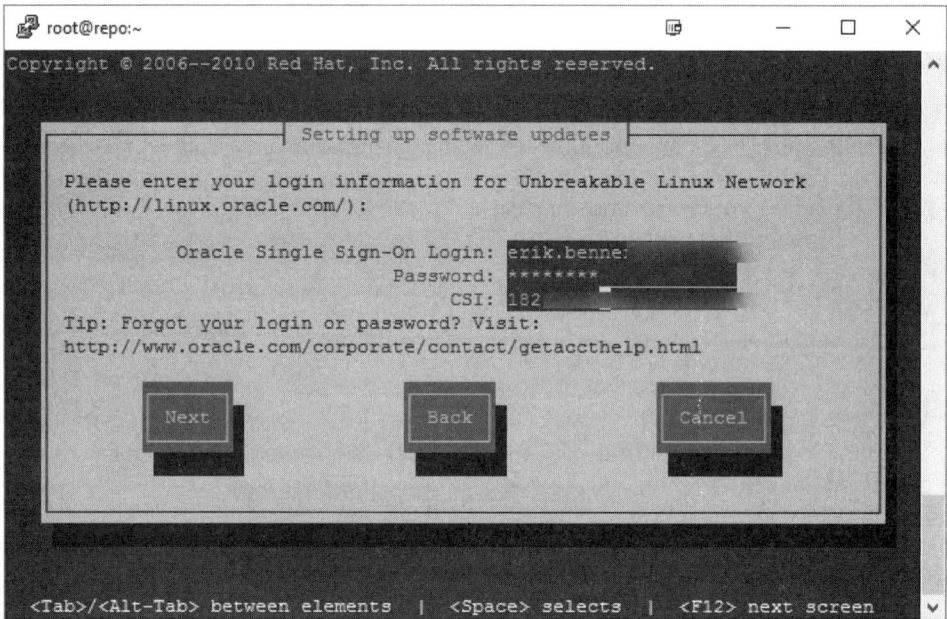

In the next step, shown here, you verify the profile name for this repository. By default, it will be the fully qualified domain name (FQDN) on the repository.

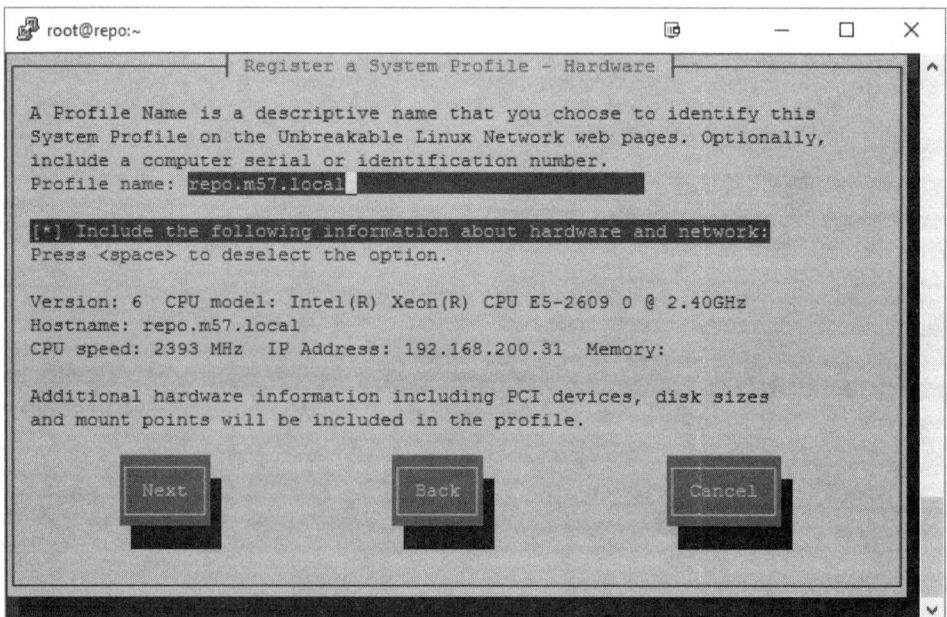

In the next step, the system automatically adds all the packages for the server. However, because this will be a repository server, you do not need to include all the RPM packages already installed on the server. In an upcoming step, the server will get a subscription to the OVM channel, which allows the repository to be populated, as shown here, with all the OVM RPMs.

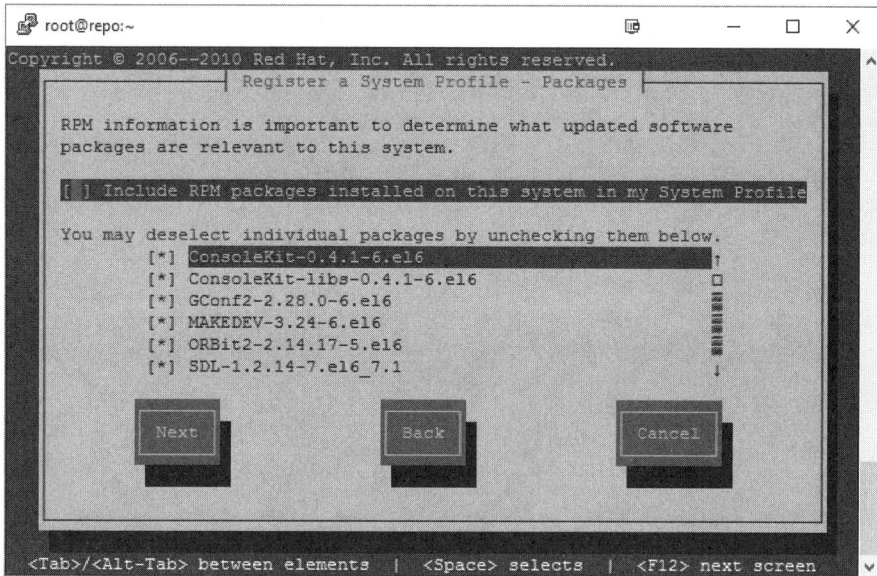

```
root@repo:~                                         □   —  □  ×
Copyright © 2006--2010 Red Hat, Inc. All rights reserved.
        ┤   Register a System Profile - Packages ├

  RPM information is important to determine what updated software
  packages are relevant to this system.

 [ ] Include RPM packages installed on this system in my System Profile

 You may deselect individual packages by unchecking them below.
            [*] ConsoleKit-0.4.1-6.el6
            [*] ConsoleKit-libs-0.4.1-6.el6
            [*] GConf2-2.28.0-6.el6
            [*] MAKEDEV-3.24-6.el6
            [*] ORBit2-2.14.17-5.el6
            [*] SDL-1.2.14-7.el6_7.1

        ┌─────┐          ┌─────┐          ┌──────┐
        │ Next│          │ Back│          │Cancel│
        └─────┘          └─────┘          └──────┘

 <Tab>/<Alt-Tab> between elements  |  <Space> selects  |  <F12> next screen
```

The final step, shown next, officially kicks off the registration process by sending the profile to the ULN servers and registering the server. The ULN profile contains the software inventory data that allows the ULN to select the appropriate packages for the system.

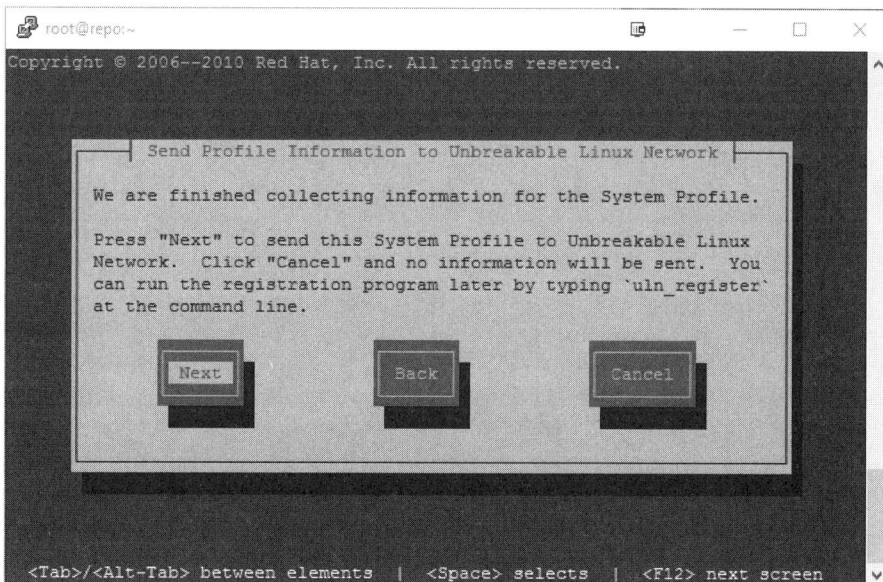

```
root@repo:~                                         □   —  □  ×
Copyright © 2006--2010 Red Hat, Inc. All rights reserved.

    ┤ Send Profile Information to Unbreakable Linux Network ├

  We are finished collecting information for the System Profile.

  Press "Next" to send this System Profile to Unbreakable Linux
  Network.  Click "Cancel" and no information will be sent.  You
  can run the registration program later by typing `uln_register`
  at the command line.

        ┌─────┐          ┌─────┐          ┌──────┐
        │ Next│          │ Back│          │Cancel│
        └─────┘          └─────┘          └──────┘

 <Tab>/<Alt-Tab> between elements  |  <Space> selects  |  <F12> next screen
```

Sending the profile can take some time, as shown next, depending on the bandwidth available.

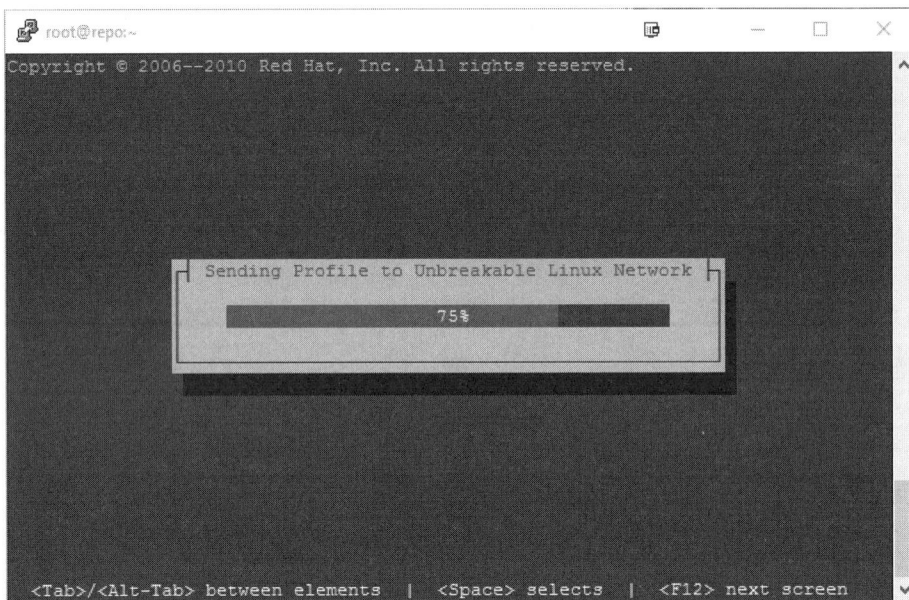

Once the registration is complete, you have the option to configure the system for Ksplice (shown next), a technology that allows the server to be patched without rebooting. For a repository, this option can be disabled because the repository server is not normally patched directly from the ULN.

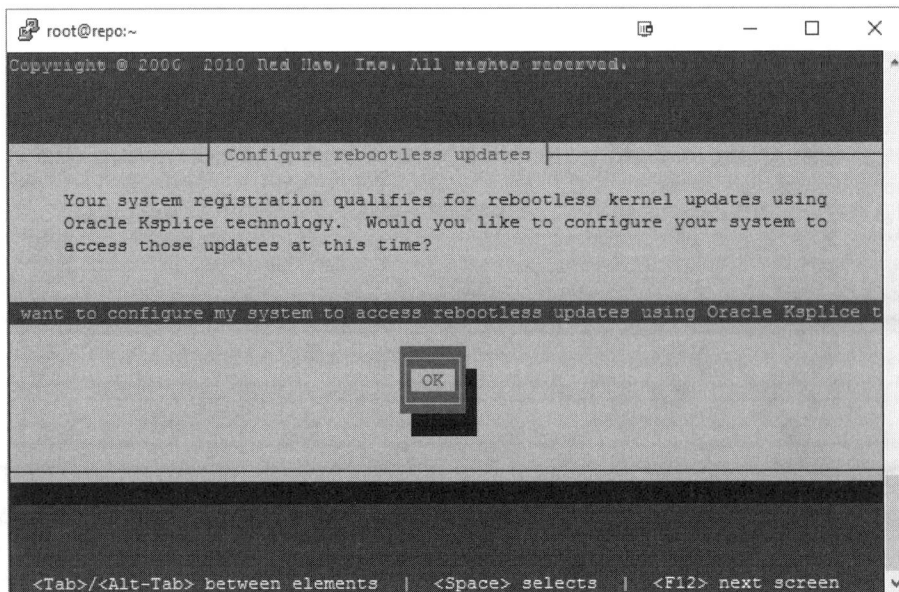

When the process is complete, as shown here, the system is ready for the next set of steps, which will subscribe the repository to the patches. This process requires a web browser pointed to https://linux.oracle.com.

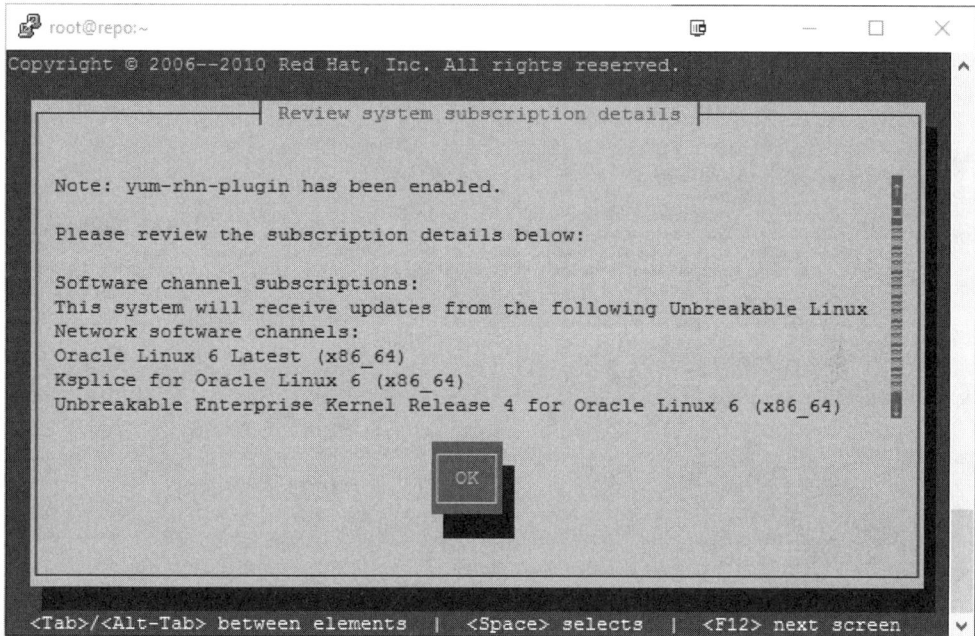

```
root@repo:~                                              — □ ×
Copyright © 2006--2010 Red Hat, Inc. All rights reserved.

          ┤ Review system subscription details ├

    Note: yum-rhn-plugin has been enabled.

    Please review the subscription details below:

    Software channel subscriptions:
    This system will receive updates from the following Unbreakable Linux
    Network software channels:
    Oracle Linux 6 Latest (x86_64)
    Ksplice for Oracle Linux 6 (x86_64)
    Unbreakable Enterprise Kernel Release 4 for Oracle Linux 6 (x86_64)

                        OK

  <Tab>/<Alt-Tab> between elements  |  <Space> selects  |  <F12> next screen
```

Channel Subscription

With the server registered to the ULN, you now need to register the server to the OVM channel, which contains the RPMs required to patch and upgrade OVM. Using a browser, log into https://linux.oracle.com using the same SSO ID you used to register the system. When you first log into the ULN, the Home tab is displayed (see Figure 27-1). It shows all the registered servers and a list of recently updated and added channels. The following tabs are also available to display additional information:

- **Channels**   Provides a list of all the channels available and the number of packages in each channel

- **Systems**   Provides a list of all systems this account supports, with the CSI number for each system, along with the number of subscribed channels for each server.

- **Errata**   Provides notifications from the ULN, announcing updates, bug fixes, as so on. These are sorted by severity, date, or advisory. This tab also links the systems affected to the server managed by this account.

- **CVE**   Provides a list of all common vulnerabilities and exposures. Common Vulnerabilities and Exposures (CVE) is a dictionary of common names for security vulnerabilities.

- **CSI Administration**   This is where you can manage the Support Identifier (SI) to which the account has access.

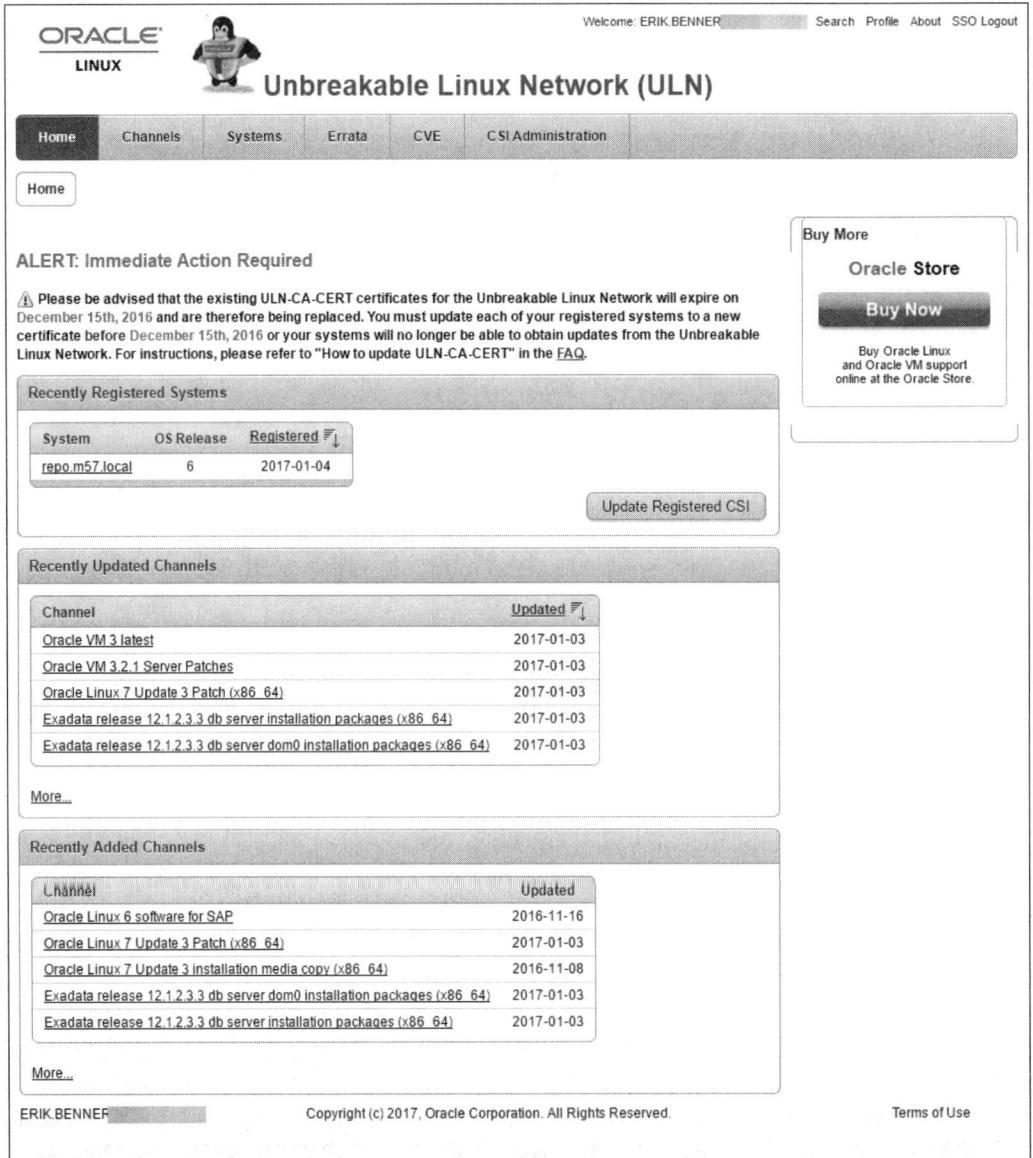

FIGURE 27-1. *The ULN Home page*

The next task is to subscribe the repository server to the Oracle VM channel. Under the Recently Registered Servers list, click the new repository server. This brings up the System Details page, shown in Figure 27-2, which shows what channels the system is subscribed to, along with system information such as operating system version, server architecture, and date registered.

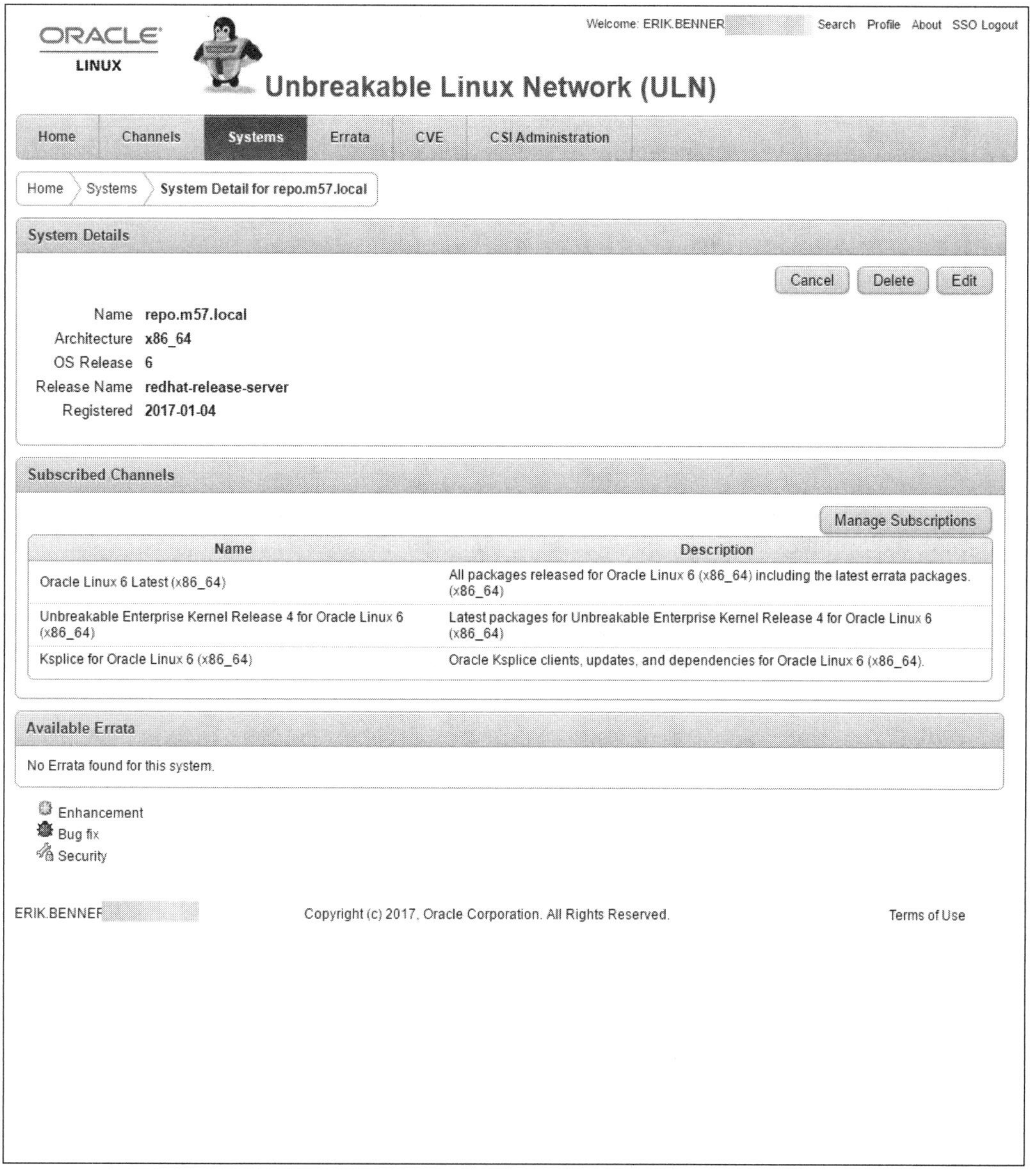

FIGURE 27-2. *The System Details page*

Next, the server must be modified to make it a yum server. To do so, click the Edit button and then check the Yum Server box (highlighted next) to apply the change. This will promote the server to being a yum server, with access to all channels.

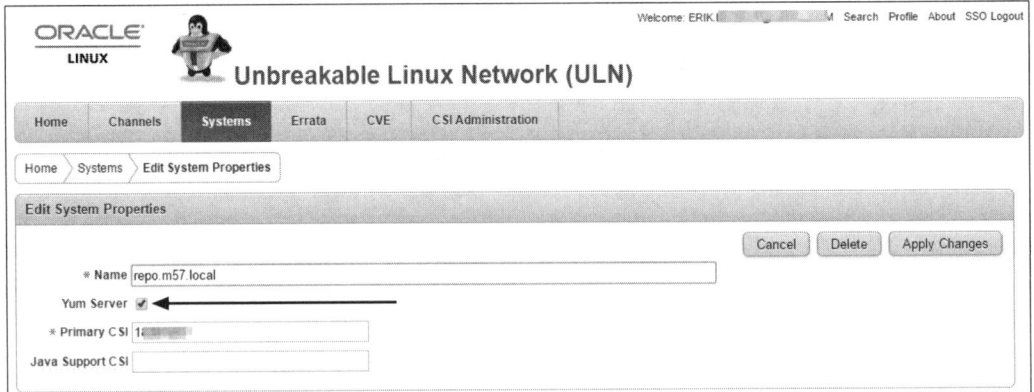

Now, back on the System Details page, click the Manage Subscriptions button. This allows you to select other channels, shown here, to subscribe the yum server to.

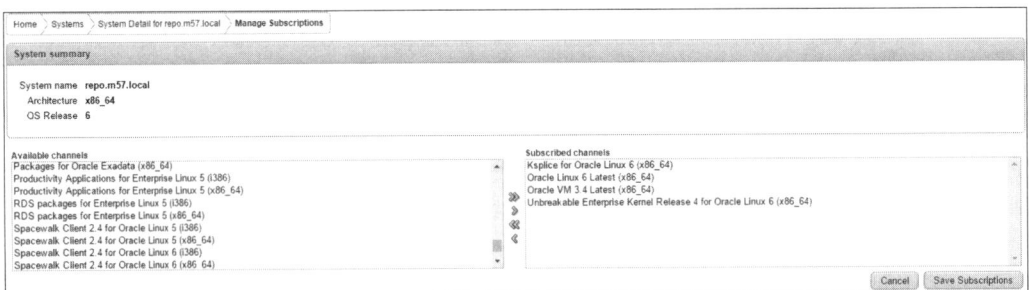

Scroll down in the Available Channels list and find the Oracle VM 3.X Latest channel, where X is the version of Oracle VM being run. Click the channel name to move it to the Subscribed Channels list. Then click Save Subscriptions. Now the server is subscribed to the Oracle VM channel. Optionally, to save space, you can unsubscribe from the Oracle Linux, Ksplice, and UEK channels, which are normally used in production environments.

In the next set of steps, you will configure the yum server to synchronize the RPMs.

YUM Server Configuration

The following steps configure the server and a yum repository (repo) for synchronizing the RPMs from the ULN to the repo server.

The first step is to edit the /etc/yum.repos.d/public-yum-ol6.repo file to enable the Oracle add-ons. This will make available several useful RPMs, including the uln-yum-mirror RPM. In the yum configuration file, find the following stanza and make sure that **enabled=1** is set:

```
[public_ol6_addons]
name=Oracle Linux $releasever Add ons ($basearch)
baseurl=http://yum.oracle.com/repo/OracleLinux/OL6/addons/$basearch/
```

```
gpgkey=file:///etc/pki/rpm-gpg/RPM-GPG-KEY-oracle
gpgcheck=1
enabled=1
```

Next, install the uln-yum-mirror RPM using the command **yum -y install uln-yum-mirror**, as shown next. Yum will automatically install all the dependencies if needed.

```
[root@repo ~]# yum -y install uln-yum-mirror
Loaded plugins: rhnplugin, security, ulninfo
This system is receiving updates from ULN.
Setting up Install Process
Resolving Dependencies
--> Running transaction check
---> Package uln-yum-mirror.noarch 0:0.3.0-2.el6 will be installed
--> Processing Dependency: createrepo >= 0.9.9-17.0.1 for package: uln-yum-
mirror-0.3.0-2.el6.noarch
--> Processing Dependency: yum-arch for package: uln-yum-mirror-0.3.0-2.el6.noarch
--> Processing Dependency: hardlinkpy for package: uln-yum-mirror-0.3.0-2.el6.noarch
--> Running transaction check
---> Package createrepo.noarch 0:0.9.9-24.el6 will be installed
--> Processing Dependency: python-deltarpm for package: createrepo-0.9.9-24.el6.noarch
---> Package hardlinkpy.noarch 0:0.0.5-1.el6 will be installed
---> Package yum-arch.noarch 0:2.2.2-9.el6 will be installed
--> Running transaction check
---> Package python-deltarpm.x86_64 0:3.5-0.5.20090913git.el6 will be installed
--> Processing Dependency: deltarpm = 3.5-0.5.20090913git.el6 for package: python-
deltarpm-3.5-0.5.20090913git.el6.x86_64
--> Running transaction check
---> Package deltarpm.x86_64 0:3.5-0.5.20090913git.el6 will be installed
--> Finished Dependency Resolution

Dependencies Resolved

================================================================================
 Package          Arch      Version                    Repository        Size
================================================================================
Installing:
 uln-yum-mirror   noarch    0.3.0-2.el6                public_ol6_addons  28 k
Installing for dependencies:
 createrepo       noarch    0.9.9-24.el6               ol6_x86_64_latest  96 k
 deltarpm         x86_64    3.5-0.5.20090913git.el6    ol6_x86_64_latest  70 k
 hardlinkpy       noarch    0.0.5-1.el6                public_ol6_addons  15 k
 python-deltarpm  x86_64    3.5-0.5.20090913git.el6    ol6_x86_64_latest  27 k
 yum-arch         noarch    2.2.2-9.el6                public_ol6_addons 331 k

Transaction Summary
================================================================================
Install       6 Package(s)

Total download size: 568 k
Installed size: 1.8 M
Downloading Packages:
(1/6): createrepo-0.9.9-24.el6.noarch.rpm                   |  96 kB     00:00
(2/6): deltarpm-3.5-0.5.20090913git.el6.x86_64.rpm          |  70 kB     00:00
(3/6): hardlinkpy-0.0.5-1.el6.noarch.rpm                    |  15 kB     00:00
(4/6): python-deltarpm-3.5-0.5.20090913git.el6.x86_64.rp    |  27 kB     00:00
```

```
(5/6): uln-yum-mirror-0.3.0-2.el6.noarch.rpm          |  28 kB   00:00
(6/6): yum-arch-2.2.2-9.el6.noarch.rpm                | 331 kB   00:00
-----------------------------------------------------------------------
Total                                  261 kB/s | 568 kB   00:02
Running rpm_check_debug
Running Transaction Test
Transaction Test Succeeded
Running Transaction
  Installing : hardlinkpy-0.0.5-1.el6.noarch                      1/6
  Installing : deltarpm-3.5-0.5.20090913git.el6.x86_64            2/6
  Installing : python-deltarpm-3.5-0.5.20090913git.el6.x86_64     3/6
  Installing : createrepo-0.9.9-24.el6.noarch                     4/6
  Installing : yum-arch-2.2.2-9.el6.noarch                        5/6
  Installing : uln-yum-mirror-0.3.0-2.el6.noarch                  6/6
  Verifying  : createrepo-0.9.9-24.el6.noarch                     1/6
  Verifying  : uln-yum-mirror-0.3.0-2.el6.noarch                  2/6
  Verifying  : yum-arch-2.2.2-9.el6.noarch                        3/6
  Verifying  : deltarpm-3.5-0.5.20090913git.el6.x86_64            4/6
  Verifying  : hardlinkpy-0.0.5-1.el6.noarch                      5/6
  Verifying  : python-deltarpm-3.5-0.5.20090913git.el6.x86_64     6/6

Installed:
  uln-yum-mirror.noarch 0:0.3.0-2.el6

Dependency Installed:
  createrepo.noarch 0:0.9.9-24.el6
  deltarpm.x86_64 0:3.5-0.5.20090913git.el6
  hardlinkpy.noarch 0:0.0.5-1.el6
  python-deltarpm.x86_64 0:3.5-0.5.20090913git.el6
  yum-arch.noarch 0:2.2.2-9.el6

Complete!
[root@repo ~]#
```

Next, you need to create the directory where all the files will be installed. By default, they go into /var/www/html/yum. It is recommended that you make this a separate filesystem, under Logical Volume Manager (lvm) control. (Note that over time, more disk space will be required. In the example, 100GB of space is used.)

```
[root@repo ~]# df -h /var/www/html/yum
Filesystem              Size  Used Avail Use% Mounted on
/dev/mapper/vg_ol6-html
                         99G   60M   94G   1% /var/www/html/yum
[root@repo ~]#
```

Next enable the httpd server:

```
[root@repo ~]# chkconfig httpd on
[root@repo ~]# service httpd start
Starting httpd: httpd:                                    [  OK  ]
[root@repo ~]#
```

Now, you can verify what channels are subscribed to by using the command **yum repolist**, as shown here:

```
[root@repo ~]# yum repolist
Loaded plugins: rhnplugin, security, ulninfo
This system is receiving updates from ULN.
repo id              repo name                                         status
ol6_x86_64_UEKR4     Unbreakable Enterprise Kernel Release 4 for Oracle Li   259
ol6_x86_64_ksplice   Ksplice for Oracle Linux 6 (x86_64)                  1,589
ol6_x86_64_latest    Oracle Linux 6 Latest (x86_64)                      36,740
ovm34_x86_64_latest  Oracle VM 3.4 Latest (x86_64)                        1,144
public_ol6_addons    Oracle Linux 6 Server Add ons (x86_64)                 427
repolist: 40,159
[root@repo ~]#
```

Because this is a yum server, the channels should be disabled in the rhnplugin.conf file. This will disable the channels from being used by the yum process when using yum to patch the server that is hosting the local copy of the yum repository. The file is /etc/yum/pluginconf.d/rhnplugin.conf. For each of the channels in the repo list, add in a stanza in the rhnplugin.conf file with the parameter **enabled=0**. If new channels are subscribed to, do not forget to add them to the rhnplugin.conf file with the channels disabled. In our example, the following lines will be added:

```
#[ol6_x86_64_UEKR4]
#enabled=0

#[ol6_x86_64_ksplice]
#enabled=0

#[ol6_x86_64_latest]
#enabled=0

[ovm34_x86_64_latest]
enabled=0

#[public_ol6_addons]
#enabled=0
```

By default, the repo is synchronized nightly, but this can be done manually using the command **uln-yum-mirror**. The first synchronization will take several hours, depending on the available Internet bandwidth.

The final step is to configure the yum server to use the local repository instead of one on the Internet. To do this, you need to create a new configuration in /etc/yum.repos.d with the yum repository configuration. You can browse to http://<repository>/yum/ to find the base URL for each repository. You can also use the **$releasever** and **$basearch** parameters. For our example, the file /etc/yum.repos.d/m57.local.repo was created:

```
[ol6_latest]
name=Oracle Linux $releasever Latest ($basearch)
baseurl=http://repo.m57.local/yum/OracleLinux/OL6/latest/$basearch/
gpgkey=file:///etc/pki/rpm-gpg/RPM-GPG-KEY-oracle
gpgcheck=1
enabled=1
```

```
[ol6_x86_64_UEKR4]
name=Oracle Linux UEK4 $releasever Latest ($basearch)
baseurl=http://repo.m57.local/yum/OracleLinux/OL6/UEK4/$basearch/
gpgkey=file:///etc/pki/rpm-gpg/RPM-GPG-KEY-oracle
enabled=1

[ol6_x86_64_ksplice]
name=Oracle Linux KSplice $releasever Latest ($basearch)
baseurl=http://repo.m57.local/yum/OracleLinux/OL6/ksplice/$basearch/
gpgkey=file:///etc/pki/rpm-gpg/RPM-GPG-KEY-oracle
enabled=1

[public_ol6_addons]
name=Oracle Linux Addons $releasever Latest ($basearch)
baseurl=http://repo.m57.local/yum/OracleLinux/OL6/addons/$basearch/
gpgkey=file:///etc/pki/rpm-gpg/RPM-GPG-KEY-oracle
enabled=1
```

The GPG key also needs to be imported using the command **rpm --import /usr/share/rhn/RPM-GPG-KEY**. To verify that the repository is working correctly, run the commands **yum clean metadata** and **yum repolist**.

Patching an Oracle VM Server

One of the most common tasks an administrator has is patching systems on a regular basis. Patching consistently using a schedule is important for both the security and health of the servers. The patches address bugs, improve features, and fix security vulnerabilities. Not patching will lead to more outages and result in significantly more exposure to the systems being compromised.

Patching Oracle VM Server requires that a yum repository be built and subscribed to the appropriate ULN channel. Once subscribed, the repository should have the latest patches from Oracle. Patching is different from upgrading: a patch is usually for servers with the same major or minor number, whereas an upgrade is generally used when the major or minor number changes. On occasion, the upgrade process can use the yum repository, but often an upgrade from a .iso file is the correct process to use. Upgrades are addressed later in this chapter.

Configuring Server Update Groups in Oracle VM Manager

Before Oracle VM servers can be patched, Oracle VM Manager needs to be configured to use the yum repository. To manage the server update setting, from OVMM navigate to the Reports and Resources tab and then select Server Update Groups, as shown next.

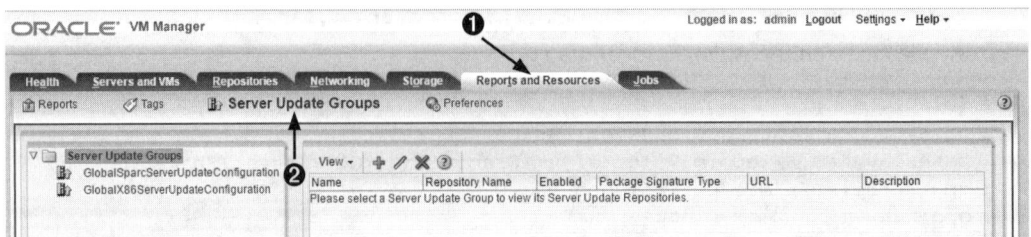

From this section, you can create a new update group. Although OVMM supports this for both SPARC and X86 systems, only X86 will be used in our example.

First, highlight the GlobalX86ServerUpdateConfiguration option and then click the green plus sign icon to add a new configuration, as shown next. This will start the dialog to create a new server update repository.

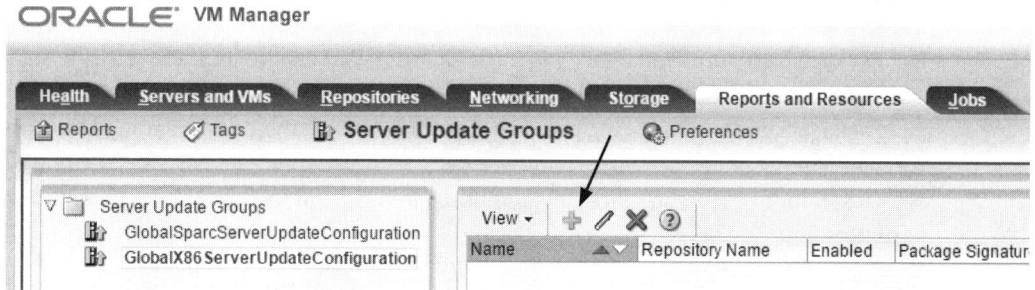

It is possible to configure multiple repositories in OVMM to allow the admin to patch against different release schedules. The most common example is to have a separate yum directory for each quarter to enable consistency when patching. This can also be done for OVS upgrades, because the administrator can make a repository specific to upgrading the OVS from one release to another. The configuration of the repository, shown next, can be edited once it has been created. The configuration includes the following parameters:

- **Name**   This is the name of the rule.
- **Repository Name**   This is the name of the repository used.

■ **URL** This is the URL to the yum repository (note that this is not the main page of the yum server, but the specific path that will be used for updates). There should be an updateinfo.xml file in the directory.

■ **Enabled** If this option is not checked, the system will ignore the update repository. This is helpful when multiple update repositories are configured, because any repositories not needed for the current patch activity can easily be disabled without configuration data being lost.

■ **Package Signature Type** GNU Privacy Guard (GPG) can be used to verify the signature of the files in the yum repository.

■ **Package Signature Key** If a package signature is used, the corresponding key must be entered.

■ **Description** You can place any additional information required to document the entry here.

Once the configuration is set, the server can be patched via yum.

Updating the Oracle VM Servers

Identifying servers that need to be patched is a straightforward process. You can see the current state of each Oracle VM server from the server's view by selecting Servers and VMs | Server Pools, as shown here.

In this view, the column Update Required shows what servers require an update. Before the server is updated (patched), it is set to maintenance mode, which triggers the live migration of running VMs from the server being updated to other Oracle VM servers in the server pool. Checking their status from this screen is helpful in large server pools. To select a server to patch, highlight the server and then click the Update Server icon, highlighted here.

This starts the upgrade process. A warning message will appear (shown next), informing you that the server will be placed into maintenance mode and that all VMs will be live migrated to other hosts, which means they will be moved with no outage.

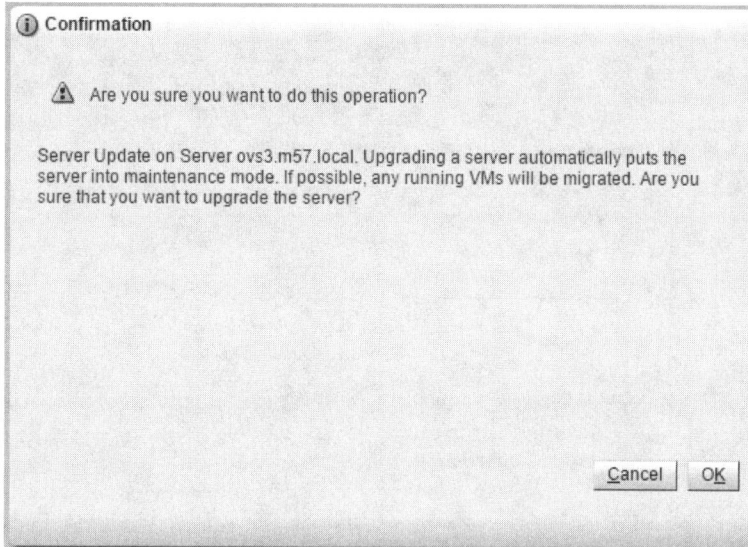

As the VMs are migrated, the servers in the pool will be locked, so it is best if no other activities are planned while the servers are being patched. The patch process also kicks off a job to upgrade the installed server. This job can be tracked in the job Summary section of the management interface. Once the OVS is patched, the system will show back online in OVMM, but the server will be in maintenance mode. No VMs can be moved to this system until the state is cleared. This gives you a chance to verify that all the network and storage is visible on the server prior to moving workloads back to the server.

To take the server out of maintenance mode, select the server and then click the edit icon (highlighted here).

Next, uncheck the Server in Maintenance Mode box (highlighted here) and then click OK. A short job will run that takes the server out of maintenance mode.

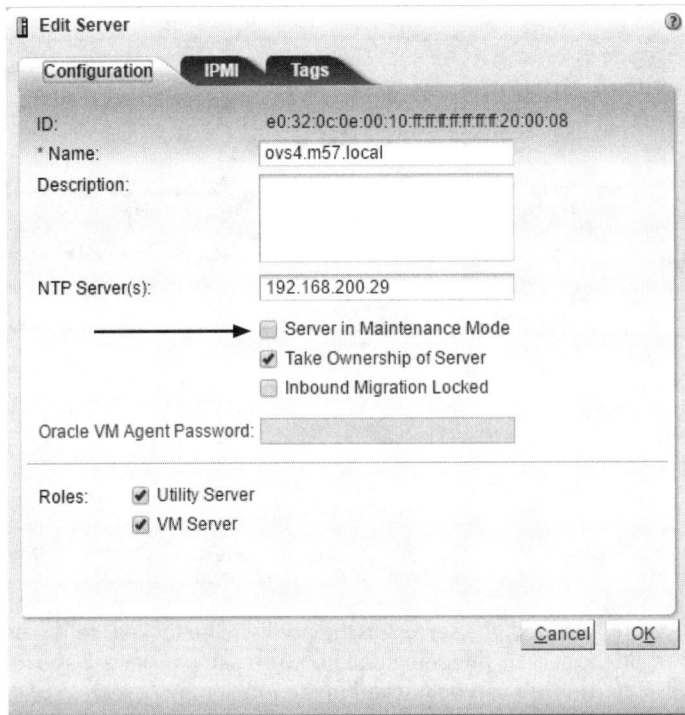

Once the server is out of maintenance mode, the process can continue with the other servers in the server pool.

Summary

This chapter covered how to prepare for and perform Oracle VM server patching. Patching is a simple process, and it is critical to the reliable operation of your private cloud. The chapter also showed you how to configure a repository server by enabling a local copy of Oracle RPMs used not only for patching Oracle VM systems but also many other Oracle technologies, including Oracle Linux. In the next chapter, you learn about some common troubleshooting tasks. The ability to troubleshoot issues with an Oracle VM installation is a critical skill to learn—not because problems happen often, but because you'll want to be able to resolve them quickly if they occur.

CHAPTER
28

Oracle VM
Troubleshooting

Things do not always go as planned, and when that happens, you, the administrator, need every tool available to troubleshoot your systems. This chapter covers troubleshooting tools and logs for the Oracle VM Server and the Oracle VM Manager.

When you're troubleshooting issues, it is best to follow a systematic method. Randomly making changes, installing patches, and not documenting changes will quickly lead to an unstable environment with any technology. Good troubleshooting practices are summed up in the six steps shown in Figure 28-1 and detailed in the following list:

1. *Identify the problem.* Question the obvious: Is this a virtualization problem? Is the storage problem an OS issue? Many factors are in play, and often a problem in one part of the stack can manifest as a symptom in an entirely different area. Verify where the errors are, and do not only look in one location. When you're dealing with error logs, modern tools that leverage machine learning to analyze logs (such as Oracle Management Cloud Log Analytics) can save you hours of effort when running down the root cause.

2. *Establish a hypothesis.* Generally in technology, when something breaks it's because a change was made. Identify all the changes made before the error occurred. Combine the changed data with the logs and develop a hypothesis on what is broken and why.

3. *Test the theory.* Once you have a working hypothesis, test whether it is the cause of the problem. Just because a log showed that the **ssh** daemon was restarted five minutes before the VM crashed does not mean there is a direct relationship between the two. Complex problems should be verified through testing whenever possible. This eliminates the danger of performing unnecessary changes that can introduce new problems into the environment. Use the test to generate a plan of action and a test plan. The *plan of action* is the change to be made to resolve the problem, and the *test plan* is how you verify that the problem is resolved.

4. *Act.* Once you have a validated plan of action, implement the plan, and only make that one change. Making multiple changes at one time can complicate troubleshooting in the future.

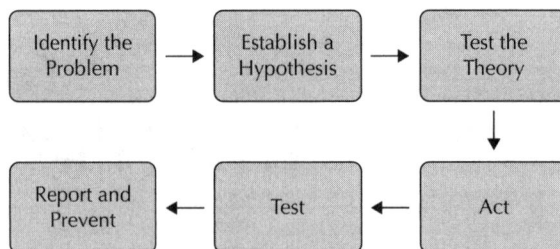

FIGURE 28-1. *Troubleshooting process flow*

5. *Test.* After the change is made, test the systems using your test plan. Verify the entire functionality of the technology stack when feasible. Often, using automated test tools helps not only in the speed at which systems can be tested but also the consistency of the tests.

6. *Report and prevent.* Document the findings, actions, and results. Then use this knowledge to prevent future issues.

The next few sections cover troubleshooting resources and tips for the Oracle VM Server and the Oracle VM Manager.

Oracle VM Server

The Oracle VM Server is the heart of your virtualized cloud. Troubleshooting in this system usually requires looking in log files as well as diagnosing network issues, storage issues, and hypervisor issues.

Directories and Log Files

Four critical directories contain configuration files and logs for Oracle VM Server. These are described in Table 28-1.

Each of these directories contains log files, as detailed in Table 28-2, that are helpful in troubleshooting any issues experienced with Oracle VM Server.

Command-Line Tools/Networking

Although almost all the management of Oracle VM is performed from within Oracle VM Manager or Oracle Enterprise Manager, you will occasionally need to access Oracle VM Server directly to troubleshoot issues. Table 28-3 details several commands in Oracle VM Server that can assist you in troubleshooting issues.

Most of these commands are simple to run and should not need more detail; however, the **xentop** command warrants a deeper look, as much of the information displayed is not well documented. **xentop** displays real-time information about the Oracle VM Server domains (see Figure 28-2).

Directory	Usage
/etc/xen	Houses the Oracle VM Server configuration files that control the low-level behavior of the hypervisor
/etc/xen/scripts	Has the networking-related scripts, including the Open vSwitch configuration files
/var/log	Holds the operating system logs as well as the logs for Oracle VM
/var/log/xen	Contains Oracle VM Server log files, QEMU logs, and xend logs

TABLE 28-1.   *Oracle VM Server Directories*

Directory	File	Use
/etc/xen	README.incompatibilities	A list of known incompatibilities between the Xen release and the guest operating systems.
	README	Description of each of the configuration files.
/var/log	ovs-agent.log	Contains a log for Oracle VM Agent. This should be one of the first places you look at when troubleshooting issues.
	osc.log	Contains a log for the installation and patching of the Oracle VM Storage Connect plug-ins.
	ovm-consoled.log	Contains a log for the Oracle VM virtual machine console.
	ovmwatch.log	Contains a log for the Oracle VM watch daemon.
	messages	Contains OS error and debug logs.
	boot.log	Contains the messages you see when the system boots.
	secure	Contains information related to authentication and authorization privileges.
	yum.log	A log that contains information about packages installed and updated using yum.
/var/log/xen	qemu-dm.*pid*.log	Contains a log for each hardware-virtualized guest created by the **quemu-dm** process. Use the **ps** command to find the PID (process identifier) and replace this in the filename.
	xend.log	Contains a log of all the actions of the Oracle VM Server daemon.
	xend-debug.log	Contains more detailed logs of the actions of the Oracle VM Server daemon.

TABLE 28-2. *Useful Log Files for Oracle VM Server*

Oracle VM Server Command	Purpose
xentop	Shows real-time information about Oracle VM Server and domains
xm dmesg	Shows the log information on the hypervisor
xm log	Shows the log of the Oracle VM Server daemon
xm uptime	Shows the uptime for dom0 and other guests

TABLE 28-3. *Oracle VM Server Troubleshooting Commands*

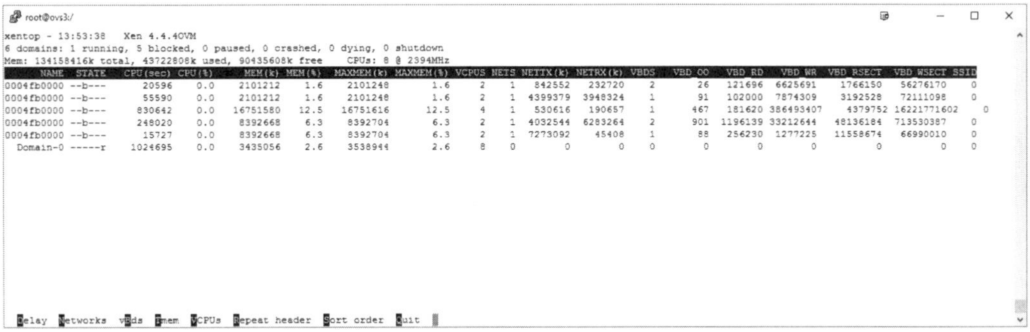

FIGURE 28-2.   *xentop*

NOTE
*To run the **xentop** command, ssh into the Oracle VM Server as root, and simply type **xentop** and press ENTER.*

The **xentop** output displays the performance information described in Table 28-4.

When **xentop** is running, you can also display more detailed information about the Networks, VBDs (Block devices), **V**CPU, and **T**mem (memory). To add in any additional details, select the corresponding letter when **xentop** is running, so **V** will show more information about the VCPUs, **T** will show memory information, and so on. The **R** will also repeat the header for each domain. This can be seen in Figure 28-3.

Troubleshooting networking on Oracle VM Server is almost the same as on a normal Oracle Linux system. Common commands used to troubleshoot the network are listed in Table 28-5.

The main difference is that on Oracle VM Server, almost all physical interfaces (such as eth0m, eth1, and so on) are normally added to bond devices (bond0, bond1, bond*X.VLAN,* and so on) and then presented to a domain as a virtual interface (vid*X.0*), also known as a *netback device* when you're looking at the network from Xen.

The **netstat** command shows interface statics when run with the **-i** option, as shown in Figure 28-4. This shows all the physical and logical components and their details.

When you're troubleshooting network issues, looking at the ERR and DRP columns is important. These columns show the number of good and bad packets:

- **RX-OK**   Correct packets received on this interface.

- **RX-ERR**   Incorrect packets received on this interface.

- **RX-DRP**   Packets that were dropped at this interface. When configured for an active-backup bond, the standby bond will show 100 percent dropped packets.

- **RX-OVR**   Packets that this interface was unable to receive.

A high number of bad packets can point to a network issue. In this case, eth1 is using a CAT5 cable but supporting 10G traffic. This is introducing network errors into eth1 and bond0, which uses the eth1 port.

Column	Description
NAME	The name of the domain. For guest domains, the Oracle VM universally unique identifier (UUID) is used.
STATE	The state of the VM: **b** Blocked domain. **c** Domain crashed. **d** Domain is dying. **p** Domain paused. **r** Domain is actively running on one of the CPU. **s** Domain shutting down.
CPU(sec)	Domain usage in seconds.
CPU(%)	Domain usage as percentage of available CPU.
MEM(k)	Current memory usage in kilobytes.
MEM(%)	Current memory usage as a percentage of available memory.
MAXMEM(k)	The maximum amount of memory, in kilobytes, that can be dynamically allocated to a guest domain.
MAXMEM(%)	The maximum amount of memory, as a percentage of available memory, that can be dynamically allocated to a guest domain.
VCPUS	The number of vCPUs assigned to the domain.
NETS	The number of networks assigned to the domain.
NETTX(k)	Total network transmitted bytes.
NETRX(k)	Total network received bytes.
VBDS	The number of virtual block devices (VBDs).
VBD_OO	The number of VBD errors, when I/O was delayed.
VBD_RD	The number of VBD read requests.
VBD_WR	The number of VBD write requests.
VBD_RSECT	The number of VBD read sectors.
VBD_WESCT	The number of VBD write sectors.

TABLE 28-4. *xentop Columns*

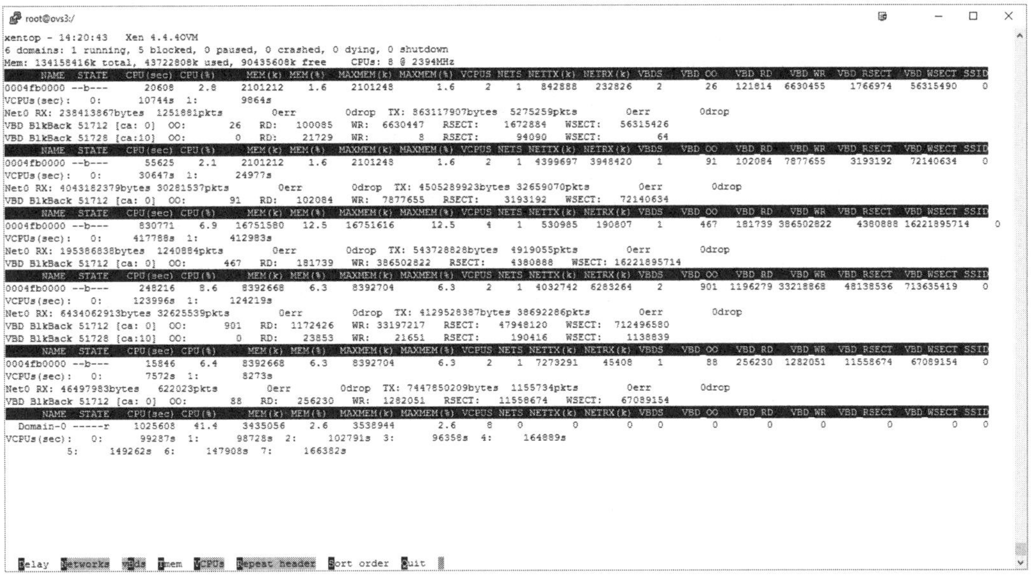

FIGURE 28-3. *xentop expanded details*

CAUTION

The cable type matters on high-speed networks. When running high-speed networks, verify that the correct category of cable is being used. 10G requires CAT6 for short runs under 40 meters, and CAT7 is needed for runs up to 100 meters.

Command	Description
netstat	The "network statics" command shows connection and routing information.
brctl	The "bridge control" command shows information about the bonds.
dig	This is a replacement for the **nslookup** command and shows DNS information.
ethtool	This command shows information about the physical ports.

TABLE 28-5. *Common Troubleshooting Commands*

```
[root@ovs3 /]# netstat -i
Kernel Interface table
Iface      MTU Met    RX-OK RX-ERR RX-DRP RX-OVR    TX-OK TX-ERR TX-DRP TX-OVR Flg
10dbdbbf7a 9000    0 686928077      0    898     0 654037891      0      0      0 BMRU
bond0      1500    0 86609403    3606 3750228     0 87919826       0      0      0 BMmRU
bond1      9000    0 688530575      0     13     0 1362506401      0      0      0 BMmRU
bond1.200  9000    0 686940153      0      0     0 654051867       0      0      0 BMRU
bond1.201  9000    0         0      0      0     0          1      0      0      0 BMRU
bond1.202  9000    0         0      0      0     0          6      0      0      0 BMRU
c0a8c800   1500    0 36648984       0 225274     0 24107945       0      0      0 BMRU
eth0       1500    0 82256653    1803      0     0 34436444       0      0      0 BMsRU
eth1       1500    0  4352757    1803 3750223     0 53483399       0      0      0 BMsRU
eth2       9000    0 688350387      0      2     0 1359895753      0      0      0 BMsRU
eth3       9000    0   180221      0      2     0  2610697        0      0      0 BMsRU
lo        65536    0   337472      0      0     0   337472        0      0      0 LRU
vif4.0     1500    0  1241099      0      0     0  4919798        0      0      0 BMRU
vif5.0     1500    0  1252037      0      0     0  5275965        0      0      0 BMRU
vif9.0     1500    0 30281738       0      0     0 32659706        0      0      0 BMRU
vif12.0    1500    0 32625539       0      0     0 38692829        0      0      0 BMRU
vif14.0    1500    0   622023      0      0     0  1156277        0      0      0 BMRU
[root@ovs3 /]#
```

FIGURE 28-4. *Network information via netstat -i*

The running configuration of each bond can be found in the /proc/net/bonding directory. Each bond will have a file in this directory that shows the running configuration of the bond. This includes the type of bond as well as connection information for each member of the bond. In the following example, we can verify that bond1 is a Link Aggregation Control Protocol (LACP) bond (dynamic link aggregation) using the physical eth2 and eth3 ports on the server. Each port is linked at 10G.

```
[root@ovs3 bonding]# more /proc/net/bonding/bond1
Ethernet Channel Bonding Driver: v3.7.1 (April 27, 2011)

Bonding Mode: IEEE 802.3ad Dynamic link aggregation
Transmit Hash Policy: layer2 (0)
MII Status: up
MII Polling Interval (ms): 250
Up Delay (ms): 500
Down Delay (ms): 500

802.3ad info
LACP rate: slow
Min links: 0
Aggregator selection policy (ad_select): stable
Active Aggregator Info:
        Aggregator ID: 2
        Number of ports: 2
        Actor Key: 13
        Partner Key: 18
        Partner Mac Address: 08:bd:43:76:0a:3d
```

```
Slave Interface: eth2
MII Status: up
Speed: 10000 Mbps
Duplex: full
Link Failure Count: 0
Permanent HW addr: 00:10:e0:39:cb:a4
Slave queue ID: 0
Aggregator ID: 2
Actor Churn State: none
Partner Churn State: none
Actor Churned Count: 0
Partner Churned Count: 0
details actor lacp pdu:
    system priority: 0
    port key: 13
    port priority: 255
    port number: 1
    port state: 61
details partner lacp pdu:
    system priority: 32768
    oper key: 18
    port priority: 128
    port number: 14
    port state: 63

Slave Interface: eth3
MII Status: up
Speed: 10000 Mbps
Duplex: full
Link Failure Count: 0
Permanent HW addr: 00:10:e0:39:cb:a5
Slave queue ID: 0
Aggregator ID: 2
Actor Churn State: none
Partner Churn State: none
Actor Churned Count: 0
Partner Churned Count: 0
details actor lacp pdu:
    system priority: 0
    port key: 13
    port priority: 255
    port number: 2
    port state: 61
details partner lacp pdu:
    system priority: 32768
    oper key: 18
    port priority: 128
    port number: 13
    port state: 63
```

Additional information about the physical ports on the server can be discovered using the **ethtool** command, which shows the link status and port type: TP (twisted pair), FIBER SFP+ interface, and so on. To use the **ethtool** command, pass the name of the port for which you need additional information, as shown in this example:

```
[root@ovs3 bonding]# ethtool eth0
Settings for eth0:
        Supported ports: [ TP ]'
        Supported link modes:   1000baseT/Full
                                10000baseT/Full
        Supported pause frame use: No
        Supports auto-negotiation: Yes
        Advertised link modes:  100baseT/Full
                                1000baseT/Full
                                10000baseT/Full
        Advertised pause frame use: No
        Advertised auto-negotiation: Yes
        Speed: 10000Mb/s
        Duplex: Full
        Port: Twisted Pair
        PHYAD: 0
        Transceiver: external
        Auto-negotiation: on
        MDI-X: Unknown
        Supports Wake-on: d
        Wake-on: d
        Current message level: 0x00000007 (7)
                                drv probe link
        Link detected: yes
```

The **brctl** command shows the Linux bridge devices, which are the bonds in the environment. This command shows each bridge and what MAC addresses are being used on each one.

To show all the bridges on an Oracle VM server, run the command **brctl show**:

```
[root@ovs3 ~]# brctl show
bridge name      bridge id                   STP enabled      interfaces
10dbdbbf7a               8000.0010e039cba4         no                  bond1.200
c0a8c800                 8000.0010e039cba2         no                  bond0
                                                                vif1.0
                                                                vif2.0
                                                                vif20.0
                                                                vif20.1
```

This example shows two bridges: 10dbdbbf7a and c0a8c800. The c0a8c800 bridge uses the bond0 interface, and the 10dbdbbf7a bridge uses the bond1.200 interface, which is VLAN200 on bond1. Also, four virtual interfaces are attached to the bridge driver; these will start with "vif."

Using **brctl**, you can see a list of all the MAC addresses used on a bridge. This command also requires the command **showmacs** and the name of the bridge, as shown here:

```
[root@ovs3 ~]# brctl showmacs 10dbdbbf7a
port no mac addr                is local?      ageing timer
   1     00:08:9b:e5:41:00      no               0.05
   1     00:10:e0:39:cb:a4      yes              0.00
   1     00:10:e0:39:cb:a4      yes              0.00
```

In this example, two MAC addresses are local to the bridge, and a third MAC address is external to the Oracle VM Server.

DNS is often critical for the network to function correctly, so Oracle includes the **dig** command in the distribution. This is the replacement command for **nslookup**, and it's easier to use. (The **nslookup** command has been deprecated, and although it is included in Oracle VM Server, it is no longer included in many Linux distributions.) To check the resolution of a name (such as the 10G interface name on a storage array), simply use the command **dig** with the DNS name, as shown in the following example:

```
[root@ovs3 bonding]# dig nas10g.m57.local

; <<>> DiG 9.8.2rc1-RedHat-9.8.2-0.47.rc1.el6_8.3 <<>> nas10g.m57.local
;; global options: +cmd
;; Got answer:
;; ->>HEADER<<- opcode: QUERY, status: NOERROR, id: 48824
;; flags: qr aa rd ra; QUERY: 1, ANSWER: 1, AUTHORITY: 1, ADDITIONAL: 1

;; QUESTION SECTION:
;nas10g.m57.local.              IN      A

;; ANSWER SECTION:
nas10g.m57.local.      86400    IN      A       192.168.210.10

;; AUTHORITY SECTION:
m57.local.             86400    IN      NS      dns.m57.local.

;; ADDITIONAL SECTION:
dns.m57.local.         86400    IN      A       192.168.200.11

;; Query time: 1 msec
;; SERVER: 192.168.200.11#53(192.168.200.11)
;; WHEN: Fri May 19 11:31:22 2017
;; MSG SIZE  rcvd: 84
```

Not only do we see that the name is resolving to the 192.168.210.10 interface, but we see the DNS server of Authority (192.168.200.11) and DNS record information.

Multipathing

The Linux **multipathd** daemon provides a critical role by enabling support for multiple paths between the Oracle VM server and the storage. Having multiple paths working protects against the failure of a storage array controller, as the Oracle VM server will automatically route the storage requests to the surviving controller. This provides storage high availability for block devices.

NOTE
*Make sure you download and install the latest multipath.conf file
from Oracle Support when adding new arrays. The Oracle-supplied
configuration is validated for Oracle Storage products. Although
Oracle includes stanzas for non–Oracle Storage technologies, these
configurations are not validated and may need to be updated based
on the individual storage vendor's requirements.*

Troubleshooting this setup requires some basic understanding of the tools. The **multipathd –k**
command starts an interactive console. After entering this command, you can enter **help** to get a
list of available commands, you can enter a command, or you can press CTRL-D to quit.

The **multipathd** interactive console can be used to troubleshoot problems you may be having
with your system. For example, the following command sequence displays the multipath
configuration, including the defaults, before exiting the console.

Command	Description
show config	Displays the current configuration file.
show topology	Shows all the mapped LUNs and their paths.
show paths	Similar to **show topology**, but only shows the paths.
reconfigure	Reloads the /etc/multipath.conf configuration file. This allows for changes to be made without a reboot.

In the following example, only one LUN is working with the multipathing: the dm-3 LUN. The
dm-1 and dm-2 LUNs are not multipathed and should have their configuration checked on the
storage array.

```
multipathd> show topology
create: 36e843b630bbdd9adee26d488ed9e51d4 dm-1 QNAP,iSCSI Storage
size=50G features='1 queue_if_no_path' hwhandler='0' wp=rw
`-+- policy='round-robin 0' prio=1 status=active
  `- 10:0:0:0 sdb 8:16 active ready running
create: 36e843b6ce263716db426d4e3edb991d1 dm-2 QNAP,iSCSI Storage
size=50G features='1 queue_if_no_path' hwhandler='0' wp=rw
`-+- policy='round-robin 0' prio=1 status=active
  `- 11:0:0:0 sdc 8:32 active ready running
create: 36e843b6b000f6c2d3e8bd4952d923ddc dm-3 QNAP,iSCSI Storage
size=50G features='1 queue_if_no_path' hwhandler='0' wp=rw
`-+- policy='round-robin 0' prio=1 status=active
  `- 12:0:0:0 sdd 8:48 active ready running
- +- policy='round-robin 0' prio=1 status=active
  `- 12:0:0:0 sde 8:52 active ready running
```

CAUTION
*Linux DM-X names can, and will, change over time. Do not use them
to identify a LUN; instead, always use the World Wide ID (WWID).*

NFS

The Network Filesystem (NFS) is also commonly used, and although a very reliable technology, it occasionally has issues with connecting to arrays that are not configured correctly. Before troubleshooting any NFS issues, first make sure each Oracle VM server can ping the NFS server.

Next, verify that NFS v3 or v4 is supported by the array. This can be done by running the **rpcinfo** command, pointing to the storage array. In this example, both NFS version 2 and version 3 are supported:

```
[root@ovs3 ~]# rpcinfo -u 192.168.200.10 nfs
program 100003 version 2 ready and waiting
program 100003 version 3 ready and waiting
[root@ovs3 ~]#
```

The next step in troubleshooting NFS shares is to use the **showmount** command to see what NFS shares are available. If **showmount** does not see the NFS export, Oracle VM will not see the export.

```
[root@ovs3 ~]# showmount -e zfs.m57.local
Export list for zfs.m57.local:
/export/test1 (everyone)
/export/test2 (everyone)
[root@ovs3 ~]#
```

Next, you can use the command **nfsstat** to check all the mount options for all NFS shares, as shown here. Verify that the NFS version used is 3 (using the **mountvers** option) and that the IP address is the one expected for the NFS server. With multihomed NFS servers, if you are not careful, the wrong IP can be accidently used.

```
[root@ovs3 ~]# nfsstat -m
/nfsmnt/ea22997c-1366-4c10-8f9e-85175b847c13 from nas10g.m57.local:/ovmm_pool0
 Flags:
rw,relatime,vers=3,rsize=524288,wsize=524288,namlen=255,hard,proto=tcp,
timeo=600,retrans=2,sec=sys,mountaddr=192.168.210.10,mountvers=3,
mountport=30000,mountproto=udp,local_lock=none,addr=192.168.210.10

/OVS/Repositories/0004fb000003000088dee23dc391c78d from nas10g.m57.local:/
ovmm_repo0
 Flags: rw,relatime,vers=3,rsize=524288,wsize=524288,namlen=255,hard,
proto=tcp,timeo=600,retrans=2,sec=sys,mountaddr=192.168.210.10,mountvers=3,
mountport=30000,mountproto=udp,local_lock=none,addr=192.168.210.10

/OVS/Repositories/0004fb0000030000c1b0fb6a3ae3940b from nas10g.m57.local:/
ovmm_flash
 Flags: rw,relatime,vers=3,rsize=524288,wsize=524288,namlen=255,soft,
nosharecache,proto=tcp,timeo=600,retrans=2,sec=sys,mountaddr=192.168.210.10,
mountvers=3,mountport=30000,mountproto=tcp,local_lock=none,addr=192.168.210.10
```

Oracle VM Manager

Even though the Oracle VM Manager has fewer components to manage, it is a critical part of the Oracle VM environment because it's the management control. However, even if the Oracle VM Manager fails, the VMs running on the Oracle VM servers will continue to run and automatically fail over if their HA flag is set. Troubleshooting the Oracle VM Manager is focused on its log files. It is also important to watch the tasks being performed in Oracle VM Manager by monitoring the Jobs panel. Finally, you should be aware that each entity in Oracle VM Manager has its own event history that can be accessed from the Oracle VM Manager.

Log Files and Directories

Oracle VM Manager error messages are displayed in the Jobs tab and in the object's Events list, and they are also available in log files. Log files are stored in the following directory on the Oracle VM Manager host computer:

`/u01/app/oracle/ovm-manager-3/domains/ovm_domain/servers/AdminServer/logs`

Here are a few files that are helpful when troubleshooting Oracle VM Manager:

- **access.log**   This log tracks HTTP access to the web interface of the Oracle VM Manager. This includes any calls to the WebLogic server's HTTP interface. This log can be used to track access and HTTP operations within Oracle VM Manager to help debug access issues and to audit access to the Oracle VM Manager. Login messages will contain the test "/ovm/console/faces/login.jspx."

- **AdminServer.log**   This log contains the events from the WebLogic Server framework, including events triggered by Oracle VM Manager. This is one of the most useful logs when you're looking for SSL/TLS certificate issues and file permission issues. It also contains actions performed within Oracle VM Manager that are usually identifiable by searching for items containing the string com.oracle.ovm.mgr.

- **AdminServer.out**   This log file contains the output from the WebLogic server, including the startup and shutdown messages. This log file is very useful for detecting problems when the Oracle VM Manager will not start, and it's helpful for troubleshooting database connectivity issues and other errors. Search for <Critical> text to rapidly find significant errors.

- **AdminServer-diagnostic.log**   The file contains exceptions from the Oracle WebLogic server, including events triggered by Oracle VM Manager such as login failures due to incorrect credentials.

Because the log file format is determined by Oracle WebLogic, many of these files may be difficult to read. One option is to leverage a log analytics tool such as Oracle Management Cloud Log Analytics, which both parses logs and leverages machine learning to correlate events between logs in all tiers of the IaaS Cloud. Another option is to use the log-parsing tool included with Oracle VM Manager. This tool is named OvmLogTool.py and is located at

/u01/app/oracle/ovm-manager-3/ovm_tools/bin

OvmLogTool.py can perform the following three useful tasks:

■ Convert and combine all the AdminServer log files into one file.

■ Create a filtered summary log file that only lists errors.

■ Display the latest contents of the AdminServer log, applying the filtering on the fly.

Usually analysis of the logs starts by generating an errorpwds summary log. The summary file can act as an index into the filtered file to investigate and analyze errors, providing you with timestamps and a shortened summary of each error that may need further investigation. To generate a summary log file, run **python OvmLogTool.py -s -o summary**, as shown here.

```
root@ovmm:/u01/app/oracle/ovm-manager-3/ovm_tools/bin
[root@ovmm ~]# cd /u01/app/oracle/ovm-manager-3/ovm_tools/bin
[root@ovmm bin]# python OvmLogTool.py -s -o summary
processing input file: /u01/app/oracle/ovm-manager-3/domains/ovm_domain/servers/AdminServer/logs/AdminServer.log00001
processing input file: /u01/app/oracle/ovm-manager-3/domains/ovm_domain/servers/AdminServer/logs/AdminServer.log
[root@ovmm bin]#
```

This generates a file named "summary" in the local directory that can then be analyzed for any errors. However, it will only contain error messages, which at times can limit your ability to understand the context of the errors. To get a full log of all events and errors within Oracle VM Manager, run the command **python OvmLogTool.py -o filteredlog**, as shown here.

```
root@ovmm:/u01/app/oracle/ovm-manager-3/ovm_tools/bin
[root@ovmm bin]# python OvmLogTool.py  -o filteredlog
processing input file: /u01/app/oracle/ovm-manager-3/domains/ovm_domain/servers/AdminServer/logs/AdminServer.log00001
processing input file: /u01/app/oracle/ovm-manager-3/domains/ovm_domain/servers/AdminServer/logs/AdminServer.log
[root@ovmm bin]#
```

This generates a file named filteredlog in the local directory. You can use this to look for all events that occurred within Oracle VM Manager.

Finally, you can use OvmLogTool.py to filter results on the fly while tailing the log, as shown in Figure 28-5.

Entities

Each entity in Oracle VM Manager has an Events tab that shows all the events and errors for a target. On the Entity, where it is a VM, Repository, Server, and so on, you can right-click the entity and select Display Events, as shown in Figure 28-6.

This displays the events for the entity, as shown in Figure 28-7, where you can see that a VM was purposely crashed several times while performing some storage testing.

```
root@ovmm:/u01/app/oracle/ovm-manager-3/ovm_tools/bin
[root@ovmm bin]# python OvmLogTool.py  -t
tailing log file: /u01/app/oracle/ovm-manager-3/domains/ovm_domain/servers/AdminServer/logs/AdminServer.log
<2017-05-07T22:33:17.464-0400> <Warning> <odof.util.PersistUtils> <Error executing query: org.eclipse.persistence.internal.jpa.querydef.CriteriaQueryImpl@15f2f030
javax.persistence.PersistenceException: Exception [EclipseLink-4002] (Eclipse Persistence Services - 2.5.2.v20140319-9ad6abd): org.eclipse.persistence.exceptions.Data
baseException
Internal Exception: weblogic.jdbc.extensions.PoolDisabledSQLException: weblogic.common.resourcepool.ResourceDisabledException: Pool ovm-jpa-ds is Suspended, cannot al
locate resources to applications..
Error Code: 0
Call: SELECT ID AS a1, ACKNOWLEDGED AS a2, ASSOCIATEDOBJECTID AS a3, ASSOCIATEDOBJECTNAME AS a4, ASSOCIATEDOBJECTTYPE AS a5, CREATETIME AS a6, DESCRIPTION AS a7, MODI
FYTIME AS a8, SEVERITY AS a9, SUMMARY AS a10, TYPE AS a11, USERACKABLE AS a12, USERVISIBLE AS a13, VERSION AS a14 FROM OVM_EVENT WHERE ((((ASSOCIATEDOBJECTID IN (?))
AND TYPE LIKE ?) AND (SEVERITY = ?)) AND (ACKNOWLEDGED = ?)) ORDER BY MODIFYTIME DESC LIMIT ?, ?
         bind => [6 parameters bound]
<2017-05-07T22:33:18.969-0400> <Warning> <odof.util.PersistUtils> <Error executing query: org.eclipse.persistence.internal.jpa.querydef.CriteriaQueryImpl@71633bba
javax.persistence.PersistenceException: Exception [EclipseLink-4002] (Eclipse Persistence Services - 2.5.2.v20140319-9ad6abd): org.eclipse.persistence.exceptions.Data
baseException
Internal Exception: weblogic.jdbc.extensions.PoolDisabledSQLException: weblogic.common.resourcepool.ResourceDisabledException: Pool ovm-jpa-ds is Suspended, cannot al
locate resources to applications..
Error Code: 0
Call: SELECT ID, ACKNOWLEDGED, ASSOCIATEDOBJECTID, ASSOCIATEDOBJECTNAME, ASSOCIATEDOBJECTTYPE, CREATETIME, DESCRIPTION, MODIFYTIME, SEVERITY, SUMMARY, TYPE, USERACKAB
LE, USERVISIBLE, VERSION FROM OVM_EVENT WHERE (((((MODIFYTIME >= ?) AND (MODIFYTIME < ?)) AND (TYPE = ?)) AND (ACKNOWLEDGED = ?)) ORDER BY MODIFYTIME ASC
         bind => [4 parameters bound]
<2017-05-07T22:33:20.980-0400> <Warning> <odof.util.PersistUtils> <Error executing query: org.eclipse.persistence.internal.jpa.querydef.CriteriaQueryImpl@5fbde0e5
javax.persistence.PersistenceException: Exception [EclipseLink-4002] (Eclipse Persistence Services - 2.5.2.v20140319-9ad6abd): org.eclipse.persistence.exceptions.Data
baseException
Internal Exception: weblogic.jdbc.extensions.PoolDisabledSQLException: weblogic.common.resourcepool.ResourceDisabledException: Pool ovm-jpa-ds is Suspended, cannot al
locate resources to applications..
Error Code: 0
Call: SELECT ID, ACKNOWLEDGED, ASSOCIATEDOBJECTID, ASSOCIATEDOBJECTNAME, ASSOCIATEDOBJECTTYPE, CREATETIME, DESCRIPTION, MODIFYTIME, SEVERITY, SUMMARY, TYPE, USERACKAB
LE, USERVISIBLE, VERSION FROM OVM_EVENT WHERE (((((ASSOCIATEDOBJECTID IN (?)) AND (MODIFYTIME >= ?)) AND (MODIFYTIME <= ?)) AND TYPE LIKE ?) AND (ACKNOWLEDGED = ?)) O
RDER BY MODIFYTIME DESC
         bind => [5 parameters bound]
<2017-05-07T22:33:20.980-0400> <Warning> <ovm.mgr.task.loadbalancer.PoolLoadBalancer> <THREAD EXIT: Load Balancer- unexpected exception: null
java.lang.NullPointerException
         at ovm.mgr.event.EventServiceImpl.getEventsForObjectIds(EventServiceImpl.java:321)
         at ovm.mgr.event.EventServiceImpl.getEventsForObjectId(EventServiceImpl.java:237)
         at ovm.mgr.event.EventServiceImpl.getEvents(EventServiceImpl.java:224)
         at ovm.mgr.task.loadbalancer.PoolLoadBalancer.ackDrsAlertEvents(PoolLoadBalancer.java:1561)
         at ovm.mgr.task.loadbalancer.PoolLoadBalancer.loadBalanceMode(PoolLoadBalancer.java:364)
         at ovm.mgr.task.loadbalancer.PoolLoadBalancer.doTask(PoolLoadBalancer.java:124)
         at ovm.mgr.util.concurrent.RunnableTask.run(RunnableTask.java:26)
```

FIGURE 28-5.   *Using OvmLogTool in real time*

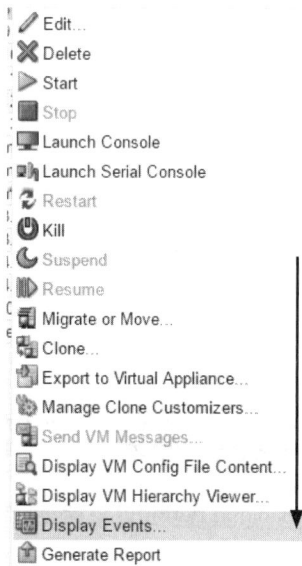

- Edit...
- Delete
- Start
- Stop
- Launch Console
- Launch Serial Console
- Restart
- Kill
- Suspend
- Resume
- Migrate or Move...
- Clone...
- Export to Virtual Appliance...
- Manage Clone Customizers...
- Send VM Messages...
- Display VM Config File Content...
- Display VM Hierarchy Viewer...
- Display Events...
- Generate Report

FIGURE 28-6.   *Display Events*

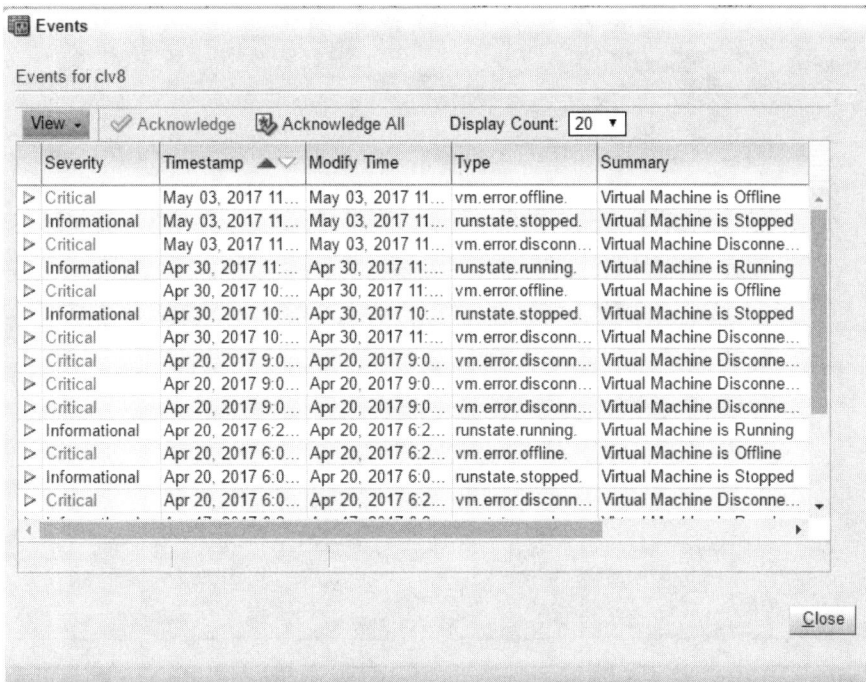

FIGURE 28-7. *Event history*

Jobs

Oracle VM Manager also displays most errors in the jobs. The Jobs panel appears in the bottom section of the screen. When each job runs, the system will notify you if there is an error with the job, as you can see in Figure 28-8, where one job has failed.

If there is an error, click the Details button to see the error, as shown in Figure 28-9. From here, you can see the job details, the queued info that's applicable, and also the individual job events.

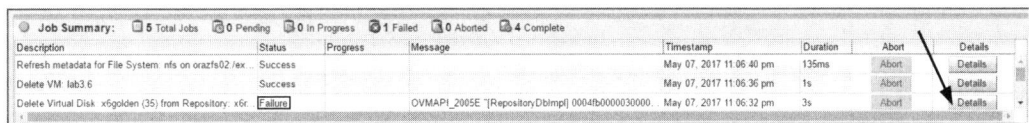

FIGURE 28-8. *Job list*

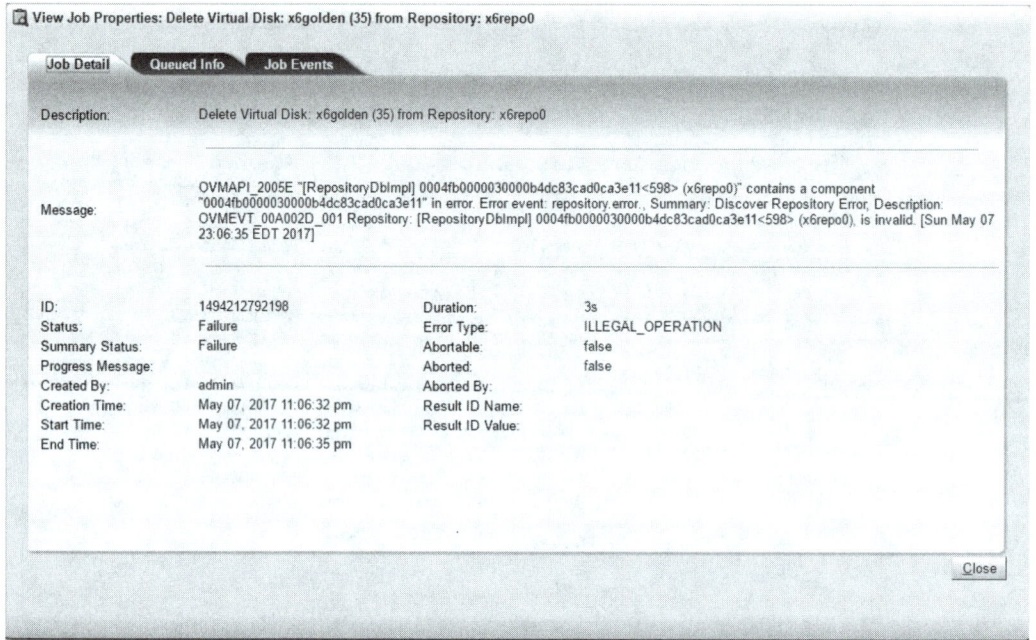

FIGURE 28-9. *Job error details*

Summary

This chapter covered the basics of the troubleshooting process—from identifying the problem to resolving the problem, documenting the issues, and implementing future actions to prevent the problem from happening again. We reviewed the common directories for Oracle VM Server as well as the critical log files and several commands that can help you gather the data needed to troubleshoot issues. We covered the Oracle VM Manager and its critical files, as well as the included Python script that can help you analyze the log files. As a reminder, although troubleshooting can be a difficult process, it does eventually get easier, especially if you follow the process, do not make multiple changes at the same time, and document what changes you made.

Index

Beta Test Oracle Software

Get a first look at our newest products—and help perfect them. You must meet the following criteria:

- ✔ Licensed Oracle customer or Oracle PartnerNetwork member

- ✔ Oracle software expert

- ✔ Early adopter of Oracle products

Please apply at: pdpm.oracle.com/BPO/userprofile

ORACLE®

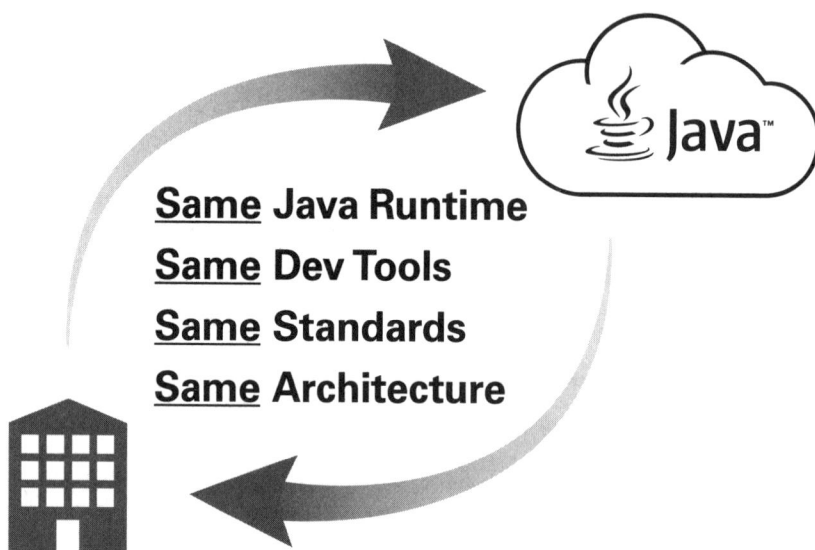

Push a Button

Move Your Java Apps to the Oracle Cloud

Same Java Runtime
Same Dev Tools
Same Standards
Same Architecture

... or Back to Your Data Center

ORACLE®

cloud.oracle.com/java